NOV 2 0 2010

P9-AZV-753

ALSO BY BARRY DAY

This Wooden "O": Shakespeare's Globe Reborn

My Life With Noël Coward (with Graham Payn)

Noël Coward: The Complete Lyrics

Noël Coward: In His Own Words

Noël Coward: Complete Sketches and Parodies

Theatrical Companion to Coward (with Sheridan Morley)

The Unknown Noël: New Writing From the Coward Archives

Coward on Film: The Cinema of Noël Coward

The Letters of Noël Coward

Oscar Wilde: A Life in Quotes

P. G. Wodehouse: In His Own Words

P. G. Wodehouse: The Complete Lyrics

The Complete Lyrics of Johnny Mercer (with Robert Kimball)

Dorothy Parker: In Her Own Words

Sherlock Holmes: In His Own Words and the Words of Those Who Knew Him

Sherlock Holmes and the Shakespeare Globe Murders

Sherlock Holmes and the Alice in Wonderland Murders

Sherlock Holmes and the Copycat Murders

Sherlock Holmes and the Apocalypse Murders

Sherlock Holmes and the Seven Deadly Sins Murders

Murder, My Dear Watson (contributor)

THE NOËL COWARD READER

THE
NOËL COWARD
READER

EDITED AND WITH COMMENTARY BY

BARRY DAY

ALFRED A. KNOPF   NEW YORK 2010

THIS IS A BORZOI BOOK PUBLISHED BY ALFRED A. KNOPF

*Introduction, chronology, and commentary copyright © 2009, 2010
by Barry Day*

Unpublished selections copyright © 2009, 2010 by N. C. Aventales AG

*All rights reserved. Published in the United States by Alfred A. Knopf,
a division of Random House, Inc., New York, and in Canada by
Random House of Canada Limited, Toronto.*

www.aaknopf.com

*Knopf, Borzoi Books, and the colophon are registered
trademarks of Random House, Inc.*

Originally publised in Great Britain in paperback in different form as
The Essential Noël Coward Compendium: The Very Best of His
Work, Life and Times *by Methuen Drama, A&C Black Publishers
Limited, London, in 2009.*

*All rights in this collection are strictly reserved and application for performance,
etc., should be made by professionals to Alan Brodie Representation Ltd.,
6th Floor, Fairgate House, 78 New Oxford Street, London WC1A 1HB, United
Kingdom (abr@alanbrodie.com); by amateurs in North America to Samuel
French Inc., 45 West 25th Street, New York, N.Y. 10010, U.S.A.
Stock rights in North America are handled by Robert Freedman Inc.,
1501 Broadway, Suite 2310, New York, N.Y. 10036. All other rights
Alan Brodie Representation Ltd. No performance of the plays in this collection
may be given unless a license has been obtained.*

*No rights in incidental music or songs contained in the work are hereby granted
and performance rights for any performance/presentation whatsoever must be
obtained from the respective copyright owners.*

*Due to limitations of space, permissions to reprint previously published material
can be found following the index.*

Library of Congress Cataloging-in-Publication Data
Coward, Noël, 1899–1973.
{Selections. 2010}
The Noël Coward reader / edited and with commentary by Barry Day. — 1st ed.
p. cm.
Includes index.
*Summary: This reader brings together the best of Noël Coward's short stories,
verse, songs, plays, screenplays, etc.*
ISBN 978-0-307-27337-6
I. Day, Barry. II. Title.
PR6005.O85A6 2010
822'.912—dc22 2010018021

Manufactured in the United States of America

First American Edition

FOR

THE MASTER

(WHO ELSE?)

CONTENTS

ILLUSTRATIONS

FOREWORD

Even though I have been able to name a lovely theatre in his memory, one of the great regrets in my life has been that I never knew Noël Coward. I did briefly meet him once, in the foyer of Sadler's Wells Theatre in 1972, not long before he died, when despite his frailty, he'd put himself out to see his beloved old friend Joyce Carey, who was appearing in the musical *Trelawny* that I was producing. I was also lucky enough to attend the glorious seventieth birthday midnight celebration for him at the Phoenix Theatre in December 1969, when it seemed every star in the Heavens had come down to pay entertaining homage—that Christmas was indeed a great Noël. Sadly, the evening, which featured such a marvelous cross section of his material, was never filmed, so Barry Day's delicious new compendium, drawn from his diaries, letters, plays, and short stories, is the next best thing.

For anyone with only a sketchy knowledge of The Master, this book contains a cross section of his work from private diaries to *Private Lives*—words leap off the page often put in marvelous context by both Barry Day's and Coward's own trenchant and illuminating observations that in themselves are hugely entertaining and superbly written. It's full of delicious little facts like *London Pride* being Coward's musical riposte to the Germans for commandeering an age-old British lavender seller's song for *Deutschland über Alles;* by using the same tune himself, it became one of the biggest hits of the War. No one today can match Coward's unique style as a performer and actor, but the cream of his writing remains surprisingly contemporary, brilliantly observed, exceptionally witty and with an underlying depth that consistently surprises anyone who only knows Coward by repute.

As a producer of musicals, I am amazed by the sheer volume and quality of work he produced and that so much of it poured out so effortlessly. However, I can't help observing that considering how many successful songs he wrote, and what an impeccable dramatist he was, his musical theatre legacy is almost non-existent and there is not one musical of his that is regularly staged. Even his greatest hit, *Bitter Sweet,* has not been done for decades, despite containing a torrent of melodies. Maybe it was because in 1934 he parted ways with the great English producer C. B. Cochran and set up his own production company. Musicals are funny things in that those that are most successful are the sum of their collaboration, rather than the single-minded vision of the author, however talented. Coward always professed to enjoy writing tunes more than wrestling with the technical aspects of lyric writing—despite being one of the great "rhymers" of all time:

> "It's one of those rules that the greatest fools obey,
> Because the sun is much to sultry
> And one must avoid its ultry-violet rays"—*sheer genius!*

The heart of a great musical is always a great book, usually adapted from an existing source—something Coward rarely did, preferring to come up with his own stories.

But how I would have loved to have had the chance to tussle with his great talent to amuse and nudge him into writing a classic musical that would be as timeless as the *Words and Music* he did leave behind. But I'll sigh no more, and just urge you to thoroughly enjoy the many Coward gems on display in Barry Day's imaginatively edited and affectionate *Noël Coward Reader*.

—SIR CAMERON MACKINTOSH

THE NOËL COWARD READER

There are probably greater painters than Noël, greater novelists than Noël, greater librettists, greater composers of music, greater singers, greater dancers, greater comedians, greater tragedians, greater stage producers, greater film directors, greater cabaret artists, greater TV stars . . . If there are, they are fourteen different people. Only *one* man combined all fourteen different talents—The Master. Noël Coward.

—LORD LOUIS MOUNTBATTEN
AT A PARTY FOR NOËL'S SEVENTIETH BIRTHDAY
(DECEMBER 1969)

Noël in his study at Chalet Coward

THE MAN THEY CALLED "THE MASTER"

> There will always be a few people . . . in every generation
> who will find my work entertaining and true.
>
> —DIARIES (APRIL 23, 1951)

NOËL COWARD. WRITER.

Of all the crafts he practiced, Noël never lost sight of the fact that he was a writer first—and everything else a not-too-distant second.

"Writing is more important than acting, for one very good reason: it lasts. Stage acting only lives in people's memories as long as they live. Writing is creative; acting is interpretive."

If some of his own plays in which he also appeared seemed to have relatively short runs, it was because the leading actor was being "goosed" by his writing muse.

It began with *Private Lives,* which ran in London for three months, when it could easily have stayed for a year or more. In his first autobiography, *Present Indicative,* Noël was unapologetic . . .

Perhaps in later years, when I'm looking for a job, I shall indeed regret those lost grosses, but I don't really think that I will. I consider myself a writer first and an actor second . . . If I play the same part over and over again for a long run, I become bored and frustrated and my performance deteriorates. In addition to this, I have no time to write. Ideas occur to me and then retreat again because, with eight performances a week to be got through, there is no time to develop them. For me, three months in London and three months in New York once in every two years is an ideal arrangement.

From his earliest days he was a writer who would try his hand at anything. His notebooks show him doing so from the age of eight, but the real impetus came three years later from a fellow child actor, Esmé Wynne, with whom he often appeared . . .

"She wrote poems. Reams and reams of them, love songs, sonnets and villanelles, alive with elves, mermaids, leafy glades and Pan (a good deal of Pan)."

Enough, certainly, to infect Noël's own budding creativity. His first completed novel was called *Cherry Pan*.

"Cherry Pan, I regret to tell you, was the daughter of the Great God Pan and was garrulous and tiresome to the point of nausea. Having materialized suddenly on a summer evening in Sussex, she proceeded with excruciating pagan archness to wreak havoc in a country parsonage before returning winsomely to her woodland glades and elfin grots."

Esmé was convinced, though, that the *moment critique* arrived when she was asked to write a three-act fairy play for a special matinée performance.

"It got a great deal of extra publicity because the censor banned it on account of its length . . . All this excitement, so dear, even then, to the heart of the youthful Noël, determined him to write himself, and he suggested that we collaborate, as we did in excruciatingly bad stories and songs for the next few years."

One particular collaboration stuck in both their minds.

One of Esmé's poems read . . .

> Our little love is dying
> On his head are lately crimson petals
> Faded quite.

Noël offered to set it to music. "I set these words to a merry lilt beginning . . . 'Our little love is dying on his head . . .' Esmé was not well pleased."

·

Time now to go it alone. And how easy it seemed. He found he had a natural gift for dialogue. Take a plot—which might possibly be a little reminiscent of, say, Shaw—sprinkle it with witty lines and you had a play.

Noël's saving grace turned out to be that, despite his creative precociousness, he knew when to listen to those who knew better and were prepared to share what they knew.

American impresario Gilbert Miller "gave me some useful pieces of advice on the art of playwriting. He said, among other things, that although my dialogue was nearly always good, my construction was 'lousy' . . . the construction of a play was as important as the foundations of a house, whereas dialogue, however good, could only, at best, be considered as interior decoration. This I recognized as being authentic wisdom . . . I will never again embark on so much as a revue sketch that is not carefully and meticulously constructed beforehand."

He was still developing that theme in the 1950s . . .

"I know this sounds like heresy in this era of highly-praised, half-formulated moods, but no mood, however exquisite, is likely to hold the attention of an audience for two hours and a half unless it is based on a solid structure . . .

"I can see no particular virtue in writing quickly; on the contrary, I am well aware that too great a facility is often dangerous and should be curbed when it shows signs of getting the bit too firmly between the teeth. No reputable writer should permit his talent to bolt with him."

But this was late in life. In earlier years his talent had taken him on many a wild ride. Very late in life he confessed that his greatest single regret was "not having taken more trouble with some of my work."

Talent, of course, has its own rules, and one of them is: You can't make rules. Yet there is a pattern when Noël's work is viewed in retrospect. The plays that are generally considered his best appear to have been produced effortlessly. A period of cogitation, certainly—conscious or unconscious—but then the piece itself was born quickly and fully formed.

Private Lives took four days to write while he was suffering from a bout of influenza in a Shanghai hotel. *Hay Fever* took three. *Blithe Spirit* took five, and only two lines of the original script were changed in production. (Shakespeare, he was pleased to note, took *six* to write *Macbeth*.)

The glory days of Coward the dramatist were from 1924 and *The Vortex* until the end of World War II. At this point his critics began to get through his defenses, although he would never admit it.

The public—the critics decided—were tired of the effete *élite*; they demanded gritty reality in their theater, although the box office often indicated otherwise. Noël Coward was *passé*. Which meant that producers who had fought to stage the latest Coward were now questioning him and asking for rewrites. Which made Noël question himself, and the later plays often show signs of creative strain and self-consciousness. He decided he should become a "better writer" and admitted, "I seem in later years to have lost my gift for economy."

Happily, the mid-1960s saw "Dad's Renaissance"—now very clearly evolved into "Dad's Restoration" or even "Coward Redux"—and the body of his work can now be seen objectively.

More to the point, it is being seen by a new audience, a young audience. Actors, directors, and the general theatergoing public are finding that this man they had assumed to be out of date and irrelevant is speaking to them.

The surface wit of the plays hides vulnerability and insecurity. And since when have *they* been out of style?

·

Noël's reputation would be secure if we had only the plays to judge him by. He was a great writer—except when he was trying to be a great writer. A conduit for greatness, rather than an intellect intent on rearranging the words just so. ("Poor Mr. Henry James who trudges and writhes and wriggles through jungles of verbiage to describe a cucumber sandwich.")

But we have much more than the plays.

There's Noël the Novelist.

Seemingly untired by the "tiresome" *Cherry Pan,* in that same year (1918) he wrote *Cats and Dogs,* the story of a brother and sister, who also talked brightly and incessantly for some eighty thousand words before Noël left them to get on with it and bore each other to death.

His next effort was over a decade later on a long trip to the Far East. On the boat between Honolulu and Yokohama he dreamed up the character of Julian Kane, a man who commits suicide because he is bored.

"I worked hard on my novel . . . but became increasingly discouraged by its obvious dullness, until I finally decided that, if it continued as it was going, the future readers of it would commit suicide from boredom long before the hero ever reached that point of defeat."

So Julian Kane lived, but *Julian Kane* died on the journey. And he also taught Noël a valuable literary lesson that would pay dividends thirty years later, when he next tried his hand at the form . . .

I am inclined to oversimplify my descriptive passages and reduce them to staccato interludes rather than letting them be part of the general structure. This is the natural result of years of dialogue writing. It is only when I have done a couple of pages of—to my mind— elaborate and drawn-out description that, on reading it over, I discover to my astonishment that it is neither elaborate nor drawn-out. On the contrary, it is usually on the skimpy side. This, I suppose, is the reason that so few playwrights write good novels and vice versa. Particularly vice versa. Most novelists overload their plays with masses of words.

Personally, I am quite determined to be good at both. I am not sure yet, judging from my short stories and autobiographies, that I have evolved a personal style. It is not a thing to pursue consciously.

—DIARIES (1957)

But three years later the personal style had evolved in the shape of *Pomp and Circumstance,* his only published novel, set in Samolo, his fictional

"A Room With a View" . . .

. . . "overlooking an absolutely ravishing tax advantage"

South Sea island and one of the few remaining minor jewels in the battered crown of British Empire.

He apologized in advance to his American publishers for its lack of either seriousness or substance. It contained, he claimed, "little sentiment and no significance."

What was significant, however, was the fact that his literary *soufflé* proved to be to the taste of both American and British readers and the book stayed near the top of the best-seller lists in both countries for many weeks.

•

The short-story form was one that had intrigued him from his earliest years, even before the Esmé episode. His childhood notebooks are full of jottings, lists of possible story titles and a number of complete, if predictably derivative, stories.

As the years went by and his stage success became apparent, a novel represented a major commitment of time, whereas a short story could provide creative punctuation and a valuable change of pace.

> Worked all the morning and came to the conclusion that I love writing fiction. It is hard going but it has the lovely satisfaction about it that good, bad or indifferent, there it is and it has not got to be translated through someone else's personality.
>
> **—DIARIES** (1949)

"Being primarily a dramatist, short stories have been an absorbing experiment in form, lying somewhere between a play and a novel. I found them fascinating to write but far from easy. They demand perhaps a little less rigid self-discipline than a play, and a great deal more than a novel. In a novel there is room for divergencies and irrelevancies, in a play, there is none; in a short story, just a little, but it must be strictly rationed."

Over the years he published several collections, all of which proved commercially successful. But the critical accolade he prized the most came from an unlikely source. He and Dame Edith Sitwell had conducted a long-standing feud, which took forty years to resolve, and it was Noël's *Collected Short Stories* that sealed their reunion . . .

"There are no short stories," Dame Edith wrote, "written in England in our time that I admire more . . . You have done more, so quietly, than most writers do by yelling at the tops of their voices.

"All the stories have that extraordinary quality of reality, so that although the endings are perfect endings, one feels the people go on living after the stories, quality stories, are finished and one wants to know what happened to them, beyond the stories."

·

Film was a medium to which Noël was a late convert.

There were reasons for his initial lack of enthusiasm.

In the late 1920s British studios were desperate for "pre-sold" material, and what better than the provocative plays of this rising young man, Noël Coward? Three of them were bought and filmed in 1927 alone. None of them was a success, for the fairly obvious reason that a Coward play of that period depended on its dialogue—and this was still the era of the silent film!

Even when sound came in, the American studio system—through a combination of censorship constraints and screenwriters' ego—managed to damage and distort his material to the point where he would write to his mother, Violet, in 1930, "I'm not very keen on Hollywood—I'd rather have a nice cup of cocoa, really."

Throughout the 1930s he appeared in only one film (*The Scoundrel*) but gave no serious thought to writing one himself. He was a playwright, and as he confided to the fan magazine *Picturegoer,* "Films are not an offshoot of the stage. They are a totally different medium."

He was to learn that lesson the hard way.

Persuaded to write and star in a wartime film about the navy, he embarked on a screenplay with his friend, the writer and artist Clemence Dane. The working title at this time was *White Ensign.*

Producer Anthony Havelock-Allan and codirector David Lean were summoned to Noël's flat to hear Noël read the result of the collaboration.

Lean remembered . . .

"It lasted for, I don't know, two-and-a-half hours. It was very rambling, contained a lot of dialogue and, at the end of reading it, he said to me—'Well, what do you think of that, my dear? What sort of film will it make?' "

"I said—'Well, it's simply wonderful, but the trouble is that what you've read me will run for five hours on the screen.'

" 'Oh, my God,' he said. 'I never thought of that. I thought you could do anything in the movies. I fear this has as many restrictions around it as the stage.' "

Lean then persuaded Noël to go and see Orson Welles's *Citizen Kane* and study the cinematic structure. It turned out to be advice on play construction every bit as key as Gilbert Miller's had been all those years earlier.

In Which We Serve—as the film became—and subsequently *Brief Encounter* are generally regarded as being two of the finest films Britain has ever produced.

·

Nor was that the whole of Noël in prose.

Two and a half autobiographies . . . diaries that started in earnest as the war ended . . . and *letters*—lots and lots of letters.

The autobiographies speak for themselves, insofar as they represent recollections in Noël's relative tranquillity. Occasionally, it must be said, they are recollections of how things should have been.

Esmé picked up this point when she read the first one, *Present Indicative* (1937). She had, after all, been a supporting actress in some of its early scenes.

She wrote to him . . .

Darling,

Even in the sense it's rather like squashing soap bubbles with a hatchet to apply the touchstone of truth to your bright and gay babblings about our early life together

. . . I can't believe you're as inaccurate when dealing with other aspects of your life as you are on the points that concern us . . . I can't think why you've got this so wrong. It's as though you invent an aspect to a case which you want to believe and then insist on believing it . . . I can understand you exaggerating, as you do in places, to make a good story—that's the showmanship coming out . . .

Still, they *were* good stories . . .

The *Diaries* began as journals that would aid his memory when it came time to continue the autobiography, but as one reads them, they evolve into something more. At a point Noël realizes that they will inevitably be read one day. He begins to take more care with the writing. He has one eye on the page and another on posterity. This is what he would like us to *think* he thought.

The *Letters* are something quite different. Of all forms of literary expression, the letter is the purest. It can't be called back and redrafted, polished. It can't be Noël Coward being "Noël Coward."

It tells what he felt at the precise moment he felt it—joy, anger, frustration. It's a form of DNA and it shows a man more insecure than we had been led to believe by the legend. Reading them, we know more about him. More to the point, we *like* him more.

•

Among the stories in his early notebooks are Noël's first attempts at the verse form . . .

Throughout most of the years of my life, since approximately nineteen hundred and eight, I have derived a considerable amount of private pleasure from writing verse . . . I find it quite fascinating to write at random, sometimes in rhyme, sometimes not. I am trying to discipline myself away from too much discipline, by which I mean that my experience and training in lyric writing has made me inclined to stick too closely to a rigid form. It is strange that technical accuracy should occasionally banish magic, but it does. The carefully rhymed verses, which I find very difficult not to do, are on the whole, less effective and certainly less moving than the free ones. The writing of free verse, which I am enjoying so very much, is wonderful exercise for my mind and for my vocabulary. Most of what I have already done I really feel is good and is opening up, for me, some new windows. My sense of words, a natural gift, is becoming more trained and selective, and I suspect, when I next sit down to write a play, things may happen that have never happened before.

When people refer to Noël the poet—which they are increasingly beginning to do as the body of his work is studied—they do him an unconscious disservice. He never claimed that anything he wrote reached the heights of poetry and insisted it be called "verse."

"I truly love writing both rhymed and unrhymed verse. It's complicated and exasperating but rewarding when it comes off."

It would also prove a temporary relief from more demanding chores—creative, personal or even political.

When World War II was finally declared, he wrote in "Personal Note" . . .

> Feeling the world so shadowed, and the time,
> Essential to clear processes of thought,
> So much accelerated, I have sought
> Relief by those excursions into rhyme.

In the context of his work as a whole it can now be seen that in some of these "excursions"—and a few of his lyrics—we find ourselves looking into his "secret heart." Nowhere is he more honest with himself than in a verse like "I Am No Good at Love." Nowhere do we see the personal insecurity behind the carefully crafted exterior more clearly than in "Nothing Is Lost," "This Is to Let You Know" or "When I Have Fears."

Whatever *Noël* chose to say, this is verse raised to poetry.

•

And then there were the songs . . .

> Where are the songs we sung
> When love in our hearts was young?

> Where, in the shadows that we have to pass among,
> Lie those songs that once we sung?
>
> —OPERETTE (1938)

Any top-ten list of lyricists from the golden age of popular song would be perverse if it didn't include (in alphabetical order) . . . Irving Berlin, Ira Gershwin, Oscar Hammerstein, Lorenz Hart, Johnny Mercer and Cole Porter. (We can argue about Yip Harburg, Frank Loesser, Hoagy Carmichael, P. G. Wodehouse, Howard Dietz and, of course, Stephen Sondheim—but some other time!)

And if the list were to be truly international, that top ten would certainly include Noël, who wrote words and music. Only Berlin and Porter did that as a matter of course.

I was born into a generation that took light music seriously. The lyrics and melodies of operetta, musical comedy, Gilbert and Sullivan were hummed and strummed into my consciousness at an early age . . . I couldn't help composing tunes, even if I wished to, and ever since a little boy they have dropped into my mind unbidden—and often in the most unlikely of circumstances!

I can only assume that the compulsion to make rhymes was born in me . . . There is no time I can remember when I was not fascinated by words "going together": Lewis Carroll, Edward Lear, Beatrix Potter, all fed my childish passion, in addition to all the usual nursery rhymes that the flesh is heir to.

Once again, "the feverish industry" of his childhood friend Esmé Wynne played a pivotal role. Early in his career he wrote about this in "How I Write My Songs" . . .

I had the edge on her because, being a natural musician, I found it easier to write to tunes jangling in my head than to devote myself to mastering iambics, trochees, anapests or dactyls. If a tune came first, I would set words to it. If the words came first, I would set them to music at the piano.

The latter process almost invariably necessitated changing the verse to fit the tune. If you happen to be born with a built-in sense of rhythm, any verse you write is apt to fall into a set pattern and remain within its set pattern until it is completed. This is perfectly satisfactory from the point of view of reading or reciting, but when you attempt to set your pattern to a tune, either the tune gives in and allows itself to be inhibited by the rigidity of your original scansion or it rebels, refusing to be dominated and displays some ideas of its own, usually in the form of unequal lines and unexpected accents. This is why I very seldom write a lyric first and set it to music later.

Much later he is giving the same advice to the young Sandy Wilson. "Don't write all the lyrics before the music. The lyric imprisons the melody. Let the music be free."
With some four hundred songs he made his case.

·

When asked why he was called—and happily answered to—"The Master," he answered, "Oh, you know—Jack of All Trades, Master of None." And then the toothy Coward grin shone through.

·

I think on the whole I am a better writer than I am given credit for being. It is fairly natural that my writing should be appreciated casually, because my personality, performances, music and legend get in the way. Someday, I suspect, when Jesus has definitely got me for a sunbeam, my works may be adequately assessed.

—DIARIES (1956)

BARRY DAY
2010

CHRONOLOGY

1899 December 16, Noël Peirce Coward born in Teddington, Middlesex, eldest surviving son of Arthur Coward, piano salesman, and Violet (*née* Veitch). A "brazen, odious little prodigy," his early circumstances were of refined suburban poverty.

1907 First public appearances in school and community concerts.

1908 Family moved to Battersea and took in lodgers.

1911 First professional appearance as Prince Mussel in *The Goldfish,* produced by Lila Field at the Little Theatre, and revived in same year at Crystal Palace and Royal Court Theatre. Cannard the page boy in *The Great Name* at the Prince of Wales Theatre, and William in *Where the Rainbow Ends* with Charles Hawtrey's Company at the Savoy Theatre.

1912 Directed *The Daisy Chain* and stage-managed *The Prince's Bride* at Savoy in series of matinées featuring the work of the children of the *Rainbow* cast. Mushroom in *An Autumn Idyll,* ballet, Savoy.

1913 An angel (Gertrude Lawrence was another) in Basil Dean's production of *Hannele.* Slightly in *Peter Pan,* Duke of York's.

1914 Toured in *Peter Pan.* Collaborated with fellow performer Esmé Wynne on songs, sketches and short stories—"beastly little whimsies."

1915 Admitted to sanatorium for tuberculosis.

1916 Five-month tour as Charley in *Charley's Aunt.* Walk-on in *The Best of Luck,* Drury Lane. Wrote first full-length song, "Forbidden Fruit." Basil Pycroft in *The Light Blues,* produced by Robert Courtneidge, with daughter Cicely also in cast, Shaftesbury. Short spell as dancer at Elysée Restaurant (subsequently the Café de Paris). Jack Morrison in *The Happy Family,* Prince of Wales.

1917 "Boy pushing barrow" in D. W. Griffith's film *Hearts of the World.* Coauthor with Esmé Wynne of one-acter "Ida Collaborates," Theatre Royal, Aldershot. Ripley Guildford in *The Saving Grace,* with Charles Hawtrey, "who . . . taught me many points of comedy acting," Garrick. Family moved to Pimlico and reopened boardinghouse.

1918 Called up for army. Medical discharge after nine months. Wrote unpublished novels *Cats and Dogs* (loosely based on Shaw's *You Never Can Tell*) and the unfinished *Cherry Pan* ("dealing in a whimsical vein with the adventures of a daughter of Pan"), and lyrics for Darewski and Joel, including "When You Come Home on Leave" and "Peter Pan." Also composed "Tamarisk Town." Sold short stories to magazines. Wrote plays *The Rat Trap, The Last Trick* (unproduced) and *The Impossible Wife* (unproduced). Courtenay Borner in *Scandal,* Strand. *Woman and Whiskey* (coauthor Esmé Wynne) produced at Wimbledon Theatre.

1919   Ralph in *The Knight of the Burning Pestle,* Birmingham Repertory, played with "a stubborn Mayfair distinction" demonstrating a "total lack of understanding of the play." Collaborated on *Crissa,* an opera, with Esmé Wynne and Max Darewski (unproduced). Wrote *I'll Leave It to You.*

1920   Bobbie Dermott in *I'll Leave It to You,* New Theatre. Wrote play *Barriers Down* (unproduced). *I'll Leave It to You* published, London.

1921   On holiday in Alassio, met Gladys Calthrop for the first time. Clay Collins in American farce *Polly With a Past:* during the run "songs, sketches, and plays were bursting out of me." Wrote *The Young Idea, Sirocco* and *The Better Half.* First visit to New York, and sold parts of *A Withered Nosegay* to *Vanity Fair* and short-story adaptation of *I'll Leave It to You* to *Metropolitan.* Houseguest of Laurette Taylor and Hartley Manners, whose family rows inspired the Bliss household in *Hay Fever.*

1922   "Bottles and Bones" (sketch) produced in benefit for Newspaper Press Fund, Drury Lane. *The Better Half* produced in "Grand Guignol" season, Little Theatre. Started work on songs and sketches for *London Calling!* Adapted Louis Verneuil's *Pour Avoir Adrienne* (unproduced). Wrote *The Queen Was in the Parlor* and *Mild Oats.*

1923   Sholto Brent in *The Young Idea,* Savoy. Juvenile lead in *London Calling!* Wrote *Weatherwise, Fallen Angels* and *The Vortex.*

1924   Wrote *Hay Fever* (which Marie Tempest at first refused to do, feeling it was "too light and plotless and generally lacking in action") and *Easy Virtue.* Nicky Lancaster in *The Vortex,* produced at Everyman by Norman MacDermott.

1925   Established as a social and theatrical celebrity. Wrote *On With the Dance* with London opening in spring followed by *Fallen Angels* and *Hay Fever. Hay Fever* and *Easy Virtue* produced, New York. Wrote silent-screen titles for Gainsborough Pictures.

1926   Toured U.S.A. in *The Vortex.* Wrote *This Was a Man,* refused a license by Lord Chamberlain but produced in New York (1926), Berlin (1927) and Paris (1928). *Easy Virtue, The Queen Was in the Parlor* and *The Rat Trap* produced, London. Played Lewis Dodd in

The Constant Nymph, directed by Basil Dean. Wrote *Semi-Monde* and *The Marquise.* Bought Goldenhurst Farm, Kent, as country home. Sailed for Hong Kong on holiday but trip broken in Honolulu by nervous breakdown.

1927 *The Marquise* opened in London while Coward was still in Hawaii, and *The Marquise* and *Fallen Angels* produced, New York. Finished writing *Home Chat. Sirocco* revised after discussions with Basil Dean and produced, London.

1928 Clark Storey in Behrman's *The Second Man,* directed by Dean. Gainsborough film productions of *The Queen Was in the Parlor, The Vortex* (starring Ivor Novello) and *Easy Virtue* (directed by Alfred Hitchcock) released—but only the latter, freely adapted, a success. *This Year of Grace!* produced, London, and with Coward directing and in cast, New York. Made first recording, featuring numbers from this show. Wrote *Concerto* for Gainsborough Pictures, intended for Ivor Novello, but never produced. Started writing *Bitter Sweet.*

1929 Played in *This Year of Grace!* (U.S.A.) until spring. Directed *Bitter Sweet,* London and New York. Set off on traveling holiday in Far East.

1930 On travels wrote *Private Lives* (1929) and song "Mad Dogs and Englishmen," the latter on the road from Hanoi to Saigon. In Singapore joined The Quaints, company of strolling English players, as Stanhope for three performances of *Journey's End.* On voyage home wrote *Post-Mortem,* which was "similar to my performance as Stanhope: confused, underrehearsed and hysterical." Directed and played Elyot Chase in *Private Lives,* London, and Fred in *Some Other Private Lives.* Started writing *Cavalcade* and unfinished novel *Julian Kane.*

1931 Elyot Chase in New York production of *Private Lives.* Directed *Cavalcade,* London. Film of *Private Lives* produced by MGM. Set off on trip to South America.

1932 On travels wrote *Design for Living* (hearing that Alfred Lunt and Lynn Fontanne finally free to work with him) and material for new revue including songs "Mad About the Boy," "Children of the Ritz" and "The Party's Over Now." Produced in London as *Words and Music,* with book, music and lyrics exclusively by Coward and directed by him. The short-lived Noël Coward Company, independent company that enjoyed his support, toured U.K. with *Private Lives, Hay Fever, Fallen Angels* and *The Vortex.*

1933 Directed *Design for Living,* New York, and played Leo. Films of *Cavalcade, Tonight Is Ours* (remake of *The Queen Was in the Parlor*) and *Bitter Sweet* released. Directed London revival of *Hay Fever.* Wrote *Conversation Piece* as vehicle for Yvonne Printemps, and hit song "Mrs. Worthington."

1934   Directed *Conversation Piece* in London and played Paul. Cut links with C. B. Cochran and formed own management in partnership with John C. Wilson and the Lunts. Appointed President of the Actors' Orphanage, in which he invested great personal commitment until resignation in 1956. Directed Kaufman and Ferber's *Theatre Royal,* Lyric, and Behrman's *Biography,* Globe. Film of *Design for Living* released, London. *Conversation Piece* opened, New York. Started writing autobiography, *Present Indicative.* Wrote *Point Valaine.*

1935   Directed *Point Valaine,* New York. Played lead in film *The Scoundrel* (Astoria Studios, New York). Wrote *Tonight at 8:30.*

1936   Directed and played in *Tonight at 8:30,* London and New York. Directed *Mademoiselle* by Jacques Deval, Wyndham's.

1937   Played in *Tonight at 8:30,* New York, until second breakdown in health in March. Directed (and subsequently disowned) Gerald Savory's *George and Margaret,* New York. Wrote *Operette,* with hit song "The Stately Homes of England." *Present Indicative* published, London and New York.

1938   Directed *Operette,* London. *Words and Music* revised for American production as *Set to Music.* Appointed adviser to newly formed Royal Naval Film Corporation.

1939   Directed New York production of *Set to Music.* Visited Soviet Union and Scandinavia. Wrote *Present Laughter* and *This Happy Breed:* rehearsals stopped by declaration of war. Wrote for revue *All Clear,* London. Appointed to head Bureau of Propaganda in Paris, to liaise with French Ministry of Information, headed by Jean Giraudoux and André Maurois. This posting prompted speculative attacks in the press, prevented by wartime secrecy from getting a clear statement of the exact nature of his work. Troop concert in Arras with Maurice Chevalier. *To Step Aside* (short-story collection) published.

1940   Increasingly "oppressed and irritated by the Paris routine." Visits U.S.A. to report on American isolationism and attitudes to war in Europe. Return to Paris prevented by German invasion. Returned to U.S.A. to do propaganda work for Ministry of Information. Propaganda tour of Australia and New Zealand, and fund-raising for war charities.

1941   Mounting press attacks in England because of time spent allegedly avoiding danger and discomfort of home front. Wrote *Blithe Spirit,* produced in London (with Coward directing) and

New York. MGM film of *Bitter Sweet* (which Coward found "vulgar" and "lacking in taste") released, London. Wrote screenplay for *In Which We Serve*, based on the sinking of HMS *Kelly*. Wrote songs including "London Pride," "Could You Please Oblige Us With a Bren Gun?," and "Imagine the Duchess's Feelings." Wrote play *Time Remembered* (unproduced).

1942   Produced and codirected (with David Lean) *In Which We Serve*, and appeared as Captain Kinross (Coward considered the film "an accurate and sincere tribute to the Royal Navy"). Played in countrywide tour of *Blithe Spirit, Present Laughter* and *This Happy Breed*, and gave hospital and factory concerts. MGM film of *We Were Dancing* released.

1943   Played Garry Essendine in London production of *Present Laughter* and Frank Gibbons in *This Happy Breed*. Produced *This Happy Breed* for Two Cities Films. Wrote "Don't Let's Be Beastly to the Germans," first sung on BBC Radio (then banned on grounds of lines "that Goebbels might twist"). Four-month tour of Middle East to entertain troops.

1944   February–September, toured South Africa, Burma, India and Ceylon. Troop concerts in France and "Stage Door Canteen Concert" in London. Screenplay of "Still Life," as *Brief Encounter*. *Middle East Diary*, an account of his 1943 tour, published, London and New York, in which a reference to "mournful little boys from Brooklyn" inspired formation of a lobby for the "Prevention of Noël Coward Reentering America."

1945   *Sigh No More*, with hit song "Matelot," completed and produced, London. Started work on *Pacific 1860*. Film of *Brief Encounter* released.

1946   Started writing *Peace in Our Time*. Directed *Pacific 1860*, London.

1947   Garry Essendine in London revival of *Present Laughter*. Supervised production of *Peace in Our Time*. *Point Valaine* produced, London. Directed American revival of *Tonight at 8:30*. Wrote *Long Island Sound*.

1948   Replaced Graham Payn briefly in American tour of *Tonight at 8:30*, his last stage appearance with Gertrude Lawrence. Wrote screenplay for Gainsborough film of *The Astonished Heart*. Max Aramont in *Joyeux Chagrins* (French production of *Present Laughter*). Built house at Blue Harbour, Jamaica.

1949   Christian Faber in film of *The Astonished Heart*. Wrote *Ace of Clubs* and *Home and Colonial* (produced as *Island Fling* in U.S.A. and *South Sea Bubble* in U.K.).

1950   Directed *Ace of Clubs*, London. Wrote "Star Quality" (short story) and *Relative Values*.

1951   Deaths of Ivor Novello and C. B. Cochran. Paintings included in charity exhibition in London. Wrote *Quadrille.* One-night concert at Theatre Royal, Brighton, followed by season at Café de Paris, London, and beginning of new career as leading cabaret entertainer. Directed *Relative Values,* London, which restored his reputation as a playwright after run of postwar flops. *Island Fling* produced, U.S.A.

1952   Charity cabaret with Mary Martin at Café de Paris for Actors' Orphanage. June cabaret season at Café de Paris. Directed *Quadrille,* London. "Red Peppers," "Fumed Oak" and "Ways and Means" (from *Tonight at 8:30*) filmed as *Meet Me Tonight.* September, death of Gertrude Lawrence: "No one I have ever known, however brilliant . . . has contributed quite what she contributed to my work."

1953   Completed second volume of autobiography, *Future Indefinite.* King Magnus in Shaw's *The Apple Cart.* Cabaret at Café de Paris, again "a triumphant success." Wrote *After the Ball.*

1954   *After the Ball* produced, U.K. July, mother died. September, cabaret season at Café de Paris. November, Royal Command Performance, London Palladium. Wrote *Nude With Violin.*

1955   June, opened in cabaret for season at Desert Inn, Las Vegas, and enjoyed "one of the most sensational successes of my career." Played Hesketh-Baggott in film of *Around the World in Eighty Days,* for which he wrote own scene. October, directed and appeared with Mary Martin in TV spectacular *Together With Music* for CBS, New York. Revised *South Sea Bubble.*

1956   Charles Condomine in television production of *Blithe Spirit,* for CBS, Hollywood. For tax reasons took up Bermuda residency. Resigned from presidency of the Actors' Orphanage. *South Sea Bubble* produced, London. Directed and played part of Frank Gibbons in television production of *This Happy Breed* for CBS, New York. Codirected *Nude With Violin* with John Gielgud (Ireland and U.K.), opening to press attacks on Coward's decision to live abroad. Wrote play *Volcano.*

1957   Directed and played Sébastien in *Nude With Violin,* New York. *Nude With Violin* published, London.

1958   Played Garry Essendine in *Present Laughter,* alternating with *Nude With Violin* on U.S. West Coast tour. Wrote ballet *London Morning* for London Festival Ballet. Wrote *Look After Lulu!*

1959   *Look After Lulu!* produced, New York, and by English Stage Company at Royal Court, London. Film roles of Hawthorne in *Our Man in Havana* and ex-King of Anatolia in *Surprise Package. London*

Morning produced by London Festival Ballet. Sold home in Bermuda and took up Swiss residency. Wrote *Waiting in the Wings.*

1960   *Waiting in the Wings* produced, Ireland and U.K. *Pomp and Circumstance* (novel) published, London and New York.

1961   Directed American production of *Sail Away. Waiting in the Wings* published, New York.

1962   Wrote music and lyrics for *The Girl Who Came to Supper* (adaptation of Rattigan's *The Sleeping Prince,* previously filmed as *The Prince and the Showgirl*). *Sail Away* produced, U.K.

1963   *The Girl Who Came to Supper* produced, U.S.A. Revival of *Private Lives* at Hampstead signals renewal of interest in his work. ("Dad's Renaissance")

1964   Directed New York production of *High Spirits,* musical adaptation of *Blithe Spirit,* and later "supervised" London production at Savoy. Introduced Granada TV's "A Choice of Coward" series, which included *Present Laughter, Blithe Spirit, The Vortex* and *Design for Living.* Directed *Hay Fever* for National Theatre, first living playwright to direct his own work there. *Pretty Polly Barlow* (short-story collection) published.

1965   Played the landlord in film *Bunny Lake Is Missing.* Wrote *Suite in Three Keys.* Badly weakened by attack of amoebic dysentery contracted in Seychelles.

1966   Played in *Suite in Three Keys,* London, which taxed his health further. Started adapting his short story "Star Quality" for the stage.

1967   Caesar in TV musical version of *Androcles and the Lion* (score by Richard Rodgers), New York. Witch of Capri in film *Boom,* adaptation of Tennessee Williams's play *The Milk Train Doesn't Stop Here Anymore.* Lorn Loraine, Coward's secretary and friend for many years, died, London. Worked on new volume of autobiography, *Past Conditional. Bon Voyage* (short-story collection) published.

1968   Played Mr. Bridger, the criminal mastermind, in *The Italian Job.*

1970   Awarded knighthood in New Year's Honours List.

1971   Tony Award, U.S.A., for Distinguished Achievement in the Theatre.

1973   March 26, died peacefully at Firefly, his home in Jamaica. Buried on Firefly Hill.

CHAPTER ONE
"OVERTURE. BEGINNERS . . .":
THE EARLY YEARS

I was truculent apparently about being born and made, with
my usual theatrical acumen, a delayed entrance.

—DIARIES (1954)

"Seated one day at the organ, / I was weary and
ill at ease / And my fingers wandered idly /
Over the noisy keys"

—ADELAIDE ANNE PROCTER,
"The Lost Chord," 1858

N OËL WAS ALWAYS an early and eager beginner, and the past never left him.

To the end of his life long-gone faces, places, sounds and images would be an inextricable part of his present . . .

"PERSONAL REMINISCENCE"

I cannot remember
I cannot remember
The house where I was born
But I know it was in Waldegrave Road
Teddington, Middlesex
Not far from the border of Surrey
An unpretentious abode
Which, I believe,
Economy forced us to leave
In rather a hurry.
But I *can* remember my grandmother's Indian shawl
Which, although exotic to behold,
Felt cold.
Then there was a framed photograph in the hall
Of my father wearing a Norfolk jacket,
Holding a bicycle and a tennis racket
And leaning against a wall
Looking tenacious and distinctly grim
As though he feared they'd be whisked away from him.
I can also remember with repulsive clarity
Appearing at a concert in aid of charity
At which I sang, not the 'Green Hill Far Away'
                      that you know
But the one by Gounod.
I remember a paperweight made of quartz.
And a somber Gustave Doré engraving
Illustrating the 'Book of Revelations'
Which, I am told, upset my vibrations.
I remember, too, a most peculiar craving
For 'Liquorice All-Sorts'

Then there was a song, 'Oh that we two were Maying'
And my uncle, who later took to the bottle, playing

And playing very well
An organ called the 'Mustel'
I remember the smell of rotting leaves
In the Autumn quietness of suburban roads
And seeing the Winter river-flooding
And swirling over the tow-path by the lock.
I remember my cousin Doris in a party frock
With 'broderie anglaise' at the neck and sleeves
And being allowed to stir the Christmas pudding
On long ago, enchanted Christmas Eves.
All this took place in Teddington, Middlesex
Not far from the Surrey border
But none of these little episodes
None of the things I call to mind
None of the memories I find
Are in chronological order
Is in chronological order.

In later life he would often reflect on the cards Life had dealt him in those first formative years.

Oh, how fortunate I was to be born poor. If Mother had been able to afford to send me to private school, Eton and Oxford or Cambridge, it would probably have set me back years.

—**DIARIES** (1967)

The young Noël's vision of female *haute couture*

I have always distrusted too much education and intellectualism; it seems to me that they are always dead wrong about things that really matter.

—DIARIES (1967)

My good fortune was to have a bright, acquisitive, but not, *not* an intellectual mind, and to have been impelled by circumstances to get out and earn my living.

—DIARIES (1969)

So he became the Boy Actor.

"THE BOY ACTOR"

I can remember, I can remember.
The months of November and December
    Were filled for me with peculiar joys
So different from those of other boys.
    For other boys would be counting the days
Until end of term and holiday times
    But I was acting in Christmas plays
While they were taken to pantomimes.
    I didn't envy their Eton suits,
Their children's dances and Christmas trees.
    My life had wonderful substitutes
For such conventional treats as these.
    I didn't envy their country larks,
Their organized games in panelled halls;
    While they made snow-men in stately parks
I was counting the curtain calls.

I remember the auditions, the nerve-racking auditions:
Darkened auditorium and empty, dusty stage,
Little girls in ballet dresses practicing "positions"
Gentlemen with pince-nez asking you your age.
Hopefulness and nervousness struggling within you,
Dreading that familiar phrase, "Thank you dear, no
    more."
Straining every muscle, every tendon, every sinew

To do your dance much better than you'd ever done
    before.
Think of your performance. Never mind the others,
Never mind the pianist, talent must prevail.
Never mind the baleful eyes of other children's mothers
Glaring from the corners and willing you to fail.

I can remember. I can remember.
The months of November and December
    Were more significant to me
Than other months could ever be
    For they were the months of high romance
When destiny waited on tip-toe,
    When every boy actor stood a chance
Of getting into a Christmas show,
    Not for me the dubious heaven
Of being some prefect's protégé!
    Not for me the Second Eleven.
For me, two performances a day.

Ah those first rehearsals! Only very few lines:
Rushing home to mother, learning them by heart,
"Enter left through window"—Dots to mark the cue
    lines:
"Exit with the others"—Still it *was* a part.
Opening performance; legs a bit unsteady,
Dedicated tension, shivers down my spine,
Powder, grease and eye-black, sticks of makeup ready
Leichner number three and number five and number
    nine.
World of strange enchantment, magic for a small boy
Dreaming of the future, reaching for the crown,
Rigid in the dressing room, listening for the call-boy
"Overture Beginners—Everybody Down!"

I can remember. I can remember.
The months of November and December,
    Although climatically cold and damp,
Meant more to me than Aladdin's lamp.
I see myself, having got a job,
Walking on wings along the Strand,
Uncertain whether to laugh or sob

And clutching tightly my mother's hand,
    I never cared who scored the goal
Or which side won the silver cup,
    I never learned to bat or bowl
But I heard the curtain going up.

I was, I believe, one of the worst boy actors ever inflicted on a paying public . . . I was a brazen, odious little prodigy, overpleased with myself and precocious to a degree . . . I am certain that, could my adult self have been present . . . he would have crept out, at the first coy gurgle, and been mercifully sick outside.

—PRESENT INDICATIVE (1937)

•

Nineteen thirteen and a booking to appear in Manchester and Liverpool in a rather turgid German drama in which he was an angel. On the train north he met a fellow child actor "to whom I took an instant fancy. She wore a black satin coat and a black velvet military hat with a peak. Her face was far from pretty, but tremendously alive. She was very *mondaine,* carried a handbag with a powder-puff and frequently dabbed her generously turned-up nose. She confided to me that her name was Gertrude Lawrence, but that I was to call her Gert because everybody else did, that she was fourteen . . . She then gave me an orange and told me a few mildly dirty stories, and I loved her from then onward."

•

From there he graduated to regular appearances in two pieces that became integral to the Christmas theatrical season, *Where the Rainbow Ends* and

ROYAL COURT THEATRE
SLOANE SQUARE.
Monday, April 17th, 1911, for Six Nights

Miss
LILA
FIELD'S
Company

"The
Goldfish"

SPECIAL MATINEES
Wednesday, Thursday and Saturday, April 19th, 20th and 22nd

Noël's first-ever role, as Prince Mussel in *The Goldfish,* 1911

Peter Pan. In the latter he specialized in the part of Slightly, one of the Lost Boys, causing critic Kenneth Tynan to say of the mature Noël: "Forty years ago he was Slightly in *Peter Pan* and you might say that he has been wholly in *Peter Pan* ever since."

•

PERRY: I *love Peter Pan.*
ZELDA: That's because you've got a mother-fixation. All sensitive lads with mother-fixations worship *Peter Pan.*

        —WAITING IN THE WINGS (1960)

•

In between his acting chores he was busy writing sketches, stories, plots for plays, songs and verse.

> I can only assume that the compulsion to make rhymes was born in me. It cannot have been hereditary for neither my mother nor my father nor any of my forebears on either side of the family displayed, as far as I know, the faintest aptitude for writing poetry or verse.
>
> There is no time I can remember when I was not fascinated by words "going together": Lewis Carroll, Edward Lear, Beatrix Potter, all fed my childish passion, in addition to all the usual nursery rhymes that the flesh is heir to, beginning, to the best of the belief, with "Pat-a-Cake, Pat-a-Cake, Baker's Man." I can still distinctly recall being exasperated when any of these whimsical effusions were slipshod in rhyming or scansion. One particularly was liable to send me into a fury. This was "Little Tommy Tucker."

> > Little Tommy Tucker
> > Sings for his supper
> > What shall he have
> > But brown bread and butter?

That "Tuck" and that "sup" and that "but" rasped my sensibilities to such a degree that a deep scar must have formed in my subconscious, for many many years later the untidy little verse sprang, unbidden by me, from the lips of one of my favourite characters, Madame Arcati, in *Blithe Spirit.* She recites it irritably in the séance scene in order to catch the attention of her "child control" on "the other side." "I despise that," she says, "because it doesn't rhyme at all, but Daphne loves it."

And as a personal P.S., Noël would add, "Bad rhyming sets my teeth on edge."

Some years later when I was rushing headlong toward puberty I wrote a series of short couplets under the general heading "Vegetable Verse." These, I am relieved to say, have disappeared. I remember at the time of writing them I read them to my mother, who was immensely struck by their brilliance. Apart from her and a few contemporary cronies nobody set eyes on them. Even my own memory, which is retentive to an extraordinary degree, has refused to hold on to them. I can recall only two tantalizing fragments:

> In a voice of soft staccato
> We will speak of the tomato

And

> The sinful aspaRAGus
> To iniquity will drag us.

Significantly, neither appeared in his *Collected Verse*!

·

In 1916 he composed the first song he considered "whole and complete."

"FORBIDDEN FRUIT"

> Ordinary man invariably sighs
> Vainly for what cannot be,
> If he's in an orchard he will cast his eyes
> Up the highest tree,
> There may be a lot of windfalls
> Lying around,
> But you'll never see a man enjoy the fruit
>   that's on the ground.
>
> Every peach out of reach is attractive
> 'Cos it's just a little bit too high,
> And you'll find that every man
> Will try to pluck it if he can
> As he passes by.
> For the brute loves the fruit that's forbidden

And I'll bet you half a crown
He'll appreciate the flavor of it much much more
If he has to climb a bit to shake it down.

If a man's engaged and feels that he is loved,
Blasé he will quickly be,
Often on one side his ladylove is shoved
While he goes upon the spree.
Then perhaps she'll marry,
And you can bet your life
He'll want her very badly when she's someone else's wife.

Every peach out of reach is attractive
'Cos it's just a little bit too high,
Though it isn't very sane
To make the things you can't attain,
Still you always try.
If you find that you're blind with devotion
For delightful Mrs. Brown,
You'll appreciate eloping with her much much more
If her husband comes along and knocks you down.

Women haven't altered since the days of Eve,
Anxiously through life they prowl,
Always trying to better what their friends achieve,
Either by fair means or foul.
A girl may be quite careful
Of the sort of life she picks,
But to be a real success she's got to know a lot of tricks.

Every peach out of reach is attractive
'Cos it's just a little bit too high,
Even well-brought-up young girls
Will look at other women's pearls
With a yearning eye
If they fight day and night persevering
And a small string they collect,
They'll appreciate the colour of them much much more
If they've sacrificed a little self-respect.

In later years Noël came to question at least one phrase in this novice
lyric.

"The suggested wager of half a crown rather lets down the tone. One cannot help feeling that a bet of fifty pounds, or at least a fiver, would be more in keeping with the general urbanity of the theme; for a brief moment the veneer is scratched and Boodle's, White's and Buck's are elbowed aside by the Clapham Tennis Club, but this perhaps is hypercriticism and it must be remembered that to the author half a crown in 1916 was the equivalent of five pounds in 1926. Also, it rhymes with 'down.' "

Never less than ambitious, Noël then determined to write the definitive war song for "the war to end all wars" that was raging around his countrymen.

On tour in Manchester in August 1917 he wrote to his mother, Violet . . .

My Darling,
At the moment I am nearly mad with excitement . . . I am collaborating with [producer] Max Darewski in a new song. I wrote the lyric yesterday after breakfast, I hummed it to him in the Midland Hotel lounge at 12 o'clock, we at once rushed up to his private room and he put harmonies to it . . . Max leapt off the piano stool and danced for joy and said it was going to take London by storm . . . I shall probably make a lot of money out of it. It is called "When You Come Home on Leave."

"WHEN YOU COME HOME ON LEAVE"

Dear one, I want you just to know
That I am carrying on
Tho' life's at best a dreary show
Now that you have gone.
I'd like you just to realize
That tho' we're far apart
Where 'ere you go on land or sea
You have with you my heart.
Tho' days for me are dull and drear
You need not have the slightest fear
For
When you come home on leave
I'll still be waiting
Waiting to greet you with a smile
To charm away your pain

And make you feel again
That life is going to be worthwhile.
I love you so my heart is simply yearning
And this is what I want you to believe
That tho' sorrows there may be
There'll be one glad day for me   .
On the day you come home on leave.

I dream of you the whole night through
I think of you all day
I'm weary for the sight of you
You've been so long away.
The weeks for me are very sad
And happy days are few
Remember when you're feeling bad
That I am lonely too.
But as I gaze across the sea
I know that you'll return to me
And
When you come home on leave . . . etc.

At the bottom of the manuscript Noël had scribbled, "Good old pot-boiling words, but what of it?"

In the event, it *didn't* take London by storm. Nor did he make a lot of money out of it, since it was never published. Ivor Novello's "Keep the Home Fires Burning" (1914) was all the British public seemed to need to see them through World War I.

•

"The Theatre must be treated with respect. It is a house of strange enchantment, a temple of dreams."

But of all the forms of literary expression he attempted, the play was always the thing. In his notebooks the first references are dated 1915, but 1918 was the vintage year for the young playwright.

"I conceived a passably good plot for a play, and as, in those days, conception was only removed from achievement by the actual time required for putting the words on paper, it was completed inside a week."

The play was *The Last Trick,* "a melodrama in four acts. The first and second acts were quite amusing, the third act good, and the last act weak and amateurish. The plot hinged on the 'revenge' motif and wasn't particularly original, but the dialogue was effective, and showed a marked improvement on my other work."

In the same year he wrote "two bad plays"—*The Impossible Wife* and *The Unattainable,* a play significant not only for the fact that it introduced the name Elvira but because it gave us embryo-Coward epigrams:

SHE: Man always sighs after the unattainable.
HE: What about Woman?
SHE: Oh, Woman never admits even to herself that anything *is* unattainable.

Quite apart from the modern woman, the modern novel caught the youthful Coward eye . . .

MRS. ASTON-HOOPER: I get so tired of the usual modern novels. They nearly always end with the hero having been married forty years to the heroine, gazing down the vista of his life and saying, "I wonder," until a dotted line cuts his rather aimless musings short.

A later scene anticipates *The Vortex* crossed with *Private Lives.* The date on the handwritten transcript is May 15, 1918 . . .

THE UNATTAINABLE

MRS. HOUGHTON-NALGRILL: I rather agree with Elvira—it must be a wonderful sensation.
MAJOR CARRINGTON: Damned unhealthy form of amusement, I call it.
MRS. HOUGHTON-NALGRILL: One wouldn't expect a man like you to be in the least interested in drug taking, dear Major—it naturally appeals to the more degenerate natures.
NORMAN CRAST: I should love to try it.
LADY CARRINGTON: My dear boy, your panting efforts to be decadent are almost pathetic . . . you're foolish to endeavour to follow in the footsteps of your ancestors. In so many cases it's much more commendable to live down tradition than live up to it.
ALICE POTTINGE: Poor Norman, you're always snubbing him, Lady Carrington.
LADY CARRINGTON: I feel it my duty, being his only living aunt.
IRENE COURTE: I should love to smoke just one little pipe of opium to see what happens.
KAY SAVILLE: You'd probably be able to obtain the same result by crossing the Channel on a rough day.
IRENE COURTE: Oh, how disgusting. But I'm really a splendid sailor.
MRS. HOUGHTON-NALGRILL: I thought you said you'd never been further than Ryde?

CHAPTER TWO
THE 1920s

Were we happy in the Twenties? On the whole I think that most of us were but we tried to hide it by appearing to be as blasé, world-weary and "jagged with sophistication" as we possibly could. Naturally, we had a lot of fun in the process.

—NOËL IN A LETTER TO BEVERLEY NICHOLS (1957)

"As we stroll down Picc-Piccadilly / In the bright morning air, / All the girls turn and stare." Noël and Gertie Lawrence as The Red Peppers in "Men About Town" (*Tonight at 8:30*, 1936).

Cocktails and laughter
But what comes after?
Nobody knows.

—"POOR LITTLE RICH GIRL" (1925)

ONE THING that made him happy as the decade began was his first acquaintance with the United States. It was, indeed, a whole New World to be conquered, and he had not the slightest doubt that, one way or another, he would do so.

Of all the things that delighted him on the first poverty-stricken visit to New York in the summer of 1921, the most delightful was his instant and lasting friendship with Alfred Lunt and Lynn Fontanne, two other actors beginning to make their name on Broadway and living in extremely close proximity in a West Side boardinghouse.

> We projected ourselves into future eminence. We discussed, the three of us, over delicatessen potato salad and dill pickles, our most secret dreams of success. Lynn and Alfred were to be married. That was the first plan. They were to become definitely idols of the public. That was the second plan. Then, all of this being successfully accomplished, they were to act exclusively together. This was the third plan. It remained for me to supply the fourth, which was that when all three of us had become stars of sufficient magnitude to be able to count upon an individual following of each other, then, poised serenely upon that enviable plane of achievement, we would meet and act triumphantly together.

Which, of course, is precisely what they did in the 1933 *Design for Living,* which Noël wrote specifically for the three of them.

•

Broadway in the early 1920s was a revelation . . . He wrote to Violet . . .

> The theatre here is something to wonder at . . . The *speed*! Everybody seems to say their lines at such a rate you'd think you wouldn't understand a word—but you do! And then it suddenly struck me—

that's the way people actually *talk*. Wait till I get back to Shaftesbury Avenue!!

I remembered the beauty of New York at night, viewed not from a smart penthouse on Park Avenue, but from a crowded seat in Washington Square. And it seemed, in spite of its hardness and irritating, noisy efficiency, a great and exciting place.

It was the start of a lifelong love affair—and down payment on what was to be his second emotional "home."
Thirty years later he would reflect . . .

"I LIKE AMERICA"

I don't care for China,
Japan's far too small,
I've rumbled the Rio Grande,
I hate Asia Minor,
I can't bear Bengal
And I shudder to think
Of the awful stink
On the road to Samarkand.

The heat and smell
Must be sheer hell
On the road to Samarkand.

I like America,
I have played around
Every slappy-happy hunting ground
But I find America—okay.
I've been about a bit
But I must admit
That I didn't know the half of it
Till I hit the U.S.A.
No likely lass
In Boston, Mass.
From passion will recoil.
In Dallas, Tex.
They talk of sex
But only think of oil.

New Jersey dames
Go up in flames
If someone mentions—bed.
In Chicago, Illinois
Any girl who meets a boy
Giggles and shoots him dead!
But I like America
Its Society
Offers infinite variety
And come what may
I shall return someday
To the good old U.S.A.

I've loathed every acre
From Cannes to Canton,
I also deplore Bombay,
I've jeered at Jamaica
And seen through Ceylon,
And exploded the myth
Of those Flying Fith
On the Road to Mandalay.

We'll never mith
Those blasted fith
On the Road to Mandalay.

But I like America,
I have travelled far
From Northumberland to Zanzibar
And I find America—okay.
I've roamed the Spanish Main
Eaten sugar-cane
But I never tasted cellophane
Till I struck the U.S.A.
All delegates
From Southern States
Are nervy and distraught.
In New Orleans
The wrought-iron screens
Are dreadfully overwrought.
Beneath each tree in Tennessee
Erotic books are read.
And when alligators thud
Through the Mississippi mud

Sex rears its ugly head.
But—I like America,
Every scrap of it,
All the sentimental crap of it
And come what may
Give me a holiday
In the good old U.S.A.

—ACE OF CLUBS (1950)

The lot of the young actor was to take engagements when and where he could . . . and that inevitably meant touring the English provinces, where in those far-off days every town had at least one theatre. You crisscrossed the country endlessly in the hope that someone influential would spot your blazing talent and take you to the West End—so that you wouldn't *have* to tour the provinces.

Noël looked back in nostalgia, from the safety of a London theatrical foothold . . .

"TOURING DAYS" (1923)

GIRL: I've often wondered if it's possible to recapture
       The magic of bygone days.
       I feel one couldn't quite resuscitate
       All the rapture and joy of a youthful phase.
       But still, it's nice to remember
       The things we used to do.
BOY: When you were on tour with me, my dear,
       And I was on tour with you.
BOTH: Touring days, touring days,
       What ages it seems to be.
GIRL: Since the landlady at Norwich
       Served a mouse up in the porridge.
BOY: And a beetle in the morning tea.
BOTH: Touring days, alluring days,
       Far back into the past we gaze.
GIRL: We used to tip the dressers every Friday night.
BOY: And pass it over lightly when they came in tight.
BOTH: But somehow to us it seemed all right,
       Those wonderful touring days.

•

In "Red Peppers"—one of the ten one-act plays in *Tonight at 8:30* (1936)—he re-creates a typical music-hall act of the period.

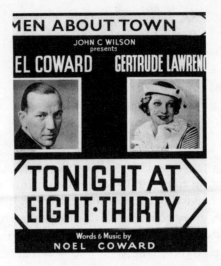

George and Lily Pepper have been touring the provincial halls using an act devised by George's father and mother and reeking with mothballs even then. Every year they drop further down the bill.

"RED PEPPERS"
AN INTERLUDE WITH MUSIC

"Red Peppers" was produced in London at the Phoenix Theatre on January 9, 1936, with the following

CAST

GEORGE PEPPER	MR. NOËL COWARD
LILY PEPPER	MISS GERTRUDE LAWRENCE
BERT BENTLEY	MR. ANTHONY PELISSIER
MR. EDWARDS	MR. ALAN WEBB
MABEL GRACE	MISS ALISON LEGGATT
ALF	MR. KENNETH CARTEN

The action of the play takes place on the stage, a dressing room and the stage again of the Palace of Varieties in one of the smaller English provincial towns.

TIME: Saturday night, the present day.

GEORGE and *LILY PEPPER* are a singing and dancing comedy act. They are both somewhere in their thirties. They have been married for many years and in the Profession since they were children. Their act consists of a "Man About Town" Dude number for which they wear smooth red wigs, tails, silk hats and canes, and a "Sailor" number for which they wear curly red wigs, sailor clothes with exaggerated bell-bottomed trousers and carry telescopes. They are first discovered performing "in one" before a back-cloth on which is painted an ordinary street scene.

"HAS ANYBODY SEEN OUR SHIP?"

VERSE 1

What shall we do with the drunken sailor?
So the saying goes.
We're not tight but we're none too bright
Great Scott! I don't suppose!
We've lost our way
And we've lost our pay,
And to make the thing complete,
We've been and gone and lost the bloomin' fleet!

REFRAIN 1

Has anybody seen our ship?
The HMS *Peculiar.*
We've been on shore
For a month or more,
And when we see the Captain we shall get "what for."
Heave ho, me hearties,
Sing Glory Hallelujah,
A lady bold as she could be
Pinched our whistles at "The Golden Key."
Now we're in between the devil and the deep blue sea
Has anybody seen our ship?

Ad-lib from orchestra.

GEORGE (*singing*): La la la la—la la la la—
LILY: Here, what are you singing about?
GEORGE: What am I singing about?
LILY: Yes, what are you singing about?
GEORGE: What's the matter with my singing?
LILY: What isn't the matter with it!

GEORGE: Don't you think I could ever do anything with my voice?

LILY: Well, it might be useful in case of fire!

GEORGE: Oi! Skip it.

LILY: Who was that lady I saw you walking down the street with the other morning?

GEORGE: That wasn't a lady, that was my wife!

LILY: Keep it clean. Keep it fresh. Keep it fragrant!

GEORGE: Was that your dog I saw you with in the High Street?

LILY: Yes, that was my dog.

GEORGE: What's his name?

LILY: Fruit Salts.

GEORGE: Fruit Salts?

LILY: Yes, Fruit Salts.

GEORGE: Why?

LILY: Ask him—Eno's.

GEORGE: Keep it clean. Keep it fresh. Keep it fragrant!

BOTH: La la la la—la la la la.

GEORGE: Why did you leave school?

LILY: Appendicitis.

GEORGE: Appendicitis?

LILY: Yes, appendicitis.

GEORGE: What do you mean, appendicitis?

LILY: Couldn't spell it!

GEORGE: I heard you had adenoids.

LILY: Adenoids?

GEORGE: Yes, adenoids.

LILY: Don't speak of it.

GEORGE: Why not?

LILY: Adenoids me!

GEORGE: Oi! Skip it! Skip it!

BOTH: La la la la—la la la la.

GEORGE: I saw a very strange thing the other day.

LILY: What was it?

GEORGE: Twelve men standing under one umbrella and they didn't get wet.

LILY: How's that?

GEORGE: It wasn't raining! (Wait for it—wait for it.)

LILY: Do you know what a skeleton is?

GEORGE: Do I know what a skeleton is?

LILY: Do you know what a skeleton is?

GEORGE: Yes.

LILY: Well, what is it?

GEORGE: A lot of bones with the people scraped off!

LILY: Keep it clean. Keep it fresh. Keep it fragrant.

GEORGE: Why is twelve midnight like the roof of a house?

LILY: Why is twelve midnight like the roof of a house?

GEORGE: Yes, why is twelve midnight like the roof of a house?

LILY: S'late!

BOTH: La la la la—la la la la.

LILY: Where did you go last night?

GEORGE: The cemetery.

LILY: Anyone dead?

GEORGE: All of 'em.

LILY: Are we going fishing?

GEORGE: Yes, we're going fishing.

LILY: We're not taking the dog with us, are we?

GEORGE: Of course we're taking the dog with us.

LILY: Why?

GEORGE: He's got the worms!

REFRAIN 2

Has anybody seen our ship?
The HMS *Disgusting.*
We've three guns aft
And another one fore
And they've promised us a funnel for the next world war.
Heave ho, me hearties,
The quarter-deck needs dusting.
We had a binge last Christmas year,
Nice plum puddings and a round of beer,
But the Captain pulled his cracker and we cried 'Oh
   dear!
Has anybody seen our ship?'

REFRAIN 3

Has anybody seen our ship?
The HMS *Suggestive.*
She sailed away
Across the bay,
And we haven't had a smell of her since New Year's Day.
Heave ho, me hearties,
We're getting rather restive,
We pooled our money, spent the lot,
The world forgetting by the world forgot.

Now we haven't got a penny for the you know what!
Has anybody seen our ship?

VERSE 2 (IF NECESSARY)

What's to be done with the girls on shore
Who lead our tars astray?
What's to be done with the drinks galore
That make them pass away?
We got wet ears
From our first five beers—
After that we lost control,
And now we find we're up the blinking pole!

Their exit consists of a neat walk off together, one behind the other, with their telescopes under their arms. Unfortunately, in the course of this snappy finale, LILY, who is behind GEORGE, drops her telescope and hurriedly retrieves it, thereby ruining the whole effect. GEORGE shoots her a look of fury and mutters something to her out of the corner of his mouth. The curtain falls and they take a call before it breathless and smiling, but with a certain quality of foreboding behind their smiles.

The curtain rises on the interior of their dressing room. It is a fairly squalid room, for although they are comparatively well known in the provinces, they have never, to date, achieved the dignity of the star dressing room or the pride of topping the bill. The room is three sides of a square. There is a wooden shelf all the way around it, above it, mirrors and lights at set intervals.

Downstage on the right there is a door leading to the passage. Downstage on the left there is a lavatory basin with a screen around it. In the center is a wooden hanging arrangement for clothes.

GEORGE's dressing place is on the right and LILY's is on the left.

As the curtain rises on the scene they both enter in silence but wearing expressions of set rage. They are still breathless and extremely hot. GEORGE goes to his dressing place and LILY goes to hers. They both take off their wigs and fling them down, then, still in silence, they proceed to rip off their sailor clothes. These are made with zippers in order to facilitate their quick change. LILY is wearing a brassiere and silk knickers, and GEORGE a vest and drawers. They both have black shoes with taps on them and black socks and sock suspenders.

GEORGE: Now then.
LILY: Now then what?

GEORGE (*contemptuously*): Now then what!

LILY: I don't know what you're talking about.

GEORGE: Oh, you don't, don't you?

LILY: No I don't, so shut up.

GEORGE: I suppose you don't know you mucked up the whole exit!

LILY: It wasn't my fault.

GEORGE: Whose fault was it then, Mussolini's?

LILY (*with sarcasm*): Funny, hey?

GEORGE (*witheringly*): I suppose you didn't drop your prop, did you? And having dropped it, you didn't have to go back for it, leaving me to prance off all by meself—who d'you think you are, Rebla?

LILY: The exit was too quick.

GEORGE: It was the same as it's always been.

LILY: It was too quick, I tell you, it's been too quick the whole week, the whole number's too quick—

GEORGE: Bert Bentley takes that number at the same tempo as he's always done.

LILY: You and your Bert Bentley, just because he stands you a Welsh rarebit at the Queen's you think he's God Almighty.

GEORGE: Bert Bentley's the best conductor in the North of England and don't you make any mistake about it.

LILY: Best conductor my foot! I suppose he thinks it's funny to see us leaping up and down the stage like a couple of greyhounds.

GEORGE: If you're a greyhound I'm Fred Astaire.

LILY: Oh, you're Fred Astaire all right, with a bit of Pavlova thrown in—you're wonderful, you are—there's nothing you can't do, except behave like a gentleman.

GEORGE: Oh, so you expect me to behave like a gentleman, do you? That's a good one, coming from you.

LILY: Oh, shut up, you make me tired.

GEORGE: I make *you* tired! I suppose it was me that mucked up the exit—I suppose it was me that dropped me bloody telescope!

LILY (*heated*): Now look here, George Pepper—

GEORGE: Stop George Peppering me—why can't you admit it when you're in the wrong?—You mucked up the exit—nobody else did—you did!

LILY: Well, what if I did? It was an accident, wasn't it? I didn't do it on purpose.

GEORGE: It doesn't matter how you did it or why you did it, you did it.

LILY (*screaming*): All right, I did it!

GEORGE (*triumphantly*): Well, don't do it again.

There is a knock on the door.

LILY: Who is it?

ALF (*outside*): Me, Alf.

LILY: All right, come in.

ALF, the callboy, enters. He is laden with the *PEPPERS'* discarded evening suits, silk hats and canes. He plumps them down.

ALF: There!

GEORGE: Thanks. (*He gets some money out of his coat pocket.*) Here, tell Fred to pop out and get me twenty Player's and a large Guinness.

LILY: Why can't you wait and have it with your steak?

GEORGE: You mind yours and I'll mind mine.

ALF: You'll have to wait until Mabel Grace is finished.

LILY: She's been finished for years as far as I'm concerned.

GEORGE: What's the matter with Mabel Grace?

LILY: Ask the public, dear, just ask the public.

ALF (*about to leave*): Same as usual, I suppose, between the houses?

GEORGE: Yes, and tell 'em not to forget the salt, like they did last night.

ALF: Righto.

ALF goes out. *LILY* starts to pack various things into a large hamper which has emblazoned on it in large black letters: "The Red Peppers."

GEORGE: What did you want to say that about Mabel Grace for in front of him?

LILY (*grandly*): It happens to be my opinion.

GEORGE: Well, in future you'd better keep your opinions to yourself in front of strangers.

LILY (*mumbling*): If you're so fond of Mabel Grace I wonder you don't go and ask her for her autograph—she'd drop dead if you did—I bet nobody's asked her for one since *Trelawny of the Wells.*

GEORGE: Mabel Grace is an artist and don't you forget it—she may be a bit long in the tooth now but she's a bigger star than you'll ever be, so there!

LILY: You make me sick, sucking up to the topliners.

GEORGE: Who sucks up to the topliners?

LILY: You do—look at Irene Baker!

GEORGE: What's the matter with Irene Baker?

LILY: When last heard from she was falling down drunk at the Empire, Hartlepool.

GEORGE: That's a dirty lie, Irene never touches a drop till after the show and well you know it.

LILY (*contemptuously*): Irene! It was Miss Baker this and Miss Baker that, the last time you saw her.

GEORGE: That's all you know.

LILY: Trying to make me think you got off with her, eh? What a chance!

GEORGE: Oh, shut up nagging!

LILY (*muttering*): Irene—!

GEORGE: If a day ever dawns when you can time your laugh like Irene Baker does, I'll give you a nice red apple!

LILY: Time my laughs! That's funny. Fat lot of laughs I get when you write the gags.

GEORGE (*grandly*): If you're dissatisfied with your material you know what you can do with it.

LILY: I know what I'd like to do with it.

GEORGE: You can't even do a straight walk off without balling it up.

LILY: Oh, we're back at that again, are we?

GEORGE: Yes we are, so there!

LILY (*coming over to him*): Now look here, just you listen to me for a minute . . .

GEORGE: I've been listening to you for fifteen years, one more minute won't hurt.

LILY: I've had about enough of this. I'm sick of you and the whole act. It's lousy, anyway.

GEORGE: The act was good enough for my mum and dad and it's good enough for you.

LILY (*with heavy sarcasm*): Times have changed a bit since your mum and dad's day, you know. There's electric light now and telephones and a little invention called Moving Pictures. Nobody wants to see the 'Red Peppers' for three bob when they can see Garbo for ninepence!

GEORGE: That's just where you're wrong, see! We're flesh and blood we are—the public would rather see flesh and blood any day than a cheesy photograph. Put Garbo on on a Saturday night in Devonport, and see what would happen to her!

LILY: Yes, look what happened to us!

GEORGE: That wasn't Devonport, it was Southsea.

LILY: Well, wherever it was, the Fleet was in.

GEORGE: If you think the act's so lousy it's a pity you don't rewrite some of it.

LILY: Ever tried going into St. Paul's and offering to rewrite the Bible?

GEORGE: Very funny! Oh, very funny indeed! You're wasted in the Show Business, you ought to write for *Comic Cuts* you ought.

LILY: At that I could think up better gags than you do—'That wasn't a lady, that was my wife!'—'D'you mind if I smoke?' 'I don't care if you burn!'—hoary old chestnuts—they were has-beens when your grandmother fell off the high wire.

GEORGE: What's my grandmother got to do with it?

LILY: She didn't fall soon enough, that's all.

GEORGE (*furiously*): You shut your mouth and stop hurling insults at my family. What were you when I married you, I should like to know! One of the six Moonlight Maids—dainty songs and dances, and no bookings!

LILY (*hotly*): When we did get bookings we got number one towns which is more than your mum and dad ever did!

GEORGE: Who wants the number one towns, anyway? You can't get a public all the year round like my mum and dad by doing a parasol dance twice a year at the Hippodrome Manchester!

LILY: The Moonlight Maids was just as good an act as the "Red Peppers" any day, and a bloody sight more refined at that!

GEORGE: You've said it. That's just what it was—refined. It was so refined it simpered itself out of the bill—

LILY: A bit of refinement wouldn't do you any harm—

GEORGE: Perhaps you'd like to change the act to "Musical Moments" with me playing a flute and you sitting under a standard lamp with a 'cello?

There is a knock at the door.

LILY: Who is it?

BERT (*outside*): Me—Bert Bentley.

GEORGE: Come in, old man.

LILY (*under her breath*): Old man—

BERT BENTLEY enters. He is the musical director, a flashy little man wearing a tail suit and a white waistcoat that is none too clean.

BERT (*cheerfully*): Well, well, well, how's tricks?

GEORGE: Mustn't grumble.

BERT: Anybody got a Gold Flake?

GEORGE: Here's a Player's, that do?

BERT (*taking one*): It's your last?

GEORGE: I've sent Fred out for some more.

BERT: Okay—thanks.

GEORGE: Sketch on?

BERT: Yes, the old cow's tearing herself to shreds.

GEORGE: It's a pretty strong situation she's got in that sketch—I watched it from the side first house on Wednesday—

BERT: She nearly got the bird second house.

LILY: Too refined, I expect. For this date.

BERT: Well, they're liable to get a bit restless, you know, when she stabs herself—she takes such a hell of a time about it—that's legits all over—

we had Robert Haversham here a couple of months ago—what a make-up—stuck together with stamp paper he was—Robert Haversham the famous tragedian and company! You should have seen the company: a couple of old tats got up as Elizabethan pages with him doing a death scene in the middle of them—he died all right.

GEORGE: Did he buy it?

BERT: He bought it—three and eightpence in coppers and a bottle of Kola.

LILY: Poor old man, what a shame!

BERT: Well, what did he want to do it for? That sort of stuff's no good. They're all alike—a few seasons in the West End and they think they're set.

LILY: Lot of hooligans birding the poor old man.

BERT (*with slight asperity*): This is as good a date as you can get, you know!

LILY: I've played better.

GEORGE: Oh, dry up, Lil, for heaven's sake! (*To* BERT.) Sorry I can't offer you a drink, old man, Fred hasn't brought it yet.

BERT: That's all right, George—I'll have one with you in between the houses. By the way, don't you think that exit of yours is dragging a bit?

LILY (*explosively*): Dragging?

GEORGE: Lil thinks it was a bit too quick.

BERT: Whatever you say, it's all the same to me.

GEORGE: Maybe you could pep it up a little.

LILY: Maybe it would be better if we did the whole act on skates!

GEORGE (*conciliatorily*): Bert's quite right, you know, Lil.

LILY: I don't know any such thing.

BERT: All right, all right, all right—there's no need to get nasty.

GEORGE: Oh, don't take any notice of her, she don't know what she's talking about.

LILY (*with overpowering sweetness*): My husband's quite right, Mr. Bentley, my husband is always quite right. You don't have to pay any attention to me, I don't count—I'm only a feed.

GEORGE: Oh, dry up.

LILY (*continuing*): But I should just like to say one thing, Mr. Bentley, if you'll forgive me for stepping out of my place for a minute, and that is, that if you take that exit any quicker at the second house, I shall not drop my telescope—Oh no—I shall sock you in the chops with it!

BERT: Who the hell d'you think you are, talking to me like that!

GEORGE: You ought to be ashamed of yourself.

LILY: You and your orchestra—orchestra! More like a hurdy-gurdy and flat at that!

BERT: What's wrong with my orchestra?

LILY: Nothing, apart from the instruments and the men what play 'em.

BERT: My orchestra's played for the best artists in the business—

LILY: Yes, but not until they were too old to care.

BERT: I didn't come up here to be insulted by a cheap little comedy act.

GEORGE (*incensed*): What's that! What's that? What's that?

BERT: You heard. You're damned lucky to get this date at all!

GEORGE: Lucky! My God, it's a fill-in—that's all—a fill-in!

BERT: I suppose Nervo and Knox use it as a fill-in, and Lily Morris and Flanagan and Allen?

LILY: They probably have friends living near.

BERT (*making a movement to go*): Before you start saucing me just take a look at your place on the bill—that's all—just take a look at it.

GEORGE: We're in the second half, anyway.

BERT: Only because the acrobats can't make their change.

LILY: It's in our contract—after the interval's in our contract.

BERT: Well, make the most of it while you've got it.

GEORGE: Get the hell out of here, you twopenny-halfpenny little squirt—lucky for you we've got another show to play.

BERT: Not so damned lucky—I've got to look at it.

LILY: Well, it'll be the first time—maybe we'll get the tempos right for a change!

BERT: You set your tempos Monday morning and they haven't been changed since.

LILY: That's your story, but don't forget you were sober on Monday morning.

BERT: Are you insinuating that I drink during the show?

LILY: Insinuating! That's a laugh. I'm not insinuating, I'm stating a fact. I can smell it a mile off.

BERT: What a lady! And what an artist, too—I don't suppose!

GEORGE: Don't you talk in that tone to my wife.

LILY: Send for the manager, George. Send for Mr. Edwards.

BERT: I'm the one that's going to send for Mr. Edwards—

GEORGE: Get out of here before I crack you one—

ALF knocks at the door.

LILY: Come in.

ALF pushes open the door with his foot and comes in carrying a tray on which are two plates of steak and chips with other plates over them to keep them hot, a bottle of A1 Sauce and three bottles of Guinness.

ALF: You're wanted, Mr. Bentley, the sketch is nearly over.

BERT (*grimly to the* PEPPERS): I'll be seeing you later.

He goes out, slamming the door after him.

GEORGE (*after him*): Lousy son of a—Lounge Lizard.
LILY (*to* ALF): Here, put it down on the hamper.
ALF (*doing so*): I've got the Player's in me pocket.
LILY (*feeling for them*): All right.
GEORGE: Come back later for the tray.
ALF: Righto.

He goes out.

GEORGE: Mr. Edwards—I'll have something to say to Mr. Edwards.
LILY: Lucky to play this date, are we? We'll see about that.
GEORGE: You were right, old girl.
LILY: What about—him?
GEORGE: Yes—dirty little rat.
LILY (*dragging up two chairs to the hamper*): Well, we all make mistakes
  sometimes—open the Guinness, there's a dear—
GEORGE: He's a little man, that's his trouble, never trust a man with short
  legs—brains too near their bottoms.
LILY: Come and sit down.
GEORGE (*opening a bottle of Guinness*): 'Alf a mo'—
LILY: That exit was too quick, you know!
GEORGE: All right—all right—

They both sit down and begin to eat.

GEORGE: They've forgotten the salt again—
LILY: No, here it is in a bit of paper—
GEORGE: Well, thank God for that anyway—

The lights fade on the scene.
  When the lights come up on the scene, *GEORGE* and *LILY* are sitting at
the dressing places freshening their makeup. They both have a glass of
Guinness within reach, and they are both wearing the rather frowsy dressing gowns that they had put on during the preceding scene. The tray, with
the remains of their dinner on it, is on the floor beside the hamper.
  GEORGE gets up, opens the door and listens.

LILY: What's on?
GEORGE: The Five Farthings.
LILY: That's the end of the first half—we'd better get a move on—
GEORGE (*returning to his place*): Fancy putting an act like that on at the end
  of the first half—you'd think they'd know better, wouldn't you?

LILY: I wouldn't think they'd know better about anything in this hole.
GEORGE: It's a badly run house and it always has been.

He proceeds to put on his dress shirt, collar and tie, which are all in one with a zipper up the back. *LILY* is doing the same on her side of the room. They stuff wads of Kleenex paper in between their collars and their necks to prevent the makeup soiling their ties.
There is a knock at the door.

LILY: Who is it?
MR. EDWARDS (*outside*): Mr. Edwards.
LILY (*pulling on her trousers*): Just a minute—
GEORGE (*under his breath*): Go easy—Bert Bentley's been at him.
LILY: I'll have something to say about that.
GEORGE: You leave it to me—I'll do the talking.
LILY: That'll be nice—Come in!

MR. EDWARDS enters. He is the house manager and very resplendent. He is smoking a large cigar.

GEORGE (*rising and offering him a chair*): Good evening, Mr. Edwards.
MR. EDWARDS (*disdaining it*): Good evening.
LILY (*amiably*): How's the house?
MR. EDWARDS: Same as usual—full.
GEORGE: That's fine, isn't it?
MR. EDWARDS (*grimly*): I watched your act tonight, first house.
GEORGE (*gaily*): There you are, Lil, what did I tell you—I had a sort of hunch you was out there—I said to my wife—what's the betting Mr. Edwards is out front?—you know—you have a sort of feeling—
LILY: Went well, didn't it?
MR. EDWARDS: I've seen things go better.
GEORGE: We follow Betley Delavine, you know—a ballad singer—they always take a bit of warming up after a ballad singer.
LILY: I'd defy Billy Bennett to get away with it in our place on the bill— I'd defy him—see?
MR. EDWARDS: There isn't anything wrong with your place on the bill.
GEORGE: Well, I'd be willing to make a little bet with you—put the Five Farthings on before us and change Betley Delavine to the end of the first half and see what happens!
LILY: You'd send them out to the bars and they'd stay there.
MR. EDWARDS: I did not come here to discuss the running of my theatre.
GEORGE: Oh—sorry, I'm sure.

MR. EDWARDS: That exit of yours killed the whole act.

GEORGE: A little mishap that's all—anybody might drop a telescope—

LILY: Even a sailor.

MR. EDWARDS: It looked terrible.

GEORGE: The tempo was all wrong, Mr. Edwards.

MR. EDWARDS: Sounded all right to me.

GEORGE: Maybe it did, but we know our own numbers, you know.

MR. EDWARDS: It didn't look like it from the front.

GEORGE: We've never had any trouble before—that exit's stopped the show in every town we've played.

LILY: A musical director can make or mar an act, you know—make or mar it.

MR. EDWARDS: Mr. Bentley is one of the finest musical directors in the business.

LILY: Then he's wasted here, that's all I can say.

GEORGE (warningly): Lily!

LILY: Well, if he's so wonderful, why isn't he at the Albert Hall—doing Hiawatha—

MR. EDWARDS: I understand you had words with Mr. Bentley.

GEORGE: We did, and we will again if he starts any of his funny business.

MR. EDWARDS: I understand that you accused him of drinking during the show.

LILY: Getting quite bright, aren't you?

GEORGE: Shut up, Lil, leave this to me.

MR. EDWARDS: Did you or did you not?

GEORGE: Look here, who d'you think you are—coming talking to us like this?

MR. EDWARDS: Did you or did you not accuse Mr. Bentley of drinking during the show?

LILY (heatedly): Yes, we did, because he does, so there!

MR. EDWARDS: That's serious, you know—it's slander!

LILY: I don't care if it's arson, it's true!

MR. EDWARDS: Now look here, Mrs. Pepper, I think it only fair to warn you—

LILY: And I think it's only fair to warn you that unless you get a better staff in this theatre and a better orchestra and a better musical director, you'll find yourself a cinema inside six months!

MR. EDWARDS: You won't gain anything by losing your temper.

GEORGE: And you won't gain anything by coming round backstage and throwing your weight about—your place is in the front of the house— my theatre this and my theatre that—it's no more your theatre than what it is ours—you're on a salary same as us, and I'll bet it's a damn sight less, too, and don't you forget it—

MR. EDWARDS (*losing his temper*): I'm not going to stand any more of this—

LILY: Oh, go and play with yourself and shut up—

MR. EDWARDS: I'll guarantee one thing, anyhow, you'll never play this date again as long as I'm in charge—

GEORGE: In charge of what, the Fire Brigade!

LILY: Play this date—anybody'd think it was the Palladium to hear you talk—

GEORGE: You'd better be careful, Mr. Edwards—you don't want a scandal like this to get round the profession—

MR. EDWARDS: What are you talking about?

GEORGE: I'm talking about the way this house is run.

MR. EDWARDS (*working up*): You mind your own business.

LILY: More than one act's been mucked up here, you know, by that orchestra of yours—it's beginning to get a name—

MR. EDWARDS: Oh, it is, is it?

GEORGE: They're all over the shop—no discipline.

LILY: What can you expect with a drunk in charge of it!

MR. EDWARDS (*raising his voice*): Look here—you stop talking like that or it'll be the worse for you.

GEORGE: His tempos are wrong and he hasn't got any authority over his men—

LILY: This date's only a fill-in for us, you know—

GEORGE: You ask our agents.

MR. EDWARDS: I shall report this conversation.

LILY: Do—report it to the Lord Mayor—if you're sober enough to remember the lyrics.

GEORGE: Shut up, Lil.

MR. EDWARDS: I will not stay here and argue—

GEORGE: You're dead right, you won't—

MR. EDWARDS: You were a flop last time you played here and you've been a flop this time and that's enough for me—

LILY (*screaming*): Flop! What d'you mean flop! We're a bigger draw than anybody on the bill—

There is a knock on the door.

GEORGE (*loudly*): Come in—

MISS MABEL GRACE enters. She is a faded ex–West End actress wearing a towel round her head to keep her hair in place, and an elaborate dressing gown.

MABEL GRACE (*acidly*): Good evening—I'm sorry to intrude—but you're making such a dreadful noise I'm quite unable to rest—

MR. EDWARDS: I'm very sorry, Miss Grace—

MABEL GRACE: I find it hard enough to play a big emotional scene twice a night in any case—

LILY: Oh, that's an emotional scene, is it? I wondered what it was—

MABEL GRACE: I am not accustomed to being spoken to in that tone, Mrs. Whatever your name is—

LILY: Pepper's the name—Pepper—P E P P E R—same as what you put in your soup.

MABEL GRACE (*coldly*): Very interesting.

MR. EDWARDS: I apologise, Miss Grace.

MABEL GRACE (*grandly*): Thank you, Mr. Edwards.

GEORGE (*in an affected voice*): What you must think of us, Miss Grace—so common—we're mortified, we are really—and you fresh from His Majesty's.

LILY: Fairly fresh.

MABEL GRACE: Mr. Edwards, I'm really not used to dressing-room brawls—I'll leave it to you to see that there is no further noise—

LILY: Except for the raspberries at the end of your sketch—even Mr. God Almighty Edwards can't control those—

MABEL GRACE: You're almost as vulgar off the stage as you are on, I congratulate you.

LILY (*very loudly*): Vulgar, are we! I'd like to ask you something. If you're so bloody West End why the hell did you leave it?

GEORGE: There'll be an answer to that in next Sunday's edition.

LILY: Thank you, George.

MR. EDWARDS: Look here, you two, I've had about enough of this—

GEORGE: You've had about enough, have you? What about us?

The conversation becomes simultaneous.

LILY: You and your cigar and your shirtfront and your Woolworth studs! Alfred Butt with knobs on—

GEORGE: You get out of here, you fat fool, before I throw you out!—

MABEL GRACE: Thank you for your courtesy, Mr. Edwards—

MR. EDWARDS: I'll see you don't play this date anymore or any other date either—

GEORGE: Oh, put it where the monkey put the nuts—

LILY:—Play this date again—thank you for the rabbit—I'd sooner play Ryde Pier in November—

In the middle of the pandemonium ALF puts his head around the door.

ALF (*yelling*): Red Peppers—three minutes—
GEORGE: Good God! We're off—
LILY (*wildly*): Get out, all of you—get out—

GEORGE takes MR. EDWARDS by the shoulders, and shoves him out of the room. MABEL GRACE, laughing affectedly, follows him.

LILY and GEORGE put on their wigs, powder their makeup, tweak their ties into place, grab their hats and canes—then, muttering curses under their breath, they collect their sailor clothes and sailor wigs and telescopes and rush out of the room as the lights fade.

The lights come up on the curtain as the orchestra is playing their introduction music. The curtain rises on the street scene again. They make their entrance for the Dude number, "Men About Town."

ROUTINE

"MEN ABOUT TOWN"

VERSE

We're two chaps who
Find it thrilling
To do the killing
We're always willing
To give the girls a treat.
Just a drink at the Ritz
Call it double or quits
Then we feel the world is at our feet.
Top hats white spats
Look divine on us,
There's a shine on us
Get a line on us
When we come your way.
Gad! Eleven o'clock!
Let's pop into the Troc:
Ere we start the business of the day.

REFRAIN 1

As we stroll down Picc—Piccadilly
In the bright morning air,
All the girls turn and stare

We're so nonchalant and frightfully debonair.
When we chat to Rose, Maud or Lily
You should see the way their boyfriends frown,
For they know without a doubt
That their luck's right out,
Up against a couple of men about town.

REFRAIN 2

As we stroll down Picc—Piccadilly
All the girls say "Who's here?
Put your hat straight, my dear,
For it's Marmaduke and Percy Vere de Vere."
As we doff hats, each pretty filly
Gives a wink at us and then looks down
For they long with all their might
For a red-hot night
When they see a couple of men about town.

They proceed to execute a complicated tap dance, during which BERT BENTLEY vengefully takes the music faster and faster. They try vainly to keep up with it, finally GEORGE slips and falls, whereupon LILY loses her temper and flings her hat at BERT BENTLEY.

LILY (*screaming*): You great drunken fool!

THE CURTAIN FALLS AMID DISCORD.

Noël allowed fellow Brit, Lynn Fontanne, to read the script before its production, and she wrote, " 'Red Peppers' is very fine and very funny. Their utter third-ratedness is so awfully pathetic. You know exactly why (aside from the pitiful business of their act) they have never been and never could be successful."

A few short years later television presumably brought down the curtain on George and Lily. Or perhaps it gave them a new lease of third-rate life . . .

When all else failed, they might even have tried their luck on the Continent, like Georgie Banks & His Six Bombshells.

(And if you feel you detect a few autobiographical Coward stories in the story . . .)

"ME AND THE GIRLS"

Tuesday

I like looking at mountains because they keep changing, if you know what I mean; not only the colours change at different times of the day but the shapes seem to alter too. I see them first when I wake up in the morning and Sister Dominique pulls up the blind. She's a dear old camp and makes clicking noises with her teeth. The blind rattles up and there they are— the mountains I mean. There was fresh snow on them this morning, that is on the highest peaks, and they looked very near in the clear air, blue and pink as if someone had painted them, rather like those pictures you see in frame shops in the King's Road, bright and a bit common but pretty.

Today was the day when they all came in: Dr. Pierre and Sister Françoise and the other professor with the blue chin and a gleam in his eye, quite a dish really he is, hairy wrists but lovely long slim hands. He was the one who actually did the operation. I could go for him in a big way if I was well enough, but I'm not and that's that, nor am I likely to be for a long time. It's going to be a slow business. Dr. Pierre explained it carefully and very very gently, not at all like his usual manner which is apt to be a bit offish. While I was listening to him I looked at the professor's face: he was staring out at the mountains and I thought he looked sad. Sister Françoise and Sister Dominique stood quite still except that Sister Françoise was fiddling with her rosary. I got the message all right but I didn't let on that I did. They think I'm going to die and as they've had a good dekko inside me and I haven't, they probably know. I've thought of all this before of course before the operation, actually long before when I was in the other hospital. I don't know yet how I feel about it quite, but then I've had a bit of a bashing about and I'm tired. It's not going to matter to anyone but me anyway and I suppose when it does happen I shan't care, what with being dopey and one thing and another. The girls will be sorry, especially Mavis, but she'll get over it. Ronnie will have a crying jag and get pissed and wish he'd been a bit nicer, but that won't last long either. I know him too well. Poor old Ron. I expect there were faults on both sides, there always are, but he was a little shit and no two ways about it. Still I brought it all on myself so I mustn't complain. It all seems far away now anyhow. Nothing seems very near except the mountains and they look as if they wanted to move into the room.

When they had all filed out and left me alone Sister D. came back because she'd forgotten my temperature chart and wanted to fill it in or something, at least that was what she said, but she didn't fool me: what she really came back for was to see if I was all right. She did a lot of teeth clicking and fussed about with my pillows and when she'd finally buggered off

I gave way a bit and had a good cry, then I dropped off and had a snooze and woke up feeling quite spry. Maybe the whole thing's in my imagination anyhow. You never know really do you?—I mean when you're weak and kind of low generally you have all sorts of thoughts that you wouldn't have if you were up and about. All the same there *was* something in the way Dr. Pierre talked. The professor squeezed my hand when he left and smiled but his eyes still looked sad. It must be funny to be a doctor and always be coping with ill people and cheering them up even if you have to tell them a few lies while you're at it. Not that he said much. He just stood there most of the time like I said, looking at the mountains.

This is quite a nice room as hospital rooms go. There is a chintzy armchair for visitors and the walls are off-white so as not to be too glarey. Rather like the flat in the rue Brochet which Ronnie and I did over just after we'd first met. If you mix a tiny bit of pink with the white it takes the coldness out of it but you have to be careful that it doesn't go streaky. I can hardly believe that all that was only three years ago, it seems like a lifetime.

All the girls sent me flowers except Mavis and she sent me a bottle of Mitsouko toilet water which is better than flowers really because it lasts longer and it's nice to dab on at night when you wake up feeling hot and sweaty. She said she'd pop in and see me this afternoon just for a few minutes to tell me how the act's getting on. I expect it's a bit of a shambles really without me there to bound on and off and keep it on the tracks. They've had to change the running order. Mavis does her single now right after the parasol dance so as to give the others time to get into their kimonos for the Japanese number. I must remember to ask her about Sally. She was overdue when I left and that's ten days ago. She's a silly little cow that girl if ever there was one, always getting carried away and losing her head. A couple of drinks and she's gone. Well if she's clicked again she'll just have to get on with it and maybe it'll teach her to be more careful in the future. Anyway Mavis will know what to do, Mavis always knows what to do except when she gets what she calls "emotionally disturbed," then she's hell. She ought to get out of the act and marry somebody and settle down and have children, she's still pretty but it won't last and she'll never be a star if she lives to be a hundred, she just hasn't got that extra something. Her dancing's okay and she can put over a number all right but that dear little *je ne sais quoi* just isn't there poor bitch and it's no good pretending it is. I know it's me that stands in her way up to a point but I can't do anything about it. She knows all about me. I've explained everything until I'm blue in the face but it doesn't make any difference. She's got this "thing" about me not really being queer but only having caught it like a bad habit. Would you mind! Of course I should never have gone to bed with her in the first place. That sparked off the whole business. Poor old Mavis. These girls really do drive me round the bend sometimes. I will say one thing though, they *do* behave like ladies, outwardly at least. I've never let them get off a plane or a train without lipstick and the proper clothes and shoes. None of those ponytails and tatty slacks for George Banks Esq.: not on your Nelly. My girls have got to look dignified whether they like it or not. To do them justice they generally do. There have been one or two slip-ups like that awful Maureen. She was a slut from the word go. I was forever after her about one thing or another. She always tried to dodge shaving under the arms because some silly bitch had told her that the men liked it. Imagine! I told her that that lark went out when the Moulin Rouge first opened in eighteen-whatever it was but as she'd never heard of the Moulin Rouge anyway it didn't make much impression on her. This lot are very good on the whole. Apart from Mavis there's Sally, blond and rather bouncy; Irma, skin a bit sluggish but comes up a treat under the lights; Lily-May, the best dancer of the lot but calves a bit on the heavy side; and Beryl and Sylvia Martin. They're our twins and they're planning to work up a sister act later on. They're both quite pretty but that ole deb-bil talent has failed to touch either of them with his fairy wings so I shouldn't think the sister act will get much further than the Poland Rehearsal Rooms. The whole show closes here next Saturday week then God knows what will happen. I wrote off to Ted before my operation telling him that the act would have to be disbanded and asking him what he could do for them, but you know what agents are, all talk and no do as a rule. Still he's not a bad little sod taken by and large so we shall see.

Wednesday

Mavis came yesterday as promised. I didn't feel up to talking for long but I did my best. She started off all right, a bit overcheerful and taking the "Don't worry everything's going to be all right" line, but I could see she was in a bit of a state and trying not to show it. I don't know if she'd been talking to any of the Sisters or whether they'd told her anything or not. I don't suppose they did, and her French isn't very good anyhow. She said the act was going as well as could be expected and that Monsieur Philippe had come backstage last night and been quite nice. She also asked if I'd like her to write to Ronnie and tell him about me being ill but I jumped on that double-quick pronto. It's awful when women get too understanding. I don't want her writing to Ronnie any more than I want Ronnie writing to me. He's got his ghastly Algerian *and* the flat so he can bloody well get on with it. I don't mind anymore anyway. I did at first, of course, I couldn't help myself, it wasn't the Algerian so much, it was all the lies and scenes. Fortunately I was rehearsing all through that month and had a lot to keep my mind occupied. It was bad I must admit but not so bad that it couldn't have been worse. No more being in love for me thank you very

much. Not I expect that I shall have much chance. But if I do get out of
this place all alive-o there's going to be no more of that caper. I've had it,
once and for all. Sex is all very well in its way and I'm all for it but the next
time I begin to feel that old black magic that I know so well I'll streak off
like a bloody greyhound.

When Mavis had gone Sister Clothilde brought me my tea. Sister
Clothilde's usually on in the afternoons. She's small and tubby and has a
bit of a guttural accent having been born in Alsace-Lorraine; she also has
bright, bright red cheeks which look as if someone had pinched them hard
just before she came into the room. She must have been quite pretty in a
dumpy way when she was a girl before she took the veil or whatever it is
you have to take before you give yourself to Jesus. She has quite a knowing
look in her eye too as though she wasn't quite so far away from the wicked
world as she pretended to be. She brought me a madeleine with my tea but
it was a bit dry. When she'd gone and I'd had the tea and half the
madeleine I settled back against the pillows and relaxed. It's surprising
what funny things pop into your mind when you're lying snug in bed and
feeling a bit drowsy. I started to try to remember everything I could from
the very beginning like playing a game, but I couldn't keep dead on the
beam: I'd suddenly jump from something that happened fifteen years ago
to something that happened two weeks back. That was when the pain had
begun to get pretty bad and Monsieur Philippe came into the dressing
room with Dr. Pierre and there was I writhing about with nothing but a
jockstrap on and sweating like a pig. That wasn't so good that bit because
I didn't know what was going to happen to me and I felt frightened. I
don't feel frightened now, just a bit numb as though some part of me was
hypnotized. I suppose that's the result of having had the operation. My
inside must be a bit startled at all that's gone on and I expect the shock has
made my mind tired. When I try to think clearly and remember things I
don't seem able to hold on to any subject for long. The thing is to give up
to the tiredness and not worry. They're all very kind, the Sisters and the
doctors, even the maid who does the room every morning gives me a
cheery smile as if she wanted to let me know she was on my side. She's a
swarthy type with rather projecting eyes like a pug. I bet she'll finish up as
a concierge with those regulation black stockings and a market basket.
There's a male orderly who pops in and out from time to time and very
sprightly he is too, you'd think he was about to take off any minute. He's
the one who shaved me before the operation and that was a carry-on if ever
there was one. I wasn't in any pain because they'd given me an injection
but woozy as I was I managed to make a few jokes. When he pushed my
old man aside almost caressingly with his hand I said "*Pas ce soir Josephine,
demain peut-être*" and he giggled. It can't be much fun being an orderly in a
hospital and have to shave people's privates and give them enemas and sit

them on bedpans from morning till night, but I suppose they must find it interesting otherwise they'd choose some other profession. When he'd finished he gave my packet a friendly little pat and said, "*Vive le sport.*" *Would you mind!* Now whenever he comes in he winks at me as though we shared a secret and I have a sort of feeling he's dead right. I suppose if I didn't feel so weak and seedy I'd encourage him a bit just for the hell of it. Perhaps when I'm a little stronger I'll ask him to give me a massage or something just to see what happens—as if I didn't know! On the other hand of course if what I suspect is true, I shan't get strong again so the question won't come up. Actually he reminds me a bit of Peter when we first met at Miss Llewellyn's Dancing Academy, stocky and fair with short legs and a high colour. Peter was the one that did the Pas de Deux from *Giselle* with Coralie Hancock and dropped her on her head during one of the lifts and she had concussion and had to go to St. George's Hospital. It's strange to think of those early days. I can see myself now getting off the bus at Marble Arch with my ballet shoes in that tatty old bag of Aunt Isobel's. I had to walk down Edgware Road and then turn to the left and the dancing academy was down some steps under a public house called the Swan. There was a mirror all along the one wall with a barre in front of it and Miss Adler used to thump away at the upright while we did our bends and kicks and positions. Miss Llewellyn was a character and no mistake. She had frizzed-up hair, very black at the parting; a heavy stage makeup with a beauty spot under her left eye if you please and a black velvet band around her neck. She always wore this rain or shine. Peter said it was to hide the scar where someone had tried to cut her throat. She wasn't a bad old tart really and she did get me my first job in a Christmas play called *Mr. Birdie.* I did an audition for it at the Garrick Theatre. Lots of other kids had been sent for and there we were all huddled at the side of the stage in practice clothes waiting to be called out. When my turn came I pranced on followed by Miss Adler, who made a beeline for the piano, which sounded as if someone had dropped a lot of tin ashtrays inside it, you know, one of those diabolical old uprights that you only get at auditions. Anyhow I sang "I Hear You Calling Me"—it was before the poor darlings dropped so I was still a soprano—and then I did the standard sailor's hornpipe as taught at the academy, a lot of hopping about and hauling at imaginary ropes and finishing with a few quick turns and a leap off. Mr. Alec Sanderson, who was producing *Mr. Birdie,* then sent for me to go and speak to him in the stalls. Miss Adler came with me and he told me I could play the heroine's little brother in the first act, a gnome in the second and a frog in the third, and that he'd arrange the business side with Miss Llewellyn. Miss Adler and I fairly flew out into Charing Cross Road and on wings of song to Lyons' Corner House where she stood me tea and we had an éclair each. I really can't think about *Mr. Birdie* without laughing and when I laugh it hurts my stitches. It really was a fair bugger, whimsical as all get-out. Mr. Birdie, played by Mr. Sanderson himself, was a lovable old professor who suddenly inherited a family of merry little kiddos of which I was one. We were all jolly and ever so mischievous in act one and then we all went to sleep in a magic garden and became elves and gnomes and what have you for acts two and three. Some of us have remained fairies to this day. The music was by Oliver Bakewell, a ripsnorting old queen who used to pinch our bottoms when we were standing round the piano learning his gruesome little songs. Years later when I knew what was what I reminded him of this and he whinnied like a horse.

Those were the days all right, days of glory for child actors. I think the boys had a better time than the girls on account of not being so well protected. I shall never forget those jovial wet-handed clergymen queuing up outside the stage door to take us out to tea and stroke our knees under the table. Bobby Clews and I used to have bets as to how much we could get without going too far. I once got a box of Fuller's soft-centers and a gramophone record of *Casse Noisette* for no more than a quick grope in a taxi. After my voice broke I got pleurisy and a touch of TB and had to be sent to a sanatorium near Buxton. I was cured and sent home to Auntie Iso after six months but it gave me a fright I can tell you. I was miserable for the first few weeks and cried my eyes out, but I got used to it and quite enjoyed the last part when I was moved into a small room at the top of the house with a boy called Digby Lawson. He was two years older than me, round about seventeen and a half. He died a short time later and I really wasn't surprised. It's a miracle that I'm alive to tell the tale, but I must say we had a lot of laughs.

It wasn't until I was nineteen that I got into the chorus at the Palladium and that's where I really learnt my job. I was there two and a half years in all and during the second year I was given the understudy of Jackie Foal. He was a sensational dancer and I've never worked so hard in my life. I only went on for him three times but one of the times was for a whole week and it was a thrill I can tell you when I got over the panic. One night I got round Mr. Lewis to let me have two house seats for Aunt Iso and Emma, who's her sort of maid-companion, and they dressed themselves up to the nines and had a ball. Emma wore her best black with a bead necklace she borrowed from Clara two doors down and Auntie Iso looked as though she were ready for tiara night at the opera: a full evening dress made of crimson taffeta with a sort of lace overskirt of the same colour; a dramatic headdress that looked like a coronet with pince-nez attached and the Chinese coat Uncle Fred had brought her years ago when he was in the merchant navy. I took them both out to supper afterward at Giovanni's in Greek Street. He runs the restaurant with a boy friend of his, a sulky-looking little sod as a rule but he played up that night and both he and

Giovanni laid on the full VIP treatment, cocktails on the house, a bunch of flowers for the old girls and a lot of hand kissing. It all knocked me back a few quid but it was worth it to see how they enjoyed themselves. They both got a bit pissed on Chianti and Emma laughed so much that her upper plate fell into the zabaglione and she had to fish it out with a spoon. Actually it wasn't long after that that Auntie Iso died and Emma went off to live with her sister in Lowestoft. I hated it when Auntie Iso died and even now after all these years it still upsets me to think of it. After all she was all I'd got in the way of relations and she'd brought me up and looked after me ever since I was five. After she'd gone I shared a flat with Bunny Granger for a bit in Longacre which was better than nothing but I'd rather have been on my own. Bunny was all right in his way; he came to the funeral with me and did his best to cheer me up but he didn't stay the course very long really if you know what I mean and that flat was a shambles, it really was. Nobody minds fun and games within reason but you can have too much of a good thing. There was hardly a night he didn't bring someone or other home and one night if you please I nipped out of my room to go to the bathroom which was up one flight and there was a policeman scuffling back into his uniform. I nearly had a fit but actually he turned out to be quite nice. Anyway I didn't stay with Bunny long because I met Harry and that was that. Harry was the first time it ever happened to me seriously. Of course I'd hopped in and out of bed with people every now and again and never thought about it much one way or another. I never was one to go off into a great production about being queer and work myself up into a state like some people I know. I can't think why they waste their time. I mean it just doesn't make sense does it? You're born either hetero, bi or homo and whichever way it goes there you are stuck with it. Mind you people are getting a good deal more hep about it than they used to be but the laws still exist that make it a crime and poor bastards still get hauled off to the clink just for doing what comes naturally as the song says. Of course this is what upsets some of the old magistrates more than anything, the fact that it *is* as natural as any other way of having sex, leaving aside the strange ones who get excited over old boots or used knickers or having themselves walloped with straps. Even so I don't see that it's anybody's business but your own what you do with your old man providing that you don't make a beeline for the dear little kiddies, not, I am here to tell you, that quite a lot of the aforesaid dear little kiddies don't enjoy it tiptop. I was one myself and I know. But I digress as the bride said when she got up in the middle of her honeymoon night and baked a cake. That's what I mean really about the brain not hanging on to one thing when you're tired. It keeps wandering off. I was trying to put down about Harry and what I felt about it and got sidetracked. All right—all right—let's concentrate on Harry-boy and remember what he looked like and not only what he looked like, but him, him himself. To begin with he was inclined to be moody and when we first moved into the maisonette in Swiss Cottage together he was always fussing about whether Mrs. Fingal suspected anything or not, but as I kept explaining to him, Mrs. Fingal wouldn't have minded if we poked Chinese mice providing that we paid the rent regularly and didn't make a noise after twelve o'clock at night. As a matter of fact she was quite a nice old bag and I don't think nor ever did think that she suspected for a moment, she bloody well knew. I don't mean to say that she thought about it much or went on about it to herself. She just accepted the situation and minded her own business and if a few more people I know had as much sense the world would be a far happier place. Anyway, Harry-boy got over being worried about her or about himself and about us after a few months and we settled down, loved each other good and true for two and a half years until the accident happened and he was killed. I'm not going to think about that because even now it still makes me feel sick and want to cry my heart out. I always hated that fucking motorbike anyhow but he was mad for it, forever tinkering with it and rubbing it down with oily rags and fiddling about with its engine. But that was part of his character really. He loved machinery and engineering and football matches and all the things I didn't give a bugger about. We hadn't a thing in common actually except the one thing you can't explain. He wasn't even all that good-looking now I come to think of it. His eyes were nice but his face wasn't anything out of the ordinary: his body was wonderful, a bit thick-set but he was very proud of it and never stopped doing exercises and keeping himself fit. He never cared what the maisonette looked like and once when I'd bought a whole new set of loose covers for the divan and the two armchairs, he never even noticed until I pointed them out to him. He used to laugh at me too and send me up rotten when I fussed about the place and tried to keep things tidy. But he loved me. That's the shining thing I like to remember. He loved me more than anyone has ever loved me before or since. He used to have affairs with girls every now and again, just to keep his hand in, as he used to say. I got upset about this at first and made a few scenes but he wouldn't stand for any of that nonsense and let me know it in no uncertain terms. He loved me true did Harry-boy and I loved him true, and if the happiness we gave each other was wicked and wrong in the eyes of the Law and the Church and God Almighty, then the Law and the Church and God Almighty can go dig a hole and fall down it.

Thursday

I had a bad night and at about two in the morning Sister Jeanne-Marie gave me a pill and I got off to sleep all right and didn't wake until seven. I couldn't see the mountains at all because the clouds had come down and wiped them away. My friend the orderly came in at eight o'clock and gave me an enema on account of I hadn't been since the day before yesterday and then only a few goat's balls. He was very cheery and kiss-me-arse and kept on saying "*Soyez courageux*" and "*Tenez-le*" until I could have throttled him. After it was all over he gave me a bath and soaped me and then, when he was drying me, I suddenly felt sort of weak and despairing and burst into tears. He at once stopped being happy-chappy and good-time-Charlie and put both his arms round me tight. He'd taken his white coat off to bath me and he had a stringy kind of vest and I could feel the hairs on his chest against my face while he held me. Presently he sat down on the loo seat and took me on to his lap as though I were a child. I went on crying for a bit and he let me get on with it without saying a word or trying to cheer me up. He just patted me occasionally with the hand that wasn't holding me and kept quite still. After a while the tears stopped and I got hold of myself. He dabbed my face gently with a damp towel, slipped me into my pyjama jacket, carried me along the passage and put me back into bed. It was already made, cool and fresh and the flowers the girls had sent me had been brought back in their vases and put about the room. I leant back against the pillows and closed my eyes because I was feeling fairly whacked, what with the enema and the crying jag and one thing and another. When I opened them he had gone.

I dozed on and off most of the morning and in the afternoon Sally came to see me. She brought me last week's *Tatler* and this week's *Paris Match,* which was full of Brigitte Bardot as usual. If you ask me, what that poor girl needs is less publicity and more discipline. Sally was wearing her beige two-piece with a camp little red hat. She looked very pretty and was in high spirits having come on after all nearly ten days late. She said the Hungarian had come to the show the night before and given her a bottle of Bellodgia. I asked her if she'd been to bed with him again and she giggled and said, "Of course not, for obvious reasons." Then I asked her if she really had a "thing" about him and she giggled some more and said that in a way she had because he was so aristocratic and had lovely muscular legs but that it wasn't serious and that anyhow he was going back to his wife in Vienna. She said he went into quite an act about this and swore that she would be forever in his heart but that she didn't believe a word of it. I told her that she'd better be more careful in the future and see to it that another time she got more out of a love affair than a near miss and a bottle of Bellodgia. She's a nice enough kid really, our Sally, but she just doesn't think or reason things out. I asked her what she was going to do when the act folds on Saturday week and she said she wasn't sure but that she'd put a phone call through to London to a friend of hers who thinks he can get some modeling for her, to fill in for the time being. She said that all the girls sent me their love and that one or other of them was coming to see me every day, but Mavis had told them not more than one at a time and not to stay long at that. Good old Mavis. Bossy to the last.

Sally had brought me a packet of mentholated filter-tip cigarettes and when she'd gone I smoked one just for a treat and it made me quite dizzy because I've not been smoking at all for the last few days, I somehow didn't feel like it. During the dizziness the late afternoon sun came out and suddenly there were the mountains again, wobbling a bit but as good as new. I suppose I've always had a "thing" about mountains ever since I first saw any, which was a great many too many years ago as the crow flies and I'd just got my first "girl" act together and we had a booking on the ever so gay continent. Actually it was in Zurich in a scruffy little dive called Die Kleine Maus or something. There were only four girls and me and we shared a second-class compartment on the night train from Paris. I remember we all got nicely thank you on a bottle of red wine I bought at the station buffet and when we woke up from our communal coma in the early hours of the morning there were the mountains with the first glow of sunrise on them and everyone did a lot of oohing and aahing and I felt as though suddenly something wonderful had happened to me. We all took it in turns to dart down the corridor to the lav and when we'd furbished ourselves up and I'd shaved and the girls had put some slap on, we staggered along to the restaurant car and had large bowls of coffee and croissants with butter and jam. The mountains were brighter then, parading past the wide windows and covered in snow and I wished we weren't going to a large city but could stay off for a few days and wander about and look at the waterfalls. However we *did* go to a large city and when we got there we laid a great big gorgeous egg and nobody came to see us after the first performance. It was a dank little room we had to perform in with a stage at one end, then a lot of tables and then a bar with a looking glass behind it so we could see our reflections, which wasn't any too encouraging I can tell you. A handful of square-looking Swiss gentlemen used to sit at the tables with their girlfriends and they were so busy doing footy-footy and gropey-gropey that they never paid any attention to us at all. One night we finished the Punch and Judy number without a hand except from one oaf in the corner on the right, and he was only calling the waiter. There were generally a few poufs clustered round the bar hissing at each other like snakes, apart from them that was it. The manager came round after the third performance and told us we'd have to finish at the end of the week. He was lovely he was, bright red in the face and shaped like a pear. I had a grand upper and downer with him because we'd been engaged on a two weeks' contract. His English wasn't up to much and in those days I couldn't speak a word of German or French so the scene didn't exactly flow. There was a lot of arm waving and banging on the dressing table and the girls sat round giggling, but I finally made him agree to pay us half our next week's salary as compensation. The next morning I had another upper and downer with Monsieur Huber, who was the man who had booked the act through Ted Bentley, my agent in London. Monsieur Huber was small and sharp as a needle with a slight cast in his eye like Norma Shearer only not so pretty. As a matter of fact he wasn't so bad. At least he took our part and called up the red pear and there was a lot of palaver in Switzer-Deutsch which to my mind is not a pretty language at all and sounds as if you'd got a nasty bit of phlegm in your throat and were trying to get rid of it. At any rate the upshot of the whole business was that he, Monsieur Huber, finally got us another booking in a small casino on the Swiss side of Lake Lugano and we all drove there in a bus on the Sunday and opened on the Monday night without a band call or even a dress rehearsal. I can't truthfully say that we tore the place up but we didn't do badly, anyway we stayed there for the two weeks we'd been booked for. We lived in a pension, if you'll excuse the expression, up a steep hill at the back of the town which was run by a false blond Italian lady who looked like an all-in wrestler in drag. She wasn't a bad sort and we weren't worried by the other boarders on account of there weren't any. The girls shared two rooms on the first floor and I had a sort of attic at the top like *La Bohème,* which had a view, between two houses, of the lake and the mountains. I used to watch them, the mountains, sticking up out of the mist in the early mornings, rather like these I'm looking at now. Madame Corelli, the all-in wrestler, took quite a fancy to us and came to see the show several times with her lover, who was a friend of the man who ran the casino. I wish you could have seen the lover. He was thick and short and bald as a coot and liked wearing very tight trousers to prove he had an enormous packet which indeed he had: it looked like an entire Rockingham tea service, milk jug and all. His name was Guido Mezzoni and he could speak a little English because he'd been a waiter in Soho in the dear dead days before the War. He asked us all to his place one night after the show and put on a chef's hat and made spaghetti Bolognese and we all got high as kites on vino rosso and a good time was had by *tutti* until just before we were about to leave when he takes Babs Mortimer, our youngest, into the bathroom, where she wanted to go and instead of leaving her alone to have her Jimmy Riddle in peace and quiet, he whisked her inside, locked the door and showed her all he'd got. Of course the silly little cow lost her head and screamed bloody murder whereupon Madame Corelli went charging down the passage baying like a bloodhound. That was a nice ending to a jolly evening I must say. Nice clean fun and no questions asked. You've never heard such a carry-on. After a lot of banging on the bathroom door and screaming he finally opened it and Babs came flying into the room in hysterics and I had to give her a sharp slap in the face to quiet her, meanwhile the noise from the passage sounded as though the Mau Maus had got in. We all had another swig all round at the vino while the battle was going on and I couldn't make up my mind whether to grab all the girls and bugger off home or wait and see what happened, then I remembered that Madame Corelli had the front-door key anyhow so there wouldn't be much point in going back and just sitting on the curb. Presently the row subsided a bit and poor old Guido came back into the room looking very hangdog with a nasty red scratch all down one side of his face. Madame followed him wearing what they call in novels a "set expression" which means that her mouth was in a straight line and her eyes looked like black beads. We all stood about and looked at each other for a minute or two because nobody could think of anything to say. Finally Madame hissed something to Guido in Italian and he went up miserably to Babs and said, "I am sawry, so sawry and I wish beg your pardon." Babs shot me a look and I nodded irritably and she said "Granted I'm sure" in a very grand voice and minced over to look out of the window which was fairly silly because it looked out on a warehouse and it was pitch dark anyway. Madame Corelli then took charge of the situation. Her English wasn't any too hot at the best of times and now that she was in the grip of strong emotion it was more dodgy than ever, however she made a long speech most of which I couldn't understand a word of, and gave me the key of the front door, from which I gathered that she was going to stay with Guido and that we were expected to get the hell out and leave them to it. I took the key, thanked Guido for the evening and off we went. It was a long drag up the hill and there was no taxi in sight at that time of the morning so we had to hoof it. When we got to the house the dawn was coming up over the lake. I stopped to look at it for a moment, the air was fresh and cool and behind the mountains the sky was pale green and pink and yellow like a Neapolitan ice, but the girls were grumbling about being tired and their feet hurting so we all went in and went to bed.

The next day I had a little set-to with Babs because I thought it was necessary. I took her down to a café on the lakefront and gave her an iced coffee and explained a few of the facts of life to her. Among other things I told her that you can't go through life shrieking and making scenes just because somebody makes a pass at you. There are always ways of getting out of a situation like that without going off into the second act of *Tosca*. In any case Guido hadn't really made a pass at her at all, he was obviously the type who's overproud of his great big gorgeous how-do-you-do and can't resist showing it to people. If he'd grabbed her and tried to rape her it would have been different, but all the poor little sod wanted was a little honest appreciation and probably if she'd just said something ordinary like "Fancy" or "What a whopper!" he wouldn't have wanted to go any further and all would have ended happily. She listened to me rather sullenly and mumbled something about it having been a shock and that she wasn't used to that sort of thing having been brought up like a lady, to which I replied that having been brought up like a lady was no help in cabaret and that if she was all that refined she shouldn't have shoved her delicate nose into show business in the first place. Really these girls make me tired sometimes. They prance about in bikinis showing practically all they've got and then get hoity-toity when anyone makes a little pounce. What's so silly about it really is that that very thing is what they want more than anything only they won't admit it. Anyway she had another iced coffee and got off her high horse and confessed, to my great relief, that she wasn't a virgin and had had several love affairs only none of them had led to anything. I told her that it was lucky for her that they hadn't and that if at any time she got herself into trouble of any sort that she was to come straight to me. After that little fireside chat we became quite good friends and when she left the act, which was about three months later, I missed her a lot. She finally got into the chorus of a musical at the Coliseum and then got married. I sometimes get a postcard from her but not very often. She must be quite middle-aged now. Good old Babs.

The other three were not so pretty as Babs but they danced better. Moira Finch was the eldest, about twenty-six, then there were Doreen March and Elsie Pendleton. Moira was tall and dark with nice legs and no tits to speak of. Doreen was mousy, mouse-coloured hair, mouse-coloured eyes and a mouse-coloured character, she also had a squeaky voice just to make the whole thing flawless. I must say one thing for her though, she *could* dance. Her kicks were wonderful, straight up with both legs and no faking and her turns were quick as lightning. Elsie was the sexiest of the bunch, rather pallid and languorous with the sort of skin that takes makeup a treat and looks terrible without it. They were none of them very interesting really, but they were my first lot and I can remember them kindly on the whole. We were together on and off for nearly a year and played different dance halls and casinos all over Italy, Spain, Switzerland and France. I learnt a lot during that tour and managed to pick up enough of the various languages to make myself understood. Nothing much happened over and above a few rows. Elsie got herself pregnant in Lyons, where we were appearing in a sort of nightclub-cum-knocking-shop called Le Perroquet Vert. A lot of moaning and wailing went on but fortunately the old tart who ran the joint knew a character who could do the old crochet hook routine and so she and I took Elsie along to see him and waited in a sitting room with a large chandelier, a table with a knitted peacock blue cloth on it and a clanking old clock on the mantelpiece set between two pink china swans, the neck of one of them was broken and the head had been stuck on again crooked. After quite a long while during which Violette Whatever-her-name-was told me a long saga about how she'd first been seduced at the age of thirteen by an uncle by marriage, Elsie came back with the doctor. He was a nasty piece of work if ever I saw one. He wore a greasy alpaca jacket with suspicious-looking stains on it and his eyes seemed to be struggling to get at each other over one of the biggest bonks since Cyrano de Bergerac. Anyway I paid him what he wanted, which was a bloody sight more than I could afford, and we took Elsie back to the hotel in a taxi and put her to bed. She looked pale and a bit tearful but I suppose that was only to be expected. Violette said she'd better not dance that night so as to give her inside time to settle down after having been prodded about and so I had to cut the pony quartet which couldn't be done as a trio and sing "The Darktown Strutters' Ball" with a faked-up dance routine that I invented as I went along. Nobody seemed to care anyway.

When we finally got back to London I broke up the act and shopped around to see if I could get a job on my own. I had one or two chorus offers but I turned them down. A small part, yes, even if it was only a few lines, but not the chorus again. I had a long talk with Ted Bentley and he advised me to scratch another act together, this time with better material. I must say he really did his best to help and we finally fetched up with quite a production. There was a lot of argle-bargle about how the act should be billed and we finally decided on "Georgie Banks and His Six Bombshells." Finding the six bombshells wasn't quite so easy. We auditioned hundreds of girls of all sorts and kinds until at long last we settled on what we thought were the best six with an extra one as a standby. In all fairness I must admit they were a bright little lot, all good dancers and pretty snappy to look at. Avice Bennet was the eldest, about twenty-seven with enormous blue eyes and a treacherous little gold filling which only showed when she laughed. Then there was Sue Mortlock, the sort of bouncy little blonde that the tired businessmen are supposed to go for. Jill Kenny came next on the scroll of honor, she was a real smasher, Irish with black hair and violet blue eyes and a temper of a fiend. Ivy Baker was a red-head just for those who like that sort of thing, she ponged a bit when she got overheated like so many redheads do and I was always after her with the Odorono, but she was a good worker and her quick spins were sensational. Gloria Day was the languid, sensuous type, there always has to be one of those, big charlies and hair like kapok, but she could move when she had to. (Her real name was Betty Mott but her dear old whiteheaded mum who was an ex-Tiller girl thought Gloria Day would look better on the bills.) The last, but by no means the least, was Bonny Macintyre—if you please—she was the personality kid of the whole troupe, not exactly pretty but cute—God help us all—and so vivacious that you wanted to strangle her, however she was good for eccentric numbers and the audiences always liked her. The standby, Myrtle Kennedy, was a bit horsey to look at but thoroughly efficient and capable of going on for anyone which after all was what she was engaged for. This was the little lot that I traipsed around the great big glorious world with for several years on and off, four and a half to be exact. Oh dear! On looking back I can hardly believe it. I can hardly believe that *Io stesso—Io mismo—Je, moi-même, Il signore—El señor—*Monsieur George Banks Esq., lying here rotting in a hospital bed really went through all that I did go through with that merry little bunch of egomaniacs. I suppose I enjoyed quite a lot of it but I'm here to say I wouldn't take it on again, not for all the rice in Ram Singh's Indian restaurant in the Brompton Road.

Friday

The loveliest things happen to yours truly and no mistake. I'm starting a bedsore! Isn't that sweet? Dr. Pierre came in to see me this morning and Sister Dominique put some ointment and lint on my fanny and here I am sitting up on a hot little rubber ring and feeling I ought to bow to people like royalty.

There was quite a to-do in the middle of the night because somebody died in number eleven, which is two doors down the passage. I wouldn't have known anything about it except that I happened to be awake and having a cup of Ovaltine and heard a lot of murmuring and sobbing going on outside the door. It was an Italian man who died and the murmuring and sobbing was being done by his relatives. Latins aren't exactly tight-lipped when it comes to grief or pain are they? I mean they really let go and no holds barred. You've never heard such a commotion. It kind of depressed me all the same, not that it was all that sad. According to Sister Jeanne-Marie the man who died was very old indeed and a disagreeable old bastard into the bargain, but it started me off thinking about dying myself and wondering what it would feel like, if it feels like anything at all. Of course death's got to come sometime or other so it's no use getting morbid about it but I can't quite imagine not being here anymore. It's funny to think there's going to be a last time for everything: the last time I shall go to the loo, the last time I shall eat a four-minute egg, the last time I shall arrive in Paris in the early morning and see waiters in shirtsleeves setting up the tables outside cafés, the last time I shall ever feel anybody's arms round me. I suppose I can count myself lucky in a way not to have anybody too close to worry about. At least when it happens I shall be on my own with no red-eyed loved ones clustered round the bed and carrying on alarming. I sometimes wish I was deeply religious and could believe that the moment I conked out I should be whisked off to some lovely place where all the people I'd been fond of and who had died would be waiting for me, but as a matter of fact this sort of wishing doesn't last very long. I suppose I'd like to see Auntie Iso again and Harry-boy but I'm not dead sure. I've got sort of used to being without them and they might have changed or I might have changed and it wouldn't be the same. After all nothing stays the same in life does it? And I can't help feeling that it's a bit silly to expect that everything's going to be absolutely perfect in the after-life, always providing that there is such a thing. Some people of course are plumb certain of this and make their plans accordingly, but I haven't got any plans to make and I never have had for the matter of that, anyway not those sort of plans. Perhaps there is something lacking in me. Perhaps this is one of the reasons I've never quite made the grade, in my career I mean. Not that I've done badly, far from it. I've worked hard and had fun and enjoyed myself most of the time and you can't ask much more than that can you? But I never really got to the top and became a great big glam-orous star which after all is what I started out to be. I'm not such a clot as not to realize that I missed out somewhere along the line. Then comes the question of whether I should have had such a good time if I *had* pulled it off and been up there in lights. You never really know do you? And I'm buggered if I'm going to sit here on my rubber ring sobbing my heart out about what might have been. To hell with what might have been. What *has* been is quite enough for me, and what *will* be will have to be coped with when the time comes.

Another scrumptious thing happened to me today which was more upsetting than the bedsore and it was all Mavis's fault and if I had the strength I'd wallop the shit out of her. Just after I'd had my tea there was a knock on the door and in came Ronnie! He looked very pale and was wear-ing a new camel's-hair overcoat and needed a haircut. He stood still for a moment in the doorway and then came over and kissed me and I could tell from his breath that he'd had a snifter round the corner to fortify himself before coming in. He had a bunch of roses in his hand and the paper they were wrapped in looked crinkled and crushed as though he'd been holding them too tightly. I was so taken by surprise that I couldn't think of any-thing to say for a minute then I pulled myself together and told him to drag the chintz armchair nearer the bed and sit down. He did what I told him after laying the flowers down very carefully on the bed table as though they were breakable and said, in an uncertain voice, "Surprise—surprise!" I said "It certainly is" a little more sharply than I meant to and then sud-denly I felt as if I was going to cry, which was plain silly when you come to analyze it because I don't love him anymore, not really, anyhow not like I used to at first. Fortunately at this moment Sister Françoise came in and asked if Ronnie would like a cup of tea and when he said he didn't want anything at all thank you she frigged about with my pillows for a moment and then took the roses and went off to find a vase for them. This gave me time to get over being emotional and I was grateful for it I can tell you. I asked after the Algerian and Ronnie looked sheepish and said he wasn't with him anymore, then he told me about the flat and having to have the bathroom repainted because the steam from the geyser had made the walls peel. We went on talking about this and that and all the time the feeling of emptiness seemed to grow between us. I don't know if he felt this as strongly as I did, the words came tumbling out easily enough and he even told me a funny story that somebody had told him about a nun and a parrot and we both laughed. Then suddenly we both seemed to realize at the same moment that it wasn't any good going on like that. He stood up and I held out my arms to him and he buried his head on my chest and started to cry. He was clutching my left hand tightly so I stroked his hair with my right hand and cried too and hoped to Christ Sister Françoise wouldn't come flouncing in again with the roses. When we'd recovered from this little scene he blew his nose and went over to the window and there wasn't any more strain. He stayed over an hour and said he'd come and see me again next weekend. He couldn't make it before because he was starting rehearsals for a French TV show in which he had a small part of an English sailor. I told him he'd better have a haircut before he began squeezing himself into a Tiddley suit and he laughed and said he'd meant to have it done ages ago but somehow or other something always seemed to get in the way. He left at about five-thirty because he was going to have a drink with Mavis at the L'Éscale and then catch the seven forty-five back to Paris. When he'd gone I felt somehow more alone than I had felt before he came so I had another of Sally's mentholated cigarettes just to make me nonchalant but it didn't really. Him coming in like that so unexpectedly had given me a shock and it was no good pretending it hadn't. I wriggled myself into a more comfortable position on the rubber ring, looked out at the view and tried to get me and Ronnie and everything straight in my mind but it wasn't any use because suddenly seeing him again had started up a whole lot of feelings that I thought weren't there anymore. I cursed Mavis of course for being so bloody bossy and interfering and yet in a way I was glad she had been. The sly little bitch had kept her promise not to write to him but had telephoned instead. I suppose it was nice of her really considering that she'd been jealous as hell of him in the past and really hated his guts. You'd have thought that from her point of view it would have been better to let sleeping dogs lie. She obviously thought that deep down inside I wanted to see him in spite of the way I'd carried on about him and the Algerian and sworn I never wanted to clap eyes on him again. After all she *had* been with me all through the bad time and I *had* let my hair down and told her much more than I should have. I don't believe as a rule in taking women too much into your confidence about that sort of thing. It isn't exactly that they're not to be trusted but it's hard for them to understand really, however much they try, and it's more difficult still if they happen to have a "thing" about you into the bargain. I never pretended to be in love with Mavis. I went to bed with her every now and again mainly because she wanted me to and because it's always a good thing to lay one member of the troupe on account of it stops the others gabbing too much and sending you up rotten. I leant back against the pillows which had slipped down a bit like they always do and stared out across the lake at the evening light on the mountains and for the first time I found myself hating them and wishing they weren't there standing between me and Paris and the flat and Ronnie and the way I used to live when I was up and about. I pictured Mavis and Ronnie sitting at L'Éscale and discussing whether I was going to die or not and her asking him how he thought I looked and him asking her what the doctor had said and then of course I got myself as low as a snake's arse and started getting weepy again and wished to Christ I *could* die, nice and comfortably in my sleep, and have done with it.

I must have dropped off because the next thing I knew was Sister Françoise clattering in with my supper tray and the glow had gone from the fucking mountains and the lights were out on the other side of the lake and one more day was over.

Saturday

Georgie Banks and His Six Bombshells I am here to tell you began their merry career together by opening a brand-new nightspot in Montevideo which is in Uruguay or Paraguay or one of the guays and not very attractive whichever it is. The name of the joint was La Cumparsita and it smelt of fresh paint and piddle on account of the lavatories not working properly. We'd had one hell of a voyage tourist class in a so-called luxury liner which finished up in a blaze of misery with a jolly ship's concert in the first-class lounge. We did our act in its entirety with me flashing on and off every few minutes in my new silver lamé tail suit which split across the bottom in the middle of "Embraceable You." The girls were nervous and Jill Kenny caught her foot in the hem of her skirt in the Edwardian quartet and fell arse over apple cart into a tub of azaleas which the purser had been watering with his own fair hands for weeks. She let out a stream of four-letter words in a strong Irish brogue and the first-class passengers left in droves. The purser made a speech at the end thanking us all very much indeed but it didn't exactly ring with sincerity. Anyhow our opening at La Cumparsita went better and we got a rave notice in one local paper and a stinker in the other which sort of leveled things out. The Latin Americanos were very friendly on the whole if a bit lecherous and the girls had quite a struggle not to be laid every night rain or shine. Bonny Macintyre, vivacious to the last, was the first to get herself pregnant. This fascinating piece of news was broken to me two weeks after we'd left Montevideo and moved on to Buenos Aires. Fortunately I was able to get her fixed up all right but it took a few days to find the right doctor to do it and those few days were a proper nightmare. She never stopped weeping and wailing and saying it was all my fault for not seeing that she was sufficiently protected. *Would* you mind! When it was all over bar the shouting she got cuter than ever and a bit cocky into the bargain and I knew then and there that out of the whole lot our Bonny was the only one who was going to cause me the most trouble, and baby was I right! The others behaved fairly well taken by and large. Jill was a bit of a troublemaker and liable to get pissed unless carefully watched. Ivy Baker got herself into a brawl with one of the local tarts when we were working in the Casino at Viña del Mar. The tart accused her of giving the come-on to her boy friend and slapped her in the face in the ladies' john, but she got as good as she gave. Ivy wasn't a redhead for nothing. The manager came and complained to me but I told him to stuff it and the whole thing died away like a summer breeze.

On looking back on that first year with the bombshells I find it difficult to remember clearly, out of all the scenes and dramas and carry-ons, what happened where and who did what to who. It's all become a bit of a jumble in my mind like one of those montages you see in films when people jump from place to place very quickly and there are shots of pages flying off a calendar. This is not to be surprised at really because we did cover a lot of territory. It took us over seven months to squeeze Latin America dry and then we got a tour booked through Australia and New Zealand. By this time all the costumes looked as though we'd been to bed in them for years and so they had to be redone. We had a layoff for a week in Panama City and we shopped around for materials in the blazing heat and then went to work with our needles and thread. Avice was the best at this lark. I know I nearly went blind sewing sequins onto a velvet bodice for Sue Mortlock, who had to do a single while we were all changing for "The Darktown Strutters' Ball" which we had to do in homemade masks because there wasn't any time to black up.

The voyage from Panama City to Australia was wonderful. The ship was quite small, a sort of freighter, but we had nice cabins and the food wasn't bad. It was the first time we'd had a real rest for months and we stopped off at various islands in the South Seas and bathed in coral lagoons and got ourselves tanned to a crisp all except poor Ivy, who got blistered and had to be put to bed with poultices of soda-bicarb plastered all over her. She ran a temperature poor bitch and her skin peeled off her like tissue paper. All the girls behaved well nearly all the time and there were hardly any rows. There was a slight drama when Bonny was found naked in one of the lifeboats with the chief engineer. It would have been all right if it hadn't been the captain who found them. The captain was half-Norwegian and very religious and he sent for me to his cabin and thumped the table and said I ought to be ashamed of myself for traipsing round the world with a

lot of harlots. I explained as patiently as I could that my girls were not harlots but professional artistes and that in any case I was not responsible for
their private goings-on and, I added, that harlots were bloody well paid for
what they did in the hay whereas all Bonny got out of the chief engineer
was a native necklace made of red seeds and a couple of conch shells which
were too big to pack. After a while he calmed down and we had two beers
sitting side by side on his bunk. When he'd knocked back his second one
he rested his hand a little too casually on my thigh and I thought to myself
"'Allo 'allo! Religious or not religious we now know where we are!" From
then on we lived happily ever after as you might say. It all got a bit boring
but anything for a quiet life.

The Australian tour believe it or not was a wow particularly in Sydney,
where we were booked for four weeks and had to stay, by popular demand,
for another two. It was in Sydney that Gloria Day fell in love with a life-
guard she met on the beach, really in love too, not just an in and out and
thank you very much. I must say I saw her point because he had a body like
a Greek god. Unfortunately he also had a wife and two bouncing little kiddies tucked away somewhere in the bush and so there was no future in it
for poor Gloria, and when we went away finally there was a lot of wailing
and gnashing of teeth and threats of suicide. I gave her hell about this and
reeled off a lot of fancy phrases like life being the most precious gift and
time being a great healer, etc., etc., and by the time we'd got to Singapore,
which was our next date, she'd forgotten all about him and was working
herself up into a state about the ship's doctor who, apart from being an
alcoholic, was quite attractive in a battered sort of way.

It was on that particular hop that things came to a head between me and
Avice. We'd been in and out of bed together on and off for quite a long
while but more as a sort of convenience than anything else. Then suddenly
she took it into her head that I was the one great big gorgeous love of her
life and that she couldn't live without me and that when we got back home
to England we'd get married and have children and life would blossom
like a rose. Now all this was cock and I told her so. In the first place I had
explained, not in detail but generally, what I was really like and that
although I liked girls as girls and found them lovely to be with that they
didn't really send me physically, anyway not enough to think of hitching
myself up forever. Then of course there was a big dramatic scene during
which she trotted out all the old arguments about me not really being like
that at all and that once I'd persevered and got myself into the habit of
sleeping with her regularly that I'd never want to do the other thing again.
After that snappy little conversation I need hardly say that there was a
slight strain between us for the rest of the tour. Poor old Avice. I still hear
from her occasionally. She finally married an electrician and went to
Canada. She sent me a snapshot of herself and her family about a year ago.

I could hardly recognize her. She looked as though she'd been blown up with a bicycle pump.

After Singapore we played various joints in Burma and Siam and one in Sumatra which was a bugger. It was there that Myrtle Kennedy, the standby, got amoebic dysentery and had to be left behind in a Dutch hospital where she stayed for nearly four weeks. She ultimately rejoined us in Bombay looking very thin and more like a horse than ever.

Bonny Macintyre's big moment came in Calcutta. She'd been getting more and more cock-a-hoop and pleased with herself mainly I think because her balloon dance always went better than anything else. It was our one unfailing showstopper and even when there was hardly anyone in front she always got the biggest hand of the evening with it. In Calcutta she started ritzing the other girls and complaining about her hotel accommodation and asking for new dresses. She also had a brawl in the dressing room with Jill and bashed her on the head so hard with her hairbrush that the poor kid had concussion and had to miss two performances. This was when I stepped in and gave our Bonny a proper walloping. I usually don't approve of hitting women but this was one of those times when it had to be done. She shrieked bloody murder and all the waiters in the joint came crowding into the room to see what was going on. The next day all was calm again, or outwardly so at least. That night however when I arrived at the club in time to put my slap on I was met by Avice wearing her tragedy queen expression. She went off into a long rigmarole which I couldn't help feeling she was enjoying a good deal more than she pretended to. There was always a certain self-righteous streak in Avice. Anyway what had happened was that Bonny had bolted with a Parsee radio announcer who she'd been going with for the last ten days. She'd left me a nasty little note which she had put into Avice's box in the hotel explaining that she was never coming back again because I wasn't a gentleman and that she'd cabled home to her mother in High Wycombe to say she was going to be married. She didn't say where she and the Parsee had bolted to and so that was that. There wasn't really anything to be done. I knew she couldn't possibly leave India because I'd got her passport—one of the first rules of traveling around with a bunch of female artistes is to hang on to their passports—however, we were all due to leave India in a few weeks' time and I couldn't see myself setting off to search the entire bloody continent for Bonny Macintyre. Nor could I very well leave her behind. I was after all responsible for her. It was a fair bitch of a situation I can tell you. Anyhow there I was stuck with it and the first thing to do was to get the show reorganized for that night's performance. I sent Avice haring off to get Sue into the balloon dance dress; sent for the band leader to tell him we were altering the running order; told Myrtle to be ready to go on in all the concerted numbers. I then did a thing I never never do before a performance. I had myself a zonking great whiskey and soda and pranced out gallantly onto the dance floor ready to face with a stiff upper lip whatever further blows destiny had in store for me.

The next week was terrible. No word from Bonny and frantic cables arriving every day from her old mum. Avice I must say was a Rock of Gibraltar. She kept her head and came with me to the broadcasting station where we tried to trace the Parsee. We interviewed lots of little hairy men with green faces and high sibilant voices and finally discovered that Bonny's fiancé—to coin a phrase—had been given two weeks off to go up to the hills on account of he'd had a bad cough. Nobody seemed to know or care what part of the hills he'd gone to. We sat about for a further few days worrying ourselves silly and wondering what to do. Our closing date was drawing nearer and we had all been booked tourist class on the homeward-bound P&O. Finally, to cut a dull story short, our little roving will-o'-the-wisp returned to us with a bang. That is to say she burst into my room in the middle of the night and proceeded to have hysterics. All the other girls came flocking in to see what the fuss was about and stood around in their nightgowns and dressing gowns and pyjamas with grease on their faces looking like Christmas night in the whorehouse. I gave Bonny some Three Star Martell in a tooth glass which gave her hiccups but calmed her down a bit. Presently, when Jill had made her drink some water backward and we'd all thumped her on the back she managed to sob out the garbled story of her star-crossed romance, and it was good and star-crossed believe me. Apparently the Parsee had taken her in an old Ford convertible which broke down three times to visit his family, a happy little group consisting of about thirty souls in all, including goats, who lived in a small town seventy miles away. The house they lived in was not so much a house as a tenement and Bonny was forced to share a room with two of the Parsee's female cousins and a baby that was the teeniest bit spastic. She didn't seem to have exactly hit it off with the Parsee's dear old mother who snarled at her in Hindustani whenever she came within spitting distance. There was obviously no room for fun and games indoors so whatever sex they had had to take place on a bit of wasteland behind the railway station. She didn't enjoy any of this very much on account of being scared of snakes but being so near the railway station often *did* actually give her the idea of making a getaway. Finally after one of the usual cozy evenings *en famille* with Mum cursing away in one corner and the spastic baby having convulsions in the other, she managed to slip out of the house without her loved one noticing and run like a stag to the station. It was a dark night but she knew the way all right having been in that direction so frequently. After waiting four hours in a sort of shed a train arrived and she got onto it and here she was more dead than alive.

By the time she'd finished telling us all this the dawn had come up like thunder and she began to get hysterical again so Avice forced a couple of aspirins down her throat and put her to bed. Three days after this, having given our last triumphant performance to a quarter-full house, we set sail for England, home and what have you, and that was really the end of Georgie Banks and His Six Bombshells.

Sunday

It's Sunday and all the church bells are ringing and I wish they wouldn't because I had a bad night and feel a bit edgy and the noise is driving me crackers.

It wasn't a bad night from the pain point of view although I felt a little uncomfortable between two and three and Sister Clothilde came in and gave me an injection which was a new departure really because I usually get a pill. Anyway it sent me off to sleep all right but it wasn't really sleep exactly, more like a sort of trance. I wasn't quite off and I wasn't quite on if you know what I mean and every so often I'd wake up completely for a few minutes feeling like I'd had a bad dream and couldn't remember what it was. Then I'd float off again and all sorts of strange things came into my mind. I suppose it was thinking yesterday so much about me and the bombshells that I'd got myself kind of overexcited. I woke up at about eight-thirty with a hangover but I felt better when I'd had a cup of tea. The orderly came in and carried me to the bathroom and then brought me back and put me in the armchair with an eiderdown wrapped round me while the bed was being made and the room done. One of the nicest things about being ill is when you're put back into a freshly made bed and can lie back against cool pillows before they get hot and crumpled and start slipping. The orderly stayed and chatted with me for a bit. He's quite sweet really. He told me he'd got the afternoon and evening off and that a friend of his was arriving from Munich who was a swimming champion and had won a lot of cups. He said this friend was very "*costaud*" and had a wonderfully developed chest but his legs were on the short side. They were going to have dinner in a restaurant by the lake and then go to a movie. I wished him luck and winked at him and wished to God I was going with them.

Later. It's still Sunday but the bells have stopped ringing and it's started to rain. The professor with the blue chin came to see me after I'd had my afternoon snooze. He looked different from usual because he was wearing quite a snappy sports coat and gray flannel trousers. He told me he'd had lunch in a little restaurant in the country and had only just got back. I watched him looking at me carefully while he was talking to me as though he wanted to find out something. I told him about having had the injection and how it made me feel funny and he smiled and nodded and lit a cigarette. He then asked me whether I had any particular religion and

when I said I hadn't he laughed and said that he hadn't either but he supposed it was a good thing for some people who needed something to hang
on to. Then he asked me if I had ever talked to Father Lucien who was a
Catholic priest who was sort of attached to the *clinique*. I said he'd come in
to see me a couple of times and had been quite nice but that he gave me the
creeps. Then he laughed again and started wandering about the room sort
of absentmindedly as though he was thinking of something else, then he
came back, stubbed his cigarette out in the ashtray on my bed table and sat
down again, this time on the side of the bed. I moved my legs to give him
a bit more room. There was a fly buzzing about and a long way off one of
those bloody church bells started ringing again. I looked at him sitting
there so nonchalantly swinging his legs ever so little but frowning as
though something were puzzling him. He was a good-looking man all
right, somewhere between forty and fifty I should say, his figure was slim
and elegant and his face thin with a lot of lines on it and his dark hair had
gone gray at the side. I wondered if he had a nice sincere wife to go home
to in the evenings after a busy day cutting things out of people, or whether
he lived alone with a faithful retainer and a lot of medical books and kept
a tiny vivacious mistress in a flashy little apartment somewhere or other or
even whether he was queer as a coot and head over heels in love with a sun-
tanned ski instructor and spent madly healthy weekends with him in cozy
wooden chalets up in the mountains. He looked at me suddenly as though
he had a half guess at what I was thinking and I giggled. He smiled when
I giggled and very gently took my hand in his and gave it a squeeze, not in
the least a sexy squeeze but a sympathetic one and all at once I realized,
with a sudden sinking of the heart, what the whole production was in aid
of, why he had come in so casually to see me on a Sunday afternoon, why he
had been drifting about the room looking ill at ease and why he had asked
me about whether I was religious or not. It was because he knew that I was
never going to get well again and was trying to make up his mind whether
to let me know the worst or just let me go on from day to day hoping for
the best. I knew then, in a sort of panic, that I didn't want him to tell me
anything, not in so many words, because once he said them there I'd be
stuck with them in my mind and wake up in the night and remember
them. What I mean is that although I knew that I knew and had actually
known, on and off, for a long time, I didn't want it settled and signed and
sealed and done up, gift wrapped, with a bow on top. I still wanted not to
be quite sure so that I could get through the days without counting. That
was a bad moment all right, me lying there with him still holding my
hand and all those thoughts going through my head and trying to think of
a way to head him off. I knew that unless I did something quickly he'd
blurt it out that I'd be up shit creek without a paddle and with nothing to
hang on to and no hope left and so I did the brassiest thing I've ever done

in my life and I still blush when I think of it. I suddenly reared myself up on my pillows, pulled him toward me and gave him a smacking kiss. He jumped back as if he'd been shot. I've never seen anyone so surprised. Then before he could say anything, I went off into a long spiel—I was a bit hysterical by then and I can't remember exactly what I said—but it was all about me having a "thing" about him ever since I'd first seen him and that that was the way I was and there was nothing to be done about it and that as he was a doctor I hoped he would understand and not be too shocked and that anyway being as attractive as he was he had no right to squeeze people's hands when they were helpless in bed and not expect them to lose control and make a pounce at him and that I'd obeyed an impulse too strong to be resisted—yes I actually said that if you please—and that I hoped he would forgive me but that if he didn't he'd just have to get on with it. I said a lot more than this and it was all pretty garbled because I'd worked myself into a proper state, but that was the gist of it. He sat there quite still while I was carrying on, staring at me and biting his lip. I didn't quite know how to finish the scene so I fell back on the old ham standby and burst into tears and what was so awful was that once I'd started I couldn't stop until he took out his cigarette case, shoved a cigarette into my mouth and lit it for me. This calmed me down and I was able to notice that he had stopped looking startled and was looking at me with one of his eyebrows a little higher than the other, quizzically as you might say, and that his lips were twitching as though he was trying not to laugh. Then he got up and said in a perfectly ordinary voice that he'd have to be getting along now as he had a couple more patients to see but that he'd come back and have a look at me later. I didn't say anything because I didn't feel I could really without starting to blub again, so I just lay puffing away like crazy at the cigarette and trying not to look too like Little Orphan Annie. He went to the door, paused for a moment, and then did one of the kindest things I've ever known. He came back to the bed, put both his arms round me and kissed me very gently, not on the mouth but on the cheek as though he were really fond of me. Then he went out and closed the door quietly after him.

Monday

I woke up very early this morning having slept like a top for nearly nine hours. I rang the bell and when Sister Dominique came clattering in and pulled back the curtains it was a clear, bright morning again, not a bit like yesterday. When she'd popped off to get me my tea I lay quite still watching a couple of jet planes flying back and forth over the mountains and making long trails of white smoke in the pale blue sky. They went terribly quickly and kept on disappearing and coming back into view again. I tried to imagine what the pilots flying them looked like and what they were thinking about. It must be a wonderful feeling whizzing through the air at that tremendous speed and looking down at the whole world. Every now and then the sun caught one of the planes and it glittered like silver. I had some honey with my toast but it was a bit too runny. When the usual routine had been gone through and I was back in bed again I began to think of the professor yesterday afternoon and what I'd done and I felt hot with shame for a minute or two and then started to laugh. Poor love, it must have been a shock and no mistake. And then I got to wondering if after all it had been quite such a surprise to him as all that. Being a doctor he must be pretty hep about the so dainty facts of life and, being as dishy as he is, he can't have arrived at his present age without someone having made the teeniest weensiest pass at him at some time or other. Anyway by doing what I did I at least stopped him from spilling those gloomy little beans, if of course there were any beans to spill. Now, this morning, after a good night, I'm feeling that it was probably all in my imagination. You never know do you? I mean it might have been something quite silly and unimportant that upset me, like those bloody church bells for instance. They'd been enough to get anybody down. Anyway there's no sense in getting morbid and letting the goblins get you. Maybe I'll surprise them all and be springing about like a mountain goat in a few weeks from now. All the same I shan't be able to help feeling a bit embarrassed when the professor comes popping in again. Oh dear—oh dear!

Here it is only half past eight and I've got the whole morning until they bring me my lunch at twelve-thirty to think about things and scribble my oh so glamorous memories on this pad which by the way is getting nearly used up so I must remember to ask Mavis to bring me another one. She'll probably be coming in this afternoon. It's funny this wanting to get things down on paper. I suppose quite a lot of people do if you only knew, not only professional writers but more or less ordinary people, only as a rule of course they don't usually have the time, whereas I have all the time in the world—or have I? Now then, now then none of that. At any rate I've at least had what you might call an *interesting life* what with flouncing about all over the globe with those girls and having a close-up of the mysterious Orient and sailing the seven seas and one thing and another. Perhaps when I've finished it I shall be able to sell it to the *Daily Express* for thousands and thousands of pounds and live in luxury to the end of my days. What a hope! All the same it just might be possible if they cut out the bits about my sex life and some of the four-letter words were changed. Up to now I've just been writing down whatever came into my mind without worrying much about the words themselves. After all it's the thought that counts as the actress said to the bishop after he'd been bashing away at her for three hours and a half.

When I got back to London after that first tour with the bombshells I let them all go their own sweet ways and had a long talk to Ted about either working up an act on my own or trying to get into a West End show. Not a lead mind you. I wasn't so silly as to think I'd get more than a bit part, but if I happened to hit lucky and got a *good* bit part and was noticed in it then I'd be on the up and up and nothing could stop me. All this unfortunately came under the heading of wishful thinking. As a matter of fact I *did* get into a show and it *was* a good part with a duet in act one and a short solo dance at the beginning of act two, but the whole production was so diabolical that Fred Astaire couldn't have saved it and we closed after two weeks and a half. Then I decided that what I really needed was acting experience. After all nobody can go on belting out numbers and kicking their legs in the air forever whereas acting, legitimate acting that is, can last you a lifetime providing you're any good at it. Anyhow Ted managed to get me a few odd jobs in reps dotted over England's green and pleasant land and for two whole years, on and off, I slogged away at it. I had a bang at everything. Young juveniles—"Anyone for tennis"—old gentlemen, dope addicts, drunks. I even played a Japanese prisoner-of-war once in a ghastly triple bill at Dundee. My bit came in the first of the three plays and I was on and off so quickly that by the end of the evening none of the audience could remember having seen me at all. Somewhere along the line during those two years it began to dawn on me that I was on the wrong track. Once or twice I did manage to get a good notice in the local paper but I knew that didn't count for much and finally I found myself back in London again with two hundred and ten pounds in the bank, no prospects and a cold. That was a bad time all right and I can't imagine now, looking back on it, how I ever lived through it. Finally, when I was practically on the breadline and had borrowed forty pounds from Ted, I had to pocket my pride and take a chorus job in a big American musical at the Coliseum which ran for eighteen months and there I was, stuck with it. Not that I didn't manage to have quite a good time one way or another. I had a nice little "combined" in Pimlico—Lupus Street to be exact—and it had a small kitchenette which I shared with a medical student on the next floor. He was quite sweet really but he had a birthmark all down one side of his neck which was a bit off-putting, however one must take the rough with the smooth is what I always say. When the show closed I'd paid back Ted and got a bit put by but not enough for a rainy day by any manner of means, so back I went into the chorus again and did another stretch. This time it lasted two years and I knew that if I didn't get out and do something on my own again I'd lose every bit of ambition I'd ever had and just give up. Once you really get into a rut in show business you've had it. All this was nearly five years ago and I will say one thing for myself, I *did* get out of the rut and although I nearly starved in the process and spent all

I'd saved, I was at least free again and my own boss. I owe a great deal to Ted really. Without him I could never have got these girls together and now of course, just as we were beginning to do really nicely I have to get ill and bugger up the whole thing. This is where I come to a full stop and I know it and it's no good pretending any more to myself or anybody else. Even if I do get out of this *clinique* it'll take me months and months to get well enough to work again and by that time all the girls will have got other jobs and I shall have to shop around and find some new ones and redo the act from the beginning, and, while we're at it, I should like to know how I'm going to live during those jolly months of languid convalescence! This place and the operation and the treatment must be costing a bloody fortune. Ted and Mavis are the only ones who know exactly what I've got saved and they're coping, but it can't go on for much longer because there just won't be anything left. I tried to say something to Mavis about this the other day but she said that everything was all right and that I wasn't to worry and refused to discuss it any further. I've never had much money sense I'm afraid, Ted's always nagging me about it, but it's no use. When I've got it I spend it and when I haven't I don't because I bloody well can't and that's that. All the same I have been careful during the last few years, more careful than I ever was before, and there must still be quite a bit in the bank, even with all this extra expense. I must make Mavis write to Ted and find out just exactly how things are. He's got power of attorney anyhow. Now you see I've gone and got myself low again. It's always the same, whenever I begin to think about money and what I've got saved and what's going to happen in the future, down I go into the depths. I suppose this is another lack in me like not having had just that extra something which would have made me a great big glamorous star. I must say I'm not one to complain much as a rule. I've had my ups and downs and it's all part of life's rich pattern as some silly bitch said when we'd just been booed off the stage by some visiting marines in Port Said. All the same one can't go on being a cheery chappie forever can one? I mean there are moments when you have to look facts in the face and not go on kidding yourself, and this, as far as I'm concerned, is one of them. I wish to Christ I hadn't started to write at all this morning, I was feeling fine when I woke up, and now, by doing all this thinking back and remembering and wondering, I've got myself into a state of black depression and it's no use pretending I haven't. As a matter of fact it's no use pretending ever, about anything, about getting to the top, or your luck turning, or living, or dying. It always catches up with you in the end. I don't even feel like crying which is funny because I am a great crier as a rule when things get bad. It's a sort of relief and eases the nerves. Now I couldn't squeeze a tear out if you paid me. That really is funny. Sort of frightening. That's the lot for today anyway. The *Daily Express* must wait.

Tuesday

Mavis came yesterday as promised and I forgot to ask her about getting another writing pad, but it doesn't matter really as there's still quite a lot of this one left. I didn't feel up to talking much so I just lay still and listened while she told me all the gossip. Lily-May had sprained her ankle, fortunately in the last number, not a bad sprain really, not bad enough that is for her to have to stay off. She put on cold compresses last night and it had practically gone down by this morning. Beryl and Sylvia were taken out after the show on Saturday night by a very rich banking gentleman from Basel who Monsieur Philippe had brought backstage. He took them and gave them a couple of drinks somewhere or other and then on to an apartment of a friend of his which was luxuriously furnished and overlooked the lake except that they couldn't see much of it on account of it being pitch dark and there being no moon. Anyway the banker and his friend opened a bottle of champagne and sat Beryl and Sylvia down as polite as you please on a sofa with satin cushions on it and while they were sipping the champagne and being thoroughly piss-elegant, which they're inclined to be at the best of times, the banker, who'd gone out of the room for a minute, suddenly came in again stark naked carrying a leather whip in one hand and playing with himself with the other. The girls both jumped up and started screaming and there was a grand old hullabaloo for a few minutes until the friend managed to calm them down and made the banker go back and put on a dressing gown. While he was out of the room he gave the girls a hundred francs each and apologized for the banker saying that he was a weeny bit eccentric but very nice really and that the whip was not to whack them with but for them to whack him, the banker, with, which just happened to be his way of having fun. Then the twins stopped screaming and got grand as all get-out and said that they were used to being treated like ladies. They didn't happen to mention who by. Then the banker came back in a fur coat not having been able to find a dressing gown and said he was sorry if he had frightened them and would they please not say a word to Monsieur Philippe. They all had some more champagne and the banker passed out cold and the friend brought them home in a taxi without so much as groping them. Anticlimax department the whole thing. Anyway they got a hundred francs each whichever way you look at it and that's eight pounds a head for doing fuck all. I must say I couldn't help laughing when Mavis told me all this but she wasn't amused at all, oh dear me no. There's a strong governessy streak in our Mavis. She went straight to Monsieur Philippe and carried on as if she were a mother superior in a convent. This made me laugh still more and when she went she looked quite cross.

Friday

I haven't felt up to writing anything for the last few days and I don't feel too good now but I suppose I'd better make an effort and get on with it. I began having terrible pains in my back and legs last Tuesday night I think it was, anyway it was the same day that Mavis came, and Dr. Pierre was sent for and gave me an injection and I've felt sort of half asleep ever since, so much so that I didn't even know what day it was. I've just asked Sister Dominique and she told me it was Friday. Imagine! That's two whole days gone floating by with my hardly knowing anything about it. I've been feeling better all day today, a bit weak I must admit, but no more pain. The professor came in to see me this afternoon and brought me a bunch of flowers and Mavis brought me a little pot of pâté-de-foie-gras, or maybe it was the other way round, anyway I know that they both came. Not at the same time of course but at different times, perhaps it was the day before yesterday that the professor came. I know he held my hand for quite a long time so he can't have really been upset about me behaving like that. He's a wonderful man the professor is, a gentle and loving character and I wish, I wish I could really tell him why I did what I did and make him understand that it wasn't just silly camping but because I was frightened. I expect he knows anyhow. He's the sort of man who knows everything that goes on in people's minds and you don't have to keep on saying you're sorry and mak- ing excuses to him any more than you'd have to to God if God is anything like what he's supposed to be. The act closes tomorrow night if today really is Friday and all the girls have promised to come to say good-bye to me on Sunday before they catch the train, at least that's what Mavis said. I had the funniest experience last night. I saw Harry-boy. He was standing at the end of the bed as clear as daylight wearing his blue dungarees and holding up a pair of diabolical old socks which he wanted me to wash out for him. Of course I know I didn't really see him and that I was dreaming, but it did seem real as anything at the time and it still does in a way. Harry never could do a thing for himself, like washing socks I mean, or anything useful in the house. I'm not being quite fair because he did fix the tap in the lava- tory basin once when it wouldn't stop running, but then he was always all right with anything to do with machinery, not that the tap in the lavatory basin can really be called machinery but it's the same sort of thing if you know what I mean. All the girls are coming to say good-bye to me on Sun- day before they catch the train, at least that's what Mavis said. Good old Mavis. I suppose I'm fonder of her than anybody actually, anybody that's alive I mean. If she doesn't come before Sunday I can tell her then. The weather's changed with a vengeance and it's raining to beat the band which is a shame really because I can't see the mountains anymore except every now and then for a moment or two when it lifts. I wonder whatever became of Bonny Macintyre. I haven't had so much as a postcard from her in all these years. She was a tiresome little bitch but she had talent and there's no doubt about it and nobody else ever did the balloon dance quite the way she did it. It wasn't that she danced all that brilliantly, in fact Jill could wipe her eye any day of the week when it came to speed and technique. But she had something that girl.

Sister Clothilde pulled the blinds down a few minutes ago just before Dr. Pierre and Father Lucien came in. Dr. Pierre gave me an injection which hurt a bit when it went in but felt lovely a few seconds later, a sweet warm feeling coming up from my toes and covering me all over like eiderdown. Father Lucien leant over me and said something or other I don't remember what it was. He's quite nice really but there *is* something about him that gives me the creeps. I mean I wouldn't want him to hold my hand like the professor does. The act closes on Saturday and the girls are all coming to say good-bye to me on Sunday before they catch the train. I do hope Mavis gets a job or meets someone nice and marries him and settles down. That's what she ought to do really. It isn't that she's no good. She dances well and her voice is passable, but the real thing is lacking. Hark at me! I should talk. I wish Sister Clothilde hadn't pulled the blinds down, not that it really matters because it's dark by now and I shouldn't be able to see them anyhow.

•

Acts like "The Bombshells" began to raise a question that undermined one of the sacred tenets of show business, and it would be many years before even Noël plucked up the courage to express it . . .

"WHY MUST THE SHOW GO ON?" (1954)

The world for some years
Has been sodden with tears
On behalf of the Acting profession,
Each star playing a part
Seems to expect the Purple Heart.
It's unorthodox
To be born in a box
But it needn't become an obsession,
Let's hope we have no worse to plague us
Than two shows a night at Las Vegas.
When I think of physicians
And mathematicians
Who don't earn a quarter the dough,

When I look at the faces
Of people in Macy's
There's one thing I'm burning to know:

Why must the show go on?
It can't be all that indispensable,
To me it really isn't sensible
On the whole
To play a leading role
While fighting those tears you can't control,
Why kick up your legs
When draining the dregs
Of sorrow's bitter cup?
Because you have read
Some idiot has said,
"The Curtain must go up!"
I'd like to know why a star takes bows
Having just returned from burying her spouse.
Brave boop-a-doopers,
Go home and dry your tears,
Gallant old troupers,
You've bored us all for years
And when you're so blue,
Wet through
And thoroughly woe-begone,
Why must the show go on?
Oh Mammy!
Why must the show go on?

We're asked to condole
With each tremulous soul
Who steps out to be loudly applauded,
Stars on opening nights
Sob when they see their names in lights,
Though people who act
As a matter of fact
Are financially amply rewarded,
It seems, while pursuing their calling,
Their suffering's simply appalling!
But butchers and bakers
And candlestick makers
Get little applause for their pains
And when I think of miners

And waiters in "Diners"
One query forever remains:

Why must the show go on?
The rule is surely not immutable,
It might be wiser and more suitable
Just to close
If you are in the throes
Of personal grief and private woes.
Why stifle a sob
While doing your job
When, if you use your head,
You'd go out and grab
A comfortable cab
And go right home to bed?
Because you're not giving us much fun,
This "Laugh Clown Laugh" routine's been overdone,
Hats off to Show Folks
For smiling when they're blue
But more *comme-il-faut* folks
Are sick of smiling through,
And if you're out cold,
Too old
And most of your teeth have gone,
Why must the show go on?
I sometimes wonder
Why must the show go on?

Why must the show go on?
Why not announce the closing night of it?
The public seem to hate the sight of it,
Dear, and so
Why you should undergo
This terrible strain we'll never know,
We know that you're sad,
We know that you've had
A lot of storm and strife
But is it quite fair
To ask us to share
Your dreary private life?
We know you're trapped in a gilded cage
But for Heaven's sake relax and be your age,
Stop being gallant

And don't be such a bore,
Pack up your talent,
There's always plenty more
And if you lose hope
Take dope
And lock yourself in the john,
Why must the show go on?
I'm merely asking
Why must the show go on?

•

After several plays, which attracted little attention—other than the fact
that they were written by a young man in his early twenties—Noël seized
public attention with *The Vortex,* in which he also starred.

It was the night of November 25, 1924, at Hampstead's Everyman
Theatre, that the breakthrough occurred—though it took William Shakespeare to make it happen. The Censor—the Lord Chamberlain's Office—
was all for banning it altogether, until one of its inspectors pointed out
ruefully, "If we ban this, we shall have to ban *Hamlet*!"

The Vortex was the story of a mother, Florence Lancaster, clinging desperately to the illusion of youth by having affairs with young men—young
enough to be her son. Her own son, Nicky, has taken to drugs. In the last
act—like Hamlet with Gertrude—he confronts her with the truth about
both of them . . .

THE VORTEX (1924)

CAST

FLORENCE LANCASTER	LILIAN BRAITHWAITE
NICKY LANCASTER	NOËL COWARD

DIRECTED BY NOËL COWARD
EVERYMAN THEATRE, HAMPSTEAD, NOVEMBER 25, 1924

The door opens and *NICKY* enters. He is in dressing gown and pajamas.
His face looks strained and white.

FLORENCE: Nicky!
NICKY: Helen, I want to talk to Mother, please.
HELEN: All right, Nicky.
FLORENCE: What is it?

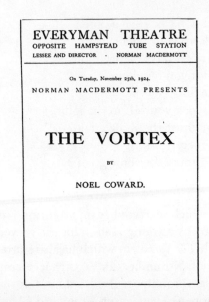

EVERYMAN THEATRE
OPPOSITE HAMPSTEAD TUBE STATION
LESSEE AND DIRECTOR · NORMAN MACDERMOTT

On Tuesday, November 25th, 1924.

NORMAN MACDERMOTT PRESENTS

THE VORTEX

BY

NOEL COWARD.

Noël (Nicky) and Lilian Braithwaite (Florence) in the final
confrontation between mother and son. So reminiscent
was it of a certain Shakespearean scene that the Lord
Chamberlain's Office concluded, "If we ban this,
we shall have to ban *Hamlet*!"

NICKY: I couldn't sleep.

HELEN: Florence dear—good night.

FLORENCE: No—no, Helen—don't go yet—

HELEN: I must.

FLORENCE: Helen—stay with me.

NICKY: Please go.

HELEN: I can't stay, Florence—it's quite impossible.

She goes out.

FLORENCE: I don't know what you mean—by coming here and ordering Helen out of my room.

NICKY: I'm sorry, Mother. I felt I had to talk to you alone.

FLORENCE: At this hour of the night—you're mad!

NICKY: No, I'm not, I think I'm probably more unhappy than I've ever been in my life.

FLORENCE: You're young—you'll get over it.

NICKY: I hope so.

FLORENCE: I knew the first moment I saw her—what sort of a girl she was.

NICKY: Oh, Mother!

FLORENCE: It's true. I had an *instinct* about her.

NICKY: It's all been rather a shock, you know—

FLORENCE (*becoming motherly*): Yes, dear—I know—I know—but you mustn't be miserable about her—she isn't worth it. (*She goes to kiss him.*)

NICKY (*gently pushing her away*): Don't, Mother!

FLORENCE: Listen, Nicky—go back to bed now—there's a dear—my head's splitting.

NICKY: I can't yet.

FLORENCE: Take some aspirin—that'll calm your nerves.

NICKY: I'm afraid I'm a little beyond aspirin.

FLORENCE: I don't want you to think I don't sympathize with you, darling—my heart *aches* for you—I know so well what you're going through.

NICKY: Do you?

FLORENCE: It's agony—absolute agony—but, you see—it will wear off— it always does in time. (NICKY *doesn't answer.*) Nicky, please go now!

NICKY: I want to talk to you.

FLORENCE: Tomorrow—we'll talk tomorrow.

NICKY: No, now—*now!*

FLORENCE: You're inconsiderate and cruel—I've told you my head's bursting.

NICKY: I want to sympathize with you, too—and try to understand everything—as well as I can—

FLORENCE: Understand everything?

NICKY: Yes, please.

FLORENCE: I don't know what you mean—

NICKY: Will you tell me things—as though I were somebody quite different?

FLORENCE: What kind of things?

NICKY: Things about you—your life.

FLORENCE: Really, Nicky—you're ridiculous—asking me to tell you stories at this hour!

NICKY (*with dead vehemence*): Mother—sit down quietly. I'm not going out of this room until I've got everything straight in my mind.

FLORENCE (*sinking down—almost hypnotized*): Nicky—please—I—

NICKY: Tom Veryan has been your lover, hasn't he?

FLORENCE (*almost shrieking*): Nicky—how dare you!

NICKY: Keep calm—it's our only chance—keep calm.

FLORENCE (*bursting into tears*): How dare you speak to me like that—suggest such a thing—I—

NICKY: It's true, isn't it?

FLORENCE: Go away—go away!

NICKY: It's true, isn't it?

FLORENCE: No—no!

NICKY: It's true, isn't it?

FLORENCE: No—I tell you—no—no—no!

NICKY: You're lying to me, Mother. What's the use of that?

FLORENCE: You're mad—mad—

NICKY: Does Father know?

FLORENCE: Go away!

NICKY: Does Father know?

FLORENCE: Your father knows nothing—he doesn't understand me any more than you do.

NICKY: Then it's between us alone.

FLORENCE: I tell you I don't know what you're talking about.

NICKY: Mother—don't go on like that, it's useless—we've arrived at a crisis, wherever we go—whatever we do we can't escape from it. I know we're neither of us very strong-minded or capable, and we haven't much hope of coming through successfully—but let's try—it's no good pretending anymore—our lives are built up of pretenses all the time. For years—ever since I began to think at all, I've been bolstering up my illusions about you. People have made remarks not realizing that I was your son, and I've pretended that they were inspired by cattiness and jealousy. I've noticed things—trivial incriminating little incidents, and I've brushed them aside and not thought any more about them because you were my mother—clever and beautiful and successful—and naturally people *would* slander you *because* you were so beautiful—and now I *know*—they were right!

FLORENCE: Nicky—I implore you—go away now—leave me alone.

NICKY: No, I can't.

FLORENCE: You're cruel—cruel to torment me—

NICKY: I don't want to be cruel—

FLORENCE: Go to bed then, and we'll talk everything over quietly another time.

NICKY: It is true about Tom Veryan, isn't it?

FLORENCE: No. No—

NICKY: We're on awfully dangerous ground—I'm straining every nerve to keep myself under control. If you lie to me and try to evade me anymore—I won't be answerable for what might happen.

FLORENCE (*dropping her voice—terrified*): What do you mean?

NICKY: I don't know—I'm frightened.

FLORENCE: Nicky—darling Nicky—I—

She approaches him.

NICKY: Don't touch me, please.

FLORENCE: Have a little pity for me.

NICKY: Was Tom Veryan your lover?

FLORENCE (*in a whisper*): Yes.

NICKY: I want to understand why—

FLORENCE: He loved me.

NICKY: But you—did you love him?

FLORENCE: Yes.

NICKY: It was something you couldn't help, wasn't it—something that's always been the same in you since you were quite, quite young—?

FLORENCE: Yes, Nicky—yes—

NICKY: And there have been others, too, haven't there?

FLORENCE (*with her face in her hands*): I won't be cross-questioned anymore—I won't—I won't—

NICKY: I wish you'd understand I'm not blaming you—I'm trying to help you—to help us both—

FLORENCE: What good can all this possibly do?

NICKY: Clear things up, of course. I can't go on anymore half knowing—

FLORENCE: Why should that side of my life be any concern of yours?

NICKY: But, Mother!

FLORENCE: I'm different from other women—completely different—and you expect me to be the same—why can't you realize that with a temperament like mine it's impossible to live an ordinary humdrum life—you're not a boy any longer—you're a man—and—

NICKY: I'm nothing—I've grown up all wrong.

FLORENCE: It's not my fault.

NICKY: Of course it's your fault, Mother—who else's fault *could* it be?

FLORENCE: Your friends—the people you mix with—

NICKY: It wouldn't matter *who* I mixed with if only I had a background.

FLORENCE: You've got as much money as you want—you've got your home—

NICKY (*bitterly*): Home! That's almost funny—there's no peace anywhere—nothing but the ceaseless din of trying to be amused—

FLORENCE: David never complains.

NICKY: I don't suppose you've looked at Father during the last few years—or you wouldn't say that.

FLORENCE: He's perfectly happy because he's sensible—he lives his own life and doesn't try to interfere with mine.

NICKY: It must be your vanity that makes you so dreadfully blind—and foolish.

FLORENCE: Understand once and for all, I *won't* be spoken to like this—

NICKY: You've had other lovers besides Tom Veryan—haven't you?

FLORENCE: Yes, I have—I have. Now then!

NICKY: Well, anyhow—that's the truth—at last—

He rises, turns his back on her and stands looking out the window.

FLORENCE (*after a pause—going to him*): Nicky—don't be angry—please don't be angry with me.

NICKY: I'm not angry a bit—I realize that I'm living in a world where things like this happen—and they've got to be faced and given the right value. If only I'd had the courage to realize everything before—it wouldn't be so bad now—it's the sudden shock that's thrown the whole thing out of focus for me—but I mean to get it right—please help me!

FLORENCE (*dully*): I don't know what to do.

NICKY: It's your life, and you've lived it as you've wanted to live it—that's fair—

FLORENCE: Yes—yes.

NICKY: You've wanted love always—passionate love, because you were made like that—it's not your fault—it's the fault of circumstances and civilization—civilization makes rottenness so much easier—we're utterly rotten—both of us—

FLORENCE: Nicky—don't—don't—

NICKY: How can we help ourselves?—We swirl about in a vortex of beastliness—this is a chance—don't you see—to realize the truth—our only chance.

FLORENCE: Oh, Nicky, do stop—go away!

NICKY: Don't keep on telling me to stop when our only hope is to hammer it out.

FLORENCE: You're overwrought—it isn't as bad as you think.

NICKY: Isn't it?

FLORENCE: No, no. Of course it isn't. Tomorrow morning you'll see things quite differently.

NICKY: You haven't understood.

FLORENCE: Yes, I have—I have.

NICKY: You haven't understood. Oh, my God, you haven't understood! You're building up silly defences in your mind. I'm overwrought. Tomorrow morning I shall see things quite differently. That's true—that's the tragedy of it, and you won't see—Tomorrow morning I *shall* see things differently. All this will seem unreal—a nightmare—the machinery of our lives will go on again and gloss over the truth as it always does—and our chance will be gone forever.

FLORENCE: Chance—chance? What are you talking about—what chance?

NICKY: I must make you see somehow.

FLORENCE: You're driving me mad.

NICKY: Have patience with me—please—please—

FLORENCE (*wildly*): How can I have patience with you?—You exaggerate everything.

NICKY: No I don't—I wish I did.

FLORENCE: Listen—let me explain something to you.

NICKY: Very well—go on.

FLORENCE: You're setting yourself up in judgment on me—your own mother.

NICKY: No, I'm not.

FLORENCE: You are—you are—let me speak—you don't understand my temperament in the least—nobody does—I—

NICKY: You're deceiving yourself—your temperament's no different from thousands of other women, but you've been weak and selfish and given way all along the line—

FLORENCE: Let me speak, I tell you—!

NICKY: What's the use—you're still pretending—you're building up barriers between us instead of helping me to break them down.

FLORENCE: What are you accusing me of having done?

NICKY: Can't you see yet?

FLORENCE: No, I can't. If you're preaching morality you've no right to—that's my affair—I've never done any harm to anyone.

NICKY: Look at me.

FLORENCE: Why—what do you mean?

NICKY: You've given me *nothing* all my life—nothing that counts.

FLORENCE: Now you're pitying yourself.

NICKY: Yes, with every reason.

FLORENCE: You're neurotic and ridiculous—just because Bunty broke off your engagement you come and say wicked, cruel things to me—

NICKY: You forget what I've seen tonight, Mother.

FLORENCE: I don't care what you've seen.

NICKY: I've seen you make a vulgar, disgusting scene in your own house, and on top of that humiliate yourself before a boy half your age. The misery of losing Bunty faded away when that happened—everything is comparative after all.

FLORENCE: I didn't humiliate myself—

NICKY: You ran after him up the stairs because your vanity wouldn't let you lose him—it isn't that you love him—that would be easier—you never love anyone, you only love them loving you—all your so-called passion and temperament is false—your whole existence had degenerated into an endless empty craving for admiration and flattery—and then you say you've done no harm to anybody. Father used to be a clever man, with a strong will and a capacity for enjoying everything—I can remember him like that, and now he's nothing—a complete nonentity because his spirit's crushed. How could it be otherwise? You've let him down consistently for years—and God knows I'm nothing for him to look forward to—but I might have been if it hadn't been for you—

FLORENCE: Don't talk like that. Don't—don't—it can't be such a crime being loved—it can't be such a crime being happy—

NICKY: You're not happy—you're never happy—you're fighting—fighting all the time to keep your youth and your looks—because you can't bear the thought of living without them—as though they mattered in the end.

FLORENCE (*hysterically*): What does anything matter—ever?

NICKY: That's what I'm trying to find out.

FLORENCE: I'm still young inside—I'm still beautiful—why shouldn't I live my life as I choose?

NICKY: You're not young or beautiful; I'm seeing for the first time how old you are—it's horrible—your silly fair hair—and your face all plastered and painted—

FLORENCE: Nicky—Nicky—stop—stop—stop!

She flings herself face downward on the bed. NICKY goes over to her.

NICKY: Mother!

FLORENCE: Go away—go away—I hate you—go away—

NICKY: Mother—sit up—

FLORENCE (*pulling herself together*): Go out of my room—

NICKY: Mother—

FLORENCE: I don't ever want to see you again—you're insane—you've said wicked, wicked things to me—you've talked to me as though I were a woman off the streets. I can't bear any more—I can't bear any more!

NICKY: I have a slight confession to make—

FLORENCE: Confession?

NICKY: Yes.

FLORENCE: Go away—go away—

NICKY (*taking a small gold box from his pocket*): Look—

FLORENCE: What do you mean—what is it—?

NICKY: Don't you know?

FLORENCE takes the box with trembling fingers and opens it. She stares at it for a moment. When she speaks again her voice is quite dead.

FLORENCE: Nicky, it isn't—you haven't—?

NICKY: Why do you look so shocked?

FLORENCE (*dully*): Oh, my God!

NICKY: What does it matter?

FLORENCE suddenly rises and hurls the box out of the window.

NICKY: That doesn't make it any better.

FLORENCE (*flinging herself on her knees beside him*): Nicky, promise me, oh, promise you'll never do it again—never in your life—it's frightful—horrible—

NICKY: It's only just the beginning.

FLORENCE: What can I say to you—what can I say to you?

NICKY: Nothing—under the circumstances.

FLORENCE: What do you mean?

NICKY: It can't possibly matter—now.

FLORENCE: Matter—but it's the finish of everything—you're young, you're just starting on your life—you must stop—you must swear never to touch it again—swear to me on your oath, Nicky—I'll help you—I'll help you—

NICKY: You!

He turns away.

FLORENCE (*burying her face in her hands and moaning*): Oh—oh—oh!

NICKY: How could you possibly help me?

FLORENCE (*clutching him*): Nicky!

NICKY (*almost losing control*): Shut up—shut up—don't touch me—

FLORENCE (*trying to take him in her arms*): Nicky—Nicky—

NICKY: I'm trying to control myself, but you won't let me—you're an awfully rotten woman, really.

FLORENCE: Nicky—stop—stop—stop—

She beats him with her fists.

NICKY: Leave go of me!

He breaks away from her, and going up to the dressing table he sweeps everything off on to the floor with his arm.

FLORENCE (*screaming*): Oh—oh—Nicky—!

NICKY: Now then! Now then! You're not to have any more lovers; you're not going to be beautiful and successful ever again—you're going to be my mother for once—it's about time I had one to help me, before I go over the edge altogether—

FLORENCE: Nicky—Nicky—

NICKY: Promise me to be different—you've got to promise me!

FLORENCE (*sinking on to the end of couch, facing audience*): Yes—yes—I promise—(*the tears are running down her face*).

NICKY: I love you, really—that's why it's so awful.

He falls on his knees by her side and buries his face in her lap.

FLORENCE: No. No, not awful—don't say that—I love you, too.

NICKY (*sobbing hopelessly*): Oh, Mother—!

FLORENCE (*staring in front of her*): I wish I were dead!

NICKY: It doesn't matter about death, but it matters terribly about life.

FLORENCE: I know—

NICKY (*desperately*): Promise me you'll be different—promise me you'll be different—

FLORENCE: Yes, yes—I'll try—

NICKY: We'll both try.

FLORENCE: Yes, dear.—Oh, my dear—!

She sits quite still, staring in front of her—the tears are rolling down her cheeks, and she is stroking NICKY's hair mechanically in an effort to calm him.

CURTAIN.

The reaction to the piece was startling.

"Success took me to her bosom like a maternal boa constrictor."

"No Press interviewer, photographer, or gossip writer had to fight in order to see me. I was wide open to them all, smiling and burbling bright witticisms, giving my views on this and that, discussing such problems as whether or not the modern girl would make a good mother. I was photographed in every conceivable position.

"I was unwise enough to be photographed in bed wearing a Chinese dressing gown and an expression of advanced degeneracy. This last was accidental and was caused by blinking at the flashlight, but it emblazoned my unquestionable decadence firmly in the minds of all who saw it. It even brought forth a letter of indignant protest from a retired Brigadier-General in Gloucestershire."

Noël grew confident enough to tease his questioners . . .

"I really have a frightfully depraved mind. I am never out of opium dens, cocaine dens and other evil places. My mind is a mass of corruption."

"The legend of my modesty grew. I became extraordinarily unspoiled by my great success. As a matter of fact, I still am."

"I was in an enviable position. Everyone except Somerset Maugham said I was the second Somerset Maugham, with the exception of a few who preferred to describe me as a second Sacha Guitry."

Noël took *The Vortex* to Broadway, where it enjoyed even greater success. The production then made a short U.S. tour, and it was in Chicago where reality hit.

"They seemed unappreciative of the comedy in the first act, but we struggled manfully across the damp patches where the laughs should have been, deciding in our minds that they were a dramatic audience rather than a comedy one."

But by the end of the second act, Chicagoans had decided they had got the hang of the thing and started to unleash their belly laughs.

The last act was worse than I could ever have imagined it to be. The sight of me in pyjamas and dressing-gown started them off happily, and from then onwards they laughed without ceasing . . . The curtain fell to considerable applause and I even had to make a speech, which, remembering that I was English, was a model of grateful restraint.

Before leaving . . . I wrote on the wall of my dressing-room in indelible pencil, "Noël Coward died here," and when I visited Clifton Webb in the same room years later, I was delighted to see that the inscription was still there.

•

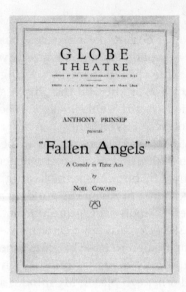

FALLEN ANGELS (1925)

CAST

JULIA STERROLL	TALLULAH BANKHEAD
JANE BANBURY	EDNA BEST
SAUNDERS	MONA HARRISON

DIRECTED BY STANLEY BELL

GLOBE THEATRE, LONDON, APRIL 21, 1925

Noël wrote *Fallen Angels* in 1923 around the same time as *The Vortex,* but it didn't get produced until the following year. The success of *The Vortex* turned the Coward bottom drawer into a treasure trove (or so it seemed).

The piece was shocking for its time. Julia Sterroll and Jane Banbury are two women reluctantly approaching middle age. They've been best friends forever and they share one guilty secret. Years back each of them, unbeknownst to the other at the time, had a brief affair with the same Frenchman, Maurice Duclos. Since then, each of them has married, safely if not exactly ecstatically.

Now they hear from Maurice. He is coming to town and would like to call on them.

Girlish *angst* ensues . . .

JULIA: Listen, Jane, we're in for a bitter time—we must summon up all our courage and face it properly.

JANE: Yes, give me another cigarette.

JULIA (*handing her box*): We must get the whole situation laid out quite clearly, like Patience, then we shall know where we are.

JANE (*lighting both cigarettes*): Yes—oh, yes!

JULIA (*sitting back on sofa*): Now then.

JANE: Now then what?

JULIA (*in businesslike tones*): Two wretchedly happy married women—

JANE: Yes.

JULIA: Both during the first two years of their married lives having treated their exceedingly nice husbands to the requisite amount of passion and adoration—

JANE: Yes.

JULIA: As is usual in such cases—after a certain time the first ecstasies of passionate adoration subside, leaving in some instances an arid waste of discontent—

JANE: Lovely, darling!

JULIA: In some instances rank boredom and rampant adultery on both sides—

JANE: Don't be gross, dear.

JULIA: And in other rarer instances such as ours—complete happiness and tranquillity devoid of violent emotions of any kind with the possible exception of golf.

JANE: Quite.

JULIA: And there lies the trouble—the lack of violent emotion, fireworks, etc.

JANE: I don't want fireworks.

JULIA: Neither do I—not the nice part of me, but there's an unworthy, beastly thing in both of us waiting to spring—it sprang once before our marriage, and it will spring again—it hasn't been fed for a long, long time—

JANE (*shocked*): Julia!

JULIA: To put it mildly, dear, we're both ripe for a lapse.

JANE (*going into peals of laughter*): A *Relapse*, Julia.—Oh, dear!

JULIA (*also collapsing*): It's perfectly appalling, and we're laughing on the very edge of an abyss!

JANE: I can't help it, it's hysteria.

JULIA: By a semi-humorous malignity of fate we both happened to throw our respective bonnets over the same windmill—

JANE (*giggling weakly*): Oh, do stop—!

JULIA (*relentlessly*): And now, at a critical moment in our matrimonial careers, that windmill is coming to wreck us.

JANE (*wailing*): I don't want to be wrecked! I don't want to be wrecked!

JULIA: Shhh, dear! Saunders will hear you.

JANE (*panic-stricken*): Don't you see? What I suggested in the first place, it's the only way—we must go—at once—anywhere out of London.

JULIA: I shall do nothing of the sort, it would be so cowardly.

JANE: A blind goat could see through that, dear!

JULIA: All the same, I shall stay and face it.

JANE: If you do, I shall.

JULIA: There is not the least necessity for us both to suffer.

JANE: If you imagine I should enjoy being by myself in Brighton while you were gallivanting about London with Maurice—

JULIA: I should be too much upset to gallivant.

JANE: No, dear, it won't do.

JULIA: What do you mean, "It won't do"?

JANE: We stand or fall together.

JULIA: I don't mind standing together, but I won't fall together, it would be most embarrassing.

JANE: Whatever happens, I am not going to be left out.

JULIA: Very well, then I'll go away and you stay.

JANE (*eagerly*): All right.

JULIA: What about standing or falling together?

JANE (*nobly*): I'm willing to sacrifice myself for you.

JULIA: Liar!

JANE: Julia, how can you—?

JULIA: I thought so.

JANE (*airily*): I don't know what you mean.

JULIA: Oh, yes, you do.

JANE: If you're going to be bad-tempered I shall go.

JULIA: I'm not in the least bad-tempered, I'm only seeing through you, that's all.

JANE: Seeing through me, indeed? What about you not going away because it would be cowardly? Huh!

JULIA (*sweetly*): Are you insinuating, dear, that I *want* to stay?

JANE: Not insinuating—I'm dead certain of it.

JULIA (*laughing forcedly*): Ha ha! Really, Jane—

JANE: You're simply longing for him.

JULIA: Jane!

JANE: You are, you know you are!

JULIA: So are you.

JANE: Certainly I am.

JULIA: Oh, Jane, we must be very careful.

JANE: I'm always careful.

JULIA: I don't mean about him, I mean about us.

JANE: Oh!

JULIA: Don't you see what's going to happen?

JANE: Yes—yes, I do.

JULIA: It's always the way, when sex comes up it wrecks everything. It's a beastly rotten thing—

JANE: It didn't wreck us before.

JULIA: We weren't together before—if we had been we should have been the blackest enemies in five minutes.

JANE: Yes, as it was you were a bit upset when I met him afterwards.

JULIA: I was awfully sweet about it.

JANE: It was too late for you to be anything else—I took jolly good care not to let you know until it was all over.

JULIA: Yes, that's true.

JANE: We've been friends, real friends, ever since we were eight and nine respectively—

JULIA: And in all probability this will break all that up.

JANE: Certainly—unless we circumvent it.

JULIA (*firmly*): I won't go away.

JANE: Neither will I—we're both firmly agreed on that point.

JULIA: It's only natural, after all, that we should want to see him again.

JANE: And it's also only natural that when we do see him again we shall fight like tigers.

JULIA: I wonder if we shall—really?

Inevitably they do . . .

Reenter *SAUNDERS* with sweet—*profiteroles au chocolat.*

JANE: I've eaten much too much already.

JULIA: So have I, but we must go on, it will keep up our strength.

JANE: They look lovely.—Tinker, tailor, soldier, sailor—

JULIA (*giggling*): No, you do that with cherry stones.

JANE (*also giggling*): I like doing it with these.

JULIA: Have some more champagne?

JANE: No, thank you.

JULIA: Here you are. (*She pours it out.*)

JANE: Thanks, darling.

JULIA: What's so silly is that I'm beginning to feel sleepy.

JANE: I'm not—exactly—just cosy.

JULIA: Bring the coffee straightaway, Saunders.

SAUNDERS: Yes, ma'am.

Exit *SAUNDERS.*

JULIA (*suddenly bursting out laughing*): Oh, dear—!

JANE: What are you laughing at?

JULIA: You look frightfully funny!

JANE: What's the matter with me? (*She gets up just a little unsteadily and looks at herself in the glass.*)

JULIA (*giggling hopelessly*): I don't know—you just do!

JANE: So do you.

JULIA (*also getting up and looking in glass*): It's our heads, I think—they're far too big.

JANE: We've had too much champagne.

JULIA (*agreeably*): Much too much.

JANE: Let's sit down again.

JULIA: All right.

They return to the table.

JANE: I feel awfully warm and comfortable.

JULIA: A child could play with me.

Enter SAUNDERS with coffee. JULIA and JANE both sit down at the table again.

JANE: I don't mind what happens now—I'm just past everything.

JULIA: Have some coffee.

JANE (*taking it from* SAUNDERS): Thank you.

JULIA: A liqueur?

JANE (*giggling*): Don't be ridiculous.

JULIA: Cordial Médoc, Saunders.

JANE: Shall we have it in tumblers?

JULIA: I ordered it specially—it rounds off a dinner so nicely.

JANE: It certainly will.

SAUNDERS goes to sideboard, pours out two liqueurs and puts them down on the table.

JULIA: Thank you, Saunders—that will do now.

SAUNDERS: Very good, ma'am.

SAUNDERS goes out with the remains of the sweet on a tray.

JANE (*sipping her liqueur*): It's terribly strong!

JULIA (*airily*): It's supposed to make one feel rather—rather— (*She waves her hand vaguely.*)

JANE: How thoughtful of you, dear.

JULIA: Have some fruit?

JANE: I couldn't.

JULIA: Do, it rounds off the dinner so nicely.

JANE: For heaven's sake stop rounding off the dinner, it's getting on my nerves.

JULIA: Don't be temperamental.

JANE: Do you think it would matter if I took off my shoes?

JULIA: Not at all—they always do in Japan, I believe.

JANE (*kicking off her shoes*): If Maurice had any instincts at all he'd arrive at this moment—looking marvellous.

JULIA: And make the most lovely sort of baffled scene!

JANE: What would baffle him?

JULIA: Us, of course, because we'd be so gloriously aloof and stately.

JANE: I shouldn't—I should give in without a murmur.

JULIA: Then he'd want me more.

JANE: If you feel that's the only way to make him, you'd better encourage me.

JULIA: You don't need any encouraging.

JANE: What do you mean by that?

JULIA: What I say.

JANE: Oh!

JULIA: Anyhow, I should never let you cheapen yourself.

JANE (*affronted*): How dare you, Julia.

JULIA: How dare I what?

JANE: Insult me.

JULIA: I didn't.

JANE: You did—you went too far—it was past a joke.

JULIA: It wasn't intended to be a joke—I hate jokes, bitterly.

JANE: Then you meant it?

JULIA: Meant what?

JANE: How can anyone carry on a conversation when you keep on saying what, what, what, what, what, what, what all the time! If you can't quite grasp what I say, you'd better go to bed.

JULIA: That was exceedingly rude, Jane.

JANE: I'm sorry, Julia, but you're annoying me.

JULIA: Unfortunately, this happens to be my flat.

JANE (*looking around*): Never mind, dear, you'll get used to it in time.

JULIA: Stop bickering, Jane.

JANE: How can you expect me not to bicker when you sit there abusing me.

JULIA: I never abused you.

JANE: Yes, you did—you insinuated that I was brazen.

JULIA: Well, so you are—sometimes—we all are, it's human nature.

JANE: Nothing of the sort.

JULIA: Don't contradict everything I say—it infuriates me.

JANE: Brazen! It was you who refused to run away this morning, anyhow.

JULIA: Why should I run away?

JANE (*laughing loudly*): That's funny.

JULIA (*coldly*): I'm glad you think so.

JANE: Why should you run away—ha-ha!

JULIA: I think you must be going to have a cold, Jane.

JANE: Why?

JULIA: Your voice is so strident.

JANE: I shall whisper for the rest of the evening.

JULIA: Do, it's more soothing.

JANE (*in a hoarse whisper*): Anyhow, there's this to be said—if you hadn't met Maurice first and gone on with him like that in Pisa—

JULIA: You're being insufferable.

JANE: Not at all—I'm merely pointing out that it's no use riding a high horse now because the whole affair's been entirely your fault from beginning to end.

JULIA (*rising*): I'm awfully disappointed in you Jane,—I thought you had a nicer mind than that.

JANE: Mind! What about yours? I suppose you imagine it's a lovely gilt basket filled with mixed fruit and a bow on the top!

JULIA: Better than being an old sardine tin with a few fins left in it!

JANE (*rising*): You'll regret that remark in your soberer moments.

JULIA: Have a cigarette.

JANE (*taking one*): Thank you.

JULIA (*striking a match*): Here!

JANE (*with dignity*): Thank you.

JULIA (*grandly*): Perhaps you'd like a little music? Shall I put the gramophone on?

JANE: Do, if you feel it would put you in a better temper.

JULIA (*ignoring her—conversationally*): I had such an amusing letter from Aunt Harriet this morning.

JANE (*rudely*): Did you really? I thought she was dead.

JULIA (*with a superior frown*): I'm afraid you must be muddling her up with someone else.

JANE: Go on, dear—tell me some more news. I love you when you're offended.

JULIA (*sadly*): I'm not offended, Jane. A little hurt, perhaps, and surprised—

JANE (*suddenly furious*): How dare you draw yourself up and become the outraged hostess with *me!*

JULIA: I'm sorry—I must have lost my sense of humour—perhaps because I'm tired—we've been together so much lately, we've probably grated on one another's nerves.

JANE: Yes, you're right there. Where are my shoes?

JULIA (*disdainfully*): I really don't know—they can't have gone far.

JANE: I should like to shake you, Julia, shake you and shake you and shake you until your eyes dropped out!

JULIA: Indeed?

JANE: Yes, when you're superior and grand like that you rouse the very worst in me—

JULIA: Obviously.

JANE: You make me feel like a French Revolution virago. I'd like to rush up and down Bond Street with your head on a pole!

JULIA: You'd better pull yourself together and I'll ask Saunders to help you to your flat.

JANE: If she comes near me I'll throttle her.

JULIA: I've never seen you violent before—it's very interesting psychologically.

JANE (*with sudden determination*): I could bring you down to earth in one moment if I liked.

JULIA: Vulgarity always leaves me unmoved.

JANE: This is not vulgarity—it's something I was more ashamed of than vulgarity, but I'm not ashamed of it anymore—I'm glad! I've kept something from you, Julia.

JULIA: I wish you'd go home, Jane.

JANE: I must have realised subconsciously all the time that you were going to turn out false and beastly—

JULIA: What are you talking about?

JANE: Where are my shoes?

JULIA: Never mind about your shoes—what do you mean?

JANE: Give me my shoes.

JULIA (*moving over to the mantelpiece*): They're probably under the table—you'd better get them and go.

JANE (*finding them and putting them on savagely*): And now I'm thankful to God I *did* keep it to myself.

JULIA: That's right.

JANE: You're still too grand to be curious, I suppose.

JULIA: Don't be cheap, Jane.

JANE: It concerns Maurice.

JULIA (*turning*): Oh! it concerns Maurice, does it?

JANE: Yes, I thought that would rouse you!

JULIA: I think you'd better tell me—if you don't want to wreck our friendship for ever.

JANE: It will wreck our friendship all right when I *do* tell you—and I don't care. It's this—*I know where he is!*

JULIA: It's a lie!

JANE: No, it isn't. He rang me up while I was dressing tonight.

JULIA: Jane!

JANE: Yes, I didn't want to tell you because I thought it would have hurt your feelings. But now I know that you haven't got any feelings to hurt—only a shallow sort of social vanity—

JULIA: Where is he, then? Tell me!

JANE: I shall do nothing of the sort. I don't want you to rush round there and make a fool of yourself.

JULIA (*losing all control*): How dare you! How dare you! I'll never speak to you again as long as I live. You're utterly completely contemptible! If it's true, you're nothing but a snivelling hypocrite! And if it's false, you're a bare-faced liar! There's not much to choose between you. Please go at once!

JANE: Go—I'm only too delighted. You must curb your social sense, Julia, if it leads you to drunken orgies and abuse!

JULIA (*in tears*): Go—go—go away—!

JANE: Certainly I shall—and it may interest you to know that I'm going *straight* to Maurice!

JULIA (*wailing*): Liar—Liar!

JANE: I'm not lying—it's true. And I shall go away with him at once, and you and Fred and Willy can go to hell, the whole lot of you!

JANE flounces out. *JULIA* hurls herself onto the sofa in screaming hysterics.

CURTAIN.

Eventually the two husbands discover what may be about to happen and are waiting for Maurice to arrive. When he does—clever Frenchman that he is—he explains that the whole thing has been a "put-up job" with the ladies to make their husbands jealous. The simple fact is that, since he has taken the flat immediately above, he wanted the ladies to advise him on his choice of curtains.

The husbands stay there bemused as Julia, Jane and Maurice go upstairs. Then they hear a man's voice singing . . .

> *Même les Anges succombent à l'amour,*
> *Parce que follement je t'aime—je t'aime—je t'aime.*

Some playgoers professed themselves scandalized, which did wonders for the box office. On the last night an officious woman stood up in her box and berated both play and author, before the orchestra struck up "I Want to Be Happy."

·

Another play written in that creative *annus mirabilis* of 1923–1924 was *Easy Virtue,* the first of Noël's plays to have its premiere in New York, with American actress Jane Cowl in the lead role of Larita. The plan was then to transfer to London via a Manchester tryout, and producer/director Basil Dean was occupied in doing just that while Noël was in New York.

On April 22, 1925, Dean is writing to him . . .

A curious position has arisen with regard to Manchester by John Hare, who owns the theatre, refusing to sign the contract for a play of the title *Easy Virtue.* He says he thought the title was *Easy Money*! As I am committed to Jane, the Duke of York's Theatre and all the other artists, I had to insist on the date. The only way I could insist on it temporarily was to agree that we should produce the play in Manchester under another name . . . I am informed the reason for the objection is because the Watch Committee [the local censors] would not allow a play with such a title . . . I can see a good deal of mischief in your eye as I dictate this letter!

It finally opened in May 1926 with the title *A New Play in Three Acts* by Noël Coward.

Ironically, at a cinema next door to the theatre—presumably outside the jurisdiction of the Watch Committee—the featured attraction was *Flames of Passion.*

Not being one to let a good joke go begging, Noël saved it up for twenty years until he had Celia Johnson and Trevor Howard leave the cinema in *Brief Encounter,* where they have been watching—*Flames of Passion*!

Easy Virtue tells the story of how the Whittakers, a hidebound English middle-class family, react when their son, John, brings home his new bride—a sophisticated older woman, Larita.

The sound of culture clash is soon in the air, and then it comes to light that Larita had been charged with—but acquitted of—the death of her previous husband. Mrs. Whittaker confronts her in the presence of her prim older daughter, Marion, and her infinitely more understanding husband . . .

EASY VIRTUE

LONDON CAST

MRS. WHITTAKER	MABEL TERRY-LEWIS
MARION	MARDA VANNE
COLONEL WHITTAKER	MARCUS BARRON
LARITA	JANE COWL
CHARLES BURLEIGH	VERNON KELSO
SARAH HURST	JOYCE CAREY
JOHN WHITTAKER	JAMES RAGLAN
FURBER	CLAUDE GRAHAM

DIRECTED BY BASIL DEAN

Presented by Charles Frohman at the Empire Theatre, New York, on November 23, 1925 (147 performances).

Presented by Basil Dean at the Opera House, Manchester, on May 31, 1926, and subsequently at the Duke of York's Theatre, London, on June 9, 1926 (124 performances).

LARITA: I haven't the faintest intention of making excuses or trying to conceal anything—that newspaper cutting was perfectly accurate—as far as it went. I *was* concerned in that peculiarly unpleasant case. I changed my name afterward for obvious reasons. The papers rather overreached themselves in publishing the number of my lovers—only two of the list really loved me.

MRS. WHITTAKER: You were responsible for a man killing himself.

LARITA: Certainly not. It was his weakness and cowardice that were responsible for that—not I.

MRS. WHITTAKER: It's incredible—dreadful—I can hardly believe it.

LARITA: I felt like that at the time, but it's a long while ago.

MARION: Fifteen years! John was a child.

LARITA: Thank you. I quite realise that.

MRS. WHITTAKER: And how have you lived since this—this—scandal?

LARITA: Extremely well.

MRS. WHITTAKER: Your flippancy is unpardonable.

LARITA: So was your question. I've only explained so far because, as you're John's mother, I felt I owed it to you; but if you persist in this censorious attitude I shall say no more.

MRS. WHITTAKER: Do you realise what you've done?

LARITA: Perfectly, and I regret nothing. The only thing that counts in this instance is my relationship with John. Nothing that has occurred in the past affects that in the least.

MRS. WHITTAKER: Your marrying him was an outrage.

LARITA: Why? I've told you before, I love him.

MRS. WHITTAKER: You prove your love by soiling his name irreparably.

LARITA: Nonsense.

COLONEL: Do you think it's quite fair, Mabel, to set ourselves up in judgment on Larita? We know none of the circumstances which led to these bygone incidents.

MRS. WHITTAKER: You've failed me too often before, Jim, so I'm not surprised that you fail me now.

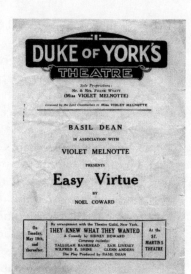

LARITA: The Colonel's not failing you— it's just as bad for him as for you. You don't suppose he *likes* the idea of his only son being tied up to me, after these—revelations? But somehow or other, in the face of overwhelming opposition, he's managed to arrive at a truer sense of values than you could any of you ever understand. He's not allowed himself to be cluttered up with hypocritical moral codes and false sentiments—he sees things as they are, and tried to make the best of them. He's tried to make the best of me ever since I've been here.

MARION: That hasn't astonished us in the least.

LARITA: No doubt, with your pure and unsullied conception of human nature, you can only find one meaning for the Colonel's kindness to me.

MARION: I didn't say that.

LARITA: You think it, though, don't you? Only this afternoon you asked me not to encourage him.

MRS. WHITTAKER: Marion!

LARITA: You disguised your unpleasant lascivious curiosity under a cloak of hearty friendship—you were pumping me to discover some confirmation of your pretty suspicions. One thing my life has taught me, and that is a knowledge of feminine psychology. I've met your type before.

MARION: How dare you! How dare you!

MRS. WHITTAKER (*rising*): This is insupportable.

LARITA (*sharply*): Yes, it is.—Sit down.

MRS. WHITTAKER (*impotently*): I—I—

She sits down.

LARITA: I want you to understand one thing—I deny nothing. I have a perfect right to say what I like and live how I choose—whether I've married John or whether I haven't, my life is my own, and I don't intend to be browbeaten.

MARION: I hope God will forgive you.

LARITA: Don't you rather overrate the Almighty's interest in the situation?

MRS. WHITTAKER: In the face of your brazen attitude, there's nothing more to be said.

LARITA: You're wrong. There's a good deal more to be said. According to you, I ensnared John in my toils in order to break away from my old life and better my position. If that were the case, what do you mean by deliberately trying to crush down my efforts to reform myself? How do you reconcile that with your stereotyped views of virtue and charity? But you needn't worry; I didn't marry John to reform myself. I don't consider my position in this house a step up, socially or spiritually. On the contrary, it's been probably the most demoralising experience that's ever happened to me.

MRS. WHITTAKER: You're a wicked, wicked woman.

LARITA: That remark was utterly fatuous and completely mechanical. You didn't even think before you said it—your brain is so muddled up with false values that you're incapable of grasping anything in the least real. Why am I a wicked woman?

MRS. WHITTAKER: You betrayed my son's honour by taking advantage of his youth and mad infatuation for you. He'd never have married you if he'd known.

LARITA: I suppose you wouldn't consider it betraying his honour if he'd had an affair with me and not married me?

MRS. WHITTAKER: It would certainly have been much more appropriate.

LARITA: Unfortunately, I don't consider John worthy of me in either capacity—I realised a long time ago that our marriage was a mistake, but not from your point of view—from my own.

MARION: It's easy to talk like that now.

LARITA: It isn't easy—it's heartbreaking. I love John more than I can ever say, but it's not blind love—unfortunately—I can see through him. He's charming and weak and inadequate, and he's brought me down to the dust.

MRS. WHITTAKER: How dare you say such vile things! How dare you!

LARITA: It's true. You can't appreciate my feelings about it. I don't expect you to.

MARION: I should think not.

LARITA: Your treatment of all this shows a regrettable lack of discrimination. You seem to be floundering under the delusion that I'm a professional *cocotte.* You're quite, quite wrong—I've never had an affair with a man I wasn't fond of. The only time I ever sold myself was in the eyes of

God to my first husband—my mother arranged it. I was really too young to know what I was doing. You approve of that sort of bargaining, don't you?—it's within the law.

MARION (*contemptuously*): Huh!

LARITA: Why do you make that peculiar noise, Marion? Does it indicate approval, contempt, or merely asthma?

MARION: Do you think this is the moment to be facetious?

LARITA: You're an unbelievable prig.

MARION: I hope you don't imagine that your insults could ever have any effect on me?

LARITA: If only you knew it, I'm at your mercy completely, but you're too silly to take advantage of it—you choose the wrong tactics.

MARION: We're certainly not experienced in dealing with women of your sort, if that's what you mean.

LARITA: It *is* what I mean—entirely. I'm completely outside the bounds of your understanding—in every way. And yet I know you, Marion, through and through—far better than you know yourself. You're a pitiful figure, and there are thousands like you—victims of convention and upbringing. All your life you've ground down perfectly natural sex impulses, until your mind has become a morass of inhibitions—your repression has run into the usual channel of religious hysteria. You've played physical purity too high and mental purity not high enough. And you'll be a miserable woman until the end of your days unless you readjust the balance.

MARION (*rising impetuously*): You're revolting—horrible!

LARITA: You need love and affection terribly—you'd go to any lengths to obtain it except the right ones. You swear and smoke and assume an air of spurious heartiness because you're not sure of your own religion and are afraid of being thought a prude. You try to establish a feeling of comradeship by sanctimonious heart-to-heart talks. All your ideals are confused and muddled—you don't know what to ask of life, and you'll die never having achieved anything but physical virtue. And God knows I pity you.

MARION, with as much dignity as she can command, walks into the library without a word, and slams the door.

MRS. WHITTAKER: You're achieving nothing by all this.

LARITA: How do you know?

MRS. WHITTAKER: Because you're a moral degenerate—lost to all sense of right and wrong.

LARITA: I respect you for one thing, anyhow—you *are* sure of yourself.

MRS. WHITTAKER: I don't want your respect.

LARITA: You're the only one here with the slightest grip. You've risen up like a phœnix from the ashes of your pride. It's quite, quite excellent— and infinitely pathetic.

MRS. WHITTAKER: I don't wish to speak to you anymore—until tomorrow. I shall be very grateful if you will remain upstairs this evening—I will make suitable excuses for your absence.

LARITA: You mean you're frightened that I should make a scene?

MRS. WHITTAKER: That is neither here nor there—I certainly don't desire an open scandal.

LARITA: You've run to cover again. I was afraid you would.

MRS. WHITTAKER: This has been painful beyond belief.

COLONEL: You're right—it has.

MRS. WHITTAKER: I don't feel capable of bearing any more.

LARITA: You intend to confine me to my room like a naughty child?

MRS. WHITTAKER: The simile is hardly appropriate, but I hope you will have the decency to remain there.

She goes upstairs in silence.

COLONEL: Lari—

LARITA: Please go away—I don't want anyone to speak to me at all for a little. I must think—think—

She is trembling hopelessly and making a tremendous effort to control her nerves.

COLONEL: Very well.

He goes out into the garden.
HILDA, who has been standing aghast throughout the entire scene, suddenly bursts into floods of tears and rushes at *LARITA.*

HILDA (*hysterically*): Lari—Lari—forgive me! I didn't mean it—I didn't mean it—

LARITA (*pushing her gently away*): Don't be a little toad, Hilda. Try to have the courage of your convictions.

HILDA rushes out into the garden, weeping hysterically.
LARITA bites her lip; then, still trembling violently, she lights a cigarette and takes *Sodom and Gomorrah* off the bureau. She settles herself on the sofa, obviously exerting every ounce of control, and opens the book methodically; she attempts to read, but her eyes can't focus on the page; she is acutely conscious of an imperfect statuette of the Venus de Milo

which is smirking at her from a pedestal by the dining-room doors. Suddenly, with all her force, she hurls the book at it, knocking it to the floor and smashing it.

LARITA: I've always hated that damned thing!

CURTAIN FALLS.

When it rises once, she has buried her face in the sofa cushion, and her shoulders are heaving, whether with laughter or tears it is difficult to say.

Larita soon realizes the situation is hopeless. She determines to leave John but not before she entrusts him to Sarah, the local girl who has loved him all along.

LARITA comes in . . . She sits down on the sofa . . .
CHARLES, another guest, enters.

LARITA (*to* CHARLES): Come and talk to me.
CHARLES: I've been wanting to do that.
LARITA: How sweet of you. Where's Sarah?
CHARLES: With John—having supper.
LARITA: Oh!

She opens her cigarette case and offers him one.

CHARLES: Thanks.

He lights hers and his own.

LARITA: Such a good floor, don't you think?
CHARLES: Perfectly awful.
LARITA: I wonder if your attention has been called to those fascinating Japanese lanterns?
CHARLES: Several times.
LARITA: You must admit it's a fine night, anyhow.
CHARLES: How you've changed.
LARITA: Changed?
CHARLES: Yes. Meeting you just now and then, as I've done, makes it easier to observe subtle differences.
LARITA: In what way have I changed?
CHARLES: You're dimmer.
LARITA: Dimmer!—with all these?

She jingles her bracelets.

CHARLES: Yes, even with those.

LARITA: You wouldn't have thought me dim if you'd seen me this afternoon.

CHARLES: Why, what happened?

LARITA: Several things.

CHARLES: I don't want you to think I'm angling for your confidence, but I *am* interested.

LARITA: I know that. It's interesting enough. Do you remember saying, the first day I met you, that one was disillusioned over everything?

CHARLES: You've been disillusioned lately?

LARITA: Yes—I didn't know I was capable of it.

CHARLES: That's one of the greatest illusions of all.

LARITA: You've been awfully nice to me.

CHARLES: Why not? We speak the same language.

LARITA: Yes—I suppose we do.

CHARLES: And naturally one feels instinctively drawn—particularly in this atmosphere.

LARITA: English country life. (*She smiles.*)

CHARLES: Yes, English country life.

LARITA: I wonder if it's a handicap having our sort of minds?

CHARLES: In what way?

LARITA: Watching ourselves go by.

CHARLES: No, it's a comfort in the end.

LARITA: I'm face-to-face with myself all the time—specially when I'm unhappy. It's not an edifying sensation.

CHARLES: I'm sorry you're unhappy.

LARITA: It can't be helped—you can't cope adequately with your successes unless you realise your failures.

CHARLES: It requires courage to do either.

LARITA: I've always had a definite ideal.

CHARLES: What is it?

LARITA: One should be top dog in one's own particular sphere.

CHARLES: It's so difficult to find out what *is* one's own particular sphere.

LARITA: I'm afraid that's always been depressingly obvious to me.

CHARLES: You feel you've deviated from your course.

LARITA: Exactly—and it's demoralised me.

CHARLES: Why did you do it?

LARITA: Panic, I believe.

CHARLES: What sort of panic?

LARITA: A panic of restlessness and dissatisfaction with everything.

CHARLES: That's a black cloud which descends upon everyone at moments.

LARITA: Not everyone—just people like us.

CHARLES: When you live emotionally you must expect the pendulum to swing both ways.

LARITA: It had swung the wrong way with a vengeance when I met John. Marrying him was the most cowardly thing I ever did.

CHARLES: Why did you?

LARITA: I loved him quite differently. I thought that any other relationship would be cheapening and squalid—I can't imagine how I could have been such a fool.

CHARLES: Neither can I.

LARITA: Love will always be the most dominant and absorbing subject in the world because it's so utterly inexplicable. Experience can teach you to handle it superficially, but not to explain it. I can look round with a nice clear brain and see absolutely no reason why I should love John. He falls short of every ideal I've ever had—he's not particularly talented or clever; he doesn't *know* anything, really; he can't talk about any of the things I consider it worth while to talk about; and, having been to a good school—he's barely educated.

CHARLES: Just a healthy young animal.

LARITA: Yes.

CHARLES: Perhaps that explains it.

LARITA: If my love were entirely physical, it would; but it isn't physical at all.

CHARLES: That *is* a bad sign.

LARITA: The worst.

CHARLES: What do you intend to do?

LARITA: I haven't decided yet.

CHARLES: I think I know.

LARITA: Don't say that.

CHARLES: Very well; I'll tell you afterwards if I guessed right.

LARITA: Go, and send Sarah to me—alone; will you?

CHARLES (*rising*): All right.

LARITA (*putting out her hand*): We shall meet again, perhaps, some day.

CHARLES: I *was* right.

LARITA (*putting her finger to her lips*): Sshhh!

CHARLES goes out . . . SARAH enters.

SARAH: Hello! Lari.

LARITA: I want to talk to you, Sarah—importantly. There isn't much time.

SARAH: Why? What do you mean?

LARITA: I'm going away—tonight.

SARAH: Lari!

LARITA: For good.

SARAH: Oh, my dear!—what on earth's the matter?

LARITA: Everything. Where's John?

SARAH: In the supper tent.

LARITA: Listen. There was a dreary family fracas this afternoon.

SARAH: What about?

LARITA: Hilda had unearthed a newspaper cutting, disclosing several of my past misdemeanours—

SARAH: The unutterable little beast! I made her swear—

LARITA: You knew about it?

SARAH: Yes, she showed it to me three days ago.

LARITA (*slightly overcome*): Oh, Sarah!—

SARAH: I said I'd never speak to her again if she showed it to anybody, and I shan't.

LARITA: It was all very unpleasant. The Colonel stood by me, of course— John wasn't there—he doesn't know anything yet.

SARAH: But, Lari dear, don't give in like this and chuck up everything.

LARITA: I must—you see, they're right; it's perfectly horrible for them. I'm entirely to blame.

SARAH: But what does it matter? The past's finished with.

LARITA: Never. Never, never, never. That's a hopeless fallacy.

SARAH: I'm most frightfully sorry.

LARITA: I wouldn't give in at all—unless I was sure. You see, John's completely sick of me—it was just silly calf love, and I ought to have recognised it as such. But I was utterly carried away—and now it's all such a hopeless mess.

SARAH: John's behaved abominably.

LARITA: No—not really. I expected too much. When you love anybody, you build in your mind an ideal of them—and it's naturally terribly hard for them to play up, not knowing—

SARAH: But, Lari, don't do anything on the impulse of the moment.

LARITA: It isn't the impulse of the moment—I realised it weeks ago.

SARAH: It may all come right yet.

LARITA: Be honest, Sarah—how can it?

SARAH: Where are you going?

LARITA: London tonight, and Paris tomorrow. I've ordered a car. Louise is packing now.

SARAH: Where will you stay?

LARITA: The Ritz. I always do.

SARAH: I wish I could do something.

LARITA (*pressing her hand*): You can.

SARAH: What?

LARITA: Look after John for me.

SARAH (*turning away*): Don't, Lari.

LARITA: I mean it. You're fond of him—you ought to have married him, by rights. He needs you so much more than me. He's frightfully weak, and a complete damn fool over most things, but he has got qualities— somewhere—worth bringing out. I'm going to arrange for him to divorce me, quietly, without any fuss.

SARAH: I don't love him nearly as well as you do.

LARITA: All the better. Women of my type are so tiresome in love. We hammer at it, tooth and nail, until it's all bent and misshapen. Promise me you'll do what I ask.

SARAH: I can't promise; but if circumstances make it possible, I'll try.

LARITA: All right—that'll do.

SARAH: Shall I see you again—ever?

LARITA: Yes, please.

SARAH: Well, we won't say good-bye, then.

LARITA: It's such a silly thing to say.

She gets up.

SARAH: Good luck, anyhow.

LARITA: I'm not sure that that's not sillier.

JOHN comes in.

JOHN: Sarah, I've been looking for you everywhere.

SARAH: Well, you've found me now.

JOHN: Lari, I'm sorry I was beastly just now—about your dress. You are rather a Christmas tree, though, aren't you?

LARITA: It was done with a purpose.

JOHN: What purpose?

LARITA: It was a sort of effort to reestablish myself—rather a gay gesture— almost a joke!

JOHN: Oh!

SARAH: You'll find me in the garden, John.

LARITA (*quickly*): Don't go, Sarah—please. (SARAH *stops.*) I'm rather tired, so I'll say good night.

JOHN: The dance will go on for hours yet—this is only a lull.

LARITA: Yes, I know; but I'm dead.

JOHN: Oh, very well.

LARITA: Good night, darling.

She kisses him.

JOHN: I'll try not to disturb you.

LARITA: I'm afraid you won't be able to help it.

SARAH: Come and dance, John.
JOHN: What's the matter, Lari? Why are you looking like that?
LARITA: I think I'm going to sneeze . . .

JOHN and *SARAH* go into the dance room. *FURBER* enters from veranda.

LARITA: Is the car ready, Furber?
FURBER: Yes, ma'am. Your maid is waiting in it.
LARITA: Get my cloak from her, will you, please?
FURBER: Very good, ma'am. (*He goes off.*)

LARITA, left quite alone, leans up against one of the windows and looks out into the garden. The light from the lanterns falls on her face, which is set in an expression of hopeless sadness. She fans herself, then lets her fan drop. *FURBER* reenters with her cloak, and helps her on with it.

LARITA: Thank you very much, Furber. You won't forget what I asked you, will you?
FURBER: No, ma'am.
LARITA: Then good-bye.
FURBER: Good-bye, ma'am.

He holds open the door for her, and she walks out. There is a burst of laughter from the veranda. The band continues to play with great enthusiasm.

CURTAIN.

•

HAY FEVER (1925)

CAST

JUDITH BLISS	MARIE TEMPEST
SIMON BLISS	ROBERT ANDREWS
SOREL BLISS	HELEN SPENCER
RICHARD GREATHAM	ATHOLE STEWART

DIRECTED BY NOËL COWARD
AMBASSADORS THEATRE, LONDON, SEPTEMBER 17, 1925

Hay Fever was based upon Noël's experience in the somewhat frenzied New York home of American actress Laurette Taylor. When Taylor realized that she was the model for the heroine, she refused to speak to Noël for several years before friendly relations were finally resumed. Today—thanks to the play— the character is better remembered than the original. But that—as someone once wittily said—is show business . . .

When I tapped out this little comedy so exuberantly onto my typewriter in the year 1924, I would indeed have been astonished if anyone had told me that it was destined to emerge, fresh and blooming, forty years later. One of the reasons it was hailed so warmly in 1925 was that there happened to be at that time an ardent journalistic campaign being conducted against "sex" plays, and *Hay Fever,* as I remarked in my first night speech, was, whether good, bad or indifferent, at least it was clean as a whistle.

I enjoyed writing it and producing it, and I have frequently enjoyed watching it.

The idea came to me suddenly in the garden and I finished it in about three days, a feat which later on when I had become news value, seemed to excite gossip writers inordinately, although why the public would care whether a play takes three days or three years to write I shall never understand. Perhaps they don't. However, when I had finished it and had it neatly typed and bound up, I read it through and was rather unimpressed with it. This was an odd sensation for me, as in those days I was almost always enchanted with everything I wrote. I knew certain scenes were good, especially the breakfast scene in the last act and the dialogue between the giggling flapper and the diplomat in the first act, but apart from these it seemed to me a little tedious. I think the reason for this was that I was passing through a transition stage as a writer; my dialogue was becoming more natural and less elaborate and I was beginning to concentrate more on the comedy values of situation rather than the comedy values of actual lines. I expect that when I read through *Hay Fever* that first time, I was subconsciously bemoaning its lack of snappy epigrams.

In her day Judith Bliss was a resplendent star on the London stage—the Grande Dame of the Matinée Tea Trays. Though reluctantly retired from the stage when the play opens, the actress in her will not be denied—as her family and guests find to their cost.

On one particular weekend she, her husband David, son Simon and daughter Sorel have each—unbeknownst to the rest of the family—invited a guest. They then proceed to ignore them, and a degree of social chaos ensues.

Before the guests arrive, Judith confides to her children . . .

JUDITH: I made a great decision this morning.

SIMON: What kind of decision?

JUDITH: It's a secret.

SOREL: Aren't you going to tell us?

JUDITH: Of course. I meant it was a secret from your father.

SIMON: What is it?

JUDITH: I'm going back to the stage.

SIMON: I knew it!

JUDITH: I'm stagnating here. I won't stagnate as long as there's breath left in my body.

SOREL: Do you think it's wise? You retired so very finally last year. What excuse will you give for returning so soon?

JUDITH: My public, dear—letters from my public!

SIMON: Have you had any?

JUDITH: One or two. That's what decided me, really—I ought to have had hundreds.

SOREL: We'll write some lovely ones, and you can publish them in the papers.

JUDITH: Of course.

SOREL: You will be dignified about it all, won't you, darling?

JUDITH: I'm much more dignified on the stage than in the country—it's my milieu. I've tried terribly hard to be "landed gentry," but without any real success. I long for excitement and glamour. Think of the thrill of a first night; all those ardent playgoers willing one to succeed; the critics all leaning forward with glowing faces, receptive and exultant—emitting queer little inarticulate noises as some witty line tickles their fancy. The satisfied grunt of the *Daily Mail,* the abandoned gurgle of the *Sunday Times,* and the shrill, enthusiastic scream of the *Daily Express*! I can distinguish them all—

SIMON: Have you got a play?

JUDITH: I think I shall revive *Love's Whirlwind.*

SOREL: Oh, Mother!

SIMON (*weakly*): Father will be furious.

JUDITH: I can't help that.

SOREL: It's such a fearful play.

JUDITH: It's a marvellous part. You mustn't say too much against it, Sorel. I'm willing to laugh at it a little myself, but, after all, it *was* one of my greatest successes.

SIMON: Oh, it's appalling—but I love it. It makes me laugh.

JUDITH: The public love it too, and it doesn't make them laugh—much. "You are a fool, a blind pitiable fool. You think because you have bought my body that you have bought my soul!" You must say that's dramatic—"I've dreamed of love like this, but I never realized, I never knew how beautiful it could be in reality!" (*Wipes away imaginary tears.*) That line always brought a tear to my eye.

SIMON: The second act *is* the best, there's no doubt about that.

JUDITH: From the moment Victor comes in it's strong—tremendously strong. . . . Be Victor a minute, Sorel—

SOREL: Do you mean when he comes in at the end of the act?

JUDITH: Yes. You know—"Is this a game?"

SOREL: "Is this a game?"

JUDITH: "Yes—and a game that must be played to the finish."

SIMON (*speaking in deep dramatic voice*): "Zara, what does this mean?"

JUDITH: "So many illusions shattered—so many dreams trodden in the dust!"

SOREL: I'm George now—"I don't understand! You and Victor—My God!" (*Strikes dramatic pose.*)

JUDITH (*listening*): "Sssh! Isn't that little Pam crying?"

SIMON (*savagely*): "She'll cry more, poor mite, when she realizes her mother is a—"

The front-door bell rings.

JUDITH: Damn! There's the bell!

Then the guests arrive and Judith finds herself alone with Sorel's guest, the rather stuffy civil servant, Richard Greatham. The opportunity for a little improvisational "performance" is a temptation too strong to resist . . .

JUDITH: You'll get used to us in time, and then you'll feel cosier. Why don't you sit down? (*She sits on sofa.*)

RICHARD (*sits beside her*): I'm enjoying myself very much.

JUDITH: It's very sweet of you to say so, but I don't see how you can be.

RICHARD (*laughing suddenly*): But I am!

JUDITH: There now, that was quite a genuine laugh! We're getting on. Are you in love with Sorel?

RICHARD (*surprised and embarrassed*): In love with Sorel?

Hay Fever at the Ambassadors Theatre, London, 1925. The Bliss family and their
beleaguered weekend guests. Judith Bliss (Marie Tempest) far right.

The National Theatre, London, revival of *Hay Fever* in 1964, directed by Noël with
"a cast that could have played the Albanian telephone directory."
Judith Bliss (Edith Evans) far right.

JUDITH (*repentantly*): Now I've killed it—I've murdered the little tender feeling of comfort that was stealing over you, by sheer tactlessness! Will you teach me to be tactful?

RICHARD: Did you really think I was in love with Sorel?

JUDITH: It's so difficult to tell, isn't it?—I mean, you might not know yourself. She's very attractive.

RICHARD: Yes, she is—very.

JUDITH: Have you heard her sing?

RICHARD: No, not yet.

JUDITH: She sings beautifully. Are you susceptible to music?

RICHARD: I'm afraid I don't know very much about it.

JUDITH: You probably are, then. I'll sing you something.

RICHARD: Please do.

JUDITH (*rises and crosses to piano; he rises*): It's awfully sad for a woman of my temperament to have a grown-up daughter, you know. I have to put my pride in my pocket and develop in her all the charming little feminine tricks which will eventually cut me out altogether.

RICHARD: That wouldn't be possible.

JUDITH: I do hope you meant that, because it was a sweet remark. (*She is at the piano, turning over music.*)

RICHARD (*crosses to piano*): Of course I meant it.

JUDITH: Will you lean on the piano in an attentive attitude? It's such a help.

RICHARD (*leaning on piano*): You're an extraordinary person.

JUDITH (*beginning to play*): In what way extraordinary?

RICHARD: When I first met Sorel, I guessed what you'd be like.

JUDITH: Did you, now? And am I?

RICHARD (*smiling*): Exactly.

JUDITH: Oh, well! . . . (*She plays and sings a little French song.*)

There is a slight pause when it is finished.

RICHARD (*with feeling*): Thank you.

JUDITH (*rising from the piano*): It's pretty, isn't it?

RICHARD: Perfectly enchanting.

JUDITH (*crosses to sofa*): Shall we sit down again? (*She reseats herself on sofa.*)

RICHARD (*moving over to her*): Won't you sing any more?

JUDITH: No, no more—I want you to talk to me and tell me all about yourself, and the things you've done.

RICHARD (*sits beside her*): I've done nothing.

JUDITH: What a shame! Why not?

RICHARD: I never realize how *dead* I am until I meet people like you. It's depressing, you know.

JUDITH: What nonsense! You're not a bit dead.

RICHARD: Do you always live here?

JUDITH: I'm going to, from now onwards. I intend to sink into a very beautiful old age. When the children marry, I shall wear a cap.

RICHARD (*smiling*): How absurd!

JUDITH: I don't mean a funny cap.

RICHARD: You're far too full of vitality to sink into anything.

JUDITH: It's entirely spurious vitality. If you troubled to look below the surface, you'd find a very wistful and weary spirit. I've been battling with life for a long time.

RICHARD: Surely such successful battles as yours have been are not wearying?

JUDITH: Yes, they are—frightfully. I've reached an age now when I just want to sit back and let things go on around me—and they do.

RICHARD: I should like to know exactly what you're thinking about—really.

JUDITH: I was thinking of calling you Richard. It's such a nice uncompromising name.

RICHARD: I should be very flattered if you would.

JUDITH: I won't suggest you calling me Judith until you feel really comfortable about me.

RICHARD: But I do—Judith.

JUDITH: I'm awfully glad. Will you give me a cigarette?

RICHARD (*producing case*): Certainly.

JUDITH (*taking one*): Oh, what a divine case!

RICHARD: It was given to me in Japan three years ago. All those little designs mean things.

JUDITH (*bending over it*): What sort of things?

He lights her cigarette.

RICHARD: Charms for happiness, luck, and—love.

JUDITH: Which is the charm for love?

RICHARD: That one.

JUDITH: What a dear!

RICHARD kisses her gently on the neck. (She sits upright, with a scream.)

JUDITH: Richard!

RICHARD (*stammering*): I'm afraid I couldn't help it.

JUDITH (*dramatically*): What are we to do? What are we to do?

RICHARD: I don't know.

JUDITH (*rises, thrusts the case in his hand and crosses to* RIGHT CENTER): David must be told—everything!

RICHARD (*alarmed*): Everything?

JUDITH (*enjoying herself*): Yes, yes. There come moments in life when it is necessary to be honest—absolutely honest. I've trained myself always to shun the underhand methods other women so often employ—the truth must be faced fair and square—

RICHARD (*extremely alarmed*): The truth? I don't quite understand. (*He rises.*)

JUDITH: Dear Richard, you want to spare me, I know—you're so chivalrous; but it's no use. After all, as I said before, David has been a good husband to me, according to his lights. This may, of course, break him up rather, but it can't be helped. I wonder—oh, I wonder how he'll take it! They say suffering's good for writers, it strengthens their psychology. Oh, my poor, poor David! Never mind. You'd better go out into the garden and wait—

RICHARD (*flustered*): Wait? What for?

JUDITH: For me, Richard, for me. I will come to you later. Wait in the summer house. I had begun to think that Romance was dead, that I should never know it again. Before, of course, I had my work and my life in the theatre, but now, nothing—nothing! Everything is empty and hollow, like a broken shell. (*She sinks onto form below piano, and looks up at* RICHARD *with a tragic smile, then looks quickly away.*)

RICHARD: Look here, Judith, I apologize for what I did just now. I—

JUDITH (*ignoring all interruption, she rises*): But now you have come, and it's all changed—it's magic! I'm under a spell that I never thought to recapture again. Go along—

She pushes him towards the garden.

RICHARD (*protesting*): But, Judith—

JUDITH (*pushing him firmly until he is off*): Don't—don't make it any harder for me. I am quite resolved—and it's the only possible way. Go, go!

She pushes him into the garden and waves to him bravely with her handkerchief; then she comes back into the room and powders her nose before the glass and pats her hair into place.

If Judith Bliss had lived to be a hundred, she would still have been acting and incorporating the advancing years seamlessly into the character she was creating. In Noël's experience not every senior female thespian was so resilient . . .

Costume design for Myra
in *Hay Fever* by Motley

Edith Evans and Maggie Smith by Hewison

"EPITAPH FOR AN ELDERLY ACTRESS"

She got in a rage
About age
And retired, in a huff, from the stage.
Which, taken all round, was a pity
Because she was still fairly pretty
But she got in a rage
About age.

She burst into tears
It appears
When the rude, inconsiderate years
Undermined her once flawless complexion
And whenever she saw her reflection
In a mirror, she burst into tears
It appears.

She got in a state
About weight
And resented each morsel she ate.
Her colon she constantly sluiced
And reduced and reduced and reduced
And, at quite an incredible rate
Put *on* weight.

She got in a rage
About age
But she still could have played Mistress Page
And she certainly could have done worse
Than *Hay Fever* or Juliet's Nurse
But she got in a terrible rage
About age.

And she moaned and she wept and she wailed
And she roared and she ranted and railed
And retired, very heavily veiled,
From the stage.

•

The Play-That-Got-Away—for over fifty years—was conceived and written while Noël was touring the United States with *The Vortex*.

Long runs in which he was personally involved as an actor bored him, and he was glad when the tour ended in Cleveland.

I had played the part [of Nicky] over 450 times, and although during the tour I had forced myself to write a play, it had been a tremendous strain, and I felt that many months of creative impulse had been frustrated.

The play was called *Semi-Monde,* and the whole action of it took place in the public rooms of the Ritz Hotel in Paris over a period of three years. [Its working title had been *Ritz Bar.*] It was well constructed and, on the whole, well written; its production in London or New York seemed unlikely as some of the characters, owing to lightly suggested abnormalities, would certainly be deleted by the Censor.

Almost as soon as he had written the piece, Noël felt the need to write his *apologia,* which incidentally expressed his views on the state of the post–World War I English theatre . . .

"PREFACE TO *SEMI-MONDE*" (1926)

I feel that a few words of explanation are necessary to exculpate *Semi-Monde* from the charges of "licentiousness," "decadence" and "sensationalism." Several times before with regard to my earlier plays these three qualities have been accredited to me in addition to several others equally vituperative. Therefore, in this case I wish to forestall the inevitable by laying at the disposal of whosoever cares to read it a brief outline of my real motives in writing of types and characters which, although constituting a comparatively small section of civilized society, are nevertheless just as valuable as factors in Human Drama as Gentlemen Burglars, Lancashire Homicides and Elizabethan Harlots.

At the time of writing this there is being waged in England a passionate campaign against what are described as "unpleasant" plays—that is, plays which utilize (perhaps a little more frankly than usual)—conflicting sex relationships for the furtherance of their dramatic values. There have been several hysterical demands—generally, it must be admitted, from elderly clergymen in Norfolk—that sex be abolished from the stage altogether. This suggestion, though too fatuous to be considered seriously, serves to illustrate the distressing trend of public opinion at a moment when the British Drama is tottering so visibly that artificial restoration has to be resorted to in the shape of imported American farces and musical comedies in increasing numbers.

•

The British nation since its deliverance from the horrors of war in 1918 appears in its attitude towards art to have become more and more lethargic—a comatose smugness seems to have swept over the land. In other countries tremendous efforts are being made in the progress of literature and drama. And for each forward step registered in America, Germany, France and Italy, England falls back two, completely undismayed in its serene and idiotic complacency. The younger writers are forced to compromise, because in most cases they are not in a position to fight and have a living to make. The slightest break away from tradition is greeted with fear and suspicion by the Church and State. Sincerely written plays by unknown young authors are turned down in feverish haste by the Lord Chamberlain, thereby being denied the judgment of the public, which is after all their right, solely because—in so many cases quite unwittingly—they present problems comic or tragic of the present day as contrasted with the standards of twenty-five years ago. These being unfortunately the only standard by which those in authority seem to be capable of judging.

During the years between 1914 and 1918 the general nerve tension was so great that with the sudden cessation of strain a complete psychological reaction was inevitable and it is in the midst of this reaction that we are living now. Moral values as they were have long since lost all significance. Ideals and ambitions as they were have changed likewise. This does not in any way mean abolishment, merely readjustment and it is this all important fact that the older generation seems incapable of grasping.

In 1909 the *Oxford English Dictionary* included a meaning for the word "camp" over and above "a row of tents." It quoted "ostentatious, exaggerated, affected, theatrical, effeminate, homosexual."

So, while Noël could hardly claim to have invented the concept, he certainly embodied it in parts of *Semi-Monde.* Whether he was dealing with the "boys" . . .

BEVERLEY FORD and CYRIL HARDACRE come through the swing doors, carrying small bags and followed by the DAY PORTER, carrying their larger ones. BEVERLEY is about forty, extremely well dressed. CYRIL is in his twenties—good-looking and slim.

BEVERLEY (*to the* DAY PORTER): Pay the taxi, will you? I haven't any change.
DAY PORTER (*putting down the bags*): Yes, sir.
CYRIL: I have.
BEVERLEY: No—he'll do it.

The DAY PORTER goes out.

Thelma Holt, Karl Sydow & Bill Kenwright
present

Noël Coward's
SEMI-MONDE

Directed and Designed by
PHILIP PROWSE

Lighting Designer
GERRY JENKINSON

LYRIC THEATRE
Shaftesbury Avenue, London W1V 7HA

Production sponsored by The Ritz, London

BEVERLEY: Well, my dear—here we are at last. Paris is a virgin for you, unsullied by memories. Are you happy?

CYRIL (*with faint impatience*): Of course I am.

BEVERLEY (*with a giggle*): You blush so beautifully when I make affected remarks.

CYRIL: Oh shut up, Beverley.

BEVERLEY: That's why I make them.

ALBERT HENNICK enters from the direction of the lounge. He is a dapper little man of about twenty-eight. His voice is rather shrill.

ALBERT: Beverley—by God, it *is* you. I was having tea with Violet; she saw you first. This is divine—how *are* you?

The *DAY PORTER* has returned by this time and gives *BEVERLEY* his change. *BEVERLEY* tips him.

BEVERLEY: Leave the bags while I go and see about our rooms. Talk to Cyril for a moment, Albert.

He goes to the Bureau.

ALBERT: I've seen you before somewhere, haven't I?
CYRIL: In London, perhaps.
ALBERT: How long are you staying?
CYRIL: Not long. Beverley wants to go down to Cannes.
ALBERT: Are you going with him?
CYRIL (*frowning slightly*): Yes.
ALBERT: My dear, how marvelous! You must both come to a party a friend of mine is giving on Thursday—Nicco Benelli—d'you know him?
CYRIL: No, I'm afraid I don't.
ALBERT: He's completely mad—you'll love him. Italian you know—dark and flashy eyes and plays the piano like an angel. Eric Burnett always says—D'you know Eric?
CYRIL: No.
ALBERT (*giggling*): Well, you will soon—he's terribly funny.

BEVERLEY rejoins them.

BEVERLEY: We're on the Rue Gilon side.
ALBERT: You must talk to Violet on the way through. She's dying to see you.
BEVERLEY: All right. (*To the* DAY PORTER) Have the bags sent over as soon as possible.
DAY PORTER: Yes, sir.
BEVERLEY: Come along.

CYRIL walks off a few paces in front.

ALBERT (*to* BEVERLEY *as they go off*): Where did you find that? It's divine!

INEZ ZULIETTA and *CYNTHIA GABLE* come through the swing doors. *INEZ* is slightly older than *CYNTHIA*. They are both dressed with rather affected simplicity.

INEZ (*coming forward and sitting by the table*): I'll wait here.
CYNTHIA: Don't be silly.
INEZ: I'll be quite happy. You needn't worry about *me*. (*She assumes a martyred expression.*)
CYNTHIA: I do wish you wouldn't be so difficult.

INEZ: I'm not being in the least difficult.

CYNTHIA: There are moments when you're infuriating.

INEZ: Thank you.

CYNTHIA (*lowering her voice*): What is there to be jealous about?

INEZ: Everything—you don't know her like I do.

CYNTHIA (*sharply*): That's true enough.

INEZ: Why say things like that?

CYNTHIA: Well, you told me yourself.

INEZ: That was all over years ago.

CYNTHIA: I didn't say it wasn't.

INEZ: You're damnably cruel sometimes.

CYNTHIA: Why don't you trust me?

INEZ: Trust you—

CYNTHIA: Yes; I feel as though I were in a cage.

INEZ: Cynthia, darling—

CYNTHIA: What?

INEZ: I do trust you—really—but don't go and see her now.

CYNTHIA: Why not?

INEZ: You know perfectly well.

CYNTHIA: Just because you've worked yourself up into a ridiculous state . . .

INEZ: I haven't done anything of the sort.

CYNTHIA: You have.

INEZ: I wish you'd give me back my pride.

CYNTHIA: Don't be melodramatic.

INEZ: And with it the courage never to see you again.

She gets up abruptly and goes out.

CYNTHIA (*following her*): Inez—Inez—

She goes out after her.

Then later . . .

MARION FAWCETT enters. She is somewhere between thirty and forty and dressed smartly. She has almost reached the kiosk when *INEZ* and *CYNTHIA* enter.

MARION: Hello, Inez. How are you?

INEZ: Exhausted, dear. You know Cynthia, don't you?

MARION: Of course. (*She shakes hands with* CYNTHIA.) You haven't seen a dark little American girl with a sort of wood violet face loitering about, have you?

INEZ: Yes, hundreds.

MARION: Gloria Craig gave her a letter of introduction to me. I must find her and give her lunch.

CYNTHIA: Well, if you don't succeed, come and lunch with us.

INEZ: I'm not lunching.

CYNTHIA (*warningly*): Inez!

INEZ: I have to go to Chanel.

CYNTHIA (*to* MARION): Well, lunch with *me* then. I'll be in the restaurant.

MARION: Thanks, my dear. See you later, Inez.

She goes off.

INEZ (*as they walk across*): I suppose it's too much to expect that you should ever wish to lunch with me alone.

CYNTHIA: Don't be ridiculous.

INEZ: I'm *not* ridiculous. You know I loathe Marion Fawcett.

CYNTHIA: I don't know anything of the sort.

INEZ (*angrily*): Go and lunch with her then—lunch and dine and sup with all the people I hate most—and discuss me with them and break up everything.

CYNTHIA (*quickly*): I will—if you're not careful!

As they are about to go off, CYRIL walks on.

CYRIL: Oh, how do you do?

INEZ (*shaking hands*): I'd no idea you were in Paris.

CYRIL: I'm over here with Beverley.

INEZ: My dear boy, how unoriginal.

All of which makes the serial heterosexual philandering that occurs elsewhere in the play seem positively conventional by comparison.

·

Since his first visit to New York five years earlier, Noël had been impressed by the speed of actors' delivery onstage, and this use of naturalistic overlapping dialogue was surely what he had in mind with the opening of this scene.

When the curtain rises the bar is crowded. Apart from the characters already familiar to the audience there are several other groups of people smoking and talking. At a table DOWN LEFT are DOROTHY and BERYL. CYNTHIA and ELISE are sitting against the wall UP RIGHT. MARION FAWCETT, SUZANNE FELLINI and GEORGE HUDD are seated together just below ELISE and *CYNTHIA*. *JEROME* is seated just above *DOROTHY* and *BERYL* reading a paper and sipping a cocktail. *ALBERT HENNICK* is devoting himself assiduously to a rich old lady who is slightly deaf but determined to be vivacious. The ensuing scene must be played simultaneously by everybody, the dialogue being immaterial to the play but the general effect of noise essential. *INEZ* and *CYRIL* are sitting silently in a corner.

CYNTHIA: I waited for twenty-five minutes.

ELISE: How infuriating!

CYNTHIA: And when she arrived with that dreadful Merrivale woman.

ELISE: Why didn't you go?

CYNTHIA: How could I—it would have been too pointed.

DOROTHY: My dear, you needn't worry about that.

BERYL: I haven't got your perfectly wonderful poise.

DOROTHY: Nonsense!

BERYL: It's true—I get embarrassed terribly easily.

DOROTHY: I wish you'd telephoned me.

ALBERT: It's really worth seeing.

OLD LADY: What?

ALBERT: I say it's really worth seeing—she's entrancing.

OLD LADY: I didn't know it was a musical play.

ALBERT: It isn't.

OLD LADY: You said she was dancing—

MARION: Never again as long as I live.

GEORGE: It was damn funny though.

MARION: It may have been to you—I was furious.

SUZANNE: She always gets bad-tempered when she's drunk.

GEORGE: I couldn't help laughing.

ELISE: I can't understand what she sees in her.

CYNTHIA: Neither can anyone else.

ELISE: It's that sort of mind that prevents her being a good artiste.

CYNTHIA: She's never real for a moment.

ELISE: She deceives a lot of people though—Freddie Carrol was raving about her—

BERYL: I will another time.

DOROTHY: You see I've known him for years.

BERYL: Yes, he said heavenly things about you.

DOROTHY: That's damn nice of him.

BERYL: But he did—honestly.

ALBERT: No—entrancing—marvelous.

OLD LADY: I love anything a little *risqué.*

ALBERT: Well, it's certainly that.

OLD LADY: What?

ALBERT: I say it's certainly that.

OLD LADY: What a pity—she used to be so lovely.

SUZANNE: I must say I see Marion's point.

GEORGE: Who was the little fair girl who sang?

MARION: I don't know—she made me feel uncomfortable.

SUZANNE: Marie something or other—she used to be at the Casino de Paris.

GEORGE: Damned attractive looking!

ALBERT: Shall we go and have lunch now?

OLD LADY: What?

ALBERT: Lunch?

OLD LADY: Oh yes—I'm dieting, you know—I shan't eat much.

ALBERT (*rising*): I'm not particularly hungry.

OLD LADY: We might walk through to the restaurant.

ALBERT pilots her out.

SUZANNE: Thanks for the cocktail, George—I wish you were eating with us.

GEORGE: I shall wait ten minutes more.

MARION (*rising*): Come on, Suzanne.

SUZANNE: Give us a call when you get back.

GEORGE: We'll have a party.

MARION: Lovely. Good-bye.

GEORGE: I shall probably be at the Crillon—I'm sick of this place.

SUZANNE: So am I—but it's a sort of habit one can't shake off.

In the event, Noël's prediction proved to be true. London and New York were out of the question. Producer Max Reinhardt, though, was enthusiastic about it, had it translated into German and taken to Berlin, "where for years it escaped production by a hairsbreadth until eventually Vicki Baum wrote *Grand Hotel,* and *Semi-Monde,* being too closely similar in theme, faded gently into oblivion."

It was finally produced by the Glasgow Citizens' Theatre in 1977 and had a short West End run in 2001, but by that time it was a period piece that carried no shock value—other than the fact that it had been written in those far-off days by—Noël Coward.

·

Unable to pitch his "camp" in 1926, Noël revisited it in 1929 —in a musical comedy of all settings. The limp-wristed flippancy of the young men in *Bitter Sweet* was daring for its time, at least onstage. But then it was a parody of the late Oscar Wilde, who affected the flower. So *that* was all right.

"GREEN CARNATION"

Blasé boys are we,
Exquisitely free
From the dreary and quite absurd
Moral views of the common herd.
We like porphyry bowls,
Chandeliers and stoles,
We're most spirited,
Carefully filleted "souls."

Pretty boys, witty boys, too, too, too
Lazy to fight stagnation,
Haughty boys, naughty boys, all we do
Is to pursue sensation.
The portals of society
Are always opened wide,
The world our eccentricity condones,
A note of quaint variety
We're certain to provide,
We dress in very decorative tones.
Faded boys, jaded boys, womankind's
Gift to a bulldog nation,

In order to distinguish us from less
                 enlightened minds,
We all wear a green carnation.

We believe in Art,
Though we're poles apart
From the fools who are thrilled by Greuze.
We like Beardsley and Green Chartreuse.
Women say we're too
Bored to bill and coo,
We smile wearily,
It's so drearily true!

Pretty boys, witty boys, you may sneer
At our disintegration,
Haughty boys, naughty boys, dear, dear, dear!
Swooning with affectation,
Our figures sleek and willowy,
Our lips incarnadine,
May worry the majority a bit.
But matrons rich and billowy
Invite us out to dine,
And revel in our phosphorescent wit,
Faded boys, jaded boys, come what may,
Art is our inspiration
And as we are the reason for the "Nineties" being gay,
We all wear a green carnation.

Pretty boys, witty boys, yearning for
Permanent adulation,
Haughty boys, naughty boys, every pore
Bursting with self-inflation.
We feel we're rather Grecian,
As our manners indicate,
Our sense of moral values isn't strong.
For ultimate completion
We shall really have to wait
Until the Day of Judgment comes along.
Faded boys, jaded boys, each one craves
Some sort of soul salvation,
But when we rise reluctantly but gracefully
                       from our graves,
We'll all wear a green carnation.

•

Encouraged by the breakthrough of *The Vortex, Hay Fever* and *Easy Virtue,* he made the crucial mistake of rummaging through his creative "bottom drawer" and pulling out some of his earlier plays. Managements were keen to stage them. Unfortunately, audiences, when they saw them, did not share their enthusiasm. Perhaps Young Mr. Coward was something they'd seen too often in the past—the proverbial flash in the pan. And what audiences determined was good—or bad—was enough for producers and critics alike.

Noël took it all very much to heart.

"I opened my arms a little too wide to everything that came, and enjoyed it. Later on, just a little while later, circumstances showed me that my acceptance had been a thought too credulous. The 'darling' of the London Theatre received what can only be described as a sharp kick in the pants."

When asked in later years what was his single biggest regret, his answer—"Not having taken more trouble with some of my work."

When faced with any major reversal—professional or personal—it was at this time that Noël evolved a philosophy to cope with it.

Escape.

Just as so many of the characters in his plays are inclined to make a hasty exit before the final curtain to resolve a tricky situation—Elyot and Amanda in *Private Lives* . . . Garry and Liz in *Present Laughter* . . . Charles in *Blithe Spirit* . . . the benighted houseguests in *Hay Fever*—so would Noël be inclined to leave a scene that didn't please.

I have always believed in putting geographical distance between myself and a flop.

—DIARIES (1948)

"SAIL AWAY"

A different sky,
New worlds to gaze upon,
The strange excitement of an unfamiliar shore,
One more good-bye,
One more illusion gone,
Just cut your losses
And begin once more.

When the storm clouds are riding through a winter sky
Sail away—sail away.
When the love-light is fading in your sweetheart's eye
Sail away—sail away.
When you feel your song is orchestrated wrong
Why should you prolong
Your stay?
When the wind and the weather blow your dreams
                                 sky high
Sail away—sail away—sail away!

When the friends that you've counted on have let you
   down
Sail away—sail away!
But when soon or late
You recognize your fate
That will be your great,
Great day.
On the wings of the morning with your own true love
Sail away—
Sail away—
Sail away!

—SAIL AWAY (1961)

"I TRAVEL ALONE" (1934)

The world is wide, and when my day is done
I shall at least have traveled free,
Led by this wanderlust that turns my eyes to
   far horizons.
Though time and tide won't wait for anyone,
There's one illusion left for me
And that's the happiness I've known alone.

I travel alone,
Sometimes I'm East,
Sometimes I'm West,
No chains can ever bind me;
No remembered love can ever find me;
I travel alone.
Fair though the faces and places I've known,

When the dream is ended and passion has flown
I travel alone.
Free from love's illusion, my heart is my own:
I travel alone.

My body has certainly wandered a good deal, but I have an uneasy suspicion that my mind has not wandered nearly enough!!

—PRESENT INDICATIVE (1937)

Traveling alone . . . Noël's British passport from the 1940s

·

After a nervous breakdown in the early 1920s his doctor advised Noël to sit down and conduct an honest self-analysis of his strengths and weaknesses. He did so, and called it a "Mental Purge" . . .

DEFECTS

Overemotional and hysterical
Overanxiety to attain popularity
Jealousy fostered by overintrospection
Intolerance
Lack of restraint—particularly emotionally
Self-pitying
Predatory
Sentimental
Almost complete ignorance upon many subjects that I should know
    thoroughly, and a facility for faking knowledge
Physical cowardice
Histrionic in private life
Given to mental gymnastics at cost of other people's peace of mind
Domineering
Overemphatic in argument and practically everything

ASSETS

An excellent knowledge of psychology when unaffected by emotion
Strong sense of humour
Facility in conversation
Power of demanding and holding affection
Loyalty to friends and personal standards
Generosity and kindness of heart
Power of concentration
Several talents
Moral courage
Strength of will when unaffected by emotion
Common sense
Personality

·

Among his other talents Noël had a particularly strong and instinctive sense of the times he was living in and the way they were changing . . .

This is a changing world, my dear,
New songs are sung—new stars appear,
Though we grow older year by year,
Our hearts can still be gay.

—PACIFIC 1860 (1946)

While he himself was in many ways a creation of the 1920s, he was also able to stand back and sense the *angst* all too close to the surface of the frenzied gaiety.

As early as 1922 he would write a song that Cecil Beaton firmly declared to be "the signature tune of the late 1920s."

"The idea came to me in a nightclub in Berlin. A frowsy blonde, wearing a sequin chest-protector and a divided skirt, appeared in the course of the cabaret with a rag Pierrot doll dressed in black velvet. She placed it on a cushion where it sprawled in pathetic abandon while she pranced around it emitting guttural noises. Her performance was unimpressive but the doll fascinated me."

It seemed to him to symbolize something of the gaudy pointlessness of the postwar age.

"The title 'Parisian Pierrot' slipped into my mind and in the taxi on the way back to the hotel the song began."

"PARISIAN PIERROT"

Fantasy in olden days
In varying and different ways
Was very much in vogue,
Columbine and Pantaloon,
A wistful Pierrot 'neath the moon,
And Harlequin a rogue.
Nowadays Parisians of leisure
Wake the echo of an old refrain,
Each some ragged effigy will treasure
For his pleasure,
Till the shadows of their story live again.

Mournfulness has always been
The keynote of a Pierrot scene,
When passion plays a part,
Pierrot in a tragic pose

Gertie as the Parisian Pierrot in the 1923 revue
London Calling!

Will kiss a faded silver rose
With sadness in his heart.
Some day soon he'll leave his tears behind him,
Comedy comes laughing down the street,
Columbine will fly to him
Admiring and desiring,
Laying love and adoration at his feet.

Parisian Pierrot,
Society's hero,
The lord of a day,
The Rue de la Paix
Is under your sway,
The world may flatter
But what does that matter,
They'll never shatter
Your gloom profound,

Parisian Pierrot,
Your spirit's at zero,
Divinely forlorn,
With exquisite scorn
From sunset to dawn,
The limbo is calling,
Your star will be falling,
As soon as the clock goes round.

—LONDON CALLING! (1923)

As the years went by and the evidence of social malaise became more obvious, Noël's comment on it became more explicit. Yes, women were now free to bob their hair, raise their hemlines—and even smoke cigarettes. But were they really any happier? Were *any* of us?

By 1925, in *On With the Dance,* he had summed it up. In a sophisticated little sketch "Hermione Baddeley stood about in evening dress looking drained and far from healthy, while [Alice] Delysia, as her French governess, lectured her in a worldly manner about the debauched life she was all too obviously leading."

As Baddeley herself remembered, "These poor little rich girls were part of the scene in 1923 and there were always some, with their doomed and mournful eyes, in the society of the Bright Young Things. I had seen many of them . . ."

Noël recalled, "I thought of the tune while I was having tea. The usual dash for the piano and the thing was done. But for some reason I wrote the song in four flats, whereas I had always kept to three flats previously."

"POOR LITTLE RICH GIRL"

You're only
A baby.
You're lonely
And maybe
Some day soon you'll know
The tears
You are tasting
Are years
You are wasting,
Life's a bitter foe,
With fate it's no use competing,

Youth is so terribly
    fleeting;
By dancing
Much faster,
You're chancing
Disaster
Time alone will show.

Poor little rich girl,
You're a bewitched girl,
Better beware!
Laughing at danger,
Virtue a stranger,
Better take care!
The life you lead sets
    all your nerves
    a-jangle,
Your love affairs are in a hopeless tangle,
Though you're a child, dear,
Your life's a wild typhoon,
In lives of leisure
The craze for pleasure
Steadily grows.
Cocktails and laughter,
But what comes after?
Nobody knows.
You're weaving love into a mad jazz pattern,
Ruled by Pantaloon.
Poor little rich girl, don't drop a stitch too soon.

The role you are acting,
The toll is exacting,
Soon you'll have to pay.
The music of living,
You lose in the giving,
False things soon decay.
These words from me may surprise you,
I've got no right to advise you,
I've known life too well, dear,
Your own life must tell, dear,
Please don't turn away.

And in the 1928 *This Year of Grace!* his warning was even more specific. ("The high tone of moral indignation implicit in the lyric impressed a number of people, notably the late Aimee Semple McPherson.")

"DANCE. LITTLE LADY"

Though you're only seventeen
Far too much of life you've seen,
Syncopated child.
Maybe if you only knew
Where your path was leading to
You'd become less wild.
But I know it's vain
Trying to explain
While there's this insane
Music in your brain.

Dance, dance, dance little lady,
Youth is fleeting—to the rhythm beating
In your mind.
Dance, dance, dance little lady,
So obsessed with second best,
No rest you'll ever find,
Time and tide and trouble
Never, never wait.
Let the cauldron bubble
Justify your fate.
Dance, dance, dance little lady,
Leave tomorrow behind.

When the saxophone
Gives a wicked moan,
Charleston hey hey,
Rhythms fall and rise,
Start dancing to the tune,
The band's crooning—
For soon
The night will be gone,
Start swaying like a reed
Without heeding
The speed
That hurries you on.

Gladys Calthrop, a friend from the 1920s and
Noël's designer for many years. Painted in oils
by Sir John Rothenstein.

Nigger melodies
Syncopate your nerves
Till your body curves
Drooping—stooping,
Laughter some day dies
And when the lights are starting to gutter
Dawn through the shutter
Shows you're living in a world of lies.

•

In 1928 the critical pendulum began to swing back decisively in Noël's
favor. The idea for what was to be his most successful musical came to him
unbidden. At the end of a weekend visit to mutual friends with his
designer, Gladys Calthrop, they were listening to a new orchestral recording of *Die Fledermaus* . . .

"Immediately a confused picture of uniforms, bustles, chandeliers and
gas-lit cafés formed in my mind and later, when we were driving over

Wimbledon Common, we drew the car to a standstill by the roadside and in the shade of a giant horse-chestnut tree mapped out roughly the story of Sari Linden."

Bitter Sweet was produced the following year in London and New York—a triumphant success in both.

It also happened to contain some of his most enduring love songs. Sari, the young heroine, asks the age-old and unanswerable question . . .

"WHAT IS LOVE?"

Tell me—tell me—tell
  me, what is love?
Is it some consuming
  flame;
Part of the moon, part
  of the sun,
Part of a dream barely
  begun?
When is the moment of
  breaking—waking?
Skies change, nothing
  is the same,
Some strange magic is
  to blame;
Voices that seem to
  echo round me and above,
Tell me, what is love, love, love?

—BITTER SWEET (1929)

Manon, the cynical café diseuse, can tell her that whatever it is—it's not enough . . .

"IF LOVE WERE ALL"

Life is very rough and tumble,
For a humble
Diseuse,
One can betray one's troubles never,
Whatever

Occurs.
Night after night,
Have to look bright,
Whether you're well
   or ill
People must laugh
   their fill.
You mustn't sleep
Till dawn comes
   creeping.
Though I never really
   grumble
Life's jumble.
Indeed—
And in my efforts to
   succeed
I've had to formulate a
   creed—

Ivy St. Helier as Manon
by Max Beerbohm

I believe in doing
   what I can,
In crying when I must,
To laughing when I choose.
Heigh-ho, if love were all
I should be lonely,
I believe the more you love a man,
The more you give your trust,
The more you're bound to lose.
Although when shadows fall
I think if only—
Somebody splendid really needed me,
Someone affectionate and dear,
Cares would be ended if I knew that he
Wanted to have me near.
But I believe that since my life began
The most I've had is just
A talent to amuse.
Heigh-ho, if love were all!

Though life buffets me obscenely,
It serenely
Goes on.

Although I question its conclusion,
Illusion
Is gone.
Frequently I
Put a bit by
Safe for a rainy day.
Nobody here can say
To what, indeed,
The years are leading.
Fate may often treat me meanly,
But I keenly
Pursue
A little mirage in the blue,
Determination helps me through.

Sari, of course—being a classic heroine—knows that true love will last through eternity, and she had the show's theme song to prove it.

Noël was convinced that there must be a waltz at the heart of each of his book musicals, and that was often to prove a problem for him, as it was in this case.

"The book had been completed long since, but the score had been causing me trouble, until one day, when I was in a taxi on my way back to the [New York] apartment after a matinée [of his revue, *This Year of Grace!*] the 'I'll See You Again' waltz dropped into my mind, whole and complete, during a twenty-minute traffic block."

"Brass bands have blared it, string orchestras have swooned it, Palm Court quartets have murdered it, barrel organs have ground it out in London squares and swing bands have tortured it beyond recognition . . . It has proved over the years to be the greatest song hit I have ever had or am ever likely to have . . . and I am still very fond of it and very proud of it."

"I'LL SEE YOU AGAIN"

CARL: All my life I shall remember knowing you,
All the pleasures I have found in showing you
The different ways
That one may phrase
The changing light, and changing shade;
Happiness that must die,

Melodies that must fly,
Memories that must fade,
Dusty and forgotten by and by.

SARAH: Learning scales will never seem so sweet again
Till our Destiny shall let us meet again.

CARL: The will of Fate
May come too late.

SARAH: When I'm recalling these hours we've had
Why will the foolish tears
Tremble across the years,
Why shall I feel so sad,
Treasuring the memory of these days
Always?

CARL: I'll see you again,
Whenever Spring breaks through again;
Time may lie heavy between,
But what has been
Is past forgetting.

SARAH: This sweet memory,
Across the years will come to me;
Though my world may go awry,
In my heart will ever lie
Just the echo of a sigh,
Good-bye.

REPRISE:
SARAH/SARI:

I'll see you again,
I live each moment through again.
Time has lain heavy between,
But what has been
Can leave me never;
Your dear memory
Throughout my life has guided me.
Though my world has gone awry,
Though the years my tears may dry
I shall love you till I die,
Good-bye!

Though my world has gone awry,
Though the end is drawing nigh,
I shall love you till I die,
Good-bye!

•

In writing the 1934 *Conversation Piece* he encountered a similar block . . .

"I knew I could never complete the score without a main theme, and sat for ten days at the piano gloomily facing the fact that my talent had withered . . . I finally decided to give up, poured myself a stiff whisky, switched off the piano light and was about to go up to bed in despair when 'I'll Follow My Secret Heart' suddenly emerged in the key of G flat, a key I had never played before."

Paul, the *soi-disant* Duc de Chaucigny-Varennes, has brought his "ward," Melanie, to Regency England Brighton with the intention of finding her a rich husband. Being a mere man, he is unaware of what is perfectly obvious to the audience from the outset—that she is in love with *him* . . .

"I'LL FOLLOW MY SECRET HEART"

MELANIE:

> A cloud has passed across the sun,
> The morning seems no longer gay.
> With so much business to be done,
> Even the sea looks gray.
> *C'est vrai. C'est vrai.*
> It seems that all the joy has faded from the day
> As though the foolish world no longer wants to play.

PAUL (*speaking*):

> Go and dress.

MELANIE (*speaking*):

> What shall I wear? A black crepe with a little bonnet?

PAUL: What on earth is the matter with you this morning?

MELANIE: White, white for a bride. But the sun ought to shine on a bride.

PAUL: You're not a bride yet.

MELANIE: But I shall be soon, shall I not? A very quiet aristocratic bride with a discreet heart!

> (*Sings*)
> You ask me to have a discreet heart
> Until marriage is out of the way
> But what if I meet
> With a sweetheart so sweet
> That my wayward heart cannot obey
> A single word that you may say?

PAUL (*speaking*): Then we shall have to go away.
MELANIE (*sings*):
> No. For there is nowhere we could go
> Where we could hide from what we know
> Is true.
> Don't be afraid I'll betray you
> And destroy all the plans you have made,
> But even your schemes
> Must leave room for my dreams.
> So when all I owe to you is paid
> I'll still have something of my own,
> A little prize that's mine alone.
>
> I'll follow my secret heart
> My whole life through,
> I'll keep all my dreams apart
> Till one comes true.
> No matter what price is paid,
> What stars may fade
> Above,
> I'll follow my secret heart
> Till I find love.

•

More than anywhere else, Noël seems to reveal his own "secret heart" in his lyrics and verse.

Love, he confessed, defeated him. "How idiotic people are when they're in love. What an age-old devastating disease . . . To me passionate love has been like a tight shoe rubbing blisters on my Achilles' heel."

As he wrote to his friend Marlene Dietrich when her torrid affair with Yul Brynner was unraveling . . .

"To hell with Goddamned 'L'Amour'! It always causes far more trouble than it is worth. Don't run after it. Don't court it. Keep it waiting off stage until you're good and ready for it and even then treat it with the suspicious disdain that it deserves."

"I AM NO GOOD AT LOVE"

> I am no good at love
> My heart should be wise and free
> I kill the unfortunate golden goose

Whoever it may be
With over-articulate tenderness
And too much intensity.
I am no good at love
I batter it out of shape
Suspicion tears at my sleepless mind
And, gibbering like an ape,
I lie alone in the endless dark
Knowing there's no escape.

I am no good at love
When my easy heart I yield
Wild words come tumbling from my mouth
Which should have stayed concealed;
And my jealousy turns a bed of bliss
Into a battlefield.

I am no good at love
I betray it with little sins
For I feel the misery of the end
In the moment that it begins
And the bitterness of the last good-bye
Is the bitterness that wins.

He may or may not have been "good at love," but he was extremely good at *writing* about it in its quieter moments . . .

About the wonder of *falling* in love . . .

"SOMETHING VERY STRANGE"

This is not a day like any other day,
This is something special and apart,
Something to remember
When the coldness of December
Chills my heart.

Something very strange
Is happening to me,
Every face I see
Seems to be smiling.

All the sounds I hear,
The buses changing gear,
Suddenly appear
To be beguiling.
Nobody is melancholy,
Nobody is sad,
Not a single shadow on the sea.
Some Magician's spell
Has made this magic start
And I feel I want to hold each shining moment
                                in my heart.
Something strange and gay
On this romantic day
Seems to be
Happening to me.

Something very strange
Is happening to me,
Every cat I see
Seems to be purring,
I can clearly tell
In every clanging bell
Some forgotten melody
Recurring.
Tinker, tailor, soldier, sailor,
Beggar-man or thief,
Every single leaf
On every tree
Seems to be aware
Of something in the air.
And if only I were younger I'd put ribbons in my hair.
Something strange and gay
On this romantic day
Seems to be
Happening to me!

—SAIL AWAY (1961)

In his later shows Noël was in the habit of making his own recording, and this lyric gave him a problem. Somehow he couldn't see himself singing about having "ribbons" in his hair. He substituted . . .

And I know that tired old nightingale
Still sings in Berkeley Square.

There were songs about the acceptance of *being* in love.

"A ROOM WITH A VIEW"

HE: I've been cherishing
Through the perishing
Winter nights and days
A funny little phrase
That means
Such a lot to me
That you've got to be
With me heart and soul
For on you the whole
Thing leans.

SHE: Won't you kindly tell me
      what you're driving at,
What conclusion you're
      arriving at?

HE: Please don't turn away
Or my dream will stay
Hidden out of sight
Among a lot of might-
have-beens!

Sonnie Hale and Jessie Matthews in
their "Room With a View"

A room with a view—and you,
With no one to worry us,
No one to hurry us—through
This dream we've found,
We'll gaze at the sky—and try
To guess what it's all about,
Then we will figure out—why
The world is round.

SHE: We'll be as happy and contented
As birds upon a tree,
High above the mountains and the sea.

BOTH: We'll bill and we'll coo-oo-oo
And sorrow will never come,

> Oh, will it ever come—true,
> Our room with a view.

SHE: I'm so practical
> I'd make tactical
> Errors as your wife,
> I'd try to set your life
> To rights.
> I'm upset a bit
> For I get a bit
> Dizzy now and then
> Following your mental flights.

HE: Come with me and leave behind the noisy crowds,
> Sunlight shines for us above the clouds.

SHE: My eyes glistened too
> While I listened to
> All the things you said,
> I'm glad I've got a head
> For heights.

> A room with a view—and you
> And no one to give advice,
> That sounds a paradise—few
> Could fail to choose,
> With fingers entwined we'll find
> Relief from the preachers who
> Always beseech us to—mind
> Our P's and Q's.

HE: We'll watch the whole world pass before us
> While we are sitting still
> Leaning on our own windowsill.

BOTH:
> We'll bill and we'll coo-oo-oo,
> And maybe a stork will bring
> This, that and t'other thing—to
> Our room with a view.

—THIS YEAR OF GRACE! (1928)

Ironically—for what was to become a sentimental classic—Noël's original intention had been quite otherwise. In 1927 he had started to write a musical comedy to be called *Star Dust*, which contained a pastiche show-within-a-show satirizing the current genre.

"A Room With a View" was intended to be tongue-in-cheek, but when

it became a genuine hit in its own right, Noël quickly—and profitably—
took the tongue out of his cheek.

•

"THIS IS TO LET YOU KNOW"

This is to let you know
That there was no moon last night
And that the tide was high
And that on the broken horizon glimmered the lights
                                                    of ships
Twenty at least, like a sedate procession passing by.

This is to let you know
That when I'd turned out the lamp
And in the dark I lay
That suddenly piercing loneliness, like a knife,
Twisted my heart, for you were such a long long
                                            way away.

This is to let you know
That there are no English words
That ever could explain
How, quite without warning, lovingly you were here
Holding me close, smoothing away the idiotic pain.

This is to let you know
That all that I feel for you
Can never wholly go.
I love you and miss you, even two hours away,
With all my heart. This is to let you know.

Or of having *been* in love . . .

"I KNEW YOU WITHOUT ENCHANTMENT"

I knew you without enchantment
And for some years
We went our usual ways
Meeting occasionally

Finding no heights nor depths among our days
Shedding no tears
Every so often when we felt inclined
Lying like lovers in each other's arms
Feeling no qualms
In our intimacy
So resolute we were in heart and mind
So steeled against illusion, deaf and blind
To all presentiment, to all enchantment
(I knew you without enchantment.)

It is so strange
Remembering that phase
Those unexacting, uneventful days
Before the change
Before we knew this seriocomic, tragic
Most unexpected, overwhelming magic.
I knew you without enchantment.

And to-day I cannot think of you without my heart
Suddenly stopping
Or, in those long grey hours we spent apart
Dropping, dropping
Down into desolation like a stone.
To be alone
No longer means to me clear time and space
In which to stretch my mind.

I see your face
Between me and the space I used to find
Between me and the other worlds I seek
There stands your sleek
And most beloved silhouette
And yet
I can remember not so long ago
We neither of us cared
Nor dared
To know
How swiftly we were nearing the abyss
(This foolish, quite ungovernable bliss)
Let's not regret
That empty life before. It was great fun
And hurt no one

There was no harm in it
At certain moments there was even charm in it.

But oh, my dearest love, there was no spell
No singing heaven and no wailing hell.
I knew you without enchantment.

But it wasn't all tears for the lost years. Love could be ludicrous, especially
when it happened to *other* people . . .

"MAD ABOUT THE BOY"

SOCIETY WOMAN: I met
 him at a party just a
 couple of years ago,
He was rather over-hearty
 and ridiculous
But as I'd seen him on
 the Screen
He cast a certain spell.
I basked in his attraction
 for a couple of hours
 or so,
His manners were a fraction
 too meticulous,
If he was real or not I
 couldn't tell
But like a silly fool, I fell.

Mad about the boy,
I know it's stupid to be mad about the boy,
I'm so ashamed of it
But must admit
The sleepless nights I've had about the boy.
On the silver screen
He melts my foolish heart in every single scene.
Although I'm quite aware
That here and there
Are traces of the cad about the boy,
Lord knows I'm not a fool girl,
I really shouldn't care,
Lord knows I'm not a schoolgirl

In the flurry of her first affair.
Will it ever cloy
This odd diversity of misery and joy?
I'm feeling quite insane
And young again
And all because I'm mad about the boy.

SCHOOLGIRL: Homework, homework,
Every night there's homework,
While Elsie practises the gas goes pop,
I wish, I wish she'd stop,
Oh dear, oh dear,
Here it's always "No, dear,
You can't go out again, you must stay home,
You waste your money on that common Picturedrome,
Don't shirk—stay here and do your work."

Yearning, yearning,
How my heart is burning.
I'll see him Saturday in *Strong Man's Pain*
And then on Monday and on Friday week again.
To me he is the sole man
Who can kiss as well as Colman
I could faint whenever there's a close-up of his lips,
Though John Barrymore is larger
When my hero's on his charger
Even Douglas Fairbanks Junior hasn't smaller hips.
If only he could know
That I adore him so.

Mad about the boy,
It's simply scrumptious to be mad about the boy,
I know that quite sincerely
Housman really
Wrote *The Shropshire Lad* about the boy.
In my English Prose
I've done a tracing of his forehead and his nose
And there is, honour bright,
A certain slight
Effect of Galahad about the boy.
I've talked to Rosie Hooper,
She feels the same as me,
She says that Gary Cooper

Doesn't thrill her to the same degree.
In *Can Love Destroy?*
When he meets Garbo in a suit of corduroy,
He gives a little frown
And knocks her down.
Oh dear, oh dear, I'm mad about the boy.

COCKNEY: Every Wednesday afternoon
I get a little time off from three to eleven,
Then I go to the Picture House
And taste a little of my particular heaven.
He appears
In a little while,
Through a mist of tears
I can see him smiling
Above me.
Every picture I see him in,
Every lover's caress,
Makes my wonderful dreams begin,
Makes me long to confess
That if ever he looked at me
And thought perhaps it was worth the trouble to
Love me,
I'd give in and I wouldn't care
However far from the path of virtue he'd
Shove me,
Just supposing our love was brief,
If he treated me rough
I'd be happy beyond belief,
Once would be enough.

Mad about the boy,
I know I'm potty but I'm mad about the boy.
He sets me 'eart on fire
With love's desire,
In fact I've got it bad about the boy.
When I do the rooms
I see 'is face in all the brushes and the brooms.
Last week I strained me back
And got the sack
And 'ad a row with Dad about the boy.
I'm finished with Navarro,
I'm tired of Richard Dix,

I'm pierced by Cupid's arrow
Every Wednesday from four till six.
'Ow I should enjoy
To let 'im treat me like a plaything or a toy,
I'd give my all to him
And crawl to him
So 'elp me Gawd I'm mad about the boy.

TART: It seems a little silly
For a girl of my age and weight
To walk down Piccadilly
In a haze of love.
It ought to take a good deal more to get a bad
                        girl down,
I should have been exempt, for
My particular kind of Fate
Has taught me such contempt for
Every phase of love,
And now I've been and spent my last half-crown
To weep about a painted clown.

Mad about the boy,
It's pretty funny but I'm mad about the boy,
He has a gay appeal
That makes me feel
There's maybe something sad about the boy.
Walking down the street,
His eyes look out at me from people that I meet,
I can't believe it's true
But when I'm blue
In some strange way I'm glad about the boy.
I'm hardly sentimental,
Love isn't so sublime,
I have to pay my rental
And I can't afford to waste much time,
If I could employ
A little magic that would finally destroy
This dream that pains me
And enchains me,
But I can't because I'm mad about the boy.

There was—and remains—great speculation as to the identity of the "boy." On the textual evidence the specific references to Ronald Colman,

John Barrymore, Richard Dix, Ramon Novarro, Gary Cooper and Douglas Fairbanks Jr. (heavily favored in some quarters!) would appear to rule them out, and Rudolph Valentino had been dead for some years when the song was introduced in the revue *Words and Music* (1932). Noël's life partner, Graham Payn, was inclined to believe that the "boy" was an idealized composite version of all these and more. He was whoever you *wanted* him to be—which is as it should be.

There was almost an extra verse when the song was included in the New York version of the revue *Set to Music* (1938). It was to have been sung by a soberly suited businessman . . .

> Mad about the boy,
> It's most peculiar but I'm mad about the boy.
> No one but Dr. Freud
> Could have enjoyed
> The vexing dreams I've had about the boy.
> When I told my wife
> She said she'd never heard such nonsense in her life.
> Her lack of sympathy
> Embarrassed me
> And made me, frankly, glad about the boy!
> My doctor can't advise me,
> He'd help me if he could.
> Three times he's tried to psychoanalyze me
> But it's just no good.
> People I employ
> Have the impertinence to call me Myrna Loy.
> I rise above it,
> Frankly love it,
> For I'm absolutely mad about the boy!

Fortunately, wiser councils prevailed. It was only 1938. And it *was* Boston . . .

And finally, there is love that's passed its "sell-by date" . . .

"BRONXVILLE DARBY AND JOAN"

> We do not fear the verdict of posterity,
> Our lives have been too humdrum and mundane,
> In the twilight of our days
> Having reached the final phase

In all sincerity
We must explain:

We're a dear old couple and we *hate* one another
And we've hated one another for a long, long time.
Since the day that we were wed, up to the present,
Our lives, we must confess,
Have been progressively more unpleasant.
We're just sweet old darlings who despise one another
With a thoroughness approaching the sublime,
But through all our years
We've been affectionately known

As the Bronxville Darby and Joan.
Our Golden Wedding passed with all our family,
An orgy of remembrance and rue,
In acknowledgment of this we exchanged a loving kiss
A trifle clammily
Because we knew:

We're a dear old couple who *detest* one another,
We've detested one another since our bridal night,
Which was squalid, unattractive and convulsive
And proved, beyond dispute,
That we were mutually repulsive.
We're just sweet old darlings who torment one another
With the utmost maliciousness and spite,
And through all our years
We've been inaccurately known
As the Bronxville Darby and Joan.

We're a dear old couple and we *loathe* one another
With a loathing that engulfs us like a tidal wave,
With our deep subconscious minds we seldom dabble
But something *must* impel
The words we spell
When we're playing "Scrabble."
We're just sweet old darlings who abhor one another
And we'll bore each other firmly to the grave,
But through all our years we've been referred to
                                        more or less
As the Bronxville Porgy and Bess.

—SAIL AWAY (1961)

•

It was a subject that in its simplest form occupied him to the end.

In a late TV interview he was asked to sum up his life in a single word. After an uncharacteristically long pause, he replied . . .

"Well, now comes the terrible decision as to whether to be corny or not.

"The answer *is* one word. Love.

"To know that you are among people you love and who love you. That has made all the successes wonderful—much more wonderful than they'd have been anyway.

"And I don't think there's anything more to be said on that. That's it."

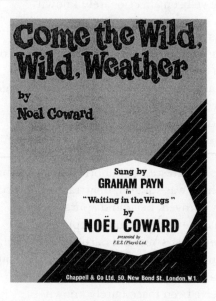

"COME THE WILD, WILD WEATHER"

Time may hold in store for us
Glory or defeat,
Maybe never more for us
Life will seem so sweet.
Time will change so many things,
Tides will ebb and flow,
But wherever fate may lead us
Always we shall know—

Come the wild, wild weather,
Come the wind and the rain,
Come the little white flakes of snow,

Come the joy, come the pain,
We shall still be together
When our life's journey ends,
For wherever we chance to go
We shall always be friends.
We may find while we're travelling through the years
Moments of joy and love and happiness,
Reason for grief, reason for tears.
Come the wild, wild weather,
If we've lost or we've won,
We'll remember these words we say
Till our story is done.

—WAITING IN THE WINGS (1961)

CHAPTER THREE
THE 1930s

Why is it that civilized humanity
Must make the world so wrong?
In this hurly-burly of insanity
Our dreams cannot last long . . .

It's getting me down.
Blues,
I've got those weary Twentieth Century Blues.

—CAVALCADE (1931)

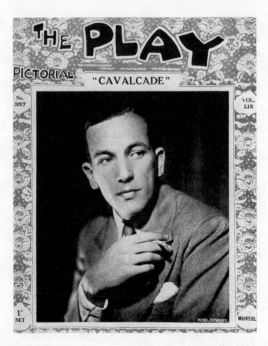

T HE FLAMBOYANT '20s finally fizzled out and gave way to a new and
increasingly apprehensive decade. Noël—like anyone with half an eye
to see it—sensed that another "war to end all wars" was likely, if not
inevitable. Those in authority had theirs firmly shut.

Once again he reflected and even anticipated the times he was living
through. In the 1931 *Cavalcade,* with the century less than a third over, he
would pin down its essential psychology . . .

"TWENTIETH CENTURY BLUES"

Why is it that civilized humanity
Must make the world so wrong?
In this hurly-burly of insanity
Our dreams cannot last long.
We've reached a deadline—
The Press headline—every sorrow,
Blues value
Is News value
Tomorrow.

Blues,
Twentieth Century Blues,
Are getting me down.
Who's
Escaped those weary
Twentieth Century Blues.
Why,
If there's a God in the sky,
Why shouldn't He grin?
High
Above this dreary
Twentieth Century din,
In this strange illusion,
Chaos and confusion,
People seem to lose their way.
What is there to strive for,
Love or keep alive for? Say—
Hey, hey, call it a day.
Blues,

Nothing to win or to lose.
It's getting me down.
Blues,
I've got those weary Twentieth Century Blues.

The song was, he felt, "ironic in theme and musically rather untidy. It is also exceedingly difficult to sing, but in the play it achieved its purpose. It struck the right note of harsh discordance and typified . . . the curious hectic desperation I wished to convey."

•

The '30s marked the peak of Noël's professional success—a period that continued through the mid-'40s.

Nineteen thirty gave us what is now generally considered to be his best play—*Private Lives.*

He wrote it on a trip to the Far East and intended it as a vehicle for himself and Gertrude Lawrence.

He recalled in his first autobiography, *Present Indicative* (1937) . . .

The Imperial Hotel, Tokyo, was grand and comfortable and was renowned for having stood firm during the big earthquake. A wire was handed me from Jeffery [Amherst, his traveling companion] saying that he had missed a boat in Shanghai and wouldn't be with me for three days which, although disappointing, was a relief, as I had begun to think I was never going to hear from him at all.

The night before he arrived I went to bed early as I wanted to greet him as brightly as possible at seven in the morning, but the moment I switched out the lights, Gertrude appeared in a white Molyneux dress on a terrace in the South of France and refused to go again until 4 a.m., by which time *Private Lives,* title and all, had constructed itself.

In 1923 the play would have

Edward Molyneux's design
for Gertie's dress

been written and typed within a few days of my thinking of it, but in 1929 I had learned the wisdom of not welcoming a new idea too ardently, so I forced it into the back of my mind, trusting to its own integrity to emerge again later on, when it had become sufficiently set and matured.

A bout of influenza laid me low in Shanghai, and I lay, sweating gloomily, in my bedroom in the Cathay Hotel for several days. The ensuing convalescence, however, was productive, for I utilized it by writing *Private Lives.* The idea by now seemed ripe enough to have a shot at, so I started it, propped up in bed with a writing-block and an Eversharp pencil, and completed it, roughly, in four days. It came easily, and with the exception of a few of the usual "blood and tears" moments, I enjoyed writing it. I thought it a shrewd and witty comedy, well constructed on the whole, but psychologically unstable; however, its entertainment value seemed obvious enough, and its acting opportunities for Gertie and me admirable, so I cabled to her immediately in New York . . .

HAVE WRITTEN DELIGHTFUL NEW COMEDY STOP GOOD PART FOR YOU STOP WONDERFUL ONE FOR ME STOP KEEP YOURSELF FREE FOR AUTUMN PRODUCTION.

To which the lady subsequently replied . . .

HAVE READ NEW PLAY STOP NOTHING WRONG THAT CAN'T BE FIXED STOP GERTIE.

Noël's response was sharp and to the point . . .

THE ONLY THING THAT WILL NEED TO BE FIXED IS YOUR PERFORMANCE STOP NOËL.

PRIVATE LIVES

AN INTIMATE COMEDY

CAST

ELYOT CHASE	NOËL COWARD
AMANDA PRYNNE	GERTRUDE LAWRENCE
VICTOR PRYNNE	LAURENCE OLIVIER
SIBYL CHASE	ADRIANNE ALLEN

DIRECTED BY NOËL COWARD

The play opened at London's new Phoenix Theatre on September 24, 1930, and they became "Noël&Gertie" overnight and forever after. Noël himself came to see that "the parts are practically synonymous."

"I am deeply attached to it. It has been enthusiastically and profitably patronized by the public wherever and in whatever language it has been played."

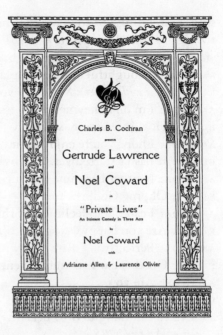

Charles B. Cochran

presents

Gertrude Lawrence

and

Noel Coward

in

"Private Lives"

An Intimate Comedy in Three Acts

by

Noel Coward

with

Adrianne Allen & Laurence Olivier

•

Elyot Chase and Amanda were married to each other, then divorced. Now they have both remarried— Elyot to Sibyl and Amanda to Victor Prynne. In a coincidence permitted only to playwrights, both couples find themselves staying on their wedding night not only at the same hotel in France but in adjoining terrace rooms—a fact they discover in suitably dramatic fashion.

•

ELYOT saunters down to the balustrade. He looks casually over onto the next terrace, and then out at the view. He looks up at the moon and sighs, then he sits down in a chair with his back toward the line of tubs, and lights a cigarette. AMANDA steps gingerly onto her terrace carrying a tray with two champagne cocktails on it. She is wearing a charmingly simple evening gown; her cloak is flung over her right shoulder. She places the tray carefully on the table, puts her cloak over the back of a chair, and sits down with her back toward ELYOT. She takes a small mirror from her handbag, and scrutinizes her face in it The orchestra downstairs strikes up a new melody. Both ELYOT and AMANDA give a little start. After a moment, ELYOT pensively begins to hum the tune the band is playing. It is a sentimental, romantic little tune ["Someday I'll Find You"]. AMANDA hears him, and clutches at her throat suddenly as though she were suffocating. Then she jumps up noiselessly, and peers over the line of tubs. ELYOT, with his back to her, continues to sing obliviously. She sits down again, relaxing with a gesture almost of despair. Then she looks anxiously over her shoulder at the window in case VICTOR should be listening, and then, with a little smile, she takes up the melody herself, clearly. ELYOT stops dead and gives a gasp, then he jumps up, and stands looking at her. She continues to sing, pretending not to know that he is there. At the end of the song, she turns slowly, and faces him.

AMANDA: Thoughtful of them to play that, wasn't it?
ELYOT (*in a stifled voice*): What are you doing here?
AMANDA: I'm on honeymoon.
ELYOT: How interesting, so am I.
AMANDA: I hope you're enjoying it.
ELYOT: It hasn't started yet.
AMANDA: Neither has mine.
ELYOT: Oh, my God!
AMANDA: I can't help feeling that this is a little unfortunate.
ELYOT: Are you happy?
AMANDA: Perfectly.
ELYOT: Good. That's all right, then, isn't it?
AMANDA: Are you?
ELYOT: Ecstatically.
AMANDA: I'm delighted to hear it. We shall probably meet again some-time. *Au revoir!* (*She turns.*)
ELYOT (*firmly*): Good-bye.

She goes indoors without looking back. He stands gazing after her with an expression of horror on his face.

The shock of their meeting causes Elyot to have a row with Sibyl and Amanda with Victor. The new spouses storm off, and Elyot and Amanda retreat to the terrace . . .

ELYOT stamps down to the balustrade and lights a cigarette, obviously try-ing to control his nerves. *AMANDA* sees him, and comes down too.

AMANDA: Give me one for God's sake.
ELYOT (*hands her his case laconically*): Here.
AMANDA (*taking a cigarette*): I'm in such a rage.
ELYOT (*lighting up*): So am I.
AMANDA: What are we to do?
ELYOT: I don't know.
AMANDA: Whose yacht is that?
ELYOT: The Duke of Westminster's, I expect. It always is.
AMANDA: I wish I were on it.
ELYOT: I wish you were too.
AMANDA: There's no need to be nasty.
ELYOT: Yes there is, every need. I've never in my life felt a greater urge to be nasty.

AMANDA: And you've had some urges in your time, haven't you?

ELYOT: If you start bickering with me, Amanda, I swear I'll throw you over the edge.

AMANDA: Try it, that's all, just try it.

ELYOT: You've upset everything, as usual.

AMANDA: I've upset everything! What about you?

ELYOT: Ever since the first moment I was unlucky enough to set eyes on you, my life has been insupportable.

AMANDA: Oh do shut up, there's no sense in going on like that.

ELYOT: Nothing's any use. There's no escape, ever.

Adrianne Allen (the original Sibyl) by Oliver Messel

AMANDA: Don't be melodramatic.

ELYOT: Do you want a cocktail? There are two here.

AMANDA: There are two over here as well.

ELYOT: We'll have my two first. (AMANDA *crosses over into* ELYOT's *part of the terrace. He gives her one, and keeps one himself.*)

AMANDA: Shall we get roaring screaming drunk?

ELYOT: I don't think that would help, we did it once before and it was a dismal failure.

AMANDA: It was lovely at the beginning.

ELYOT: You have an immoral memory, Amanda. Here's to you. (*They raise their glasses solemnly and drink.*)

AMANDA: I tried to get away the moment after I'd seen you, but he wouldn't budge.

ELYOT: What's his name.

AMANDA: Victor, Victor Prynne.

ELYOT (*toasting*): Mr. and Mrs. Victor Prynne. (*He drinks.*) Mine wouldn't budge either.

AMANDA: What's her name?

ELYOT: Sibyl.

AMANDA (*toasting*): Mr. and Mrs. Elyot Chase. (*She drinks.*) God pity the poor girl.

ELYOT: Are you in love with him?

AMANDA: Of course.

ELYOT: How funny.

AMANDA: I don't see anything particularly funny about it, you're in love with yours aren't you?

ELYOT: Certainly.

AMANDA: There you are then.

ELYOT: There we both are then.

AMANDA: What's she like?

ELYOT: Fair, very pretty, plays the piano beautifully.

AMANDA: Very comforting.

ELYOT: How's yours?

AMANDA: I don't want to discuss him.

ELYOT: Well, it doesn't matter, he'll probably come popping out in a minute and I shall see for myself. Does he know I'm here?

AMANDA: Yes, I told him.

ELYOT (*with sarcasm*): That's going to make things a whole lot easier.

AMANDA: You needn't be frightened, he won't hurt you.

ELYOT: If he comes near me I'll scream the place down.

AMANDA: Does Sibyl know I'm here?

ELYOT: No, I pretended I'd had a presentiment. I tried terribly hard to persuade her to leave for Paris.

AMANDA: I tried too, it's lucky we didn't both succeed, isn't it? Otherwise we should probably all have joined up in Rouen or somewhere.

ELYOT (*laughing*): In some frowsy little hotel.

AMANDA (*laughing too*): Oh dear, it would have been much, much worse.

ELYOT: I can see us all sailing down in the morning for an early start.

AMANDA (*weakly*): Lovely, oh lovely.

ELYOT: Glorious! (*They both laugh helplessly.*)

AMANDA: What's happened to yours?

ELYOT: Didn't you hear her screaming? She's downstairs in the dining room I think.

AMANDA: Mine is being grand, in the bar.

ELYOT: It really is awfully difficult.

AMANDA: Have you known her long?

ELYOT: About four months, we met in a house party in Norfolk.

AMANDA: Very flat, Norfolk.

ELYOT: How old is dear Victor?

AMANDA: Thirty-four, or five; and Sibyl?

ELYOT: I blush to tell you, only twenty-three.

AMANDA: You've gone a mucker all right.

ELYOT: I shall reserve my opinion of your choice until I've met dear Victor.

AMANDA: I wish you wouldn't go on calling him "Dear Victor." It's extremely irritating.

ELYOT: That's how I see him. Dumpy, and fair, and very considerate, with glasses. Dear Victor.

AMANDA: As I said before I would rather not discuss him. At least I have good taste enough to refrain from making cheap gibes at Sibyl.

ELYOT: You said Norfolk was flat.

AMANDA: That was no reflection on her, unless she made it flatter.

ELYOT: Your voice takes on an acid quality whenever you mention her name.

AMANDA: I'll never mention it again.

ELYOT: Good, and I'll keep off Victor.

AMANDA (*with dignity*): Thank you.

There is silence for a moment. The orchestra starts playing the same tune that they were singing previously.

ELYOT: That orchestra has a remarkably small repertoire.

AMANDA: They don't seem to know anything but this, do they?

She sits down on the balustrade, and sings it, softly. Her eyes are looking out to sea, and her mind is far away.

"SOMEDAY I'LL FIND YOU"

When one is lonely the days are long;
You seem so near
But never appear.
Each night I sing you a lover's song;
Please try to hear,
My dear, my dear.

Can't you remember the fun we had?
Time is so fleet,
Why shouldn't we meet
When you're away from me days are sad;
Life's not complete,
My sweet, my sweet.

Someday I'll find you,
Moonlight behind you,
True to the dream I am dreaming
As I draw near you
You'll smile a little smile;

For a little while
We shall stand
Hand in hand.
I'll leave you never,
Love you for ever,
All our past sorrow redeeming,
Try to make it true,
Say you love me too.
Someday I'll find you again.

ELYOT watches her while she sings. When she turns to him at the end, there are tears in her eyes. He looks away awkwardly and lights another cigarette.

ELYOT: You always had a sweet voice, Amanda.
AMANDA (*a little huskily*): Thank you.
ELYOT: I'm awfully sorry about all this, really I am. I wouldn't have had it happen for the world.

The original London cast of *Private Lives,* 1930. Laurence Olivier (Victor), Adrianne Allen (Sibyl), Noël (Elyot) and Gertrude Lawrence (Amanda).

AMANDA: I know. I'm sorry too. It's just rotten luck.

ELYOT: I'll go away tomorrow whatever happens, so don't you worry.

AMANDA: That's nice of you.

ELYOT: I hope everything turns out splendidly for you, and that you'll be very happy.

AMANDA: I hope the same for you, too.

The music, which has been playing continually through this little scene, returns persistently to the refrain. They both look at one another and laugh.

ELYOT: Nasty insistent little tune.

AMANDA: Extraordinary how potent cheap music is.

ELYOT: What exactly were you remembering at that moment?

AMANDA: The Palace Hotel Skating Rink in the morning, bright strong sunlight, and everybody whirling round in vivid colours, and you kneeling down to put on my skates for me.

ELYOT: You'd fallen on your fanny a few moments before.

AMANDA: It was beastly of you to laugh like that, I felt so humiliated.

ELYOT: Poor darling.

AMANDA: Do you remember waking up in the morning, and standing on the balcony, looking out across the valley?

ELYOT: Blue shadows on white snow, cleanness beyond belief, high above everything in the world. How beautiful it was.

AMANDA: It's nice to think we had a few marvellous moments.

ELYOT: A few: We had heaps really, only they slip away into the background, and one only remembers the bad ones.

AMANDA: Yes. What fools we were to ruin it all. What utter, utter fools.

ELYOT: You feel like that too, do you?

AMANDA (*wearily*): Of course.

ELYOT: Why did we?

AMANDA: The whole business was too much for us.

ELYOT: We were so ridiculously over in love.

AMANDA: Funny wasn't it?

ELYOT (*sadly*): Horribly funny.

AMANDA: Selfishness, cruelty, hatred, possessiveness, petty jealousy. All those qualities came out in us just because we loved each other.

ELYOT: Perhaps they were there anyhow.

AMANDA: No, it's love that does it. To hell with love.

ELYOT: To hell with love.

AMANDA: And yet here we are starting afresh with two quite different people. In love all over again, aren't we? (ELYOT *doesn't answer.*) Aren't we?

ELYOT: No.

AMANDA: Elyot.

ELYOT: We're not in love all over again, and you know it. Good night, Amanda. (*He turns abruptly, and goes towards the French windows.*)

AMANDA: Elyot—don't be silly—come back.

ELYOT: I must go and find Sibyl.

AMANDA: I must go and find Victor.

ELYOT (*savagely*): Well, why don't you?

AMANDA: I don't want to.

ELYOT: It's shameful, shameful of us.

AMANDA: Don't: I feel terrible. Don't leave me for a minute, I shall go mad if you do. We won't talk about ourselves anymore, we'll talk about outside things, anything you like, only just don't leave me until I've pulled myself together.

ELYOT: Very well. (*There is a dead silence.*)

AMANDA: What have you been doing lately? During these last years?

ELYOT: Travelling about. I went around the world you know after—

AMANDA (*hurriedly*): Yes, yes, I know. How was it?

ELYOT: The world?

AMANDA: Yes.

ELYOT: Oh, highly enjoyable.

AMANDA: China must be very interesting.

ELYOT: Very big, China.

AMANDA: And Japan—

ELYOT: Very small.

AMANDA: Did you eat sharks' fins, and take your shoes off, and use chopsticks and everything?

ELYOT: Practically everything.

AMANDA: And India, the burning Ghars, or Ghats, or whatever they are, and the Taj Mahal. How was the Taj Mahal?

ELYOT (*looking at her*): Unbelievable, a sort of dream.

AMANDA: That was the moonlight I expect, you must have seen it in the moonlight.

ELYOT (*never taking his eyes off her face*): Yes, moonlight is cruelly deceptive.

AMANDA: And it didn't look like a biscuit box did it? I've always felt that it might.

ELYOT (*quietly*): Darling, darling, I love you so.

AMANDA: And I do hope you met a sacred elephant. They're lint white I believe, and very, very sweet.

ELYOT: I've never loved anyone else for an instant.

AMANDA (*raising her hand feebly, in protest*): No, no, you mustn't—Elyot—stop.

ELYOT: You love me, too, don't you? There's no doubt about it anywhere, is there?

AMANDA: No, no doubt anywhere.

ELYOT: You're looking very lovely you know, in this damned moonlight. Your skin is clear and cool, and your eyes are shining, and you're growing lovelier and lovelier every second as I look at you. You don't hold any mystery for me, darling, do you mind? There isn't a particle of you that I don't know, remember, and want.

AMANDA (*softly*): I'm glad, my sweet.

ELYOT: More than any desire anywhere, deep down in my deepest heart I want you back again—please—

AMANDA (*putting her hand over his mouth*): Don't say any more, you're making me cry so dreadfully.

He pulls her gently into his arms and they stand silently, completely oblivious to everything but the moment, and each other. When finally, they separate, they sit down, rather breathlessly, on the balustrade.

AMANDA: What now? Oh darling, what now?

ELYOT: I don't know, I'm lost, utterly.

AMANDA: We must think quickly, oh quickly—

ELYOT: Escape?

AMANDA: Together?

ELYOT: Yes, of course, now, now.

AMANDA: We can't, we can't, you know we can't.

ELYOT: We must.

AMANDA: It would break Victor's heart.

ELYOT: And Sibyl's too probably, but they're bound to suffer anyhow. Think of the hell we'd lead them into if we stayed. Infinitely worse than any cruelty in the world, pretending to love them, and loving each other, so desperately.

AMANDA: We must tell them.

ELYOT: What?

AMANDA: Call them, and tell them.

ELYOT: Oh no, no, that's impossible.

AMANDA: It's honest.

ELYOT: I can't help how honest it is, it's too horrible to think of. How should we start? What should we say?

AMANDA: We should have to trust to the inspiration of the moment.

ELYOT: It would be a moment completely devoid of inspiration. The most appalling moment imaginable. No, no, we can't, you must see that, we simply can't.

AMANDA: What do you propose to do then? As it is they might appear at any moment.

ELYOT: We've got to decide instantly one way or another. Go away together now, or stay with them, and never see one another again, ever.

AMANDA: Don't be silly, what choice is there?

ELYOT: No choice at all, come— (*He takes her hand.*)

AMANDA: No, wait. This is sheer raving madness, something's happened to us, we're not sane.

ELYOT: We never were.

AMANDA: Where can we go?

ELYOT: Paris first, my car's in the garage, all ready.

AMANDA: They'll follow us.

ELYOT: That doesn't matter, once the thing's done.

AMANDA: I've got a flat in Paris.

ELYOT: Good.

AMANDA: It's in the Avenue Montaigne. I let it to Freda Lawson, but she's in Biarritz, so it's empty.

ELYOT: Does Victor know?

AMANDA: No, he knows I have one but he hasn't the faintest idea where.

ELYOT: Better and better.

AMANDA: We're being so bad, so terribly bad, we'll suffer for this, I know we shall.

ELYOT: Can't be helped.

AMANDA: Starting all those awful rows all over again.

ELYOT: No, no, we're older and wiser now.

AMANDA: What difference does that make? The first moment either of us gets a bit nervy, off we'll go again.

ELYOT: Stop shilly-shallying, Amanda.

AMANDA: I'm trying to be sensible.

ELYOT: You're only succeeding in being completely idiotic.

AMANDA: Idiotic indeed! What about you?

ELYOT: Now look here Amanda—

AMANDA (*stricken*): Oh my God!

ELYOT (*rushing to her and kissing her*): Darling, darling, I didn't mean it—

AMANDA: I won't move from here unless we have a compact, a sacred, sacred compact never to quarrel again.

ELYOT: Easy to make but difficult to keep.

AMANDA: No, no, it's the bickering that always starts it. The moment we notice we're bickering, either of us, we must promise on our honour to stop dead. We'll invent some phrase or catchword, which when either of us says it, automatically cuts off all conversation for at least five minutes.

ELYOT: Two minutes dear, with an option of renewal.

AMANDA: Very well, what shall it be?

ELYOT (*hurriedly*): Solomon Isaacs.

AMANDA: All right, that'll do.

ELYOT: Come on, come on.

AMANDA: What shall we do if we meet either of them on the way downstairs?

ELYOT: Run like stags.

AMANDA: What about clothes?

ELYOT: I've got a couple of bags I haven't unpacked yet.

AMANDA: I've got a small trunk.

ELYOT: Send the porter up for it.

AMANDA: Oh this is terrible—terrible—

ELYOT: Come on, come on, don't waste time.

AMANDA: Oughtn't we to leave notes or something?

ELYOT: No, no, no, we'll telegraph from somewhere on the road.

AMANDA: Darling, I daren't, it's too wicked of us, I simply daren't.

ELYOT (*seizing her in his arms and kissing her violently*): Now will you behave?

AMANDA: Yes, but Elyot darling—

ELYOT: Solomon Isaacs!

They rush off together through ELYOT's suite. After a moment or so, VICTOR steps out onto the terrace and looks around anxiously. Then he goes back indoors again, and can be heard calling "Mandy." Finally he again comes out onto the terrace and comes despondently down to the balustrade. He hears SIBYL's voice calling "Elli" and looks around as she comes out of the French windows. She jumps slightly upon seeing him.

VICTOR: Good evening.

SIBYL (*rather flustered*): Good evening—I was—er—looking for my husband.

VICTOR: Really, that's funny. I was looking for my wife.

SIBYL: Quite a coincidence. (*She laughs nervously.*)

VICTOR (*after a pause*): It's very nice here isn't it?

SIBYL: Lovely.

VICTOR: Have you been here long?

SIBYL: No, we only arrived to-day.

VICTOR: Another coincidence. So did we.

SIBYL: How awfully funny.

VICTOR: Would you care for a cocktail?

SIBYL: Oh no thank you—really—

VICTOR: There are two here on the table.

SIBYL glances at the two empty glasses on the balustrade, and tosses her head defiantly.

SIBYL: Thanks very much, I'd love one.

VICTOR: Good, here you are. (SIBYL *comes over to* VICTOR's *side of the terrace. He hands her one and takes one himself.*)

SIBYL: Thank you.

VICTOR (*with rather forced gaiety*): To absent friends. (*He raises his glass.*)

SIBYL (*raising hers*): To absent friends. (*They both laugh rather mirthlessly and then sit down on the balustrade, pensively sipping their cocktails and looking at the view.*) It's awfully pretty isn't it? The moonlight, and the lights of that yacht reflected in the water—

VICTOR: I wonder who it belongs to.

THE CURTAIN SLOWLY FALLS.

•

Noël was pleased to note that the critics variously described the play as "tenuous," "thin," "brittle," "gossamer," "iridescent" and "delightfully daring." "All of which connoted, to the public mind, 'cocktails,' 'evening dress,' 'repartee,' and irreverent allusions to copulation, thereby causing a gratifying number of respectable people to queue up at the box office."

He went on to say that "there is actually more to the play than this . . . but on the whole not very much. It is a reasonably well-constructed dualogue for two experienced performers, with a couple of extra puppets thrown in to assist the plot and to provide contrast."

In this he misses a good part of his own point. For most productions over the years the "thin" and "brittle" wit has been the keynote, and another clue that Noël himself seemed to pass over has been picked up only recently by directors coming to the text with a fresh eye.

AMANDA: Selfishness, cruelty, hatred, possessiveness, petty jealousy. All those qualities came out in us just because we loved each other.

On an anything-but-superficial level it can be claimed that the play is really about the impossibility of sustaining love. The wit is merely the surface coating to conceal the hurt.

Of the song he said in a 1970 interview: "Personally, from the point of view of lighting, I think I would always prefer the moonlight in front of me. It's not a lyric of high intellectual content, but it's a good opening phrase . . . Gertie Lawrence and I always liked a little sing occasionally, and as we were going to do a straight comedy, we thought we might have a song. You see, I was trained when I was very young as a show-off, and I've continued."

He could also parody his own work, as he did in a contemporary sketch . . .

"STRICTLY PRIVATE LIVES"

GERTIE and *NOËL* are discovered lying on the sofa in *Private Lives* attitude. The gramophone is playing their own record. It finishes.

NOËL: Darling, you oughtn't to have whistled just there—it sounds tinny.
GERTIE: Tinny, my foot.
NOËL: I beg your pardon.
GERTIE: I said—"Tinny, my foot."
NOËL: I do hope you're not going to turn out to be disagreeable.
GERTIE: I'm not in the least disagreeable, but it's silly to go on about that whistling; everybody adores that record, and they write to me from all over the country saying they particularly like the whistling—it gives a sense of intimacy.
NOËL: Intimacy, my grandmother.
GERTIE: My foot and your grandmother ought to get together.
NOËL: That would mean your having one foot in the grave.
GERTIE: Very funny. I can't imagine how you always think of those swift witty replies—it's wonderful, it is, really.
NOËL: Be quiet.
GERTIE: What!
NOËL: I said—"Be quiet."
GERTIE: You should never have written *Cavalcade.* It was a grave mistake.
NOËL: Why?
GERTIE: Because it's blown you up like a frog, a pompous National Frog.
NOËL: Look here . . .

GERTIE: You're so damned pleased with yourself.

NOËL: Pleased with myself! I should like to say one thing—

GERTIE: Sollocks, darling—oh, Sollocks.

Two minutes' pause. NOËL puts on a dance record.

NOËL: Do you feel like dancing?

GERTIE: Not at all.

They dance.

NOËL: Why are we doing this?

GERTIE: Charity.

NOËL: What charity?

GERTIE: I haven't the slightest idea, I believe it's something to do with angry old governesses.

NOËL: I thought it was a Fresh Air Fund for the waiters at the Café de Paris.

GERTIE: Anyhow, it doesn't matter, does it?

NOËL: Not a bit.

They dance in silence for a moment or two.

NOËL: A pretty thing about the financial situation.

GERTIE: Very pretty.

NOËL: Looks as though there might be a revolution among the Welsh miners.

GERTIE: You'd better write a play about it.

NOËL (leaving her and stopping the gramophone): That was rude.

GERTIE: I don't see why.

NOËL: Cigarette?

GERTIE: No.

NOËL (lighting one): Are you going to sing in your new play?

GERTIE: No.

NOËL: Good.

GERTIE: How dare you say that?

NOËL: I think you left musical comedy in the nick of time.

GERTIE: Nick, nick, nick. What do you mean—nick?

NOËL: Your voice is not what it was.

GERTIE: Yours is, and that's what's wrong with it.

NOËL: At least I don't sing flat.

GERTIE: Meaning that I do?

NOËL: Knowing that you do.

GERTIE: Flat, indeed!
NOËL: *Very* flat.
GERTIE: You're insufferable.
NOËL: Darling—Sollocks!

NOËL goes in silence to the piano. They sing a few songs. During the last one he stops just as she is taking a top note.

NOËL: There you are—*flat!*

He bangs the note.

·

The Far East seemed to inspire him. Without it we should not have his most famous song, "Mad Dogs and Englishmen."

On a motor trip in early 1930 from Hanoi to Saigon "a song popped into my head."

This drive took about a week and while jungles and river and mountain and rice fields were unrolling by the window of the car, I wrestled in my mind with the complicated rhythms and rhymes of the song until finally it was complete, without even the aid of pencil and paper. I sang it triumphantly and unaccompanied to my travelling companion, Jeffery Amherst, on the veranda of a small jungle guesthouse. Not only Jeffery but the gecko lizards and the tree frogs gave every vocal indication of enthusiasm.

Noël's own enthusiasm was somewhat tempered on the eve of World War II. Asking Winston Churchill's advice on how he (Noël) could best contribute to the war effort:

It was, on the whole, an unsuccessful little interview. I was aware throughout that he was misunderstanding my motives and had got it firmly into his mind that I wished to be a glamorous secret agent. I tried vainly to disabuse him of this by assuring him that nothing was further from my thoughts, and that even if my heart were set on such a course, the very fact of my celebrity value would prove an insuperable obstacle. I emphasized repeatedly my firm conviction that my brain and creative intelligence could be of more service to the government than my theatrical ability. I think the word "intelligence" must have been the monkey wrench, because at the mere mention of it he said irascibly, "You'd be no good in the Intelligence Service." I endeavoured, with growing inward irritation, to explain that I didn't mean "the Intelligence" in inverted commas, but my own *personal* intelligence, which was not in inverted commas. He would have none of it, however, and went off at a great tangent about the Navy (which in any event was preaching to the already converted). Finally, warming to his subject, he waved his hand with a bravura gesture and said dramatically: "Get into a warship and see some action! Go and sing to them when the guns are firing—that's your job!" With, I think, commendable restraint, I bit back the retort that if the morale of the Royal Navy was at such low ebb that the troops were unable to go into action without my singing "Mad Dogs and Englishmen" to them, we were in trouble at the outset and that, although theoretically "singing when the guns are firing" sounds extremely gallant, it is, in reality, impracticable, because during a naval battle all ship's companies are at action stations, and the only place for me to sing would be in the wardroom by myself.

—FUTURE INDEFINITE (1950)

The song later very nearly became the cause of an Anglo-American *détente*. When Churchill and Roosevelt met on the British battleship HMS *Prince of Wales* to draw up the Atlantic Charter, their respective aides were troubled to hear what seemed to be a "heated altercation" during a private session.

The argument turned out to be about the sequence of the words in "Mad Dogs." Did "In Bangkok at twelve o'clock / They foam at the mouth and run" come at the end of the first refrain or the second?

Noël was later asked by Churchill to adjudicate. "I'm afraid, Prime Minister," he said, "the President was right and *you* were wrong." Churchill gave him that bulldog glare and finally said, "Bwitain can take it!"

"MAD DOGS AND ENGLISHMEN"

In tropical climes there are certain times of day
When all the citizens retire
To tear their clothes off and perspire.
It's one of those rules that the greatest fools obey,
Because the sun is much too sultry
And one must avoid its ultry-violet ray.

Papalaka papalaka papalaka boo,
Papalaka papalaka papalaka boo,

Digariga digariga digariga doo,
Digariga digariga digariga doo.

The natives grieve when the white men leave their huts,
Because they're obviously definitely nuts!

Mad dogs and Englishmen
Go out in the midday sun,
The Japanese don't care to,
The Chinese wouldn't dare to,
Hindoos and Argentines sleep firmly from twelve to one,
But Englishmen detest a siesta.
In the Philippines
There are lovely screens
To protect you from the glare.
In the Malay States
There are hats like plates
Which the Britishers won't wear.
At twelve noon
The natives swoon
And no further work is done.

But mad dogs and Englishmen
Go out in the midday sun.

It's such a surprise for the Eastern eyes to see
That though the English are effete,
They're quite impervious to heat.
When the white man rides every native hides in glee,
Because the simple creatures hope he
Will impale his solar topee on a tree.

Bolyboly bolyboly bolyboly baa,
Bolyboly bolyboly bolyboly baa,
Habaninny habaninny habaninny haa
Habaninny habaninny habaninny haa.

It seems such a shame
When the English claim
The earth
That they give rise to such hilarity and mirth.

Mad dogs and Englishmen
Go out in the midday sun.
The toughest Burmese bandit
Can never understand it.
In Rangoon the heat of
    noon
Is just what the natives
    shun.
They put their Scotch or
    Rye down
And lie down.
In a jungle town
Where the sun beats
    down
To the rage of man and
    beast,
The English garb
Of the English sahib
Merely gets a bit more
    creased.
In Bangkok
At twelve o'clock
They foam at the mouth
    and run,

Noël always claimed that in early
photographs he looked like "a
heavily-doped Chinese illusionist."
Osbert Lancaster obviously agreed.

But mad dogs and Englishmen
Go out in the midday sun.

Mad dogs and Englishmen
Go out in the midday sun.
The smallest Malay rabbit
Deplores this stupid habit.
In Hong Kong
They strike a gong
And fire off a noonday gun
To reprimand each inmate
Who's in late.
In the mangrove swamps
Where the python romps
There is peace from twelve to two,
Even caribous
Lie around and snooze,
For there's nothing else to do.
In Bengal
To move at all
Is seldom, if ever done,
But mad dogs and Englishmen
Go out in the midday sun.

·

By now Noël was often heavily involved in producing and directing his own plays. This created several new problems.

There were the auditions.

"The nicest words I know in the theatre are 'That's all, sir,' which signify the end of a mass audition. It means that we shan't have to hear 'Phil the Fluter's Ball' again that morning."

There was the Stage Mother—a subject Noël was thoroughly familiar with, since he had the archetypal one himself . . .

"MRS. WORTHINGTON"

Regarding yours, dear Mrs. Worthington,
Of Wednesday the twenty-third,
Although your baby
May be,
Keen on a stage career,
How can I make it clear,

That this is not a good idea.
For her to hope,
Dear Mrs. Worthington,
Is on the face of it absurd,
Her personality
Is not in reality
Inviting enough,
Exciting enough
For this particular sphere.

Don't put your daughter on the stage, Mrs. Worthington,
Don't put your daughter on the stage,
The profession is overcrowded
And the struggle's pretty tough
And admitting the fact
She's burning to act,
That isn't quite enough.
She has nice hands, to give the wretched girl her due,
But don't you think her bust is too
Developed for her age,
I repeat

MRS. WORTHINGTON

DON'T PUT YOUR DAUGHTER ON THE STAGE

SCHOOL OF ACTING

WORDS & MUSIC

by NOEL COWARD

Price 2/- net   CHAPPELL

Mrs. Worthington,
Sweet
Mrs. Worthington,
Don't put your daughter on the stage.

Don't put your daughter on the stage,
     Mrs. Worthington,
Don't put your daughter on the stage,
She's a bit of an ugly duckling
You must honestly confess,
And the width of her seat
Would surely defeat
Her chances of success,
It's a loud voice, and though it's not exactly flat,
She'll need a little more than that
To earn a living wage,
On my knees,
Mrs. Worthington,
Please
Mrs. Worthington,
Don't put your daughter on the stage.

Don't put your daughter on the stage,
     Mrs. Worthington,
Don't put your daughter on the stage,
Though they said at the school of acting
She was lovely as Peer Gynt,
I'm afraid on the whole
An ingenue role
Would emphasize her squint,
She's a big girl, and though her teeth are fairly good
She's not the type I ever would
Be eager to engage,
No more buts,
Mrs. Worthington,
Nuts!
Mrs. Worthington,
Don't put your daughter on the stage.

Don't put your daughter on the stage,
     Mrs. Worthington,
Don't put your daughter on the stage,
One look at her bandy legs should prove

She hasn't got a chance,
In addition to which
The son of a bitch
Can neither sing nor dance,
She's a *vile* girl and uglier than mortal sin,
One look at her has put me in
A tearing bloody rage,
That sufficed,
Mrs. Worthington,
Christ!
Mrs. Worthington,
Don't put your daughter on the stage.

•

"Its universal appeal lies, I believe, in its passionate sincerity. It is a genuine *cri de coeur* and as such cannot fail to ring true. Unhappily, its effectiveness, from the point of view of propaganda, has been negligible. I had hoped, by writing it, to discourage misguided maternal ambition, to deter those dreadful eager mothers from making beasts of themselves, by boring the hell out of me and wasting their own and my time, but I have not succeeded. On the contrary, the song seems to have given them extra impetus and ninety-nine out of a hundred of the letters they write to me refer to it with roguish indulgence, obviously secure in the conviction that it could not in any circumstance apply to them. This is saddening, of course, but realizing that the road of the social reformer is paved with disillusion I have determined to rise above it."

•

There was the Inevitable Party Guest, who couldn't wait to get back to suburban Surbiton or Staines to tell her social circle, "Oh, I had a *long* chat with Noël Coward . . ."

"SOCIAL GRACE"

I expect you've heard this a million times before
But I absolutely adored your last play
I went four times—and now to think
That I am actually talking to you!
It's thrilling! Honestly it is, I mean,
It's always thrilling isn't it to meet someone
                              really celebrated?

I mean someone who really does things.
I expect all this is a terrible bore for you.
After all you go everywhere and know everybody.
It must be wonderful to go absolutely everywhere
And know absolutely everybody and—oh dear—
Then to have to listen to someone like me,
I mean someone absolutely ordinary just one of your
    public.
No one will believe me when I tell them
That I have actually been talking to the great man
    himself.
It must be wonderful to be so frightfully brainy
And know all the things that you know.
I'm not brainy a bit, neither is my husband,
Just plain humdrum, that's what we are.
But we do come up to town occasionally
And go to shows and things. Actually my husband
Is quite a critic, not professionally of course,
What I mean is that he isn't all that easily pleased.
He doesn't like everything. Oh no, not by any means.
He simply hated that thing at the Haymarket
Which everybody went on about. "Rubbish" he said,
Straight out like that, "Damned Rubbish!"
I nearly died because heaps of people were listening.
But that's quite typical of him. He just says what he
    thinks.
And he can't stand all this highbrow stuff—
Do you know what I mean?—All these plays about
    people being miserable
And never getting what they want and not even
    committing suicide
But just being absolutely wretched. He says he goes to
    the theatre
To have a good time. That's why he simply loves all your
    things.
I mean they relax him and he doesn't have to think.
And he certainly does love a good laugh.
You should have seen him the other night when we went
    to that film
With what's-her-name in it—I can't remember the title.
I thought he'd have a fit, honestly I did.
You must know the one I mean, the one about the man
    who comes home

And finds his wife has been carrying on with his best
    friend
And, of course, he's furious at first and then he decides
    to teach her a lesson.
You must have seen it. I wish I could remember the name
But that's absolutely typical of me, I've got a head
    like a sieve,
I keep on forgetting things and as for names—well!
I cannot for the life of me remember them.
Faces yes, I never forget a face because I happen to be
    naturally observant
And always have been since I was a tiny kiddie
But names —oh dear! I'm quite hopeless.
I feel such a fool sometimes
I do honestly.

Which inspired him to write . . .

"I'VE GOT TO GO OUT AND BE SOCIAL"

I've got to go out and be social,
I've got to go out and be social,
I've got to be bright
And extremely polite
And refrain from becoming too loose or too tight
And I mustn't impose conversational blight
On the dolt on my left
And the fool on my right.
I must really be very attractive tonight
As I have to go out and be social.

I have to go out and be social,
I've got to go out and be social,
I have to forget
The Bohemian set
And discuss with the flower of *Burke* and *Debrett*
The fall of the franc and the National Debt,
I have to regret
That the weather is wet
There's so much that I can't afford to forget—
As I have to go out and be social.

—UNPUBLISHED VERSE

·

Having studied the female of the species over the years—particularly those of "a certain age"—Noël became something of an amateur psychiatrist himself.

With P. G. Wodehouse it was aunts that were anathema. Noël was more clinical and dispassionate, but one can see elements of his passive aunts Ida, Vida and Dora and a great deal of his aggressive mother, Violet, in Mrs. Mallory and Mrs. Radcliffe . . .

"MRS. MALLORY"

Mrs. Mallory went to a Psychiatrist
On the advice of Mrs. Silvera
Who had been twice divorced
And considered herself to be maladjusted.
Mrs. Mallory, who had never been divorced at all,
Considered that she also was maladjusted
Not for any specific reason, really
Nothing you could put your finger on
But a definite feeling of dissatisfaction
With life in general and Mr. Mallory in particular,
And Deidre too who was no comfort and solace
    to her mother
Though at her age she should have been
But she was an unpredictable character
Who devoted too much time to rock 'n' roll
And none at all to domestic science
And helping in the house and keeping a wary eye open
For Mr. Right to come along and sweep her away
To a series of social triumphs
In Washington possibly, or at least Baltimore,
Which Mrs. Mallory could read about in the gossip
    columns
And then send the cuttings to Irma in Minneapolis
Who would have to read them whether she liked it or not.

Mrs. Mallory lay on the Psychiatrist's sofa
With her arms relaxed at her sides
And her feet sticking up, one to the right and
    one to the left
Like a mermaid's tail.

The Psychiatrist sat behind her out of range
And waited politely for her to begin to talk
Which she was only too eager to do
After the first shyness had worn off
And he had asked her a few routine questions.
But she talked and talked and talked and talked.
So much, so much came tumbling out of her,
More than she would ever have believed possible,
But then, of course, unlike Mrs. Silvera, he didn't
    interrupt
And say things like, "That reminds me of when
    I went to Atlantic City
With my first husband" or "I feel exactly the same,
    dear, naturally
But I have to control my feelings on account of being
    so strictly raised."
The Psychiatrist didn't seem to be reminded of anything
    at all.
He sat there so quietly that once Mrs. Mallory looked
    around
To see if he had dropped off, but he hadn't;
There he was scribbling away on a pad and
    occasionally nodding his head.
She told him all about Deidre
And Mr. Mallory coming home from the Rotarian lunch
And taking his pants off on the landing
And shouting "Everything I have is yours,
    you're part of me!"
So loudly that Beulah had come out of the kitchen
And seen him with his lower parts showing
And his hat still on.
She also told the Psychiatrist about the man
    in the subway
Who had pressed himself against her from behind
And said something that sounded like "Ug Ug"
Which was the one thing she had never told Mrs. Silvera
Perhaps on account of her having been so strictly raised.
She told him as well about the extraordinary dream
    she had had
On the night following the Beedmeyers' anniversary
    party
But when she was in the middle of it,
Before she had even got to the bit about the horse,

He suddenly rose and smiled and said that he hoped
   to see her next Friday.
At the same time.
And much less maladjusted
And when Mr. Mallory came home from the office
She had put on her new hostess gown
Which she had worn only twice
Once at the Beedmeyers and the other time
   at the Palisades Country Club
On Christmas Eve.
Also she had rubbed some "Shalimar" behind her ears
And greeted him with an all-embracing welcoming
   smile
But it was none of it any use really
When dinner was over they looked at television
   as they always did
Until it was time to go to bed.
Mr. Mallory spent longer in the bathroom than usual
And the "Shalimar" began to wear off.
But when he did come back in his pyjamas
It didn't seem to matter much anyway
Because he merely belched and said "Excuse
   me" automatically,
Blew her a perfunctory kiss and got into his own bed,
Later on, after he had read *McCall's* for a little,
He switched off the light.

Mrs. Mallory lay in the darkness
With her arms relaxed at her sides
And her feet up, one to the right and one to the left
Like a mermaid's tail
And a tear rolled down her face all the way to her chin.

•

And then there was Mrs. Radcliffe . . .

"THE KINDNESS OF MRS. RADCLIFFE"

Mrs. Radcliffe always awoke on the dot of half-past seven. It was a habit of years and from this regularity she derived a certain pride. It signified a disciplined mind in a disciplined body, and Mrs. Radcliffe was a great one for discipline. Life was a business that had to be handled with efficiency and dispatch otherwise where were you? She had a poor opinion of those, and alas there were all too many of them, who allowed themselves to be swayed this way and that by emotions and circumstances over which they had little or no control. To have little or no control over emotions and circumstances was, to Mrs. Radcliffe, anathema. Not only did she consider it was foolish to succumb to the manifold weaknesses inherent in our natures, and after all there are many of these in even the sternest of us, it was downright dangerous. Mrs. Radcliffe could quote several instances of people of her acquaintance, occasionally even relatives, who, owing either to self-indulgence, lack of sense of responsibility or, in some cases, willful stubbornness—such as Cousin Laura for example—had completely degenerated and failed. It must not be imagined that Mrs. Radcliffe, who heaven knows was a broad-minded and kindly woman, referred to failure merely in the worldly sense; many of those who from her point of view had "failed" had, on basely materialistic counts, done exceedingly well for themselves. Failure was a hydra-headed monster. You could be shrewd and businesslike, marry well and become a senior partner in no time and still fail. You could bear children, bring them up firmly, embark them on promising careers, keep your figure, wear smart clothes and play bridge as well as Mrs. Poindexter and still fail. On the other hand you could be poor and of no account, an insignificant cog in the great wheel of life and succeed, succeed triumphantly, for surely success in the eyes of God is of more ultimate importance than the glittering transient satisfaction of success in the eyes of the world. This, to sum it up briefly, was Mrs. Radcliffe's philosophy and she was delighted with it. She felt herself to be on a footing with the Almighty which was, to say the least of it, cordial. She referred to Him frequently in her mind and even more frequently in her conversation, not, it must be understood, with the slightest trace of sanctimoniousness. Hers was far too healthy and sane a character for that, rather more in a spirit of reverend friendliness. Occasionally she even blasphemed mildly to the extent of saying "Good Lord" or "My God" in moments of light stress. This, she considered in her secret heart, to be rather amusingly racy provided she didn't allow it to become a habit.

On this particular morning in early April Mrs. Radcliffe awoke as usual and lay for a few moments in dreamy awareness of the comfort of her bed, the translucent greenish charm of her bedroom, and the fact that it was a sunny day. This was apparent from the bars of strong light shining

through the venetian blind and making stripes on the corner of the dressing table and the chaise longue by the window. Presently she heard Mildred approaching with her early tea; a swift glance at the clock on the table
by her bed informed her that Mildred was four and a half minutes late. She
decided, however, not to mention it this time. Mildred's unpunctuality
was, unfortunately, the least of her defects; in fact there were moments
when Mrs. Radcliffe genuinely regretted her generous impulse in taking
her from the orphanage when she might quite easily have found a girl from
the Registry Office with a certain amount of previous training in domestic
service. The training of Mildred presented many problems and showed
every sign of being an uphill struggle. But still Mrs. Radcliffe in her
capacity as one of the esteemed Vice-Presidents of the Orphanage Committee had felt it her bounden duty to set an example to some of the other
members, who, although volubly free with suggestions for the future of
their charges when the moment came to launch them onto the world, were
singularly unresponsive when it came to the point of doing anything practical about it themselves. Mrs. Radcliffe often smiled whimsically as she
recalled the various expressions on the faces of the committee when she
had burst her bombshell. "I will take Mildred myself," she had said, quite
simply, without undue emphasis on the magnanimity of her gesture,
just like that, "I will take Mildred myself!" She remembered that Mrs.
Weecock, who was overemotional and effusive, had risen impulsively and
kissed her, and that Doctor Price had immediately proposed a vote of
thanks which had been carried unanimously with the greatest enthusiasm.

Mildred, after several months of strenuous effort, had, as yet, only managed to scrape the surface of what was ultimately expected of her; however
she was willing, sometimes almost too eager to please, all of which was
natural enough, poor little thing; nobody could accuse Mrs. Radcliffe of
being unable to recognize pathetic, overwhelming gratitude, however
nervous.

At this moment the object of her reflections entered the room. She was
an uncouth girl of eighteen. Her abundant sandy hair straggled widely
away from her neat cap, giving it the appearance of a small white fort set in
the middle of a desert. Her hands were large and pink and her feet, encased
in cotton stockings and strap shoes, were larger still. Her face, however,
apart from a few freckles, was pleasing. She had a generous mouth and
well-set grayish-green eyes. She said "Good morning, 'um," in a breathy
voice and, having deposited the tray temporarily on the chest of drawers,
went over and pulled up the blind. She also closed the window, which during Mrs. Radcliffe's slumbers had been open a fraction at the top, rather
too sharply, so that the panes rattled.

"Gently, Mildred, gently," said Mrs. Radcliffe as she hoisted herself up
on her pillows preparatory to receiving the tea tray. Mildred, by drawing

in her breath and clicking her tongue against her teeth several times, made a noise which, although intended to express bitter self-reproach, merely succeeded in being irritating. Mrs. Radcliffe winced and waited for her tray in silence. The tray was a complicated affair designed for the comfort of invalids. By pressing lightly with the hands, two pairs of wooden legs shot out from each side thereby forming a neat little bridge across the patient's knees. This was one of the banes of Mildred's life. If the eiderdown were rumpled or Mrs. Radcliffe had not arranged herself in a completely symmetrical position, the whole thing was liable to tip sideways causing everything on it to slide alarmingly and hover on the brink of disaster. This morning, aware that she had transgressed over the window shutting, Mildred was even more nervous than usual. Her large hands were trembling and she breathed heavily. She set the tray across Mrs. Radcliffe's legs with laborious care; so far so good, only a few drops slopped out of the milk jug. She straightened herself with a sigh of relief and in the moment of triumph God struck her down. The corner of her apron, unbeknownst to her, had been caught by the left legs of the tray and the straightening of her body jerked it free with just sufficient force to overbalance the teapot. It was one of those moments in life when Time ceases to exist, years of fear and agony are endured in the passing of a brief instant. Mildred watched, with dilating eyes, the fat blue teapot with the willow-pattern design on it wobble from side to side and then slowly, slowly, with the slowness of protracted death, fall off the tray, roll over twice on the smooth slope of the counterpane, shedding its lid on the way, and finally crash to the floor, emptying its contents with devilish exultance into Mrs. Radcliffe's ostrich feather bedroom slippers. In the deadly silence that ensued a train whistled in the cutting a mile away, causing Mildred to jump violently as though the last trump had sounded for her.

Mrs. Radcliffe, who as a rule could be relied upon to assume an attitude of splendid calm in any crisis, for once lost control and fairly let fly. Mildred stood before her wretchedly twisting her hands, dumb with misery, too frightened even to take in half of what was being said to her. Disjointed words flashed across her consciousness like those moving electric light signs which tell of immediate events but which, if your attention is not wholly concentrated on them, become a series of meaningless phrases. A few invectives like "Idiot," "Fool," "Clumsy" and "Stupid" seared her mind for a moment and then were gone with the rest, leaving her shivering in a void of hopelessness and shame.

Presently Mrs. Radcliffe regained control and, after a slight pause, spoke with icy precision: "Pick it up," she said, and then again: "PICK IT UP!" using each word as a sword. Mildred stooped and picked up the teapot and stood with it in her hands, only vaguely aware of its heat. "The tray," said Mrs. Radcliffe. "Take the tray." Mildred put the teapot down on the floor again and took the tray.

The next ten minutes were devoted, insofar as was possible, to restoring order to chaos. Mildred, galvanized suddenly into feverish activity, flew down to the kitchen, blurted out the disaster in a few stumbling words to Cook, flew upstairs again with a cloth, rubbed and scrubbed with hot water out of the silver-plated jug to erase the tea stains from the carpet amid a hail of frigidly patient directions from her mistress. Finally, when the best that could be done had been done, she blurted out, "I'm sure I'm very sorry, 'um, it was an accident," and made for the door. Mrs. Radcliffe halted her.

"Just a moment, Mildred."

Mildred waited, standing first on one foot then on the other. Mrs. Radcliffe's voice was cold and just, she was now in full command again and sailing to victory.

"To explain that it was an accident, Mildred," she said, "was unnecessary. I should hardly have imagined that you had done such a thing on purpose. But what I wish to point out to you is that the accident would never have occurred if you had not been both careless and slovenly. I have spoken to you, Heaven knows often enough, about your clumsiness, and if you don't try to improve I very much fear I shall have to give you your notice. This time, however, and it is the last time, I shall excuse you." Mildred's heart leapt with relief like a bird in her breast. "But," continued Mrs. Radcliffe, "in order that this shall be a lesson to you, in order that you shall think and be more careful in future, I intend to punish you." There was a slight pause. The small gilt clock on the mantelpiece gave a little whir and struck eight. Mrs. Radcliffe waited portentously until it had finished. "I understand that today is your afternoon out?" The bird in Mildred's breast dropped like a stone to the earth and through the earth into deep caverns of despair. "Yes, 'um," she said huskily. "Well," went on the voice of doom, "you will stay in this afternoon and help with the silver. That is all, thank you." A tear coursed down the side of Mildred's nose. "Very good, 'um," she said in a voice so low as to be almost inaudible, and went out of the room.

The fact that every minute of every hour of every day of Mildred's week had been concentrated on the anticipatory bliss of that afternoon out was of course hidden from Mrs. Radcliffe. How could she possibly know that Fred, thrilling wonderful Fred, assistant to Mr. Lewis the chemist in the High Street, had arranged to meet Mildred at two-thirty outside Harvey Brown's and take her to see Spencer Tracy, Clark Gable and Myrna Loy in *Test Pilot*? How could she possibly know that Messrs. Tracy and Gable and Miss Loy would be up and away by next Thursday and their sacred screen occupied by an English historical picture featuring Sir Cedric Hardwicke?

How also could she guess that as Fred would be out on his rounds all the morning there was no possible way of letting him know that Mildred would be unable to meet him and that, after waiting for a half an hour or so on the pavement outside Harvey Brown's, he would probably be so furious that he would never speak to her again?

Fortunately for Mrs. Radcliffe's peace of mind she was ignorant of all this and, in consequence, her sense of exhilaration at having handled a difficult and annoying domestic drama with her usual consummate calm and decision was in no way impaired.

2

Mr. Stanley Radcliffe stood five foot six inches and a half in his socks which, no matter with what fickleness the weather might change, were invariably of austere gray worsted. His hair, thin on the top but happily bushy at the sides, was of the same color as his socks. As a character he was amiable, temperate and industrious but, if criticize we must, a trifle lacking in spirit. This defect, however, could be understood, if not altogether excused, by the fact that he had been married to Mrs. Radcliffe for thirty-three years. It is a well-known sociological truism that two dominant personalities become ill-at-ease when compelled by force of circumstance to inhabit the same house for a long period of time. It is possible that Mr. Radcliffe wisely realized this early on in his married life and, being a man of peaceful and sensible disposition, relinquished the ever dubious joys of domestic authority to his wife. It must not be supposed, however, that outside his home he was anywhere near as weak as he was in it. On the contrary, in his office—he was a partner in the firm of Eldridge, Eldridge and Black, Solicitors-at-Law—in his office he was often a veritable martinet. Times out of number Miss Hallett, his secretary, would emerge from taking the morning letters with pursed lips and a spread of scarlet stretching from her neck up to her ears that spoke volumes.

On the morning of the teapot tragedy he was feeling cheerful. It was a cheerful day. The birds were twittering in the garden. He had received a letter from Henry Boulder, a more or less private client, that is to say a client who combined the transaction of legal business with a pleasant personal relationship, inviting him to visit him that afternoon at his house near Bromley to discuss the details of a new building contract that Eldridge, Eldridge and Black were drawing up for him, and perhaps play a round of golf afterward. A game of golf to Stanley Radcliffe was as steel is to a magnet, or rather a magnet to steel. He loved golf deeply and truly with all the passion of his nature. He was also fond of Mrs. Boulder, not in any way lasciviously, Mr. Radcliffe's sex impulses had atrophied from neglect at least fifteen years ago, but with a warm sense of comradeship.

She was a gay, vivacious creature in the early forties, given to telling rather risqué stories, and she had a loud, infectious laugh. Life at the Boulders' home seemed to consist of one long joke. Henry Boulder laughed a lot too, and frequently said the most outrageous things, but with such an air of worldly geniality that no offense could possibly be taken.

Mr. Radcliffe looked at his wife sipping her coffee and opening letters at the other side of the table. She had her glasses on and appeared to be in a tranquil mood. He wondered if the moment was at last ripe for him to suggest what he had been longing to suggest for weeks. Why not take the plunge? He cleared his throat. Mrs. Radcliffe looked up. "Such a nice let-ter from Mrs. Riddle," she said. "They've just come back from a cruise to the Holy Land."

A fleeting vision of Mrs. Riddle, a formidable woman of vicious piety, blustering through the Church of the Holy Sepulcher, flashed across Mr. Radcliffe's mind for a moment and was obliterated. Now or never.

"How nice, dear," he said. "I wanted to——"

"They bathed in the Dead Sea," went on Mrs. Radcliffe, glancing at a closely written page of thin notepaper. "And it was so salt that they couldn't sink."

"I shouldn't have thought," said Mr. Radcliffe with a bold chuckle, "that they would have wished to."

Mrs. Radcliffe looked at him suspiciously and then smiled, but without mirth, and went on reading the letter. Humor was not her strong suit and flippancy definitely irritated her.

Mr. Radcliffe, realizing that he had made a tactical error, cleared his throat again. "Adela," he said, "I have just had a letter from Henry Boul-der." This, he realized the moment the words were out of his mouth, was another tactical error implying as it did that a letter from Henry Boulder was on a par with a letter from Mrs. Riddle. Mrs. Radcliffe ignored him completely and went on reading. Then Mr. Radcliffe, in a determined effort to get what was in his mind out of it, committed the gravest blun-der of all. He advanced recklessly into the open. "I thought of inviting the Boulders to dinner tonight," he said.

Mrs. Radcliffe slowly lowered her letter and stared at him. If he had sug-gested inviting two naked Zulus to dinner she could not have expressed more shocked surprise. "My dear Stanley!" she said in the exasperated tone one might use in addressing a particularly fractious invalid. "The Dukes are coming."

"I don't see that that would make any difference," he said suddenly.

Mrs. Radcliffe, scenting mutiny, decided to scotch it once and for all. She leant across the table and smiled. "I fully appreciate," she said, "that they are great friends of yours," the emphasis on the word "yours" implied just enough subtle contempt, "but they are certainly not great friends of mine, in fact I barely know them. Also, my dear, although I am sure they are very useful to you in business, they are hardly"—here she gave a little laugh—"hardly the sort of people I would invite to meet the Dukes!"

Mr. Radcliffe opened his mouth to speak, to speak sharply, to say with firmness and conviction that the Reverend Francis Duke, vicar or no vicar, was an overbearing, pretentious bore, and his wife a giggling fool, and that for good humor and pleasant company and making a dinner party a success Mr. and Mrs. Henry Boulder could knock spots off them any day of the week. All this and more was bubbling in his mind, clamoring to be said, but the habit of years was too strong for him. He met the unwinking stare of his wife's slightly protuberant blue eyes for a moment and then wavered, the game was up. "Very well, my dear," he said, and resumed his toast and marmalade. Mrs. Radcliffe relaxed and smiled indulgently, poor old Stanley! She, who was so used to triumph, could afford to be magnanimous. She leant across the table and patted his hand affectionately then, generously wiping the episode from her mind, she embarked on the fourth page of Mrs. Riddle's letter about the Holy Land.

Mr. Radcliffe, half an hour later, sat in the corner of a third-class smoking compartment on the train to London puzzling out in his mind the most tactful way in which he could repay some of the Boulders' hospitality. He could, of course, invite them to dine at a restaurant and perhaps get seats for a play afterward, but even so he was terribly afraid that the absence of Adela and the fact that they had never been asked to the house might hurt their feelings. People were extremely touchy about things like that. The last time he had visited them Mrs. Boulder had dropped a few hints. Suddenly, with a rush of blood to his face, he remembered that that same evening, just after dinner, he had, in a moment of expansion, definitely invited them. He remembered his very words: "You must come and dine one night soon and we'll have some bridge—my wife is so anxious to get to know you better."

When the train arrived at Cannon Street he went straight to the telegraph office, walking slowly as if he were tired. He wrote out the telegram carefully. "Boulder, 'The Nook,' Bromley. Very disappointed unable accept your kind invitation for this afternoon regards Radcliffe."

3

Mrs. Radcliffe rose from her desk in the morning room with a sigh and patted her hair in front of a mirror on the wall. She had been absentmindedly disarranging it while writing that difficult letter to Cousin Laura. She looked at her reflection for a moment and then, smiling, shook her head sorrowfully at herself. "You must really break yourself of that bad habit," she said with mock firmness, and then looked hurriedly to see if Mildred had happened to come in without her noticing. It would be too ridiculous to be caught by a servant talking to oneself. All was well, however Mildred had not come in. As a matter of fact Mildred was at that moment in her bedroom at the top of the house crying her eyes out.

That letter to Laura had certainly been difficult, but Mrs. Radcliffe felt a sense of great relief at having at last written it. It had been hanging over her for days. Laura was her Aunt Marion's daughter and they had been at school together. Laura's whole life, in Mrs. Radcliffe's opinion, had been untidy, inefficient and annoying. To begin with she had married a drunkard with no money who had finally deserted her and died in Rio de Janeiro. After that for several years and with two young children on her hands she had contrived to run a tea shop at Hove and carry on a scandalous affair with a married man at the same time. In the year 1912 she had married again, a handsome but vague young man also with no money to speak of, who had later been killed in the retreat from Mons. In the intervening years between the Armistice and 1930 she had fortunately been abroad running a pension in some dead-and-alive seaside town in Northern Italy. Meanwhile the children of her first marriage had grown up. The boy, Frank, had married and gone off to plant rubber in Burma and was seldom heard from, while the girl, Estelle, had also married and, with an inefficiency obviously inherited from her mother, had died in childbirth, having misjudged her time and been caught in labour on a Channel Island steamer in the middle of a storm. Laura, now a woman of over sixty, had been living ever since in a small house in Folkestone only just managing to pay the rent every quarter by taking in paying guests. Almost the most irritating thing about her was her unregenerate cheerfulness. Even in the begging letter Mrs. Radcliffe had received from her a few days back there had been an irrepressible note of flippancy. Mrs. Radcliffe picked it up from the desk and re-read it for the third time. "My dear Adela," she read, "I am in the soup this time and no mistake. Please forgive me for worrying you with my troubles, but I really don't know where to turn. Mr. Roland, one of my extra quality streamlined P.G.'s, upped and left me on Saturday without paying his month's board and lodging and I was counting on it to pay off the last instalment on my dining-room set. I owe eighteen pounds on it and unless I pay it by Friday they'll come and take every stick away and poor Mr. Clarence Sims and Mr. Brackett, my other two gents, will have to sit on the bare floor. I do feel dreadful asking you to lend me ten pounds temporarily. I can raise eight all right on mother's silver, but if you possibly can spare it do please help me as I am in a flat spin and worried to death. I promise to pay it back within the next three months. Your distracted but affectionate cousin, Laura." Mrs. Radcliffe replaced Laura's letter in its envelope and read once more her own firm and admirable answer to it.

My dear Laura, your letter was a great surprise to me, not having heard from you for so long. Believe me, I sympathize with you more than I can say in all your worries. If you will remember I always have. (Underlined.) How very disgraceful of your lodger to leave without paying you. Wasn't it a little unwise to take in that sort of man in the first place? However, it's no use crying over spilt milk, is it? With regard to your request for ten pounds, I am afraid that is quite out of the question at the moment. As you know I have many calls upon my purse in these trying times especially now that the Orphanage, of which I am vice-president, is becoming so overcrowded that we find ourselves forced to build a new dormitory for the little ones to which we all, that is the committee and myself, have had to subscribe a great deal more than we can afford. You see we all have our little troubles! However, as we are such old friends, let alone actual blood relations—I always think that sounds so unpleasant, don't you?— I cannot bear to think of you in such dire straits, so I am enclosing a check for three guineas. This is most emphatically not a loan as I cannot bear the thought of money transactions between friends. Please, dear Laura, accept it in the spirit in which it is offered. Stanley joins me in the warmest greetings. I remain, your affectionate cousin, Adela Radcliffe.

Mrs. Radcliffe sat down at the desk again and wrote out the check, then having placed it with the letter in an already addressed envelope, she licked it down and stuck a stamp on it with an authoritative thump of her fist. This done she sat back in her chair and relaxed for a moment. What a pleasant thing it is, she reflected, to be in the fortunate position of being able to help those who, owing to defects in character and general fecklessness, are so pitifully unable to help themselves. In this mood of justifiable satisfaction, and humming a little tune, she went down into the kitchen to interview the Cook.

4

Mrs. Brodie had cooked for Mrs. Radcliffe for nearly three years and had, on the whole, proved satisfactory. Mrs. Radcliffe's tastes were simple. She disapproved of high seasoning, rich sauces, and the complicated flubdubbery of the French school. She designated any dish that was not strictly in accordance with the wholesome English culinary tradition as "Messy," and nobody who knew Mrs. Radcliffe even casually could visualize her for a moment sitting down to anything messy. Mrs. Brodie filled the bill perfectly. True, there were times when she displayed a certain tendency to flightiness. There had been one or two slipups. The Malayan curry, for instance (Mrs. Brodie's brother was a sailor), and the dreadful time the Piggots came to dinner and had been offered soufflé en surprise, the cold middle part of which had so surprised Mrs. Piggot's wisdom tooth that she had had to lie down on Mrs. Radcliffe's bed and have her gum painted with oil of cloves. All that, however, was in the past, although an occasional reminder of it came in handy as a curb whenever Mrs. Brodie showed signs of rebellion.

This morning there was no spirit in Mrs. Brodie at all, she had her own private troubles, as indeed who has not, and today they had come to a head. In the first place her widowed sister had been whisked off to the hospital to be operated on for gallstones, thereby leaving no one to look after Mrs. Brodie's husband who had had two strokes in the last nine months and was due for another one at any moment. This had necessitated some quick thinking and the sending of a telegram first thing to a niece in Southampton, together with a money order for fare and expenses. Mrs. Brodie devoutly hoped that at this moment the niece was already in the train. In the meantime she had telephoned to Mrs. Marsh, her next-door neighbor, asking her to pop in from time to time during the day and see that Mr. Brodie was all right. She planned to slip over herself during the afternoon to see that the niece was safely installed, and call at the hospital for news of her sister. This obviously meant asking Mrs. Radcliffe's permission, as Mrs. Brodie's home was in Maidstone, twenty miles away by bus, and in order for her to get there and back dinner would have to be later than usual and a scratch meal at that. At Mrs. Radcliffe's first words her heart sank. "Good morning, Cook. I want a particularly nice dinner tonight. The Vicar and Mrs. Duke are coming, also Miss Layton and Mr. Baker. Have you any suggestions?" Mrs. Radcliffe spoke kindly, in the special smooth voice she reserved for the Lower Orders. The Lower Orders, she knew, appreciated differences in class as keenly as anybody, that was one of the fundamental virtues of the English social structure and the reason that no nonsensical experiments such as Bolshevism or Communism or anything like that could ever take root in the British Isles. Class was class and there was no getting away from it, you only had to look at the ineffectiveness of those little men who shouted from sugar boxes in Hyde Park to realize how secure England was from disintegration. Everybody knew that they were paid by the Russians anyhow.

Mrs. Brodie looked at her mistress's gentle, pale face and pleasant smile and, for one wild instant, contemplated telling her about her sister's gallstones and Mr. Brodie's imminent and probably final stroke and imploring her to cancel her dinner party for tonight. The impulse died as soon as it was born and she found herself trembling at her temerity in even having thought of such a thing.

"Very good, 'um," she said. "We might start with cream of tomato"—

Mrs. Radcliffe nodded—"then fillets of plaice?" Mrs. Radcliffe pursed her lips thoughtfully and then shook her head. "Lemon sole," she said. Mrs. Brodie wrote "lemon sole" down on a slate; the slate pencil squeaked causing Mrs. Radcliffe to draw in her breath sharply and close her eyes. Mrs. Brodie went on—

"Rack of lamb, mint jelly, new potatoes, beans or peas?"

"Peas," said Mrs. Radcliffe laconically.

Here Mrs. Brodie, having gallantly consigned her personal sorrows to the back of her mind and feeling oppressed by the uncompromising ordinariness of the menu, ventured a daring suggestion—

"I read a lovely new receipt for a sweet in *Woman and Home* the other day," she said eagerly, doubtless feeling subconsciously that the thrill of a new experiment might drug her mind into forgetfulness of her troubles—"it's called 'Mousse Napoleon' and—"

Mrs. Radcliffe cut her short. "I would rather we took no risks tonight, Cook," she said firmly. "We will have apple charlotte and a baked custard for Mrs. Duke who, as you know, has only recently recovered from influenza"; then, detecting in Mrs. Brodie's eye a fleeting but unmistakable expression of defiance, she thought it advisable to show the whip, not use it, just show it. She laughed indulgently and with the suspicion of an edge in her voice said, "We don't want any repetition of that unfortunate experience we had with the soufflé for Mr. and Mrs. Piggot, do we?"

Mrs. Brodie lowered her head. "No, 'um," she murmured.

"Then that will be all," said Mrs. Radcliffe lightly. "I shall be out to lunch."

Mrs. Brodie watched the door close behind her and sat down at the kitchen table. She felt low, dispirited, as though the hand of God were against her. It wasn't only Alice's gallstones and Mr. Brodie and the nuisance of Eileen having to be sent for and boarded and fed. Those were the sort of things in life that had to be faced. It was less than that and yet somehow more. Suddenly her whole being was shaken by a blind, vindictive hatred for Mrs. Piggot. "Silly old bitch!" she said out loud. "Wisdom tooth indeed! I'd like to yank the whole lot out with the pliers!" In a moment her rage subsided and she felt ashamed. She sat there idly for a moment wondering whether or not it would do her good to give way and have a nice cry. She was a great believer in a nice cry from time to time when things got on her nerves, it sort of loosened you up; however, the fact that Mildred had been crying steadily for two hours dissuaded her. "It would never do for all of us to be mooching about the house with red eyes," she reflected. "Whatever would happen if someone came to the front door! A nice thing that would be!" The clock on the dresser struck half-past ten, at the same moment Mildred came into the kitchen, pink and swollen, but calm.

"Cheer up, Mildred," said Mrs. Brodie comfortingly. "There's just as good fish in the sea as ever come out of it. Let's make ourselves a nice hot cup of tea."

5

After her successful interview with Mrs. Brodie, Mrs. Radcliffe went upstairs to put on her hat. She debated in her mind whether she should catch the eleven o'clock train to London which would get her to Charing Cross at twelve-five, thus giving her a whole hour to fill in before she was due to lunch with Marjorie and Cecil, or wait for the twelve o'clock which would get her to Victoria at twelve-fifty. She could certainly utilize that extra hour in town by doing Swan and Edgar's before lunch instead of afterward, but on the other hand as she had arranged to spend the entire afternoon shopping with Marion anyhow, perhaps an hour in the morning as well might be too much of a good thing. Also, if she took the twelve o'clock she would have time to call in at the Orphanage on the way to the station and have a little chat with Matron. She made one of her characteristically quick decisions. The twelve o'clock.

Mrs. Radcliffe's little chats with Matron took place on an average of about once a fortnight. They were unofficial and the other members of the executive committee, who met on the first Tuesday of every month, were unaware that they took place at all. If they had they might conceivably have been a trifle annoyed, people were like that, reluctant to take a practical personal interest themselves over and above their official capacities and yet oddly resentful of anyone who did. This regrettable human weakness was clearly recognized by both Matron and Mrs. Radcliffe, and, without saying so in so many words, they had tacitly agreed upon a policy of discreet silence. As Matron boldly remarked one day, "What the eye doesn't see the heart doesn't grieve over." These clandestine meetings were very useful to Mrs. Radcliffe. The various tidbits of information and gossip concerning members of the staff, the oddities of the children, etc.—some of them not always pleasant—all combined to give her a knowledge of the inner workings of the institution that came in handy at meetings. Had it not been for Matron she would never have been able to unmask that most distressing business last year of Hermione Blake and Mr. Forrage, a hirsute young man who tended the garden and did any other odd manual jobs that were required of him. She remembered how, fortified by her private information, she had swayed the whole committee. Mr. Forrage, due to her eloquence, had been summarily dismissed, while Hermione Blake, a sullen girl obviously devoid of moral principles, had, after a long cross-examination and ultimate confession, been justly robbed of her status as a prefect and forbidden, on the threat of being sent to a Reformatory, to speak to anybody whatsoever for three months. This punishment had not worked out quite as effectively as had been hoped, for apparently, according to Matron, the girl, after moping and crying for a week or so, had decided to treat it as a sort of game and invented a series of extravagant gestures and signs that caused so much laughter in the dormitory that Matron had been forced to send her to sleep in one of the attics by herself.

A plump, spotty girl, Ivy Frost by name, ushered Mrs. Radcliffe into Matron's private sanctum. It was a small room congested with personal effects. There were a great number of photographs of Matron's friends and relatives; a varied selection of ornaments, notably a small china mandarin whose head wobbled if you trod on the loose board by the table on which he sat, and a procession of seven ivory elephants on the mantelpiece, graded in size, and being led by the largest one toward a forbidding photograph of Matron's mother sitting under a lamp.

"Well, Ivy," said Mrs. Radcliffe benevolently as she ensconced herself in a creaking cane armchair by the fireplace and loosened her furs, "and how are you?"

"Very well, thank you, mum."

"That's right." Mrs. Radcliffe put her head a little to one side and scrutinized her through half-closed eyes as though measuring the perspective in a watercolor with which she was not completely satisfied.

"Your spots seem to be worse than ever," she said.

Ivy blushed and looked down. Her spots were the curse of her existence. Nothing she did for them seemed to do any good. A whole pot of Cuticura ointment in three weeks, to say nothing of hot compresses and boracic powder, had achieved no signs of improvement; on the contrary, two new ones had appeared within the last few days, one small, on her chin, and the other large, on the side of her nose. She had been teased about them a good deal by the other girls, Mabel Worsley in particular, who, on one occasion, had persuaded all her dormitory mates to shrink away from her shielding their faces with their hands for fear of contamination. This joke had lasted a long while and provided much merriment. Mrs. Radcliffe went on, kindly, but with a note of reproof: "You're at an age now when you should take an interest in your appearance. I expect you eat too many sweets and don't take enough exercise—isn't that so?"

"Yes, mum," muttered Ivy, her eyes still fixed on the carpet.

"Well there you are then," said Mrs. Radcliffe with finality.

Ivy shifted her feet unhappily. It was not true that she had been eating too many sweets. No sweet had crossed her lips for months. Nor was it true that she didn't take enough exercise. She took as much exercise as the other girls and, being a member of the hockey team, more than a great many of them. But she had learned from bitter experience that it was never any use denying anything to those in authority. Authority was always in the right and you were always in the wrong. Much better keep quiet and say as little as possible.

Mrs. Radcliffe, feeling that further discussion would be unproductive, spoke the longed-for words of dismissal:

"Run along now, child, and tell Matron I'm here."

Ivy darted to the door with alacrity and vanished through it, but not quickly enough to escape Mrs. Radcliffe's parting shot—"And the next time I come I expect to see a nice, clean, healthy skin!"

Ivy, safely in the passage with the door closed behind her, contorted her face into the most hideous grimace she could manage and then, with a deep sigh, went off in search of Matron.

The Matron was a small, faded woman of fifty. Her sight was poor, which necessitated her wearing glasses with very strong lenses. These gave her a sinister expression which sometimes had a scarifying effect on the smaller children. However, she was a kind enough creature on the whole, that is to say as kind as it is possible to be without imagination. This deficiency occasionally caused her to be crueler in the discharging of her duties than she really intended to be. A few of her charges liked her, the majority tolerated her, while only a very small number actually detested her.

She was in the middle of her weekly locker inspection when Ivy Frost burst in and told her that Mrs. Radcliffe had arrived, and notwithstanding the fact that she had just found a lipstick together with a packet of "papier poudré" in Beryl Carter's locker, cunningly concealed in the leg of a pair of combinations, and had already sent for Beryl in order to confront her with her guilt, she immediately decided that, shocking and urgent though the matter undoubtedly was, it would have to be dealt with later. Mrs. Radcliffe, not only in her capacity as vice-president, but by virtue of her social position in the town, was not the sort of person to be kept waiting for a moment. Also her visits were a great pleasure to Matron. It was, indeed, flattering to be on terms of almost conspiratorial intimacy with anyone so aristocratic and imposing. She hurried along the passages and down the stairs with the eagerness of a romantic girl on the way to meet her lover. By the time she arrived she was quite breathless. Mrs. Radcliffe shook hands cordially, but without rising, Matron pulled the chair away from her writing desk and sat down on it, quite close to her visitor as though to emphasize the confidential character of the interview.

"Well, well, well," she said, flushing with pleasure. "This *is* a nice surprise!"

"I am on my way up to town," said Mrs. Radcliffe, "to lunch with my daughter and her husband and do a little shopping, and I thought as I had a little time to spare, I would drop in and ask you if everything was running smoothly and satisfactorily."

Matron smiled deprecatingly and replied in a tone of bright resignation:

"As well as can be expected."

"You look a little tired, Matron. I hope you haven't been overdoing it?"

"Oh no, Mrs. Radcliffe." Matron shook her head. "Of course, there *is* a lot to be done and with such a small staff we all get a bit fagged sometimes, but still it's no use complaining, is it? After all, that's what we're here for."

Mrs. Radcliffe smiled understandingly and there was silence for a moment. These preliminaries had by now become almost a ritual, the actual phrasing might vary with different visits, but the essence remained the same. Mrs. Radcliffe was always on her way to somewhere else and just happened to drop in casually, and Matron was always overcome with flattered surprise. Mrs. Radcliffe unfailingly commented upon Matron's tiredness, and Matron invariably denied it with an air of gallant stoicism. This over, they wasted no time in getting down to brass tacks.

"How is Elsie Judd?" said Mrs. Radcliffe, lowering her voice and leaning forward in her chair, which gave an ominous crack as though anticipating the worst. The adolescent processes of Elsie Judd, an overdeveloped girl of fourteen, had been causing some anxiety.

"Better," replied Matron, also lowering her voice. "I thought it advisable to call in Doctor Willis. He examined her most thoroughly and told me afterward that if we kept her quiet and watched her carefully for a few months that it would all blow over."

Mrs. Radcliffe nodded approvingly. "Is the new gardener satisfactory?"

Matron gave a little shrug. "In a way he is," she said. "I mean, he keeps everything quite tidy, but he's very slow over odd jobs and, of course, he can't drive the Ford like Mr. Forrage could."

The truth of the matter was that Matron secretly regretted Mr. Forrage. She often reproached herself for having divulged the Hermione Blake business to Mrs. Radcliffe. There might not have been very much in it really, although everybody seemed to think there was, and if she had only kept her mouth shut, and perhaps spoken to Mr. Forrage privately, a great deal of fuss and trouble might have been avoided. The new man, viewed as a possible menace to the chastity of older girls, was, of course, as safe as houses! In addition to having a wall eye, he was seventy-three and suffered from rheumatism. This, together with his age, not unnaturally restricted the field of his activities somewhat. Running errands, chopping wood, and the various odd jobs of domestic plumbing and carpentry at which his predecessor had been so invaluable, were obviously out of the question. Apart from this, he was disagreeable, which Mr. Forrage had never been. Yes, Matron definitely regretted Mr. Forrage, and although nothing would have persuaded her to admit it to Mrs. Radcliffe, whose moral indignation had been the cause of his dismissal, she made an inward vow to be a little more wary of her disclosures in the future. However, no major upheaval could possibly result from her discussing with Mrs. Radcliffe the perfidy of Beryl Carter. On the contrary, Mrs. Radcliffe's advice, which was always sensible and the epitome of kindly justice, might prove very useful in helping her to deal with the situation.

"I am very worried," she said, lowering her voice still further, "about Beryl Carter!"

Mrs. Radcliffe rustled expectantly. "Beryl Carter? Isn't that the rather fast-looking girl we had trouble with at the theatricals?"

"It is," said Matron. "And she's been a nuisance ever since. I don't know what's to be done with her, really I don't. Only just now I found a lipstick and one of those 'papier poudré' things in her locker—wrapped up in her combinations," she added, as though that made the whole affair more shameful than ever. Mrs. Radcliffe assumed a judicial expression.

"How old is the girl?"

"Getting on for sixteen."

"Hum—" Mrs. Radcliffe thought for a moment. "What was her mother?"

Matron had her answer ready to this, clear and accurate. She had looked up Beryl's dossier in the files only the other day. "A prostitute," she said. "She died when Beryl was three. The child was looked after by a char-woman, some sort of relative I think until she was eight, then she was sent here."

"There's no doubt about it," said Mrs. Radcliffe sagely, "heredity accounts for a great deal. You'd better send for the girl and let me talk to her."

This was rather more than Matron had bargained for. A little wise advice was one thing, but cross-examination in her presence might conceivably undermine her own personal authority, and in defence of her personal authority Matron was prepared to fight like a tigress.

"I don't think that would be altogether advisable," she said, and observing Mrs. Radcliffe stiffen slightly, added hurriedly, "She's rather an unruly girl, I'm afraid, and she might be rude. I should hate there to be any unpleasantness."

"You needn't be afraid of that," said Mrs. Radcliffe in a voice that brooked no argument. "I flatter myself that I am capable of dealing with a child of fifteen, however unruly. Kindly send for her at once, Matron. We can decide what is to be done with her after I have talked to her."

It may have been the unexpected peremptoriness of Mrs. Radcliffe's tone, or it may have been that Matron, having passed a sleepless night owing to neuralgia, was inclined to be more irritable than usual that morning. It may have been the weather or it may even have been some obscure cosmic disturbance. Whatever it was; whatever the cause; what took place was shocking to a degree. Matron lost her temper. To do her justice, she felt it happening and made a tremendous effort to control it; but alas! to no purpose. She felt herself go scarlet and then white again. She was aware of a strange singing in her ears, of great forces at work, rumbling through the room, pushing her over the precipice. She looked Mrs. Radcliffe fair and square in the eye and said, "No!" Not even: "No, Mrs. Radcliffe." Not even: "I'm very sorry, Mrs. Radcliffe, but what you ask is quite impossible." Just a plain unequivocal: "No," spoken more loudly than she intended and without adornment. There ensued a silence so profound that even the infinitesimal creaking of Mrs. Radcliffe's stays as she breathed, could plainly be heard. So charged with tension was the atmosphere, that Matron felt numbed, robbed of all sensation, as though she had been electrocuted. She continued to stare at Mrs. Radcliffe's face, because there didn't seem to be anywhere else to look, also she couldn't have moved a muscle if you had paid her. She watched a small nerve in the region of Mrs. Radcliffe's right eyebrow twitch spasmodically and her expression of blank astonishment slowly give place to one of glacial anger. Still the silence persisted. From the world beyond those four walls, the ordinary, unheeding outside world, a few familiar sounds penetrated; the grinding gears of a car; a dog barking in the distance; a tram clanking around the corner of Cedar Avenue into the High Street; but Matron heard them vaguely, remotely, as though they belonged to another existence. She experienced the strange sensations of one who is coming to from an anesthetic. That unutterable fatigue. That reluctance to take up the threads of life again. That deadly, detached lassitude. At last Mrs. Radcliffe spoke. "I beg your pardon?" she said, with such terrifying emphasis on the "beg" that Matron jumped as though someone had fired off a revolver in her ear. Again, to her own amazement, anger seized her. How dare Mrs. Radcliffe speak to her in that tone as though she were a menial? What right had she to come here and demand to interview Beryl Carter, or anybody else for that matter? It was nothing more nor less than an unwarrantable liberty, that's what it was. "I'm very sorry, I'm sure," she said, "but I'm afraid I cannot allow you to interview any of the girls without the authority of the committee." This was shrewd of Matron, although not an entirely true statement of fact. Mrs. Radcliffe, as vice-president, was perfectly within her rights in asking to see any of the girls, and Matron knew it as well as she did, but Matron also knew, owing to Mrs. Radcliffe's expansiveness on one or two occasions, that the committee would be far from pleased if it discovered that she was in the habit of making surreptitious visits to the Orphanage behind its back. Mrs. Poindexter in particular who was also a vice-president and who, in addition, was well known to be on far from cordial terms with Mrs. Radcliffe, would undoubtedly take full advantage of such an excellent opportunity of attacking her in front of everyone. Mrs. Poindexter had a sharp tongue as Matron knew to her cost. If anyone could floor Mrs. Radcliffe she could. All this and more had already passed through Mrs. Radcliffe's mind and, angry as she was, she fully realized that an open quarrel with Matron would be impolitic to a degree. There were other ways, she reflected, of dealing with a woman of that type. Matron, after all, was not indispensable. She was efficient within her limits, but she was certainly getting on in years, the committee might well be persuaded in the course of the next few months to replace her with somebody younger and more in tune with modern ideas of hygiene. Obviously, poor thing, she had been denied the benefits of breeding and education over and above the regulation course of hospital training, but still an ignorant woman, in such a very responsible position, was perhaps just a trifle dangerous? She was convinced that the Hermione Blake affair could never have occurred had there been a younger, more authoritative Matron in charge. Observing the palpable vulnerability of her adversary as she sat there opposite her, strained and tense on the edge of her chair, her eyes staring through her spectacles immovably, as though they had been stuck into them from the back, she almost felt it in her heart to be sorry for her. In fact, she definitely was sorry for her; poor stupid woman, having the impertinence to say "No," to her in that shrill hysterical voice, the temerity of referring to the authority of the committee! Authority of the committee, indeed! Mrs. Radcliffe almost snorted, but restrained herself. She rose from her chair slowly and grandly, complete mistress of the situation, captain of her soul. "Matron," she said, and Matron, also rising, quivered at the sound of her voice as a small fish will quiver when transfixed by a spear. "I must admit I am very surprised, very surprised indeed." She spoke evenly and pleasantly without heat. "Not that you should consider it inadvisable to send for this girl when I asked you to, in that you are perfectly justified, after all, you are in charge here and I am sure we are all only too willing to accede you the fullest authority that your position entitles you to—but—" Here she paused for a moment and adjusted her silver fox— "that you should adopt an attitude that I'm afraid can only be described as downright rude is quite frankly beyond me—"

"Mrs. Radcliffe," began Matron cravenly. The grand manner had triumphed, all anger had evaporated, all passion spent, she felt abject and ashamed—Mrs. Radcliffe overruled her by holding up her hand and smiling, a smile in which there was worldly understanding with just a soupçon of grief—

"Please let me go on," she said gently. "The whole thing has been the most absurd misunderstanding. It was exceedingly tactless and foolish of me to suggest sending for Beryl Carter. I am sure you are perfectly capable of dealing with the matter as it should be dealt with. It was only that I allowed myself to be carried away by my very real interest in this Orphanage and all the young lives for which we are responsible. I only wish sometimes that some of my fellow members of the committee felt as personally about it as I do, but doubtless they are too occupied with their own worries. But one thing I must say, Matron, before I leave, and I must go in a moment, otherwise I shall miss my train, and you really won't take offense at this will you?—you are a little touchy you know, sometimes—" She laughed lightly—Matron quivered again and braced herself. Mrs. Radcliffe went on. "It's this—I really hardly know how to put it—but for some time, and this I assure you has nothing to do with this morning whatever, for some time I have been rather concerned about you, in fact only the other day I mentioned it to Mrs. Weecock and Doctor Price at the end of the meeting. You see," here Mrs. Radcliffe paused again as though really at a loss to know how to handle a situation of such appalling delicacy, "you see, you really are a little old to be doing work which demands such an immense amount of physical energy. I am often amazed that you mange as well as you do—and I have noticed, especially just lately, that you have been looking very, very seedy—"

"I assure you, Mrs. Radcliffe—" began Matron again, but once more Mrs. Radcliffe silenced her—"We were wondering whether it wouldn't be a good idea for you to have a little change," she said. "Of course, I haven't mentioned this in full committee yet, I felt that I should like to discuss it with you first—what do you think?"

Here it was, retribution, the axe! Matron saw it there above her head suspended by a hair. A series of sickening pictures flashed across her mind—a letter from the committee containing her dismissal with, at best, a minute pension. The dismantling of her room, the packing of her things. The confused squalor of her married sister's house at Whitby, she wouldn't be able to afford to live anywhere else. All very well for Mrs. Radcliffe to talk about "a little change," she knew what that meant all right; the thin end of the wedge. She made a gallant effort to speak calmly, to prove by perfect poise that she was in the best of health and fit to manage a dozen orphanages for at least another twenty years, but her nerves, which for considerable time had been stretched beyond endurance, betrayed her. Her humiliation was complete. She burst into floods of tears. Mrs. Radcliffe regarded her pityingly for a moment and then put her arm round her. Matron, her glasses misted with tears and knocked half off her nose by Mrs. Radcliffe's bosom, was unable to see and could only hear and smell. She could hear Mrs. Radcliffe's heart beating and her even, comfortable breathing, and smell a sharp tang of eau de cologne and the rather animal, fusty scent of her fur. Presently she withdrew herself and dabbed blindly at her eyes with her handkerchief. She heard, as though from a long way off, Mrs. Radcliffe's voice saying with a trace of impatience: "Come, come, Matron, there's nothing to cry about. The whole episode is forgiven and forgotten." Then she heard the shutting of the door and a brisk retreating step in the passage and realized that she was alone. Still sobbing, she sank down to her knees on the floor, groping for her glasses which had finally fallen off entirely. The small china mandarin nodded at her.

6

Mrs. Radcliffe walked to the station with a springy tread. It was a radiant morning. The air was balmy, the sun was shining and a procession of large white clouds was advancing across the sky. They looked beautiful, she thought, so majestic, so removed from the pettiness, the insignificant sorrows and joys of human existence. Mrs. Radcliffe often derived great pleasure from the changing sky. Times out of number she had sat at her window just gazing up into that vast infinity and allowing her thoughts to wander whither they would, occasionally chiding herself humorously for the extravagant fancies that took shape in her mind. How fortunate to be blessed with imagination, to possess that inestimable gift of being able to distinguish beauty in the ordinary. Many of her acquaintances, she knew for a fact, hardly glanced at the sky from one year's end to the other unless to see if it was going to rain. She remembered once saying to Cecil, Marjorie's husband, who after all was supposed to be a painter, when they were standing in the garden one summer evening before dinner, that sunset and sunrise were God's loveliest gifts to mortals if only they were not too blind to be able to appreciate them. Cecil had laughed, that irritating, cynical laugh of his, and replied that many thousands of people would appreciate them more if they were edible. She recalled how annoyed she had been, she could have bitten her tongue out for betraying a fragment of her own private self to someone who was obviously incapable of understanding it. On looking back, she realized that that was the first moment that she really knew that she disliked Cecil. Of course, she had never let Marjorie suspect it for an instant, and never would. What was done, was done, but still it was no use pretending. "Know thyself," was one of the cornerstones of her philosophy. Poor Marjorie. Poor willful, disillusioned Marjorie. That Marjorie was thoroughly disillusioned by now, Mrs. Radcliffe hadn't the faintest doubt. Nobody could be married for seven years to a man like Cecil with his so-called artistic temperament, his casualness about money, her money, and his complete inability to earn any for himself, without being disillusioned. Mrs. Radcliffe sighed as she turned into Station Road. What a tragedy!

Marjorie Radcliffe had met Cecil Garfield at a fancy-dress ball at the Albert Hall in 1930. She was up in town for a few days visiting a married school friend, Laura Courtney. There had been a buffet dinner before the ball, in Laura's house in St. John's Wood, and Marjorie, dressed as Cleopatra, a very effective costume that she had designed and made herself, was escorted to the Albert Hall by Roger Wood, a cousin of Laura's who was in the air force. Roger was not dressed as anything in particular. He was a hearty young man and balked at the idea of tidying himself up; the most he had conceded to the carnival spirit of the occasion was a false moustache and a dark blue cape lined with scarlet which he wore over his ordinary evening clothes. Marjorie had been rather bored with him and was much relieved when, upon arrival at the ball, they had been accosted in the foyer by a group of hilarious young people none of whom she knew, but all of whom seemed to know Roger. They were whirled off to the bar immediately to have a drink before even attempting to find Laura and the rest of their party. Among the group was Cecil Garfield, and Cecil was dressed as Mark Antony. This coincidence provided an excuse for a great deal of playful comment from everybody. It would be useless to deny that Cecil looked very attractive as Mark Antony. His physique, much of which was apparent, was magnificent. He had a quick wit and a charming smile and Marjorie danced several dances with him.

At about three in the morning everybody, Laura and her husband included, adjourned to Cecil's studio in Glebe Place to cook eggs and bacon. It was there that Marjorie first realized that he was an artist. Now the word "Artist," to Marjorie, held an imperishable glamour. She had long ago decided that a life such as her mother would have wished her to lead with a conventional husband, a cook and a baby, was out of the question. Marjorie wholeheartedly detested her suburban existence and, if the truth were known, was none too fond of her mother. Of this unnatural state of affairs, Mrs. Radcliffe was mercifully unaware, and if Mr. Radcliffe occasionally had an inkling of it, he was wise enough to keep his suspicions to himself. Marjorie's predilection for the artistic life had originally started when she was in her teens. Miss Lucas, her drawing mistress at school, had, perhaps unsuitably, lent her *The Life of Van Gogh*. Profoundly impressed by this, Marjorie had gone from bad to worse. *My Days with the French Romantics, The Beardsley Period, Isadora Duncan's Autobiography,* and *The Moon and Sixpence* had followed each other in quick succession. By the time she was twenty, she had assimilated a view of life so diametrically opposed to her mother's, that existence at home became almost insupportable. She was an intelligent girl, however, wise beyond her years and practiced in deceit. A certain proficiency in this direction being essential with a mother like Mrs. Radcliffe, and with a secretiveness that could only be described as downright sly, she kept her own counsel.

When Marjorie first met Cecil she had just turned twenty-one. She was a tall girl with a pale, almost sallow skin, dark hair, and keen, well-set blue eyes. Her figure was good although, as Mrs. Radcliffe frequently remarked, her movements were inclined to be a little coltish; however, she would doubtless soon grow out of that. With common sense unusual in one so young, she had faced the fact that, though she longed for it above all things, she had no creative ability whatsoever. This does not mean that she had not explored every possibility. She had written poems and begun novels—she had taken a course of line drawing at the Slade School, this only after a series of endless arguments with her mother, who had finally given way on condition that she traveled back and forth to London in company with Phyllis Weecock who was taking a stenography course at the Polytechnic. She had sat at the piano for hours trying to string chords together into a tune but alas, with no success, as she invariably forgot the ones she had started with and was incapable of remembering any of it at all the next day. She had, of course, made a bid for the stage, but on this Mrs. Radcliffe had put her foot down firmly. Poor Marjorie. None of it was any good. Her musical ear was nonexistent, her drawing commonplace, and her writing devoid of the faintest originality. However, undaunted by all this, she flatly refused two offers of marriage, one from Kenneth Eldridge, the son of one of the partners in her father's firm, and, worse still, Norman Freemantle, whose aunt, Lady Walrond, was not only the widow of a baronet, but owned an enormous mansion near Dorking and was as rich as Croesus.

Mrs. Radcliffe had risen above Kenneth Eldridge, but the rejection of Norman Freemantle went through her like a knife.

Cecil and Marjorie had sat in a corner together that night after the ball and talked. A few days later they met by the Peter Pan statue in Kensington Gardens and talked a lot more. They talked of literature, music, religion and morals and agreed on all points. Of painting they talked more than anything. Cecil's gods were Cézanne, Van Gogh, Matisse and Manet. He considered Picasso an intrinsically fine painter, but misguided. Cecil, when he talked of painting, betrayed his heart. Marjorie watched him fascinated. She noted the way his body became tense, the swift, expressive movements of his hands, how, when he was describing some picture that meant much to him, he would screw up his eyes and look through her, beyond her, beyond the trees of the park and the red buses trundling along on the other side of the railings, beyond the autumn sunshine and the people and the houses, beyond the present into the future. It was himself he was staring at through those half-closed eyes, himself having painted a successful picture, several successful pictures. Not successful from other people's points of view, perhaps, but from his own. It was when she first saw him like that, unself-conscious, almost arrogant, demanding so much of life and of himself and of anybody who had anything to do with him, that she knew she loved him. More than this, she knew that she could help him and comfort him and look after him. At last she had found someone in whom she could sublimate her passionate, unresolved yearning for creativeness. Five months later she had crept out of the house early on a bleak wet morning in February, traveled to London by the seven-forty-five train, met him under the clock at Victoria Station and married him at nine-thirty at a Registry Office in Fulham.

Needless to relate, this insane headstrong gesture left a wake of sorrow and suffering in the Radcliffe household only comparable to the darkest moments of Greek tragedy. However, after bitter letters had been exchanged and after over a year had passed, during which time Marjorie and Cecil had endured a penurious hand-to-mouth existence in a small flat in Yeoman's Row, a fortunate miscarriage of Marjorie's, if such an inefficient catastrophe could ever be called fortunate, and her subsequent illness, had at last effected a reunion. Mrs. Radcliffe had come to London. Still grieving, still shocked by filial ingratitude, still licking the wounds in her mother's heart, nevertheless she came. About a month later it was arranged that Mr. Radcliffe should resume the small allowance that he had given to his daughter before her disastrous marriage. This generosity undoubtedly owed something to a remark of Mrs. Poindexter's at a bridge party, when she was heard to say loudly to Mrs. Newcombe that the manners and cruelty of the Radcliffes in permitting their only child to live in abject poverty was nothing short of medieval.

All this had taken place six years ago. Since then the allowance had been raised, on the stubborn insistence of Mr. Radcliffe, to almost double. Consequently, the Garfields were enabled to live in comparative comfort in a small house behind Sloane Square with a studio at the back converted, at certain expense, from a conservatory.

The fact that Cecil only very rarely managed to sell a picture was a source of great irritation to Mrs. Radcliffe. Having at last, soothed by the passage of time, consented to bury the hatchet and accept her artistic son-in-law, it was extremely frustrating not to be able to refer to his work with any conviction. To say "My son-in-law is quite a well-known painter, you know," was one thing, but it was quite another to say, "My son-in-law is a painter," and upon being asked what kind of a painter, to be unable to explain. If only he would do portraits that had some resemblance to the sitter, or landscapes which gave some indication, however faint, of what they were supposed to be. It was all very fine to argue that a painter painted through his own eyes and nobody else's, and that what was green to one person might very possibly be bright pink to another. All that sort of talk smacked of affectation and highbrowism. What was good enough for Landseer and Alma Tadema was good enough for Mrs. Radcliffe, and, she would have thought, good enough for anybody who had their heads screwed on the right way.

With these reflections she settled herself into the corner seat of a first-class compartment and opened a copy of *Vogue* that she had bought at the bookstall. Just at the instant of the train's starting three people clambered into the carriage. Now it is an odd frailty in the human character that however benevolent and kindly you may be by nature, the influx of strangers into an empty compartment that you have already made your own by getting there first, is very annoying. Mrs. Radcliffe was no exception to this rule. She looked up testily and was shocked to observe that the interlopers, apart from the initial tiresomeness of their interloping, were quite obviously of the lower classes. Now one of the reasons that Mrs. Radcliffe, who was naturally thrifty, always paid without regret the extra money for a first-class ticket instead of a third, was in order to avoid contact with the lower classes. Not that she had anything against the lower classes, she hadn't. She defied anyone to be more democratic spirited, to have a warmer, more genuine sympathy and understanding for those who happened to be in less fortunate circumstances than herself. But when she bought a first-class ticket she demanded the first-class privileges that the ticket entitled her to. Therefore she was perfectly justified in regarding these three most unprepossessing-looking people, with marked disapproval. The man, who wore a cloth cap and a dirty handkerchief round his neck, was smoking a cigarette. The woman, probably his wife, was pasty and dressed in a shabby gray coat and skirt, a pink blouse, a mustard-colored beret and black button boots. The third interloper was a boy of about eleven. He had no hat, unbrushed hair, a sore on his lip and a long mackintosh with one of the pockets hanging out.

Mrs. Radcliffe gathered herself together. "I think you have made a mistake," she said. "This is a first-class carriage."

The man and woman looked guilty. The little boy didn't look anything at all, he just stared at her. The woman spoke in a husky, whining voice.

"The third class is full," she said. "If we 'adn't of 'opped in 'ere double-quick we'd 'ave missed the train."

"In that case," said Mrs. Radcliffe, "you will be able to get out at the next station and change."

"I don't see 'ow it's any of your business any'ow," muttered the man sullenly.

Mrs. Radcliffe ignored him and looked out of the window. There was silence for a moment which was broken by the little boy saying loudly, "'Oo does she think she is?"

The woman giggled.

"Never you mind," she said. "The Queen of Roumania as like as not!"

"Shut up!" said the man. There was another pause and then the woman spoke again. "I will say it's a treat to be able to take yer weight off yer feet for a minute," she murmured. "I'm worn out and that's a fact."

"Shut up grumbling," said the man.

"I wasn't grumbling," she replied with spirit. "Just talking to pass the time." The man shot a baleful glance at Mrs. Radcliffe. "Well, pass the time some other way," he said, "you might upset 'er ladyship."

Mrs. Radcliffe peered out of the window as though she had suddenly recognized a horse that was grazing in a field.

"That would never do," said the woman with another giggle. "She might 'ave us sent to jail, I shouldn't wonder. Be quiet, Ernie, and stop fiddling with that mac, you'll 'ave the button off in a minute."

Presently the train drew into a station. Mrs. Radcliffe withdrew her gaze from the window and looked the man straight in the eye. He held his ground for a moment and then quailed. Nobody moved. The train stopped.

"I don't wish to have to complain to the guard," said Mrs. Radcliffe.

A thunderous look passed over the man's face, he spat out his cigarette violently so that it fell at Mrs. Radcliffe's feet, then he jumped up.

"Come on, Lil," he said. "Look lively." He opened the door and they all three clattered out onto the platform. He slammed the door and then pushed his face in at the window causing Mrs. Radcliffe to shrink back.

"I'll tell you what your sort need," he snarled. "And that's a nice swift kick up the whatsit!"

The woman giggled shrilly again and they were gone. Mrs. Radcliffe fanned herself with *Vogue*. What a very unpleasant experience.

7

When Mrs. Radcliffe arrived, Marjorie opened the door to her herself. They had a maid but she was in the kitchen preparing the lunch. Cecil was still working in the studio and so Marjorie and her mother sat in the drawing room to wait for him. The drawing room was on the ground floor and the dining room opened out of it. The house was small and rather dark and smelt of cooking. Marjorie had tried to mitigate it by burning some scent in a heated iron spoon, but she had done this a little too early, and by now the scent had mostly evaporated whereas the cooking had not. Mrs. Radcliffe glanced around the room with a scarcely perceptible sigh of regret. It was simply furnished and neat enough, and there was a profusion of flowers, but it was far far removed from the setting her maternal imagination had originally painted for her only daughter. Mrs. Radcliffe looked at her only daughter curled up in the corner of the sofa, so unlike her in every respect, with her dark cropped hair, her large horn-rimmed glasses and her serviceable oatmeal-colored frock over which she wore a flamboyant bolero jacket of bright scarlet, and marveled that from her loins should ever have sprung such a baffling disappointment. Marjorie at the same time was observing her mother with equal wonderment. It was always like this.

They always met as strangers, and it usually took quite a while to establish a point of contact. Mrs. Radcliffe's visits were fortunately rare. Marjorie wholeheartedly dreaded them, and it is possible that her mother did too, but immutable forces insisted on them taking place. It is doubtful whether Marjorie would have shed a tear had she been told that she was never going to set eyes on her mother again. It is also doubtful whether Mrs. Radcliffe would have minded either. She would shed a tear certainly, many tears. She would be, for a time, inconsolable, but genuine grief, the desolate heart, would be lacking.

"How's Father?" asked Marjorie.

"Very well indeed. He had one of his liver attacks last week but it didn't last too long. He made a great fuss about it, you know what Father is."

Marjorie nodded understandingly, the ice thawed slightly in the warmth of their both knowing what Father was. Marjorie jumped up from the sofa and went over to a table by the window.

"Let's have some sherry," she said. "Cecil will be here in a minute." She poured out two glasses and brought them over carefully. "I'm afraid I've filled them rather too full."

Mrs. Radcliffe took hers and held it away from her for the first sip in case a drop should fall on her knees.

"How is Cecil?"

"Bright as a button. He's been working like a dog for the last two weeks."

"Really?" The vision of Cecil working like a dog did not impress Mrs. Radcliffe. In the first place she didn't believe it. She didn't consider that painting away in that studio constituted work at all. It was just dabbing about. Cecil, as far as she could see, spent his whole life dabbing about. She naturally didn't say this to Marjorie. Marjorie was inclined to be overvehement in defense of her husband's activities.

"Has he managed to sell any more pictures lately?" she inquired. The "any more" was purely courtesy. As far as she could remember Cecil had only sold one picture in the last eighteen months and for that he had received only twenty pounds.

An expression of irritation passed over Marjorie's face, but she answered amiably enough. "He's planning to have an exhibition in June. Lady Bethel is lending him her house for it."

This caused Mrs. Radcliffe to sit up as Marjorie had intended that it should.

"Is that the Lady Bethel who organized that charity pageant just before Christmas?"

"Yes," said Marjorie. "She's a darling, there was a lovely picture of her in the *Tatler* last week: going to a Court ball," she added wickedly.

Mrs. Radcliffe was clearly puzzled. Lady Bethel was certainly an important figure. If she was willing to lend her house for an exhibition of Cecil's paintings it might mean—here her reflections were disturbed by Cecil himself coming into the room. He had washed and tidied himself for lunch, but for all that he looked ill-groomed. His hair was too long, he wore no tie and there were paint stains on his very old gray flannel trousers. He bent down and kissed Mrs. Radcliffe on the cheek and then poured himself out some sherry.

"How are you, Marm?" he said breezily. He always addressed her as "Marm" and there was a suggestion in his tone of mock reverence which never failed to annoy her. "You look shining and beautiful."

Mrs. Radcliffe deplored extravagance of phrase. She answered rather tartly, "Very well indeed, thank you, Cecil."

Cecil came over and leant against the mantelpiece, looking down at her. She was forced to admit to herself that he was handsome in a loose, slovenly sort of way, but she could never be reconciled to that hair, never, if she lived to be a thousand.

"I've been telling Mother about Lady Bethel promising to lend her house for your exhibition," said Marjorie a trifle loudly.

Was it Mrs. Radcliffe's fancy or did Cecil give a slight start of surprise?

"Yes," he said with marked nonchalance. "It's sweet of the old girl, isn't it?"

Something in Mrs. Radcliffe revolted at Lady Bethel, *The* Lady Bethel, being referred to as an old girl, but she didn't betray it.

"It certainly is very nice of her," she said. "But she has a great reputation, hasn't she for giving a helping hand to struggling artists?"

Cecil, disconcertingly, burst out laughing. "Touché, Marm," he said. "Come along and let's have some lunch." He helped her out of her chair with elaborate solicitude and led the way into the dining room.

Lunch passed off without incident. The conversation, although it could not be said to sparkle, was at least more or less continuous. Cecil was in the best of spirits. He was extremely attentive to Mrs. Radcliffe, always it is true with that slight overture of mockery, that subtle implication in his voice and his gestures that she was a great deal older than she was, and had to be humored at all costs. He insisted, with playful firmness, that she drink some Chianti which she didn't really want, as wine in the middle of the day was apt to make her headachy in the afternoon. He displayed the most flattering interest when she described her visit to the Orphanage and the tact and kindliness she had had to exert in dealing with Matron, and when she told of her unpleasant adventure in the train, he was shocked beyond measure and said that that sort of thing was outrageous and that something ought to be done about it. During this recital Mrs. Radcliffe observed that Marjorie was bending very low over her plate, and wondered whether her nearsightedness was getting worse. Although fully aware that her long experience and inherent social sense were responsible for the success of the lunch party, Mrs. Radcliffe was not too occupied to notice that the soup was tepid, the fillet of steak much too underdone and that there was garlic in the salad. All of this saddened her. It was indeed depressing to reflect that Marjorie, with the lifelong example of her mother's efficiency before her, was still unable to turn out a simple, well-cooked meal. However, with her usual good-humored philosophy she rose above it. It took all sorts to make a world and if, by some caprice of Fate, her own daughter had turned out to be one of the less competent sorts, so much the worse.

After lunch was over and they had had their coffee (lukewarm), in the drawing room, Mrs. Radcliffe expressed a desire to see Cecil's pictures. This request was made merely in the spirit of conventional politeness. She had no real wish to see his pictures, as she knew from experience that there was little or no chance of her admiring them. Cecil and Marjorie were also perfectly aware of this, but nevertheless, after a little hemming and hawing Cecil led the way into the studio. Marjorie walked behind with a rather lagging tread. The untidiness of Cecil's studio always struck Mrs. Radcliffe with a fresh shock of distaste. It was inconceivable that anyone, however artistic, could live and breathe amid so much dirt and squalor. The table alone, which stood under the high window, was a sight to make the gorge rise. On it were ashtrays overflowing with days-old cigarette ends, two or three used and unwashed teacups, a bottle of gin, a noisome conglomeration of paint tubes of all shapes and sizes, many of them cracked and broken so that their contents was oozing out and all of them smeared with a brownish substance that looked like glue, a pile of books and magazines, countless pencils and crayons and pieces of charcoal and, most disgusting of all, a half-full glass of milk, around the rim of which a fly was walking delicately. The rest of the room was equally repulsive. There was a model throne draped with some dusty material, a gas fire with a bowl of water in front of it, in which floated several more cigarette ends, two easels, several canvases stacked against the wall, a large divan covered in red casement cloth and banked with paint-stained cushions and a pedestal supporting a sculpture in bronze of a woman's breast. It was only by the greatest effort of self-control that Mrs. Radcliffe repressed a cry of horror.

The picture on which Cecil was working stood on the bigger of the two easels in the middle of the room. It represented a man, or what passed for a man, sitting in a crooked rocking chair without any clothes on. His legs, which were fortunately crossed, were enormously thick. Upon a slanting table at the right-hand side of the picture was what appeared to be a guitar together with a vase of flowers, a bottle and a fish. The paint on the canvas looked as though it had been flung at it from the other side of the room. There was not a trace of what Mrs. Radcliffe had been brought up to recognize as "fine brushwork." In fact there didn't appear to be any brushwork at all. She regarded in silence for a moment and then shook her head. "It's no use," she said, trying to keep the irritation out of her voice. "I don't understand it."

"Never mind, Marm," said Cecil cheerfully. "It's not really finished yet, anyhow."

"But what does it mean?"

"It's called *Music,*" said Marjorie as though that explained everything.

"I still don't understand what it *means,*" said Mrs. Radcliffe.

Cecil exchanged a quick look with Marjorie, who shrugged her shoulders. This annoyed Mrs. Radcliffe. "I'm sure you think I'm very ignorant and old-fashioned," this time making no attempt to control her irritation, "but I don't approve of this modern futuristic art and I never shall. To my mind a picture should express beauty of some sort. Heaven knows, there is enough ugliness in the world without having to paint it—"

"But we don't think that picture is ugly, Mother," said Marjorie with an edge on her voice. Cecil looked at her warningly. Mrs. Radcliffe sniffed.

"You may not think it's ugly and your highbrow friends may not think so either, but I do," she said.

"Our friends are not particularly highbrow, Marm," he said gently. "And as a matter of fact, nobody has seen this picture yet at all. You're the first, you should feel very honored," he added with a disarming smile. Unfortunately, however, the smile was not quite quick enough and failed to disarm. Mrs. Radcliffe was by now thoroughly angry. The Chianti at lunch had upset her digestion as she had known it would and, having endured that inferior, badly cooked food and done her level best to be pleasant and entertaining into the bargain, to be stood in front of a daub like this and expected to admire it was really too much. In addition to this, both Cecil and Marjorie had a note of patronage in their voices which she found insufferable. All very fine for them to be patronizing when they were living entirely on her money, or rather Mr. Radcliffe's which was the same thing. All very fine for a strong, healthy young man of Cecil's age to fritter his time away painting these nonsensical pictures when he ought to be in some steady job shouldering his responsibilities and supporting his wife in the luxury to which she had been accustomed. All very fine to allude to Lady Bethel as an "old girl" and a "darling" in that casual intimate manner and boast that she was going to lend her house for an exhibition of Cecil's paintings. If Lady Bethel considered that that sort of nonsense was worthy of being exhibited she must be nothing short of an imbecile. In any case, she strongly doubted that Lady Bethel had promised any such thing. She recalled the swift look that had passed between Cecil and Marjorie before lunch, and the rather overdone nonchalance of Cecil's tone. The whole thing was nothing but a lie in order to impress her. The suspicion of this, which had lain dormant at the back of her mind throughout the whole of lunch, suddenly became a conviction. Of course that was what it was. A deliberate lie calculated to put her in the wrong, to make her feel that her criticisms of Cecil's painting in the past had been unjust, and to try to deceive her into the belief that he was appreciated and understood by people who really knew, whereas all the time he was nothing more nor less than the complete and utter failure he always had been and always would be. Mrs. Radcliffe decided to speak her mind.

"Cecil," she said in an ominous voice, "I have something to say to you that I have been wishing to say for some time past."

The smile faded from Cecil's face, and Marjorie walked across purposefully and slipped her arm through his.

"Fire away, Marm," he said with a certain bravado, but she saw him stiffen slightly.

"I want to suggest," went on Mrs. Radcliffe, "that you give up this absurd painting business once and for all and find some sort of job that will bring you in a steady income—"

"Give up his painting, Mother, you must be mad!" said Marjorie angrily.

Cecil patted her arm. "Shut up, darling," he said.

Mrs. Radcliffe ignored the interruption and continued: "I have talked the matter over with my husband." This was untrue, but she felt that it solidified her position. "And we are both in complete agreement that it is nothing short of degrading that a young man of your age should be content to live indefinitely on his wife's money."

There was dead silence for a moment. Mrs. Radcliffe's face was flushed and the corners of Cecil's mouth twitched.

"I'm sure Father said no such thing," said Marjorie.

"Kindly let me speak, Marjorie." Mrs. Radcliffe looked at her daughter coldly.

"I think, Marm," interposed Cecil, "that anything more you said might be redundant."

"Nevertheless," went on Mrs. Radcliffe, "I would like to say this—"

Marjorie broke away from Cecil and came close to her mother. Her face was white with anger. "You will not say another word," she said. "You will go away now out of this house and you will never set foot in it again!"

Mrs. Radcliffe fell back a step, genuinely horrified at the passionate fury in her daughter's face. "Marjorie!"

"I mean it," Marjorie was clenching and unclenching her hands. Cecil stepped forward and put his arm around her, but she shook him off.

"No, Cecil, this is between Mother and me. She says that for a long time she's been wishing to say those cruel, insulting things to you. Well, I've been waiting a longer time to say a few things to her. I've been waiting all my life and now I'm going to—"

"Darling!" Cecil put his arm round her again and this time held her. He spoke gently, but with an unaccustomed note of sternness. "For God's sake don't. It won't do any good, really it won't, and you'll only regret it afterward. Whatever you said she'd never understand, never in a thousand years."

Marjorie looked up at his face and he gave a little smile, her lip trembled. "All right," she said in a low voice. "You needn't hang on to me, I won't do anything awful—"

He let her go and she went quickly over to the window and stood with her back turned looking out on to the narrow stretch of garden that separated their house from the house next door. For a moment, while he had been talking, something had pierced Mrs. Radcliffe. She was shocked, outraged, angry; all that her affronted pride demanded her to be, but in addition to this, for a brief instant, the flash of a second, she had been aware of a sharp, overwhelming sense of loneliness. It passed as swiftly as it had come and she was secure again, secure in righteous indignation, wounded as only a mother can be wounded by her daughter's base ingratitude. She closed her lips in a tight line and surveyed Cecil and Marjorie and the studio and everything in it with an expression of withering contempt. Cecil put his hand under her elbow and piloted her to the door. "I think it's time we put an end to this distressing scene," he said. "Come along, Marm, I'll see you to the front door."

They walked through the yard and in through the French windows of the dining room without a word. She collected her bag and fur from the sofa in the drawing room.

"Shall I telephone for a taxi?" he asked.

"Thank you no," she replied with frigid politeness. "I prefer to walk."

He held the front door open for her and she descended into the street. A child bowling an iron hoop nearly cannoned into her. She drew aside as an empress might draw aside from some unmentionable offal in her path and, with a barely perceptible nod to Cecil, walked away.

When Cecil got back into the studio Marjorie was smoking a cigarette. She looked swiftly at him as he came in the door and noted, with a little tug at her heartstrings, that his face was white and drawn.

"Sorry, darling," she said as lightly as she could.

He looked at his unfinished picture for a moment and then flung himself on to the divan. "Well!" He spoke in a taut, strained voice. "That was highly instructive, I must say."

"Mother's a very stupid woman," Marjorie said perfectly evenly, there was no anger in her anymore. "She doesn't know anything about anything. The fact that we're happy together infuriates her."

"Are we!" said Cecil.

"Oh, Cecil!" Marjorie's eyes filled with tears and she turned away. "How can you be such a bloody fool!"

"There's a certain element of truth in what she says," went on Cecil, intent on masochism. "After all, I do live on your money, don't I?"

"And why in the name of God shouldn't you?" Marjorie flared. "What's money got to do with it? We love each other and trust each other, isn't that enough?"

"It would be nicer though," he said with fine sarcasm, "if *somebody* apart from you and Bobbie Schulter thought I was a good painter! It would be nicer, really a great deal nicer, if I could sell just one Goddamned picture occasionally."

"Oh, darling!" Marjorie came over and sat by him on the divan. "Please, please don't go on like that. It's absolutely idiotic and you know it as well as I do. It hurts me terribly when you lash out and say bitter, foolish things that I know in my heart that you don't really mean. Look at me—please look at me and snap out of it."

Cecil looked at her and made a gallant effort to smile. It wasn't entirely successful, but it was the best he could do. Marjorie flung both her arms round him and drew his head down onto her shoulder. She stroked his hair gently and he wouldn't have known she was crying if a tear hadn't happened to drop on to his neck.

8

Mrs. Radcliffe's blood was boiling and continued to boil through several quiet squares and streets until she turned into Brompton Road. Here she stopped for a moment and consulted her watch which hung from a little gold chain on her bosom. The watch said twenty minutes past two. Marion was meeting her in the piano department at Harrods at half-past, not that either she or Marion intended to buy a piano, but it was as good a place to meet as anywhere else and less crowded. It would never do for Marion to suspect that her blood was boiling, because she would inevitably ask why, and Mrs. Radcliffe would have either to tell her or invent a convincing lie, neither of which she felt inclined to do. She sauntered very slowly toward Harrods in order to give herself time to deal efficiently with her unruly emotions. It was no use pretending one way or the other, she reflected. Marjorie was no daughter of hers. This, of course, was rhetorical rather than accurate, her memories of the pain and indignity of Marjorie's arrival, even after thirty years, were still clear, but still the fact of disowning Marjorie in her mind, of denying her very existence in relation to herself, somehow reassured her. Mrs. Radcliffe searched in vain through the past to find one occasion on which Marjorie had proved to be anything but a disappointment. Even as a child she had been unresponsive and sometimes actually belligerent. She recalled still with a blush of shame, the dreadful tea party when Marjorie, age four, had spat a whole mouthful of Madeira cake at poor kind old Mrs. Woodwell, who had bent down to kiss her. She recalled how a few years later she had, quite unnecessarily, been sick over the edge of the dress circle during a matinee of *Peter Pan*. She remembered the countless times during adolescence that she had been rebellious, sly, untruthful and sulky. Heaven knew it had been explained to her often enough and with the utmost patience and kindness that an only daughter's primary duty was to be a comfort and support to her mother, and a fat lot of good it had done. Marjorie had never been even remotely a comfort to her mother. On the contrary she had been a constant source of grief and pain to her ever since she was born. Then, of course, the secretiveness and cruelty of running off and marrying Cecil without a word of warning, turning her back on her parents and her home and all the love and affection of years without a regret, without a shred of gratitude. No, Marjorie was certainly no daughter of hers. Much better to face the truth fair and square. The reconciliation a year after the marriage had been a great mistake, she realized that now; in any case, the miscarriage and illness and everything had probably been greatly exaggerated in order to play upon her sympathy and get the allowance renewed. There was no love in Marjorie, no gentleness, no affection. That was what was so heartbreaking. If she had been merely self-willed and obstinate. If she had done all she had done and yet betrayed at moments just a scrap of sweetness and understanding, an indication that there was just a little soft womanliness in her character somewhere, then Mrs. Radcliffe would have forgiven her and stood by her and done everything she could to mitigate the disastrous mess she had made of her life, but no, there was no love in Marjorie, not a speck of softness, she was as hard as nails. Better to cut the knot once and for all rather than compromise, rather than humiliate her spirit by making any further bids for a love and affection that, she knew now, had never existed and never could exist, and proceed in pride and loneliness to the grave. Mrs. Radcliffe stopped by a confectioner's at the corner of Ovington Street and wiped away a tear, then she blew her nose and proceeded in pride and loneliness to Harrods.

Marion was dutifully waiting in the cathedral quiet of the piano department. She was the type of woman who is always a little too early for everything, not from any pronounced sense of punctuality so much as an innate determination not to miss a moment. Life to Marion was a glorious adventure. Her zest for enjoyment even after fifty-seven years of strict virginity was unimpaired. She had a small income bequeathed by her father, who had been a colonel in the Indian Army, the top part of a house in Onslow Gardens, a collection of theatre programs dating back to 1898, and a parrot called Rajah, upon which she lavished a great deal of brusque affection. She smoked incessantly and belonged to a small ladies' club in Dover Street which was rather dull, but useful to pop into from time to time and write letters. Her friendship with Mrs. Radcliffe went back to their schooldays and was based on romance. Adela Radcliffe, Adela Wyecroft as she had been then, had captained the lacrosse team and had been revered and adored by most of the school and by Marion Kershaw most of all. She still possessed a snapshot of Adela taken when she was sixteen, standing against a background of fierce waves, wearing a small boater, a white dress with high, puffed sleeves and holding an anchor. It was a striking photograph and although the dust of ages lay over the tears that Marion had once shed over it, she cherished it with a certain merry nostalgia.

Adela's attitude to Marion had been then, and was still, one of affectionate tolerance, not entirely free from patronage. In her opinion, Marion was a good sort, but rather a fool and definitely unstable emotionally. She could have married quite well if she had only concentrated a little more. Mrs. Radcliffe could remember several occasions when a little common sense and proper management could have achieved the altar; that young Critchley boy for instance, he had been quite keen on her, and even Admiral Mortimer's son, although on the whole it was just as well she hadn't married him as he had had to be sent out of the Navy for something or other when he was twenty-four. But Marion was hopeless. She was always getting these wild enthusiasms for people and then dropping them like hot cakes. Look at that Sylvia Bale! A tiresome whining creature if ever there was one. Marion had gone on about how wonderful she was in the most ridiculous way and even went so far as to share a flat with her but not for long. Mrs. Radcliffe remembered how she had chuckled inwardly when Marion, trembling with rage, had recounted to her the beastly behavior of Sylvia Bale. Mrs. Radcliffe had refrained from saying "I told you so," she was not one to rub it in, but she certainly had known all along and warned her into the bargain.

Today, Marion was at her most exuberant. She was wearing a tailor-made, none too well cut, a white blouse with rather an arty-looking colored scarf tied in a knot in front and one of those newfangled hats perched much too far forward. She was smoking, needless to say. Mrs. Radcliffe was aware of the strong smell of tobacco as she kissed her. Marion, who had nearly finished her cigarette, couldn't find anywhere to crush it out and so before anything could be discussed at all they had to wander about among the Steinways in search of an ashtray. This was typical of Marion. Finally, of course, she had to stamp it out on the carpet and one of the assistants gave her a most disagreeable look.

Marion was full of conversation. She hadn't seen Adela for ages, but not for *ages!* and there was really so much to tell her that she couldn't think where to begin. Mrs. Radcliffe was really rather grateful for this volubility, for although by now she had regained complete command of herself and had contrived, at God alone knew what cost to her nerves, to present an outward mien as unruffled and tranquil as usual, the fact remained, she was still upset. However strong in character you may be, however bitterly you may have learned through sad experience to discipline yourself to withstand the cruel bludgeonings of Chance, you are after all but human. And Mrs. Radcliffe felt, in justice to herself, that in view of all she had recently gone through, to say nothing of the courage with which she had faced to the full the whole agonizing tragedy of the situation, she might be forgiven a little inward weakness, a little drooping of the spirit. There were not many others, she reflected, who were capable of cutting their only child out of their hearts at one blow and go out shopping with Marion as though nothing had happened.

Marion, unaware of the abyss of suffering so close to her, continued to chatter like a magpie. "You'd never believe it," she said. "But I did the most idiotic thing the other night. I'd been to the Old Vic with Deidre Waters, you remember Deidre Waters, she married Harry Waters and then he left her and now they're divorced and she's living with Nora Vines and they're doing those designs for textiles, some of them are damned good too, I can tell you. Well, Deidre arrived to call for me and kept the taxi waiting, fortunately, I was ready, but she rushed me out of the house so quickly that I forgot to take my latchkey out of my other bag. Well, my dear, of course I didn't think a thing about it, it never even crossed my mind, how I could have been such a fool I can't think and, of course, when I got home there I was! Can you imagine? Thank Heaven it wasn't raining but it was bitterly cold and I was in evening dress with only that Chinese coat between me and the elements." She laughed hilariously and went on. "Well, I really was in the most awful state, I couldn't think *what* to do. I knew it wouldn't be any use banging on Mrs. Bainbridge's window, she has the downstairs part you know, for even if I could have climbed across the area railings and reached it she'd never have heard, she's deaf as a post and sleeps at the back anyway. I was absolutely flummoxed. I looked up and down the street and there wasn't a soul in sight and then I walked to the corner to see if I could see a policeman. Of course I couldn't, you can never find one when you want one. I was in despair. I could have gone to the Club of course, but it would have meant waking up the night porter and I hadn't any night things or anything and anyhow there probably wouldn't have been a room, it's awfully small you know. Then I thought of Deidre and Nora, but you can't swing a cat in their flat and the vision of spending the night on their sofa didn't appeal to me very much I can tell you."

She paused for breath as they turned into the scent department. "Well—just as I was about to just sit down on the pavement and cry I saw a man, quite a youngish-looking man in a silk hat! I rushed up to him and I must say he looked horrified, but *horrified;* I daren't imagine what he must have thought but I explained and he was absolutely charming. He walked back with me to the house and my dear, would you believe it? He noticed something that I hadn't noticed at all. Mrs. Bainbridge's window was open a little bit at the top! Well, what did he do but take off his coat and hat and put them on the top step and then climb over the railings and break into the house. I was terrified of course that old Mother Bainbridge would think it was a burglar and have a stroke or something but I couldn't help laughing. In a minute or two—I was shivering by this time as you can imagine—I saw the light go up in the hall and he opened the front door and let me in. Of course I asked him to come up and have a whiskey and soda but he refused; then I helped him on with his coat and hat and off he went! There now. Wasn't that fantastic? I mean the luck of him just coming along at that moment. I couldn't get over it honestly I couldn't. All the time I was undressing and going to bed I kept on saying to myself: 'Well, really!' " The recital might have continued even longer if Mrs. Radcliffe had not interrupted it by demanding of an assistant the price of a bottle of Elizabeth Arden vanishing cream. She had paid scant attention to what Marion had been saying, her thoughts being elsewhere. Even if Marion had known this it is doubtful whether she would have minded much. Talking, with Marion, was an automatic process like breathing. She didn't talk to inform, or to entertain, or to be answered. She just talked.

They visited several departments and made several minor purchases, Mrs. Radcliffe leading the way, dignified and decisive, with Marion in full spate, yapping at her heels. When finally they emerged into the warm spring sunshine Mrs. Radcliffe was feeling distinctly better. The business of pricing things and buying things had occupied her mind and soothed her. Marion of course was still talking—"And when he walked up to the cage," she was saying, "Rajah put his head on one side and gave him a look and, my dear, if looks could kill that one would have! Needless to say I was *terrified!* You see he's always perfectly all right with women and of course he adores me but he hates *men.* Parrots are like that, you know, always much more affectionate with the opposite sex to what they are themselves; it is extraordinary, isn't it? I mean how sex instincts come out even in birds. Not of course that I ever look on Rajah as a bird, he's a person and a very definite person at that I can tell you. Well, my dear, poor Mr. Townsend said 'Poll, Pretty Poll,' or something and put his finger between the bars of the cage if you please. I gave a little scream. 'Oh, do be careful, Mr. Townsend,' I said. 'He takes a lot of knowing, he does really.' 'I'm used to parrots,' said Mr. Townsend, 'we had one at Epsom for years.' The Townsends live at Epsom you know, and my dear as he said it, before the words were out of his mouth Rajah bit his finger through to the bone! Now can you imagine?" Marion paused dramatically, this time evidently demanding some sort of response. Mrs. Radcliffe looked at her absently and with an effort wrenched her mind from wondering whether it would be better to do Swan and Edgar's now or leave it until another day.

"How dreadful," she said.

"I didn't know what to do—" Marion was off again having used Mrs. Radcliffe's perfunctory comment as a sort of springboard. Mrs. Radcliffe, still undecided, led the way up Knightsbridge toward Hyde Park Corner. Perhaps on the whole it would be wiser to leave Swan and Edgar's until next week. She felt she really couldn't face the exertion of getting into a crowded bus and going all that way. The most sensible thing to do would be to have a cup of tea somewhere. Just as they were crossing Sloane Street Marion broke off in the middle of a description of Mr. Townsend's obstinate refusal to allow her to telephone for a doctor. "Adela," she cried, "I'd nearly forgotten. I'd promised to go to Maud Fearnley's shop just for a minute, it's only a few doors down and she'd so love it if you came too. She's the one I told you about you know, whose husband was killed in that motor accident, not that she cared for him very much, but he left her without a penny and so she started this hat shop. I do think people are awfully plucky, don't you? I mean it takes a lot of grit to do a thing like that. Anyway she calls herself 'Yolande et Cie' and gets a lot of the newest models from Paris, at least, between you and me, I believe what she really does is to pop over there from time to time and just copy the models but for heaven's sake don't say I said so. She's a very old friend of mine and she really is having a terribly uphill struggle. Do come, she'd be so thrilled!"

Mrs. Radcliffe hesitated for a moment and then, swayed by the thought of the obvious pleasure she would be bestowing upon Yolande et Cie by visiting her shop and also by the reflection that if Yolande et Cie was having such an uphill struggle as all that she wasn't likely to be very expensive and it might be possible to find a smart new hat at a lower price than elsewhere, she consented benevolently and they turned down Sloane Street.

Maud Fearnley was a vague, faded woman in the early forties. Marion's enthusiastic allusion to pluck and spirit and her picture of her as a shrewd, capable businesswoman dashing back and forth between Paris and London, gallantly fighting step by step to conquer misfortune, was unhappily a trifle inaccurate. True she had been left penniless by the death of her husband and, bolstered up by the energy and financial support of a few strongminded friends, she certainly had taken over the lease and "goodwill" of Yolande et Cie, but for all that Maud Fearnley was not the stuff of which conquerors are made. She was a drifter. She had drifted into marriage, drifted into widowhood, and now she had drifted into a milliner's shop in Sloane Street. On the one occasion when she had happened to drift over to Paris, the results, commercially speaking, had been so far from successful that her friends had implored her never to do it again.

She rose from a small desk when Mrs. Radcliffe and Marion entered the shop and advanced toward them with the incredulous smile of a lonely traveler who unexpectedly happens upon two old school friends in a jungle clearing. She embraced Marion gratefully and was introduced to Mrs. Radcliffe. Mrs. Radcliffe sized her up at a glance. Her quick eye noted the dejected beige dress, the blue knitted wool jacket slung around the shoulders with the sleeves hanging, the mouse-colored hair and the amiable, rather silly expression. The woman's a fool she decided immediately, probably another of Marion's ridiculous enthusiasms, likely as not they had both planned this casual visit to the shop in order to get her to spend some money. Mrs. Radcliffe, in common with a great many other women of her social position, cherished a firm belief that there existed a sort of tacit conspiracy among those not as comfortably situated as herself to get at her money. This was not meanness on her part, she knew herself to be generous to a fault, it was merely a resigned acceptance of the frailties of human nature. No one could accuse her of being disillusioned. She was an idealist first and last, but in her wide and varied experience of life she had been forced to admit that if you allowed people to suspect that you had an assured income it was often liable to bring out the worst in them. One of her complaints against Marion had always been that she never, if she could possibly help it, made the slightest gesture toward paying for anything. Not that she would have permitted her to for a moment, she was perfectly aware of her financial situation and anyhow to be paid for by Marion would have been somehow incongruous, as well imagine a bird of paradise being entertained by a woodpecker. No, it wasn't that she wished Marion to pay for a thing but if she just occasionally made the effort she would have respected her a good deal more. Now in this dim little shop, its whole atmosphere charged with genteel failure, Mrs. Radcliffe scented danger. Mrs. Fearnley's greeting of Marion had been a little too surprised, a tiny bit overdone. The whole thing had probably been arranged over the telephone that morning. To do Marion and Mrs. Fearnley justice it is only fair to say that Mrs. Radcliffe's suspicions on this occasion were unfounded. Mrs. Fearnley had been quite genuinely surprised to see them come into the shop; in fact, poor thing, she was always surprised if anyone came in, and one of her fundamental weaknesses as a saleswoman was her inability to control it. She betrayed too desperate an eagerness, too flagrant an anxiety to please her infrequent customers. She wooed them and fawned upon them to such an extent that they sometimes left the shop in extreme embarrassment without buying a thing. Today, confronted by the majesty

of Mrs. Radcliffe, she could hardly contain herself. She gave a series of little gasps and cries of pleasure and one of pain when she happened to pinch
her finger in the sliding glass door of one of the showcases. She showed
Mrs. Radcliffe several hats, offering them to her with the despairing subservience of a beggar displaying the stump of an amputated arm and
imploring charity. Marion kept up a running fire of comment on each
model as it appeared—"There," she said, "isn't that sweet?"—"Ah, now
that one I really *do* like." "Look, Adela, at the way that's turned up at the
back! Isn't that the smartest thing you've ever seen?" Mrs. Radcliffe
looked at them all but without enthusiasm. She even agreed to try two or
three on after a lot of coaxing from both Mrs. Fearnley and Marion. They
both fluttered about behind her as she stood in front of the glass, heading
this way and that and regarding her ecstatically from all angles. Finally she
discovered one that really wasn't so bad. It was perfectly plain, which was
more than could be said for most of the others, made of black straw with
just one greenish-blue quill in it. It really was quite stylish. Mrs. Radcliffe
tried it on twice and then returned to it and tried it on once more. She
revolved slowly before the mirror holding a hand glass and scrutinizing it
from the back and from both sides. It certainly suited her, there was no
doubt about that. The excitement of Mrs. Fearnley and Marion rose to
fever pitch. At last she turned to Mrs. Fearnley.

"How much is it?" she asked.

Mrs. Fearnley was foolish enough to shoot a triumphant look at Marion.

"Four guineas," she said self-consciously.

"Four guineas!" Mrs. Radcliffe stared at her as though she had gone out
of her mind. "Four guineas—for this!"

"It's my very latest model," said Mrs. Fearnley. "It came over from Paris
only last week by airplane."

Mrs. Radcliffe took it off with a gesture that implied that it could cir-
cumnavigate the globe by airplane for all she cared and still not be worth
four guineas.

"I'm afraid that's far beyond my poor resources!" she said with a cold
smile.

"Oh, Adela!" wailed Marion. "It suits you down to the ground."

"I would be willing to make a slight reduction," ventured Mrs. Fearnley.

"I fear that it would have to be a great deal more than a *slight* reduction
to satisfy me," said Mrs. Radcliffe with an acid note in her voice. She had
not failed to note Mrs. Fearnley's exultant look at Marion before she had
quoted the price and it had annoyed her profoundly. It was just as she
suspected, nothing more nor less than a put-up job, she wouldn't be at all
surprised if this Mrs. Fearnley hadn't agreed to pay Marion a commission.
A nice state of affairs when you couldn't even trust your oldest friends. It
really was too disheartening the way people behaved, always on the make;

it was degrading. But they would find to their cost that it was not so easy to swindle her as they thought. She looked Mrs. Fearnley steadily in the eye. "To ask four guineas for that hat, Mrs. Fearnley," she said, "is nothing short of outrageous. You know as well as I do that it isn't worth a penny more than a guinea if that!"

Mrs. Fearnley, quailing before this onslaught, was about to speak when Marion forestalled her. Marion's face was quite pink and she looked furious.

"Really, Adela," she said, "I don't think there's any necessity to talk to Mrs. Fearnley like that."

"I resent being swindled," said Mrs. Radcliffe picking up her own hat and putting it on carefully in front of the glass.

"Oh, Mrs. Radcliffe," Mrs. Fearnley burst out in horror, "how *can* you say such a thing. I'm sure I never—"

"Well, really," exclaimed Marion, "I never heard of such a thing, honestly I didn't, never in all my life. Adela, you should be ashamed of yourself, honestly you should. I mean—you can't behave like that, really you can't—"

Mrs. Radcliffe looked at her crushingly. "Don't talk to me like that, Marion," she said. "And don't imagine that I can't read you like an open book because I can. I know perfectly well why you're in such a state. I'm not quite such a fool as you and your friend seem to think I am. I should be interested to know how much commission you expected to receive if I had been stupid enough to pay four guineas for this, this monstrosity." There now, it was out, she had said it and a good job too. She looked coolly at Marion in the shocked silence that ensued and was gratified to observe that her eyes were filling with tears. Serve her right, that would teach her not to take advantage of a generous lifelong friendship.

Marion, making a tremendous effort not to cry, spoke with dignity. "If it was your intention to hurt me," she said, "you have succeeded beyond your wildest dreams. I am very sorry you said what you did, Adela, more sorry than I can say . . ."

"I must say," interposed Mrs. Fearnley, gaining a sort of bleak courage from Marion's obvious distress, "I have never been so insulted in all my life, never," she said bridling. "If it were not for the fact that you are a friend of dear Marion's, I should be forced to ask you to leave my shop."

"I have no wish to stay," said Mrs. Radcliffe with hauteur, "and I shall certainly never set foot in it again, nor, I assure you, will any of my friends." She glanced at Marion. "I mean naturally my real friends," she added. "Good afternoon."

Mrs. Fearnley and Marion watched the door swing shut behind her and her stately figure pace along by the window and disappear from view; then Marion gave up to the tears she had been so gallantly trying to restrain and sank down onto a small gilt chair with her face buried in her hands.

"Oh dear," she wept. "Oh dear, oh dear—how dreadful—how absolutely dreadful."

Mrs. Fearnley placed her arms around her for a moment and patted her sympathetically and then, with commendable tact, let her to have her cry out while she put the offending hat back into the showcase.

9

Those who knew Mrs. Radcliffe only slightly would have been surprised, whereas those who knew her well would have been downright amazed had they chanced to be strolling through Hyde Park between the hours of four o'clock and six o'clock and observed her sitting on a seat, not even a twopenny green chair, but a seat alone! The amazement would have been justifiable because with all her failings and after all Mrs. Radcliffe was not perfect, she was no loiterer. One could imagine other people, Mrs. Weecock for instance or even, on occasion, the redoubtable Mrs. Poindexter, idling away an hour or so, but Mrs. Radcliffe, never. Hers was far too energetic and decisive a character for it to be conceivable that, in the admirable organization of her days, she should have an hour to spare. But there she was, sitting alone, leaning a trifle against the back of the seat, with her hands folded on her lap. She had taken off her glasses for a moment and on each side of the bridge of her nose there was a little pink line. Before her, in the mellow afternoon light, the unending pageant of London life passed by. Nurses with perambulators and straggling children; dim-looking gentlemen in bowler hats; a few soldiers arrogant in their uniforms; neatly dressed young women of uncertain profession; various representatives of the lower orders, their children making a great deal more noise than those of higher birth; occasionally somebody's paid companion walking along meekly with a dog, all parading before her weary eyes. In Knightsbridge the constant procession of taxis, private cars, lorries, bicycles and buses provided a soothing orchestration to the scene while every now and then a common London sparrow flew down from the trees and chirruped shrilly quite close to her.

Mrs. Radcliffe however was aware of all this only subconsciously, her conscious mind being occupied, to the exclusion of everything else, with the cruelty and ingratitude of human behavior. What a day! What a disillusioning day she had had, beset on all sides by ignorance, stupidity, defiance, deceit, rudeness and, in the case of Marion and Mrs. Fearnley, sheer treachery. Why, she wondered without anger—she was no longer angry—why should all this be visited on her? What had she done to deserve it? She put on her glasses and looked up at the sky, beyond which her indestructible faith envisaged a kindly God, in the vague hope that she might receive some miraculous sign, some indication of where she had erred to merit such harsh treatment. Perhaps, it was just within the bounds of possibility, she had unwittingly committed some trifling sin, some thoughtless act of omission which had brought down this avalanche of suffering upon her. She scanned the heavens humbly, supplicatingly, but no sign was forthcoming. True there was an airplane flying high over in the direction of Westminster Abbey, and for a moment the light of the sun caught it so that it shone like burnished silver before disappearing behind a cloud, but that could hardly be construed as a sort of reassuring wink from the Almighty. She lowered her eyes again. It was, she reflected without bitterness, inevitable that a woman of her temperament should feel things more keenly, with more poignance than ordinary people. It was one of the penalties of being highly strung. After all, that awareness of beauty, that unique sensitiveness to the finer things of life, had to be paid for. Everything had to be paid for. Your capacity for joy was inexorably balanced by your capacity for sorrow. Other people, such as Stanley for instance, just existed. Stanley really couldn't be said to live, really live, for a moment. Sometimes, she gave a wry smile, she almost envied him. No ups and downs for Stanley. No ecstasies, no despairs. Just an even, colorless monotony from the cradle to the grave. How extraordinary to be like that and, in some ways, how fortunate. Here she gave herself a little shake, she was becoming morbid. It was surely better to live life to the full and to pay the price, however high it might be, than to be a drone without punishment and without reward.

At this rather more comforting stage of her reflections her attention was diverted by a handsome, well-dressed woman in the middle forties and a distinguished gray-haired man in a silk hat and frock coat, who sat down on a seat almost immediately opposite her. They were unmistakably of high breeding, possibly even titled. They were talking with animation and every now and then, obviously in response to something amusing he had said, she gave a pleasant laugh. Mrs. Radcliffe looked at them with great interest. They had probably been to some grand social function, a reception perhaps or a wedding, although it was a little late for it to have been a wedding. The woman's face seemed familiar to her somehow, she racked her brains for a minute and then suddenly remembered, of course, it was Lady Elizabeth Vale, *The* Lady Elizabeth Vale, she was almost certain it was. Mrs. Radcliffe made no effort to repress a feeling of rising excitement. Lady Elizabeth Vale was one of the most famous women in London society, or in fact any society. An intimate friend of royalty and the wife of one of the most brilliant of the younger Cabinet Ministers, she was well known to combine impeccable breeding with considerable wealth. She was much photographed and she travelled extensively. Her moral reputation was as untarnished as could be expected with such a glare of limelight beating upon her. Her most ordinary activities received the closest attention in the gossip columns but so far no definite hint of scandal had stained her name. It was possible that even if it had Mrs. Radcliffe would have forgiven it. People of the social position of Lady Elizabeth Vale could demand from Mrs. Radcliffe, should they so wish, an inexhaustible meed of Tolerance and Christian Charity. As she sat there watching the couple out of the corner of her eye, she indulged in a few fleeting fancies. That capacity for reverie so soothing to the bruised ego was strongly developed in Mrs. Radcliffe. She often admonished herself with a lenient smile. "There you go," she'd say, "dreaming again!"

Today, possibly owing to the disillusionment she had suffered, her imagination was especially vivid. The real world was too pitiless, too sharply cruel. Was it not natural enough that she should seek refuge for a while in the rich gardens of her mind? She gave fantasy full rein. How pleasant it would be for instance if Fate, in the guise of some minor accident such as a child falling down and having to be picked up, should enable her to establish a friendship with Lady Elizabeth Vale. It would of course begin quite casually. "There dear, don't cry." "Poor little thing, I wonder where its mother is." Something quite simple and ordinary like that. Then, the child disposed of somehow or other, a little desultory conversation during which Lady Elizabeth would swiftly recognize what a charming, delightful creature Mrs. Radcliffe was and, with one of those graceful impulses that were so typical, invite her to tea! Mrs. Radcliffe saw herself clearly ensconced in a luxurious drawing room in Belgrave Square; discreet footmen hovering about with delicacies; the light from the fire gleaming on priceless old family silver; the conversation cozy and intimate—

"Dear Mrs. Radcliffe, I know you'll think it fearfully unconventional of me on the strength of such a short acquaintance, but I would so like it if you would call me Elizabeth, Lady Elizabeth sounds so stuffy somehow between friends and I'm sure we're going to be real friends, I felt it at once, the moment I saw you—" Here Mrs. Radcliffe paused for a moment in her flight to ponder the likelihood of it being "Elizabeth" or "Betty." "My dear Elizabeth." "My dear Betty." Betty won. "My dear Betty, of course I should be charmed, and you must call me Adela." Her mind jumped to a bridge party at Mrs. Poindexter's which she had accepted for next Wednesday. "I'm so sorry, I can't start another rubber, really I can't. I must fly home and dress, I'm dining with Betty Vale and going to the Opera—"

At this point her attention was dragged back to reality by the consciousness that a figure was standing close to her. She looked up and saw the most dreadful old woman. Mrs. Radcliffe positively jumped. The old woman was wearing a threadbare jacket, a skirt literally in rags, gaping boots and a man's old straw hat from under which straggled wisps of greasy white hair. Her face was gray and her eyes red-rimmed and watery.

"Please lady," she murmured hoarsely, "spare us a copper, I 'aven't 'ad a bite to eat all day, honest I 'aven't." Mrs. Radcliffe's first instinct naturally was to tell her to go away at once. These beggars were everywhere nowadays, it was really disgraceful. She glanced round to see if there were a policeman in sight and in doing so observed Lady Elizabeth Vale looking full at her. Automatically, without thinking, like the reflex action of a motorist who suddenly swerves to avoid a dog that has run out into the road, she plunged her hand into her bag and gave the woman half-a-crown. The woman looked at it incredulously and then burst into a wail of gratitude. "God bless yer, lady," she cried. "God bless yer kind 'eart"; she wandered away clutching the coin and still mumbling her blessings. Mrs. Radcliffe, with a smile of mingled pity and good-natured tolerance, looked across at Lady Elizabeth Vale for her reward. They would exchange a glance of mutual understanding, a glance expressing a subtle acknowledgment of what had passed, of the bonds of class and distinction that bound them together. That reciprocal glance would imply so much, administer such balm to Mrs. Radcliffe's battered spirit. Unfortunately, however, Lady Elizabeth didn't look at her again, she was immersed in conversation. After a little while she got up, her escort helped her to arrange her sable cape more comfortably around her shoulders and, still talking, they walked away. Mrs. Radcliffe only distinguished a few words as they passed her seat. The man, placing his hand protectively under Lady Elizabeth's elbow said, in an intimate tone of mock exasperation—"My *dear* Elizabeth—"

10

At a quarter to eleven that evening Mrs. Radcliffe went upstairs to bed. The dinner had been a success on the whole, marred only by the clumsiness of Mildred who had banged against Mrs. Duke's chair while proferring her the baked custard and caused the spoon, with a certain amount of custard in it, to fall onto her dress. Stanley had, as usual, not contributed very much, but the Vicar had been splendid, he had kept everyone highly amused with his imitation of Miss Lawrence trying not to sneeze while she was playing the organ at choir practice, and, after dinner, he had sung "Now Sleeps the Crimson Petal," by Roger Quilter, with great charm and feeling. Miss Layton of course had been rather silly, but then she always was, making sheep's eyes at Mr. Baker all the evening and laughing in that affected way, as though he'd ever look twice at a dried-up frump like her. That dress! Mrs. Radcliffe, as she was taking the pins out of her hair, paused for a moment to smile at the memory of Miss Layton's dress. It really was too absurd, a woman of her age, she must be fifty if she was a day, dolling herself up with all those frills and folderols. She'd have been much better advised to wear a plain black frock. Mrs. Radcliffe remembered having whispered this naughtily to Mr. Baker who had been on her left, and smiled again.

Presently Stanley came upstairs, she heard him go into his room on the other side of the landing. Stanley really was a very peculiar man. Fancy asking Miss Layton to play like that the moment the Vicar had sat down, indeed, before Mrs. Duke had even left the piano stool. How unobservant men were. Couldn't he have noticed that the one thing she had been trying to avoid was the possibility of Miss Layton playing. To begin with she had a very heavy touch and no style whatsoever, also she always insisted upon the piano being opened fully which was a great nuisance as it meant taking off the shawl, the vase and the photographs. In any case it was quite obvious that she only wanted to play at all in order to make an impression on Mr. Baker; however, she certainly hadn't succeeded. Mr. Baker had paid very little attention, even when she had embarked upon "The Golliwog's Cakewalk" by Debussy with all that banging in the bass, he had only nodded politely and raised his voice a trifle.

Presently Stanley came in to say "Good night." She came out of the bathroom and there he was, fiddling about with the things on her dressing table. Poor Stanley, he was undoubtedly beginning to show his age, she wished he'd learn to stand up a little straighter, stooping like that made him look much older than he really was. If only he had a little more grit, more strength of character. If only he were the sort of man upon whom she could lean occasionally when she felt weary and sick at heart, the sort of man who would put his arms around her and comfort her and bid her be of good cheer. But no; no use expecting any sympathy or demonstrativeness from Stanley. He was utterly wrapped up in himself and always had been. She had contemplated for a moment, while she was dressing for dinner, telling him about Marjorie's behavior, but she had quickly put the thought out of her mind. Stanley always stood up for Marjorie, he would be sure to have twisted the whole thing around into being her fault and then said something sarcastic. He had one of those blind, uncritical adorations for Marjorie that so many elderly fathers have for their only daughters. It was sometimes quite ridiculous the way he went on about her. He even liked Cecil, and said that in his opinion he was a damned intelligent, straightforward young fellow. Straightforward, if you please! Mrs. Radcliffe knew better.

Hearing his wife enter, Mr. Radcliffe stopped fiddling with the things on the dressing table and looked at her. She was in her nightdress and pink quilted silk dressing gown; on her feet were her ostrich feather bedroom slippers, looking a trifle draggled; on her large pale face was a layer of Elizabeth Arden cold cream which made it even paler. Her gray hair was tortured into several large curling pins.

"Stanley," she said. "What a fright you gave me." This was untrue. He hadn't given her a fright at all, she had known perfectly well he was there as she had heard him come in when she was in the bathroom, but still it was something to say.

"Sorry, dear," he replied. "I just came in to say good night."

Mrs. Radcliffe kissed him absently. "Good night, Stanley." This being said she turned away expecting him to have gone by the time she turned around again, but when she did he was still there, kicking at the edge of the rug with the toe of his shoe. He looked at her again, his forehead was wrinkled, he obviously had something on his mind.

"What's the matter, Stanley?" she asked, a little impatiently.

"I think you were a bit hard on poor Miss Layton tonight," he suddenly blurted out. "Talking to Mr. Baker like that all the time she was playing. She noticed, you know, and it upset her very much. I walked to the corner with her and she was nearly crying."

"Really, Stanley," said Mrs. Radcliffe with extreme exasperation, "you are too idiotic."

"Idiotic I may be," retorted her husband with unwonted spirit, "but you were unkind and that's worse!"

Mrs. Radcliffe opened her mouth to reply, to give full vent to the annoyance he had caused her, not only at this moment, but the whole evening long, but before she could utter a word he had gone out of the room and shut the door, almost slammed it, in her face. She stood quite still for an instant with her eyes closed and her hands tightly clenched at her sides. This was too much. At the end of a dreadful day like she'd had, for Stanley, her own husband, to fly at her and accuse her of being unkind. After a little she moved over to her bed quivering at the injustice of it all. She knelt down automatically to say her prayers, but it was quite a while before she was able to will herself into a suitable frame of mind. Suddenly, like a ray of light in the dark cavern of her unhappiness, the incident of the beggar woman in the park flashed into her memory, and with that all disquiet left her. It was like a miracle. When she had finished her prayers and got into bed she was smiling. Unkind indeed!

•

Noël often referred to *Design for Living* as his favorite play.

It had its origins in that first visit to New York. Here he met fellow actors Alfred Lunt and Lynn Fontanne—not yet "The Lunts."

He wrote to Violet . . .

Darling,
Do you remember Lynn Fontanne? She played some small parts in London and came to New York. Well, she's had a huge success in a

play called *Dulcy* (she's Dulcy). I went to see her opening night with her fiancé, an actor called Alfred Lunt and, my dear, a star was born. Well, *two* stars, actually, as Alfred is also making a name for himself in these parts.

They're quite wonderful and couldn't have been kinder to me. They haven't any money either—though they soon will have, I'm sure—and they helped me keep body and soul together by sharing their last crust (not quite that, really). They're going to be huge stars and, since we all know that yours truly is going to be one too, we've decided that, when that great day arrives, we shall act together in a play I shall write for us and the cosmos will have a new galaxy.

His prediction would catch up with him a decade later toward the end of a trip around South America. In Santiago a cable reached him from the Lunts, who had been working exclusively for the Theatre Guild for some years . . .

OUR CONTRACT WITH THEATRE GUILD UP IN JUNE STOP WE'RE FREE STOP WHAT ABOUT IT?

Noël traveled back to the United States on a Norwegian freighter. By the time he arrived in San Francisco, he had the draft of the play under his arm.

Portrait of Lynn Fontanne when she appeared in *Design for Living* (*The Stage* magazine, March 1933)

"All three of us gave the worst performances of our careers every
night for months and managed to be very good indeed."

DESIGN FOR LIVING

ALFRED LUNT, NOEL COWARD AND LYNN FONTANNE

ETHEL BARRYMORE
THEATRE

Otto (Alfred Lunt) is a painter who lives with Gilda (Lynn Fontanne), an interior decorator. When asked why she doesn't marry him, she replies simply, "Because I love him." Marriage would spoil their relationship. The only problem is that she also loves Leo (Noël), a writer, who loves her in return. And they *both* love Otto, who loves both of them.

DESIGN FOR LIVING (1933)

CAST

GILDA	LYNN FONTANNE
OTTO	ALFRED LUNT
LEO	NOËL COWARD

DIRECTED BY NOËL COWARD
ETHEL BARRYMORE THEATRE, NEW YORK, JANUARY 24, 1933

The play revolves around the complications this perilous *ménage à trois* creates for them and the people around them, as they realize once and for all that, while they can't live *with* each other, they can't live without each other, either. *Private Lives* (continued):

ACT 1. Paris. Otto returns from a business trip, overjoyed to see Gilda again but she immediately tells him he must go to the Hotel George V. Leo has just arrived and can't wait to see him. Otto leaves . . .

GILDA stands quite still for a moment or two; then she sits down at a table. *LEO* comes out of the bedroom. He is thin and nervous and obviously making a tremendous effort to control himself. He walks about aimlessly for a little and finishes up looking out of the window, with his back to *GILDA*.

LEO: What now?
GILDA: I don't know.
LEO: Not much time to think.
GILDA: A few minutes.
LEO: Are there any cigarettes?
GILDA: Yes, in that box.
LEO: Want one?
GILDA: No.
LEO (*lighting one*): It's nice being human beings, isn't it? I'm sure God's angels must envy us.
GILDA: Whom do you love best? Otto or me?

Sketches by Galbraith

LEO: Silly question.

GILDA: Answer me, anyhow.

LEO: How can I? Be sensible! In any case, what does it matter?

GILDA: It's important to me.

LEO: No, it isn't—not really. That's not what's important. What we did was inevitable. It's been inevitable for years. It doesn't matter who loves who the most; you can't line up things like that mathematically. We all love each other a lot, far too much, and we've made a bloody mess of it! That was inevitable, too.

GILDA: We must get it straight, somehow.

LEO: Yes, we must get it straight and tie it up with ribbons with a bow on the top. Pity it isn't Valentine's Day!

GILDA: Can't we laugh a little? Isn't it a joke? Can't we make it a joke?

LEO: Yes, it's a joke. It's a joke, all right. We can laugh until our sides ache. Let's start, shall we?

GILDA: What's the truth of it? The absolute, deep-down truth? Until we really know that, we can't grapple with it. We can't do a thing. We can only sit here flicking words about.

LEO: It should be easy, you know. The actual facts are so simple. I love you. You love me. You love Otto. I love Otto. Otto loves you. Otto loves me. There now! Start to unravel from there.

GILDA: We've always been honest, though, all of us. Honest with each other, I mean. That's something to go on, isn't it?

LEO: In this particular instance, it makes the whole thing far more complicated. If we were ordinary moral, high-thinking citizens we could carry on a backstairs affair for weeks without saying a word about it. We

could lunch and dine together, all three, and not give anything away by
so much as a look.

GILDA: If we were ordinary moral, high-thinking citizens we shouldn't
have had an affair at all.

LEO: Perhaps not. We should have crushed it down. And the more we
crushed it down the more we should have resented Otto, until we hated
him. Just think of hating Otto—

GILDA: Just think of him hating us.

LEO: Do you think he will?

GILDA (*inexorably*): Yes.

LEO (*walking about the room*): Oh, no, no—he mustn't! It's too silly. He
must see how unimportant it is, really.

GILDA: There's no question of not telling him, is there?

LEO: Of course not.

GILDA: We could pretend that you just arrived here and missed him on
the way.

LEO: So we could, dear—so we could.

GILDA: Do you think we're working each other up? Do you think we're
imagining it to be more serious than it really is?

LEO: Perhaps.

GILDA: Do you think, after all, he may not mind quite so dreadfully?

LEO: He'll mind just as much as you or I would under similar circumstances. Probably a little bit more. Imagine that for a moment, will
you? Put yourself in his place.

GILDA (*hopelessly*): Oh, don't!

LEO: Tell me one thing. How sorry were you last night, when once you
realized we were in for it?

GILDA: I wasn't sorry at all. I gave way utterly.

LEO: So did I.

GILDA: Very deep inside, I had a qualm or two. Just once or twice.

LEO: So did I.

GILDA: But I stamped on them, like killing beetles.

LEO: A nice way to describe the pangs of a noble conscience!

GILDA: I enjoyed it all, see! I enjoyed it thoroughly from the very first
moment. So there!

LEO: All right! All right! So did I.

GILDA (*defiantly*): It was romantic. Suddenly, violently romantic! The
whole evening was "Gala." You looked lovely, darling—very smooth
and velvety—and your manner was a dream! I'd forgotten about your
French accent and the way you move your hands, and the way you
dance. A sleek little gigolo!

LEO: You must try not to be bitter, dear.

GILDA: There seemed to be something new about you: something I'd never realized before. Perhaps it's having money. Perhaps your success has given you a little extra glamour.

LEO: Look at me now, sweet! It's quite chilly, this morning light. How do I appear to you now?

GILDA (*gently*): The same.

LEO: So do you, but that's because my eyes are slow at changing visions. I still see you too clearly last night to be able to realize how you look this morning. You were very got up—very got up, indeed, in your green dress and your earrings. It was "Gala," all right—strong magic!

GILDA: Coloured lights, sly music, overhanging trees, paper streamers—all the trappings.

LEO: Champagne, too, just to celebrate, both of us hating it.

GILDA: We drank to Otto. Perhaps you remember?

LEO: Perfectly.

GILDA: How could we? Oh, how could we?

LEO: It seemed quite natural.

GILDA: Yes, but we knew in our hearts what we were up to. It was vile of us.

LEO: I'll drink Otto's health until the day I die! Nothing could change that ever.

GILDA: Sentimentalist!

LEO: Deeper than sentiment: far, far deeper. Beyond the reach of small enchantments.

GILDA: Was that all it was to you? A small enchantment?

LEO: That's all it ever is to anybody, if only they knew.

GILDA: Easy wisdom. Is it a comfort to you?

LEO: Not particularly.

GILDA (*viciously*): Let's have some more! "Passion's only transitory," isn't it? "Love is ever fleeting!" "Time is a great healer." Trot them all out, dear.

LEO: Don't try to quarrel with me.

GILDA: Don't be so wise and assured and knowing, then. It's infuriating.

LEO: I believe I was more to blame than you, really.

GILDA: Why?

LEO: I made the running.

GILDA: *You* made the running! (*She laughs.*)

LEO: A silly pride made me show off to you, parade my attraction for you, like a mannequin. New spring model, with a few extra flounces!

GILDA: That's my story, Leo; you can't steal it from me. I've been wallowing in self-abasement, dragging out my last night's femininity and spitting on it. I've taken the blame onto myself for the whole thing. Ernest was quite shocked; you should have been listening at the door.

LEO: I was.

GILDA: Good! Then you know how I feel.

LEO: Lot of damned hysteria.

GILDA: Possibly, but heartfelt at the moment.

LEO: Can't we put an end to this flagellation party now?

GILDA: We might just as well go on with it; it passes the time.

LEO: Until Otto comes back.

GILDA: Yes. Until Otto comes back.

LEO (*walking up and down*): I expect jealousy had something to do with it, too.

GILDA: Jealousy?

LEO: Yes. Subconscious and buried deep, but there all the same; there for ages, ever since our first meeting when you chose Otto so firmly.

GILDA: Another of those pleasant little galas! The awakening of spring! Romance in a café! Yes, sir! "Yes, sir, three bags full!"

LEO: A strange evening. Very gay, if I remember rightly.

GILDA: Oh, it was gay, deliriously gay, thick with omens!

LEO: Perhaps we laughed at them too hard.

ACT 2 . . . and now Gilda and Leo are living together in London. It's the morning after the opening night of Leo's play, *Change and Decay,* and he is reading his reviews . . .

LEO (*rolling over on his back and flinging the paper in the air*): It's a knockout! It's magnificent! It'll run a year.

GILDA: Two years.

LEO: Three years.

GILDA: Four years, five years, six years! It'll run forever. Old ladies will be trampled to death struggling to get into the pit. Women will have babies regularly in the upper circle bar during the big scene at the end of the second act—

LEO (*complacently*): Regularly as clockwork.

GILDA: The *Daily Mail* says it's daring and dramatic and witty.

LEO: The *Daily Express* says it's disgusting.

GILDA: I should be cut to the quick if it said anything else.

LEO: The *Daily Mirror,* I regret to say, is a trifle carping.

GILDA: Getting uppish, I see. Naughty little thing!

LEO (*reading the* Daily Mirror): "*Change and Decay* is gripping throughout. The characterization falters here and there, but the dialogue is polished and sustains a high level from first to last and is frequently witty, nay, even brilliant—"

GILDA: I love "Nay."

LEO (*still reading*): "But"—here we go, dear!—"But the play, on the whole, is decidedly thin."

GILDA: My God! They've noticed it.

LEO (*jumping up*): Thin—thin! What do they mean, "thin"?

GILDA: Just thin, darling. Thin's thin all the world over and you can't get away from it.

LEO: Would you call it thin?

GILDA: Emaciated.

LEO: I shall write fat plays from now onwards. Fat plays filled with very fat people!

GILDA: You mustn't let your vibrations be upset by the *Daily Mirror.* It means to be kind. That's why one only looks at the pictures.

LEO: The *Daily Sketch* is just as bad.

GILDA (*gently*): Just as good, dear—just as good.

LEO: Let's have another look at Old Father *Times.*

GILDA: It's there, behind the *Telegraph.*

LEO (*glancing through it*): Noncommittal, but amiable. A minute, if slightly inaccurate, description of the plot.

GILDA (*rising and looking over his shoulder*): Only a few of the names wrong.

LEO: They seem to have missed the main idea of the play.

GILDA: You mustn't grumble; they say the lines are provocative.

LEO: What *could* they mean by that?

GILDA: Anyhow, you can't expect a paper like the *Times* to be really interested in your petty little excursions in the theatre. After all, it is the organ of the nation.

LEO: That sounds vaguely pornographic to me.

·

Eventually Gilda leaves them both. Leo and Otto commiserate over a few drinks . . .

Design for Living fashion drawing

LEO: Where is Gilda?

OTTO: She's gone out.

LEO: Out! Why? Where's she gone to?

OTTO: I don't know.

LEO (*turning away*): How vile of you! How unspeakably vile of you both!

OTTO: It was inevitable.

LEO (*contemptuously*): Inevitable!

OTTO: I arrived unexpectedly; you were away; Gilda was alone. I love her; I've always loved her—I've never stopped for a minute, and she loves me, too.

LEO: What about me?

OTTO: I told you I was sorry about hurting you.

LEO: Gilda loves me.

OTTO: I never said she didn't.

LEO (*hopelessly*): What are we to do? What are we to do now?

OTTO: Do you know, I really haven't the faintest idea.

LEO: You're laughing inside. You're thoroughly damned well pleased with yourself, aren't you?

OTTO: I don't know. I don't know that either.

LEO (*savagely*): You are! I can see it in your eyes—so much triumph—such a sweet revenge!

OTTO: It wasn't anything to do with revenge.

LEO: It was. Of course it was—secretly thought out, planned for ages— infinitely mean!

OTTO: Shut up! And don't talk such nonsense.

LEO: Why did you do it, then? Why did you come back and break every- thing up for me?

OTTO: I came back to see you both. It was a surprise.

LEO: A rather cruel surprise, and brilliantly successful. You should be very happy.

OTTO (*sadly*): Should I?

LEO: Perhaps I should be happy, too; you've set me free from something.

OTTO: What?

LEO (*haltingly*): The—feeling I had for you—something very deep, I imag- ined it was, but it couldn't have been, could it?—now that it has died so easily.

OTTO: I said all that to you in Paris. Do you remember? I thought it was true then, just as you think it's true now.

LEO: It is true.

OTTO: Oh, no, it isn't.

LEO: Do you honestly believe I could ever look at you again, as a real friend?

OTTO: Until the day you die.

LEO: Shut up! It's too utterly beastly—the whole thing.

OTTO: It's certainly very, very uncomfortable.

LEO: Is Gilda going to leave me? To go away with you?

OTTO: Do you want her to?

LEO: Yes, I suppose so, now.

OTTO: We didn't make any arrangement or plans.

LEO: I came back too soon. You could have gone away and left a note for me—that would have been nice and easy for you, wouldn't it?

OTTO: Perhaps it would, really. I don't know that I should have done it, though.

LEO: Why not?

OTTO: If I had, I shouldn't have seen you at all, and I wanted to see you very much.

LEO: You even wanted to see me, hating you like this? Very touching!

OTTO: You're not hating me nearly as much as you think you are. You're hating the situation: that's quite different.

LEO: You flatter yourself.

OTTO: No. I'm speaking from experience. You forget, I've been through just what you're going through now. I thought I hated you with all my heart and soul, and the force of that hatred swept me away on to the high seas, too far out of reach to be able to come back when I discovered the truth.

LEO: The truth!

OTTO: That no one of us was more to blame than the other. We've made our own circumstances, you and Gilda and me, and we've bloody well got to put up with them!

LEO: I wish I could aspire to such a sublime God's-eye view!

OTTO: You will—in time—when your acids have calmed down.

LEO: I'd like so very much not to be able to feel anything at all for a little. I'm desperately tired.

OTTO: You want a change.

LEO: It seems as if I'm going to get one, whether I want it or not.

OTTO (*laughing*): Oh, Leo, you really are very, very tender!

LEO: Don't laugh! How dare you laugh! How *can* you laugh!

OTTO: It's a good joke. A magnificent joke.

LEO (*bitterly*): A pity Gilda chose just that moment to go out, we could all have enjoyed it together.

OTTO: Like we did before?

LEO: Yes, like we did before.

OTTO: And like we shall again.

LEO (*vehemently*): No, *never* again—never!

OTTO: I wonder.

The telephone rings. *LEO* goes over mechanically to answer it; he lifts up the receiver, and as he does so he catches sight of the two letters propped

Otto (Alfred Lunt) and Leo (Noël) try to console each other over a few
drinks. They can manage without Gilda (Lynn Fontanne), can't they?
Can't they?

up against the brandy bottle. He stares at them and slowly lets the receiver
drop on to the desk.

LEO (*very quietly*): Otto.
OTTO: What is it?
LEO: Look.

OTTO comes over to the desk, and they both stand staring at the letters.

OTTO: Gilda!
LEO: Of course.
OTTO: She's gone! She's escaped!
LEO: Funny word to use, "escaped."
OTTO: That's what she's done, all the same, escaped.
LEO: The joke is becoming richer.
OTTO: Escaped from both of us.
LEO: We'd better open them, I suppose.
OTTO (*slowly*): Yes—yes, I suppose we had.

They both open the letters, in silence, and read them.

LEO (*after a pause*): What does yours say?

OTTO (*reading*): "Good-bye, my clever little dear! Thank you for the keys of the city."

LEO: That's what mine says.

OTTO: I wonder where she's gone?

LEO: I don't see that that matters much.

OTTO: One up to Gilda!

LEO: What does she mean, "Keys of the city"?

OTTO: A lot of things.

LEO: I feel rather sick.

OTTO: Have some sherry?

LEO: That's brandy.

OTTO: Better still.

He pours out a glass and hands it to LEO.

LEO (*quietly*): Thank you.

OTTO (*pouring one out for himself*): I feel a little sick, too.

LEO: Do you think she'll come back?

OTTO: No.

LEO: She will—she must—she must come back!

OTTO: She won't. Not for a long time.

LEO (*drinking his brandy*): It's all my fault, really.

OTTO (*drinking his*): Is it?

LEO: Yes. I've, unfortunately, turned out to be successful. Gilda doesn't care for successful people.

OTTO: I wonder how much we've lost, with the years?

LEO: A lot. I think, practically everything now.

OTTO (*thoughtfully*): Love among the artists. Very difficult, too difficult.

LEO: Do you think we could find her?

OTTO: No.

LEO: We could try.

OTTO: Do you want to?

LEO: Of course.

OTTO: Why? What would be the use?

LEO: She might explain a little—a little more clearly.

OTTO: What good would that do? We know why she's gone perfectly well.

LEO: Because she doesn't want us anymore.

OTTO: Because she thinks she doesn't want us anymore.

LEO: I suppose that's as good a reason as any.

OTTO: Quite.

LEO: All the same, I should like to see her just once—just to find out, really, in so many words—

OTTO (*with sudden fury*): So many words! That's what's wrong with us! So many words—too many words, masses and masses of words, spewed about until we're choked with them. We've argued and probed and dragged our entrails out in front of one another for years! We've explained away the sea and the stars and life and death and our own peace of mind! I'm sick of this endless game of three-handed, spiritual ping-pong—this battling of our little egos in one another's faces! Sick to death of it! Gilda's made a supreme gesture and got out. Good luck to her, I say! Good luck to the old girl—she knows her onions!

OTTO refills his glass and drains it at a gulp.

LEO: You'll get drunk, swilling down all that brandy on an empty stomach.
OTTO: Why not? What else is there to do? Here, have some more as well.

He refills LEO's glass and hands it to him.

LEO: All right! Here goes.

He drains his glass.

LEO: Now we start fair.

He refills both their glasses.

OTTO (*raising his glass*): Gilda! (*He drains it.*)
LEO (*doing the same*): Gilda! (*He drains it.*)
OTTO: That's better, isn't it? Much, much better.
LEO: Excellent. We shall be sick as dogs!
OTTO: Good for our livers.
LEO: Good for our immortal souls.

He refills the glasses, and raises his.

LEO: Our Immortal Souls!
OTTO (*raising his*): Our Immortal Souls!

They both drain them to the last drop.

LEO: I might have known it!
OTTO: What?
LEO: That there was going to be a break. Everything was running too smoothly, too well. I was enjoying all the small things too much.

OTTO: There's no harm in enjoying the small things.

LEO: Gilda didn't want me to.

OTTO: I know.

LEO: Did she tell you so?

OTTO: Yes, she said she was uneasy.

LEO: She might have had a little faith in me, I think. I haven't got this far just to be sidetracked by a few garlands.

OTTO: That's what I said to her; I said you wouldn't be touched, inside.

LEO: How about you?

OTTO: Catching up, Leo! Popular portraits at popular prices.

LEO: Good work or bad work?

OTTO: Good. An occasional compromise, but essentials all right.

LEO (*with a glint in his eye*): Let's make the most of the whole business, shall we? Let's be photographed and interviewed and pointed at in restaurants! Let's play the game for what it's worth, secretaries and fur coats and de luxe suites on transatlantic liners at minimum rates! Don't let's allow one shabby perquisite to slip through our fingers! It's what we dreamed many years ago and now it's within our reach. Let's cash in, Otto, and see how much we lose by it.

He refills both glasses and hands one to OTTO.

LEO: Come on, my boy!

He raises his glass.

LEO: Success in twenty lessons! Each one more bitter than the last! More and better Success! Louder and funnier Success!

They both drain their glasses.
They put down their glasses, gasping slightly.

OTTO (*agreeably*): It takes the breath away a bit, doesn't it?

LEO: How astonished our insides must be—all that brandy hurtling down suddenly!

OTTO: On Sunday, too.

LEO: We ought to know more about our insides, Otto. We ought to know why everything does everything.

OTTO: Machines! That's what we are, really—all of us! I can't help feeling a little discouraged about it every now and then.

LEO: Sheer sentimentality! You shouldn't feel discouraged at all; you should be proud.

OTTO: I don't see anything to be proud about.

LEO: That's because you don't understand; because you're still chained to stale illusions. Science dispels illusions; you ought to be proud to be living in a scientific age. You ought to be proud to know that you're a minute cog in the vast process of human life.

OTTO: I don't like to think I'm only a minute cog—it makes me sort of sad.

LEO: The time for dreaming is over, Otto.

OTTO: Never! I'll never consent to that. Never, as long as I live! How do you know that science isn't a dream, too? A monstrous, gigantic hoax?

LEO: How could it be? It proves everything.

OTTO: What does it prove? Answer me that!

LEO: Don't be silly, Otto. You must try not to be silly.

OTTO (*bitterly*): A few facts, that's all. A few tawdry facts torn from the universe and dressed up in terminological abstractions!

LEO: Science is our only hope, the only hope for humanity! We've wallowed in false mysticism for centuries; we've fought and suffered and died for foolish beliefs, which science has proved to be as ephemeral as smoke. Now is the moment to open our eyes fearlessly and look at the truth!

OTTO: What is the truth?

LEO (*irritably*): It's no use talking to you—you just won't try to grasp anything! You're content to go on being a romantic clod until the end of your days.

OTTO (*incensed*): What about you? What about the plays you write? Turgid with romance; sodden with true love; rotten with nostalgia!

LEO (*with dignity*): There's no necessity to be rude about my work—that's quite separate, and completely beside the point.

OTTO: Well, it oughtn't to be. It ought to be absolutely in accord with your cold, incisive, scientific viewpoint. If you're a writer it's your duty to write what you think. If you don't you're a cheat—a cheat and a hypocrite!

LEO (*loftily*): Impartial discussion is one thing, Otto. Personal bickering is another. I think you should learn to distinguish between the two.

OTTO: Let's have some more brandy.

LEO: That would be completely idiotic.

OTTO: Let's be completely idiotic!

LEO: Very well.

They both refill their glasses and drain them in silence.

OTTO: There's a certain furtive delight in doing something consciously that you know perfectly well is thoroughly contemptible.

LEO: There is, indeed.

OTTO: There isn't much more left. Shall we finish it?

LEO: Certainly.

OTTO refills both glasses.

OTTO (*handing* LEO *his*): Now what?

LEO: Now what what?

OTTO (*giggling slightly*): Don't keep on saying, "what, what, what"—it sounds ridiculous!

LEO: I wanted to know what you meant by "Now what."

OTTO: Now what shall we drink to?

LEO (*also giggling*): Let's not drink to anything—let's just drink!

OTTO: All right.

He drinks.

LEO (*also drinking*): Beautiful!

OTTO: If Gilda came in now she'd be surprised all right, wouldn't she?

LEO: She'd be so surprised, she'd fall right over backwards!

OTTO: So should we.

They both laugh immoderately at this.

LEO (*wiping his eyes*): Oh, dear! Oh, dear, oh, dear, how silly! How very, very silly.

OTTO (*with sudden change of mood*): She'll never come back. Never.

LEO: Yes, she will—when we're very, very old, she'll suddenly come in— in a bath chair!

OTTO (*sullenly*): Damn fool.

LEO (*with slight belligerence*): Who's a damn fool?

OTTO: You are. So am I. We both are. We were both damn fools in the first place, ever to have anything to do with her.

LEO (*admiringly*): You're awfully strong, Otto! Much, much stronger than you used to be.

OTTO: I've been all over the world; I've roughed it—that's what's made me strong. Every man ought to rough it.

LEO: That's the trouble with civilized life—it makes you soft. I've been thinking that for a long time. I've been watching myself getting softer and softer and softer—it's awful!

OTTO: You'd soon be all right if you got away from all this muck.

LEO: Yes, I know, but how?

OTTO (*putting his arm around his shoulders*): Get on a ship, Leo—never mind where it's going! Just get on a ship—a small ship.

LEO: How small?

OTTO: Very small indeed; a freighter.

LEO: Is that what you did?

OTTO: Yes.

LEO: Then I will. Where do very small ships sail from?

OTTO: Everywhere—Tilbury, Hamburg, Havre—

LEO: I'm free! I've suddenly realized it. I'm free!

OTTO: So am I.

LEO: We ought to drink to that, Otto. It's something worth drinking to. Freedom's been lost to us for a long, long time and now we've found it again! Freedom from people and things and softness! We really ought to drink to it.

OTTO: There isn't any more brandy.

LEO: What's that over there?

OTTO: Where?

LEO: On the thing.

OTTO (*going to it*): Sherry.

LEO: What's the matter with sherry?

OTTO: All right.

He brings over the bottle and fills their glasses.

LEO (*raising his*): Freedom!

OTTO (*doing the same*): Freedom!

They both drink.

LEO: Very insipid.

OTTO: Tastes like brown paper.

LEO: I've never tasted brown paper.

OTTO: Neither have I.

They roar with laughter.

LEO: Sherry's a very ludicrous word, isn't it, when you begin to analyse it?

OTTO: Any word's ludicrous if you stare at it long enough. Look at "macaroni."

LEO: That's Italian; that doesn't count.

OTTO: Well, "rigmarole" then, and "neophyte" and "haddock."

LEO: And "wimple"—wimple's the word that gets me down!

OTTO: What is a wimple?

LEO: A sort of medieval megaphone, made of linen. Guinevere had one.

OTTO: What did she do with it?

LEO (*patiently*): Wore it, of course. What did you think she did with it?

OTTO: She might have blown down it.

LEO (*with slight irritation*): Anyhow, it doesn't matter, does it?

OTTO (*agreeably*): Not in the least. It couldn't matter less. I always thought Guinevere was tedious, wimple or no wimple.

LEO: I'm beginning to float a little, aren't you?

OTTO: Just leaving the ground. Give me time! I'm just leaving the ground—

LEO: Better have some more sherry.

OTTO: I'm afraid it isn't very good sherry.

LEO (*scrutinizing the bottle*): It ought to be good; it's real old Armadildo.

OTTO: Perhaps we haven't given it a fair chance.

He holds out his glass; *LEO* refills it and his own.

LEO (*raising his glass*): *Après moi le déluge!*

OTTO: *Après* both of us the deluge!

They drain their glasses.

LEO: I think I shall sit down now. I'm so terribly sick of standing up.

OTTO: Human beings were never meant to stand up, in the first place. It's all been a grave mistake.

They both sit on the sofa.

LEO: All what?

OTTO: All this stamping about.

LEO: I feel ever so much happier. I don't feel angry with you or with Gilda or with anybody! I feel sort of at peace, if you know what I mean.

OTTO (*putting his arm around him*): Yes, I know—I know.

LEO: Keys of the city, indeed!

OTTO: Lot of damned nonsense.

LEO: Too much sense of drama, flouncing off like that—

OTTO: We've all got too much sense of drama, but we won't have anymore—from now onwards, reason and realism and clarity of vision.

LEO: What?

OTTO (*very loudly*): I said "Clarity of vision."

LEO: I wouldn't have believed I could ever feel like this again—so still and calm, like a deep, deep pool.

OTTO: Me, too—a deep pool, surrounded with cool green rushes, with the wind rustling through them—

This flight of fancy is disturbed by a faint hiccough.

LEO (*resting his head on* OTTO's *shoulder*): Will you forgive me—for—for everything?
OTTO (*emotionally*): It's I who should ask you that!
LEO: I'm glad Gilda's gone, really—she was very wearisome sometimes. I shall miss her, though.
OTTO: We shall both miss her.
LEO: She's the only really intelligent woman I've ever known.
OTTO: Brilliant!
LEO: She's done a tremendous lot for us, Otto. I wonder how much we should have achieved without her?
OTTO: Very little, I'm afraid. Terribly little.
LEO: And now she's gone because she doesn't want us anymore.
OTTO: I think she thinks we don't want her anymore.
LEO: But we do, Otto—we do—
OTTO: We shall always want her, always, always, always—
LEO (*miserably*): We shall get over it in time, I expect, but it will take years.
OTTO: I'm going to hate those years. I'm going to hate every minute of them.
LEO: So am I.
OTTO: Thank God for each other, anyhow!
LEO: That's true. We'll get along, somehow—(*his voice breaks*)—together—
OTTO (*struggling with his tears*): Together—
LEO (*giving way to his, and breaking down completely*): But we're going to be awfully—awfully—lonely—

They both sob hopelessly on each other's shoulders as the curtain slowly falls.

•

At one performance Alfred and Noël accidentally swapped lines. Realizing what had happened, they continued to play each other's lines. "Since it was a drunk scene," Noël recalled, "nobody noticed. But then I realized that Leo [now Alfred] would come to a line where he had to burp. And I knew Alfred couldn't burp—so I took the line back and we finished the scene mightily pleased with ourselves. Until we exited, only to be confronted with an icy Lynn. 'Nothing either of you did on that stage tonight was even *remotely* funny!' "

Despite that, he would conclude that "all three of us gave the worst performances of our careers every night for months and managed to be very good indeed."

And, of course, Gilda *does* return—to them both.

·

One of the problems created by some young directors in approaching this particular piece is to emphasize what they see as a hidden "gay agenda." (If only darling Noël could have written it the way he *wanted* to write it.)

The clear rebuttal to that is in Noël's own words . . . "Suggestion is always more interesting than statement."

At the time of *Design for Living* the Lunts had been acting almost exclusively together for some years and perfected a style of naturalism that other actors appearing with them found difficulty getting used to. Even Noël, who knew them so well but had never acted with them before.

The preparation for the play was not without the occasional *crise* and— successfully over—he made the process the subject of a satirical sketch . . .

"DESIGN FOR REHEARSING"

CAST

NOËL COWARD	SIMON JONES
ALFRED LUNT	BARRIE INGHAM
LYNN FONTANNE	ROSEMARY HARRIS

FIRST PERFORMED IN A CONCERT VERSION AT TEN CHIMNEYS
(THE LUNTS' HOME AT GENESEE DEPOT, WISCONSIN) APRIL 13, 2003

The scene is a bare stage with a few chairs and benches dotted about and a prompt table with a script, cigarettes and chewing gum. *ALFRED* and *LYNN* are discovered sitting upstage opposite each other mumbling indistinctly. *NOËL* enters in hat and coat.

NOËL: Hello, my little dears. I thought I was early.
ALFRED: We hadn't anything else to do so we got here at 10:15.
LYNN: Darling, I had a marvellous idea.
NOËL (*taking off hat and coat*): What?
LYNN: I'm not going to say "strawberry jam" like I did yesterday at all.

NOËL: How are you going to say it?

LYNN: Like this: "Strawberry Jam."

NOËL: Lovely. What scene shall we start with?

LYNN: You see, it's such an obvious change of mood there that it's better not to mark it too much, so if I tack "strawberry jam" onto the rest of it and then say it quite casually like this: "strawberry jam."

NOËL: Ever so much better.

LYNN: I'll do it the old way if you want me to but I did feel . . .

NOËL: Try it anyhow.

LYNN: You see, I think *she* would. You be Alfred for a moment and I'll show you what I mean. (*She grips his wrists.*) "Strawberry jam." There!

NOËL: That's quite, quite magnificent, dear. Now what are we going to start with—you and Alfred in the second act?

ALFRED: Oh, God, I was so *awful* in that scene yesterday—just an old stodgy Scandinavian Pudding.

NOËL: I thought you were so excellent.

ALFRED: No. No. No. I was awful—dreadful. I didn't sleep a wink all night—tossing about and turning I was, and pacing the floor.

LYNN: Do you know what he did to me at 4:30 this morning?

NOËL: I tremble to think.

LYNN: His whole First Act and then we cooked some eggs.

ALFRED: I loathe my face, you know—it's horrible—no bone structure. I'd like to have a face like yours.

LYNN: He's always wanted to have a face like yours.

NOËL: Let's do your scene in the Second Act with Alfred.

LYNN: No, darling. We can do that at home. Let's do one of your scenes.

NOËL: All right. I'd like to say one thing, Alfred, before we begin. You're raving to say you were bad in that scene yesterday—it was perfectly enchanting, all through.

ALFRED (*wailing*): Oh, no. No. No. No. It was terrible.

LYNN: I was a shell, an empty shell, that's all I was, and I had a stom-achache.—You wait until I get my words slick.

ALFRED: Do you know, Noël, this is the most *extraordinary* play! It's got a sort of—you know—an underneath—quality. It's fascinating—when I first read the script I got the most extraordinary feeling of *satisfaction*—like when I read *Karl and Anna*.

LYNN: Never mind that now, darling. We must begin.

NOËL: My entrance?

LYNN: Yes.

ALFRED: By the way, Noël, you did the most superb bit of business with the lid of the cigarette box yesterday. Don't change it—for God's sake don't change it!

NOËL: Well, I wasn't quite sure—I thought it might be a little overdone.

ALFRED: No. No. No. It was enchanting. Larry noticed it—he said it was perfect.

LYNN: Larry does the most marvellous imitation of you. He did it last night in Alfred's hat.

ALFRED: I suppose you know this is the best play you've ever written.

LYNN: Do you realise we've never in our lives had a complete script to work on. We're quite dazed—we really are—dazed.

ALFRED: You remember, *Caprice?*

LYNN: Oh, my God!

NOËL: Come on, my entrance.

LYNN (*kissing him*): Darling, you won't be disheartened about yesterday, will you? It was the first time I'd touched the last Act without my book.

ALFRED: And don't worry about her making her entrance through the fireplace. The old girl has no bump of locality at all. She's walked through fireplaces for years—just the Santa Claus of Fifty-second Street.

NOËL: Let's not start with my entrance. We're very slick there. It's the end of the act that's so ragged.

ALFRED: That's my fault—I'm awful.

NOËL: No, it isn't—it's mine.

LYNN: I'll be all right when I get my words slick. God knows I realise I'm slow, but I've never been as slow as this. We're tired, you know—all those years learning part after part.

NOËL: Alfred's entrance.

ALFRED: All right.

They take their places. LYNN and NOËL laugh hysterically—ALFRED enters.

ALFRED: Hello, Leo.

NOËL: Hello, Otto.

ALFRED: Why did you stop laughing so suddenly?

NOËL: It's funny how lovely it is to see you.

ALFRED: Why funny?

(Pause)

NOËL: Come on, Lynn.

LYNN: Oh, God! let's go back. I shall always forget that line—always—always—always.

They go back.

ALFRED: Hello, Leo.

NOËL: Hello, Otto.

ALFRED: Why did you stop laughing so suddenly?

NOËL: It's funny how lovely it is to see you.

ALFRED: Why funny?

(Pause)

LYNN: It's no use looking at me like that. I can't do anything if you look at me like that.

ALFRED: I wasn't looking at you at all.

LYNN: Oh yes, you were—you had a sneer on your face.

ALFRED: She always picks on me when she forgets her lines.

LYNN: I was word perfect in this scene last night and now Alfred's put me off entirely.

ALFRED: Nonsense.

LYNN: No. No. It's no good. When you're in this mood I can't act with you. It's not fun.

NOËL: Will you both of you shut up and get on with it?

LYNN: We're always like this, darling. You mustn't be disheartened. What's my line?

NOËL: "Where's Ernest?"

LYNN: Where's Ernest?

Etc., Etc., Etc., until:

ALFRED: Oh, did you?

NOËL: Yes I did.

ALFRED: I see.

(Pause)

LYNN and NOËL (*together*): If only you wouldn't look like that.

LYNN: I shall never remember that line—never—never—never—

NOËL: I'll say it, then.

LYNN: No, I'll say it.

NOËL: All right—say it.

LYNN: Give it to me.

ALFRED: I see.

LYNN: If only you wouldn't look like that. You sat down there yesterday, Alfred.

ALFRED: Well, I'm standing up today.

LYNN: That's what's putting me off.

ALFRED: I don't see that it matters very much how I look.

Etc., Etc., Etc., until:

LYNN: . . . It's overbalancing and disrupting everything.

NOËL: "Distorting."

LYNN: It's disrupting my part.

NOËL: I bet it isn't.

LYNN: I'll show you. Where's my bag.

They look for it.

LYNN: Here. (*She produces part.*)

NOËL (*finding place*): There you are—"distorting."

LYNN: Funny, I could have sworn it was disrupting.

NOËL: Never mind.

ALFRED: I *knew* it was distorting.

LYNN: Why didn't you say so?

ALFRED: Because you've already snapped my head off once this morning.

LYNN: It's silly to say things like that just because you're nervous about going to the dentist at four-thirty.

ALFRED: It's nothing to do with the dentist.

LYNN: Oh, yes it is. (*To* NOËL) It upsets him, you know.

ALFRED: I think you must be sickening for something. You haven't behaved like this since *Strange Interlude.*

LYNN: Now, Alfred.

ALFRED: So disagreeable and snappy.

NOËL (*shouting them down*): Listen, both of you—listen—

LYNN: What?

NOËL: I shall never be able to play this part—

ALFRED: Don't be so silly.

LYNN: It's our fault—we're worrying him.

NOËL: No. It's nothing to do with you—it's me—I'm wrong—I haven't got the feel of it—when I watch you—you're so meticulous, so superb it takes the ground from under my feet.

ALFRED and LYNN: No. No. No.

NOËL: Yes. Yes. Let's get somebody else and I'll just direct. Honestly— I'm so wretched—I shall never—

ALFRED: You're wonderful. You're going to be better than you've *ever been in your life.*

LYNN: You're so fluid and assured—you're an actor.

NOËL: No. No. No.

ALFRED: Yes. Yes. Yes. I'm the one who's going to let the play down.

NOËL: No. No. No.

LYNN: No. No. No.

ALFRED: Yes. Yes. Yes. I'm awful.

LYNN: No, darling, no. It's me not knowing my lines.

NOËL: What does it matter about the lines?

ALFRED: Let's go back and start all over again.

LYNN: Yes. From the very beginning.

NOËL: Don't you think we'd better start from my entrance.

LYNN: Yes, darling—your entrance.

ALFRED: It's my entrance that it gets so ragged.

NOËL: All right.

ALFRED: Hello, Leo.

NOËL: Hello, Otto.

ALFRED: Why did you stop laughing so suddenly?

NOËL: It's funny how lovely it is to see you.

ALFRED: Why funny?

(Pause)

ALFRED. Come on, Lynn.

LYNN (*absently*): Where's Ernest?—I was wrong about that reading in the Second Act—it ought to be like this: Listen—"Strawberry *jam*"!

CURTAIN.

•

Nineteen thirty-six brought a letter that surprised even the imperturbable Mr. Coward.

It was from Greta Garbo, proposing marriage. Of course, it *was* Leap Year . . .

And it's Tuesday.

Dear Little Coward,

Received your very loved, small and tiny letter. Dear person, it almost makes me wish the newspapers in this country was right. I am so dreadfully fond of you, that I wish I could forget you. Can't think of anything more terrific than to fall in love with you. Eternally occupied as you are and in need of absolutely no one and looking forward to splendid loneliness completely immune to any female charm!!! Well, this might be an English lesson. Anyhow, I take the opportunity to ask if you will be my little bride (it's Leap Year, you know). Don't accept, please, I would have to come and get you right away. How you must dislike my writing this way—but—that fluttering, tired and sad heart of mine has been in such a peculiar state since a few weeks ago, but I don't suppose I know you well enough to go into that too much.

I have a very humbling wish that you would write a story for me (us), if you ever have time from the theatre. I can't beg you any harder, as you will do as fits you anyhow—naturally. Besides that I would like, horribly I think, to go on dusty roads with you and tell

you little fairy tales—beautiful ones about solitary figures living in
white castles on top of moonlit mountains (permanent moonlight).
And as finish I must tell you that what I really would like to tell you
I haven't told—Darling, you are so flippantly serious.

Noël claimed he was tempted to accept—but he just *knew* Garbo would
demand top billing!

•

Nineteen thirty-six was also Noël and Gertie Revisited. Audiences had
responded to them in *Private Lives,* and Noël felt they would like them
even more in a variety of roles.

Tonight at 8:30 was a series of ten one-act plays in which he and Gertie
would play all the leading roles. As he described them to his Algonquin
Round Table friend, Aleck Woollcott, "They are all brilliantly written,
exquisitely directed, and I am bewitching in all of them."

In the event, the number was reduced to nine. The tenth—"Star Cham-
ber"—played only one matinée and was dropped. After a provincial tour
the show opened at London's Phoenix Theatre on January 13, 1936—
a lucky venue for them, since they had opened it in 1930 with *Private
Lives.* It played for 157 performances. At the end of the year they would
take it to Broadway, where it played at the National Theatre from November 24 for 118 performances.

TONIGHT AT 8:30 (1936)

"FUMED OAK"

CAST

HENRY GOW	NOËL COWARD
DORIS (HIS WIFE)	GERTRUDE LAWRENCE
ELSIE (HIS DAUGHTER)	MOYA NUGENT
MRS. ROCKETT (MOTHER-IN-LAW)	ALISON LEGGATT

DIRECTED BY WILLARD STOKER

It never ceased to irritate Noël that the general perception was that he
could only write about duchesses, gilded youth and the general froth of
Society. And to be fair, the chattering classes did tend to dominate in his
early plays, as they did in so many of his contemporaries'. In later years,
though, he was able to show that—having been born into a lower-middle-
class family himself—he could understand "ordinary" people and speak for

The worm turns. Henry Gow (Noël) tells his daughter, Elsie (Moya Nugent),
and his wife, Doris (Gertrude Lawrence), that he is leaving them to start
a new life on his own. "Good-bye, one and all. Nice to have known you!"
("Fumed Oak," from *Tonight at 8:30*, 1936)

them, as he did in parts of *Cavalcade* (1931), *This Happy Breed* (1939) and
In Which We Serve (1942).

But perhaps the most inspiring of his proletarian principals was Henry
Gow in "Fumed Oak"—the part in the sequence that Noël claimed he
most enjoyed playing.

Henry lives a life of quiet desperation in a South London house, "indis-
tinguishable from several thousand others," with his shrewish wife, Doris;
his cantankerous mother-in-law, Mrs. Rockett; and his adenoidal daughter, Elsie. As we meet them all in the first scene it is obvious that he is hen-
pecked by all of them. Despite their incessant nagging, he says not a word.

But in the *second* scene . . . the worm turns . . .

[Note: I have eliminated the interjections from the three women to give
Henry his monologue.]

HENRY (*to* DORIS): Fifteen, no sixteen years ago tonight, Dorrie, you and
    me had a little rough and tumble in your Aunt Daisy's house in Stans-
    field Road, do you remember?

    We had the house to ourselves, it being a Sunday, your Aunt had
    popped over to the Golden Calf with Mr. Simmonds, the lodger, which,
    as the writers say, was her wont. You'd been after me for a long while,
    Dorrie.

I didn't know it then, but I realized it soon after, you had to have a husband, what with one sister married and the other engaged, both of them younger than you, you had to have a husband, and quick, so you fixed on me. You were pretty enough and I fell for it hook, line and sinker. Then a couple of months later you'd told me you'd clicked. You cried a hell of a lot, I remember, said the disgrace would kill your mother if she ever found out. I didn't know then that it'd take a sight more than that to kill that leathery old mare.

(*To Grandma*) I expect you were in on the whole business, in a refined way of course. You knew what was going on all right, you knew that Dorrie was no more in the family way than I was, but we got married; you both saw to that, and I chucked up all the plans I had for getting on. Perhaps being a steward on a ship and seeing a bit of the world. Oh yes, all that had to go, and we settled down in rooms and I went into Ferguson's Hosiery.

I was the innocent one, not you. I found out you'd cheated me a long, long time ago, and when I found out, realized it for certain, I started cheating on you. Prepare yourself, Dorrie, my girl, you're going to be really upset this time. I've been saving! Every week for over ten years I've been earning a little bit more than you thought I was. I've managed, by hook and by crook, to put by five hundred and seventy-two pounds—d'you hear me? *Five hundred and seventy-two pounds!*

I haven't got it on me, it's in the bank. And it's not for you, it's for me—all but fifty pounds of it, that much is for you, just fifty pounds, the last you'll ever get from me—I've done what I think's fair and what I think's fair is a damn sight more than you deserve. I've transferred the freehold of this house into your name, so you'll always have a roof over your head—you can take in lodgers at a pinch, though God help the poor bastards if you do!

I'm going away. I've got my ticket here in my pocket, and my passport. My passport photo's a fair scream. I wish I could show it to you, but I don't want you to see the nice new name I've got.

Where am I going? Wouldn't you like to know? Maybe Africa, maybe China, maybe Australia. There are lots of places in the world you know nothing about, Dorrie. You've often laughed at me for reading books, but I found out a hell of a lot from books. There are islands in the South Seas for instance with cocoa palms and turtles and sunshine all the year round, you can live there for practically nothing, then there's Australia or New Zealand. With a little bit of capital I might start in a small way sheep-farming. Think of it, miles and miles of open country stretching as far as the eye can see, good fresh air, that might be very nice, might suit me beautifully. Then there's South America. There are coffee plantations there and sugar plantations and banana plantations. If

I go to South America I'll send you a whole crate. 'Ave a banana, Dorrie! 'Ave a banana!

Then there's the sea. Not the sea we know at Worthing with the tide going in and out regular and the band playing on the pier. The *real* sea's what I mean. The sea that Joseph Conrad wrote about, and Rudyard Kipling and lots of other people, too, a sea with whacking great waves and water spouts and typhoons and flying-fish and phosphorus making the foam look as it was lit up. Those people knew a thing or two I can tell you. They knew what life could be like if you give it a chance. They knew there was a bit more to it than refinement and fumed oak and lace curtains and getting old and miserable with nothing to show for it. I'm getting on a bit now, but my health's not too bad, taken all round. There's still time for me to see a little bit of real life before I conk out. I'm still fit enough to do a job of work, real work, mind you, not bowing and scraping and wearing meself out showing fussy old cows the way to the lace and chinaware and the bargain basement.

And don't start weeping and wailing either, that won't cut any ice with me. I know what you're like, I know you through and through. You're frightened now, scared out of your wits, but give you half a chance and you'd be worse than ever you were. You're a bad lot, Dorrie, not what the world would call a bad lot, but what *I* call a bad lot. Mean and cold and respectable.

And don't talk to me about "poor little Elsie." Poor little Elsie, my eye! I think Elsie's awful. I always have ever since she was little. She's never done anything but whine and snivel and try to get something for nothing.

Elsie can go to work in a year or so, in the meantime, you can go to work yourself, you're quite a young woman still and strong as an ox.

I'm taking my last look at you, Dorrie. I shall never see you again as long as I live.

And look what I'm looking at!

Three generations, Grandmother, Mother and Kid. Made of the same bones and sinews and muscles and glands, millions of you, millions just like you. You're past it now, Mother, you're past the thick of the fray, you're nothing but a music-hall joke, a mother-in-law with a bit of money put by. Dorrie, the next few years will show whether you've got guts or not. Maybe what I'm doing to you will save your immortal soul in the long run, that'd be a bit of all right, wouldn't it? I doubt it, though, your immortal soul's too measly.

You're a natural bully and a cheat, and I'm sick of the sight of you; I should also like to take this opportunity of saying that I hate that bloody awful slave bangle and I always have. As for you, Elsie, you've got a chance, it's a slim one, I grant you, but still it's a chance. If you learn to work and be independent and, when the time comes, give what you have to give freely and without demanding lifelong payment for it, there's just a bit of hope that you'll turn into a decent human being. At all events, if you'll take one parting piece of advice from your cruel, ungrateful father, you'll spend the first money you ever earn on having your adenoids out.

Good-bye, one and all. Nice to have known you!

•

Tonight at 8:30 fascinates by the sheer range of Noël's writing and, in the original production, the sheer versatility of Noël&Gertie's acting. As a result, it's easy to overlook the fact that one of the nine plays that make up the repertory is the most technically ambitious piece of writing he ever attempted.

"Shadow Play"—apart from being a love story—deals with the nature of time and memory, a subject that was beginning to interest a number of writers and philosophers in the mid-'30s. J. B. Priestley was to deal with it in a number of his plays, but most of them, such as *Time and the Conways* and *I Have Been Here Before,* came later.

Noël's touch was lighter but still unnerving, as he mingles what is, what was and what might have been . . .

"SHADOW PLAY"

PRODUCED IN LONDON AT THE PHOENIX THEATRE
ON JANUARY 13, 1936, WITH THE FOLLOWING CAST:

VICTORIA GAYFORTH	MISS GERTRUDE LAWRENCE
SIMON GAYFORTH	MR. NOËL COWARD
MARTHA CUNNINGHAM	MISS EVERLEY GREGG
GEORGE CUNNINGHAM	MR. ALAN WEBB
LENA	MISS MOYA NUGENT
SIBYL HESTON	MISS ALISON LEGGATT
MICHAEL DOYLE	MR. EDWARD UNDERDOWN
A YOUNG MAN	MR. ANTHONY PELISSIER
HODGE (DRESSER)	MR. KENNETH CARTEN

Time: The Present.

The scene is a well-furnished, rather luxurious bedroom in the GAY-FORTHS' house in Mayfair. There is a bed on the right with a table by the side of it on which are various bottles, books and a telephone.

Below the bed there is a door which leads to the bathroom. On the left there is a door leading to the passage and the rest of the house. Above this is a dressing table. At the foot of the bed there is a small sofa.

When the curtain rises LENA, VICTORIA's maid, is bustling about the room. It is about midnight and she is laying out a dressing gown or negligee on the bed and generally arranging the room for the night.

VICTORIA and MARTHA come in from the left. VICTORIA is about thirty; beautifully gowned. Her manner is bored and irritable. MARTHA is slightly older, also well dressed but more tranquil.

VICKY: It couldn't matter less whether I go to Alice's or not—in fact it would be infinitely more comfortable for everybody concerned if I didn't.

MARTHA: What nonsense!

VICKY: Alice's parties are always dreary, and I don't feel in the mood even for a good party tonight.

MARTHA: What's the matter?

VICKY: I've told you—I've got a headache.

MARTHA: I think you're unwise.

VICKY: What do you mean, darling?

MARTHA: You know perfectly well what I mean.

VICKY (sitting down at the dressing table): Of course I do, but I'm getting tired of everybody being subtle and hiding behind the furniture—I know that Simon will go without me and I know that Sibyl will be there and I know that if I don't go he will leave with her and if I do go he will leave with me and wish he was leaving with her. I also know that I'm bored stiff with the whole situation—let it rip—

MARTHA: Line of least resistance.

VICKY: Exactly—I have a headache—I feel thoroughly disagreeable—all I want is sleep—no more resisting—just sleep—Lena—give me three Amytal—

LENA: Three, madame?

VICKY: Yes, three—and you can go to bed.

LENA: Yes, madame.

MARTHA: Is the extra tablet a gesture of defiance?

VICKY: Don't be tiresome, Martha.

LENA brings her three tablets from a bottle by the bed and a glass of water.

MARTHA: Do you take those things every night?

VICKY (swallowing the tablets): No, darling, I don't. And even if I did it wouldn't matter a bit—they're perfectly harmless.

LENA: Are you sure that's all, madame?
VICKY: Yes, thank you, Lena—good night.
LENA: Good night, madame.

She goes out.

MARTHA: I don't like seeing people unhappy.
VICKY: I'm not in the least unhappy—just tired.
MARTHA: How much do you mind?
VICKY: Mind what?

She takes the dressing gown off the bed and goes into the bathroom, leaving the door open.

MARTHA (*firmly*): About Simon and Sibyl.
VICKY: Heartbroken, dear. (*She laughs.*) You mustn't be deceived by my gay frivolity, it's really only masking agony and defeat and despair—
MARTHA (*helping herself to a cigarette*): You're extremely irritating.
VICKY: That's what you wanted, isn't it?
MARTHA: You needn't be suspicious of me, you know—I have no axe to grind—I merely wanted to help—
VICKY: You're a noble, understanding old friend, darling, that's what you are, and I must say I should like to crack you over the head with a bottle.
MARTHA: Thank you, dear.

The telephone rings.

VICKY: Answer that, will you?—it's probably Michael—I'll be out in a minute—
MARTHA: All right. (*She goes to the telephone.*) Hello—No, it's Martha—She's in the bathroom, she'll be out in a minute—No, she's not—We've been to a play and it was so good that it gave her a headache—Hold on, here she is—

VICKY comes in in a dressing gown, flings herself on to the bed and takes the telephone.

VICKY: Hello, Michael—No, I'm not—Yes, I've doped myself to the eyes and I'm about to go off into a coma—Of course you can't, don't be so idiotic—What are you in such a state about?—I thought we'd settled all that—It's no use dropping your voice like that—Martha can hear perfectly well, she's got ears like a hawk—

MARTHA: Perhaps you'd like me to go?

VICKY (*to* MARTHA): Be quiet, darling—(*At telephone.*)—I'm tired, Michael, and I've got a headache and so will you kindly shut up—Yes, all right—tomorrow—Good God, no. I shall be sound asleep—Go away, Michael, I can't bear any more—(*She hangs up.*) It's lovely being loved, isn't it?

She rolls over on the bed face downwards.

MARTHA: You'd better get into bed—

VICKY: Perhaps you'd like to fill a hot-water bottle and take my temperature?

MARTHA (*patiently*): Have you got a book to read?

VICKY: Yes, but it's unreadable.

MARTHA: Do get into bed.

VICKY: Go to hell, darling, and don't fuss—

MARTHA (*seriously*): I really wish I could do something—

VICKY (*violently*): Stop it, I tell you—I don't want your sympathy—I don't want anybody's sympathy—whatever happens, happens—let it—what does it matter—

MARTHA: Very well. (*She turns to go.*)

VICKY (*jumping off the bed and coming to her*): I'm sorry—I know I'm beastly, but you see it's no use discussing things—the Amytal will begin to work soon and I shall have a nice long sleep and feel much better in the morning—It was the play that upset me, I think—you were quite right—everybody seemed to be having such a good time, didn't they?—it's a bit tantalizing to see everybody having quite such a good time—it would be so much easier, wouldn't it, if we had music when things go wrong—music and a little dancing and the certainty of "Happy ever after"—I hope you didn't miss the ironic twist at the end when they were married—crashing chords and complete tidiness—very convenient—Go away, darling—go and collect George and Simon and go on to Alice's—I shall go to sleep in a minute—really I will—

MARTHA: All right—I'll telephone you in the morning—

She kisses her and is about to go, when *SIMON* comes into the room. He is wearing a dressing gown over his evening clothes.

VICKY (*surprised*): Simon!

SIMON (*to* MARTHA): George is waiting for you, Martha—he's getting a bit restive.

VICKY: Aren't you going to Alice's?

SIMON: No, I didn't feel that I could face it.

VICKY: Oh, I see.

MARTHA: Do you want me to make excuses for you both, or just not say anything about it?

VICKY: Say that you haven't seen us, and why aren't we there, and is there any truth in the rumour that we're not getting on very well—(*She laughs.*)

SIMON: Don't be silly, Vicky.

VICKY: Say that I've gone to Ostend with Michael and that Simon's shot himself—but only in the leg.

SIMON (*bitterly*): Say that it's definitely true that we're not getting on very well—say that it's due to incompatibility of humour.

MARTHA: I shall say that I don't know you at all—anymore.

She goes out.

VICKY (*calling after her*): Give my love to Sibyl!

SIMON: That was a bit cheap, wasn't it?

VICKY: I thought it was only kind—Sibyl can't live without love—like the woman in the play tonight—don't you remember—? (*She hums.*) "Nobody can live without loving somebody, nobody can love without leaving somebody!"

SIMON: You mustn't forget to sing that to Michael.

VICKY: Are we going to bicker? There's nothing like a nice bicker to round off a jolly evening.

SIMON: I'm getting a little tired of bickering.

VICKY: Let's not then, let's be absolutely divine to each other—let's pretend.

SIMON: I didn't go to Alice's party on purpose—

VICKY: I didn't think it was a sudden attack of amnesia.

SIMON: I want to talk to you.

VICKY: Do you, Simon? What about?

SIMON: Lots of things.

VICKY: Name fifteen.

SIMON: Seriously.

VICKY: There you are, you see—our moods are clashing again—it really is most unfortunate.

SIMON: I failed to notice during the evening that your spirits were so abnormally high.

VICKY: A sudden change for the better, dear, let's make the most of it.

SIMON: There's something I want to say to you—I've been wanting to say it for quite a while.

VICKY: Take the plunge, my darling—we're alone in the swimming bath.

SIMON: Would you consider divorcing me?

VICKY: Oh, Simon!

SIMON: If I made everything easy—

VICKY: Naming Sibyl?

SIMON: Of course not.

VICKY: You mean you'd prefer to be implicated with a professional home-breaker as opposed to an amateur one?

SIMON: I would like, if possible, to keep this conversation impersonal.

VICKY: We might put on fancy dress for it.

SIMON: I'm serious, Vicky.

VICKY: I'm told that all really funny comedians are serious.

SIMON: You haven't answered my question yet.

VICKY: I thought perhaps I hadn't heard it quite clearly.

SIMON: I want you to divorce me.

VICKY: Yes, now I hear—it's a beastly question, isn't it?

SIMON: Not so very beastly if you analyze it—quite sensible really.

VICKY: It oughtn't to be such a shock—but somehow it is—it makes me feel a little sick.

SIMON: I'm sorry.

VICKY: Don't worry about being sorry—feeling a little sick doesn't matter that much.

SIMON: I've thought it all over very carefully.

VICKY: Oh, Simon, have you? Have you really?

SIMON: Of course I have. It's been on my mind for a long time.

VICKY: How sinister that sounds—surely not for a very long time?

SIMON: Long enough.

VICKY: You're cruelly definite.

SIMON: It's less cruel to be definite—in the long run.

VICKY: It's been an awfully short run—really.

SIMON: You haven't answered me yet.

VICKY: An amicable divorce—everything below board?

SIMON: Yes.

VICKY: Where will you go with your temporary light of love? The South of France, or just good old Brighton?

SIMON: I don't think we need discuss that.

VICKY: It's a nasty business, isn't it—a very nasty business.

SIMON: Not necessarily, if it can be arranged discreetly and without fuss.

VICKY: Do you love her so much? Sibyl, I mean.

SIMON: I'd rather not discuss that either.

VICKY: Perhaps you'd prefer to conduct the whole thing by signs—sort of Dumb Crambo.

SIMON: You're unbelievably irritating.

VICKY: When did you first begin to hate me?—When did I first begin to get on your nerves?—What did I say?—What did I do?—Was it a dress I wore—the way I laughed at somebody's joke?—Was I suddenly gay when you were sad?—Was I insensitive?—Was I dull? When did it start—tell me if you can remember—please tell me.

SIMON: Don't be so foolish.

VICKY: I won't be irritating anymore, Simon—I'll try to be sensible—really I will—but I must know why—why things change—I wish to God I hadn't taken those sleeping tablets—my head's going round—I would so love to be clear, just at this moment, but nothing's clear at all.

SIMON: I didn't know you'd taken anything.

VICKY: Don't be alarmed—I'm not becoming a drug fiend—it's an amiable, gentle prescription, just to make me sleep when I have a headache, or when I'm overtired or unhappy—

SIMON: There's the overture—we shall be late.

VICKY: What did you say?

SIMON: —You really ought not to get into the habit of taking things to make you sleep—however harmless they are—

VICKY: We've only been married five years—it seems longer at moments—then it seems no time at all—

The music begins, and, after a few chords, stops again.

SIMON: There it is again—listen.

VICKY: If you really love Sibyl, deeply and truly, it's different, but I have an awful feeling that you don't—anyhow, not enough—

SIMON: We will wander on together—
Through the sunny summer weather—
To our cosy little château
Like a pastoral by Watteau.

TOGETHER: To our cosy little château on the Rhine.

SIMON: —It isn't that I don't love you—I always shall love you—but this is something else—I don't know what started it, but I do know that it's terribly strong—and then there's Michael—I've been awfully angry about Michael—

VICKY: That's idiotic—Michael doesn't mean a thing to me—you know perfectly well he doesn't—

The music begins again, this time more loudly.

SIMON: There it is again—do hurry. (*He dances a few steps.*)

VICKY (*calling*): Lena—Lena—hurry up—I was miserable anyhow tonight—all the time we were in the theatre—everybody was having such a good time—and then they were married in the end—that was funny, wasn't it?—about them being married in the end . . .

SIMON: —It isn't that I want to make you unhappy, but you must admit we haven't been hitting it off particularly well during the last year—if we're not comfortable together surely it would be much more sensible to separate—

The scene darkens. The side flats move off and upstage away from the center flat.

VICKY: I feel so sad inside about it—I wish I could make you understand—it was so lovely in the beginning—
SIMON: Things never stay the same—you can't expect what was lovely then to be lovely now—
VICKY (*almost crying*): Why not—why not?—Then we were happy—
SIMON: But, darling, you must see—

"THEN"

SIMON: Here in the light of this unkind familiar now
    Every gesture is clear and cold for us,
    Even yesterday's growing old for us,
        Everything changed somehow.
        If some forgotten lover's vow
    Could wake a memory in my heart again,
    Perhaps the joys that we knew would start again.
        Can't we reclaim an hour or so
        The past is not so long ago.
VICKY: Then, love was complete for us
    Then, the days were sweet for us
    Life rose to its feet for us
        And stepped aside
        Before our pride.
    Then, we knew the best of it
    Then, our hearts stood the test of it.
    Now, the magic has flown
    We face the unknown
    Apart and alone.

SIMON: Hodge—where's Hodge?—I must change—quick—we're going back.

The orchestra swells. *FLORRIE (LENA)* comes hurrying in with an evening gown over her arm and a pair of shoes, a mirror, a powder puff, etc., in her hands. *VICKY* sinks onto the bed.

SIMON: You can't sit there—we're going back—

FLORRIE: Here, dear—here's a chair.

VICKY: I'm not sure that I want to—I'm not at all sure—maybe it won't be as lovely as I think it was—

SIMON: Don't be such a fool—grab it while you can—grab every scrap of happiness while you can—Hodge—come on—

HODGE, a dresser, comes in with a dinner jacket. *SIMON* takes off his dressing gown and puts on the dinner jacket. *VICKY* is changing on the opposite side of the stage. Meanwhile the whole scene is changing. The lights in the foreground fade except for the two spotlights on *SIMON* and *VICKY.*

VICKY (*breathlessly*): Play—go on playing—we must have music—

SIMON comes down to the footlights and begins to sing to the conductor. He sings

"PLAY, ORCHESTRA, PLAY"

SIMON: Listen to the strain it plays once more for us,
    There it is again, the past in store for us.
        Wake in memory some forgotten song
        To break the rhythm—driving us along
    And make harmony again a last encore for us.
        Play, orchestra, play
        Play something light and sweet and gay
           For we must have music
           We must have music
        To drive our fears away.
    While our illusions swiftly fade for us,
        Let's have an orchestra score.
    In the confusions the years have made for us
        Serenade for us, just once more.
    Life needn't be grey,
    Although it's changing day by day,
        Though a few old dreams may decay,
        Play, orchestra, play.

VICKY joins him and they finish it together. Meanwhile all the lights fade entirely except for two pin-spots on the two of them. The spot on *SIMON* goes out and *VICKY* is left singing almost hysterically "We Must

Have Music." The orchestra rises to a crescendo and there is a complete blackout.

To measured music and in a pool of light, SIBYL HESTON appears. She lights a cigarette and glances at her wristwatch. SIMON appears from the opposite side of the stage. He stands a little apart from her. The music stops.

SIBYL: I'm waiting—I'm waiting—why don't you tell her?

SIMON: It will hurt her, you know.

SIBYL: She can weep on Michael's shoulder—it's a very attractive shoulder.

SIMON: I don't want to hurt her.

SIBYL: She'll have to know sooner or later. Nobody can live without loving somebody, nobody can love without leaving somebody.

SIMON: I saw you in the theatre tonight—you looked marvellous.

SIBYL: Sweet Simon.

SIMON: Very cool and green and wise.

SIBYL: Not wise—oh, my dear, not wise at all. I happen to love you.

SIMON: Is that so unwise?

SIBYL: Let's say—indefinite!

SIMON: It's less cruel to be indefinite in the long run.

SIBYL: Tell her the truth—you must tell her the truth.

SIMON: I have been awfully angry about Michael.

SIBYL: Why be angry, darling? It's such waste of energy.

SIMON: I don't like Vicky making a fool of herself.

SIBYL: I don't like Vicky making a fool of you.

SIMON: I didn't know she took things to make her sleep.

SIBYL: You must tell her the truth—sleep or no sleep.

The music starts again. MICHAEL walks on. He passes SIBYL and SIMON, stops, lights a cigarette and glances at his wristwatch. The music stops.

MICHAEL: I'm waiting—I'm waiting—why don't you tell her?

SIMON: I don't want to hurt her.

MICHAEL: Give her my love.

SIMON: That was a bit cheap, wasn't it?

SIBYL (*laughing*): When did she first begin to get on your nerves, Simon? What started it? Was it a dress she wore? Was it the way she laughed at somebody's joke? Was she suddenly gay when you were sad? Was she insensitive? Was she dull?

MICHAEL: Was she dull?

SIBYL: Was she dull?

SIMON: It was so lovely in the beginning.

SIBYL: Things never stay the same—you can't expect what was lovely then to be lovely now.

SIMON: We're going back all the same—it's our only chance—

SIBYL: Was she dull?

MICHAEL: Was she dull?

SIMON: Shut up—shut up both of you—we're going back—

He begins to sing and as he sings the lights fade on SIBYL and MICHAEL.

> Life needn't be grey
> Though it is changing day by day.
> Though a few old dreams may decay
> Play, orchestra—play, orchestra—play, orchestra—
> Play—

Blackout.

The lights come up on a moonlit garden. There is a stone seat on the left of the stage. VICKY and a YOUNG MAN are sitting on it.

VICKY: It's nice and cool in the garden.

YOUNG MAN: It's nice and cool in the garden.

VICKY: Country house dances can be lovely when the weather's good, can't they?

YOUNG MAN: Rather—rather—yes, of course—rather.

VICKY: I'm waiting for something.

YOUNG MAN: Country house dances can be lovely when the weather's good, can't they?

VICKY: This is where it all began.

YOUNG MAN: It's nice and cool in the garden.

VICKY: Please hurry, my darling, I can't wait to see you for the first time.

YOUNG MAN: Do you know this part of the country?

VICKY: Intimately. I'm staying here with my aunt, you know.

YOUNG MAN: Does she ride to hounds?

VICKY: Incessantly.

YOUNG MAN: That's ripping, isn't it?—I mean it really is ripping.

VICKY: Yes. She's a big woman and she kills little foxes—she's kind *au fond,* but she dearly loves killing little foxes.

YOUNG MAN: We're getting on awfully well—it's awfully nice out here—I think you're awfully pretty.

VICKY: This is waste of time—he should be here by now—walking through the trees—coming towards me.

YOUNG MAN: I think you're an absolute fizzer.

VICKY: Yes, I remember you saying that—it made me want to giggle—but I controlled myself beautifully.

YOUNG MAN: I think you know my sister—she's in pink.

VICKY: I remember her clearly—a beastly girl.

YOUNG MAN: In pink.

VICKY (*suddenly*): In pink—in pink—
> Your sister's dressed in pink
> It wasn't very wise I think
> To choose that unbecoming shade
> Of pink—

YOUNG MAN: I'm so glad you like her—you must come and stay with us—my mother's an absolute fizzer—you'd love her.

VICKY: God forbid!

YOUNG MAN: That's absolutely ripping of you.

VICKY: Now—now—at last—you're walking through the trees—hurry—

SIMON comes through the trees. He is smoking a cigarette.

VICKY: I thought you'd missed your entrance.

SIMON: Are you engaged for this dance?

VICKY: I was, but I'll cut it if you'll promise to love me always and never let anything or anybody spoil it—never—

SIMON: But of course—that's understood.

YOUNG MAN: Will you excuse me—I have to dance with Lady Dukes.

VICKY: Certainly.

YOUNG MAN: Good hunting.

VICKY: Thank you so much—it's been so boring.

YOUNG MAN: Not at all—later perhaps.

He goes.

SIMON: Well—here we are.

VICKY: The first time—we knew at once, didn't we? Don't you remember how we discussed it afterwards?

SIMON: I saw you in the ballroom—I wondered who you were.

VICKY: My name's Victoria—Victoria Marden.

SIMON: Mine's Simon Gayforth.

VICKY: How do you do?

SIMON: Quite well, thank you.

VICKY: I suppose you came down from London for the dance?

SIMON: Yes, I'm staying with the Bursbys—

VICKY: What do you do?

SIMON: I'm in a bank.

VICKY: High up in the bank? Or just sitting in a cage totting up things?

SIMON: Oh, quite high up really—it's a very good bank.

VICKY: I'm so glad.

SIMON: How lovely you are.

VICKY: No, no, that came later—you've skipped some.

SIMON: Sorry.

VICKY: You're nice and thin—your eyes are funny—you move easily—I'm afraid you're terribly attractive—

SIMON: You never said that.

VICKY: No, but I thought it.

SIMON: Stick to the script.

VICKY: Small talk—a lot of small talk with quite different thoughts going on behind it—this garden's really beautiful—are you good at gardens?—

SIMON: No, but I'm persevering—I'm all right on the more straightforward blooms—you know—snapdragons, sweet william, cornflowers and tobacco plant—and I can tell a Dorothy Perkins a mile off.

VICKY: That hedge over there is called *Cupressus macrocapa.*

SIMON: Do you swear it?

VICKY: It grows terrifically quickly but they do say that it goes a bit thin underneath in about twenty years—

SIMON: How beastly of them to say that—it's slander.

VICKY: Did you know about valerian smelling of cats?

SIMON: You're showing off again.

VICKY: It's true.

SIMON: I can go one better than that—lotuses smell of pineapple.

VICKY (*sadly*): Everything smells of something else—it's dreadfully confusing—

SIMON: Never mind, darling—I love you desperately—I knew it the first second I saw you—

VICKY: You're skipping again.

They sing a light duet, "You Were There," after which they dance.

"YOU WERE THERE"

SIMON: Was it in the real world or was it in a dream?
Was it just a note from some eternal theme?

Was it accidental or accurately planned?
　　How could I hesitate
　　Knowing that my fate
Led me by the hand?

REFRAIN

　　You were there
I saw you and my heart stopped beating
　　You were there
And in that first enchanted meeting
　　Life changed its tune, the stars, the moon came near to me.
Dreams that I dreamed, like magic seemed to be clear to me, dear
to me.
　　You were there.
Your eyes looked into mine and faltered.
　　Everywhere
The colour of the whole world altered.
　　False became true
　　My universe tumbled in two
The earth became heaven, for you were there.

VICKY: How can we explain it—the spark, and then the fire?
　　How add up the total of our hearts' desire?
　　Maybe some magician, a thousand years ago—
　　Wove us a subtle spell—so that we could tell—so that
　　　we could know—
　　You were there—(etc.)

During the dance the lights fade on the scene and they finish in each
other's arms in a spotlight. The spotlight fades and in the darkness a voice
is heard singing "Then they knew the best of it—then their hearts stood
the test of it," etc.
　　A spotlight picks up LENA—singing, holding the tablets and a glass of
water. After song fade again.

　　　　Then love was complete for them
　　　　Then the days were sweet for them
　　　　Life rose to its feet for them
　　　　And stepped aside
　　　　Before their pride.
　　　　Then they knew the best of it

Then their hearts stood the test of it.
Now the magic has flown
They face the unknown
Apart and alone.

The lights go up again on the interior of a limousine. MARTHA and
GEORGE CUNNINGHAM are sitting in it.

GEORGE: On the whole this has been one of the most uncomfortable
evenings I've ever spent.

MARTHA: There, there, dear, I know, but for heaven's sake don't go on
about it.

GEORGE (*petulantly*): Why, if they had to take us to dinner and a play,
should they have chosen that particular dinner and that particular play?

MARTHA: What was wrong with the dinner?

GEORGE: Gastronomically speaking it was excellent, but the atmosphere
reeked with conjugal infelicity—when people are at loggerheads they
should refrain from entertaining—it's bad for the digestive tract.

MARTHA: For an elderly barrister you're unduly sensitive.

GEORGE: I expected the grouse to sit up on its plate and offer me a brief.

MARTHA: Never mind, when we get to Alice's you'll be able to have a nice
drink and talk to some lovely young things and feel much better.

GEORGE: And why that play? Sentimental twaddle.

MARTHA: The music was lovely.

GEORGE: That's no good to me. You know perfectly well I can't distinguish "Abide With Me" from "God Save the King."

MARTHA: Concentrate on "God Save the King."

GEORGE: I couldn't even go to sleep with those idiotic people loving each
other for ever all over the stage.

MARTHA: Well we'll go to a nice soothing gangster picture tomorrow
night and you can watch people killing each other all over the screen.

GEORGE: What's wrong with them, anyway?

MARTHA: Who, Simon and Vicky?

GEORGE: Yes.

MARTHA: They're unhappy.

GEORGE: Well, they oughtn't to be—they've got everything they want.

MARTHA: Sibyl Heston's got hold of Simon and Vicky's trying to pretend
that she doesn't mind a bit and everything's in a dreary muddle—
women like Sibyl Heston ought to be shot.

GEORGE: Sometimes they are.

MARTHA: Not often enough.

GEORGE: I suppose Vicky's got a young man hanging around, hasn't she?

MARTHA: No, not really—she's been encouraging Michael Doyle a bit but it doesn't mean anything—it's just part of the pretending.

GEORGE: Damn fools—they're all damn fools—

VICKY runs on from the side of the stage. She is picked up by a blue spotlight.

VICKY: Go away, you're spoiling it all—I know what you're saying— I know what everybody's saying—

MARTHA: I was only trying to help.

VICKY: I know—I know—you're very kind—but it isn't any use—

GEORGE: People were so much more sensible twenty years ago—take my sister, for instance—look how brilliantly she managed her life   you ought to have known my sister—

VICKY: In pink.

GEORGE: In brilliant pink.

VICKY (*singing*): In pink—in pink
>Your sister's dressed in pink,
>It wasn't very wise I think
>To choose that unbecoming shade
>Of pink—!

SIMON enters and is picked up in a blue spot.

SIMON: This compartment is reserved—we're going back.

GEORGE: I'm most awfully sorry.

VICKY: There are probably some empty ones farther along the train.

MARTHA: But of course—we quite understand—George, help me with my dressing case—

SIMON: Allow me—

He helps them to remove imaginary luggage from the rack.

GEORGE: I suppose you don't happen to know what time we reach Milan?

SIMON: I know we arrive in Venice at about six-thirty—I think there's about four hours' difference.

VICKY: It's really charming of you to be so considerate—you see we are on our honeymoon.

MARTHA: Grab every scrap of happiness while you can.

GEORGE: We shall meet later.

SIMON: I hope so.

MARTHA and *GEORGE* step out of the car and walk off. *SIMON* and *VICKY* climb in. The spotlights follow them into the cab.

SIMON: Well, here we are.

VICKY: My name's Victoria.

SIMON: Victoria what?

VICKY: Victoria Gayforth.

SIMON: What a silly name.

VICKY: I adore it.

SIMON: That's because you're sentimental.

VICKY: Fiercely sentimental—overromantic too.

SIMON: Dearest darling.

VICKY: The wedding went off beautifully, didn't it?

SIMON: Brief, to the point, and not unduly musical.

VICKY: Didn't Mother look nice?

SIMON: Not particularly.

VICKY: Oh, Simon!

SIMON: It was her hat, I think—it looked as though it were in a hurry and couldn't stay very long.

VICKY: Was that man who slapped you on the back your uncle?

SIMON: Yes, dear—that was my uncle.

VICKY: I'm so sorry.

SIMON: He ran away to sea, you know, when he was very young, and then, unfortunately, he ran back again.

VICKY: Your sister looked charming.

SIMON: In pink.

VICKY: In pink—in pink—

SIMON: Stop it—stop it—you'll wake yourself up.

VICKY: It was that rhyme in the play tonight—it keeps coming into my mind.

SIMON: Do concentrate—we're on our honeymoon.

VICKY: Happy ever after.

SIMON: That's right.

VICKY: Do you think that those people we turned out of the carriage ever loved each other as much as we do?

SIMON: Nobody ever loved each other as much as we do with the possible exception of Romeo and Juliet, Héloïse and Abélard, Paolo and Francesca, Dante and Beatrice—

VICKY: I wish she hadn't been called Beatrice—it's such a smug name.

SIMON: Antony and Cleopatra, Pelléas and Mélisande—

VICKY: I've always felt that Mélisande was rather a silly girl—so vague.

SIMON: All right—wash out Mélisande.

VICKY (*looking out the window*): Look at all those little houses flashing by—think of all the millions of people living in them—eating and drinking—dressing and undressing—getting up and going to bed—having babies—

SIMON: When I was a young bride I never mentioned such things on my honeymoon.

VICKY: Things never stay the same.

SIMON: It was considered immodest to do anything but weep gently and ask for glasses of water.

VICKY: I'm abandoned, darling—I can't wait to be in your arms—

SIMON: Dear heart—

He takes her in his arms.

VICKY (*struggling*): No no—this isn't right—my clothes are all wrong—I must go—

SIMON: Don't go.

VICKY: I must—this dressing gown's all wrong I tell you—when we arrived in Venice I was wearing a blue tailor-made—and then later we dined—and I was in grey—

SIMON: In grey—in grey
Your dress was soft and grey
It seems a million years away
The ending of that sweet and happy day.

VICKY: Oh darling—

SIMON: Don't go—

VICKY: I must—I must—

She steps out of the carriage and disappears into the darkness.

SIMON left alone, sings a reprise of "You Were There," and the lights fade completely.

When the lights go up *SIMON* and *VICKY* are sitting at a little table with a shaded light on it. They are just finishing dinner.

SIMON: We can sit on the piazza for a little and then we can drift . . .

VICKY: Let's call the gondola right away and cut out the piazza—I'm a big drifting girl.

SIMON: I think the band on the piazza will be awfully disappointed.

VICKY: It's funny, isn't it, to be so frightfully in love that you feel as if you were going mad?

SIMON: Ever so funny.

VICKY: Do you think our front gondolier is nicer than our back one?

SIMON: Not altogether—he has better teeth, of course, but then he's about fifty years younger.

VICKY: Let's come here again in fifty years' time.

SIMON: All right.

VICKY: We can arrange to be carried on to the train—it will be quite simple.

SIMON: It won't be a train, darling—it will be a pointed silver bullet leaving Croydon at four and arriving here at twenty-past three.

VICKY: Oh dear!

SIMON: What's the matter?

VICKY: We haven't quarrelled yet.

SIMON: Never mind.

VICKY: We'll have a nice quarrel when we get back to London, won't we?

SIMON: I shall sulk for the first few days, anyhow—I'm the sulky type, you know.

VICKY: That's why I married you.

SIMON: Oh, darling—I'm going to be terribly serious for a minute—will you bear with me?

VICKY: Of course.

SIMON: There's something I want to say to you—I've been wanting to say it for quite a while—

VICKY (*with panic in her voice*): Oh, Simon, don't—what is it? What is it?

SIMON: I love you.

VICKY (*putting her head down on the table*): You mustn't make people cry on their honeymoons—it's not cricket.

SIMON (*tenderly*): Dearest—everything's cricket if only you have faith.

VICKY: When did you know you loved me—the very first minute, I mean?

SIMON: In the garden—during the dance—I saw you and my heart stopped beating—

VICKY: It was a most enchanted meeting.

SIMON: Life changed its tune—the stars and moon came near to me—

VICKY: Dreams that I'd dreamed, like magic seemed to be clear to me—dear to me—

SIMON: False became true—my universe tumbled in two—the earth became heaven—for you were there—

VICKY: Stop it—stop it—it's that damned musical comedy again—going round and round in my head—listen—before the dream breaks say what you said that night in Venice—say it from your heart as you said it then—say it, please—please—

SIMON: I'm not sure that I can remember—it's a long while ago—

VICKY: Please, Simon—please—

SIMON: It's this, darling—we're here together close as close and it's the beginning—but we're going to be together for a long time—probably all our lives, so we must be careful—I want to reassure you now about later on—about any tricks the future might play on us—I know I love you with all my heart—with every bit of me—it's easy now, because it's summer weather and there isn't a cloud in the sky and we're alone—but there'll be other people presently—we can't live our whole lives on this little island—other people are dangerous—they spoil true love, not consciously because they want to, but because they're themselves—out for all they can get—mischievous—you do see what I mean, don't you—?

VICKY: You mean they might make us want them one day instead of each other.

SIMON: Yes, but only a little—not like this—not all the way round—

VICKY: I can't imagine even that—I'm very single-tracked.

SIMON: Don't look sad—don't even have a flicker of unhappiness not for ages yet, anyway—but whenever you do—if I'm bad or foolish or unkind, or even unfaithful—just remember this, because this is what really matters—this lovely understanding of each other—it may be a jumping off place for many future journeys—but however long the journey one's got to come back some time, and this is the white cliffs of Dover—hang on to the white cliffs of Dover—

VICKY: I'll try—

They hold hands for a moment across the table.

There is a burst of music which dies away on a discord. Then a dance tune starts and keeps up a steady rhythm during the ensuing scene. The light on SIMON and VICKY fades a little. They are sitting quite still gazing at each other. SIBYL HESTON and MICHAEL DOYLE dance on together out of the shadows. They are in a brilliant spotlight.

MICHAEL: We're a bit early, aren't we? They're still on their honeymoon.

SIBYL: Nonsense. The curtain will be lowered between scenes two and three to denote a lapse of four years—

The light on SIMON and VICKY goes out completely.

MICHAEL (over his shoulder): I'm so sorry.

SIBYL: It's impossible to dance here.

MICHAEL: They put so many tables on the floor.

SIBYL: There's no room at all.

MICHAEL: Let's go on to the Florida.

SIBYL: And the Coconut Grove.

MICHAEL: And the Four Hundred.

SIBYL: And the Blue Train.

SIMON and VICKY dance on in another spotlight.

SIMON: There's always the Florida.

VICKY: And the Coconut Grove.

SIMON: And the Four Hundred.
VICKY: And the Blue Train.

The rhythm gets slightly faster. The two couples circle round each other.

SIBYL: The Florida.
SIMON: The Coconut Grove.
MICHAEL: The Four Hundred.
VICKY: The Blue Train.
SIBYL: The Florida.
VICKY: The Coconut Grove.
MICHAEL: The Four Hundred.
SIMON: The Blue Train.

The music gets faster still. They change partners. SIMON dances with SIBYL and MICHAEL with VICKY—then they change back to each other again—then once more—all saying together: "The Florida," "The Coconut Grove," "The Four Hundred," "The Blue Train." MICHAEL and VICKY disappear and SIBYL and SIMON are left dancing round and round together, faster and faster. From the darkness can be heard voices shouting rhythmically: "The Florida," "The Coconut Grove," "The Four Hundred," "The Blue Train," coming to a crescendo and then a blackout.

LENA appears on the right-hand side of the stage with a telephone. MARTHA appears on the opposite side, also with a telephone. Both in spotlights.

MARTHA: Hello—who is it?
LENA: It's Lena, madame.
MARTHA: Oh, Lena—yes—what is it?
LENA: Mr. Gayforth asked me to telephone to you, madame—
MARTHA: Is anything wrong?
LENA: It's Mrs. Gayforth, madame—those sleeping tablets—Mr. Gayforth wants to know if you can leave the party and come at once—
MARTHA: Good heavens! Is she ill?
LENA: Yes, madame—that is—she's not exactly ill but—
MARTHA: Have you sent for a doctor?
LENA: No, madame—Mr. Gayforth didn't want to send for a doctor until he'd seen you.
MARTHA: I'll come at once.
LENA: It was that extra Amytal tablet, madame—I knew she shouldn't have taken it—
MARTHA: I'll be there in a few minutes—in the meantime—give her some strong black coffee—

The lights fade.

In the darkness VICKY's voice is heard.

VICKY: Simon, Simon—where are you?—I'm lonely—I'm frightened—
don't go away from me yet—in spite of what they say there is still time
if only we're careful—

SIMON: There's something I want to say to you—I've been wanting to say
it for quite a while—

VICKY: Don't say it—don't say it yet.

SIMON: I would like if possible to keep this conversation impersonal.

VICKY: I would so love to be clear at this moment. But nothing's clear at
all—

SIMON: I didn't know you had taken anything—

VICKY: It was only to make me sleep—whenever I'm tired or unhappy, oh,
Simon—Simon—come back—the white cliffs of Dover—I'm trying so
hard—I'm trying to hold on—don't leave me—don't leave me—

SIMON: Give her a little more, Lena.

LENA: Yes, sir.

SIMON: You don't think we ought to send for a doctor?

MARTHA: No, she'll be all right.

SIMON: It was awfully sweet of you to come back, Martha—I got in a
panic—you were the only one I could think of—

VICKY: I shall be sick if I have any more of that damned coffee.

SIMON: That's a very good idea—be sick.

VICKY: No, no—I hate being sick—it's mortifying—I'm perfectly all
right now—really I am.

The lights slowly go up on the bedroom.

VICKY is sitting on the edge of the bed. SIMON is sitting by her side with
one arm around her, holding a cup of coffee in his other hand. MARTHA is
kneeling on the floor at her feet. LENA is standing anxiously at the foot of
the bed holding a coffee pot.

SIMON: There, darling—won't you lie down a bit?

VICKY: Don't fuss.

SIMON: You ought to be ashamed of yourself.

VICKY: What are you rolling about on the floor for, Martha? It looks very
silly.

MARTHA (rising): You may well ask.

VICKY: I think I should like a cigarette.

SIMON: Then you will be sick.

VICKY: No, it's passed off.

LENA (handing her a cigarette): Here, madame.

VICKY: Thank you, Lena. Match, please.
SIMON: Here, Martha, take this cup, will you?

He gives MARTHA the coffee and lights VICKY's cigarette.

VICKY: That's lovely. (*She puffs.*)
SIMON: It's all right, Lena—you can go to bed again.
LENA: Are you sure, sir?
SIMON: Yes, thank you, Lena.
LENA: Good night, sir.
SIMON: Good night.

LENA goes out.

VICKY: Now perhaps somebody will explain. What happened to me?
SIMON: You just went mad, that's all—raving.
VICKY (*interested*): Did I froth at the mouth?
SIMON: I don't know—I was too agitated to notice.
MARTHA: I think I'd better go back to Alice's.
VICKY: Alice's! Oh yes, of course. Oh, Simon—I remember now.
SIMON: Don't think of anything—just relax.
MARTHA (*kissing her*): Good night, darling.
VICKY (*absently—her thoughts a long way away*): Good night.
MARTHA: Good night, Simon.
SIMON: Thanks awfully, Martha.

MARTHA goes out.

VICKY: I'm so sorry, Simon—I'm feeling quite tranquil now—let's talk about the divorce in the morning.
SIMON: Divorce? What do you mean?
VICKY: You asked me to divorce you, didn't you?
SIMON: Certainly not.
VICKY: Are you trying to make me believe that that was part of the dream?
SIMON: I don't know what you're talking about.
VICKY: It's sweet of you to lie—but it won't wash.

SIMON sits on the bed again and puts his arms around her.

SIMON: Please forgive me.
VICKY (*sleepily*): We'll talk it all over calmly—tomorrow.
SIMON: All right.
VICKY (*resting her head on his shoulder*): If you really love her all that much I'll try not to be beastly about it—

Victoria Gayforth (Gertrude Lawrence) and Simon Gayforth (Noël)
in "Shadow Play," from *Tonight at 8:30*

SIMON: I don't love anybody that much.

VICKY: What did I do when I went mad? I'm so interested.

SIMON: You talked a lot—I thought it was nonsense at first and then I
realised that it was true—then you began dancing about the room—
then you really did go mad—and I got very frightened and told Lena to
ring up Martha—

VICKY: It was certainly a very strange feeling—

She closes her eyes and the music starts again very softly.

SIMON: It will be all right now—it really will—I promise.

VICKY: The music's beginning again.

Preparing for the Hollywood all-star production of *Tonight at 8:30.*
Basil Rathbone *(left)* and Gladys Cooper *(extreme right),* who appeared in
"The Astonished Heart." (September 1940)

Binnie Barnes and Reginald Gardiner as
"The Red Peppers" (Hollywood, 1940)

The music swells. *SIMON* lifts her gently onto the bed and covers her over with the counterpane. Then he kisses her, disentangles her cigarette from her fingers, tiptoes across the room and switches off the lights, all but a little lamp by the bed, and stretches himself on the sofa at her feet.

The music reaches a crescendo as—

THE CURTAIN FALLS.

There have been innumerable productions of *Tonight at 8:30* over the years—the quality invariably variable, once the originals, Noël&Gertie, no longer played all the leading parts.

But perhaps the most unusual was staged in Hollywood in 1940 in aid of British War Relief. Noël reported to his secretary, Lornie . . .

I didn't see the first bill, which was young Doug [Fairbanks] and Constance Bennett in "We Were Dancing," Basil Rathbone and Gladys Cooper in "The Astonished Heart" and Binnie Barnes and Reginald Gardiner in "Red Peppers." All the reports say that Binnie was marvelous. I saw, however, the second and third bills. Roland Young in "Fumed Oak," who played it like a dim Foreign Office attaché and was awful, "Family Album" with Joan [Fontaine], Claire Trevor, Philip Merivale, etc., and Aubrey Smith as "Burrows"—this was charmingly done and the success of the series, "Hands Across the Sea" with Judith Anderson, Isobel Jeans, Nigel Bruce, Ian Hunter, etc., was a lash-up on account of Zazu Pitts never having been on the stage before and playing "Mrs. Wadhurst." Every laugh she got went to her head and she did more and more clowning until not one word of the play was heard. The third bill was pretty horrible except for Bart [Herbert] Marshall, Rosalind Russell, Una O'Connor and Edmund Gwynn [Gwenn] in "Still Life." "Ways and Means" was played by Brian Aherne and Greer Garson with all the lightness and speed of a performance of *King Lear* given by a church social. But the pearl of the whole evening was "Shadow Play" with Georges Metaxa and a rather aging Jewish actress called Dorothy Stone; this was terribly macabre. Georges, who is now quite square, was completely incomprehensible and sang very loudly indeed. Dorothy Stone danced so much that I was afraid she would have heart failure; unfortunately she didn't.

•

February 1937, and Noël and Gertie are playing *Tonight at 8:30* in New York—three different roles every night, several of them involving singing and dancing as well as acting. By now the effort was taking its toll, particularly on Noël.

So when society hostess Cobina Wright—a *doppelgänger* Elsa Maxwell with money—invited him for a quiet weekend in the Hamptons, he unthinkingly accepted.

He should have been warned by the car ride there, where he was accompanied by Clifton Webb—who was also in a Broadway show—drinking brandy and wearing "earmuffs and a camel's hair beret."

"All in all the journey seemed longer than the one on the Trans-Siberian railway, though without the amusing frontier stations." When they arrived, he found himself in the next room to Webb, who proceeded to snore "in the exact rhythm of the 'Hallelujah Chorus.' "

The next day he awoke to see from his window "a long caravan of Rolls-Royces and Pierce-Arrows—like a funeral cortège for some eminent gangster, except minus the flowers." The "just us" had arrived. What predictably happened over the next several hours he turned into a 1939 story called "What Mad Pursuit?" . . .

Since many of the real-life characters were still alive at the time, Noël was careful not to be too specific, but readers who moved in those circles would have little difficulty in recognizing Cobina Wright in Louise Steinhauser, Clifton Webb in Lester Gaige, Carole Lombard (Carola Binney) and Grace Moore (Irene Marlow) and various others "who shall be nameless."

He later turned the story into a play, *Long Island Sound* (1947).

·

"WHAT MAD PURSUIT?"

1

Evan Lorrimer's celebrity value was unquestionably high. In the course of twenty years he had written no less than eleven novels; a volume of war poems, tinged with whimsical bitterness; one play which had been much praised by the London critics and run nearly two months; a critical survey of the life and times of Madame de Staël entitled *The Life and Times of Madame de Staël;* sundry essays and short stories for the more literary weeklies, and an autobiography. The autobiography had been on the whole the least successful of his works, but he in no way regretted having written it. For years he had been aware that incidents, journeys, and personal experiences had been accumulating in his mind until it had come to a point when he could no longer feel free to pursue his historical researches. He felt himself to be congested, or, to put it more crudely, constipated, and that unless he could get rid of this agglomeration of trivia, his real genius, which was writing graphically of the past in terms of the present, would atrophy. The autobiography, therefore, was a sort of cathartic and as such achieved its object. Hardly had the corrected and revised manuscript been delivered to the publishers before he was at work again, drafting out with renewed energy and clarity of thought his great novel of the Restoration, *A London Lady.* There was no doubt in his mind that if *My Steps Have Faltered,* which was the title of the autobiography, had not been written when it was, *A London Lady* would never have been written at all. The success of *A London Lady* transcended by far everything else he had ever written. It went into several editions within the first few weeks of its publication. It was elected, without one dissentient vote, as the Book Society's choice for the month of February. The most important moving picture company in Hollywood acquired the film rights of it at an even higher price than they had paid for *The Life of Saint Paul,* which had been awarded the Pulitzer Prize for the year before, and in addition to all this, its sales in America surpassed those of England a hundredfold before it had been out six weeks. It was on the suggestion of Evan's New York publisher, Neuman Bloch, that he had agreed to do a short lecture tour in the States. He had been naturally apprehensive of the idea at first, but after a certain amount of coaxing, and tempted by the prospect of visiting America for the first time in such singularly advantageous circumstances—full expenses there and back, a tour of only eight weeks visiting the principal towns, and a guaranteed fee for each lecture that appeared to be little short of fantastic—he gathered his courage together, made exhaustive notes on the subjects on which he intended to speak, and set sail in the *Queen Mary.*

Now it would be foolish to deny that Evan Lorrimer enjoyed publicity. Everyone enjoys publicity to a certain degree. It is always pleasant to feel that your name is of sufficient interest to the world to merit a prominent position in the daily newspapers. For many years past, Evan had been privately gratified to read such phrases as "Of course Evan Lorrimer was there, suave and well-groomed as usual," or "That inveterate first-nighter, Evan Lorrimer, arrived a few minutes before the curtain rose and was seen chatting laughingly to Lady Millicent Cawthorne in the foyer," or "Evan Lorrimer whose new novel, *A London Lady,* has caused such a sensation, was the guest of honour at the Pen and Pencil Club on Sunday evening." Such allusions, guileless and dignified, are immensely agreeable. Unimportant perhaps in their essence, but in their implication very important indeed. Just as millions of little coral animals in so many years construct a barrier reef against the sea, so can these small accolades, over a period of time, build, if not quite a barrier reef, at least a fortification against the waves of oblivion. Evan felt this very strongly. His reviews he read as a matter of course, regarding them rightly as part of the business. Naturally he was pleased when they were good and pained when they were bad, but the gossip columns were different. They were both unprejudiced and uncritical; they contented themselves with the simple statement that he was here or there with so-and-so, or accompanied by such-and-such, and by their repetitious banality did more to consolidate his reputation than all the carefully phrased opinions of the literati put together. But Evan, well used as he was to being photographed and interviewed and occasionally signing a few autograph books, was certainly unprepared for the violence of his reception in New York. From the moment the ship paused at Quarantine turmoil engulfed him. He was belaboured with questions by over a dozen reporters at the same time, photographed waving to mythical friends by no less than fifteen cameras simultaneously, hurried on to the dock where he was met by Neuman Bloch, Mrs. Bloch, the firm's publicity agent, several more reporters and, most surprisingly, a man who had been at school with him and whom he hadn't clapped eyes on for twenty-six years. In the flurry of Customs examination, interviews, and the effort to sustain a reasonably intelligent flow of conversation with the Blochs, he was completely unable to recall the man's name; however, it didn't matter, for after wringing his hand warmly, and standing by his side in silence for a few minutes, he disappeared into the crowd and Evan never saw him again.

Evan Lorrimer at the age of forty-three was, both in appearance and behaviour, a model of what an eminent Englishman of letters should be. He was five-foot-ten, his figure was spare but well-proportioned, he had slim, expressive hands, dark hair greying slightly at the temples, deep-set grey eyes, a small, neat moustache and an urbane smile. Perhaps his greatest asset was his voice which was rich in tone and, at times, almost caressing, particularly when, with his slyly humorous gift of phrase, he was describing somebody a trifle maliciously. Lady Cynthia Cawthorne, who in Lowndes Square had achieved the nearest approach to a London salon since Lady Blessington, was wont to say, with her loud infectious laugh, that had she only been younger she'd have married Evan Lorrimer out of hand if only to hear him repeat over and over again his famous description of being taken, at the age of fifteen, to the Musée Grevin by Marcel Proust.

Evan, like so many people who have attained fame and fortune by their own unaided efforts, was a firm self-disciplinarian. He apportioned his time with meticulous care: so many hours for writing, so many for reading. He ate and drank in moderation and indulged in only enough exercise to keep himself fit. He contrived, although naturally of a highly strung, nervous temperament, to maintain an agreeable poise both physically and mentally and to derive a great deal of enjoyment from life, admittedly without often scaling the heights of rapture, but also without plumbing the depths of despair. This self-adjustment, this admirable balance, was dependent upon one absolute necessity and that necessity was sleep. Eight solid hours per night minimum, with a possible snooze during the day, was his deadline. Without that he was lost, his whole organism disintegrated. He became jumpy and irascible, unable to concentrate. In fact on one occasion, owing to an emotional upheaval when the pangs of not sufficiently requited love gnawed at his vitals for nearly four months, he became actively ill and had to retire to a nursing home. Realizing this one weakness, this Achilles' heel, he arranged his life accordingly.

At home, in his small house in Chesham Place, his two servants had been trained to a mouselike efficiency. Until he was called in the morning the house was wrapped in the silence of death. The knocker had been taken off the front door, and both bells, front and back, muffled down to the merest tinkle; the telephone by his bed was switched off nightly and rang in the basement, and even there, after a series of dogged experiments by Albert his valet, it had been reduced to nothing more than a purr. Naturally, taking all this into consideration, the first few nights in New York were a torture to him. He had, of course, been warned that the sharpness of the climate and the champagne quality of the air would enable him to do with less sleep than he was accustomed to in the older, more stagnant atmosphere of England, and although he discovered this to be true to a certain extent, he was unable to repress a slight feeling of panic. If only, he reflected, he could get away into the country for two or three days, to relax, to give himself time to adjust himself, he might come to view the so much swifter tempo of American life with more equanimity.

It was on the fourth day after his arrival, towards the end of a strenuously literary cocktail party given in his honour by the Neuman Blochs that he met Louise Steinhauser. He was introduced to her by his hostess and immediately taken out on to the terrace to look at the view. This had already happened to him five times, and although he had been deeply impressed by the view the first two times, it was now beginning to pall a little; however Louise was adamant. "Look at it," she said in a husky, rather intense voice. "Isn't it horrible?"

Evan gave a slight start of surprise. Louise went on, "Every time I look at New York from a height like this, I positively shudder. All those millions of people cooped up in those vast buildings give me such a feeling of claustrophobia that I think I'm going mad. If I didn't live out in the country most of the time I really should go mad. My husband, poor darling, comes in every day of course, and we have an apartment at the Pierre—you can just see it from here behind that tower that looks like a pencil with india-rubber on top—but really I hardly ever use it unless I happen to come in for a late party or an opening night or something, and even then I often drive down home afterwards, however late it is."

"How far away is your home in the country?" enquired Evan.

"About an hour in the automobile; at night of course, it's much quicker and I can't begin to tell you how lovely it is to arrive at about two in the morning and smell the sea—my house is right on the sea—and just go to sleep in that wonderful silence—you'd think you were miles away from anywhere, and yet it's actually only a little way from New York. There are no houses near us, we're completely isolated—You really must come down for a weekend, except that I warn you there isn't a thing to do except lie about and relax. Bonwit, that's my husband, plays golf occasionally or a little tennis, but I don't play anything. I find at my age—I shall be forty-four next month, imagine!"—she laughed disarmingly, "I never try to hide my age, it's so silly, after all what *does* it matter. Anyhow, as I was saying, at my age I find that all I want are my comforts, nice books, a few real friends, not just acquaintances, and good food. I'm afraid that's all I can offer you, peace and good food, but if you would like to slip away from all this," she indicated the remainder of the cocktail party milling about inside with a wave of her hand, "and really lead the simple life for a couple of days, you don't even have to bring dinner clothes if you don't want to. Please come, both Bonwit and I would be absolutely enchanted."

Evan had been looking at her carefully while she was talking, carefully and critically. Being a writer, he was naturally observant, his mind was trained to perceive small indicative details. Being a celebrity he was also cautious. He noted Louise's clothes first; they were obviously expensive, the ruby and diamond clip in her small cloche hat could only have come from Cartier. Her pearls might or might not be real, but the clasp most certainly was. In addition to these external advantages he liked her. She was vivacious, humorous and friendly. She also seemed to have a sensible appreciation of the values of life.

"You're most kind," he said. "There's nothing I should like better."

"Now isn't that lovely," cried Louise. "How long are you going to be here?"

"Alas, only until next Wednesday, then I have to lecture in Chicago."

"I suppose you're booked up for this next weekend?"

Evan shook his head. He had been tentatively invited to the Neuman Blochs' house at Ossining, but he hadn't definitely accepted. "I was supposed to go to the Blochs'," he said, "but I can get out of it."

"Then that's settled," said Louise gaily. "I'm coming in on Saturday to go to *Starlight,* that's a musical comedy that Lester Gaige is in. He's one of my greatest friends, you'll adore him. Why don't you dine with me and come too, and we'll all three drive down afterwards. He's the only person I've invited for this weekend. I daren't have a lot of people when he comes because he insists on being quiet. He says he gives out so much at every performance during the week that he's damned if he'll give a social performance on Sundays. He really is divine, and he certainly won't bother you because he does nothing but sleep."

As they rejoined the cocktail party, Evan felt that the much-vaunted American hospitality was a very genuine and touching trait.

2

Lester Gaige was certainly amusing. At first, watching him on the stage, Evan had been unsure as to whether or not he was going to like him; he seemed to be too debonair, almost arrogant in the manner in which he moved through the bewildering intricacies of *Starlight*. True, he danced beautifully, sang, with no voice but compelling charm, and dominated by sheer force of personality every scene he was in; but there was a something about him, a mocking veneer that made you a trifle uneasy as to what you might discover underneath. However, in the car driving down to the country, he was much more human. His clothes were inclined to be eccentric. He had on suede shoes, thin silk socks, very pale grey flannel trousers of exquisite cut, a bois de rose sweater with a turtle neck, a tweed sports jacket of extravagant heartiness and a fur-lined overcoat with an astrakhan collar. In addition he wore a small beret basque and a pair of the largest horn-rimmed glasses Evan had ever seen. The conversation between him and Louise was stimulating if a little local in allusion. They referred to so many people in such a short space of time that Evan became quite confused; but he sat back in the corner of the luxurious Packard and gave himself up to being agreeably soothed and entertained. It was obvious that Louise and Lester had been intimate friends for several years; their talk, generally in a gaily reminiscent vein, jumped from London to Paris, from Antibes back to New York, from New York to Venice and from Venice to California. "That amazing party of Irene's when Broddie got blind and had that awful scene with Carola." "That terrible night in Salzburg when Nada refused to go home and finally disappeared into the mountains with Sonny Boy for three days." Occasionally Evan, not wishing to appear out of it, ventured a question as to who So-and-so was, and was immediately rewarded by a vivid, if not always entirely kind, description of So-and-so's life, activities and morals. On the whole he enjoyed himself very much. To begin with, they had all three had a Scotch highball (ridiculous expression) in Lester's dressing room before they started and then another one at "21" where they had had to stop for a moment because Lester had to give some message to Ed Bolingbroke, who had been apparently too drunk to understand it, then not long after they had crossed the Fifty-ninth Street Bridge, Lester had produced a bottle of Scotch from his overcoat pocket, and they had all had a little extra swig to keep them warm. It was necessary to keep warm for the night was bitterly cold; there had been a blizzard the day before and the snow was several inches thick and freezing over.

When they finally reached the Steinhauser home Evan got out of the car, stretched his cramped legs and gave an exclamation of pleasure. It really was most attractive. A large low white house built on three sides of a square and looking out over Long Island Sound. It was a clear moonlight night and far away on the Connecticut coast lights twinkled across the water. Behind the house was nothing but snow, and a few bleak winter trees. Above all, there was silence, complete and soul-satisfying silence, broken only by the soft lap of the waves on the shore.

Inside, the house was the acme of comfort, a large fire was blazing away in a wide open fireplace in the main living room; before it was set a table laid for supper. A pleasant, coloured butler in a white coat met them at the front door. Evan sighed a deep sigh of relief. This was even better than he had imagined.

They sat up until very late over the fire talking. The supper had been delicious, a simple but tasty dish of spaghetti, tomatoes and eggs, a well-mixed green salad with cream cheese and Bar-le-Duc and further Scotch highballs. Evan had had two since his arrival and although he was far from intoxicated, he felt enjoyably mellow. Lester, who was really a great deal more intelligent than one would expect a musical comedy actor to be, displayed a flattering interest in Evan's work. He had read *A London Lady,* and been thrilled with it, he was also one of the few people who had read and enjoyed *My Steps Have Faltered.* Evan dismissed his praise of this with a deprecatory laugh, but he was pleased none the less. Louise was a good hostess and, more than that, Evan decided, an extremely good sort. She talked with vivacity and her sense of humour was true and keen. She appeared to be one of those rare types, a rich woman who is completely unaffected by her wealth. She was downright, honest, and withal very attractive. She alluded to her husband frequently, and it was apparent that although they might not quite see eye to eye over certain things, she was deeply attached to him. They had a son at Harvard to whom they were both obviously devoted. Louise showed Evan a photograph of him dressed in the strange robotish armour of an American footballer. He was a husky, fine-looking lad. Lester was highly enthusiastic about him. "That boy is fantastic," he said, "you'd never believe it to look at him, but he paints the most remarkable watercolours! He gave me one when I was playing Boston in *And So What.* It's a seascape, rather Japanesey in quality, almost like a Foujita." Evan looked again at the photograph, slightly puzzled. Really Americans were most surprising. It was difficult to imagine that six feet of brawn and muscle painting demure seascapes, and even more difficult to understand how Lester Gaige playing in *And So What* in Boston could ever have heard of Foujita. Perhaps there was something to be said after all for that American culture that Europeans referred to with such disdain.

It wasn't until nearly four o'clock that Louise suddenly jumped up from the sofa on which she had been lying and cried, "Really this is terrible— I bring you down here to rest and keep you up to all hours talking. We simply *must* go to bed." She led the way through the hall and along a little passage. "I've given you the quietest room in the house," she said over her shoulder, "it's on the ground floor and you'll have to share a bathroom with Lester. I would have given you a room upstairs with a bath to yourself but it isn't nearly so shut away and you might be disturbed by Bonwit getting up early or the servants or something." She opened the door leading into a charmingly furnished bedroom. "This is Lester's," she said, "you're along here." They passed through a gleaming, well-equipped bathroom, along another little passage and there was Evan's room. It was large, with two beds and decorated in a pale, restful green. In addition to the two beds there was a chaise longue piled with cushions in front of the fire which, although it must have been lit hours ago, was still burning cosily. Evan smiled with pleasure. "What a perfect room," he said gratefully. Louise gave the fire a poke. "I know how English people loathe central heating," she said, "and I've told them to have a fire for you all the time you're here, but if you'll take my advice you'll have the heat on a little bit as well, because the weather's really freezing."

After Louise had said good night and gone up to bed, and Lester and Evan had smoked one more cigarette and exchanged the usual politeness as to which of them should use the bathroom first, Evan, at last alone, opened the window, and, cold as it was, stood for a moment looking up at the stars and listening to the silence. He sniffed the icy air into his lungs, and with a sigh of utter contentment climbed into bed and was asleep in five minutes.

3

Evan woke at ten-thirty, which was rather early considering how late he had gone to bed. He counted up in his mind, four-thirty to ten-thirty, only six hours, but still it didn't matter, he could easily make up for it that night. He lay there idly looking at the reflection of the sea on the ceiling and contemplating, with a slight sinking of the heart, his lecture on Monday night. It was drawing very near and he was naturally nervous, but still he had certainly been wise to give himself this breathing space immediately before it. He planned to go over his notes sometime during the day. He was aware, of course, that he spoke well and that his subject "History and the Modern Novel" was pretty certain to interest his American audience. He intended to start with the middle ages, the period of his first two novels, then jump to French eighteenth century, bringing in his *Porcelaine Courtesan, Madame Is Indisposed* and *The Sansculotte,* then to the Directoire and *Madame de Staël,* leaving the Restoration and *A London Lady* to the last. He was determined, in spite of the cautious advice of Neuman Bloch, to deliver a few well-deserved slaps at some of the more successful American writers who so impertinently twisted European history to their own ends. Evan detested slang and the use of present-day idiom in describing the past. Not that he was a believer in the "Odd's Boddikins" "Pish Tush-ery" school of historical writing; he himself eschewed that with the great-est contempt, but he did believe in being factually accurate insofar as was possible, and in using pure English. Had not the exquisite literacy of *A London Lady* been one of the principal reasons for its success with the Book Society? And not only the Book Society, with the reviewers of both conti-nents and with the general public. One of Evan's most comforting convic-tions was that the general public had a good deal more discrimination and taste than it was given credit for, and that all this careless, slipshod, *soi-disant* modern style with its vulgarity of phrase and cheap Americanisms would, in a very little while, be consigned to the oblivion it so richly deserved.

At this point in his reflections he broke off to wonder whether or not he should ring for some fruit juice and coffee. He remembered from last night that the only entrance to his room was through Lester's and the bathroom and it would be inconsiderate to wake Lester if he were still sleeping. Evan, with a little sigh not entirely free from irritation, decided to go and see. He tiptoed out into the passage and into the bathroom and opened the door leading to Lester's room very quietly. Lester *was* still sleeping in a pair of pastel blue silk pyjamas with his head buried in the pillow. Evan stood there regarding him uncertainly for a moment. It would, of course, be unkind to wake him, and yet on the other hand he might possibly sleep until lunchtime and Evan would have to wait nearly three hours for his coffee. He retired into the bathroom, closing the door softly after him, and pondered the situation. Presently, renouncing indecision once and for all, he flushed the toilet and then listened carefully with his ear to the door. He was rewarded by hearing a few grunts and then the creaking of the bed. Quick as a flash he darted across to the lavatory basin and turned the tap on full, once embarked he intended taking no chances. After a few moments he opened the door again and peeped in. Lester was sitting up looking, he was glad to observe, quite amiable. Evan coughed apologetically. "I'm awfully sorry," he said, "I'm afraid I woke you up. I'd no idea the tap would make such a row."

"It wasn't the tap," said Lester without rancour, "it was the Lulu."

"How does one get coffee, do you suppose?"

"Let's ring," said Lester. "We can either have it here or put on our dress-ing gowns and go into the sun porch—which do you prefer?"

"I don't mind a bit." Evan, his plan having succeeded so easily, was feel-ing a little guilty and determined to be amenable at all costs.

"I think the sun porch is nicer." Lester jumped out of bed, rang the bell and went into the bathroom to brush his teeth.

While they were breakfasting on the sun porch, an agreeable glass-enclosed room at the side of the house commanding a wide view of the sea and the drive, Bonwit Steinhauser appeared in elaborate plus-fours. He was a red-faced, rather dull-looking man, with a large body that had once been muscular but was now just fat. He said "good morning" affably and after a little desultory conversation went away. When he had gone Lester pushed his coffee cup out of his way and leant across the table almost furtively.

"You know I like Bonwit," he whispered as though by such a confession he was straining credulity to the utmost. "There's something really awfully kind about him. Of course everyone says he's a bore and I suppose he is in a way, but when he's had a few drinks, my dear!" He did one of his characteristic gestures of pawing the air with his right hand. "He can be terribly, terribly funny! I shall never forget when I was up here one weekend with Ida Wesley, she's dead as a doornail now, poor sweet, and Bonwit, who shall be nameless, got so fried—" Here he broke off abruptly and said, "My God!" Evan turned around to see what had startled him and saw a car coming slowly up the drive. He jumped to his feet. Lester got up too, and, after looking out carefully for a moment, gave a laugh. "It's all right," he said, "it's only Irene and Suki and Dwight and Luella—I thought for a minute it was strangers."

"Are they coming for lunch?" asked Evan apprehensively.

"I expect so," replied Lester, sitting down again. "But you'll love Irene, she's divine, but *divine*—you've heard her sing, haven't you?"

Evan shook his head.

"You've never heard Irene Marlow sing!" Lester was horrified. "You haven't lived, that's all, you just haven't lived! We'll make her sing after lunch, Suki's with her fortunately, he always plays for her. It really is the most lovely voice and there's somebody with an amazing sense of humour! I mean, she really gets herself, which is more than you can say for most prima donnas, and if you could hear her when she's in a real rage with Dwight—that's Dwight Macadoo who shall be nameless—my God! it's wonderful: bang goes the Italian accent and out pops Iowa!"

"We'd better go and dress, hadn't we?" suggested Evan, feeling unequal to greeting a famous Iowan prima donna in his pyjamas.

"You go and dress," said Lester. "And you might turn on a bath for me when you've finished. I'll go and deal with the visiting firemen."

Evan retired to his room, shattered. It was really appalling luck that these people should have selected today of all days to come to lunch. How cross Louise would be. But still, he comforted himself, she'd be sure to get rid of them all as soon as possible.

When he emerged, bathed, shaved and dressed in perfectly cut English country clothes, he found everybody in the large living room. Apparently, while he had been dressing, some more people had arrived. Bonwit was mixing cocktails behind a little bar in the far corner of the room. There was no sign of Louise.

Seeing Evan come in, Lester, who was sitting on the sofa with a fattish little man and two women, jumped up. "This is my friend," he cried, "I don't think you know my friend! Who shall be nameless," he added with a light laugh. Evan smiled sheepishly, he was unused to being nameless, but Lester came over and took him affectionately by the arm. "I must introduce you to everybody," he said. "We'd better begin right here and work round the whole God-damned circle." He raised his voice. "Listen, everybody—this is Evan Lorrimer, one of the greatest living English novelists, he's my friend and I'm mad about him!" He turned enquiringly to Evan. "Aren't I, honey?"

Evan summoned up enough poise to give a little smile and say, "I hope so," whereupon Lester, holding him firmly by the arm, walked him around the room. A slight hush fell while this tour was in progress. Evan shook hands with everyone and responded pleasantly to their assurances of how glad they were to know him, but he was unable to catch more than a few names as he went along, and finally sat down feeling rather confused, in the place on the sofa that Lester had vacated. The fattish little man, he discovered, was Otis Meer, who wrote a famous gossip column for one of the daily papers, and the two women were Irene Marlow and Luella Rosen. Irene was flamboyant, but attractively so, she was dressed in a scarlet sports suit, with a vivid green scarf, her brown hair was done in clusters of curls and her hat—it couldn't have been anyone else's—was on the mantelpiece. Luella Rosen was sharp and black, like a little Jewish bird, she also was wearing sports clothes, but of a more sombre hue.

Irene smiled, generously exposing a lot of dazzlingly white teeth. "Lester had been telling us all about you," she said—her voice had a trace of a foreign accent—"and you've no idea how thrilled we are to meet you. I haven't read your book yet, but I've got it."

"Mr. Lorrimer has written dozens of books, dear," said Luella.

Irene sat back and closed her eyes in mock despair. "Isn't Luella horrible?" she said. "I'm never allowed to get away with a thing—anyway, I meant your last one, and I know it couldn't matter to you whether I've read it or not; but I really am longing to, particularly now that I've met you." She winked at Evan, a gay, confiding little wink, and nudged him with her elbow. Luella gave a staccato laugh. "Irene's our pet moron," she said. "She's never read a book in her life except *Stories of the Operas.* She's just an Iowa girl who's made good, aren't you, darling?"

"Listen, lamb pie," said Irene, "you leave Iowa out of this. What's the matter with Iowa, anyway?"

"Nothing apart from Julia de Martineau," said Otis Meer, and went into a gale of laughter. Irene and Luella laughed too. Evan was naturally unaware of the full piquancy of the joke. At this point an exceedingly handsome man came up and handed him an old-fashioned.

"This is my dream prince," said Irene. "Dwight, you know Mr. Evan Lorrimer, don't you?"

"We've met already," said Evan, nodding to Dwight who nodded back with a grin and sat down on the floor at their feet, balancing his own drink carefully in his right hand as he did so. "Where the hell's Louise?" he asked.

"Louise has never been known to be on time for anything," said Luella.

Irene turned to Evan. "Isn't Louise a darling? You know she's one of the few really genuine people in the world. I can't bear people who aren't genuine, can you?" Evan made a gesture of agreement and she went on. "Being a writer must be just as bad as being a singer in some ways, having to meet people all the time and look pleased when they say nice things about your books."

"Tough," said Luella. "My heart goes out to you both." She got up and went over to the bar.

"You mustn't pay any attention to Luella," said Irene, comfortingly, observing that Evan looked a trifle nonplussed. "She always goes on like that, she's actually got the kindest heart in the world, sometimes I really don't know what I'd do without her, she's one of our few really genuine friends, isn't she, Dwight?" Dwight looked up and nodded and then stared abstractedly into the fire. At this moment, Louise came into the room with a scream.

"I'm so terribly sorry, everybody—" she wailed. "I overslept." While she was being swamped with greetings, Evan looked at her in horror. She seemed to be a totally different person. Could this be the same woman whose friendly tranquillity and wise, philosophical outlook had so charmed him last night? Could she have known all these people were coming or was she merely masking her dismay at their appearance and trying to carry everything off with a high hand? If so, she was certainly doing it very convincingly. She seemed to be wholeheartedly delighted to see them. Her eye lighted on him and she came over with her arms around a red-haired woman in black and a small fair man. "My dear," she said, "you really must forgive me—I do hope you slept all right—" She broke off and turned to the red-haired woman. "He's a sleep maniac just like me," she said. Then to Evan again: "You have met everyone, haven't you, and been given a drink and everything?" Evan held up his glass in silent acknowledgment, he was bereft of words, whereupon she snatched it out of his hand. "You must have another at once," she cried. "That looks disgusting," and led him vivaciously to the bar.

During the next half an hour, which Evan spent leaning against the bar, he managed to sort out people a little in his mind. The red-haired woman in black was the Countess Brancati, she had been a Chicago debutante a few years back and had married into the Italian aristocracy. The thin grey man by the window talking to Luella Rosen was her husband. The little fair man was Oswald Roach, commonly known as Ossie. Ossie was a cabaret artist whose specialty was to sing rather bawdy monologues to his own improvisations on the ukelele. The source of this information was Bonwit, who, although sweating copiously from the efforts of mixing different sorts of drinks for everybody, was willing, almost grateful, for an opportunity to talk. "Who is the thin boy with the pale face?" Evan asked him. Bonwit shook the cocktail shaker violently. "That's Suki," he said with obvious distaste. "He's a Russian fairy who plays the piano for Irene, he's all right until he gets tight, then he goes cuckoo."

Evan was regarding this phenomenon with interest, when there was a loud commotion in the hall, and two enormous Alsatians sprang into the room followed by a neatly dressed girl in jodhpurs and a fur coat. "I came just as I was," she said, as Louise advanced to kiss her. "I was riding this morning and Shirley wouldn't wait, she's gone into the kitchen to see about food for Chico and Zeppo." She indicated the Alsatians who were running around the room wagging their tails and barking. "I do hope you didn't mind us bringing them, but we couldn't leave them all alone in the apartment for the whole day." Louise gaily assured her that she didn't mind a bit and brought her over to the bar. "Here's someone who's been dying to meet you," she said to Evan. "Leonie Crane, she's written three plays herself, she's one of my closest friends and she's read everything you've ever written." Leonie Crane blushed charmingly and wrung Evan's hand with considerable force. "Not quite all," she said in a well-modulated deep voice. "Louise always exaggerates, but I did think *A Lady of London* was swell. Shirley and I read it in Capri in the summer."

"*A London Lady,*" Evan corrected her gently and she blushed again. "That's typical of me," she said. "I'm so vague that Shirley says she wonders how I've lived as long as I have without being run over—Hello, Bonny," she leaned over the bar and patted Bonwit's wet hand. "What about a little hard liquor—I'm dying!"

Leonie was undeniably attractive, she radiated health and a sort of jolly schoolboyish vitality; her canary-colored silk shirt was open at the neck and her curly brown hair was cut close to her head. She was a little shy and tried to conceal it with a certain lazy gaucherie. Evan found her most sympathetic, and they talked for several minutes and then Shirley appeared. Leonie presented her to Evan with brusque matter-of-fact dispatch.

"This is Evan Lorrimer, Shirley—Shirley Benedict." They shook hands. Shirley was on the same lines as Leonie but older and a little more heavily built. She had jet black hair, clear blue eyes, and was wearing a perfectly plain grey flannel coat and skirt. She wore no jewellery except a pair of pearl button earrings. Both girls were singularly free from trifling adornments.

Presently Lester reappeared dressed in an entirely new colour scheme so far as tie and sweater went, but with the same strong, garish sports coat that he had worn the night before. He kissed Leonie and Shirley affectionately, and told Evan that they were both angels and that when he'd got to know them a little better he'd worship them. They all four had an old-fashioned on the strength of this prophecy and Evan began to feel a little drunk. It was not part of his usual routine to drink three tumblers of practically neat whisky in the middle of the day on an empty stomach, but he had now become sufficiently light-headed not to care. After all, there was no sense in just sitting about in corners looking sulky, just because some rather odd people had happened to come over for lunch. It would be both disagreeable and silly. Everyone seemed disposed to be most gay and friendly, why not relax and enjoy himself. Comforted by this successful disposal of his conscience, he agreed with cheerful resignation when Louise suggested that they should all go over to the Hughes-Hitchcocks for one more tiny drink before lunch. He had not the remotest idea who the Hughes-Hitchcocks were, but it was apparent from the enthusiastic assent of everyone present and from Lester's glowing description of them that they were an entrancing young married couple who lived only just down the road. Evan accepted an offer to go in Leonie's car and together with her and Shirley and Lester—the Alsatians were left behind—he went.

Lester's assurance that the Hughes-Hitchcocks lived only just down the road proved to be inaccurate. Evan, wedged between Shirley, who was driving, and Leonie in a small Duesenberg roadster, with Lester on his lap, suffered cramp and terror simultaneously for a full half an hour's fast going. Shirley drove well, there was no doubt about that, if she had not they would all have been dead within the first five minutes; but it was the sort of driving that is liable to react unfavourably on the nerves of anyone who happens to drive himself. Evan had driven for years. He owned a sedate Studebaker in faraway green England and frequently conveyed himself back and forth through the country in it, but not at a pace like this, not at seventy miles an hour over an ice-covered road that had frozen so hard that it was like glass. The fact that he was also unaccustomed to a right-hand drive added considerably to his agony. His instinct time and time again was to seize the wheel and swerve over to the left to avoid what seemed to be imminent destruction. Fortunately, however, he restrained himself and sat in frozen misery until at last they turned into a large driveway under tall trees.

On the terrace outside the Hughes-Hitchcocks' house, which was a vast grey structure built on the lines of a French château, stood several cars. It was obviously quite a large party. Once inside, his legs felt so shaky after Lester's weight and the rigours of the drive that he accepted with alacrity the first drink that was offered to him, which was a dry martini in a glass larger than the cocktail glasses he was used to. After a little he relaxed sufficiently to look about him. There were at least twenty people in the room apart from his own party which was arriving in groups. His host, a good-looking hearty young man, brought up a fair girl whom he introduced as Mrs. Martin. Evan, as he shook hands with her, was unable to avoid noticing that she was in an advanced stage of pregnancy. She seemed quite unembarrassed over the situation and looked at him with vague brown eyes. He observed that her fragile young hand was clasping a highball. "Don't be frightened," she said with a simper, "it's not due until Wednesday, and if it doesn't come then I'm going to have a Cæsarian." Evan felt at a loss to know how to reply to such compelling candour, so he smiled wanly. She gave a slight hiccough and said, "Excuse me." Evan fidgeted awkwardly.

"Is that necessary?" he asked, and then flushed to the roots of his hair at the thought that she might imagine he was referring to the hiccough, but she either hadn't noticed or was too drunk to care. "Not necessary," she replied with a little difficulty, "not exactly necessary, but nice work if you can get it," then she drifted away. Presently Lester came up and they went over and sat down together in a window seat. "It's always like this in this house," he said. "Thousands of people milling around—I can't think how they stand it. They're such simple people themselves too, and grand fun, you know, there's no chichi about them, that's what I like and Hughsie—" Here Lester chuckled—"Hughsie's a riot, my dear, if you get Hughsie alone sometimes and get him to tell you some of his experiences in the Navy, he'll slay you; of course he's settled down now, and mind you he adores Sonia, and they've got two of the most enchanting children you've ever seen, but still what's bred in the bone comes out in the what have you . . ."

At this moment Otis Meer joined them. "Christ," he whispered to Lester, "Charlie Schofield's still trailing round with that bitch. I thought they were all washed up weeks ago."

"You should know," replied Lester, "if anybody should."

Evan asked for this interesting couple to be pointed out to him.

"That man over by the fireplace, the tall one with the blonde. He's Charlie Schofield, one of our richest playboys. She's Anita Hay, she used to be in 'The Vanities.' Otis hates her," he added, Evan thought, rather unnecessarily.

"She's one of these high-hatting dames," said Otis. "She'd high hat her own father if she knew who he was."

"Is she invited everywhere with Mr. Schofield?" enquired Evan, who was puzzled by the social aspects of the situation.

"If she's not he just takes her," replied Lester laconically. "He's been crazy about her for years."

Presently Louise came up with Luella Rosen. "I must apologize for dragging you over here," she said to Evan, "but I absolutely promised we'd come, and they're such darlings really, but I'd no idea there was going to be this crowd—have another drink and we'll go in five minutes."

"Can I drive back with you?" asked Evan wistfully.

"Of course," said Louise. "We'll meet in the hall in about five minutes."

During the next hour Evan was forced to the conclusion that the time sense, in the wealthier strata of American society, was lacking. Louise showed no indication of wanting to leave. Almost immediately after she had promised to meet Evan in the hall in five minutes, she sat down with Mr. Hughes-Hitchcock and began to play backgammon; her laugh rang out several times and Evan wondered bleakly if "Hughsie" were retailing some of his experiences in the Navy.

Lester had disappeared. Otis Meer, Ossie and the Russian pianist were sitting in a corner engrossed in an intense conversation. Irene Marlow was entertaining a large group of people with a description of her first meeting with Geraldine Farrar—a few disjointed sentences came to Evan's ear— "That vast empty stage—" "My clothes were dreadful, after all I was completely unknown then, just an ambitious little girl from Iowa—" "She said with that lovely gracious smile of hers 'My child—' " What Miss Farrar had said was lost to Evan for at that moment Charles Schofield came and spoke to him.

"We haven't been formally introduced," he said amiably, "but I think you know a great friend of mine, the Prince of Wales?" Evan, endeavouring not to betray surprise, nodded casually. "Of course," he said, "although I fear I don't know him very well." Actually he had met the Prince of Wales twice, once at a charity ball at Grosvenor House and once at a supper party at Lady Cynthia Cawthorne's. On both occasions he had been presented and the Prince had been charming, if a trifle vague; neither conversation could truthfully be said to have established any degree of intimacy.

"He's a grand guy," went on Charlie Schofield, "absolutely genuine. I've played polo with him a lot. Do you play polo?"

"No—I don't ride well enough."

"It's a grand game," said Charlie. "I used to play on Boots Leavenworth's team—you know Boots Leavenworth, of course?"

Evan did not know the Earl of Leavenworth except by repute, but he felt it would sound churlish to go on denying everything. "Rather," he said, "he's awfully nice."

"I suppose you don't know what's happened about him and Daphne?"

"I think things are much the same," hazarded Evan.

"You mean Rollo's still holding out?"

"When I left England," said Evan boldly, "Rollo was still holding out."

"God!" said Charlie with vehemence. "Aren't people extraordinary!

You'd think after all that business at Cannes last summer he'd have the decency to face facts and come out into the open. As a matter of fact, I've always thought he was a bit of a bastard, outwardly amusing enough you know, but something shifty about him. As a matter of fact poor Tiger's the one I'm sorry for, aren't you?"

"Desperately," said Evan.

"Where is Tiger now?"

"I don't know." Evan wildly racked his brains for an appropriate place for Tiger to be. "Africa, I think."

"Jesus!" cried Charlie aghast, "you don't mean to say he's thrown his hand in and left poor Iris to cope with everything?"

The strain was beginning to tell on Evan. He took refuge in evasion. "Rumours," he said weakly. "One hears rumours, you know how people gossip!"

Fortunately at this moment Shirley and Leonie came up and asked him if he'd like to play table tennis. "We can't play at all," said Shirley, "we're terrible, but it's good exercise." Evan smiled affably at Charlie and went with them into an enormous room glassed in on three sides, furnished only with the table, a few garden chairs and some large plants in pots. It was hotter than a Turkish bath. On the way he confided to them that he didn't play, but would be enchanted to watch them. He sat down, lit a cigarette and they started. They hadn't been playing a minute before he realised how wise he had been to refuse. They played like lightning, grimly, with an agility and concentration that was nothing short of ferocious. He watched them amazed. These two attractive young women, smashing and banging, occasionally muttering the score breathlessly through clenched teeth. Sometimes Leonie gave a savage grunt when she missed a shot, like a prize fighter receiving a blow in the solar plexus. Presently, they having finished one game and changed round and started another, Evan began to feel drowsy. The hypnotic effect of following the little white ball back and forth and the monotonous click of the wooden bats lulled him into a sort of coma. Vague thoughts drifted through his mind. He wondered who Rollo was and why he was probably holding out, and what Tiger might have left poor Iris to cope with—Poor Iris—Poor Tiger—Evan slept.

4

At ten minutes past four precisely the Steinhauser party rose from the lunch table and Evan went to his bedroom and shut the door. Lunch had not started until after three. There had been a certain amount of delay while Louise and Lester were rounding everybody up at the Hughes-Hitchcocks'. Then several arguments as to who should drive back with whom. Evan, with commendable tenacity, considering that he had just been awakened from a deep sleep, had clung to Louise like a leech despite all efforts of Shirley and Leonie to persuade him to go back with them, and finally succeeded in being brought home at a more reasonable speed in Louise's Packard. Lunch had been rather a scramble and consisted principally of clam chowder which he detested and veal cutlets which, not surprisingly, were so overdone as to be almost uneatable. Evan, whose head was splitting, took two aspirin, divested himself of his shoes, trousers and coat, put on his dressing gown and lay thankfully on the bed pulling the eiderdown up to his chin. If he could get a real sleep now, he reflected, not just a doze in a chair, and get up at about seven and bath and change, everyone would have assuredly gone. They must all have dinner engagements in New York, and he would be able to dine peaceably with Louise and Bonwit and Lester, allow a polite hour or so for conversation, and go to bed firmly at ten-thirty. The warmth of the eiderdown stole round him, his legs began to congeal pleasantly with a prickling sensation, the throbbing of his head gradually diminished and he fell asleep.

About an hour later he felt himself being dragged to consciousness by somebody shaking him rhythmically. With intense reluctance he opened his eyes and beheld Lester bending over him. He moaned slightly and tried to evade that inexorable hand.

"You must wake up now, honey," said Lester. "You've had over an hour and Irene's going to sing." Evan's mind, still webbed with sleep, tried unsuccessfully to grapple with this announcement. "Who's Irene?" he muttered.

"Don't be silly," said Lester. "Irene Marlow; she's mad about you, she says she won't so much as open her trap unless you're there—we've been trying to persuade her for twenty minutes—she says she'll sing for you or not at all—come on." He flicked the eiderdown off the bed and pulled Evan into a sitting posture. It was no use trying to go to sleep again now, even if Lester had allowed him to. Once wakened up like that he was done for. He went drearily into the bathroom and sponged his face, then came back and put on his trousers, coat and shoes. Lester, while he did so, lay on the chaise longue and discoursed enthusiastically upon the quality of Irene's voice, her passion for Dwight Macadoo and the fact that leaving all her success and glamour aside she was really completely genuine. "It's amazing about that boy," he said apropos of Dwight. "Really amazing— she's absolutely nuts about him and although he may be the biggest thing since *Ben-Hur* I must say I think he's just plain dumb! Of course, you can't expect him to be anything else really, he was only a cowboy in Arizona when she met him, galloping about on a horse all day in chaps, and rounding up all those God-damned steers—who shall be nameless—well, anyway, she met him out on Grace Burton's ranch and gave her all, if you know what I mean, and since that she's taken him everywhere—mind you, I'm not saying he isn't sweet, he is, but he just doesn't utter."

Lester led the way into the living room. The party was sitting around expectantly. Irene was standing by the piano while Suki, with a cigarette dangling from his lips, was playing a few introductory chords. When Lester and Evan came in everybody said "Shhh" loudly. They sank down on to the floor by the door, Irene flashed Evan a charming smile and started off on "Vissi d'Arte." She sang beautifully. Evan, whose understanding of music was superficial to say the best of it, recognized at once that the quality of her voice and the charm with which she exploited it was of a very high order indeed. When she had finished *Tosca* everyone gave little groans and cries of pleasure, and someone called for *Bohème.* Irene sang *Bohème;* then Ossie implored her to sing the waltz from *The Countess Maritza.* She started this and forgot the words halfway through, so she stopped and sang three songs of Debussy in French, and then some Schumann in German. Evan, being by the door in a draught, wished that she'd stop, the floor was beginning to feel very hard and he was afraid of catching cold. Irene, blissfully unaware that even one of her audience wasn't enjoying her performance to the utmost, went on singing for over an hour. When she finally left the piano and sat down, amid ecstasies of admiration, Evan rose stiffly and went over to the bar. Otis was leaning against it with Shirley and Leonie, Bonwit was still behind it.

"Isn't that the most glorious voice you've ever heard?" cried Ossie. "Frankly I'd rather listen to Irene than Jeritza, Ponselle and Flagstad all together in a lump." Evan, repressing a shudder at the thought of Jeritza, Ponselle and Flagstad all together in a lump, agreed wholeheartedly and asked Bonwit for a drink.

"Martini; old-fashioned, daiquiri, rye and ginger ale, Scotch highball, pay your dime and take your choice," said Bonwit cheerfully. Evan decided on a highball, not that he wished to drink anymore for the pleasure of it, but he was chilled by the draught from the door. Bonwit mixed him a strong one, and after a while he began to feel more cheerful. Louise came over, Evan noticed that she looked very flushed, and dragged Ossie away from the bar. "Darling Ossie, you must," she insisted, "everybody's screaming for you—Lester's gone to get your ukelele, you left it in the hall." Ossie, after some more persuasion, sat down in the middle of the room with his ukelele which Lester had handed to him, and began to tune it. Otis shouted out, "Do 'The Duchess,' " and Irene cried, "No, not 'The Duchess,' do 'Mrs. Rabbit.' " Louise cried, "No, not 'Mrs. Rabbit,' do 'Ella Goes to Court.' " Several other people made several other suggestions, and there was pandemonium for a few moments. Shirley whispered to Evan, "I do hope he does 'Ella Goes to Court,' you'll adore it."

Ossie silenced the clamour by striking some loud chords; then he sang "Mrs. Rabbit." "Mrs. Rabbit" was a description, half-sung and half-spoken, of the honeymoon night of an elderly lady from Pittsburgh. It was certainly amusing, while leaving little to the imagination. Ossie's rendering of it was expert. He paused, raised his eyebrows, lowered and raised his voice, and pointed every line with brilliantly professional technique. Everyone in the room shouted and wept with laughter. When he had finished with a vivid account of the death of Mrs. Rabbit from sheer excitement, the clamour started again. This time he sang "The Duchess." It was rather on the same lines as "Mrs. Rabbit" although the locale was different. It described a widow from Detroit who married an English Duke and had an affair with a gondolier during their honeymoon in Venice. Evan permitted himself to smile tolerantly at Ossie's somewhat stereotyped version of an English Duke. Finally, when he had sung several other songs, all of which varied only in the degree of their pornography, he consented to do "Ella Goes to Court." Evan, having finished his highball and noticing another close to his elbow, took it hurriedly and braced himself for the worst. "Ella Goes to Court" was, if anything, bawdier than the others had been. It was a fanciful description of a middle-aged meat packer's wife from Chicago who, owing to the efforts of an impecunious English Countess, is taken to a Court at Buckingham Palace and becomes intimately attached to a Gentleman-in-Waiting on her way to the Throne Room. The whole song was inexpressibly vulgar, and to an Englishman shocking beyond words. Fortunately the references to the Royal Family were comparatively innocuous; if they had not been Evan would undoubtedly have left the room, but still, as it was, the whole thing, with its sly implications, its frequent descents to barroom crudeness, and above all the ignorance and inaccuracy with which Ossie endeavoured to create his atmosphere, irritated Evan profoundly. Aware that several people were covertly watching him to see how he would take this exhibition, he debated rapidly in his mind whether to look as disgusted as he really felt or to pretend to enjoy it. He took another gulp of his highball and forced an appreciative smile onto his face. A diversion was caused by the noisy entrance of four newcomers. "My God!" cried Lester. "It's Carola!" There was a general surge towards a smartly dressed woman with bright eyes and still brighter hair who walked in a little ahead of the others. Lester kissed her, Louise kissed her, everybody kissed her except Evan, who was formally introduced a little later by Otis Meer.

Her name was Carola Binney and she was, according to Leonie and Shirley, the most famous and gifted comedienne on the New York stage. Evan vaguely remembered having heard of her at some time or other. She certainly possessed abundant vitality and seemed to be on the most intimate terms with everybody present. The people with her, Evan learned, were Bob and Gloria Hockbridge who were scenario writers from Holly-wood, and Don Lucas. There was probably no one in the world, even Evan, who had not heard of Don Lucas. Evan looked at him and really experi-enced quite a thrill. He was even handsomer in real life than he was on the screen. His young finely modelled face healthily tanned by the sun; his wide shoulders and long curling lashes; his lazy, irresistible charm. There it all was. "It was exactly," thought Evan, "as tho' some clear-eyed, vital young god from the wider spaces of Olympus had suddenly walked into a nightclub." Lester brought him over. "This is Don Lucas," he said exul-tantly. "He's just a struggling boy who's trying to make a name for himself and got sidetracked by somebody once saying he was good-looking."

"Nuts, Les," said the clear-eyed Olympian as he shook hands. "Glad to know you, Mr. Lorrimer."

Lester, Don and Evan drifted over to the bar where Bonwit, after greet-ing Don, gave them each a highball. Evan tried to refuse but Lester insisted. "Phooey!" he cried, placing his arm around Evan's shoulders. "This is a party and life's just one big glorious adventure—which shall be nameless!"

Don, it appeared, was on a three weeks' vacation from Hollywood; he had just completed one picture, *The Loves of Cardinal Richelieu,* and was going back on Thursday to start another which was to be called *Tumult,* and was based on Tolstoy's *War and Peace.* The Hockbridges were writing it and had apparently done a swell job. Evan glanced across at the Hock-bridges. Mr. Hockbridge was a plump bald man in the early forties, while his wife was much younger, possibly not more than twenty-five, with enormous wide blue eyes and platinum blond hair done in the style of Joan of Arc. Evan tried to imagine them sitting down together and writing the story of *War and Peace* and gave up. After three strong whiskies and sodas such fantasy was beyond him.

Don, within the first few minutes of their conversation, pressed him warmly to come and stay with him when he lectured in Los Angeles. "It's a very simple house," he said. "None of that Spanish crap—all loggias and whatnot, but I can let you have a car and an English valet." "Simple house!" Lester gave a shriek. "It's about as simple as Chartres Cathedral. It's the most gorgeous place in California." He turned to Evan. "You really must go," he went on. "Seriously, I mean it—it's an experience, if you know what I mean, and when I say experience, well!—" He laughed and dug Don in the ribs.

"It would be grand to have you if you'd come," he said. "You mustn't pay any attention to the way Les goes on—we happened to have a party when he was there and Oh boy!" He shook his handsome head and sighed as though shattered by the memory of it. "But if you came you wouldn't be disturbed. I shall be working all day anyhow—you could do exactly as you liked."

Evan thanked him very much, and said it sounded delightful. Lester went off into further eulogies about the magnificence of Don's house but was interrupted by Louise who came up and placed one arm around Don's waist and the other round Evan's.

"We're all going over to the Grouper Seligmans for just ten minutes," she said. "Carola's longing to see their house; I must say it's unbelievable what they've done with it." Evan gently disentangled himself. "I don't think I'll come if you don't mind," he said. "I've got to go over my notes for my lecture tomorrow night."

There was a shocked silence for a moment, then Louise gave a wail of distress. "Oh my dear," she cried, "please come just for a few minutes. The Grouper Seligmans will be so bitterly disappointed, they're pining to meet you and they're such darlings."

Evan shook his head. "I'd really rather not," he said firmly.

"Then I won't go either," said Lester.

"Neither will I," said Louise. "We'll none of us go."

Don Lucas patted Evan's shoulder encouragingly. "Come on," he coaxed. "Be a sport."

"They're divine people," said Lester. "They really are, you'll love them, and old Bernadine's a riot; she's Jane Grouper Seligman's mother, you know; you can't go back to Europe without having seen Bernadine Grouper."

"Only for just ten minutes," said Louise. "I shall really feel terribly badly if you don't go—it's quite near, just down the road and the house really is lovely, the most perfect taste, they've spent millions on it—"

"Don't worry him if he'd rather not," said Don. "Let's all have another drink."

Evan, touched by the sympathy in Don's voice and embarrassed by Lester's and Louise's obvious disappointment, gave in. "Very well," he said, "but I really must get back in time to go over my notes before dinner."

Louise's face lit up with pleasure. "Of course you shall," she cried. "You're an angel—the four of us shall go in my car—come on everybody."

5

It was nearly an hour's drive to the Grouper Seligmans' house, and in the car Lester suggested playing a word game to pass the time. Evan didn't care for word games but as he couldn't very well sit in morose silence he capitulated with as good a grace as possible. They played "Who am I?" and "Twenty Questions" and "Shedding Light." Evan acquitted himself favourably and, owing to his superior knowledge of history, won reverent praise for his erudition in "Twenty Questions."

"Shedding Light" bewildered him, but he was glad to see that it bewildered Don Lucas even more. As a matter of fact everything bewildered Don Lucas; his contributions consisted mainly of the names of obscure baseball players and movie directors, but he persevered with naïve charm in the face of the most waspish comments from Lester. Suddenly the games were interrupted by the chauffeur taking a wrong turning and arriving, after a few minutes of violent bumping, onto the edge of a swamp. Louise, who had been too occupied in trying to think of a Spanish seventeenth-century painter beginning with M to notice, leant forward, slid back the glass window and shouted a lot of instructions, most of which Lester contradicted. "We ought to have turned to the left by the bridge, I know we ought," she said.

"If we'd done that we should have arrived at the Witherspoons'," said Lester. "And God forbid that we should do that."

"Nonsense," cried Louise. "The Witherspoons are right over on the other side near the Caldicotts."

"If," said Lester with a trace of irritation, "we had gone up that turning just past the Obermeyers' gate and then on over the hill we should have got into the highway and been able to turn right at the crossroads."

"Left," said Louise. "If you turn right at the crossroads, you come straight to the golf course, and that's miles away, just next to the Schaeffers."

"You'd better back," said Lester to the chauffeur. "And when you get into the main road again stop at the first petrol station and ask."

Presently after some more bumping and a frightening moment when the frozen surface of the ground nearly caused the car to skid into a ditch, they emerged again onto the main road. About a quarter of an hour later, having followed the instructions of a Negro at a petrol station, and gone back the way they had come for a few miles, they turned up a small lane and arrived at the Grouper Seligmans'. The rest of their party had naturally arrived some time before and everybody was playing skittles in a luxurious skittle alley with a bathing pool on one side of it and a bar on the other. Mr. and Mrs. Grouper Seligman came forward to meet them both grasping large wooden balls. They were a good-looking young couple in bathing costume. "This is wonderful," cried Mrs. Grouper Seligman. "We thought you were dead, we're just going to finish this game, have one more drink and then go in the pool—go and talk to Mother, she's stinking!"

Mr. Grouper Seligman led them to the bar where the members of his own house party were sitting on high stools apparently having relinquished the joys of the alley and the pool to the invaders. Old Mrs. Grouper, elaborately coiffed and wearing a maroon tea-gown and a dog-collar of pearls, greeted Evan warmly. "You may or may not know it," she said in a harsh, bass voice, "but you're my favourite man!"

Evan bowed politely and tried to withdraw his hand, but she tightened her grasp and pulled him towards her. "That book of yours," she said portentously, and cast a furtive look over her shoulder as though she were about to impart some scurrilous secret, "is great literature—No, it's no use saying it isn't because I know—Henry James used to be an intimate friend of mine and I knew poor Edith Wharton too, and believe me," her voice sank to a hoarse whisper, "I *know.*" She relaxed Evan's hand so suddenly that he nearly fell over backward. At that moment his host gave him an old-fashioned with one hand and piloted him with the other up to an emaciated dark woman in a flowered dinner dress.

"Alice," he said, "you English ought to get together—this is a countryman of yours—Mr. Lorrimer—Lady Kettering." Lady Kettering shook hands with him wearily and gave an absent smile. "How do you do," she said. The sound of an English voice comforted Evan, he hoisted himself onto a vacant stool next to her. Mr. Grouper Seligman having done his duty as a host, left them. "What a lovely house," said Evan. Lady Kettering looked at him in surprise and then glanced around as though she were seeing it all for the first time. "I suppose it is," she replied, "if you like this sort of thing."

Evan felt a little crushed. "Of course I haven't seen much of it, I've only just arrived."

"I've been here for three months," said Lady Kettering, "and I must say it's beginning to get me down. I'm going to Palm Beach next week. I think Palm Beach is bloody, don't you?"

"I've never been there," said Evan.

"Well, take my advice and don't go. It's filled with the most frightening people."

"I shan't be able to anyhow," said Evan. "I'm over here to do a lecture tour."

"How horrible," said Lady Kettering. "Whatever for?"

"My publishers were very insistent that I should." Evan was slightly nettled. "And after all I think it will be interesting to see something of America. This is my first visit."

"You ought to go to Mexico," said Lady Kettering. "That's where you ought to go."

"I'm afraid I shan't have time."

"That's the one thing you don't need in Mexico—time doesn't exist—it's heaven."

"Why don't you go to Mexico instead of Palm Beach?"

"I've promised to join the Edelstons' yacht and go on a cruise in the Bahamas," said Lady Kettering. "Do you know the Edelstons?"

"No," replied Evan.

"Well, take my advice," she said, "and give them a wide berth. They're bloody."

At this moment Don Lucas came and prised Evan gently off his stool. "Come and swim," he said.

The idea of swimming on a Sunday evening in mid-February seemed fantastic to Evan. "I don't think I will."

"Come on, be a sport."

"I'd rather watch you."

"Nuts to that," cried Don. "Everybody's going to swim, it'll be swell."

Evan allowed himself to be led over to the pool, inwardly vowing that no power on earth would get him into the water. Leonie and Shirley were giving an exhibition of fancy diving from the highest board, while Louise, Lester, Carola Binney, Irene Marlow and Ossie, who were already in bathing suits, sat around the edge and applauded. "Isn't that amazing?" cried Lester as Leonie did a spectacular jackknife. "I'd give anything in the world to be able to dive like that, but everything, if you know what I mean!"

Don took Evan firmly into a richly appointed men's dressing room and handed him a pair of trunks. "Now undress," he ordered.

Once more Evan protested. "Really I'd rather not——"

"What the hell——" said Don. "The water's warm and we'll all have fun—come on, be a pal——"

"Honestly——" began Evan.

"Now listen here," Don sat down on a bench and looked at Evan reproachfully, "this is a party and we're all having a good time and you're just bent on spoiling the whole shooting match."

"Why should you be so anxious for me to swim?" asked Evan almost petulantly.

"Because I like you," said Don with a disarming smile. "I liked you from the word go and you like me too, don't you? Come on, be frank and admit it."

"Of course I like you," said Evan. "I like you very much."

"Very well then," said Don triumphantly. "Do we swim or don't we?"

"You do and I don't."

"You wouldn't like me to get tough now, would you?" said Don in a wheedling voice, but with an undertone of menace. "I could, you know!"

"I'm sure you could, but I fail to see——"

"Come on now, quit stalling." Don advanced toward him and forcibly removed his coat. For one moment Evan contemplated screaming for help, but visualizing the ridiculous scene that would ensue he contented himself with struggling silently in Don's grasp. "Please let me go," he muttered breathlessly, "and don't be so silly."

Don had succeeded in slipping Evan's braces off and was endeavouring to unbutton his shirt when Lester came in. "Boys, boys," he cried admonishingly, "do try to remember that this is Sunday—which shall be nameless," and went into gales of laughter. Don released Evan immediately.

"This guy's a big sissy," he said. "He won't swim."

"I don't blame him," said Lester. "The water's like bouillabaisse. It's got more things in it than Macy's window."

"To hell with that, I'm going to swim if it kills me."

"It probably will on top of all that liquor." Lester went over and took a packet of cigarettes out of the pocket of his coat which was hanging on a peg. Then he came and sat on the bench next to Evan who, with a flushed face, was adjusting his clothes. "Relax, honey," he said, "Don always goes on like this when he's had a few drinks. Have a Camel?"

Evan took a cigarette, meanwhile Don was tearing off his clothes with ferocious speed. When he was completely naked he stood over Lester and Evan with arms folded and regarded them with scorn. Lester looked up at him. "It's all right, Puss," he said, "we've seen all that and it's gorgeous, now go jump in the pool and sober up."

"I don't know what's the matter with you guys," he grumbled, and went toward the door.

"You'd better put on some trunks," said Lester, "or have I gone too far?"

Don came slowly back and put on a pair of trunks. "Funny, hey?" he said bitterly and went out. A moment later they heard a loud splash and a shriek of laughter.

"What about another little drinkie?" said Lester.

6

About an hour later Evan found himself in a car sitting between Carola Binney and Luella Rosen whom he hadn't spoken to since before lunch. Don and Lester were squeezed together in the front seat next to Dwight Macadoo who was driving. The car apparently belonged to Irene Marlow. Evan had had two more old-fashioneds since his struggle with Don and was drunk, but in a detached sort of way. He had lost all capacity for resistance. From now on, he decided, he would drink when he was told to, eat when he was told to and go where he was taken. There was no sense in fighting against overwhelming odds. He lay back, quite contentedly, with his head on Luella's shoulder and listened to Carola describing a man called Benny Schultz who had directed a play she had tried out in Boston last September—

"Never again—" she was saying vehemently, "would I let that rat come within three blocks of me—My God—you've no idea what I went through—he comes prancing into my dressing room on the opening night after the first Act—the first Act! believe it or not, and starts giving me notes—'Listen, Benny,' I said, 'you may have directed *Crazy Guilt* and *Mother's Day* and *The Wings of a Dove,* and you may have made Martha Cadman the actress she is, and Claudia Biltmore the actress she certainly isn't, but you're not coming to my room on an opening night and start telling me that my tempo was too fast and that I struck a wrong note by taking my hat off at my first entrance. To begin with I had to take that God-awful hat off which I never wanted to wear anyway because the elastic band at the back was slipping, and if I hadn't it would have shot up into the air and got a laugh in the middle of my scene with Edgar; in the second place if you had engaged a supporting company for me who could act and a leading man who had some idea of playing comedy, and at least knew his lines, I wouldn't have had to rush through like a fire engine in order to carry that bunch of art-theatre hams and put the play over, and in the third place I should like to remind you that I was a star on Broadway when you were selling papers on the East Side, and I knew more about acting than you when I was five, playing the fit-ups with *The Two Orphans.* And what's more, if you think I'm going to tear myself to shreds trying to get laughs in the supper scene in the pitch dark—well, you're crazy—' " She paused for a moment, Luella gave a barely audible grunt.

"You've got to have light to play comedy," she went on, "and all the phoney highbrow directors in the world won't convince me otherwise."

"For all that I think Benny's pretty good," said Luella.

"He's all right with Shakespeare. I give you that," said Carola. "His Macbeth was fine, what you could see of it, but comedy never—look at the flop he had with *Some Take It Straight.*"

"*Some Take It Straight* was the worst play I ever sat through," Luella admitted.

"It needn't have been," cried Carola. "I read the original script. They wanted me to do it with Will Farrow, it really wasn't bad apart from needing a little fixing here and there—then that rat got hold of it and bitched it entirely."

Lester let the window down. "What's Carola yelling about," he enquired.

"Benny Schultz," said Luella.

"I wouldn't trust him an inch, not an inch," said Lester. "Look what he did to Macbeth."

"Are we nearly home?" asked Evan.

"We're not going home—we're going to Maisie's."

Evan lifted his head from Luella's shoulder. "Who's she?" he asked sleepily.

"She's divine," replied Lester. "You'll worship her—I mean she's a real person, isn't she, Luella?"

"It depends what you call real," said Luella. "Personally she drives me mad."

At this point the car turned into a gateway and drew up before a low, rather rambling white-walled house. Everyone got out and stamped their feet on the frozen snow to keep warm, while they waited for the door to be opened, which it presently was by a large forbidding-looking Swedish woman who regarded them suspiciously. Lester embraced her. "It's all right, Hilda," he said, "it's only us."

She stood aside and they all trooped in, shedding their coats in the hall. Lester led the way into a sort of studio paneled in pitch pine with wide bow windows and an immense log fire. The room was luxuriously furnished in a style that Evan supposed was early American. Anyhow in spite of its being extremely overheated, its simplicity was a relief after the other houses he had visited. He felt as though he had been going from house to house all his life. A grizzled woman with fine eyes and wearing a riding habit greeted them brusquely and introduced the other people in the room. There were two girls called Peggy and Althea, one fat and the other thin, a very pale young man in green Chinese pyjamas called George Tremlett, and a statuesque Frenchwoman with raven hair who appeared to be dressed as a Bavarian peasant. The only two members of their own party present were Leonie and Shirley who were lying on the floor playing with a Siamese cat. There was a large table of drinks along one of the windows. Don Lucas made a beeline for it. "Donny wants some firewater," he said. "Donny wants to get stinking."

"You were stinking at the Grouper Seligmans'," said Luella.

"Isn't he beautiful?" said the Frenchwoman.

When everyone had helped themselves to drinks Evan found himself sitting on a small upright sofa with George Tremlett.

"You arrived in the middle of a blazing row," whispered George with a giggle. "Suzanne and Shirley haven't spoken for two years and suddenly in she walked with Leonie—"

"Which is Suzanne?"

"The dark woman, Suzanne Closanges. She writes poetry either in French or English, she doesn't care which, and she lives here with Maisie."

"Maisie who?" asked Evan.

"Maisie Todd, of course," said George with slight irritation. "This is Maisie Todd's house—I did it."

"How do you mean 'did it'?"

"Designed it," George almost squealed. "I'm George Tremlett."

"How do you do," said Evan.

"It was lovely doing this house," went on George, "because I had an absolutely free hand—Maisie's like that—we had the grandest time driving all over New England and finding bits and pieces here and there. I found this very sofa we're sitting on tucked away in a fisherman's bedroom at Cape Cod."

"How extraordinary," said Evan—he felt overpoweringly sleepy.

Leonie came over with the Siamese cat and placed it on Evan's lap. "Isn't he adorable?" she said. "I gave him to Maisie for a Christmas present in 1933 and he's grown out of all knowledge."

The cat arched its back, dug its claws into Evan's leg and with a loud snarl hurled itself to the floor. "They're very fierce," went on Leonie picking it up again by the nape of its neck so that it hung spitting and kicking in the air. "And the older they grow the fiercer they get, but Dante isn't fierce though he's older than hell—are you, my darling?" she added affectionately, kissing it on the side of the head. The cat gave a sharp wriggle and scratched her cheek, from her eye, which it missed by a fraction, to her chin. She screamed with pain and dropped it onto a table where it knocked over and smashed a photograph of a lady in fencing costume framed in glass, jumped down and disappeared behind a writing desk. Evan started to his feet, everyone came crowding over.

"The son of a bitch," wailed Leonie. "He's maimed me for life." With that she burst into tears. Maisie Todd took charge with fine efficiency. She produced a large white handkerchief to staunch the blood, dispatched George to fetch some iodine from her bathroom. Shirley flung her arms around Leonie and kissed her wildly. "Don't darling, don't cry," she besought her. "For God's sake don't cry, you know I can't bear it."

"There's nothing to cry about," said Maisie, "it's only a scratch."

"It may only be a scratch," cried Shirley, "but it's terribly deep and it's bleeding."

"Don't fuss," said Maisie.

"It's all very fine for you to say 'don't fuss,'" Shirley said furiously, "but it might very easily have blinded her—you oughtn't to keep an animal like that in the house, it should be destroyed."

"Leonie gave it to Maisie herself before she knew you," put in Suzanne with a little laugh.

"Mind your own business," snapped Shirley.

Leonie dabbed her eyes and her cheeks alternately with the bloodstained handkerchief.

"For God's sake shut up, everybody. I'm all right now, it was only the shock."

"Drink this, darling," said Lester, handing her his glass.

"We should never have come—I knew something awful would happen," said Shirley.

"There is nothing to prevent you going." Suzanne spoke with icy dignity. There was a horrified silence for a moment. Shirley left Leonie and went very close to Suzanne.

"How dare you," she said softly. Evan noticed that she was trembling with passion. "How dare you speak to me like that—"

Maisie intervened. "Now listen, Shirley," she began. Shirley pushed her aside. "I've always disliked you, Suzanne, from the first moment I set eyes on you, and I wish to say here and now that you're nothing but a fifth-rate gold digger sponging on Maisie the way you do and making her pay to publish your lousy French poems, and you're not even French at that—you're Belgian!"

Suzanne gave a gasp of fury, slapped Shirley hard in the face and rushed from the room, cannoning into George Tremlett who was coming in with the iodine and knocking the bottle out of his hand on to the floor. "Oh, dear!" he cried, sinking on to his knees. "All over the best Hook rug in the house!"

From then onwards everybody talked at once. Maisie dashed out of the room after Suzanne; Leonie started to cry again. The two girls, Althea and Peggy, who had been watching the whole scene from a corner, decided after a rapid conversation to follow Maisie and Suzanne, which they did, slamming the door after them. George was moaning over the Hook rug and trying to rub out the iodine stains with a silk scarf. Lester joined Luella and Carola by the fireplace, Carola was protesting violently at Suzanne's behaviour, while Luella smiled cynically. Lester, genuinely distressed, was sympathizing with Shirley and Leonie, while Don added to the din by strolling over to the piano with Dwight Macadoo and playing "Smoke Gets in Your Eyes" with one hand. Presently he desisted. "This piano stinks," he said. "No tone—where's the radio?" Before he could find it Luella, to Evan's intense relief, suggested that they should all go, and led the way firmly into the hall. While they were struggling into their coats and wraps the large Swedish woman watched them silently with a baleful expression. The freezing night air struck Evan like a blow between the eyes; he staggered slightly. Don quickly lifted him off the ground and deposited him in the car with infinite tenderness.

"You were wrong about that swim," he said affectionately. "It was swell, made me feel like a million dollars. Now we'll go home and have a little drinkie."

7

They had no sooner got inside the Steinhausers' front door when Irene came rushing out of the living room. "Where the hell have you been?" she cried angrily to Dwight. "I looked for you all over and when I came out you'd gone off in my car."

"Now don't be mad at me, darling—" began Dwight.

"Mad at you! I've never been madder in my life—come in here." She dragged him into the library and banged the door.

"Well," said Lester, "isn't she the cutest thing—My dear!" He waved his hand benevolently after them. "These prima donnas—who shall be nameless—"

Louise appeared with a great cry and flung her arms around Evan. He was dimly aware that she had changed into a long flowing tea-gown. "*There* you are," she said, "I couldn't think what had happened to you— you must be starving." Still holding him tightly she pulled him into the living room which had undergone a startling change. All the furniture had been pushed out on to the sun porch with the exception of the chairs which were arranged around the walls. An enormous buffet loaded with hams, turkeys, salads, bowls of fruit, bowls of cream, two large cakes and piles of plates stood along one side of the room. Another smaller table for drinks was joined on to the bar behind which Bonwit was still officiating, assisted by a Japanese in a white coat. There were at least fifty people in the room and the noise was deafening. Evan, dazed as he was, distinguished the Grouper Seligmans, Lady Kettering, and several of the people he had seen at the Hughes-Hitchcocks', including the young expectant mother who was sitting on the floor with her back against one of the piano legs, and a large plate of variegated food on her lap, apparently in a stupor, while Suki played an unending series of complicated syncopation in her ear.

Louise led Evan to the table and gave him a plate on which she piled, with professional speed, a turkey leg, Virginia ham, baked beans, a fish cake, potato salad, lettuce, a wedge of Camembert cheese and a large slice of strange-looking brown bread. "There," she said, "now sit down quietly, and eat, you poor dear." With that she whisked away from him and rushed across to Carola and Luella. He looked around for a vacant chair but there wasn't one, so he stayed where he was and ate standing against the table. The food was certainly good although there was far too much of it on his plate. He was about to slide the cheese and one of the slices of ham into an empty bowl that had held salad when he was arrested by Charlie Schofield putting his hand on his shoulder. He jumped guiltily as though he'd been caught in the act of doing something nefarious.

"I told Alice Kettering what you said about Tiger being in Africa," said Charlie, "and she's in an awful state—she was crazy about him for years you know."

Before Evan could reply Don came up and forced a glass into his hand. "I promised you a little drinkie," he said genially, "and a little drinkie you're going to have."

A big woman in yellow put her arm through Charlie Schofield's and led him away. Evan saw out of the corner of his eyes that Lady Kettering was drifting towards him. He retreated onto the sun porch followed by Don looking very puzzled.

"What's the idea?"

"Just somebody I don't want to talk to," said Evan with as much nonchalance as he could muster.

"Listen, pal," said Don. "If there's anyone you don't like just you tip me off and I'll sock 'em."

Evan, shuddering inwardly at the thought of Don socking Lady Kettering, muttered that it was of no importance really, and leant against the window. Outside the moon had come up and the sea shone eerily in its light like grey silk; far away in the distance a lighthouse flashed. It all looked so remote and quiet that Evan felt inclined to weep. Don squeezed his arm reassuringly. "You know I like you," he said, "I like you better than any Englishman I've ever met. Most Englishmen are high hat, you know, kind of snooty, but you're not high hat at all, you're a good sport."

"Thank you," said Evan dimly.

"I hope you weren't sore at me for trying to make you go in the pool," Don went on. "I wouldn't like to have you sore at me. It isn't often I get a chance to talk to anyone really intelligent—not that you're only just intelligent, you're brilliant, otherwise you wouldn't be able to write all those God-damned books, would you now?"

"Well," began Evan, feeling that some reply was demanded.

"Now don't argue." Don's voice was fierce. "Of course you're brilliant and you know you are, don't you?"

Evan smiled. "I wouldn't exactly say—"

Don patted his hand tolerantly. "Of course you do—everybody knows when they're brilliant, they'd be damned fools if they didn't. Jesus, the way you played that question game in the car—if that wasn't brilliant I should like to know what is? But what I mean to say is this: I'm just a simple sort of guy, really, without any brains at all—I've got looks, I grant you that otherwise I shouldn't be where I am today should I? But no brains, not a one. Why, the idea of sitting down and writing a letter drives me crazy let alone a book. Sometimes when I look at something beautiful like all that," he indicated the view, "or when I run across someone really brilliant like you are I feel low—honest to God I do—"

"Why?" said Evan.

"Because I'm such a damn fool of course. I couldn't write down what that looks like to me, not if you paid me a million dollars I couldn't. I couldn't paint it either, I couldn't even talk about it. What do I get out of life I ask you? Money, yes—I make a lot of dough and so what—Happiness, no—I'm one of the unhappiest sons of bitches in the whole world," he broke off.

"Cheer up," said Evan as cheerfully as he could. He was feeling depressed himself.

"It gets me down," murmured Don, pressing his forehead against the glass of the window. "It just gets me down."

Evan was pained and embarrassed to observe that he was crying. A concerted scream of laughter came from the living room. Evan peeped in.
Everyone was grouped round Carola who, with a man's Homburg hat
perched on her head, was doing an imitation of somebody. Evan glanced
back at Don, who was still staring out into the night; his shoulders were
heaving. Now was the moment to escape, everyone was far too occupied to
notice whether he was there or not; if he could get into the hall without
Louise seeing him, the rest was easy; he could get into his room, lock the
door and go to bed. He crept along behind the buffet, avoiding Mr. Hockbridge, who was asleep on a chair, and reached the hall in safety. From
behind the closed door of the library came sounds of strife, apparently
Irene's fury at Dwight had in no way abated. Evan paused long enough to
hear her scream angrily—"It was Luella's fault, was it—we'll see about
that!"—then he darted down the passage, through Lester's room and the
bathroom and reached his own room with a sigh of relief. He switched on
the lights by the door and started back in horror. Stretched out on his bed
was a woman in a heavy sleep. On closer examination he recognized the
Countess Brancati. Her black dress was rumpled and her hair was spread
over the pillow like pink hay.

A great rage shook Evan to the core. He seized her by the shoulder and
pushed her backwards and forwards violently; she continued to sleep
undisturbed. He knelt down on the floor by the bed and shouted "Wake
up—please wake up" in her face to which she replied with a low moan. He
shook her again and one of her earrings fell off; he picked it up and put it
on the bed table and stood there looking at her, his whole body trembling
with fury and frustration. He gave her one more despairing shove but she
paid no attention. Then, with an expression of set determination he
marched back to the living room. On his way he met Bonwit emerging
from the library. "My God," Bonwit said, "there's all hell breaking loose in
there," and then, noticing Evan's face, "what's happened to you?"

"There's a woman on my bed," Evan almost shouted.

"I'll bet it's Mary Lou Brancati," said Bonwit. "She always passes out
somewhere—come on—we'll get her out."

They went back together. The countess had turned over on to her face.
Bonwit slapped her behind; she wriggled slightly and he did it again
harder. Presently, after several more whacks, she turned over and muttered, "G'way and leave me alone—" Bonwit whereupon hoisted her up on
to the side of the bed and shook her. She opened her eyes and looked at him
malevolently. "Get the hell away from me," she said. "What d'you think
you're doing!"

"Come on, baby," said Bonwit, "you're missing everything. There's a
party going on."

"To hell with it," she replied. "G'way and leave me alone."

"Take her other arm," ordered Bonwit. Evan obeyed and they hauled her struggling and protesting into the bathroom. There Bonwit dabbed her face with a wet sponge; she gave a scream and tried to hit him. Finally they got her into the hall and deposited her in a chair. Bonwit slapped his hands together as though he had just felled a tree and said, "Now you're okay, fellar."

At that moment the hall suddenly filled with people. Louise came out of the library with her arms around Irene who was sobbing. Dwight followed them miserably. Unfortunately Luella and Otis Meer came out of the living room at the same instant followed by Lester, Lady Kettering and the Grouper Seligmans. Irene, catching sight of Luella, wrested herself from Louise's arms. "So you're still here," she said harshly. "I'm surprised you have the nerve!"

Luella looked at her coolly. "You're tight, Irene," she said. "You'd better go home."

"You're a snake!" cried Irene, breathing heavily. "A double-faced, rotten snake!"

Lester tried to calm her. "Look here, honey," he said, "there's no cause in getting yourself all worked up."

Irene pushed him aside. "You shut up—you're as bad as she is—you're all of you jealous of Dwight and me and always have been—Luella's been trying to get him for years, and if you think I'm so dumb that I haven't seen what's been going on you're crazy."

"Really," murmured Lady Kettering. "This is too bloody—we'd better go—"

"Go and be damned to you!" said Irene.

Louise gave a cry of distress. Lady Kettering turned and tried to make a dignified exit into the living room, but was prevented by Ossie, Suki, the Hughes-Hitchcocks and Mrs. Hockbridge, who had crowded into the doorway to see what was happening.

Luella seized Irene by the arm in a grip of steel. "Behave yourself," she hissed. "What do you mean by making a disgusting scene like this about nothing?"

"Nothing!" Irene screamed and writhed in Luella's grasp. Otis Meer gave a cackle of shrill laughter. Dwight tried to coax Irene back into the library. Louise wept loudly and was comforted by Lester and Ossie. Lady Kettering struggled valiantly through the crowd to try to find her cloak. Carola, who had joined the group with Shirley and Leonie, announced in ringing tones that in her opinion the possession of an adequate singing voice was hardly sufficient excuse for behaving like a Broadway floozy. Lester turned on her and told her to shut up and not make everything worse, and in the indescribable pandemonium that ensued, Evan fled.

8

About an hour later, Evan, sitting up rigidly in his bed, began to relax. He had brushed his teeth, taken three aspirins, undressed, tried to lock the door but discovered there was no key, and read four chapters of *Sense and Sensibility* which he always travelled with as a gentle soporific. He had left no stone unturned in his efforts to drag his aching mind away from the horrors he had endured. He had turned out the light twice and attempted to sleep but to no avail. Incidents of the day, people's names, unrelated scraps of conversation crowded into his brain, making even the possibility of lying still out of the question let alone sleep. Sleep was aeons away, he felt that it was well within the bounds of probability that he would never sleep again. The thought of the lecture he had to give that very night, it was now three a.m., tortured him. He felt incapable of uttering one coherent phrase and as for talking for an hour, his mind reeled at the very idea of it. The continual noise, the endless arrivals and departures, the impact of so many different atmospheres and personalities, the unleashing of vulgar passion he had witnessed, to say nothing of the incredible amount of alcohol he had drunk, had lacerated his nerves beyond bearing. He was outraged, shamed, exhausted and bitterly angry.

Now at last he was beginning to feel calmer. The three aspirins he had taken had made his heart thump rather, his maximum dose as a rule being two, but it was apparently taking effect. He glanced at his watch, ten minutes past three, if he could manage to sleep until eleven he would have had nearly his eight hours and probably be able to get in an extra hour at his hotel before his lecture if he wasn't too nervous. "I'll give myself another ten minutes," he reflected, "and then turn out the light, by that time it ought to be all right."

He lay there still as a mouse, resolutely emptying his mind and concentrating on gentle, peaceful things, the waves of the sea, a vast four-poster bed in some remote English country house, the cool, soft lavender-scented sheets, the soughing of the wind outside in the elms—At this moment the door opened and Bonwit came in on tiptoe. He was in his pyjamas and carrying a pillow and an eiderdown. He looked relieved when he saw that Evan wasn't asleep.

"I'm awfully sorry, fellar," he said, "but I've got to come and use your other bed—there's been all hell going on. Irene drove off in her car with Dwight, leaving Suki and Luella behind, the Brancatis went too, leaving Ossie and Otis, and we've only just found Don Lucas—he's in the living room on the sofa. Ossie and Otis are in with Lester, Luella's in with Louise and Suki's in my room. I've got to get up at seven to go into town but don't be afraid I'll disturb you—I've left my clothes in the bathroom so as I can dress in there."

"Oh," said Evan hopelessly, the blackness of despair made further utterance impossible.

Bonwit clambered into bed and switched off his light. "I'm all in," he said. "Good night, fellar."

Evan switched off his light too, and lay staring into the darkness.

In a remarkably short space of time Bonwit began to snore. Evan groaned and tried to fold the pillow over his ears, but it was no good, the snores grew louder. They rose rhythmically to a certain pitch and then died away. Occasionally the rhythm would be broken by a grunt, then there would be silence for a moment, then they'd start again. Evan, after a half an hour of it, suddenly leapt up on an impulse of pure blinding rage, switched on the light and went over to Bonwit's bed and stood looking at him. Bonwit was lying on his back with his mouth wide open—the noise issuing from it was incredible. Evan, flinging all gentleness and consideration to the winds, seized him violently by the shoulders and turned him over. Bonwit gave a terrific snort, turned back again almost immediately and went on snoring louder than ever. Evan began to cry, tears coursed down his cheeks and fell on to his pyjamas—panic assailed him—if this went on he would definitely go mad. He walked up and down the room fighting to prevent himself from losing control utterly and shrieking the house down. He went over to the window and looked out. The night was crystal clear, there wasn't a cloud in the sky. Suddenly he knew what he was going to do, the idea came to him in a flash. He was going away, that's what he was going to do. He was going to dress, telephone for a taxi and leave that horrible house for ever. It was idiotic not to have thought of it before. He would leave a note for Louise in the hall asking her to bring his suitcase into New York with her. He tore off his pyjamas and began to dress. Bonwit stopped snoring and turned over, Evan switched off the light and stood still hardly daring to breathe. If Bonwit woke up and caught him trying to escape, he'd obviously try to prevent him—there would be arguments and persuasions and protests, probably ending in the whole house being roused.

Bonwit started to snore again and Evan, with a sigh of relief, finished dressing. Holding his shoes in his hand he crept down the passage, through the bathroom and into Lester's room. He could dimly make out two forms in one bed and one in the other. He banged against a chair on his way to the door and immediately lay down flat on the floor. Lester moved in his sleep but didn't wake; finally, on hands and knees, Evan crawled out into the other passage and into the hall. Once there, he put on his shoes and went cautiously in search of the telephone; just as he was about to go into the library he remembered that it was in the bar, he had heard Bonwit using it before lunch. He went into the living room. The curtains were not drawn and moonlight was flooding through the windows. Don was sleeping soundly on a sofa, he looked rather debauched but extraordinarily hand-some. Poor Don. Evan shook his head at him sorrowfully and went over to the bar. There was a shutter down over it which was padlocked. This was a terrible blow. Evan thought for a moment of going back and waking Bon-wit; but decided against it. If there was no taxi he'd walk and if he didn't know the way he'd find it, at all events he knew he would rather die in the snow than spend one more hour in that house. He scribbled a note to Louise in the library. "Dear Mrs. Steinhauser—" He debated for a moment whether or not to address her as Louise, she had certainly kissed him several times during the day and called him Darling frequently, also he knew her to be a kindly, well-intentioned woman, although at the moment he could cheerfully have strangled her. On the whole he felt that "Mrs. Steinhauser" better expressed the manner in which he was leaving her house. "Dear Mrs. Steinhauser—Finding myself unable to sleep I have decided to go back to New York. Please forgive this unconventional departure, but it is essential, if I am to lecture with any degree of success, that I relax for several hours beforehand. Please don't worry about me, I am sure I shall find my way to the station quite easily, but if you would be so kind as to have my suitcase packed and bring it in with you tomorrow, I should be more than grateful. With many thanks for your delightful hospitality I am, yours sincerely, Evan Lorrimer." He signed his name with a flourish. "She can stick that in her damned visitors' book," he said to himself. He left the note in a promi-nent position on a table in the hall, found his hat and coat in a cupboard and let himself quietly out of the front door. The cold air exhilarated him. It was odd, he reflected, how the excitement of escape had completely ban-ished his nervous hysteria. He felt surprisingly well, all things considered. The snow shone in the moonlight and the country lay around him white and still. He noticed a glow in the sky behind a hill. That must be a village, he thought, and set off jauntily down the drive.

About an hour later, when he had walked several miles and his adven-turous spirit had begun to wilt a trifle, he was picked up by a milk van. The driver was rugged and friendly and agreed to take him to the nearest station. They had some coffee together in an all-night lunchroom when they got there; the next train for New York wasn't due for three-quarters of an hour, and the driver talked freely about his home and domestic affairs with an accent that Evan found, at moments, extremely difficult to under-stand. Finally he drove away in his van having allowed Evan to pay for the coffee, but refused to accept two dollars.

"Nuts to that," he said with a laugh. "I like you—you're not high hat and kind of snooty like most Englishmen—So long, buddy."

Buddy, warmed by this tribute, went on to the platform and waited for the train.

When he arrived in New York it was daylight. The night-porter at his hotel greeted him in some surprise and handed him a pile of telephone messages and a letter. When he got to his room he opened the letter first. "Dear Mr. Lorrimer," he read, "Although we have never met, your books have given me so much pleasure that I am taking this opportunity of welcoming you to Chicago, where I understand you are going to talk to us next week on 'History and the Modern Novel.' " My husband and I would be so pleased if you would come out to us for the weekend after your lecture. Our home is on the edge of the lake and we flatter ourselves it is the nearest approach to an English country house that you could find in the whole of the Middle West. It is peaceful and quiet, and no one would disturb you, you could just rest. If you have anyone with you we should, of course, be delighted to receive them, too. My husband joins me in the hope that you will honour us by accepting. Yours very sincerely, Irma Weinkopf." Evan undressed thoughtfully and got into bed.

•

There was another party that made a lasting impression on Noël.

During the summer of 1937 or 1938, I forget which, Elsa Maxwell gave a party in the South of France. It was a "beach" party and when she invited Grace Moore, Beatrice Lillie and me, she explained that we were to "come as we were" and that it would be "just ourselves." When we arrived (as we were) we discovered that "just ourselves" meant about a hundred of us, all in the last stages of evening dress. We also discovered that one of the objects of the party was for us to entertain. As we were on holiday and had no accompanist and were not in any way prepared to perform, we refused. Elsa was perfectly understanding, but the other guests were a trifle disgruntled. I believe Beattie was persuaded to sing, but Grace and I held firm. This whole glittering episode was my original inspiration for "I Went to a Marvellous Party." Beattie eventually sang the song in *Set to Music* wearing slacks, a fisherman's shirt, several ropes of pearls, a large sun hat and dark glasses. She has sung it a great deal since.

"I'VE BEEN TO A MARVELLOUS PARTY"

Quite for no reason
I'm here for the Season
And high as a kite,
Living in error
With Maud at Cap Ferrat
Which couldn't be right.

Everyone's here and frightfully gay,
Nobody cares what people say.
Though the Riviera
Seems really much queerer
Than Rome at its height,
Yesterday night—

I've been to a marvellous party
With Nounou and Nada and Nell,
It was in the fresh air
And we went as we were
And we stayed as we were
Which was Hell.
Poor Grace started singing at midnight
And didn't stop singing till four;
We knew the excitement was bound to begin
When Laura got blind on Dubonnet and gin
And scratched her veneer with a Cartier pin,
I couldn't have liked it more.

I've been to a marvellous party,
I must say the fun was intense,
We all had to do
What the people we knew
Would be doing a hundred years hence.
Dear Cecil arrived wearing armour,
Some shells and a black feather boa,
Poor Millicent wore a surrealist comb
Made of bits of mosaic from St. Peter's in Rome,
But the weight was so great that she had to go home,
I couldn't have liked it more.

People's behaviour
Away from Belgravia
Would make you aghast,
So much variety
Watching Society
Scampering past,
If you have any mind at all
Gibbon's divine *Decline and Fall*
Seems pretty flimsy,
No more than a whimsy,

I've been to a marvellous party
Elsie made an entrance with May!
You'd never have guessed
From her fisherman's vest
That her bust had been whittled away
Poor Lulu got fried on Chianti
And talked about esprit de corps
The French girl was dancing a fox-trot with me
When suddenly Cyril screamed Fiddle-de-dee
And ripped off his trousers and jumped in the sea
I couldn't have liked it more!

You're for no reason
I'm here for the season
And high as a kite
Living in sin
With Maud at Cap Ferrat
Which couldn't be right
Everyone here and frightfully gay
Nobody cares what people say
Tho' the Riviera
Seems really much queerer
Than Rome at its height
Yesterday night

I've been to a marvellous party
With Tiger and Boo Boo and Nell
It was in the fresh air
And we went as we were
And we stayed as we were which was Hell!
Poor Clare slarted singing at midnight
And didn't stop singing till four
Daphne Pop-Oliver got very tight
Peggie and Jane had a hand to hand fight
And Lulu struck Maud and went out like a light
I couldn't have liked it more

I've been to a marvellous party
We didn't start dinner till ten
And young Bobbie Carr
Did a stunt at the bar
With a lot of extraordinary men
Poor Lula was there looking frightful
And Michael arrived with a whore
We knew the excitement was bound to begin
When Laura demolished a bottle of gin
And scratched her veneer with a carving pin
I couldn't have liked it more!

By way of contrast
On Saturday last—

I've been to a marvellous party,
We didn't start dinner till ten
And young Bobbie Carr
Did a stunt at the bar
With a lot of extraordinary men;
Dear Baba arrived with a turtle
Which shattered us all to the core,
The Grand Duke was dancing a fox-trot with me
When suddenly Cyril screamed "Fiddle-de-dee"
And ripped off his trousers and jumped in the sea,
I couldn't have liked it more.

I've been to a marvellous party,
Elise made an entrance with May,
You'd never have guessed
From her fisherman's vest
That her bust had been whittled away.
Poor Lulu got fried on Chianti
And talked about *esprit de corps.*
Maurice made a couple of passes at Gus
And Freddie, who hates any kind of a fuss,
Did half the Big Apple and twisted his truss,
I couldn't have liked it more.

I've been to a marvellous party,
We played the most wonderful game,
Maureen disappeared
And came back in a beard
And we all had to guess at her name!
We talked about growing old gracefully
And Elsie who's seventy-four
Said, "A, it's a question of being sincere,
And B, if you're supple you've nothing to fear."
Then she swung upside down from a glass chandelier,
I couldn't have liked it more.

—SET TO MUSIC (1939)

•

"I *am* England and England is me," Noël told the *Daily Express* in 1965. And he might well have added, "Whether it likes it or not!"

Over the years there were times when much of the English press proved antipathetic and the critics cold. None of it changed his devotion to his country. And most of his country remained devoted to him.

It didn't mean that he couldn't see and make fun of some of its fading imperialistic foibles, as he did in "Mad Dogs and Englishmen." And he was perfectly aware that the aristocracy was living—somewhat impecuniously in many cases—on its storied past . . .

Note the key lines in "The Stately Homes of England":

> To prove the upper classes
> Have still the upper hand

Noël recorded it and sang it all over the world "and it has been popular with everyone with the exception of a Mayoress in New Zealand, who said it let down the British Empire."

Bea Lillie at that "marvellous party"
in the South of France

"THE STATELY HOMES OF ENGLAND"

Lord Elderley, Lord Borrowmere,
Lord Sickert and Lord Camp
With every virtue, every grace,
Ah what avails the sceptred race,
Here you see—the four of us,
And there are so many more of us
Eldest sons that must succeed.
We know how Caesar conquered Gaul
And how to whack a cricket ball;
Apart from this, our education
Lacks coordination.
Though we're young and tentative
And rather rip-representative,
Scions of a noble breed,
We are the products of those homes serene and stately
Which only lately
Seem to have run to seed!
The Stately Homes of England,
How beautiful they stand,
To prove the upper classes
Have still the upper hand;
Though the fact that they have to be rebuilt
And frequently mortgaged to the hilt
Is inclined to take the gilt
Off the gingerbread,
And certainly damps the fun
Of the eldest son—
But still we won't be beaten,
We'll scrimp and scrape and save,
The playing fields of Eton
Have made us frightfully brave—
And though if the Van Dycks have to go
And we pawn the Bechstein Grand,
We'll stand
By the Stately Homes of England.

Here you see
The pick of us,
You may be heartily sick of us,
Still with sense
We're all imbued.

Our homes command extensive views
And with assistance from the Jews
We have been able to dispose of
Rows and rows and rows of
Gainsboroughs and Lawrences,
Some sporting prints of Aunt Florence's,
Some of which were rather rude.
Although we sometimes flaunt our family conventions,
Our good intentions
Mustn't be misconstrued.

The Stately Homes of England
We proudly represent,
We only keep them up for
Americans to rent.
Though the pipes that supply the bathroom burst
And the lavatory makes you fear the worst,
It was used by Charles the First
Quite informally,
And later by George the Fourth
On a journey north.
The State Apartments keep their
Historical renown,
It's wiser not to sleep there
In case they tumble down;
But still if they ever catch on fire
Which, with any luck, they might
We'll fight
For the Stately Homes of England.

The Stately Homes of England,
Though rather in the lurch,
Provide a lot of chances
For Psychical Research—
There's the ghost of a crazy younger son
Who murdered, in thirteen fifty-one,
An extremely rowdy Nun
Who resented it,
And people who come to call
Meet her in the hall.
The baby in the guest wing,
Who crouches by the grate,
Was walled up in the west wing

In fourteen twenty-eight.
If anyone spots
The Queen of Scots
In a hand-embroidered shroud
We're proud
Of the Stately Homes of England.

REPRISE—ACT 2

Lord Elderley, Lord Borrowmere,
Lord Sickert and Lord Camp,
Behold us in our hours of ease,
Uncertain, coy and hard to please.
Reading in *Debrett* of us,
This fine Patrician quartette of us,
We can feel extremely proud,
Our ancient lineage we trace
Back to the cradle of the Race
Before those beastly Roman bowmen
Bitched our local Yeomen.
Though the new democracy
May pain the old Aristocracy
We've not winced nor cried aloud,
Under the bludgeonings of chance what will
    be—will be.
Our heads will still be
Bloody but quite unbowed!

The Stately Homes of England
In valley, dale and glen
Produce a race of charming,
Innocuous young men.
Though our mental equipment may be slight
And we barely distinguish left from right,
We are quite prepared to fight
For our principles,
Though none of us knows so far
What they really are.
Our duty to the nation,
It's only fair to state,
Lies not in procreation
But what we procreate;
And so we can cry

With kindling eye
As to married life we go,
What ho!
For the Stately Homes of England!

The Stately Homes of England,
Although a trifle bleak,
Historically speaking,
Are more or less unique,
We've a cousin who won the Golden Fleece
And a very peculiar fowling piece
Which was sent to Cromwell's niece,
Who detested it,
And rapidly sent it back
With a dirty crack.
A note we have from Chaucer
Contains a bawdy joke.
We also have a saucer
That Bloody Mary broke.
We've two pairs of tights
King Arthur's Knights
Had completely worn away.
Sing Hey!
For the Stately Homes of England!

—OPERETTE (1938)

•

I think social distinctions are very
important because they make a balance.

—INTERVIEW (1972)

CRESTWELL (the butler): I drink to the
final inglorious disintegration of the
most unlikely dream that ever troubled
the foolish heart of man—Social Equality!

—RELATIVE VALUES (1951)

We British are a peculiar breed.
Undemonstrative on the whole.
It takes a very big shock indeed
To dent our maddening self-control.

So he wrote in a verse, "Not Yet the Dodo" (1967).

It was an affectionate observation based on years of study of his fellow citizens at home and abroad, and there was nothing funnier, he felt, than the Englishman abroad. He saw plenty of them on his travels, and on a trip to India to entertain the troops during World War II he experienced a time warp called the British Raj.

It inspired a song "written and firmly sung in Calcutta in 1944. Only a very few 'Indian Colonels' protested and it was a great success."

"I WONDER WHAT HAPPENED TO HIM?"

The India that one read about
And may have been misled about
In one respect has kept itself intact.
Though "Pukka Sahib" traditions may have cracked
And thinned
The good old Indian army's still a fact.
That famous monumental man
The Officer and Gentleman
Still lives and breathes and functions from Bombay
                                    to Katmandu.

At any moment one can glimpse
Matured or embryonic Blimps
Vivaciously speculating as to what became of who.
Though Eastern sounds may fascinate your ear
When West meets West you're always sure to hear—

Whatever became of old Bagot?
I haven't seen him for a year.
Is it true that young Forbes had to marry that Faggot
He met in the Vale of Kashmir?
Have you had any news
Of that chap in the Blues.
Was it Prosser or Pyecroft or Pym?
He was stationed in Simla, or was it Bengal?
I know he got tight at a ball in Nepal
And wrote several four-letter words on the wall.
I wonder what happened to him!

Whatever became of old Shelley?
Is it true that young Briggs was cashiered

For riding quite nude on a
  push-bike through Delhi
The day the new Viceroy
  appeared?
Have you had any word
Of that bloke in the Third,
Was it Southerby, Sedgwick
  or Sim?
They had him thrown out
  of the club in Bombay
For, apart from his mess
  bills exceeding his pay,
He took to pigsticking in
  quite the wrong way.
I wonder what happened to him!

One must admit that by and large
Upholders of the British Raj
Don't shine in conversation as a breed.
Though Indian army officers can read
A bit
Their verbal wit—has rather run to seed.
Their splendid insularity
And roguish jocularity
Was echoing through when Victoria was Queen.
In restaurants and dining cars,
In messes, clubs and hotel bars
They try to maintain tradition in the way
                    it's always been
Though worlds may change and nations disappear
Above the shrieking chaos you will hear—

Whatever became of old Tucker?
Have you heard any word of young Mills
Who ruptured himself at the end of a chukka
And had to be sent to the hills?
They say that young Lees
Had a go of D.T.'s
And his hopes of promotion are slim.
According to Stubbs, who's a bit of a louse,
The silly young blighter went out on a "souse,"
And took two old tarts into Government House.
I wonder what happened to him!

Whatever became of old Keeling?
I hear that he got back from France
And frightened three nuns in a train in Darjeeling
By stripping and waving his lance!
D'you remember Munroe,
In the P.A.V.O.?
He was tallish and mentally dim.
That talk of heredity can't be quite true,
He was dropped on his head by his ayah at two,
I presume that by now he'll have reached GHQ.
I'm sure that's what happened to him!

Whatever became of old Archie?
I hear he departed this life
After rounding up ten sacred cows in Karachi
To welcome the Governor's wife.
D'you remember young Phipps
Who had *very* large hips
And whose waist was excessively slim?
Well, it seems that some doctor in Grosvenor Square
Gave him hormone injections for growing his hair
And he grew something here, and he grew
                    something there.
I wonder what happened to her—*him*?

·

As the 1930s were ending, a new and somber drama was taking shape.
Noël had no hand in writing it, but he was to play a part in acting it out.

In 1938 he was recruited by Sir Robert Vansittart at the Foreign Office
to join an unofficial team of businessmen and other prominent men whose
daily business took them to Europe. Clearly, World War II was
imminent—at least in the minds of those who took the trouble to see—
and the Vansittart faction needed "intelligence" to make the case for
Britain to re-arm. Noël and the others were asked to report back on the
attitude they found in the places they visited.

"We have nothing to worry about but the destruction of civilization,"
he wrote to Woollcott as he went off to be "Noël Coward, singing my little songs and being a bit of a silly ass." Innocent as he may have thought he
appeared, he managed to wind up on the Nazi black list that came to light
after the war. Rebecca West, who was also on the list, cabled him:

MY DEAR THE PEOPLE WE SHOULD HAVE BEEN SEEN
DEAD WITH.

The summer of 1939 had a distinctly *faux*-theatrical quality to it. On the surface, life went on as usual. Noël wrote two plays: *This Happy Breed* (a semi-sequel to *Cavalcade,* taking events in British life up to the present) and a comedy, *Such Sweet Sorrow* ("Very gay, I think," he wrote to Woollcott, "which I am going to play here this autumn"), which became *Present Laughter.*

In the event, neither achieved their planned September production, for reasons totally *non*-theatrical.

A far bigger drama was about to unfold, in which he had a personal part to play . . .

CHAPTER FOUR
THE 1940s

London Pride has been handed down to us.
London Pride is a flower that's free.
London Pride means our own dear town to us,
And our pride it forever will be . . .
Nothing ever could override
The pride of London Town.

—"LONDON PRIDE" (1941)

St. Paul's Cathedral. Amazingly
untouched at the height of the 1941
blitz. ("Stay, city / Smokily enchanted /
Cradle of our memories and
hopes and fears.")

Prime Minister Winston Churchill,
symbol of England's hopes
during these years

WORLD WAR II started on September 3, 1939. Three days later Noël was flown to Paris to set up a Bureau of Propaganda.

It was not the kind of work he had wanted or was even suited for.

Nonetheless, he composed a radio broadcast designed to emphasize the ties between the two countries that had been known to slip from time to time since Agincourt.

·

"FRIENDSHIP IN WARTIME"

In clear words Rudyard Kipling expressed our English sentiments for France many years ago—twenty-six years ago to be exact—in the month of June 1913, over a year before the Great War, before our two countries were merged together indissolubly to resist aggression, to defend those weaker than ourselves and to fight to the last to keep our ideals in a world threatened by force, arrogance and stupidity. For four long years the French and the English were side by side. Fighting together, laughing and joking together, suffering and dying together. All this they did for an ideal, an ideal that is still in their hearts today. The ideal is something worth fighting for and dying for. It is ironic that so soon after those four desolate years we should again find ourselves united in the same circumstances against the same enemy. But he who imagines that our hearts are not as one in this new struggle is storing up for himself the bitterest of illusions. We have fought together before and we know each other's mettle. The youth of both our countries have been bred on memories—memories of the gallantry and courage of our allies and of their deep unchanged and unchanging friendship.

In thousands of ordinary English homes there are today evidences of this. Perhaps a Poilu's tin hat, hung in a place of honour in the sitting room with an inscription scratched on it—or a snapshot of Father and his pal Pierre Dupont, arm in arm, laughing together somewhere in France—"Good old Pierre. His boy ought to be about twenty-two now—I'll tell our Jack to look him up when he goes over next week." All very sentimental, no doubt, but a sentiment that is based on memory and on hardship and pain endured together can never be laughed away. Its roots lie too deeply embedded in the years. Those strange years when the French and the English sacrificed themselves and fought as they are fighting now and they will fight if need be in years to come. As they will always fight, together, for their liberty and their equality and their fraternity.

·

Then reality set in . . .

"I could not avoid realising quite early on that the job I had undertaken was neither so serious nor so important as I had been led to believe."

To fill the empty hours he began writing about his colleagues as if they were characters in a play—which, in a sense, they were—like the Colonel Blimp–like figure, ever so slightly redolent of mothballs, of Lord Gerald Wellesley. When he and Lord Reay joined the team, the office was naturally christened the House of Lords. In November 1939 Wellesley was appointed Liaison Officer between the Paris office and GHQ (General Headquarters) in Arras.

"NOTES ON LIAISON"

Lord Gerald Wellesley said, "Now, see here,
I must make liaison with Commandant Reay
I'm also in need of a camouflaged car
And some *laissez-passers*—or whatever they are.
I also *must* have a large box made of tin
To put all my lack of initiative in.
I also require from the dear DMI
The reasons for which and for what and for why
And would someone kindly send off a few wires
Explaining my slightly more private desires?
If Reay or Strathallan would carry my bag
And Noël would run to the Ritz like a stag
And ask the day porter to ring up HQ
To ask what the devil they want me to do,
I then would be able to send Wilson back
To bring me the things I'd forgotten to pack.
I really would hate you to think me a bore
But *could* you procure by a quarter to four
A chauffeur-cum-batman to double the jobs;
A file and a safe for my thingamebobs,
A mosquito net and a waterproof (new)
To keep out the rain when I reach GHQ?
I really don't wish to annoy or embarrass
But what sort of car will convey me to Arras?
Or would it be better to go there by train?
Would somebody make it their job to explain
If when at Headquarters I ever arrive,

The number of miles I'm expected to drive?
And should I send Campbell a detailed report
Of all that I've seen or of what I have thought?
Or would it be better to dictate in code
Or type it myself in my country abode?
In short, will you give me instructions or not
To tell me the whys and the wherefores and what
I'm expected to say should I ever appear
Within sight of Liaison with Commandant Reay?"

A few weeks later there was a progress report of sorts . . .

"NEWS BALLAD"

Lord Gerald Wellesley, now in his stride,
Margin for error exceedingly wide.
Lord Gerald Wellesley learning a lot.
Some of it valid but most of it not.
Lord Gerald Wellesley's full of ideas,
Thereby confirming the worst of our fears.
Lord Gerald Wellesley hasn't much hope
Of dropping the droppings just dropped by the Pope.
And still dear Lord Gerald is not really clear
Regarding liaison with Commandant Reay.

As his assistant Cole Lesley recalled, Noël would take out his "Paris Poems" and re-read them with evident delight to the end of his life.

When his superiors detected "a frenzied beating of wings," Noël was sent to America to gauge opinion there.

As someone working for the British Government in what was still a neutral country, he was technically now a spy. He was recruited by William "Little Bill" Stephenson—"A Man Called Intrepid"—the U.S.-based intelligence link between Roosevelt and Churchill, to be one of "Little Bill's boys," a group that included Leslie Howard, David Niven, Alexander Korda, Cary Grant and Ian Fleming among others.

He saw where my celebrity value would be useful and he seemed to think I ought to be as flamboyant as possible, which was very smart of him. My disguise would be my own reputation as a bit of an idiot . . . a merry playboy. It was very disarming. Very clever of him . . .

In talking to people I ridiculed the whole business of intelligence, because that's the best way to get on with it—ridicule and belittle ourselves, and say what an awful lot of duffers we are, can't get the facts straight and all that sort of thing. I was awfully bewildered. I thought it would be more Mata Hari—and then I told myself, "Well, hardly that. I couldn't wear a jewel in my navel, which I believe she was given to doing . . ." I was never much good as a spy, really . . . So many career intelligence officers went around looking terribly mysterious—long black boots and sinister smiles. Nobody ever issued me with a false beard. In fact, the hush-hush side of it was frankly disappointing. I never had to do any disguises. Except occasionally I had to look rather idiotic—but that wasn't all that difficult. I'm a *splendid* actor.

Such a drastic lifestyle change would give anyone pause, and it certainly gave Noël cause to reflect . . .

"PERSONAL NOTE"

Creative impulse whether fine, austere,
Or light in texture; great in scope, or small,

Noël with his secretary, Lorn "Lornie" Loraine, in his Gerald Road flat

Owes to its owner, if it's true at all
Some moments of release in this dark year.

Feeling my spirit battered, bludgeoned, sore,
All my ideas so pale, oppressed by doom,
Like frightened children in a burning room
Scurrying round and round to find the door.

Feeling the world so shadowed, and the time,
Essential to clear processes of thought,
So much accelerated, I have sought
Relief by those excursions into rhyme.

I must confess I have no mind just now
To write gay Operettes, Reviews or Plays
Nor leisure, for these swiftly moving days
Have set my hand to quite a different plough.

And what a different plough! An office desk;
Large trays marked "In" and "Out"; a daily load
Of turgid memoranda, and a code
That lends itself too glibly to burlesque.

From this new language that I have to learn,
From these dull documents, these dry reports,
From this dank verbiage, from these cohorts
Of qualifying adjectives, I turn—

And for a while, perhaps a few brief hours,
My mental muscles gratefully expand
To form these unimportant verses and
Like Ferdinand the Bull, I sniff the flowers.

•

Wherever his wartime travels took him, Noël always hurried back to his beloved London.

"London Pride" was written in the spring of 1941. I was standing on the platform of a London railway station on the morning after a bad blitz. Most of the glass in the station roof had been blown out and there was dust in the air and the smell of burning. The train I was waiting to meet was running late and so I sat on a platform seat and watched the Londoners scurrying about in the thin spring sunshine. They all seemed to me to be gay and determined and wholly admirable and for a moment or two I was overwhelmed by a wave of sentimental pride. The song started in my head then and there and was finished in a couple of days. The tune is based on the old traditional lavender seller's song "Won't you buy my sweet blooming lavender, there are sixteen blue bunches one penny." This age-old melody was appropriated by the Germans and used as a foundation for "Deutschland über Alles," and I considered that the time had come for us to have it back in London where it belonged.

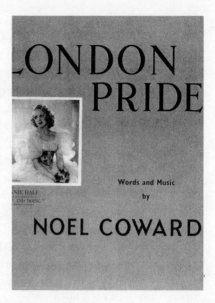

I am proud of the words of this song. They express what I felt at the time and what I still feel, i.e., London Pride.

"LONDON PRIDE"

London Pride has been handed down to us.
London Pride is a flower that's free.
London Pride means our own dear town to us,
And our pride it forever will be.
Whoa, Liza,
See the coster barrows,
Vegetable marrows
And the fruit piled high.
Whoa, Liza,
Little London sparrows,
Covent Garden Market where the costers cry.
Cockney feet
Mark the beat of history.
Every street
Pins a memory down.

Nothing ever can quite replace
The grace of London Town.

There's a little city flower every spring unfailing
Growing in the crevices by some London railing,
Though it has a Latin name, in town and countryside
We in England call it London Pride.

London Pride has been handed down to us.
London Pride is a flower that's free.
London Pride means our own dear town to us,
And our pride it forever will be.
Hey, lady,
When the day is dawning
See the policeman yawning
On his lonely beat.
Gay lady,
Mayfair in the morning,
Hear your footsteps echo in the empty street.
Early rain
And the pavement's glistening.
All Park Lane
In a shimmering gown.
Nothing ever could break or harm
The charm of London Town.

In our city darkened now, street and square
                              and crescent
We can feel our living past in our shadowed present.
Ghosts beside our starlit Thames
Who lived and loved and died
Keep throughout the ages London Pride.

London Pride has been handed down to us.
London Pride is a flower that's free.
London Pride means our own dear town to us,
And our pride it forever will be.
Grey city
Stubbornly implanted,
Taken so for granted
For a thousand years.
Stay, city,

Smokily enchanted,
Cradle of our memories and hopes and fears.
Every Blitz
Your resistance
Toughening,
From the Ritz
To the Anchor and Crown,
Nothing ever could override
The pride of London Town.

·

It turned out to be his "Keep the Home Fires Burning," the song that became the British anthem of this latest war, the song that helped us through.

LONDON. 1940.

England is a good place to be just now. This may sound affected, almost bragadoccio, but for me it is true. These are dark hours and days and weeks and months that we are living through but the very dangers that surround us, the very fears and apprehensions that lie just below the surface of our ordinary lives give a certain zest to small pleasures which, in happier times, would have passed unnoticed.

How odd to be sitting below the house just before dawn with an overcoat on over your pyjamas, drinking a cup of tea and waiting for the "All Clear" to sound! How strange, the casual, friendly conversations in dark streets; the feeling of comradeship with everybody; the little jokes! How strange and how comforting. It seems that for the first time people of all shapes and sizes and classes and creeds are getting to know one another. Never before, driving home snugly from theatres, restaurants, night-clubs or private houses, was there such richness, such awareness of adventure. Here we are on our little island and the issues have become simple. We have a good deal to grumble about which is warming to the cockles of the spirit, like stamping the feet to keep out the cold.

Thousands of stories are exchanged all over the country during the strained hours of waiting. Gay stories, sad stories, personal experiences, criticisms of the government, the Press, the A.R.P., the L.D.V.s, even the B.B.C. "Careless talk," we are informed on all sides, may cost lives and aeroplanes and ships, so we dutifully bite back what we know to be an absolute fact, that a friend of ours heard from a friend of his who lives just near Dover that a friend of his saw with his own eyes a German plane disgorge seventeen real nuns dressed as Storm Troopers! We sometimes, of course, break down and whisper this but we are learning wisdom and so we leave out the fatal word "Dover" and say "Somewhere on the South East Coast" instead, thereby salving our national conscience and enhancing the mystery of our information.

London is emptier than I have ever known it. So many people have been evacuated to the country, so many mothers have taken or sent their children to the generous hospitality of the United States and Canada. As comparatively few Governesses and Nannys can be sent, many society ladies are thus enabled to get to know their children for the first time. The old order is certainly changing. The streets in the daytime look more or less normal, except for the nobler public buildings, such as the Houses of Parliament, Westminster Abbey and Claridges which are heavily sandbagged. Whitehall, Downing Street and all Government offices have, in addition to sandbags, complicated barricades of barbed wire and are sharply guarded, sometimes by army veterans with fixed bayonets and a glint of Crimean reminiscence in their eyes, sometimes by very young men indeed who wear an expression of frightening zeal. Woe betide the eminent minister who has left his pass at the club.

On this building from which I am speaking, Broadcasting House, they are on the alert every hour of the day and night. It is comparatively easy to get in by the simple process of filling in a form at the desk; this form is duly stamped and handed to you. But getting out is quite another matter for, if you happen to drop or mislay your pass, you are incarcerated here for life! I have mine, at this moment, clutched firmly in my hand.

The spirit of the people is extraordinary. I have always had a romantic admiration for the common sense and courage of my countrymen and women. This admiration has occasionally shown itself in my writing. Perhaps in my adolescence during the last war, certain impressions became embedded in my subconscious mind. I was young then and paid little heed to what was going on but I suppose I knew, as we all knew, that we were in a tight corner. Now that I am older and have watched this danger growing year by year, until we find ourselves in the tightest corner we have been in for centuries, there is nothing subconscious about the impressions I am receiving.

The facts are clear and, as I said before, the issues are simple. We all know what we are up against and we are all prepared united and unafraid which is odd, for there is much to fear. In this fortitude which is neither stolid nor unimaginative there is a strong exhilaration. I became aware of it the moment I stepped out of the plane on my return from America four weeks ago. In the early months of the war there was a certain amount of fretfulness and scare, now there is none. Then there was uncertainty, now there is conviction.

In the year nineteen thirty-one on the opening night of *Cavalcade* I was called upon to make a speech in which I said that "It was a pretty exciting thing to be English." Later I regretted this. It seemed to me to have been too glib and theatrically patriotic. I regret it no longer, although now, of course, it almost belongs to the Understatement Department. I maintain that it is not only a pretty exciting thing to be English but essential as well, because on this side of the world it is all that there is left.

—BBC BROADCAST

•

The sights he saw, the people he encountered, made him increasingly resentful of those at home who seemed less than grateful for what was being done, the sacrifices being made for them on the front line.

One evening he lay in bed, listening to the drone of RAF bombers overhead on their way to Cologne.

"For two hours," he said, "there was a steady hum in the sky."

It inspired him to write . . .

"LIE IN THE DARK AND LISTEN"

Lie in the dark and listen,
It's clear tonight so they're flying high
Hundreds of them, thousands perhaps,
Riding the icy, moonlight sky.
Men, material, bombs and maps
Altimeters and guns and charts
Coffee, sandwiches, fleece-lined boots
Bones and muscles and minds and hearts
English saplings with English roots
Deep in the earth they've left below
Lie in the dark and let them go
Lie in the dark and listen.

Lie in the dark and listen
They're going over in waves and waves
High above villages, hills and streams
Country churches and little graves
And little citizens' worried dreams.
Very soon they'll have reached the sea
And far below them will lie the bays
And coves and sands where they used to be
Taken for summer holidays.

Lie in the dark and let them go
Lie in the dark and listen.

Lie in the dark and listen
City magnates and steel contractors,
Factory workers and politicians
Soft, hysterical little actors
Ballet dancers, "Reserved" musicians,
Safe in your warm, civilian beds.
Count your profits and count your sheep
Life is flying above your heads
Just turn over and try to sleep.
Lie in the dark and let them go
Theirs is a world you'll never know
Lie in the dark and listen.

•

The war brought front of mind that sense of patriotism that was fundamental to his nature.

Cavalcade had been the most overt and sustained expression to date. At the end of it the heroine, Jane Marryot, gives her Toast to the Future—as she has done through the decades we've shared with her in the play . . .

"Let's couple the Future of England with the Past of England. The glories and victories and triumphs that are over, and the sorrows that are over, too. Let's drink to our sons who made part of the pattern and to our hearts that died with them. Let's drink to the spirit of gallantry and courage that made a strange Heaven out of unbelievable Hell, and let's drink to the hope that one day this country of ours, which we love so much, will find dignity and greatness and peace again."

In his first-night curtain speech Noël heard himself saying, "In spite of the troublous times we are living in, it is still pretty exciting to be English," though in later years he would reflect, "Quite true, quite sincere; I felt it strongly, but I rather wished I hadn't said it, hadn't popped it onto the top of *Cavalcade* like a paper cap."

This Happy Breed (written in 1939 but not staged until 1942) is a sort of sequel to *Cavalcade*. The events lead up to the second "war to end all wars" and at the end of the play he has the working-class hero, Frank Gibbons, soliloquize to his baby grandson, who symbolizes his country's future . . .

FRANK: Frankie boy, I wonder what you're going to turn out like! You're not going to get any wrong ideas, see? That is, not if I have anything to do with it . . . There's nobody here to interrupt us, so we can talk as

Frank Gibbons (Noël) tells his infant
grandson, Frank, what it means to be
an Englishman in *This Happy Breed,*
(written in 1939 but not performed
until 1942).

man to man, can't we? There's not much to worry about really, so long
as you remember one or two things always. The first is that life isn't all
jam for anybody, and you've got to have trouble of some kind or another
whoever you are. But if you don't let it get you down, however bad it is,
you won't go far wrong . . . Another thing you'd better get into that
little bullet head of yours is that you belong to something that nobody
can't ever break, however much they try. And they'll try all right—
they're trying now. Not only people in other countries who want to do
us in because they're sick of us ruling the roost—and you can't blame
them at that! But people here, in England. People who have let 'em-
selves get soft and afraid. People who go on a lot about peace and goodwill and the ideals they believe in, but somehow don't believe in 'em
enough to think they're worth fighting for . . . The trouble with the
world is, Frankie, that there are too many ideals and too little horse
sense. We're human beings, we are—all of us—and that's what people
are liable to forget. Human beings don't like peace and goodwill and
everybody loving everybody else. However much they may think they
do, they don't really because they're not made like that. Human beings
like eating and drinking and loving and hating. They also like showing
off, grabbing all they can, fighting for their rights and bossing anybody

who'll give 'em half a chance. You belong to a race that's been bossy for years and the reason it's held on as long as it has is that nine times out of ten it's behaved decently and treated people right. Just lately, I'll admit, we've been giving at the knees a bit and letting people down who trusted us and allowing noisy little men to bully us with a lot of guns and bombs and aeroplanes. But don't worry—that won't last—the people themselves, the ordinary people like you and me, know something better than all the fussy old politicians put together—we know what we belong to, where we come from, and where we're going. We may not know it with our brains, but we know it with our roots. And we know another thing too, and it's this. We 'aven't lived and died and struggled all these hundreds of years to get decency and justice and freedom for ourselves without being prepared to fight fifty wars if need be—to keep 'em.

ETHEL comes in.

ETHEL: What in the world are you doing? Talking to yourself?
FRANK: I wasn't talking to myself—I was talking to Frankie.
ETHEL: Well, I'm sure I hope he enjoyed it.
FRANK: He's stopped dribbling anyhow!
ETHEL: Come on in—supper's ready—you'd better close the windows, he might get a chill.

ETHEL goes out.
FRANK closes the windows and goes back to the pram.

FRANK: So long, son . . .

HE GOES OUT AS THE CURTAIN FALLS.

THIS HAPPY BREED (1939)

CAST

FRANK GIBBONS   NOËL COWARD

ETHEL GIBBONS   JUDY CAMPBELL

DIRECTED BY NOËL COWARD

HAYMARKET THEATRE, LONDON, APRIL 30, 1943

·

In the early years of the war, gaps began to open between England and America that were in many ways wider than the Atlantic.

To Aleck Woollcott, a friend since the days of the Algonquin Round Table, Noël wrote—with America still neutral.

I hear that Ruth Gordon and Helen Hayes among many others have been making strong representations to persuade me to give all this up and return to the theatre! If you should see them at any time, you might explain sweetly and tenderly for me that the reason I cannot at the moment return to the theatre (madly important though I know it to be) is that I am an Englishman and my country is at war!

This is a sinister and deadly war, in many ways more so than the last one. There has not been so much bloodshed as yet but, with the kind assistance of press and radio, some very dreadful things are happening to the human spirit. There is no knowing what will survive and what we shall all feel and think. I expect a lot of things will change.

P.S. I occasionally hurtle up to the front and sing firmly to the troops who are so sunk in the mud that they can't escape.

To Jack Wilson, his former lover and now his U.S. manager safely tucked away in New York . . .

I honestly can't bear the thought of leaving England again—except for very brief periods—till the end of the war. The muddle and confusion and irritation is almost as bad as ever but the ordinary people are so magnificent that with all the discomforts and food rationing and cigarette shortage and blackouts, I want to be with them.

The other day I went to a certain very badly blitzed coastal town, Plymouth. The behaviour of the people in the midst of such appalling devastation was beyond praise and beyond gallantry. They were genuinely cheerful and philosophic and I never heard anyone even grumble. In the evenings between 7:30 and 9:30 there is a band on the front and the whole of the town—or what is left of it—come out and dance in the sunlight. The girls put on their bright-coloured frocks and dance with the sailors and marines and soldiers. The fact that they were dancing on the exact site of a certain historic game of bowls added a little extra English nostalgia to what was one of the most touching and moving scenes I have ever seen.

Looking back on those years in his second volume of autobiography, *Future Indefinite* (1959) . . .

I was a flagrant, unabashed sentimentalist and likely to remain so until the end of my days. I did love England and all it stood for. I loved its follies and apathies and curious streaks of genius; I loved standing to attention for "God Save the King"; I loved British courage, British humour, and British understatement . . . I loved the people—the ordinary, the extraordinary, the good, the bad, the indifferent, and what is more I belonged to that exasperating, weather-sodden little island with its uninspired cooking, its muddled thinking and its unregenerate pride, and it belonged to me, whether it liked it or not.

As war was declared, Noël set himself the personal mission to write the song, the play and the film that would help his fellow countrymen get through it.

The song was "London Pride." The play would be *Blithe Spirit.*

Written in five days during a visit to the Welsh resort of Portmeirion in May 1941, it was produced only a month later and he was proud to claim that "only two lines of the original script were ultimately cut."

The play ran longer than the war. Its 1,997 performances set a record for a straight play at the time.

Critic Graham Greene considered it "a weary exhibition of bad taste." And indeed, on the surface, death and the afterlife might seem an unlikely subject of humour for a country submerged in a war.

Noël himself was certainly of the opinion that few things in life—or death—were serious enough to be taken seriously.

BLITHE SPIRIT

CAST

CHARLES CONDOMINE	CECIL PARKER
RUTH CONDOMINE	FAY COMPTON
ELVIRA	KAY HAMMOND
MADAME ARCATI	MARGARET RUTHERFORD

DIRECTED BY NOËL COWARD
PICCADILLY THEATRE, LONDON, JULY 2, 1941

After his first wife, Elvira, died, author Charles Condomine married Ruth, and they appear to live a pleasant, if uneventful and conventional, life. Charles is writing *The Unseen,* a book about spiritualism, and invites Madame Arcati, a medium who lives nearby, to join them and their friends, the Bradmans, for a *séance,* so that he can acquire the suitable "local colour" an author needs.

During the *séance* Madame Arcati accidentally conjures up the ghost of Elvira, who is visible only to Charles. This, not surprisingly, causes a certain amount of confusion.

Finally, Madame Arcati and the Bradmans depart, leaving Charles with his *two* wives . . .

CHARLES: I think I'll have a drink. (*Moves upstage to drinks table and pours whisky and soda.*) Do you want one?

RUTH: No, thank you, dear.

CHARLES (*pouring himself out a drink*): It's rather chilly in this room.

RUTH: Come over by the fire.

CHARLES: I don't think I'll make any notes tonight—I'll start fresh in the morning.

CHARLES turns with glass in hand, sees *ELVIRA* and drops his glass on the floor.

CHARLES: My God!

RUTH: Charles!

ELVIRA: That was very clumsy, Charles dear.

CHARLES: Elvira!—then it's true—it was you!

ELVIRA: Of course it was.

RUTH (*starts to go to* CHARLES): Charles—darling Charles—what are you talking about?

CHARLES (*to* ELVIRA): Are you a ghost?

PICCADILLY THEATRE
PICCADILLY CIRCUS, W

Proprietors: A.S. & W. LTD.   Licensed by the Lord Chamberlain to ALBERT BILLINGS

H. M. TENNENT LTD. in association with JOHN C. WILSON
presents

FAY   KAY
COMPTON   HAMMOND

CECIL   MARGARET
PARKER   RUTHERFORD

IN

BLITHE SPIRIT
An Improbable Farce in Three Acts
BY

NOEL COWARD

THE PLAY DIRECTED BY THE AUTHOR
DECOR BY G. E. CALTHROP

The original London production (1941) and the 2009 Broadway revival, with Rupert Everett (Charles), Angela Lansbury (Madame Arcati), Jayne Atkinson (Ruth) and Christine Ebersole (Elvira) at the Shubert Theatre.

ELVIRA (*crosses below sofa to fire*): I suppose I must be—it's all very confusing.

RUTH (*comes to right of* CHARLES, *becoming agitated*): Charles—what do you keep looking over there for? Look at me—what's happened?

CHARLES: Don't you see?

RUTH: See what?

CHARLES: Elvira.

RUTH (*staring at him incredulously*): Elvira!!

CHARLES (*with an effort at social grace*): Yes—Elvira, dear, this is Ruth—Ruth, this is Elvira.

RUTH tries to take his arm. *CHARLES* retreats downstage left.

RUTH (*with forced calmness*): Come and sit down, darling.

CHARLES: Do you mean to say you can't see her?

RUTH: Listen, Charles—you just sit down quietly by the fire and I'll mix you another drink. Don't worry about the mess on the carpet—Edith can clean it up in the morning. (*She takes him by the arm.*)

CHARLES (*breaking away*): But you must be able to see her—she's there—look—right in front of you—there—

RUTH: Are you mad? What's happened to you?

CHARLES: You can't see her?

RUTH: If this is a joke, dear, it's gone quite far enough. Sit down for God's sake and don't be idiotic.

CHARLES (*clutching his head*): What am I to do—what the hell am I to do!

ELVIRA: I think you might at least be a little more pleased to see me—after all, you conjured me up.

CHARLES (*above table left centre*): I didn't do any such thing.

ELVIRA: Nonsense, of course you did. That awful child with the cold came and told me you wanted to see me urgently.

CHARLES: It was all a mistake—a horrible mistake.

RUTH: Stop talking like that, Charles—as I told you before, the joke's gone far enough.

CHARLES: I've gone mad, that's what it is—I've just gone raving mad.

RUTH (*pours out brandy and brings it to* CHARLES *below piano*): Here—drink this.

CHARLES (*mechanically—taking it*): This is appalling!

RUTH: Relax.

CHARLES: How can I relax? I shall never be able to relax again as long as I live.

RUTH: Drink some brandy.

CHARLES (*drinking it at a gulp*): There, now—are you satisfied?

RUTH: Now sit down.

CHARLES: Why are you so anxious for me to sit down—what good will that do?

RUTH: I want you to relax—you can't relax standing up.

ELVIRA: African natives can—they can stand on one leg for hours.

CHARLES: I don't happen to be an African native.

RUTH: You don't happen to be a *what*?

CHARLES (*savagely*): An African native!

RUTH: What's that got to do with it?

CHARLES: It doesn't matter, Ruth—really it doesn't matter—we'll say no more about it.

CHARLES crosses to armchair and sits. RUTH comes upstage of him.

CHARLES: See, I've sat down.

RUTH: Would you like some more brandy?

CHARLES: Yes, please.

RUTH goes up to drinks table with glass.

ELVIRA: Very unwise—you always had a weak head.

CHARLES: I could drink you under the table.

RUTH: There's no need to be aggressive, Charles—I'm doing my best to help you.

CHARLES: I'm sorry.

RUTH (*crosses to upstage of* CHARLES *with brandy*): Here—drink this—and then we'll go to bed.

ELVIRA: Get rid of her, Charles—then we can talk in peace.

CHARLES: That's a thoroughly immoral suggestion, you ought to be ashamed of yourself.

RUTH: What is there immoral in that?

CHARLES: I wasn't talking to you.

RUTH: Who were you talking to, then?

CHARLES: Elvira, of course.

RUTH: To hell with Elvira!

ELVIRA: There now—she's getting cross.

CHARLES: I don't blame her.

RUTH: What don't you blame her for?

CHARLES (*rises and backs downstage left a pace*): Oh, God!

RUTH: Now look here, Charles—I gather you've got some sort of plan behind all this. I'm not quite a fool. I suspected you when we were doing that idiotic séance . . .

CHARLES: Don't be so silly—what plan could I have?

RUTH: I don't know—it's probably something to do with the characters in your book—how they, or one of them would react to a certain situation—I refuse to be used as a guinea pig unless I'm warned beforehand what it's all about.

CHARLES (*moves a couple of paces towards* RUTH): Elvira is here, Ruth—she's standing a few yards away from you.

RUTH (*sarcastically*): Yes, dear, I can see her distinctly—under the piano with a zebra!

CHARLES: But, Ruth . . .

RUTH: I am not going to stay here arguing any longer . . .

ELVIRA: Hurray!

CHARLES: Shut up!

RUTH (*incensed*): How dare you speak to me like that!

CHARLES: Listen, Ruth—please listen—

RUTH: I will not listen to any more of this nonsense—I am going up to bed now, I'll leave you to turn out the lights. I shan't be asleep—I'm too upset. So you can come in and say good night to me if you feel like it.

ELVIRA: That's big of her, I must say.

CHARLES: Be quiet—you're behaving like a guttersnipe.

RUTH (*icily*): That is all I have to say. Good night, Charles.

RUTH walks swiftly out of the room without looking at him again.

CHARLES (*follows* RUTH *to door*): Ruth . . .

ELVIRA: That was one of the most enjoyable half-hours I have ever spent.

CHARLES (*puts down glass on drinks table*): Oh, Elvira—how could you!

ELVIRA: Poor Ruth!

CHARLES (*staring at her*): This is obviously a hallucination, isn't it?

ELVIRA: I'm afraid I don't know the technical term for it.

CHARLES (*comes downstage to centre*): What am I to do?

ELVIRA: What Ruth suggested—relax.

CHARLES: What happens if I touch you?

ELVIRA: I doubt if you can. Do you want to?

CHARLES (*sits left end of sofa*): Oh, Elvira . . . (*He buries his face in his hands.*)

ELVIRA (*to left arm of sofa*): What is it, darling?

CHARLES: I really do feel strange, seeing you again . . .

ELVIRA (*moves to right below sofa and around above it again to left arm*): That's better.

CHARLES (*looking up*): What's better?

ELVIRA: Your voice was kinder.

CHARLES: Was I ever unkind to you when you were alive?

ELVIRA: Often . . .

CHARLES: Oh, how can you! I'm sure that's an exaggeration.

ELVIRA: Not at all—you were an absolute pig that time we went to Cornwall and stayed in that awful hotel—you hit me with a billiard cue—

CHARLES: Only very, very gently . . .

ELVIRA: I loved you very much.

CHARLES: I loved you too . . . (*He puts out his hand to her and then draws it away.*) No, I can't touch you—isn't that horrible?

ELVIRA: Perhaps it's as well if I'm going to stay for any length of time . . . (*Sits left arm of sofa.*)

CHARLES: I suppose I shall wake up eventually . . . but I feel strangely peaceful now.

ELVIRA: That's right. Put your head back.

CHARLES (*doing so*): Like that?

ELVIRA (*stroking his hair*): Can you feel anything . . . ?

CHARLES: Only a very little breeze through my hair . . .

ELVIRA: Well, that's better than nothing.

CHARLES (*drowsily*): I suppose if I'm really out of my mind they'll put me in an asylum.

ELVIRA: Don't worry about that—just relax—

CHARLES (*very drowsily indeed*): Poor Ruth . . .

ELVIRA (*gently and sweetly*): To hell with Ruth.

THE CURTAIN FALLS.

Elvira decides that if she can't return to Charles's world, he should join her in hers. Knowing his regular habits, she tampers with his car—but today it is Ruth who makes the journey. Now Charles has *two* ghost wives, and any minute Ruth will appear. Elvira begs Charles to have Madame Arcati send her back . . .

ELVIRA: Please get rid of her. Ruth will be in in a minute.

CHARLES: Madame Arcati, would you think it most frightfully rude if I asked you to go into the dining room for a moment? My first wife wishes to speak to me alone.

MADAME ARCATI: Oh, must I? It's so lovely being actually in the room with her.

CHARLES: Only for a few minutes—I promise she'll be here when you come back.

MADAME ARCATI: Very well. Hand me my bag, will you—it's on the settee.

ELVIRA (*picking it up and handing it to her*): Here you are.

MADAME ARCATI (*taking it and blowing her a kiss*): Oh, you darling—you little darling.

MADAME ARCATI, humming ecstatically, goes into the dining room and shuts the door.

Program cover for the U.S. production of *Blithe Spirit*
at the Morosco Theatre, 1941

ELVIRA: How good is she really?

CHARLES: I don't know.

ELVIRA: Do you think she really could get me back again?

CHARLES: But, my dear child . . .

ELVIRA: And don't call me your dear child—it's smug and supercilious.

CHARLES: There's no need to be rude.

ELVIRA: The whole thing's been a failure—a miserable dreary failure—
and oh! what high hopes I started out with.

CHARLES: You can't expect much sympathy from me, you know. I am perfectly aware that your highest hope was to murder me.

ELVIRA: Don't put it like that, it sounds so beastly.

CHARLES: It is beastly. It's one of the beastliest ideas I've ever heard.

ELVIRA: There was a time when you'd have welcomed the chance of being
with me forever.

CHARLES: Your behaviour has shocked me immeasurably, Elvira—I had
no idea you were so unscrupulous.

ELVIRA (*bursting into tears*): Oh, Charles . . .

CHARLES: Stop crying.

ELVIRA: They're only ghost tears—they don't mean anything really—but they're very painful.

CHARLES: You've brought all this on yourself, you know.

ELVIRA: That's right—rub it in. Anyhow it was only because I loved you—the silliest thing I ever did in my whole life was to love you—you were always unworthy of me.

CHARLES: That remark comes perilously near impertinence, Elvira.

ELVIRA: I sat there, on the other side, just longing for you day after day. I did really—all through your affair with that brassy-looking woman in the South of France I went on loving you and thinking truly of you—then you married Ruth and even then I forgave you and tried to understand because all the time I believed deep inside that you really loved me best . . . that's why I put myself down for a return visit and had to fill in all those forms and wait about in draughty passages for hours—if only you'd died before you met Ruth everything might have been all right—she's absolutely ruined you—I hadn't been in the house a day before I realised that. Your books aren't a quarter as good as they used to be either.

CHARLES (*incensed*): That is entirely untrue . . . Ruth helped me and encouraged me with my work which is a damned sight more than you ever did.

ELVIRA: That's probably what's wrong with it.

CHARLES: All you ever thought of was going to parties and enjoying yourself.

ELVIRA: Why shouldn't I have fun? I died young, didn't I?

CHARLES: You needn't have died at all if you hadn't been idiotic enough to go out on the river with Guy Henderson and get soaked to the skin.

ELVIRA: So we're back at Guy Henderson again, are we?

CHARLES: You behaved abominably over Guy Henderson and it's no use pretending that you didn't.

ELVIRA: Guy adored me—and anyhow he was very attractive.

CHARLES: You told me distinctly that he didn't attract you in the least.

ELVIRA: You'd have gone through the roof if I'd told you that he did.

CHARLES: Did you have an affair with Guy Henderson?

ELVIRA: I would rather not discuss it if you don't mind.

CHARLES: Answer me—did you or didn't you?

ELVIRA: Of course I didn't.

CHARLES: You let him kiss you though, didn't you?

ELVIRA: How could I stop him—he was bigger than I was.

CHARLES (*furiously*): And you swore to me—

ELVIRA: Of course I did. You were always making scenes over nothing at all.

CHARLES: Nothing at all—

ELVIRA: You never loved me a bit really—it was only your beastly vanity.

CHARLES: You seriously believe that it was only vanity that upset me when you went out in the punt with Guy Henderson?

ELVIRA: It was not a punt—it was a little launch.

CHARLES: I didn't care if it was a three-masted schooner—you had no right to go!

ELVIRA: You seem to forget *why* I went! You seem to forget that you had spent the entire evening making sheep's eyes at that overblown harridan with the false pearls.

CHARLES: A woman in Cynthia Cheviot's position would hardly wear false pearls.

ELVIRA: They were practically all she was wearing.

CHARLES: I am pained to observe that seven years in the echoing vaults of eternity have in no way impaired your native vulgarity.

ELVIRA: That was the remark of a pompous ass.

CHARLES: There is nothing to be gained by continuing this discussion.

ELVIRA: You always used to say that when you were thoroughly worsted.

CHARLES: On looking back on our married years, Elvira, I see now, with horrid clarity, that they were nothing but a mockery.

ELVIRA: You invite mockery, Charles—it's something to do with your personality, I think, a certain seedy grandeur.

CHARLES: Once and for all, Elvira—

ELVIRA: You never suspected it but I laughed at you steadily from the altar to the grave—all your ridiculous petty jealousies and your fussings and fumings—

CHARLES: You were feckless and irresponsible and morally unstable— I realised that before we left Budleigh Salterton.

ELVIRA: Nobody but a monumental bore would have thought of having a honeymoon at Budleigh Salterton.

CHARLES: What's the matter with Budleigh Salterton?

ELVIRA: I was an eager young bride, Charles—I wanted glamour and music and romance—all I got was potted palms, seven hours every day on a damp golf course and a three-piece orchestra playing "Merrie England."

CHARLES: It's a pity you didn't tell me so at the time.

ELVIRA: I did—but you wouldn't listen—that's why I went out on the moors that day with Captain Bracegirdle. I was desperate.

CHARLES: You swore to me that you'd gone over to see your aunt in Exmouth!

ELVIRA: It was the moors.

CHARLES: With Captain Bracegirdle?

ELVIRA: With Captain Bracegirdle.

CHARLES (*furiously*): I might have known it—what a fool I was—what a blind fool! Did he make love to you?

ELVIRA (*sucking her finger and regarding it thoughtfully*): Of course.

CHARLES: Oh, Elvira!

ELVIRA: Only very discreetly—he was in the cavalry, you know . . .

CHARLES: Well, all I can say is that I'm well rid of you.

ELVIRA: Unfortunately you're not.

CHARLES: Oh yes I am—you're dead and Ruth's dead—I shall sell this house lock, stock and barrel and go away.

ELVIRA: I shall follow you.

CHARLES: I shall go a long way away—I shall go to South America—you'll hate that, you were always a bad traveller.

ELVIRA: That can't be helped—I shall have to follow you—you called me back.

CHARLES: I did *not* call you back!

ELVIRA: Well somebody did—and it's hardly likely to have been Ruth.

CHARLES: Nothing in the world was further from my thoughts.

ELVIRA: You were talking about me before dinner that evening.

CHARLES: I might just as easily have been talking about Joan of Arc but that wouldn't necessarily mean that I wanted her to come and live with me.

ELVIRA: As a matter of fact she's rather fun.

CHARLES: Stick to the point.

ELVIRA: When I think of what might have happened if I'd succeeded in getting you to the other world after all—it makes me shudder, it does honestly . . . it would be nothing but bickering and squabbling forever and ever and ever. I swear I'll be better off with Ruth—at least she'll find her own set and not get in my way.

CHARLES: So I get in the way, do I?

ELVIRA: Only because I was idiotic enough to imagine that you loved me, and I sort of felt sorry for you.

CHARLES: I'm sick of these insults—please go away.

ELVIRA: There's nothing I should like better—I've always believed in cutting my losses. That's why I died.

CHARLES: Of all the brazen sophistry—

ELVIRA: Call that old girl in again—set her to work—I won't tolerate this any longer—I want to go home.

ELVIRA starts to cry.

CHARLES: For heaven's sake don't snivel.

The spectral Ruth finally appears, and the two women gang up to nag Charles. Appalled by the prospect the future holds, he leaves them *both*.

•

The original Madame Arcati was Margaret Rutherford, who because of the subsequent film version, became everyone's conception of the part—but not Noël's.

In writing to Jack Wilson about the production, Noël said: "The great disappointment is Margaret Rutherford, whom the audience love, because the part is so good, but who is actually very, very bad indeed. She is indistinct, fussy and, beyond her personality, has no technical knowledge or resources at all. She merely fumbles and gasps and drops things and throws many of my best lines down the drain. She is . . . mortification to me, because I thought she would be marvelous. I need hardly say that she got a magnificent notice. So much for that."

Ironically, he had experienced great difficulty in persuading the lady to take the part in the first place. She respected spiritualism and felt the play was an attack on it. It took impresario Binkie Beaumont's most silken manner—and an expensive lunch—to persuade her that it was an attack on *fraudulent* mediums. "Very well"—Miss Rutherford finally nodded her several chins—"but I must warn you that I regard this as a very serious play, almost a tragedy. I don't see it as a comedy at all."

Years later Harold Pinter, directing a revival for London's National Theatre, warned his cast from the outset that although Noël may have dubbed it "an improbable farce," he personally considered it to be neither improbable nor a farce.

It wasn't the first time—nor would it be the last—that other people saw aspects of Noël's work that he had not knowingly intended.

He himself had his own very clear ideas of who should do what—and how. Judy Campbell—the only actress to play Elvira onstage opposite Noël—sent a postcard to Maria Aitken, who was playing the part in Pinter's production. "I thought you might like to know Noël's note to me. It was this—'Never forget, Elvira is a ghost in gum boots.' "

"Pretty good, isn't it?" Maria commented. "Means you don't waft about too much. She may be a ghost, but she's extremely down to earth. I pass it on to every Elvira I come across."

•

Nineteen forty-one also saw the play-that-never-was. Noël was frustrated during his trips around America by so much apparent apathy toward the European war and sometimes on the receiving end of actual vituperation. "Occasionally I ran into trouble and had to bare my teeth in a snarl; once when a purple-faced business magnate announced with fatuous conviction that Britain was done for and that I could be God-damn sure that America, having won the 1914–1918 war, was not going to be played for a sucker a second time."

Noël reached for the weapon he wielded best—his words.

He wrote a play. His working title was *Salute to the Brave,* but then he settled for *Time Remembered.*

It takes place in late September 1940 in Norma Ryerson's Connecticut home. The characters are as symbolic of their different attitudes as any in a Ben Jonson play.

Norma is a spoiled suburban matron who believes that organizing a British War Relief Ball is a more than ample contribution.

One of Noël's particular *bêtes noires* at this time was the spectacle of Brits sitting out the war in the safety of the United States. Typical were Rory Macullum, a onetime successful novelist whose future lies firmly in his past and who now affects to be a sub-IRA/Fascist and shares his opinions, wanted or not. Maxwell Drage (Eton & Oxford) is an equally pretentious professional cynic.

In the following excerpt Andy, Melody and Lindsay are fellow guests.

MAXIE: Oh, God!

RORY: What's the matter with you?

MAXIE: I don't know—I've got the jitters.

RORY: You're too sentimental, old boy.

MAXIE: This bloody war's getting me down.

RORY: It'll get you down a damn sight more before it's over, if you let it. Take a tip from me and enjoy it—the situation's funny if you look at it in the right way.

MAXIE: *I* don't see much that's funny about it.

RORY: All these people—scared out of their lives, scampering for cover— that's funny enough . . .

MAXIE: You'll get yourself into trouble, you know, if you're not careful.

RORY: Why? Just because I say what I think?

MAXIE: You don't say what you think, you don't even think anymore—all you care about is getting people hopping mad and holding the centre of the stage.

RORY: Magnificent sophistry, my dear Maxie, and if I may say so as one Englishman to another, quite typically British. You don't happen to share my opinion and so you at once pretend to yourself that it isn't an opinion at all . . . that's called rationalization by some, by others, hypocrisy. The British have been doing that for centuries and now, by God, with their whole damned Empire on the skids—they're still doing it.

MAXIE: You won't get me to rise to that bait. You don't think that any more than I do.

RORY: There you go again, old boy. As a matter of fact I do think so. I think we're done for, and I also think it serves us bloody well right.

MAXIE: And even if we are, what the hell's the use of going on about it to other people?

RORY: Aha! That's quite a different argument altogether.

MAXIE: If you really think that, if you really believe it—don't you care? Doesn't it mean anything to you?

RORY: Not a thing, why should it? I don't owe anything to England, on the contrary England owes a great deal to me—it owes me all those thousands of hours that I worked in a factory in the North—all those years of my youth when I was trapped and couldn't get out. I didn't know very much about your easy, smooth, plutocratic world then, Maxie, but my God, I hated it all right . . .

MAXIE: I don't know what you're bellyaching about—it's paid you back pretty handsomely.

RORY: Not enough.

MAXIE: Good old inferiority complex.

RORY: Call it what you like—I love to see them squirm.

MAXIE: Maybe if your books had been a bit more successful during the last few years you might feel differently.

RORY: That, old boy, is a cheap gibe and shows a fluffy, silly mind—you've never known anything really, and you never will—go on wallowing in your sentimental mush about the old country—go on bewailing the fine traditions of smugness—pomposity and conservatism that are being bombed to hell.

ANDY: Many of the Americans see things from a different—and in Norma's case—more selfish perspective. Someone suggests America herself may be at war a year from now. Norma pooh-poohs such a ridiculous idea . . .

NORMA: Oh Andy, I'm sure we shan't be—even if Roosevelt got in again and tried with all his might and main—the country would never stand for it. Of course, if he *does* get in we shan't any of us have any money left so nothing will matter anyway—Edward said to me just before he left for Florida—"A third term and I go out of business automatically!" You see we obviously shouldn't be able to keep up this house, or Sutton Place—we should just have to stay at the Waldorf for a few months every year and travel for the rest of the time.

MELODY: But my dear, *where* could you go? There isn't anywhere left to travel to.

LINDSAY: See America and die.

NORMA (*irritably*): Really, Lindsay, you know perfectly well that's not the point at all. After all we all love our country and are proud of it—it is the last refuge of peace and freedom in the world today—but you must admit that once you've exhausted Palm Beach and California, there aren't many places to go!

LINDSAY: It would be a big pioneer step to start exhausting Arizona.

Lelia Heseldyne arrives from London with her two sons, anxious to keep them safe from the bombing but concerned to be leaving her husband to carry out his military duties without her at his side. She symbolizes the dilemma faced at this time by many of her British contemporaries.

Noël introduces her in a stage direction . . .

•

LELIA is a woman of great personal charm; attractive, chic and typical of what is known as The International Set. She is witty and articulate and has more intelligence than most of her kind. Her age is about forty. For the last so many years she has accepted the values of those with whom she has mixed but not quite unquestioningly because her own innate personal honesty with herself, at moments, causes her, most uncomfortably, to see through the whole business. Instead of utilizing this intuition and really getting down to brass tacks she has allowed herself to drift with the tide with the result that she is a good deal more unhappy than she allows anyone to suspect. At the moment she is strung high; the strain in her manner is almost imperceptible.

Another guest is Marcel Thevelin. He represents the Free French movement and is in America—not unlike Noël himself—to try to put his country's case and rally support against the "quisling" government the occupying Germans have installed.

He gets into an ugly argument with Rory, which ends in Norma asking him to leave her house. This brings things to a head for Lelia . . .

LELIA (*quietly*): I know the whole business has been very upsetting for you and I agree that it was most unpleasant but I would like you to see that in taking up the attitude you have over it, you really have got hold of the wrong end of the stick.

NORMA: I haven't done any such thing. I merely maintain that if you can't have a friendly discussion without coming to blows . . .

LELIA: It was *not* a friendly discussion.

MAXIE: Lelia's quite right, Norma—it was entirely Rory's fault—he was rather tight and quite insufferable.

NORMA: The fact remains he is staying in my house and he has a perfect right to say what he pleases.

LELIA: Does that apply to all of us?

NORMA (*horrified at* LELIA'S *tone*): Why, Lelia?

LELIA: Because if it does, I have a few things I should like to say.

NORMA: Darling, you're overtired—for heaven's sake let's not argue anymore—let's play a nice word game or something . . .

LELIA: I'm not in the least overtired.

NORMA: You've been in a very strange mood ever since you arrived, darling. We've all noticed it—haven't we, Melody?

LELIA: You were quite right—it was because I was trying to make adjustments that weren't worth making.

NORMA (*with a false laugh*): I wish I knew what you were talking about, Lelia dear.

LELIA: I don't suppose you ever will really, but my conscience wouldn't allow me to leave your house without explaining—

NORMA: Leave my house? What on earth do you mean?

MELODY: My dear Lelia—I really do think it's most foolish of you to behave like this.

LELIA: I'm leaving your house tomorrow morning for the excellent reason that I couldn't bear to stay in it a moment longer.

NORMA (*furiously*): Well really . . . I'm sure I don't know what *I've* done that you should turn on me like this.

LELIA: You haven't done anything, Norma. You never have done anything of the least significance or importance in your whole life. Neither have I, neither have most of the people we know. And now something is being done for us—something tremendous and violent and quite inexpressibly vulgar. There's a war on, Norma! I grant you it's inconvenient and a grave bore because already it's interfering with our pleasures. But it's going to do worse than that before it's over, much worse.

NORMA: I think you must have gone mad, Lelia—I really do. You must be going to have a nervous breakdown.

LELIA: There's no longer any time for nervous breakdowns—I find that strangely comforting.

NORMA: I still don't understand why you should attack me—I mind about the war just as much as you do—and I've worked like a slave from morning till night ever since it started. I've done nothing but organize things and serve on committees until I've worn myself out . . .

LELIA: You don't even know what the war's about, Norma—you haven't the faintest conception of the issues at stake. If you had any real understanding of what is going on in these dangerous, tragic years, what took place tonight could never possibly have happened.

NORMA: So it was all my fault, was it? Well I must say—

LELIA: It was entirely your fault—and if there's a rousing scandal about it—which I should think is highly probable—it will serve you right.

NORMA: How dare you speak to me like that, Lelia!

LELIA: I am speaking like this because I want there to be no confusion in your mind, no misunderstanding at all as to why I am going away. I am going because I find that we no longer have anything in common and because the atmosphere in this house of muddled thinking and false values is intolerable to me.

NORMA (*with a great effort*): My dear, if you're not comfortable here, obviously you're perfectly at liberty to do whatever you like. I shall quite understand. We'll talk it all over quietly in the morning.

LELIA: There won't be time in the morning to talk over anything. I've already told you I'm leaving—anyhow there's nothing more to discuss.

NORMA: You can't be serious, Lelia—I won't believe it—I mean it doesn't make sense! After all you've only just arrived—and there are the boys and Nanny and everything—just because that tiresome scene occurred and upset everybody.

LELIA: It's nothing to do with that really. I actually decided yesterday that I wasn't going to stay. I'm going back to England.

NORMA: Going back to *England*? What on earth for?

MELODY (*putting her knitting away in a large bag*): I'm sure the wisest thing would be for us all to go to bed—everyone's on edge and I'm really not surprised—it's all been most agitating.

NORMA (*rising*): I quite agree.

LELIA: Then this is good-bye, Norma—I probably shan't see you in the morning.

NORMA (*with rather overdone poise*): Nonsense, Lelia—you're overwrought— Melody's perfectly right—we're all on edge.

LELIA: I am neither overwrought, overtired nor on edge—nor am I going to have a nervous breakdown. As a matter of fact I never felt better in my life.

The great American Public was never to be exposed to this particular piece of Coward propaganda.

On December 7, 1941, the Japanese attacked Pearl Harbor and America was in the war, like it or not. As a play *Time Remembered* was forgotten. Until now.

·

During those early years of the war new sights and sounds were all around Noël and despite his claim that he had no mind to write, it was to prove a very prolific period of his life.

Quite apart from what he actually produced, other impressions of that period were stored away at the back of his mind, ready to take shape at some future date.

In 1941 he made a lengthy goodwill tour of Australia and New

Zealand. The limited long-distance range of planes at that time obliged him to break his homeward journey on a tiny atoll called Canton Island, "a coral reef, one degree south of the equator, twenty-nine miles round and no wider than a few hundred yards at any point."

The island contained nothing but a would-be luxury American-style hotel and by way of extreme contrast, the British Residents, Frank and Lucy Fleming. While cocktails were being lifted in the hotel, the Flemings were busy raising and lowering the Union Jack and generally seeing to it that the sun never set unsaluted on their particular outpost of Empire.

Noël put his impressions of the former in the poem "Canton Island."

"CANTON ISLAND"

Accept this testimonial from one
Who's travelled far, who's travelled fairly wide
Who's sought for many an island in the sun
And breasted many a changing tropic tide
Who, in the varied course of his career,
Has journeyed North and South and West and East,
Sharing with pleasure, not unmixed with fear,
The diverse habitats of man and beast.
This testimonial need not be scorned,
Idly dismissed or casually ignored
Especially as he who writes was warned
That here on Canton Island he'd be bored.
Bored! On this self-sufficient coral reef?
Bored with this fascinating personnel?
Bored with the luxury beyond belief
Of this irrelevant and strange hotel?
Where every meal provides a different thrill
Of gay anticipation; where each dish,
No matter how it's listed on the bill,
Tastes doggedly of oranges or fish.
Where modern science has so deftly brought
Refrigeration to the finest art
That even a red snapper freshly caught
Smells unmistakably of apple tart!
Where all the bedrooms are equipped with showers
With, written on the faucets, Cold and Hot
So that the passengers can pass the hours
Endeavouring to find out which is what.
Where, when you find your bed has not been made,

Little avails your anger or your sorrow,
Swiftly you learn to let emotion fade
Then ring the bell and *wait* for a Chamorro.
(Chamorros! Children of the Southern Seas,
Natives of Guam, incapable of crime,
Uncertain, coy but striving hard to please
So vague, so blissfully unaware of time.
How they have guessed, these innocents abroad,
That service, in a Democratic State
Has in its nonchalance, its own reward?
They also serve who only ring and wait.)
Who could be bored when each new day brings forth
Some psychological or cosmic twist,
Rain from the West; a cyclone from the North;
A new bug for the Entomologist;
A Clipper zooming down out of the night,
Disgorging passengers of different sorts;
Elderly bankers blinking at the light,
Ladies in strained, abbreviated shorts,
Fat men and thin men, quiet men and loud
Out of the sky they come to rest below
Then when they've fed and slept, unshaven, cowed,
At crack of dawn, into the sky they go.
What sort of man is he who on this dot;
This speck in the Pacific; this remote
Arena full of plot and counterplot,
Could not be interested—could fail to note
The vital dramas, comedies, burlesques.
The loves, the hates, the ceaseless interplay;
The posturings, the human arabesques
Performed interminably day by day?
Who, if he's human, would not almost swoon
With pleasure as he dives from off the dock
Into the limpid depths of the lagoon
And meets an eel advancing round a rock?
Where is the witless fool who could deny
The fun of swimming gently in the dark
And wondering if that which brushed his thigh
Was just a stingray or a six-foot shark?
The man who could be bored in this strange place.
The man unable to appreciate
The anguished look on everybody's face
When told the Northbound Clipper *isn't* late.

The man too unreceptive and too slow
To be responsive to the vibrant beat,
The pulse, the Life Force, throbbing just below
The surface of this coral-bound retreat,
Dear God, that man I would not care to know!
Dear God, that man I would not wish to meet!!

As for the Flemings, Noël had been touched by the fact that the picture of the King and Queen they saluted daily was an illustration torn from a magazine. He promised them when he left that he would arrange for a real one to be sent to them from Buckingham Palace, and duly did so. He was surprised that it was never acknowledged, and it was only in 1963 that he discovered why, when Frank Fleming wrote to him . . .

Box 30
Makuluva Island
Suva
Fiji
7.1.1963
Dear Noël,
The Portrait arrived in our hands on the third . . . We have acknowledged it, as you advised, by today's date . . . We sent what we hope is a correct and seemly letter of thanks but confidentially I found it necessary to put a brake on my long-cherished desire to say something which would not perhaps be quite correct.

You see, many years ago I was one of a small body of "Returned Sailors and Soldiers," as we were called, who formed a guard of honor on the jetty when she arrived. As the Duchess passed me [Queen Elizabeth would then have been Duchess of York] I caught the full glance of her beautiful eyes and have been her devoted admirer ever since. (This is what I was tempted to say, but dared not.)

Thanks for all the work you did over the Portrait. Do try to send an occasional line to us—you know, even a comic postcard from Sarfend [Southend] "wish you were here" would be better than nothing . . . I wish you to know that Lucy and I think and talk of you frequently—that your photograph is peering down at me as I write this . . . We are naïve enough to imagine that you may sometimes give us a thought.

With affectionate regards,
Lucy and Frank (Fleming)
(Once of Canton Is.)

Noël did more than give them a thought. He turned them into "Mr. and Mrs. Edgehill" in a 1944 short story of that name.

He had been writing short stories from his earliest years, but starting in the 1930s he began to find the form attracting him more and more.

Being primarily a dramatist, short stories have been an absorbing experiment in form, lying somewhere between a play and a novel. I found them fascinating to write, but far from easy. They demand perhaps a little less rigid self-discipline than a play, and a great deal more than a novel. In a novel there is room for divergencies and irrelevancies, in a play there is none; in a short story, just a little, but it must be strictly rationed.

—DIARIES, 1949

He clearly mastered the creative challenges—to his own satisfaction and that of others. Dame Edith Sitwell wrote to him that "there are no short stories written in our time that I admire more."

The Flemings became the Edgehills and Canton Island becomes Cowrie Island in "Mr. and Mrs. Edgehill." And it can be argued that Noël himself makes a cameo appearance in the guise of Lady Cynthia Marchmont . . .

•

"MR. AND MRS. EDGEHILL"

Mrs. Edgehill had walked along to the "Split" and sat down with her back against Roper's Folly. Roper's Folly was the remains of a wooden lookout house which Mr. Roper, since deceased, had begun to build many years ago and had discarded. It was a pleasant place to sit, and she came there often in the evenings when she had washed up the tea things. It was silly of poor Mr. Roper ever to have thought of building a house on that particular spot; for one thing, it was too exposed and lay right in the path of the trade winds. Also, if he had ever completed it, it would have necessitated making a path all the way from the landing stage. There would have been no peace in the house either, stuck right out there on the edge of the surf, and in really bad weather it might quite conceivably have been washed away—indeed, bits of it already had been. Last March year, when the cyclone had passed quite close to the island, waves had broken clean over it.

Mrs. Edgehill sat there idly with her hands in her lap. She could, of course, have brought her knitting or a book, but it was nicer just to do nothing at all. On her right the vivid water swirled through the "Split" into the lagoon; when it had escaped the foam and turbulence of the surf, it flowed swiftly and smoothly and looked solid like blue-green glass.

Directly in front of her was nothing but sea and sky. The sky, as usual at this time of year, was pale and without a cloud; the line of the horizon was sharp, and the enormous rollers advanced monotonously, as though they had been strictly disciplined, to break on the outer rocks of the reef. Occasionally in the troubled water she would see the sinister dorsal fin of a shark slip by, or a school of porpoises flinging themselves through the waves just before they broke. She had a soft corner in her heart for the porpoises; they were so gay and abandoned, and seemed to enjoy life. At her feet, among the shells and seaweed and myriad pieces of broken coral, hermit crabs scuttled about; some of them were enormous and had almost outgrown their borrowed shells. She always longed to catch one in the act of changing into a larger shell, but she had never been lucky.

Her back was to the island—it was not really an island in the proper sense of the word, merely a coral reef some hundred yards wide enclosing a large lagoon—but when the sun went down she would, of course, turn round. This was a ritual. Eustace pulled the flag down at sunset, and he liked her to stand up wherever she happened to be just for those few solemn moments. She loved him for insisting on this, even if there was no one to see; even when they had been alone on the island for months, she had always stood rigidly and watched the flag slowly fluttering down the mast and Eustace in his faded khaki shorts hauling away at the ropes.

There was still half an hour or so to go before sunset, so she could afford to relax and let her thoughts wander. She was rather given to doing this; Eustace had said, years and years and years ago when they were first married, that her mind was like a ragbag. She remembered having been vaguely hurt by this at the time, but later she had had to admit that there was a certain justification for what he said. Her mind was rather like a ragbag—she viewed it quite literally as being a hotchpotch of odds and ends and bits of coloured stuff and thimbles and needles and whatnot—but the trouble was that she could never get it really tidied up, and by nature she was a tidy woman.

Here, of course, sitting by herself looking at the sea, it didn't matter how casually her mind behaved; it could jump backward and forward through time and space as much as it liked. She could even talk out loud to herself if she wanted to; there was nobody to hear her except the hermit crabs. Sometimes she tried to string together piece by piece the last twenty years, all the adventures and excitements and joys and despairs, but she nearly always got sidetracked; some particular memory would hold the stage for too long and, in reliving it, the story would become unstuck and muddled. It was quite a story, too, when you came to think of it, if you could write it for a magazine and put it down clearly, without having to worry about spelling or keep on stopping to think of the right words.

Up until she had first met Eustace, of course, there hadn't been any story at all; that is, nothing out of the ordinary. Just a girl with a mother and father and three sisters and one brother living in a country town. She closed her eyes for a moment against the bright, alien sea, and walked along Hythe High Street; she turned to the left just after passing the Red Lion, and walked across the bridge over the dike, past Mrs. Vernon's, and along for a bit until she got on to the Front. The tide was out, but only just out, because the sands still looked wet. Away to the right were the Romney Marshes and the sea wall with the Martello towers sticking up against the evening sky. There was Eustace coming toward her, arm in arm with that awful Elsie Mallet; there was her Fate walking into her life with a slight sailor's roll and his cap too much on the back of his head and a tuft of towlike hair jutting out over his forehead. She had often, in later years, felt slight conscience pangs about Elsie Mallet. After all, he was her second cousin and had come down from Chatham on weekend leave.

Mrs. Edgehill opened her eyes again, and permitted herself a complacent smile. Poor Elsie! No need to pity her really; they hadn't been actually engaged, but still . . . That had been the beginning—the very beginning—twenty-five years ago.

She turned her head, and looked back toward the hotel and the landing stage. Eustace was still fiddling with the canoe. He looked very small and thin in the distance, like a sunburned little boy. She did wish he could put on a little more weight, but still he was the thin type, and although he was over fifty he would always look young for his age.

Her mind ran lightly back to the honeymoon at Blackpool. That was 1919—she never liked thinking about it very much because she hadn't enjoyed it. It wasn't Eustace's fault—it wasn't anybody's fault really—but she hadn't known it was going to be quite like that. Later on she had to admit that she'd been a bit silly over the whole thing, but Blackpool of all places, so common and noisy and all those thousands of people and that awful bedroom in the Marine Hotel and the picture of the soldier saying good-bye to the dead horse. Waking up to that every morning was no picnic. It almost made her cry to think of it. And being sick on the scenic railway, and Eustace getting drunk on the Saturday night, and then having that dreadful quarrel on the pier . . . Then came London, and the flat in Acacia Mansions, and Eustace leaving the Navy and getting the job at Bartlett's. Whoever it was that said the first year of married life is the most difficult was dead right and no mistake.

It was funny to look back on bitterness and utter misery and not mind about it anymore. Perhaps if it had not been for the operation, and the baby dying and her being so ill for all those months, nothing would ever have come right. Eustace might have gone on at Bartlett's; they might have had other children, and gone on living in that flat and quarreling and not understanding about each other or anything. Eustace might have left her eventually—run off with somebody else (her heart contracted painfully at the very thought of it)—none of the rest might ever have happened, none of the adventures and troubles, none of the true love (she sighed and then smiled)—she wouldn't change places, not with anyone in the world, she wouldn't go back five minutes, but she wouldn't change! She looked back again. Eustace had at last left the canoe and was walking back to the house. He saw her and waved his hand. She watched him go in by the back door, followed faithfully by Sandy; Sandy probably thought that there was a bit of fish going.

The sun was getting lower and the sea colour was changing; a spider crab suddenly popped out of a hole in the sand and went dancing down to the water's edge on its high, spindly legs as though it were being blown by the wind. Mrs. Edgehill settled herself comfortably again. There was no hurry.

2

Cowrie Island is a small coral ring in the Southwest Pacific. Officially it is designated as belonging to the outer Samolan Group, but this is merely for the purpose of identification as it is entirely isolated. Actually it is nearer to Fiji than to Samolo, but it comes under the jurisdiction of the Samolan governor. It was first charted in the year 1786 by the redoubtable Captain Evangelus Cobb, who was driven by a gale onto its reefs. Fortunately the damage to his ship was comparatively slight, for there was no water on the island and had he been forced to stay there he and his crew would have died of thirst. As it was, however, he was stranded for only a few days and was able to report with lyric enthusiasm in his logbook that it was ". . . a reef of personable size o'er which fluttered small white birds of exquisite beauty . . . so tame were these gentle, fragile creatures that they were willing, nay, eager to accept biscuit crumbs from the naked hand."

In the nineteenth century, when the Samolan Group was taken over by the British, Cowrie Island was, rather casually, included in the deal. Since then it had remained uninhabited until the early 1920s, when the then governor of Samolo, Sir Vivian Cragshore, with extraordinary foresight for a colonial governor, had realized its possible potentialities as a future seaplane base.

With commendable promptitude, and in the face of considerable opposition from the Colonial Office, he had equipped an expedition consisting of ten people—three Samolans, four half-castes (all of whom had passed with honours through an engineering course at Pendarla University) and three Englishmen, or rather two Englishmen and a Scotsman named Ian Strachan.

Ian Strachan was in charge of the party, and they swiftly and efficiently set to work to build rain tanks, several huts—most of which were demolished by the weather in later years—and a flagstaff which, although it blew down every now and then, survives to this day. After a few months of extremely primitive living the expedition departed, leaving only Strachan and the hardy Samolans. These exiles were supplied with necessities by a ship which called twice a year. Strachan lived there in solitude with the exception of the Samolans, who fished incessantly, until 1935, when he died of blood poisoning, having had his heel torn off by a barracuda while swimming in the lagoon.

At this time the Trans-National Airways were already casting covetous eyes on the island with a view to using it as a convenient overnight stop for their intended Trans-Pacific Clipper service. Representations were made from Washington to the British Government for either a lease or sale of the island. Meanwhile Sir Humphrey Logan, who had succeeded Sir Vivian Cragshore in Samolo, dispatched Eustace Edgehill, who had been trying for two years, not very successfully, to run a pineapple plantation on the seacoast near Naruchi, and bade him build a house and install himself as British Resident, pending the results of the Anglo-American discussions.

In May 1936 Eustace Edgehill arrived at Cowrie Island. He brought with him adequate but not extravagant supplies and six Samolan boys of excellent physique but dubious reputation, dubious that is to say from the standpoint of the Church of England Mission School in Naruchi. They were beach boys, and beach boys, in the view of the God-fearing, were definitely lesser breeds without the law. They had spent most of their extreme youth and adolescence diving for pennies for the edification of visiting tourists. For the further edification of the tourists they were known to be obliging in many other ways. They were cheerful, amoral, and they could all play the "akula" (a local form of ukulele) with impeccable rhythm. They could also sing charmingly, although some of their native hybrid songs were not entirely guiltless of sensual implication. They were expert fishermen and were tough, willing and without malice.

It was for these latter qualifications that Eustace Edgehill chose them to accompany him. There was a certain amount of fuss in church circles in Naruchi—in fact, a question was asked in the House of Assembly in Pendarla—but Eustace, who took a bleak view of missionaries and was none too enthusiastic about the Church of England anyhow, finally got his way and, amid scenes of local jubilation, they set sail.

For Eustace the whole thing was a tremendous adventure. In the first place the title "British Resident" filled him with pride; secondly, the thought of going off into the unknown, starting as it were from scratch, building himself a house, and installing himself as monarch of all he surveyed, fluttered his heart with excitement and gratification. All his life he had been like that, not only willing but eager to cast away the substance for the shadow. Not that the pineapple plantation could in truth be called substance. It had been unsatisfactory and unremunerative from the word go, and for him, with his irrepressible spirit of adventure, far too sedentary.

For his wife, Dorrie, this new challenge to Fate was full of menace. After all, they were neither of them as young as they used to be and he, like poor Mr. Strachan, might be bitten by a barracuda or get sunstroke all by himself on an exposed coral reef. She had not enjoyed the pineapple experiment any more than he had, but at least, with all its disappointments and difficulties, they had been together. Now he was leaving her behind, by order of the governor, until the house was built and he could send for her. He swore that it would only be a question of a few months at the outside, but she remained skeptical, heavyhearted and full of dark forebodings. When he had finally sailed she went dismally back to the house, looked with distaste at the crop of undersized pineapples and had a good cry.

3

The arrival at Cowrie Island was, on the whole, discouraging. There was a heavy sea running, a seventy-mile-an-hour gale and driving rain. Three days of this had to be endured before they could come close enough in to land a boat and negotiate the "Split." After several hazardous journeys, during one of which the boats nearly capsized, they finally managed to get themselves and their supplies ashore. Eustace, wearing a pair of shorts, gum boots, a raincoat and a topee, looked around him and sighed.

The sight that met his eyes was not entirely up to what his imagination had pictured. The driving rain did little to enhance the cheerfulness of the scene. The island was about twenty-eight miles in circumference and, where he stood by the rickety landing stage, about three to four hundred yards wide; beyond the "Split" on the right, and also about a quarter of a mile away on the left, it narrowed until at certain places there was less than a hundred yards between the pounding surf and the lagoon. There were no trees or shrubs of any sort, except one large, rather sullen-looking bush that looked like a vast green hedgehog.

The huts that the Strachan expedition had built were still standing, but were in a bad state of disintegration. Over by the "Split" stood a strange stone edifice which had obviously never been finished at all. This had been started in a moment of enthusiasm by Mr. Roper, who had been Ian Strachan's second in command. The captain of the ship was standing with Eustace on the landing stage. He waved his hand contemptuously in the direction of Mr. Roper's unfulfilled dream. "Bloody silly," he said; "any fool would have known better than to try to build a house right on the point like that." Eustace smiled desolately and agreed with him.

The largest of the Strachan huts still had enough roof over half of it to keep out the rain, and so, pending further explorations, Eustace directed the boys to dump the supplies and themselves in there until the weather abated a little. The captain, who was obviously concerned about getting his boat through the "Split" and back to the ship, wrung Eustace's hand with ill-disguised sympathy, slapped him a thought too heartily on the back and departed with many shouted promises to see him again in about three months' time.

Eustace walked over to the sea side of the reef and watched the boat battling through the surf. When it had safely navigated it and was rapidly becoming a small black speck in the distance, he turned and walked back to the hut. The boys were still staggering up from the landing stage with packing cases. Ippaga, the eldest of them, was sucking at a sodden cigarette and shouting orders. He smiled broadly at Eustace, exposing two rows of perfect teeth, and shrugged his shoulders as much as to say, "Well—here we are—it's bloody awful, but all we can do is to make the best of it." Eustace smiled back at him, and suddenly felt more cheerful.

A few hours later, a little before sundown, a miracle happened. The rain stopped abruptly, the skies cleared and the whole island was bathed in soft, luminous yellow light; the lagoon was transformed from a waste of choppy grey waves into a sheet of vivid emerald and blue with multicolored coral heads pushing up above the surface of the water. The boys, who had been profitably employed in rigging up a tarpaulin over the unroofed part of the principal hut, gave loud whoops of joy and, tearing off whatever odd garments they happened to have, ran down to the landing stage, from which they dived, clean as arrows, and with hardly any splash at all.

Eustace watched them indulgently and, lighting a cigarette, sat down on one of the rotting wooden rails of the veranda. While he was sitting there a very small, delicate white bird circled twice round the hut, and then, quite unafraid, settled on his hand. The sky suddenly became a pageant; the vanished storm had left wisps of cloud that took fire from the last rays of the sun; every color imaginable flamed across the heavens. Eustace nodded his head contentedly. "Dorrie will like this," he said to himself.

4

Doris Edgehill was a woman of fortitude. She was also what has been described in a popular song as a "One-Man Girl." She had met and fallen in love with Eustace in 1917 and, in spite of the disappointments, difficulties and, in her case, actual tragedies of early married life, she had remained in love with him and would continue to love him until the end of her days. It is indeed fortunate for the sanctity of marriage vows that women of her type still exist. Not that she ever gave much thought to sanctity of any sort. Once Eustace had whisked her away from her home and family and the ambiguous religious ministrations of the local vicar, she was perfectly content to accept his views on God and man and the universe without argument and without question. She seldom troubled her mind with conjectures on the life hereafter, being far too occupied with the continued effort of adapting herself to the occasionally alarming circumstances of life as it was.

Eustace's incorrigible adventurousness and sudden inexplicable enthusiasms led her convulsively, but on the whole happily, through the years. It is true that she sometimes reflected on the strange unorthodoxy of her married life as compared with the romantic visions of it that she had cherished originally. These visions, of course, had been the natural outcome of her home environment, which was nothing if not conventional: a hardworking husband, a house or flat, several children and a tranquil old age. This perhaps was what she had hoped for, but it was so long ago that she could not really accurately remember. At all events it certainly could not have panned out more differently.

If, during those far-off early days, any prophetic instinct had so much as hinted at the shape of the years to come, she would have been aghast. Here she was, rising forty-five, with greying hair and a skin toughened by tropic suns and varied weathers, sitting, grass-widowed, on a failing pineapple plantation on one of the remoter British Colonial possessions. It really was laughable. If it weren't for being worried about Eustace and separated from him by hundreds of miles of ocean, she could have laughed with more wholehearted enjoyment. Even as it was, she could not help seeing the funny side.

This perverse but undaunted sense of humor had come to her aid in far worse situations than the one in which she now found herself. There was the time when they had first come out to the South Seas and landed themselves in Suva with that dreadful copra business. Then there was the collapsible aeroplane which Eustace had had sent out in crates from England with a view to revolutionizing the inter-island communications. That had been the worst really, on account of it being so dangerous—let alone all their savings being invested in the damn thing.

She could never remember without a shudder the black day when Eustace and Joe Mortimer and the native boys had at last managed to put the machine together and were preparing for the trial flight. Joe Mortimer had been in the Royal Flying Corps in the last war, and so he was the pilot. Eustace, poor old Eustace, apart from being the promoter of the whole enterprise, was the observer. She could see it now, that long stretch of sandy beach with the aeroplane, surrounded by giggling natives and Eustace in a cap and goggles that made him look like a beetle. Then the propeller being "revved" up; going round faster and faster, then a lot of shouting, and the natives scattering in all directions, and the machine, slowly but with gathering speed, starting off along the beach.

It was all over in less than five minutes, but it had seemed to her like five years. On it went, growing smaller and smaller in the distance until it almost reached the bluff of coco palms jutting out into the sea; then it took off—she remembered distinctly giving a loud scream—and flew out over the lagoon cumbersomely and jerkily as though it were being pulled by a string. Then, horror of horrors, wallop it went into the sea, just the other side of the reef, where there was heavy surf. She stood transfixed with misery and waited. All her life it seemed that she waited, watching the plane like a large wounded bird bobbing about in the waves. A big roller took it as lightly as though it were a paper boat, and, turning it upside down, dashed it against the reef.

It was then that she started to shout loudly. Kumani, the fisherman, had the canoe ready, and was just pushing it off when she, sobbing and breathless, jumped into it. Eustace and Joe were both on the reef when they got there. Joe looked all right, but Eustace was lying twisted up and deathly still. When they finally managed to get him into the canoe he had regained consciousness and was groaning. He had three broken ribs, a fractured thigh and a lump on his head the size of a cricket ball, and that was that. Joe's nose was bleeding pretty badly, but apart from that he was unhurt. The aeroplane, having been repeatedly dashed against the rocks, finally disappeared from view. With it disappeared their joint savings of several years.

After that there were no other adventures for quite a long time. Eustace was in the hospital at Suva for eleven months, and in a plaster cast for six of them. During this time Dorrie had managed to get a job as teacher in the mission school. She taught only the very smallest native children and hated every minute of it, but it sufficed to keep a roof over her head. A little later on, just before Eustace was well enough to leave the hospital, Providence, which always favors the reckless, obligingly arranged for Uncle Ernest to die in Cumberland, and Uncle Ernest, whom she hadn't clapped eyes on since she was fourteen, by some oversight had left her five hundred pounds in his will. On receipt of the solicitors' letter from London explaining this incredible bit of good fortune, she had gone immediately to Eustace in the hospital, and they had made plans for the future.

There had been a lot of argument and, on her part, some tears, but Eustace was quite determined. They had had enough of Fiji. They must go away somewhere quite different, and make a fresh start. Dorrie fought this gallantly, but without much conviction. She never had much conviction when Eustace was really set on something, and finally they decided that the moment he was well enough they would set sail for the Samolan

Islands. Eustace was wildly enthusiastic about this because a man who had been in the next bed to him when he first came into the hospital had been Samolan born and swore that it was a veritable paradise and full of the most fantastic opportunities for anyone who had the faintest grit and initiative. Dorrie ultimately gave up the struggle, and so to Samolo they went.

That was all ten years ago. Samolo had not turned out to be quite the heaven on earth that Eustace's bedmate had depicted, but on the whole, up until the pineapples, they had not done so badly. During the years Eustace had been respectively a barman in a new luxury hotel in Pendarla which failed; a warder in the prison, which unenviable job he relinquished voluntarily because he said it depressed his spirit; an assistant office manager in the Royal Hawaiian and Samolan Shipping Company, which lasted over three years and might have gone on indefinitely if Eustace had not had a blood row with one of the directors; and finally came the pineapple scheme, which she was now concerned with liquidating as soon as possible.

Eustace's appointment as Resident on Cowrie Island had come as a staggering surprise to them both. Dorrie privately considered it to be a wild eccentricity on the part of the governor, who had met Eustace at a Rotary luncheon and taken a fancy to him. Her innate loyalty to Eustace prevented her from ever implying, either by word or deed, that in her humble opinion he was not of the stuff of which successful Residents are made—Residents, that is to say, according to the conventional conception of what a Resident, a representative of His Majesty's Government, should really be.

Eustace was small and undistinguished physically by either height or girth; his attitude toward religion was undoubtedly tinged with mockery; he was utterly lacking in pomposity; he had a slight but quite unmistakable Cockney accent. True, his loyalty to his country and its traditions was strong and at moments downright truculent; he had an undisguised passion for four-letter words and bawdy songs, and very little tolerance of any kind. Still, if the governor thought he was suitable for the job, she would obviously be the last person to say anything against it.

Once the immediate depression of his departure was over, she set to work diligently to get rid of the pineapple plantation as soon as possible. She actually had some good luck over this, and finally managed to dispose of three-quarters of the land to a new real estate company which wished to turn the East Naruchi beach into a bathing resort. The other quarter, which was to the west and slightly elevated above sea level, she held on to, reflecting logically that land was land whichever way you looked at it and that if the Naruchi beach scheme ever amounted to anything it would probably treble its value in a few years' time. Having achieved all this, she stored all their furniture and personal belongings against the happy day when the house on Cowrie Island should be ready for her, and rented a small furnished flat in Pendarla.

Pendarla was the main town on the island and the seat of government. It was situated on the north coast, and boasted a wide and lovely harbor. A range of mountains swept straight up from the sea and, over the foothills, sprawled the town itself. Dorrie's flat was in a new building at the far end of the Mallaliea road. This meant that she was within an easy tram ride from the center of the town, with the additional advantage of being more or less in the country. Her flat was on the seventh story, one floor from the top, and she had a small balcony which commanded a view over the harbor to the right and to the left over Mano point to the open sea. She spent many hours sitting there with her sewing and gazing, a trifle forlornly, out over the curling breakers to where she imagined Cowrie Island lay. As a matter of fact, it really lay about three hundred miles directly behind her, but maps and distances and geography had never been her strong point, and it didn't really matter anyway.

After she had been there a few weeks she was astonished, and considerably shattered, to receive an invitation to lunch at Government House. It had not yet occurred to her that as the wife of the new Resident of Cowrie Island she would automatically be received into the higher Samolan social circles. This unexpected contingency upset her very much. She knew herself to be completely lacking in social graces; she had no gloves, and only one passable afternoon dress which she knew to be several years out of date. She was also oppressed with the fear that either by talking too much, or too little, or losing her head and doing something stupid, she might let Eustace down.

It was therefore in a state of miserable panic that she finally drove up in a taxi and turned into the impressive drive of Government House. An immense Samolan in a white tunic and a scarlet fez opened the door of the cab, and she was received by a cherubic young naval officer with an unmistakable twinkle in his eyes. He led her through a large hall and along a shady patio into the drawing room. She was painfully aware that her shoes were squeaking loudly on the parquet. There was a small group of people clustered round a sort of trolley table, on which were decanters and jugs and glasses. She was too nervous to notice who anybody was.

Lady Logan came forward to meet her, followed by Sir Humphrey. Lady Logan was tall, immeasurably distinguished, with rather untidy white hair and an easy, friendly smile. Sir Humphrey was large and shaggy and exuded an air of benign frowsiness; his white silk tropic suit hung on his enormous frame with the utmost casualness. He placed a vast hand under her elbow, and piloted her toward the other guests. There was a smartly dressed, drained-looking woman, Lady Something-or-Other, who was on a visit from England and staying in the house; an admiral with gentle blue eyes and aggressive eyebrows; a captain of marines, very handsome with curly hair, a curly mouth and a most curly moustache. Vivienne and Sylvia, the two Logan daughters, came forward and greeted her warmly. She, of course, knew them by sight, but had never spoken to them before. They were pretty, fresh-looking girls in cool linen frocks. Last of all she was introduced to a Professor Carmichael who, the governor explained, was making a tour of the islands at the head of an entomological mission. Dorrie had not the faintest idea what that meant, but she nodded knowingly as she shook his withered little hand. The naval ADC offered her the choice of either a dry martini, sherry or tomato juice. She chose the dry martini and then wished she'd plumped for the tomato juice. Lady Logan motioned her to a place beside her on the sofa and asked her if she had had any news of Eustace, and whether or not she was looking forward to her exile on Cowrie Island. Dorrie replied in a prim, constricted voice that she was certainly looking forward to going to the Island, but that she was afraid that it would be a long time before she got there.

Lady Whatever-It-Was chimed in and said that the whole thing sounded too entrancing for words and that she envied her with every fiber of her being.

Vivienne, the elder Logan girl, said, "Really, Aunt Cynthia, you know perfectly well you'd hate it."

Lady Logan laughed. "I'm afraid it wouldn't be quite your affair, darling," she said. "You've always been a great one for your comforts, and on Cowrie Island there is apparently nothing but coral, coral and more coral."

"But I adore coral," protested Lady Cynthia, handing her empty cocktail glass to the ADC. "I don't mean those dismal little pink necklaces that German governesses wear—they're absolutely bloody, of course—but coral qua coral is sheer heaven!"

Dorrie, who had jumped slightly at the surprising use of the word "bloody" in such high circles, was trying to decide in her mind whether Lady Cynthia really was idiotic or merely, for some obscure reason, pretending to be, when luncheon was announced and they all went into the dining room. Lady Cynthia sat on the governor's left and Dorrie on his right. As the meal progressed, Dorrie began to lose a little of her shyness. Lady Cynthia continued to talk and behave like somebody out of a back number of the *Tatler*, but Dorrie had to admit to herself that she was now and then quite amusing and apparently without guile. H. E. talked incessantly on a variety of topics. The two girls chattered gaily in high, shrill, very English voices, and flirted mildly with the captain of marines. Lady Logan, at the other end of the table, grappled gallantly with the professor, who was obviously rather heavy in the hand. The admiral uttered a short bark at intervals.

When lunch was over, they all sat out on the patio and had coffee. The afternoon sun blazed down on the smooth, perfectly kept lawn, but under cover, in the shade of the pink plaster arches, it was pleasantly cool. Dorrie relaxed and allowed the gentle, effortless atmosphere to smooth away her agitation. It was stupid, she reflected, to be shy of people and get into a state. After all, as long as you were yourself and didn't pretend or try to show off, nothing much could happen to you. Lady Cynthia, who had been upstairs to powder her nose, came back and sat down next to her on a swing seat; she rocked it languidly backward and forward with her foot, and offered Dorrie a cigarette. "I must say," she said pensively, "I really do think you're bloody brave."

"Why?" said Dorrie in surprise.

"Well"—Lady Cynthia held up her hand and scrutinized her nails with some distaste—"going off into the blue like that and settling down on a little dump and not clapping eyes on anybody from one year's end to another."

"It won't be so bad as all that," said Dorrie. She suddenly felt confident and almost superior. Perhaps she really was a good deal more dashing than she had ever thought she was. "After all, I shall be with my husband." This sounded rather flat, and she immediately wished that she hadn't said it. Lady Cynthia gave a little laugh, and then suddenly her face looked sad and much older.

"What's he like?" she said.

Dorrie stiffened as though to ward off an attack, and then, realising that there was really no offensive intent in Lady Cynthia's question but merely a frank curiosity, she relaxed and gave a little laugh. "He's not much to look at really," she said, "that is, he isn't what you'd call exactly handsome. But still it's a nice face, if you know what I mean, and he's full of go and always keen on getting things done."

"What sort of things?" said Lady Cynthia inexorably.

"All sorts . . ." There was pride in Dorrie's voice. "He can turn his hand to anything. The trouble is"—she paused—"he sometimes gets a bit carried away."

"I shouldn't imagine that he'd have many opportunities of getting carried away on Cowrie Island."

"Well, you never know," said Dorrie simply. "He's building a house at the moment, and I must say I wish I was there to keep an eye on it."

"How long have you been married?"

"Twenty-eight years next August."

"Good God!" Lady Cynthia looked genuinely astonished. "And you still love him all that much?"

Dorrie tightened up again, and Lady Cynthia, immediately realizing it, suddenly patted her hand and smiled—a charming smile, which completely banished the habitual look of weary boredom from her face. "Please forgive me," she said gently. "You mustn't think I'm being bloody. I'm always far too inquisitive about people, particularly if I happen to take a fancy to them."

The unmistakable sincerity of Lady Cynthia's tone flabbergasted Dorrie. The idea of being taken a fancy to by anyone so ineffably poised and remote from her own way of life as Lady Cynthia seemed quite fantastic. How surprised Eustace would be when she told him about it! "How did you know I loved him so much?" she asked.

"It's pretty obvious really." Lady Cynthia smiled again, but this time a trifle wryly. "I envy you. I've run through three husbands in far less time than twenty-eight years. Perhaps I'm not as lucky as you, or as sensible—or even as nice," she added.

This was plainly Dorrie's cue, and she took it unstintingly. "I'm quite sure you couldn't be nicer," she said boldly, and then was glad she had done so, because Lady Cynthia looked so obviously pleased.

"It's always pleasant, isn't it," she said, "to meet new friends? I shall be here for another two weeks—do ring me up and we might have lunch and gossip or go to a movie or something."

Dorrie, quite overcome, murmured that she'd certainly love to. Then Lady Logan made a slight but perceptible movement indicating that it really was time that the party broke up. There was a brief flurry of general conversation. The naval ADC said that he was driving into the town and would give Dorrie a lift, and, after the various good-byes had been accomplished, she followed him out through the vast, echoing hall into the hot sunshine.

5

On Christmas Eve 1936 Eustace sat down on an upturned canoe a few hundred yards away from the landing stage and lit a pipe. In order to do this he had to crouch down and bend himself almost double because there was quite a strong southwester blowing. Having lit it successfully, he sighed luxuriously, wriggled his right sandal to shake a pebble out of it and looked with pride on his achievements of the last seven months.

First and foremost there was the house. It stood about twenty yards back from the narrow beach. The last coat of bright blue paint was still drying on the doors and window frames. It was, to him, a beautiful house. It was his; he had built it, and he loved it with all his heart. It consisted of two large rooms separated by a partition that reached not quite up to the roof, so that whatever cool breeze there might be could blow through it. The kitchen, scullery and larder were built out on one side. This, although unsymmetrical from the more aesthetic architectural point of view, was undeniably convenient, as it ensured that the smell of cooking would invade the main rooms only when the wind was blowing from the north, which it very seldom did.

The lower part of the house up to the level of the windowsills was constructed of thick coral rocks, hewn roughly but efficiently by the boys. Above this was ordinary teak clapboarding stained brown and varnished in order the better to withstand the elements. The roof was pink corrugated tin and fitted snugly. He had been held up for weeks waiting for that damned roofing to arrive in the supply ship. However, there it was complete in every detail except for the crazy paving path which he intended to start work on on Boxing Day. At the moment, of course, there was no furniture beyond a camp bed, a couple of wooden tables and chairs and a Frigidaire. This worked on an oil burner and was surprisingly successful.

Dorrie was due to arrive any time within the next week with the rest of their belongings. His heart fairly jumped in his chest when he thought of showing it all to her. To the left of the house, slightly nearer to the lagoon, was the radio station (nearly complete as far as equipment went) and the flagstaff, with the Union Jack fluttering bravely in the evening sunshine. Two of the disintegrating Strachan huts had been pulled down and the materials used for bolstering up the remaining three. In one of these the boys lived in haphazard chaos, ruled authoritatively by Ippaga. The other two were used for stores. The landing stage had been reinforced and repainted, and net paths had been made so that it was possible to walk in comfort from hut to hut without crunching along through loose coral.

At the moment, work being over for the day, the boys were whooping and splashing down by the landing stage. Eustace looked at them affectionately. They were good boys and had worked well and were to have tomorrow off entirely in addition to an extra ration of beer and cigarettes. They were also, he reflected dispassionately, extremely beautiful. He watched Ayialo, who had won the native swimming championship three years running at Naruchi, do a double-back somersault into the lagoon.

Still puffing at his pipe, he sauntered down to the landing stage to join them. The water at the end of the landing stage was about twenty feet deep and crystal clear. Shoals of vividly colored coral fish glittered just below the surface like precious stones. He slipped off his shorts and dived in. The water was still a bit too warm for his liking. It would cool off a bit after the sun had gone down. He swam out a couple of hundred yards to a coral head; his swimming was of the sedentary, Margate breaststroke variety. Three of the boys accompanied him, streaking through the water like seals, their arms and legs acting apparently independently of each other but with perfect rhythm and grace; their heads seemed to be almost continually submerged as though they were able to breathe as comfortably below the surface as above it. Eustace rather envied them this easy familiarity with an element that he had always regarded with slight suspicion. They had often attempted to teach him how to "crawl" and do other aquatic contortions, but it was never any good. He invariably choked and spluttered and got too much water up his nose, and finally decided that he was too old a dog to learn such exhausting and complicated tricks.

He clambered up onto the coral head, wriggled his bottom into a comparatively comfortable position and sat looking back at the shore. Ayialo and Ippaga sprang out of the water and sat down next to him. He glanced at their sleek, glistening bodies and wondered, rather perplexedly, whether or not he ought to insist on them wearing bathing trunks when Dorrie arrived. Not that Dorrie would give a hoot, of course, but perhaps from the point of view of Christian decency . . . He suddenly laughed out loud. Ippaga looked at him questioningly. Eustace, whose Samolan was still, after several years, far from fluent, felt that the effort of explaining what he was laughing at would be too complicated, and so he waved his hand vaguely and said, "*Mo imana,*" which meant, "I am very happy." Ippaga nodded understandingly and, looking toward the house, clapped his hands violently as though to applaud their combined handiwork. Then he and Ayialo, almost in one combined movement, shot into the sea.

Eustace watched them swimming strongly down and down through the clear water, their bodies becoming increasingly paler in the blue depths; their breath control was really fantastic, and it seemed to be several minutes before their heads bobbed up above the surface again. They decided to race each other to the shore. Ippaga gave a loud cry, and off they went at an astonishing rate. Eustace sighed a trifle enviously and remembered, when he was their age, the nightmare swimming lessons he had had to endure in St. Michael's baths; the damp, dank smell; the hairy-chested, implacable swimming instructor shouting at him from the side, and the clammy nastiness of the water wings rubbing against his shoulders. This was certainly a far cry from Sydenham all right!

A few days after Christmas, Eustace was awakened from his afternoon snooze by a great commotion outside. He jumped up from the camp bed and looked out of the window. Ippaga was jumping up and down in a frenzy of excitement, and all the other boys were yelling and pointing out to sea.

His heart gave a leap, and he dashed out, hurriedly doing up the top two buttons of his shorts which he always undid before relaxing after lunch in order to give his stomach freedom to expand and help the digestion. It had often been a false alarm before, but this time it was not. There was the ship, a smudge on the horizon with a thin wisp of black smoke curling up from its funnel into the pale sky. He stood stock-still for a moment or two, and suddenly was aware that his eyes were stinging with tears. He ran back into the house again, began to find a clean shirt, then sat down on the bed and started to laugh. There was an hour at least to go before the ship came in close enough to send off a boat, and here he was carrying on as though the house were on fire! He had ample time to have a saltwater shower and a shave and get the cups out for tea. He laughed again, this time with less hysteria and more wholehearted glee, and went out to the hut where the shower was. He caught himself doing a little dance step as he went; then he stopped because he did not want to betray too much emotion in front of the boys.

An hour and a half later he was standing in clean white shorts and shirt and stockings and shoes on the edge of the "Split" by Roper's Folly, watching the ship's boat slowly, maddeningly slowly, making its way toward the surf. He had been there for three-quarters of an hour. Horrible macabre thoughts rushed through his mind. The boat might capsize; Dorrie would be flung into the sea among the sharks—there were always hundreds of them just out there beyond where the waves broke—he would see her disappearing and be powerless to do anything—perhaps he would even hear her scream—her last dying despairing shriek . . . He began to jump up and down in an agony of agitation. The boat came nearer and nearer. Just before it reached the surf he saw Dorrie.

She was sitting in the stern and she waved a white handkerchief. He waved back frantically and shouted, but she could not possibly have heard because of the wind and the sea. The boat got through the surf without any trouble at all, and slid into the smooth water of the "Split." Suddenly there she was, just a couple of yards away from him, looking very cool and calm in a pink cotton dress and a white sun helmet. He called out "Welcome, darling" in a strangled voice, quite unaware that the tears were streaming down his cheeks. He started to run, breathlessly, to the landing stage.

•

Late that evening they were sitting in deck chairs side by side just outside the house. The moon was up and made a glittering path of light across the lagoon. The furniture had been dumped, some of it in the house and the rest down by the landing stage; the captain and the first officer had gone back to the ship. The boys had all gone to bed for the night. Dorrie and Eustace had each a whiskey and soda and a cigarette, but they had to keep putting one or other of them down in order to hold hands. Dorrie had told him all about the pineapple plantation sale and Lady Cynthia and Government House and the various incidents and discomforts of her journey. Eustace had told her all about the building of the house and the setbacks and the four days' gale in November and the giant stingray that had got right into the lagoon through the "Split." Lots of other bits and pieces of news would come to light later; there was infinite time, all the time in the world. At the moment there seemed to be nothing more to say. There they were, together again; the stars were blazing down on them; they could hear the gentle lap of the small wavelets of the lagoon against the supports of the landing stage and the steady, soothing roar of the surf behind them.

Eustace flipped his cigarette away, placed his whiskey glass carefully down on a bit of rock and, kneeling by the side of Dorrie's deck chair, put his arms tightly around her and buried his face in her breast.

"Careful!" she said automatically, putting down her glass too.

"Do you like it?" he asked huskily, "the house, I mean, and the island and the whole place?"

Dorrie smiled in the darkness and stroked his hair. "I will say this for it," she said, "it's one up on Blackpool."

6

By the end of the year 1937 Washington and London had finally come to an arrangement about Cowrie Island. For months and months negotiations had been under way. Thousands of civil servants in thousands of offices had typed memoranda and filed and unfiled letters, telegrams, reports, ciphers and suggestions in duplicate, triplicate and often quadruplicate. There had been meetings, conferences and discussions; official, semiofficial and private. Clerks and secretaries and shorthand-typists and stenographers had gone wearily home evening after evening on buses in England and trolley cars in Washington, sick and tired and bored with the very name of Cowrie Island.

Finally, at long last, the decision was arrived at that America and Britain should share the island fifty-fifty. It was, in fact, to be known henceforward as a Condominion. In many high official quarters it was confidently asserted that this arrangement would have a beneficial and lasting effect on Anglo-American relations. The President of the United States was jubilant; the President of Trans-National Airways positively ecstatic, and the Colonial Minister in London relieved, resigned and, on the whole, indifferent. A few Middle Western senators asked some irrelevant questions; one of them, a slightly obtuse gentleman who had been inaccurately briefed on the situation, made a rambling speech in Des Moines, Iowa, filled with withering references to "Perfidious Albion" while Sir Humphrey Logan, His Majesty's representative in Samolo, who had been opposed to the whole business from the start, bowed his head to the inevitable.

The only people who knew nothing about the transaction whatever were the British Resident and his wife on the island itself. For them the months slipped by in peace and contentment. The crazy paving was laid down and completed. Ippaga and Ayialo were chased by a nine-foot shark in the very middle of the lagoon, but managed to clamber to safety on a coral head. (The shark was later caught by the combined efforts of all the boys together and a chunk of bleeding raw meat from the Resident's Frigidaire.)

Dorrie found a wounded love tern, one of the island's little white birds, and nursed it devotedly back to health and strength, after which it refused to leave her, and Eustace built a little dovecote for it behind the house. Sandy, the little ginger cat which had been presented to the Edgehills by the captain of the supply ship, in defiance of all apparent biological laws, suddenly produced a litter of five kittens in the middle of Roper's Folly. This, to all intents and purposes, immaculate conception, caused a profound sensation on the island.

As far as Dorrie was concerned it was the happiest year she had ever spent in her life. She learnt to float on her back without moving at all, an accomplishment that she had always envied in others. She went off with Eustace on excursions to the far side of the lagoon in a little boat which the boys had built and for which Eustace had rigged up a sail. She became a passionate collector of shells, and sometimes one or other of the boys would dive down deep enough to procure for her some lettuce coral which, when bleached by the sun, made the loveliest house decorations imaginable.

Every morning at dawn and every evening at sunset Eustace performed, with correct solemnity, the ritual of the Flag. For this all the boys, in brightly colored sarongs, the only moments of the day or night in which they wore anything, stood respectfully to attention. Dorrie stood to attention too, and, once in a while, permitted herself the luxury of a nostalgic tear or two. Thoughts of Home dropped into her mind. The soft wet green of the Romney Marshes; the brightly colored traffic in Piccadilly on a spring morning; the crowded pavements of Oxford Street; the bargain basement at Selfridge's and the Changing of the Guard.

She occasionally received letters from Home, from her sisters and her brother and one or two faithful friends. She devoured these eagerly enough, but they never moved her so much as watching Eustace hauling away at that little flag. She had been away for many years and she realized that, if she did go back, everyone she had ever known would be changed beyond all recognition. Only the aspects of England that were unchangeable would be familiar still. This thought saddened her a little sometimes, but not for long. She had Eustace and the house and the sun and the sea and the sky, and her world was at peace.

7

In March 1941 Lady Cynthia Marchmont was sitting in the American-bound Trans-Pacific Clipper reading a rather highly colored romantic novel about the American Civil War. Her mind, however, was only partially concentrated on what she was reading. She was dressed in the uniform of the Mechanized Transport Corps. It was a smart uniform, and it suited her. She took a small compact containing powder, lipstick and mirror out of her pocket, and scrutinized her face with detached interest. She decided that she looked a bit tired and that the lines were deepening under her eyes and around her mouth.

This, oddly enough, depressed her far less than it might have done a few years ago. There was every reason for her to be looking tired, as she had just completed a lecture tour of Australia and New Zealand, and the whole business had been fairly exhausting. She was perfectly aware that she was a not particularly experienced or inspired public speaker, but the lecture tour, on the whole, had been a success. Her subject had been the women of Britain in wartime and the efficiency of their contribution to the war effort. She herself since September 1939 had been working unremittingly. In the beginning she had plunged immediately into the organization of canteens and rest rooms for the troops. Later, being an excellent driver, she had enlisted in the MTC as an ordinary private and had worked her way up to her present rank of commandant. She was conscious, sometimes almost shamefacedly so, that for the first time for many years she was no longer bored. It was strange to reflect that all the distractions and small happinesses she had so assiduously sought during the twenties and the thirties were no longer attractive or even valid. On the surface, they had been gay, those years—monotonously gay. Looking back, her mind refreshed and renovated by so much violent change, she was astonished to realize that her memories even lacked poignancy. There they lay, strewn behind her, all the love affairs and parties and yachting trips and summers in the South of France and the Lido; all the trivial strains and stresses and febrile emotions that had woven the pattern of her life and the lives of her friends.

She remembered a phrase that she had read years ago in a book of historical memoirs, a phrase spoken by a dying French actress of the eighteenth century who had achieved triumph and fame and been reduced to penury. *"Ah les beaux jours, les beaux jours, j'étais si malheureuse!"* She smiled to herself and wondered how miserable she had really been? Certainly a great deal more than she had realized at the time. Not the obvious, genuine unhappinesses, like Clare dying in that frowsy little hospital in Paris, and Henry being killed in the motor smash, and poor Philip getting muddled up with that bloody woman and finally commiting suicide—those tragedies and sufferings had been real, and would have been real in any circumstances, whatever sort of life she had led—but the general tone of all those years, the perpetual, unrecognized, hectic boredom. She had lived through so much of all that, pretending to herself and to everyone else that she was enjoying it. She smiled again, and then sighed and put her compact back into her pocket. It really had been too idiotic.

She looked out of the window of the plane. They were flying at about eight thousand feet, and the evening sky was clear except for a bank of fantastic cloud formations faraway on the horizon. She glanced at her wristwatch. According to schedule they should have arrived at Cowrie Island an hour ago, but there had been a head wind nearly all day since they had left Nouméa in the gray hours of the morning. The light faded from the sky, and the empty, outside world disappeared. About an hour and a half later there was a slight commotion in the forward end of the plane, and the steward came bustling through with a tray of cocktails in little cardboard cups.

"It's all right," he said, "we've sighted the Island." There was a ring of restrained excitement in his voice, and Lady Cynthia wondered idly whether or not the pilot and observer had perhaps been getting a little agitated. She looked out of the window and there—far, far below them in the darkness—was a little cluster of twinkling lights. One of them seemed to be moving and was changing alternately, red and green and white. That would be the pilot launch.

Lady Cynthia began to collect her things, and the lighted notice flashed on: "Please fasten your belts." The Clipper, sweeping lower and lower over the lagoon, finally with an almost imperceptible bump touched down on the water; spray obscured the windows; the passengers unfastened their belts and began to move about, collecting their books and overnight bags. The engines stopped; there was a confused noise of shouting outside, and, after a considerable time, the giant machine was towed gently alongside the landing stage. The pilot went out first; then two of the officers. Lady Cynthia waited, sitting quite still in her seat. She always hated hurrying for no particular reason, and she much preferred the other passengers to disembark before her. When they had all gone she rose, a little wearily, and stepped onto the landing stage.

The hot night air seemed to strike her in the face. She walked along the wooden pier, brightly illuminated by two enormous arc lamps, and up a short rock path to the hotel. It was all on one story and on entering the main lounge she was immediately impressed by the incongruity of so much expensive luxuriousness flourishing on a small coral reef in the middle of the Pacific Ocean. She registered at the reception desk and the manageress, Mrs. Handley, a smartly dressed little American woman, insisted on showing her to her room herself. The room was pleasantly furnished with its own private shower and toilet. Mrs. Handley was both amiable and voluble and said that dinner would be ready in about half an hour, and would Lady Marchmont, when she had washed and freshened up, care to come along to her private suite and meet her husband, Robb, and have a cocktail? Lady Cynthia accepted gracefully, although inwardly she would much rather have been left alone, and Mrs. Handley departed saying that she would send one of the boys for her in ten minutes.

The Handleys were an oddly assorted couple. It would be impossible, reflected Lady Cynthia, to imagine two people more thoroughly opposite from each other in every respect. Mrs. Handley—Irma—had shrewd, sharp eyes and was impeccably soignée; her simple linen frock was perfectly cut and pressed, and her hair looked as if it had been done by an expert Fifth Avenue hairdresser that very afternoon. Robb, her husband, was entirely casual both in appearance and manner. He was nice-looking and had a certain loose-limbed charm. His eyes were a trifle too pale and his fair hair was untidy.

Captain Elliot, the pilot of the Clipper, a large, friendly, beefy man, was also present together with the airport manager, a tall, austere young man whose surname Lady Cynthia did not catch but who was referred to by everybody as "Brod."

Robb Handley mixed an excellent dry martini with the efficiency of an expert. Lady Cynthia was very grateful for it. She felt tired, and the drumming of the plane was still in her ears. Conversation was general and consisted mainly of "shop." The new hospital for the ground staff was nearly finished; the westbound clipper had been held up in Honolulu and would be a couple of days late at least; there was a cyclone about a hundred miles off, which would probably mean that the supply ship would be late too, which was irritating because they were beginning to run out of cereals and cigarettes.

Lady Cynthia allowed the talk to flow around her and, sipping her cocktail, idly took in the details of the room. It was pleasantly done, in excellent taste. There were no flowers except for one vase of zinnias on a side table. The whole atmosphere was typical of a well-run hotel or country club anywhere in the United States. The windows were shuttered; the air-conditioning plant made an occasional clicking sound, and, apart from the distant noise of the surf pounding on the reef, it was impossible to imagine that you were anywhere but in the midst of civilization.

Suddenly a name in the conversation galvanized her into attention—"Edgehill"—it struck a forgotten chord in her mind. Brod was talking.

"That guy makes me tired. He's always beefing about something or other."

Mrs. Handley laughed.

"Well"—there was a slightly amused drawl in her voice—"he hasn't got much else to do, has he?"

"But it isn't as if we didn't do all we could to be cooperative." Brod turned earnestly to Captain Elliot. "We never have a film showing without inviting them to it—Robb and Irma are constantly sending them over supplies whenever they run short . . ."

"I like her," said Irma. "I think she's just darling, but I must admit he gives me a bit of a headache now and then."

"Who are the Edgehills?" interjected Lady Cynthia.

Robb refilled her cocktail glass. "He's the British Resident, ma'am."

Lady Cynthia, flinching slightly at suddenly being addressed as royalty, remembered in a flash—Mrs. Edgehill! The nice little woman at Government House, Pendarla, when she was staying with Humphrey and Eloise. "Is she here now?" she asked.

"All of two hundred yards away," said Robb. "In the Residency." Everybody laughed at this, obviously a standard joke. Lady Cynthia felt definitely irritated. She rose and said with a sweet smile: "They're very old friends of mine. I must call on them at once."

At this there was a general outcry. Mrs. Handley protested that dinner would be ready in a few minutes—wouldn't it be better to go over afterward? Lady Cynthia was inflexible. "I had no idea they were still here," she said. "I really must go. I really don't want any dinner. I ate far too much in the plane." She smiled at the captain. "The food was delicious. I wonder if anyone would be kind enough to show me the way to"—she paused—"to the Residency?"

Robb escorted her out of the side door of the hotel. It was a very dark night, and he had brought a large electric torch with him. Hermit crabs scuttled away from the coral path as the beam of light struck them. The air was soft and a little cooler; a wind had sprung up and the noise of the surf was like thunder. In a minute or two they arrived at Edgehill's house; there was a glow of lamplight showing through the window. Robb shouted "Huroo" loudly, and then knocked on the front door. After a moment a man opened. Lady Cynthia could not see what he looked like, as he was silhouetted against the light inside.

"Here's a friend to see you," said Robb with great breeziness. Eustace peered into the darkness. "Oh, who is it?" he asked rather dimly.

Lady Cynthia, remembering that five minutes ago she had asserted that they were her oldest friends, rested her hand lightly on Robb's arm and whispered, "I want it to be a surprise—thank you so much for showing me the way." She gave him a little push, but, obtusely, he would not move. "What about you getting back?" he asked.

"I can get back perfectly all right," she said firmly.

"Okay, ma'am," he said and, to her immense relief, called out, "Good night, Mr. Edgehill," and went off into the night.

Eustace Edgehill was still standing at the door. Behind him appeared Mrs. Edgehill. Lady Cynthia really felt a little foolish; she had obeyed a sudden impulse, and now it looked as if it might all be a great failure. After all, Mrs. Edgehill had met her only once and probably wouldn't know who she was from Adam. She spoke quickly and was surprised to note that there was definitely a note of nervousness in her voice.

"I'm Lady Cynthia Marchmont," she said. "I had the pleasure of meeting your wife at Government House in Pendarla years ago. I'm just here for the night and am leaving again in the clipper at crack of dawn. I do hope I'm not disturbing you by coming so late, but I should hate to leave without seeing her again."

Mrs. Edgehill gave a little cry.

"Well!" she gasped, "isn't that extraordinary! Just fancy you remembering me."

She gave Eustace a little shove. "Get out of the way, dear."

She seized both Lady Cynthia's hands in hers. "Please come in—this is the nicest surprise I've ever had in my life." She drew her inside. "This is my husband." Her voice sounded breathless. "You never met him, did you, but I remember we talked about him."

Eustace shook hands. He was a wizened little man, deeply tanned by the sun, and wearing nothing but shorts and sandshoes. Lady Cynthia noticed that, in spite of the fact that his hair was thinning a little, he retained a slightly boyish air, as though he had never quite grown up. He shut the door carefully and led her politely to a rickety-looking but comfortable chair.

"If only I'd known," cried Mrs. Edgehill, "I'd have put on a dress instead of receiving you in old shorts and a blouse like this."

As a matter of fact, she did look rather peculiar. Her shorts had obviously originally belonged to her husband, and her blouse was of startlingly flowered printed silk. It would have been an excellent design for chintz chair covers but was a trifle overpowering as it was.

"Get out the whiskey, Eustace," she said, and then, a thought striking her, "Have you had dinner?"

Lady Cynthia's eye quickly took in the cups and plates and dishes on the table. It was obvious that they had just finished. She nodded. "Yes," she said, "I dined the moment I got off the plane, but I should love a soft drink of some sort."

"You must have some Johnnie Walker, you really must," said Mrs. Edgehill. "This is an occasion!" Lady Cynthia was touched to see that her whole face was quivering with pleasure. She called out to her husband, who had disappeared into what was probably the kitchen, "The soda's in the Frigidaire." She produced a packet of Gold Flake cigarettes. "I'm afraid these are all we have to offer you until the next supply ship comes, unless you'd rather have an American one. Eustace can pop over to the hotel in a minute."

Lady Cynthia shook her head. "I much prefer these."

Mrs. Edgehill lit her cigarette, then lit one for herself and drew up a chair. "I wish I'd known, really I do. I'd have had the house tidy for you. It does look like a pigsty, doesn't it?"

At this moment Eustace came back bearing a bottle of whiskey, two bottles of soda and an opener. Lady Cynthia looked around the room. It certainly was the strangest mix-up she had ever seen. There was an old sofa with a faded chintz cover; rather a good Spanish-looking sideboard; a gramophone, one of the old-fashioned kind with a livid green horn; two or three deck chairs; a portable radio, and a table covered with shells of different shapes and colors and some gleaming white, graceful branches of bleached coral. On the stained wooden walls there were two or three dim watercolors; a whole row of six perfectly charming old prints of London; and in the place of honor, on the wall of the partition facing the stove, a framed photograph of the King and Queen. The frame, obviously home-made, was of varnished wood and the photograph was quite dreadful. It had apparently been cut out of one of the illustrated papers, and some kind of disaster had happened to it. Mrs. Edgehill caught her looking at it and smiled sadly.

"Isn't that awful?" she asked. "We had a terrible storm about six months ago, and the rain came in and trickled all down the inside of the frame and ruined it. It makes me feel ashamed every time I look at it, but we can't take it down because it's the only one we have."

"Surely," said Lady Cynthia, "as official British Resident you should have an official portrait of the King and Queen."

"We've asked for one over and over again," said Eustace, prizing open one of the bottles of soda, "But there's a new governor in Samolo now, and nobody's ever paid any attention."

"As a matter of fact, we really do feel it a bit," said Mrs. Edgehill, with an overbright little smile. "You see, we are the only two British people here, and it's been a little difficult to keep our end up since the Americans came."

8

It was long after midnight when Lady Cynthia finally tore herself away. Eustace accompanied her back to the hotel, took her in through the side door and showed her the way to her room. When she said good night to him he gripped her hand and held it for quite a while.

"It was awfully nice of you to drop in," he said, his voice sounding rather hoarse. "It'll set Dorrie up no end. She has so often talked about you. She always wanted to ring you up, you know, when you asked her to that time at Government House, but she never dared. You've no idea how much this evening has meant to her, really you haven't."

He let go her hand, and then added shyly, "You won't forget about that photograph, will you? It isn't really for us, ourselves—we're little people and we don't matter very much—But I would like these Americans to know that we had it. You see, they don't quite understand how difficult it is sometimes for us to be the only British people here, with the war going on and everything and being such a long way away from home . . ." He broke off abruptly, and, with a muttered "Good night," turned and walked away along the passage.

Lady Cynthia went into her room and, closing the door quietly behind her, sat down at her dressing table and observed, without surprise, that her eyes were filled with tears.

"I'm getting old," she reflected, "old, and possibly rather maudlin, but all the same I'm learning a good deal more than I ever learned before."

She undressed slowly and lay on the bed without switching out the light, knowing that sleep was miles away from her. She glanced at her travelling clock: ten past one. She was to be called at three-thirty, because they were taking off just before dawn. It really wasn't any use attempting to sleep—she could sleep all day tomorrow in the plane anyway. She lit a cigarette and let her mind wander back over the evening.

She was not at all sure why it was that she had felt so highly strung and emotional all the time; perhaps because she hadn't had any dinner, or maybe it was that she was overtired and had had two strongish whiskey and sodas on top of the Handleys' dry martinis. There was nothing in the least sad about the Edgehills. They were obviously a devoted couple and serenely happy in each other's company from morning till night; whatever troubles had assailed them in their lives, they had had each other, and had been able to share them.

Perhaps this was what had given her that slight ache in her heart: the spectacle of two people who were secure in the knowledge that, whatever might happen to them, providing it was not death or separation, they could never be lonely!

Lady Cynthia sighed lightly and tried unsuccessfully to remember any one period of her life when she had felt that sense of security. There was Henry, of course, but then he had died too soon, before either of them had had time to get through the first painful ecstasies and miseries of being married and in love. There had certainly been no security there—not even a semblance of tranquillity ever. She tried to imagine what would have happened if he had lived, and their possessive, demanding passion for each other had simmered down with the passing of the years. What would have been left? Gentle domesticity, quiet acquiescence—understanding—tolerance?

She suddenly laughed aloud, and stubbed her cigarette out in the ash-tray on the table by the bed. What nonsense! They would never have had the remotest chance of it; all the cards would have been stacked against them; too much money and leisure and far too many shrill, predatory friends. The period had been against them too; those overgay, strained 1920s.

Still, the Edgehills had lived through that period also—but that was different. They belonged to another world. They had had the inestimable advantage of having to work in order to live; every bit of pleasure or happiness they ever had they had earned, striven for, and fully appreciated when they got it. That was where the difference lay, and it was a basic difference. She and Henry had had everything—everything but the essentials; an abundance of treacherous gifts poured into their laps. The Edgehills had had nothing, nothing but the essentials. Their security and gentleness and love for each other; their tranquil acceptance of life as it was; their immutable, inner convictions about themselves and each other, had not been showered on them in colored wrappings like so many wedding presents. Those things were never showered on anyone. But they were the lucky ones, luckier even than they knew.

She fixed the pillow behind her head, and stared up at the ceiling. There was a small lizard in the corner using all its wiles to catch a fly. It stalked it very, very slowly, and then, suddenly, out shot its long tongue, there was no more fly, and the lizard relaxed. Lady Cynthia relaxed too. What an extraordinary evening! After the first half hour, when they had had a drink and the initial shyness had evaporated, the whole atmosphere had changed, become intimate. Eustace Edgehill, who had hurriedly put on a clean shirt in her honor, had taken it off again, and lay back in his deck chair. Dorrie—Lady Cynthia smiled—Dorrie had put a large conch shell at her feet for cigarette ends, and turned on the news on the portable radio. There they had sat, three English people, listening to an American voice, rich in dramatic overtones, describing a heavy air raid on London. Lady Cynthia remembered watching the expression on the Edgehills' faces, or rather the lack of expression. They had sat quite still, staring straight in front of them. At one moment Dorrie had frowned, and then closed her eyes wearily. After a while Eustace had got up and turned the radio off.

"No sense in sitting here and upsetting ourselves," he said, and poured himself out another drink.

Presently they had begun to talk about "Home" and ask questions. Did Lady Cynthia know Hythe, and had it been knocked about much? Was London really as badly hit as the radio said it was? Eustace had a married sister living in Clapham who wrote to him occasionally. They had not heard from her lately, but she never said much about the blitzes in her letters—perhaps they hadn't had it very badly in Clapham?

Lady Cynthia told them all she could think of about London. She described the first dreary, anticlimactic months of the war, and then the tension when it really started; the miraculous, agonizing days when the men came pouring back from Dunkirk. She had been at Dover, running a canteen on the station. Dorrie and Eustace drank in every word with passionate eagerness; Dorrie's right hand was tapping ceaselessly on the edge of her chair, and her eyes were glistening. She said that one of her cousins had been through Dunkirk, but that she hadn't seen him since he was a little boy and didn't even know what he looked like now. Then they had sat silent for a little while; the refrigerator made a whirring sound every now and then, and the noise of the sea seemed to get louder and louder. Later on in the evening they had told her about their lives on the island from the very beginning when Eustace had come out with the boys and built the house.

They spoke eagerly, interrupting each other and passing the story back and forth. It had been a bit of a shock when the Americans had first arrived, but they had got used to it after a bit, although, of course, it wasn't half so quiet and peaceful as it had been before. They had had official instructions to do their level best to cooperate with them in every way possible. The Handleys were quite nice in their way. They had arrived just before the hotel was finished. They had been nothing if not friendly and civil from the word go really, but, of course, you couldn't get away from the fact that, being Americans, they weren't in the war and didn't really understand. All they really seemed to be interested in was Trans-National Airways.

Then Broderick Sarnton, the new airport manager, had arrived. He was all right really, but the one who had been there before had been much nicer. Inevitably there had had to be several changes. The Americans had imported a whole lot of Chamorro boys from Guam, and there had been quarrels between them and the Samolans until finally, after a lot of rows and arguments, Eustace had had to give in and send the Samolans home— except Ippaga, who helped in the radio office.

The Americans really weren't so bad. They were awfully kind about sending over cartons of Lucky Strikes and Camels, but unfortunately they didn't like Lucky Strikes or Camels very much. They also asked them regularly every week to see the newest films, which were brought by the clippers, but they accepted only once in a while because they really didn't care to put themselves too much under obligation, and they had no way of returning the hospitality.

There had been a rather unhappy incident. Lady St. Merrion, the wife of the new Governor General of Samolo, had arrived one night in the American-bound clipper. There had been bad flying weather and the plane was unable to take off the next morning as usual. Dorrie, naturally expecting that Lady St. Merrion would come to call, as Eustace was the official British Resident, had worn her one and only afternoon frock all day long for three days, and Eustace had put on a shirt and tie and white flannel trousers, but she had never come. They had watched her every morning strolling by toward the "Split" with the captain of the clipper and one or two of the other passengers. They used to fish for barracuda off the point by Roper's Folly. By the time Dorrie had finished retailing this unfortunate exposé of aristocratic bad manners, her face was quite red. "You see," she said to Lady Cynthia, "it didn't matter about us really, but it was the flag. She never once even looked up at the flag."

9

In October 1940 there was a crisis on Cowrie Island. The crisis had no international complications and was brought about entirely by the weather. For three whole weeks a gale had been blowing. No clipper had arrived, either from Honolulu or Nouméa, and the supply ship was over a month late. There were no cigarettes left on the island and very little food. The food situation, of course was not really serious, because fish could always be obtained easily from the farther side of the lagoon. It was impossible to fish in the open sea, because the waves were tumultuous, and to attempt to get a boat out through the "Split" was obviously out of the question. The lagoon fish, however, were reasonably edible although small and a trifle monotonous. Everyone's nerves became rather frayed. Brod had a row with the Handleys. Some of the mechanics fell out with each other, with the result that one of them had his head split open with a bottle and had to be put in hospital.

The hotel passed its days in echoing emptiness and acquired a greater air of incongruity than ever. Robb Handley, who had a secret store of bourbon whiskey, elected to get wildly drunk one night with the assistant airport manager, and they both swam out to one of the farther coral heads in the lagoon. Having reached it, they collapsed in complete exhaustion and had to stay there until the following morning, when they were rescued by the launch and brought back to the landing stage, stark naked and shivering violently.

The Edgehills, as usual, kept to themselves. Eustace continued to perform the ritual of the flag every morning and evening. He was fully aware that this might appear foolish to the Americans, if not somewhat irritating. On three occasions the flagstaff blew down, but he got it up again all right, assisted by Dorrie and Ippaga. They, too, were completely out of cigarettes, but Eustace had some pipe tobacco, and so they shared a pipe amicably each evening. Dorrie almost grew to enjoy it.

At last, on a dreadful day, when the rain was driving across the reef almost horizontally like staves of music, the supply ship was sighted. Everyone on the island was immediately galvanized into frenzied activity. Brod rather lost his head and, against the advice of Eustace, the assistant airport manager and several others, insisted on sending the barge out through the "Split." Eustace and Dorrie, crouching in the lee of the rock walls of Roper's Folly, watched the barge anxiously as it edged out into the surf. Miraculously, it managed to get through, or rather over, the gigantic rollers, and headed for the ship. In about two hours it returned, laden with packing cases.

This time disaster overtook it. It had just reached the entrance to the "Split" when an extra-large wave knocked it round broadside onto the reef. There was a panic-stricken shout from the seven men on board, then an agonizing pause, until another wave capsized it completely. Dorrie gave a scream and sprang to her feet. Eustace left her side and started to run over the coral to the edge of the surf. She called after him to come back. There was nothing that he could possibly do beyond just stand there in the driving wind and rain, and watch the barge being battered to matchwood. Fortunately, the men managed to get themselves ashore. They were badly cut and bruised, and three of them had to go to hospital. The worst aspect of the whole business was that all the packing cases contained food supplies and cigarettes.

Four days later the weather abated sufficiently to enable the ship to send in a boat. It made three journeys during the day and managed to land the remaining supplies, among them a mail bag for the Edgehills. It was a very small mail bag, containing two letters from Eustace's married sister; a long, rambling letter from Ena Harris, a friend of Dorrie's in Pendarla; and an impressive-looking flat parcel. They opened the parcel last. Inside it was a typewritten letter and two thick pieces of cardboard, sandwiching between them a signed photograph of Their Majesties, the King and Queen. The letter was from a lady-in-waiting and started: "Dear Mr. Edgehill: The Queen has commanded me to send you the enclosed photograph of Their Majesties. Her Majesty was most interested to hear from Lady Cynthia Marchmont . . ." Dorrie said, "Oh dear!" in a choking voice and, sinking down on the bed, burst into tears.

10

In the spring of 1942 the American authorities decided to evacuate Cowrie Island. The process took several weeks. Two destroyers appeared escorting a large freighter. The clipper service had been canceled ever since the month following Pearl Harbor. The Handleys had gone, and the hotel had been closed for some months. The Edgehills, having received no instructions of any sort, were slightly at a loss and, as the weeks passed and the island grew more and more denuded, they realized that they would have to make a decision. The captain of one of the American destroyers had called politely on arrival and offered them passage on his ship, bound for Honolulu, which offer they had felt bound to refuse pending instructions from Samolo.

Now the evacuation was nearly completed, no instructions had come, and they were faced with having to decide whether to accept passage in the American ship and pack all their belongings onto the freighter, or to stay where they were and await events. The young American captain, who was both helpful and sympathetic, strongly advised them to come with him. He explained that, since the Japanese had declared war, all radio communications in the Pacific had gone haywire, and that once they arrived in Honolulu the British consul there would advise them what to do.

Eustace, who felt that the dignity of his position demanded advice from rather higher authority than a mere consul, was torn with indecision. Finally, after an anguished discussion with Dorrie, which lasted nearly all night, he decided to go, and they started to pack. The Americans were leaving on the following evening, and the captain was to call in the morning for their final decision. They had started to pack at about 4:30 a.m. listlessly and miserably. Any thought of sleep was out of the question. Just after dawn Dorrie went into the kitchen to cook some eggs and bacon. They were both worn out with arguing and were utterly depressed, and she thought that a little sustenance might cheer them up a bit. While she was putting the kettle on for the tea, she happened to glance out of the window. The kitchen window was at the back and looked out over the reef to the open sea. There was the freighter in the same place it had been for the last few weeks. A little to the right and to the left of it lay the destroyers, but—she blinked her eyes and stared—there was a third ship, smaller than the American destroyers, but unmistakably warlike. She gave a loud cry.

Eustace came running into the kitchen. She pointed with a quivering finger.

"Look at the flag," she said breathlessly. "Look at the flag!"

From the third ship fluttered the White Ensign. Eustace gave a whoop of joy and flung his arms around her; the coffeepot went flying off the stove and broke on the floor. Still with his arm tightly around her, he rushed her out of the side door, and they started to run toward the edge of the reef. Eustace was shouting, which was very foolish, as the ship was at least a mile off shore.

Just before sundown that evening they were sitting together in the stern of a boat being rowed out through the "Split." The boat's crew were sunburned British sailors. Dorrie was clasping her handbag and a large, flat package very carefully done up in sacking and string. She glanced at poor old Roper's Folly as they passed, and felt a sudden catch in her throat. There were the hermit crabs and the little mound with the colored shells on it where the love bird was buried. There was the house, their house that Eustace had built so lovingly; the lowering sun glinted on the windows, making it look as though it were on fire. She almost wished that it was. It was hateful going away like this and leaving the house empty and alone.

The Union Jack still fluttered from the flagstaff; she wondered sadly how long it would stay there.

Eustace, after a sidelong look at her face, leant close to her and put his hand on hers. "Never mind, old girl," he said softly. "It was lovely while it lasted." She returned the pressure of his hand, and tried to smile, but it was not a great success, so she turned her face toward the open sea and did not look at the island anymore.

HMS *Rapid*
May 1944

It was good to know that in the big picture of the war there was room for small cameos such as this.

•

The song ("London Pride") . . . the play (*Blithe Spirit*) . . . and now the film.

In *Future Indefinite* Noël tells of how in mid-1941 "a deputation of three gentlemen . . . called on me at the Savoy Hotel. I received them warily because I knew that the object of their visit was to persuade me to make a film, and I had no intention of making a film then or at any other time . . . I had convinced myself, with easy sophistry, that (filmmaking) was a soul-destroying industry in which actors of mediocre talent were publicized and idolized beyond their deserts, and authors, talented or otherwise, were automatically massacred."

The "deputation" left, with Noël having promised to at least consider the proposition. The following day he happened to be having dinner with his old friend Louis Mountbatten, who was serving with the Royal Navy. Mountbatten told him how his command, the destroyer HMS *Kelly,* had recently been sunk off the coast of Crete. Noël knew at once that he had his story.

Inspiration had come quickly but implementation was infinitely harder. It took influence from Mountbatten and even King George VI himself to overcome bureaucratic resistance. One problem was that Noël intended to play the leading role of Captain Kinross—a character based almost too closely on Mountbatten—himself. Another was that his command, HMS *Torrin* (aka *Kelly*), is also lost—a fact that was considered to be negative propaganda for the war effort. It took the King to point out that "although the ship is lost, the spirit which animates the Royal Navy is clearly brought out in the men and the procession of ships coming along to take its place at the end and demonstrates the power of the Navy."

The film *In Which We Serve* went ahead—its title being taken from a

Naval "Prayer to Be Used at Sea." ("Be pleased to receive into thy Almighty and most Gracious protection the persons of us thy servants, and the Fleet in which we serve.") What set the film apart was not so much the battle scenes as the use of "thy servants." Noël—having been advised by codirector David Lean to study Orson Welles's acclaimed *Citizen Kane*—borrowed the flashback technique to create a deeper human context. We see the ship torpedoed and the survivors floating in the water, clinging to a life raft, watching her slowly sink. Then, one by one, we see something of each man's personal story.

The film was an immediate and lasting success.

Critic C. A. Lejeune concluded, "His heart has sneaked up on Mr. Coward. *In Which We Serve* never gushes, but there is a subtle warmth in the old astringency. For the first time he seems to be speaking, not to the select but to the simple."

The casting was considered to be impeccable. John Mills, Celia Johnson (as Mrs. Kinross), Bernard Miles, Joyce Carey, Michael Wilding, Kay Walsh, Kathleen Harrison and Richard Attenborough in his first film role.

IN WHICH WE SERVE (1942)
CAST

CAPTAIN "D" KINROSS	NOËL COWARD
SHORTY BLAKE	JOHN MILLS
WALTER HARDY	BERNARD MILES
ALIX (MRS. KINROSS)	CELIA JOHNSON

DIRECTED BY NOËL COWARD AND DAVID LEAN

PRODUCED BY TWO CITIES

FIRST SHOWN ON SEPTEMBER 27, 1942

NARRATOR (Leslie Howard): This is the story of a ship . . .

In early sequences we see HMS *Torrin* being built. Now it is fully commissioned and Captain Kinross addresses his new crew . . .

STUDIO EXTERIOR, PLYMOUTH QUAYSIDE, DAY.

CLOSE SHOT, CAPTAIN and NUMBER ONE.

NUMBER ONE: Ship's company present, sir.

CAPTAIN (*acknowledging salute*): Thank you—stand them at ease, please.

NUMBER ONE: Aye, Aye, sir. (*To Ship's Company*) Ship's Company—stand at—*ease*.

The CAPTAIN advances and climbs onto a bollard. He stands for a moment looking over the troops.

CAPTAIN: Break ranks and gather round me.

STUDIO EXT. PLYMOUTH QUAYSIDE. DAY.

LONG SHOT with CAPTAIN "D" in the foreground and the MEN breaking ranks. The CAPTAIN beckons them nearer.

CAPTAIN: Come a bit nearer—I don't want to have to shout. Can you hear me all right in the back row?

SAILOR (*in back row*): Yes, sir—we can hear you fine.

STUDIO EXT. PLYMOUTH QUAYSIDE. DAY.

LONG SHOT, different angle, with the MEN in foreground, and CAPTAIN in the background.

CAPTAIN: Good. You all know that it is the custom of the Service for the Captain to address the Ship's Company on Commissioning Day to give them his policy and tell them the ship's programme. Now my policy is easy and if there are any here who have served with me before, they will know what it is. Are there any old shipmates of mine here?

Noël as Captain "D." He is wearing Lord Mountbatten's cap.

About half a dozen hands go up eagerly in different parts of the crowd.

STUDIO EXT. PLYMOUTH QUAYSIDE. DAY.
CLOSE SHOT, CAPTAIN "D" as he recognizes them one by one.

CAPTAIN: Glad to see you again, Johnson.

STUDIO EXT. PLYMOUTH QUAYSIDE. DAY
MEDIUM SHOT, JOHNSON in the crowd. The camera ZIP PANS to a group that includes COOMBE.

CAPTAIN (*off*): . . . and Coombe . . .

ZIP PAN to ADAMS.

CAPTAIN (*off*): . . . and Adams . . .

ZIP PAN to REYNOLDS.

CAPTAIN (*off*): . . . and Reynolds . . .

The camera ZIP PANS to another group. We see a hand sticking up behind the heftily built CHIEF STOKER.

STUDIO EXT. PLYMOUTH QUAYSIDE. DAY.
CLOSE SHOT, the CAPTAIN.

CAPTAIN: Who's that small fellow hiding his face behind the Chief Stoker?

STUDIO EXT. PLYMOUTH QUAYSIDE. DAY.
MEDIUM SHOT, the CROWD. There is a general murmur of laughter as PARKINSON steps clear.

PARKINSON: Parkinson, sir.

STUDIO EXT. PLYMOUTH QUAYSIDE. DAY.
CLOSE-UP, the CAPTAIN.

CAPTAIN: You were cox'n of the All Comers whaler in the Valletta, weren't you?

STUDIO EXT. PLYMOUTH QUAYSIDE. DAY.
CLOSE-UP, PARKINSON.

PARKINSON: I was that, sir, when we won the All Comers cup in the 1936 regatta.

STUDIO EXT. PLYMOUTH QUAYSIDE. DAY
CLOSE-UP, the CAPTAIN.

CAPTAIN: Yes, and fell into the ditch when you got back to the ship.

STUDIO EXT. PLYMOUTH QUAYSIDE. DAY.
LONG SHOT, over the CAPTAIN's shoulder. There is loud laughter. The tension of the new Ship's Company is lightened, and a friendly, more free-and-easy air comes over them.

CAPTAIN: Well, there are enough old shipmates to tell the others what my policy has always been. Johnson, Coombe, Adams, Reynolds, Parkinson—what sort of a ship do I want the *Torrin* to be? (*There is a slight pause.*) Come on, Reynolds?

STUDIO EXT. PLYMOUTH QUAYSIDE. DAY.
CLOSE-UP, REYNOLDS.

REYNOLDS: A happy ship, sir.

STUDIO EXT. PLYMOUTH QUAYSIDE. DAY.
CLOSE-UP, the CAPTAIN.

CAPTAIN: That's right.

STUDIO EXT. PLYMOUTH QUAYSIDE. DAY
CLOSE-UP, COOMBE.

COOMBE: An efficient ship, sir.

STUDIO EXT. PLYMOUTH QUAYSIDE. DAY
MEDIUM SHOT, the CAPTAIN.

CAPTAIN: Correct. A happy and efficient ship. A very happy and a very efficient ship. Some of you might think I am a bit ambitious wanting both, but in my experience you can't have one without the other. A ship can't be happy unless she's efficient and she certainly won't be efficient unless

"There's dysentery in every ripple." Noël
being prepared for the scene in which the
survivors of the sinking of HMS *Torrin*
float in the oily Mediterranean
(replicated at Denham Studios).

she's happy. Now for our programme. You've most of you seen the commissioning programme of the *Torrin* published in Plymouth General Orders, and you will have noted that this allows the customary three weeks. In peacetime it takes all of three weeks to get a new Ship's Company together, to let them sling their hammocks and teach them their stations and various duties, to get all the cordite and shells and oil fuel and stores on board and so on and so forth.

Well, you've read your papers and you know that Ribbentrop signed a non-aggression pact with Stalin yesterday. As I see it that means war next week, so I will give you not three *weeks* but exactly three *days* to get this ship ready to sail. None of us will take off our clothes or sling our hammocks or turn in for the next three days and nights until the job is finished, then we'll send Hitler a telegram saying "The *Torrin*'s ready— you can start your war!"

•

The film experienced its normal quota of technical problems, but Noël himself encountered one he had never expected—his own *voice*. West End audiences had attuned their ears to the clipped Coward delivery but not so the Denham Studios sound technicians.

After the "happy ship is an efficient ship" speech a soundman was heard to ask if someone would please tell Mr. Coward to watch his enunciation during that "fish and chips speech."

•

Before the ship sails there is a party in the Wardroom for the immediate families of the senior crew. One of them, "Flags," has just become engaged, and Kinross (Captain "D") tries to persuade his wife, Alix, to toast the happy couple . . .

INTERIOR, WARDROOM, NIGHT.
CLOSE-UP, ALIX.

ALIX (*to FLAGS and his fiancée, MAUREEN*): Stop whispering, you two—Number One, you ought never to have put them next to each other.

INT. WARDROOM. NIGHT
CLOSE-UP, CAPTAIN "D."

CAPTAIN: We ought to drink to them. Come on, everybody—to the Newly Betrothed.

INT. WARDROOM. NIGHT
LONG SHOT, the table as seen between FLAGS and MAUREEN.

EVERYBODY: To the Newly Betrothed.

They all drink.

BOBBY: What's "betrothed," Daddy?
CAPTAIN: The beginning of the end, my boy.
FLAGS: On behalf of my fiancée and myself—thank you very kindly.

INT. WARDROOM. NIGHT.
CLOSE-UP, CAPTAIN "D."

CAPTAIN: Alix, as Flags and Maureen are so bashful—I think it only right and proper that you should make a speech.

INT. WARDROOM. NIGHT.
MEDIUM SHOT, the GROUP around ALIX.

ALIX: No—no—I can't—honestly I can't . . .
NUMBER ONE: Come on, Mrs. Kinross—I'll support you.
MRS. MACADOO: Hear! Hear!—speech.

Everybody calls for speech. Finally, still protesting, ALIX rises to her feet.

ALIX: Teddy, I swear I'll never forgive you for this. Oh dear—what am I to say?

CAPTAIN (*laughing*): Happy Christmas!

ALIX: Just you wait.

CAPTAIN: Come on now—silence, everybody—Her Worship the Lady Mayoress is about to declare the bazaar open . . .

NUMBER ONE: Don't let him get you down, Mrs. Kinross.

ALIX: Ladies and Gentlemen—I'll begin by taking my husband's advice . . .

CAPTAIN: Hurray!

ALIX: . . . and wish you all a very, very happy Christmas. I'm sure that Mrs. Farrell and Mrs. Macadoo will back me up when I say I am going to deliver a word of warning—on behalf of all wretched Naval wives—to Maureen, who has been unwise enough to decide on joining our ranks . . .

General laughter and murmurs of "Hear! Hear!" from MRS. FARRELL and MRS. MACADOO.

INT. WARDROOM. NIGHT.
CLOSE TWO shot, MAUREEN and FLAGS.

ALIX (*off*): Dear Maureen—we all wish you every possible happiness but it's only fair to tell you in advance what you're in for . . .

"TORPS" (*off*): Shame—shame!

INT. WARDROOM. NIGHT.
CLOSE-UP, ALIX.

ALIX: Speaking from bitter experience I can only say that the wife of a sailor is most profoundly to be pitied. To begin with, her home life—what there is of it—has no stability whatever. She can never really settle down—she moves through a succession of other people's houses, flats and furnished rooms. She finds herself grappling with domestic problems in Hong Kong, Bermuda, Malta, or Weymouth—we will not deal with the question of pay! That is altogether too painful, but what we will deal with is the most important disillusionment of all and that is . . .

INT. WARDROOM. NIGHT
CLOSE-UP, CAPTAIN "D."

CAPTAIN: Stop her, somebody—this is rank mutiny.

INT. WARDROOM. NIGHT
CLOSE-UP, ALIX.

ALIX (*firmly*): That is, that wherever she goes, there is always in her life a permanent and undefeated rival—her husband's ship! Whether it be a sloop or a battleship, or a submarine or a destroyer . . . it comes before home, wife, children, everything. Some of us fight this and get badly mauled in the process—others, like myself, resign themselves to the inevitable. That is what you will have to do, my poor Maureen—that is what we all have to do if we want any peace of mind at all. Ladies and Gentlemen, I give you my rival—it is extraordinary that anyone could be so fond and proud of their most implacable enemy—This Ship— God Bless this Ship and all who sail in her.

She drinks as the scene dissolves.

One of the film's most moving scenes takes place belowdecks between Walter Hardy and Shorty Blake . . .

INTERIOR, PETTY OFFICERS MESS. DAY.
In the foreground of the picture is WALTER, writing a letter. In the background are BRODIE, STEVENS, HOOPER and RIDGEWAY. BRODIE and STEVENS are reading. HOOPER is doing his accounts.
WALTER dips his pen in the ink and starts to write again.
INT. PETTY OFFICERS MESS. DAY.
CLOSE-UP, WALTER's letter.

My dear wife—well, here we are, old darling, in port again for a bit—so near and yet so far—as you might say.

INT. PETTY OFFICERS MESS. DAY.
MEDIUM SHOT, WALTER. In the background SHORTY can be seen coming into the Mess.

WALTER (*looking up and seeing SHORTY*): Hello, Shorty . . . come in.

SHORTY takes off his cap and comes up to WALTER.

SHORTY (*rather haltingly*): I—or—I just popped along to see if you'd had any news from home—
WALTER: Not so much as a PC . . . That's Kath all over—in all the years we've been married she's never got a post right yet. Have you heard from Freda?
SHORTY: Yes.
WALTER: How's she doing?
SHORTY: She's all right.
WALTER (*noticing something strained in SHORTY's manner*): What's the matter?
SHORTY: It's Kath, Walter . . . she and Mrs. Lemmon . . . you see they was all in the house together and—and it got blitzed . . .

WALTER: What do you mean?

SHORTY (*miserably*): Kath got killed . . . both of them did—Freda was all right—she was under the stairs . . .

WALTER (*after a pause*): Oh—oh, I see.

SHORTY: I thought I'd better tell you, seeing that—well—I mean . . .

WALTER: Thanks, son, I'm much obliged—thanks very much. (*He rises.*) I think I'll go out on deck for a bit . . .

SHORTY: Righto.

WALTER (*moving away, then stopping*): I'm glad Freda's all right.

SHORTY (*with an attempt at a smile*): Yes—she's fine. (*Almost apologetically*) We got a son.

WALTER (*coming back and giving* SHORTY *a pat on the shoulder*): That's good . . . Congratulations.

WALTER walks away from camera into a LONG SHOT and goes out of the Mess.

DISSOLVE TO:

STUDIO EXTERIOR, QUARTERDECK, DAY

MEDIUM SHOT, WALTER. He reaches the extreme aft of the Quarterdeck and looks toward the shore. He suddenly discovers that his unfinished letter to Kath is in his hand. He looks at it almost unseeingly for a moment, then crumples it up and throws it over the side.

STUDIO EXTERIOR, (SMALL TANK), DAY. (INSERT).

CLOSE SHOT, the water, from above. The crumpled letter falls into the water and drifts away out of picture.

•

Prior to and, indeed, all the way through production Noël and his colleagues were totally dependent on the support of the top Naval brass. Mountbatten recommended that Noël invite the Second Sea Lord—the Admiralty Head of Personnel—to come along and see some of the rushes, since the Admiralty had lent the production an entire ship's company.

He was shown the scene above, and Mountbatten recalled, "The Admiral was very emotional. 'By Jove, Coward,' he said, 'that convinces me you were right to ask for a proper ship's company, *real* sailors. No actors could possibly have done that.'"

•

The *Torrin* is sunk and most of her crew has perished with her. The survivors are taken to Alexandria to be reassigned to other ships. Kinross addresses them for the last time.

It was perhaps the most difficult scene in the film as far as Noël was concerned.

"I had to say good-bye, stand still and say good-bye to each one of them. I had written some things in and I tore up my script and said, 'Please, chaps, say what you think you would have said in this situation.' And this I could hardly take. Each of them said their own line, like 'Good luck, sir!' or 'Chin up, sir'—all these perfectly trite, ordinary phrases, spoken from the heart. Talk about improvisation. It was nothing to do with 'acting.' They were *being*."

INTERIOR, LARGE SHED, ALEXANDRIA, DAY. (MATTE)

LONG SHOT. FIVE OFFICERS and NINETY MEN are gathered. They are dressed in a variety of borrowed tropical clothing—vests, singlets, shirts, shorts or trousers, white or khaki. Not hats or caps. Several men are bandaged. The RNVR SUBLIEUTENANT calls out:

SUBLIEUT.: Ship's Company—*shun*!

INT. LARGE SHED. ALEXANDRIA. DAY

MEDIUM SHOT. CAPTAIN "D" and the SUBLIEUTENANT. The latter comes to attention, but does not salute, as he has no cap.

SUBLIEUT.: Ship's Company present, sir.
CAPTAIN: Thank you—stand easy, please.

Captain "D" says good-bye to the survivors in Alexandria. ("There isn't one of you that I wouldn't be proud and honoured to serve with again. Good-bye, good luck and thank you all from the bottom of my heart.")

SUBLIEUT.: Ship's Company—stand—*easy*!

CAPTAIN: I have come to say good-bye to the few of you who are left. We have had so many talks but this is our last . . . I have always tried to crack a joke or two before and you have all been friendly and laughed at them. But today I am afraid I have run out of jokes, and I don't suppose any of us feel much like laughing. The *Torrin* has been in one scrap after another—but even when we have had men killed, the majority survived and brought the old ship back.

Now she lies in fifteen hundred fathoms and with her more than half our shipmates. If they had to die, what a grand way to go, for now they lie all together with the ship we loved, and they are in very good company. We have lost her but they are still with her. There may be less than half the *Torrin* left but I feel that each of us will take up the battle with even stronger heart. Each of us knows twice as much about fighting and each of us has twice as good a reason to fight. You will all be sent to replace men who have been killed in other ships, and the next time you are in action, remember the *Torrin*. As you ram each shell home into the gun, shout *Torrin,* and so her spirit will go on inspiring us until Victory is won. I should like to add that there isn't one of you that I wouldn't be proud and honoured to serve with again. Good-bye, good luck and thank you all from the bottom of my heart.

INT. LARGE SHED, ALEXANDRIA. DAY
CLOSE SHOT. CAPTAIN "D." The MEN file past and he shakes hands with each one.

MEN (*mumbling*): Good luck, sir . . .
Thank you, sir . . .
(Etc., etc.)
SHORTY: Good-bye, sir . . . (*He shakes hands with the* CAPTAIN.)
WALTER (*shaking hands*): Good-bye, sir.

Camera TRACKS CLOSER and CLOSER to the CAPTAIN's FACE. The MUSIC swells and the scene FADES OUT.
FADE IN:
The MUSIC swells and the VOICE OF THE NARRATOR, who spoke the prologue to the film, says:

Here ends the story of a ship, but there will always be other ships, for we are an island race. Through all our centuries the sea has ruled our destiny. There will always be other ships and men to sail in them. It is these men, in peace or war, to whom we owe so much. Above all victories, beyond all loss, in spite of changing values in a changing world, they give, to us their countrymen, eternal and indomitable pride. God bless our ships and all who sail in them.

As he speaks, we see a series of shots of minelayers, sloops, destroyers, trawlers, aircraft carriers, submarines, cruisers, tugs, converted liners, tankers, MTBs and battleships . . . all sailing purposefully into the future.

•

Tributes poured in from all sides, but few can have pleased him more than this from his crusty colleague, Aleck Woollcott . . .

> My dear Noël, this job you have done seems to me a really perfect thing. There was no moment of it from which I drew back or dissented. I went away marveling at its sure-footedness and realizing that all the ups and downs of your life (in particular the downs) had taught you to be unerring for your great occasion. All your years were a kind of preparation for this. If you had done nothing else and were never again to do anything else they could have been well spent.
>   Of course, I have thought of all these things afterward. At the time I just sat and cried quietly. For, after all, this picture is of courage all compact and courage is the only thing that brings the honorable moisture to these eyes.

There was to be only one jarring note, and the cause of it was not decisively proved until official files were opened years later. There had been talk of a knighthood for Noël as early as *Cavalcade* (1931), but the honour was considered premature. There was plenty of time. In fact, there turned out to be forty years of it.
   In the wake of *In Which We Serve,* so to speak, Mountbatten argued the case to his cousin King George. Noël was sounded out. Should there be such an offer . . . ? Noël would be honoured to accept. But the offer never came, and a letter from Churchill, dated December 29, 1942, reveals why . . .

> With considerable personal reluctance I have therefore come to the conclusion that I could not advise Your Majesty to proceed with this proposal on the present occasion.
> With my humble duty, I remain
> Your Majesty's faithful subject and servant
> Winston S. Churchill

Although he always suspected that this was the case, Noël did his best not to bear a grudge. The relationship between the two men was always wary, but the admiration was mutual.

•

Those years of conflict found Noël at his most prolific. He was alternately sentimental and satirical.

His personal travels gave him a perspective denied to most. Country after country. One battle zone after another. Troop concerts. Hospital visits. So many faces looking hopefully towards home. He was doing all he could—but it was so little.

"I'VE JUST COME OUT FROM ENGLAND"

I've just come out from England, and I feel
Foolishly empty-handed, for I bring
Nothing to you but words. But even so,
Even mere words can now and then reveal
A little truth. I know, or think I know,
If only I had had the chance to go
To all your homes and talk to all your mothers,
Wives and sweethearts, sisters, fathers, brothers;
What they'd have said and wanted me to say,
Those messages, unspoken, wouldn't ring
With sentimental pride, they'd be restrained.
We British hate to give ourselves away,
All our traditions having firmly trained
Our minds to shun emotional display.
Our people always understate with such
Determined nonchalance, whether it's praise
Or blame, anger or joy or woe,
However moved they are, or may have been,
They'll very very seldom tell you so,
But still, beneath the crust we feel as much,
If not a great deal more than those who sob
And weep and laugh too easily. My job,
Being a writer, is to read between
The lines that others write; to look behind
The words they string together and to find
The right translation, the right paraphrase
Of what they feel rather than what they say.

What they would say, those patient people who
So very lovingly belong to you,
Would be extremely simple, almost offhand.
"Give Jack my love"—"Tell Bert to come home soon"
"Tell Fred Aunt Nora's gone, he'll understand"

"Tell Jimmy everybody's doing fine"
"Give George our love and tell him Stan's had leave
And Elsie's doing war work nine till nine."
"Tell Billy that last Sunday afternoon
We saw a newsreel and we recognized
Him on a tank—we weren't half surprised."
It wouldn't take a genius to perceive
What lies behind those ordinary phrases
But on my own responsibility
I'd like to tell you what I know to be
Deep in the hearts of all of us in Britain.
The war's been long, it's had its tragic phases,
Its black defeats, its violent ups and downs,
But now, in all the villages and towns
That lie between Land's End and John o' Groat's,
Hope is restored, new faith in victory,
New faith in more than victory, new pride
In something that deep down we always knew,
Thus, at long last, through you and all you've done,
We have been proved again. Much will be written
In future years. Historians will spew
Long treatises on your triumphant story,
They'll rightly praise your gallantry and glory
And probably embarrass you a lot.
They'll make exhaustive military notes,
Argue each battle fought, from every side,
But maybe they'll forget to say the one
Important thing. Four simple words are not
Unlikely, midst so much, to get mislaid:
For once I feel I need not be afraid
Of being sentimental. I can say
What those at home, who miss you and have such
Deep pride in you, would wish me to convey,
In four short words—note the true English touch—
The words are simply: "Thank you very much."

His satirical side was inclined to get him into trouble in these sensitive times.

In 1943 at the height of the war he wrote a song called "Don't Let's Be Beastly to the Germans."

The BBC promptly banned it as being almost treasonable—a sense of irony not being high on Director General Lord Reith's Calvinist priorities.

"DON'T LET'S BE BEASTLY TO THE GERMANS"

We must be kind—
And with an open mind
We must endeavour to find
A way—
To let the Germans know that when the war is over
They are not the ones who'll have to pay.
We must be sweet—
And tactful and discreet
And when they've suffered defeat
We mustn't let
Them feel upset

NOEL COWARD   MAKES HIS OWN   CONTRIBUTION

TO THE PROBLEM   OF HOW TO   TREAT GERMANY

Or ever get
The feeling that we're cross with them or hate them,
Our future policy must be to reinstate them.

Don't let's be beastly to the Germans
When our victory is ultimately won,
It was just those nasty Nazis who persuaded them
                                    to fight
And their Beethoven and Bach are really far worse
                            than their bite.
Let's be meek to them—
And turn the other cheek to them
And try to bring out their latent sense of fun.
Let's give them full air parity—
And treat the rats with charity,
But don't let's be beastly to the Hun

We must be just—
And win their love and trust
And in addition we must
Be wise
And ask the conquered lands to join our hands to
                                    aid them.
That would be a wonderful surprise.
For many years—
They've been in floods of tears
Because the poor little dears
Have been so wronged and only longed
To cheat the world,
Deplete the world
And beat
The world to blazes.
This is the moment when we ought to sing
                            their praises.

Don't let's be beastly to the Germans
When we've definitely got them on the run—
Let us treat them very kindly as we would a
                            valued friend—
We might send them out some Bishops as a form of
                            lease and lend,
Let's be sweet to them—
And day by day repeat to them

That "sterilization" simply isn't done.
Let's help the dirty swine again—
To occupy the Rhine again,
But don't let's be beastly to the Hun.

Don't let's be beastly to the Germans
When the age of peace and plenty has begun.
We must send them steel and oil and coal and
everything they need
For their peaceable intentions can be
always guaranteed.
Let's employ with them a sort of "strength
through joy" with them,
They're better than us at honest manly fun.
Let's let them feel they're swell again and bomb
us all to hell again,
But don't let's be beastly to the Hun.

Don't let's be beastly to the Germans
For you can't deprive a gangster of his gun
Though they've been a little naughty to the Czechs
and Poles and Dutch
But I don't suppose those countries really minded
very much.
Let's be free with them and share the BBC
with them.
We mustn't prevent them basking in the sun.
Let's soften their defeat again—and build
their bloody fleet again,
But don't let's be beastly to the Hun.

.

"I shall never cease to be surprised at the sublime silliness . . . After all, 'Let's help the dirty swine again / To occupy the Rhine again' and 'Let's give them full air parity / And treat the rats with charity' are not, as phrases, exactly oozing with brotherly love."

Ironically, it was Winston Churchill who rescued it. He insisted Noël sing it at dinner parties until he was hoarse. And on this particular point Churchill and FDR were in total accord.

.

Though his theatrical activities were restricted by his various duties, Noël did find time in 1942–1943 to tour the provinces with productions of *This Happy Breed, Blithe Spirit* and *Present Laughter* (the other play postponed by the outbreak of hostilities) and it was probably the last of these that gave him the most pleasure.

Garry Essendine is an actor just admitting to being forty—and resisting every inch of the way.

"I'm always acting—watching myself go by. I see myself all the time, eating, drinking, loving, suffering. My life is not my own. I belong to the public and my work."

It was fitting that Noël created the part, since there are distinct elements of autobiography here. (In a BBC radio interview in 1972 he admitted, "Of course, Garry Essendine is me.")

As he wrote to his U.S. manager, Jack Wilson, who was to produce the 1946 Broadway version . . .

> *Present Laughter* is not so much a play as a series of semi-autobiographical pyrotechnics, and it needs, over and above everything else, abundant physical vitality. I myself found it arduous to play and God knows I have the vitality of the devil. Clifton's method is more measured than mine and I suspect that because of this, in spite of his technical skill and wit and charm, he gives the audience time to see the wheels going round. I played it more violently than I have ever played anything, and swept everything and everybody along with me at a breakneck speed.

To Clifton Webb, who was to play Garry/Noël . . .

Darling Mr. Webb,
You poor foolish boy! Fancy attempting to play a part which being in itself small and rather thankless requires, above everything else, beauty and grace and sweetness. After all, you must remember, it was written with those qualities in mind and played with such exquisite finesse that you could have heard a bomb drop.

However, if you like, in your clumsy heavy-footed way, to go stamping through the fabric of my dreams, that's entirely your affair.

I detected in your letter a certain whining note about the number of words you had to learn.

This complaint has been verified by those funny little Lunts who I hear are strutting about in some trumpery little piece [*O Mistress Mine*] and who also have trouble with their words.

Now, my Darling Little Webb, it is a question of concentration and Mary Baker Eddy . . . You must persevere, Dear Boy, and think beautiful thoughts and if you don't make an enormous success in it, I shall come and knock the B'Jesus out of you! I consign you happily to your fate! I love you very much.

It must be admitted that there was some cause for Webb's complaint. The part has just about as many lines as Hamlet—but rather more laughs.

PRESENT LAUGHTER (1939)

CAST

GARRY ESSENDINE	NOËL COWARD
ROLAND MAULE	JAMES DONALD
LIZ ESSENDINE	JOYCE CAREY
JOANNA LYPPIATT	JUDY CAMPBELL
HENRY LYPPIATT	GERALD CASE
MORRIS DIXON	DENNIS PRICE

DIRECTED BY NOËL COWARD

HAYMARKET THEATRE, LONDON, APRIL 29, 1943

•

In Act 1 Garry has an unexpected visit from a somewhat eccentric young playwright, Roland Maule . . .

GARRY motions ROLAND into a chair.

GARRY: Do sit down, won't you?
ROLAND (*sitting*): Thank you.
GARRY: Cigarette?
ROLAND: No, thank you.
GARRY: Don't you smoke?
ROLAND: No.
GARRY: Drink?
ROLAND: No, thank you.
GARRY: How old are you?
ROLAND: Twenty-five, why?
GARRY: It doesn't really matter—I just wondered.
ROLAND: How old are you?
GARRY: Forty in December—Jupiter, you know—very energetic.
ROLAND: Yes, of course. (*He gives a nervous, braying laugh.*)
GARRY: You've come all the way from Uckfield?

ROLAND: It isn't very far.

GARRY: Well, it sort of sounds far, doesn't it?

ROLAND (*defensively*): It's quite near Lewes.

GARRY: Then there's nothing to worry about, is there?
I want to talk to you about your play.

ROLAND (*gloomily*): I expect you hated it.

GARRY: Well, to be candid, I thought it was a little uneven.

ROLAND: I thought you'd say that.

GARRY: I'm glad I'm running so true to form.

ROLAND: I mean it really isn't the sort of thing you would like, is it?

GARRY: In that case why on earth did you send it to me?

ROLAND: I just took a chance. I mean I know you only play rather trashy stuff as a rule, and I thought you just might like to have a shot at something deeper.

GARRY: What is there in your play that you consider so deep, Mr. Maule? Apart from the plot which is completely submerged after the first four pages.

ROLAND: Plots aren't important, it's ideas that matter. Look at Chekhov.

GARRY: In addition to ideas I think we might concede Chekhov a certain flimsy sense of psychology, don't you?

ROLAND: You mean my play isn't psychologically accurate?

GARRY (*gently*): It isn't very good, you know, really, it isn't.

ROLAND: I think it's very good indeed.

GARRY: I understand that perfectly, but you must admit that my opinion, based on a lifelong experience of the theatre, might be the right one.

ROLAND (*contemptuously*): The commercial theatre.

GARRY: Oh, dear. Oh, dear. Oh, dear!

ROLAND: I suppose you'll say that Shakespeare wrote for the commercial theatre and that the only point of doing anything with the drama at all is to make money! All those old arguments. What you don't realise is that the theatre of the future is the theatre of ideas.

GARRY: That may be, but at the moment I am occupied with the theatre of the present.

ROLAND (*heatedly*): And what do you do with it? Every play you appear in is exactly the same, superficial, frivolous and without the slightest intellectual significance. You have a great following and a strong personality, and all you do is prostitute yourself every night of your life. All you do with your talent is to wear dressing gowns and make witty remarks when you might be really helping people, making them think! Making them feel!

GARRY: There can be no two opinions about it. I am having a most discouraging morning.

ROLAND (*rising and standing over* GARRY): If you want to live in people's memories, to go down to posterity as an important man, you'd better do something about it quickly. There isn't a moment to be lost.

GARRY: I don't give a hoot about posterity. Why should I worry about what people think of me when I'm dead as a doornail, anyway? My worst defect is that I am apt to worry too much about what people think of me when I'm alive. But I'm not going to do that anymore. I'm changing my methods and you're my first experiment. As a rule, when insufferable young beginners have the impertinence to criticize me, I dismiss the whole thing lightly because I'm embarrassed for them and consider it not quite fair game to puncture their inflated egos too sharply. But this time my highbrow young friend you're going to get it in the neck. To begin with, your play is not a play at all. It's a meaningless jumble of adolescent, pseudo-intellectual poppycock. It bears no relation to the theatre or to life or to anything. And you yourself wouldn't be here at all if I hadn't been bloody fool enough to pick up the telephone when my secretary wasn't looking. Now that you are here, however, I would like to tell you this. If you wish to be a playwright you just leave the theatre of tomorrow to take care of itself. Go and get yourself a job as a butler in a repertory company if they'll have you. Learn from the ground up how plays are constructed and what is actable and what isn't. Then sit down and write at least twenty plays one after the other, and if you can manage to get the twenty-first produced for a Sunday night performance you'll be damned lucky!

ROLAND (*hypnotized*): I'd no idea you were like this. You're wonderful!

GARRY (*flinging up his hands*): My God!

ROLAND: I'm awfully sorry if you think I was impertinent, but I'm awfully glad too, because if I hadn't been you wouldn't have got angry and if you hadn't got angry I shouldn't have known what you were really like.

GARRY: You don't in the least know what I'm really like.

ROLAND: Oh, yes, I do—now.

GARRY: I can't see that it matters, anyway.

ROLAND: It matters to me.

GARRY: Why?

ROLAND: Do you really want to know?

GARRY: What on earth are you talking about?

ROLAND: It's rather difficult to explain really.

GARRY: What is difficult to explain?

ROLAND: What I feel about you.

GARRY: But—

ROLAND: No, please let me speak—you see, in a way I've been rather unhappy about you—for quite a long time—you've been a sort of obsession with me. I saw you in your last play forty-seven times, one week I came every night, in the pit, because I was up in town trying to pass an exam.

GARRY: Did you pass it?

ROLAND: No, I didn't.

GARRY: I'm not entirely surprised.

ROLAND: My father wants me to be a lawyer, that's what the exam was for, but actually I've been studying psychology a great deal because I felt somehow that I wasn't at peace with myself and gradually, bit by bit, I began to realise that you signified something to me.

GARRY: What sort of something?

ROLAND: I don't quite know—not yet.

GARRY: That "not yet" is one of the most sinister remarks I've ever heard.

ROLAND: Don't laugh at me, please. I'm always sick if anyone laughs at me.

GARRY: You really are the most peculiar young man.

ROLAND: I'm all right now, though, I feel fine!

GARRY: I'm delighted.

ROLAND: Can I come and see you again?

GARRY: I'm afraid I'm going to Africa.

ROLAND: Would you see me if I came to Africa too?

GARRY: I really think you'd be happier in Uckfield.

ROLAND: I expect you think I'm mad but I'm not really, I just mind deeply about certain things. But I feel much better now because I think I shall be able to sublimate you all right.

GARRY: Good. Now I'm afraid I shall have to turn you out because I'm expecting my manager and we have some business to discuss.

ROLAND: It's all right. I'm going immediately.

GARRY: Shall I get you your script?

ROLAND: No, no—tear it up—you were quite right about it—it was only written with part of myself, I see that now. Good-bye.

GARRY: Good-bye.

Richard Briers, who played Roland in the 1965 London revival, remembers . . .

Ah! Roland! A very favourite part! Acting opposite Nigel Patrick was pretty tough, as he demanded a terrific pace. I was fast, too, and on the first night we played the opening scene so fast that nobody understood a word!

I played Maule with great emotion, trying to save Garry from his awful commercial plays. After his long tirade against *my* type of plays, there was a pause and I exclaimed, "You're wonderful" and became instantly in love with him, which, of course, drove him up the wall!

After the first night Noël looked at me, paused, and said: "You frightened me to death!"

Later in the play Garry, exasperated by what he sees as the continual and unreasonable demands of his "extended family" of wife, staff and associates, expresses himself forcefully, if a little histrionically.

GARRY: I'm sick to death of being stuffed with everybody's confidences. I'm bulging with them. You all of you come to me over and over again and pour your damned tears and emotions and sentiment over me until I'm wet through. You're all just as badly behaved as I am really, in many ways a great deal worse. You believe in your lachrymose amorous hangovers whereas I at least have the grace to take mine lightly. You wallow and I laugh because I believe now and I always have believed that there's far too much nonsense talked about sex. You, Morris, happen to like taking your paltry attachments seriously. You like suffering and plunging into orgies of jealousy and torturing yourself and everyone else. That's your way of enjoying yourself. Henry's technique is a little different, he plumps for the domestic blend. That's why he got tired of Joanna so quickly. Anyhow, he's beautifully suited with poor Elvira. She's been knee-deep in pasture ever since she left Roedean! Joanna's different again. She devotes a great deal of time to sex but not for any of the intrinsic pleasures of it, merely as a means to an end. She's a collector. A go-getter and attractive, unscrupulous pirate. I personally am none of these things. To me the whole business is vastly overrated. I enjoy it for what it's worth and fully intend to go on doing so for as long as anybody's interested and when the time comes that they're not I shall be perfectly content to settle down with an apple and a good book!

MORRIS: Well, I'll be damned!

HENRY: Of all the brazen, arrogant sophistry I've ever listened to that takes the prize for all time!

MORRIS: You have the nerve to work yourself up into a state of moral indignation about us when we all know—

GARRY: I have not worked myself into anything at all. I'm merely defending my right to speak the truth for once.

HENRY: Truth! You wouldn't recognise the truth if you saw it. You spend your whole life attitudinizing and posturing and showing off—

GARRY: And I should like to know where we should all be if I didn't! I'm an artist, aren't I? Surely I may be allowed a little license!

MORRIS: As far as I'm concerned, it's expired.

LIZ: For heaven's sake stop shouting all of you, you'll have the roof off.

JOANNA (*rising*): I'm sick of this idiotic performance. I'm going.

HENRY (*furiously to* GARRY): And kindly don't start that old threadbare argument about none of us being able to live and breathe if it wasn't for your glorious talent.

GARRY: How dare you allude to my talent in that nasty sarcastic tone, you ungrateful little serpent!

MORRIS: Anyhow, if it hadn't been for our restraining influence you'd be in the provinces by now.

GARRY: And what's the matter with the provinces, may I ask? They've often proved to be a great deal more intelligent than London.

HENRY: Be careful! Someone might hear.

GARRY: I suppose you'll be saying next that it's your restraining influence that has allowed me to hold my position as the idol of the public for twenty years—

MORRIS: You're not the idol of the public. They'll come and see you in the right play and the right part, and you've got to be good at that. Look what happened to you in *Pity the Blind*!

GARRY: I was magnificent in *Pity the Blind.*

MORRIS: Yes, for ten days.

HENRY: If it hadn't been for us you'd have done *Peer Gynt.*

GARRY: If I so much as hear *Peer Gynt* mentioned in this house again I swear before heaven that I shall produce it at Drury Lane.

HENRY: Not on my money you won't!

GARRY: Your money indeed! Do you think I'm dependent on your miserable money to put on plays? Why there are thousands of shrewd old gentlemen in the city who would be only too delighted to back me in anything I choose to do.

HENRY: I think it rather depends whether they are married or not.

GARRY: Oh, so we're back to that again, are we.

HENRY: No, we're not back to anything. This has been a most disgusting, degrading scene, and if it wasn't for the fact that Morris and I signed the contract for the Forum Theatre this morning we should both of us wash our hands of you forever!

GARRY: You've what!!

GARRY (*to* HENRY): Do you mean to tell me that you signed a contract for that theatre when I particularly told you that no power on God's earth would induce me to play in it?

MORRIS: Now look here, Garry—

GARRY: I will not look there. It's nothing more nor less than the most outrageous betrayal of faith and I'm deeply, deeply angry . . .

HENRY: As I told you the other day they are doing up the whole theatre, reseating the orchestra floor which will put over a hundred on to the

Gladys Calthrop's set from the 1947 revival of *Present Laughter* at the Haymarket Theatre, London. Once again Noël starred as Garry Essendine. ("I'm always acting . . . watching myself go by . . . My life is not my own . . . I belong to the public and my work.")

capacity. In addition to that they're mad to have you there and have even consented to put a shower bath into your dressing room—

GARRY: I don't care whether they've put a swimming bath in my dressing room and a squash court and a Steinway Grand. I will not play a light French comedy to an auditorium that looks like a Gothic edition of Wembley Stadium.

It's easy to see why—when in professional doubt—Noël would reach for and frequently appear in "dear old *Present Laughter.*"

In any case, Garry was simply the distillation of the Matinée Idol. Before him there was—Ritz Berkeley . . .

"THE ONE MAN PLAY" (1921)

The scene is the office of *RITZ BERKELEY,* a matinée idol.

RITZ (*at telephone*): No, of course not . . . very well, old man . . . yes, old man . . . no, old man . . . I won't play it . . . not my type . . . dine at seven, is that all right? What did I think of the show on Saturday? Terrible, old man . . . I'll let you know . . . yes, I've got an author . . . young, brains, enthusiasm . . . thinks I'm the best actor in England . . . damn clever . . . good-bye.

CHLOË is stamping books at desk.

RITZ: What are you doing, Chloë?
CHLOË: Stamping all these autograph books with your signature.
RITZ: Well, do it outside and show Mr. Griggs up when he arrives.
CHLOË: Don't be cross, Ritzie dear—just 'cos it's Monday morning.

(Exits.)

RITZ: Damn everybody. (*Snatches up phone.*) Hello, hello, is that you, Bertram? . . . Get me Sir Alfred Butt . . . (*Hangs up receiver. Waits. Bell rings.*) That you, Butt? . . . yes . . . *what* matinée? No, Butt . . . Yes, Butt . . . Never, never, never . . . Look here, Butt, it must be something with weight . . . give and take, you know . . . very well, I won't play it . . . Elsie Janis? No . . . No . . . Delysia? No, no, no . . . I want artists, old man, artists! (*He rings off.*) The man's a total fool!

Enter *CHLOË.*

CHLOË: Mr. Griggs to see you.
RITZ: Didn't I tell you to show him up?
CHLOË: All right, Ritzie darling—don't be fractious. (*Exits.*)
RITZ: Damn everything. (*At phone*) Get me Charlot. I'll hold on (*Pause.*) That you, Charlot? . . . Yes, old man . . . about that play you sent me—terrible.

Enter *NORMAN GRIGGS,* a Dramatist.

RITZ: Sit down, old man . . . yes . . . no . . . Fay Compton? God forbid . . . Constance Collier? Not on your life . . . Irene Vanbrugh? Fearful, old boy, fearful . . . I won't play with 'em (*Rings off.*) Well?
GRIGGS: You told me to come and see you—about my play!
RITZ: So I should think—you ought to be downright ashamed of yourself . . .
GRIGGS: Why?
RITZ: It's awful, old man, awful!
GRIGGS: Oh!
RITZ: Where's your construction?

GRIGGS: *I don't know.*

RITZ: Where's your dialogue?

GRIGGS (*pointing to play on desk*): There.

RITZ: Don't be silly, old boy. Understand once and for all—this play of yours is hopeless—dreadful.

GRIGGS: May I have it back, then?

RITZ: What the hell for?

GRIGGS: To send to someone else.

RITZ: Try not to be a fool, old man. Try not to be a fool. I'm going to do it all right.

GRIGGS (*brightening*): I thought you said it was hopeless?

RITZ: So it is. We must work on it together.

GRIGGS: It's complete as it is.

RITZ: Complete, my foot. (*Telephone rings.*) Hello, hello . . . look here, what the hell did you send me that script for? You know I can't read German. What, old man? Moscovitch? Never . . . Leslie Henson. Good God, no . . . Phyllis Monkman—don't be funny (*He rings off.*) Now about this play of yours . . .

GRIGGS (*hesitant*): Yes?

RITZ: Who have you got in your mind's eye for the leading lady?

GRIGGS (*timidly*): Madge Titheradge.

RITZ: Hopeless, old man. No depth.

GRIGGS: Iris Hoey.

RITZ: Worse. No breadth.

GRIGGS: Gladys Cooper?

RITZ: Look here, old boy—I'm serious, you know—what about Lucy Wittlebot?

GRIGGS: Who's Lucy Wittlebot?

RITZ: You mean you haven't seen me dancing with her at The Embassy?

GRIGGS: Oh yes, I remember now.

RITZ: That girl's got talent. She's never had a chance yet.

GRIGGS: Is she quite the type?

RITZ: Type be damned. She's young, fresh, pretty. What more do you want!

GRIGGS: Oh, all right.

RITZ: And see here—you've got to build up that part for me. I can't play it as it is.

GRIGGS: Build it up? But . . .

RITZ: What do you think I put on plays for—to see other people act in 'em? You're a young author and you've got to learn the *right* way to do things. I'm going to *mould* you. Now then, for instance, in this script you allow me to be discovered on the stage when the curtain goes up.

GRIGGS: Well, why not?

RITZ: Try to be intelligent. Why *not*! I'm your star—I'm the crux of your show. I must have an entrance down a staircase.

GRIGGS (*in anguish*): But it's a river bungalow. You can't have staircases in a river bungalow.

RITZ: Don't argue, old boy, don't argue. I'm telling you how to make your play a success.

GRIGGS: Oh!

RITZ: Then you must give me a good comedy scene when I hide under the bed.

GRIGGS: But why should you hide under the bed in your own home?

RITZ: Ingenuous youth! I hide under the bed because I know her husband is outside.

GRIGGS: But she's unmarried?

RITZ: Don't be silly, old man—give her a husband.

GRIGGS: But . . . but . . .

RITZ: That's it . . . but-but-but-but-but! Can't you see I'm trying to help you? You've got to give me a lovely little scene when I stand in the window with the moonlight all around me. Then you must work it somehow so that I have a big scuffle with two armed men. Then you must give me the final curtain with the room in darkness and me sitting gazing into the fire and saying—"I wonder."

GRIGGS: You seem to have forgotten that this is a simple psychological comedy.

RITZ: Simple psychological poppycock. What you want is a commercial success. (*To himself*) I don't know what's happened to the theatre today. I might as well write the damn thing myself.

GRIGGS (*gulping*): Oh!

BLACKOUT.

·

Nineteen forty-five represented a peak for Noël—certainly as far as the cinema was concerned. It was the year of *Brief Encounter*, a film that has remained in just about every critic's top-ten list.

It started life as "Still Life," one of the one-act plays in the *Tonight at 8:30* sequence.

The scene is the station buffet at Milford Junction. Laura Jesson (Gertrude Lawrence), a suburban housewife with children, comes into Milford every week on a shopping trip, which is almost certainly the highlight of her very predictable week. One day she accidentally meets the equally respectable Alec Harvey (Noël), a married doctor who practices in Milford one day a week. Laura gets a piece of grit in her eye from a passing express train, Alec removes it and they strike up a conversation. They meet again the following week . . . and then the next . . . and the next. Neither is prepared to acknowledge what is obvious—that they are falling in love.

In adapting "Still Life" for the screen, Noël profited again from the lesson of *Citizen Kane.*

Whereas the stage and theatre audiences of the day traditionally expected narrative continuity, film could play with time and—with a little necessary guidance—expect its audience to follow.

In addition, you expected to look at what was going on on that stage objectively—a spectator acting as the fourth wall of the set. With film you could take a point of view and be inside the head of one of the characters.

This is what Noël chose to do with his screenplay. Instead of *observing* Laura Jesson, the film audience could see events from Laura's perspective. *Brief Encounter* was to be *her* story. As a device it would prove infinitely more emotionally involving.

BRIEF ENCOUNTER (1945)

CAST

LAURA JESSON	CELIA JOHNSON
ALEC HARVEY	TREVOR HOWARD
MYRTLE BAGOT	JOYCE CAREY
ALBERT GODBY	STANLEY HOLLOWAY
BERYL	MARGARET BARTON
DOLLY MESSITER	EVERLEY GREGG
FRED JESSON	CYRIL RAYMOND

DIRECTED BY DAVID LEAN
PRODUCED BY CINEGUILD
FIRST SHOWN NOVEMBER 26, 1945

•

The film begins with the story's ending. Social *mores* have dogged their relationship from the outset. Now, about to say good-bye in the railway buffet where they first met, suburbia intrudes yet again in the shape of a casual acquaintance of Laura's, Dolly Messiter . . .

Then, as she sits on the train with the garrulous Dolly, we hear her thought voice . . .

LAURA'S VOICE: This can't last—the misery can't last—I must remember that and try to control myself. Nothing lasts really—neither happiness or despair—not even life lasts very long—there will come a time in the

Scene from "Still Life," the original one-act play in *Tonight
at 8:30* (1936) that became *Brief Encounter*. At the station
tearoom, where they first met, Alec (Noël) and Laura
(Gertrude Lawrence) are seeing each other for the last time,
when they are interrupted by Laura's garrulous neighbor,
Dolly Messiter (Everley Gregg).

future when I shan't mind about this anymore—when I can look back
and say quite peacefully and cheerfully "How silly I was"—No, no—
I don't want that time to come ever—I want to remember every
minute—always—always—to the end of my days.

And even when she reaches the safety of home and family and looks at
her safe, predictable husband, we continue to hear what she is thinking . . .

LAURA'S VOICE: Fred—Fred—dear Fred. There's so much that I want to
say to you. You are the only one in the world with enough wisdom and
gentleness to understand—if only it were somebody else's story and not
mine. As it is you are the only one in the world that I can never tell—
never—never—because even if I waited until we were old, old people,
and told you then, you would be bound to look back over the
years . . . and be hurt and oh, my dear, I don't want you to be hurt. You
see, we are a happily married couple, and must never forget that. This is
my home . . .

A shot of FRED over LAURA's shoulder. He is engrossed in his crossword puzzle.

LAURA'S VOICE: . . . you are my husband—and my children are upstairs
in bed. I am a happily married woman—or rather, I was, until a few

weeks ago. This is my whole world and it is enough—or rather, it was, until a few weeks ago.

CLOSE SHOT of LAURA.

LAURA'S VOICE: . . . But, oh, Fred, I've been so foolish. I've fallen in love! I'm an ordinary woman—I didn't think such violent things could happen to ordinary people.

Again a shot of FRED over LAURA's shoulder.

LAURA'S VOICE: It all started on an ordinary day, in the most ordinary place in the world . . . the refreshment room at Milford Junction. I was having a cup of tea and reading a book that I'd got that morning from Boots—my train wasn't due for ten minutes . . . I looked up and saw a man come in from the platform. He had on an ordinary mac with a belt. His hat was turned down and I didn't even see his face. He got his tea at the counter and turned—then I did see his face. It was rather a nice face. He passed my table on the way to his . . .

Then, the series of accidental meetings. The following week they run into each other in the street . . . the next week he happens to come into the tea shop where Laura is having lunch, and since the place is crowded, he has to share her table . . . Laura always goes to see a film after lunch as part of her regular routine ("What exciting lives we lead, don't we?"). On this occasion Alec asks if he may join her.

And so it goes. All perfectly innocent—or so they believe.

For the first time they talk about themselves. Or, at least, Alec does . . .

CLOSE SHOT of LAURA and ALEC.

Laura (Celia Johnson) literally reflects on how her humdrum
suburban life might have been.

LAURA: Is tea bad for one? Worse than coffee, I mean?

ALEC: If this is a professional interview my fee is a guinea.

LAURA: Why did you become a doctor?

ALEC: That's a long story. Perhaps because I'm a bit of an idealist.

LAURA: I suppose all doctors ought to have ideals, really—otherwise
I should think their work would be unbearable.

ALEC: Surely you're not encouraging me to talk shop?

LAURA: Why shouldn't you talk shop? It's what interests you most,
isn't it?

ALEC: Yes—it is. I'm terribly ambitious really—not ambitious for myself
so much as for my special pigeon.

LAURA: What is your special pigeon?

ALEC: Preventative medicine.

LAURA: Oh, I see.

ALEC (*laughing*): I'm afraid you don't.

LAURA: I was trying to be intelligent.

ALEC: Most good doctors, especially when they're young, have private
dreams—that's the best part of them; sometimes, though, those get
over-professionalized and strangulated and—am I boring you?

LAURA: No—I don't quite understand—but you're not boring me.

ALEC: What I mean is this—all good doctors must be primarily enthusiastic. They must have, like writers and painters and priests, a sense of
vocation—a deep-rooted, unsentimental desire to do good.

LAURA: Yes—I see that.

ALEC: Well, obviously one way of preventing disease is worth fifty ways of curing it—that's where my ideal comes in—preventative medicine isn't anything to do with medicine at all, really—it's concerned with conditions, living conditions and common sense and hygiene. For instance, my speciality is pneumoconiosis.

LAURA: Oh, dear!

ALEC: Don't be alarmed, it's simpler than it sounds—it's nothing but a slow process of fibrosis of the lung due to the inhalation of particles of dust. In the hospital here there are splendid opportunities for observing cures and making notes, because of the coal mines.

LAURA: You suddenly look much younger.

ALEC (*brought up short*): Do I?

LAURA: Almost like a little boy.

ALEC: What made you say that?

LAURA (*staring at him*): I don't know—yes, I do.

ALEC (*gently*): Tell me.

LAURA (*with panic in her voice*): Oh, no—I couldn't really. You were saying about the coal mines.

ALEC (*looking into her eyes*): Yes—the inhalation of coal dust—that's one specific form of the disease—it's called anthracosis.

LAURA (*hypnotized*): What are the others?

ALEC: Chalicosis—that comes from metal dust—steelworks, you know . . .

LAURA: Yes, of course. Steelworks.

ALEC: And silicosis—stone dust—that's gold mines.

LAURA (*almost in a whisper*): I see.

There is the sound of a bell.

LAURA: That's your train.

ALEC (*looking down*): Yes.

LAURA: You mustn't miss it.

ALEC: No.

LAURA (*again with panic in her voice*): What's the matter?

ALEC (*with an effort*): Nothing—nothing at all.

LAURA (*socially*): It's been so very nice—I've enjoyed my afternoon enormously.

ALEC: I'm so glad—so have I. I apologize for boring you with those long medical words.

LAURA: I feel dull and stupid, not to be able to understand more.

ALEC: Shall I see you again?

There is the sound of a train approaching.

LAURA: It's the other platform, isn't it? You'll have to run. Don't worry about me—mine's due in a few minutes.

ALEC: Shall I see you again?

LAURA: Of course—perhaps you could come over to Ketchworth one Sunday. It's rather far, I know, but we should be delighted to see you.

ALEC (*intensely*): Please—please . . .

The train is heard drawing to a standstill . . .

LAURA: What is it?

ALEC: Next Thursday—the same time.

LAURA: No—I can't possibly—I . . .

ALEC: Please—I ask you most humbly . . .

LAURA: You'll miss your train!

ALEC: All right.

He gets up.

LAURA: Run . . .

ALEC (*taking her hand*): Good-bye.

LAURA (*breathlessly*): I'll be there.

ALEC: Thank you, my dear.

He leaves LAURA, and the camera tracks into a big CLOSE SHOT to hold her, smiling with joy.

LAURA collects her shopping basket and goes toward the door to Number 3 platform.

She comes out of the refreshment room onto the platform.

She looks up past camera at ALEC's train, which can be heard pulling out of the station.

A shot of ALEC, from LAURA's viewpoint. He is leaning out a carriage window, and waves to her as the train starts to pull out of the station.

CLOSE-UP of LAURA. She waves back, and her eyes follow the departing train.

LAURA'S VOICE: I stood there and watched his train draw out of the station. I stared after it until its little red taillight had vanished into the darkness. I imagined him arriving at Churley and giving up his ticket and walking through the streets, and letting himself into his house with his latchkey. Madeleine, his wife, would probably be in the hall to meet him—or perhaps upstairs in her room—not feeling very well—small, dark and rather delicate—I wondered if he'd say "I met such a nice woman in the Kardomah—we had lunch and went to the pic-

Alec (Trevor Howard) and Laura (Celia Johnson) make their way back to the railway station at Milford Junction around which their emotional life revolves.

tures"—then suddenly I knew that he wouldn't—I knew beyond a shadow of doubt that he wouldn't say a word, and at that moment the first awful feeling of danger swept over me.

Their affair is never to be consummated, and Alec makes the decision to take a job in Africa. They return to the refreshment room for the last time, and now the film replays the opening scene—except that it now carries a very different meaning.

ALEC (*quietly*): You know what's happened, don't you?
LAURA: Yes—yes, I do.
ALEC: I've fallen in love with you.
LAURA: Yes—I know.
ALEC: Tell me honestly—my dear—please tell me honestly if what I believe is true . . .
LAURA (*in a whisper*): What do you believe?
ALEC: That it's the same with you—that you've fallen in love too.
LAURA (*near tears*): It sounds so silly.
ALEC: Why?
LAURA: I know you so little.

ALEC: It is true, though—isn't it?

LAURA (*with a sigh*): Yes—it's true.

ALEC (*making a slight movement toward her*): Laura . . .

LAURA: No please . . . we must be sensible—please help me to be sensible—we mustn't behave like this—we must forget that we've said what we've said.

ALEC: Not yet—not quite yet.

LAURA (*panic in her voice*): But we must—don't you see!

ALEC (*leaning forward and taking her hand*): Listen—it's too late now to be as sensible as all that—it's too late to forget what we've said—and anyway, whether we'd said it or not couldn't have mattered—we know—we've both of us known for a long time.

LAURA: How can you say that—I've only known you for four weeks—we only talked for the first time last Thursday week.

ALEC: Last Thursday week. Hadn't it been a long time since then—for you? Answer me truly.

LAURA: Yes.

ALEC: How often did you decide that you were never going to see me again?

LAURA: Several times a day.

ALEC: So did I.

LAURA: Oh, Alec.

ALEC: I love you—I love your wide eyes and the way you smile and your shyness, and the way you laugh at my jokes.

LAURA: Please don't . . .

ALEC: I love you—I love you—you love me too—it's no use pretending that it hasn't happened because it has.

LAURA (*with tremendous effort*): Yes it has. I don't want to pretend anything either to you or to anyone else . . . but from now on I shall have to. That's what's wrong—don't you see? That's what spoils everything. That's why we must stop here and now talking like this. We are neither of us free to love each other, there is too much in the way. There's still time, if we control ourselves and behave like sensible human beings, there's still time to—to . . .

She puts her head down and bursts into tears.

ALEC: There's no time at all.

We are now back to their final moments together. Again, the station refreshment room.

ALEC: Are you all right, darling?

LAURA: Yes, I'm all right.

ALEC: I wish I could think of something to say.

LAURA: It doesn't matter—not saying anything, I mean.

ALEC: I'll miss my train and wait to see you into yours.

LAURA: No—no—please don't. I'll come over to your platform with you—I'd rather.

ALEC: Very well.

LAURA: Do you think we shall ever see each other again?

ALEC: I don't know. (*His voice breaks.*) Not for years anyway.

LAURA: The children will all be grown up—I wonder if they'll ever meet and know each other.

ALEC: Couldn't I write to you—just once in a while?

LAURA: No—please not—we promised we wouldn't.

ALEC: Laura, dear, I do love you so very much. I love you with all my heart and soul.

LAURA (*without emotion*): I want to die—if only I could die.

ALEC: If you died you'd forget me—I want to be remembered.

LAURA: Yes, I know—I do too.

ALEC (*glancing at the clock*): We've still got a few minutes.

DOLLY (*off*): Laura! What a lovely surprise!

LAURA (*dazed*): Oh, Dolly!

DOLLY joins LAURA and ALEC.

DOLLY: My dear, I've been shopping till I'm dropping. My feet are nearly falling off, and my throat's parched, I thought of having tea in Spindle's, but I was terrified of losing the train.

LAURA'S VOICE: It was cruel of Fate to be against us right up to the last minute. Dolly Messiter—poor, well-meaning, irritating Dolly Messiter . . .

The camera is slowly tracking in to a CLOSE-UP of LAURA.

DOLLY: I'm always missing trains and being late for meals, and Bob gets disagreeable for days at a time. (*Her voice is fading away.*) He's been getting those dreadful headaches, you know. I've tried to make him see a doctor but he won't.

(Her voice fades out.)

LAURA'S VOICE: . . . crashing into those last few precious minutes we had together. She chattered and fussed, but I didn't hear what she said. I was dazed and bewildered. Alec behaved so beautifully—with such perfect politeness. Nobody could have guessed what he was really feeling—then the bell went for his train.

The platform bell rings.

LAURA: There's your train.
ALEC: Yes, I know.
DOLLY: Aren't you coming with us?
ALEC: No, I go in the opposite direction. My practice is in Churley.
DOLLY: Oh, I see.
ALEC: I am a general practitioner at the moment.
LAURA (*dully*): Dr. Harvey is going out to Africa next week.
DOLLY: Oh, how thrilling.

There is the sound of ALEC's train approaching.

ALEC: I must go.
LAURA: Yes, you must.
ALEC: Good-bye.
DOLLY: Good-bye.

He shakes hands with DOLLY, and looks swiftly once only at LAURA.
CLOSE-UP of LAURA. ALEC's hand comes into the shot and gives her shoulder a little squeeze.

LAURA'S VOICE: I felt the touch of his hand for a moment and then he walked away . . .

ALEC is seen from LAURA's viewpoint. He crosses the refreshment room and goes out of the door onto the platform.

LAURA'S VOICE: . . . away—out of my life for ever.

·

On May 4, 1945, Germany surrendered, and the world that emerged from the shadows of war was dramatically different in so many ways for so many people.

Noël wrote prophetically . . .

"THIS IS A CHANGING WORLD"

The world was young
So many many years,
The passage of time must show

Some traces of change,
Love songs once sung,
Much laughter, many tears,
Have echoed down the years,
The past is old and strange.
Each waning moon,
All dawns that rise, all suns that set,
Change like the tides that flow across the sands,
Each little tune
That fills our hearts with vague regret,
Each little love duet
Fades in our hands,
Don't stray among the moments that have fled,
New days are just ahead,
New words are still unsaid.

This is a changing world, my dear,
New songs are sung—new stars appear,
Though we grow older year by year
Our hearts can still be gay,
Young love at best is a passing phase,
Charming and foolish and blind,
There may be happier, wiser days
When youth is far behind.
Where are the snows of yesteryear?
When Winter's done and Spring is here
No regrets are worth a tear,
We're living in a changing world, my dear.

This is a changing world, my dear,
New dreams are dreamed,
New dawns appear,
Passion's feckless cavalier
Who loves and rides away,
Time will persuade you to laugh at grief,
Time is your tenderest friend,
Life may be lonely and joy be brief
But everything must end.
Love is a charming souvenir,
When day is done and night draws near
No regrets are worth a tear
We're living in a changing world, my dear.

—PACIFIC 1860 (1946)

As Noël reflected, "There was still the future to be fought."

I wish I had more feeling about it. My mind seems unable to take it in. It has all been too long and too stupid and cruel. We shall see how the sweet face of peace looks. I cannot help visualizing an insane, vacuous grin.

—DIARIES (AUGUST 10, 1945)

The very deep feelings I had during the war and have since, almost deliberately, been in danger of losing. If I forget these feelings or allow them to be obscured, because they are uncomfortable, I shall be lost . . . I must hang on to those moments or I shall not have survived the war.

—DIARIES (JANUARY 20, 1946)

•

The immediate postwar years did not treat Noël kindly. Austerity Britain with its new Labour Government could see no possible merit in an effete playwright who only seemed to write about duchesses and people who did nothing for a living. His time was clearly past. For the next decade—with rare exception—everything he did was dismissed by the critics.

There was his postwar—and last—revue, *Sigh No More* (1945) that received a lukewarm reception. Even Noël admitted that he said "goodbye to it without a pang."

Then there was Mary Martin in *Pacific 1860,* his musical that opened the bomb-damaged Theatre Royal, Drury Lane. It was prewar operetta and it failed to strike a responsive chord with audiences who were in the mood for more upbeat American-style entertainment. (Symbolically, the show that took its place and ran forever was *Oklahoma!*)

Heard today, the score is charming and underrated in the Coward canon and we did get the chance to meet two of the most endearing characters in his gallery of grotesques . . .

"UNCLE HARRY"

> We all of us have relations,
> Our crosses in life we bear,
> A gloomy group of uncles, cousins and aunts,
> We meet them in railway stations,
> In Harrods or Chester Square,

And always on the Channel boat to France.
We have to be polite to them,
They sometimes send us pheasants,
We always have to write to them
To thank for Christmas presents.
These family obligations
Admittedly are a bore
But I possess one uncle that I positively adore.

Poor Uncle Harry
Wanted to be a missionary
So he took a ship and sailed away.
This visionary,
Hotly pursued by dear Aunt Mary,
Found a South Sea Isle on which to stay.
The natives greeted them kindly and invited them to
    dine
On yams and clams and human hams and vintage
    coconut wine,
The taste of which was filthy but the after-effects
    divine.
Poor Uncle Harry
Got a bit gay and longed to tarry.
This, Aunt Mary couldn't quite allow,
She lectured him severely on a number of church affairs
But when she'd gone to bed he made a getaway down
                                        the stairs,
For he longed to find the answer to a few of the
                                        maidens' prayers.
Uncle Harry's not a missionary now.

Poor Uncle Harry
After a chat with dear Aunt Mary
Thought the time had come to make a row,
He lined up all the older girls in one of the local
    sheds
And while he was reviling them and tearing himself
                                        to shreds
They took their Mother Hubbards off and tied them
    round their heads.
Uncle Harry's not a missionary now.
He's awfully happy
But he's certainly not a missionary now!

Now Uncle Harry was just a "seeker,"
A "dreamer" sincerely blest,
Of this there couldn't be a shadow of doubt.
The fact that his flesh was weaker
Than even Aunt Mary guessed
Took even her some time to figure out.
In all those languid latitudes
The atmosphere's exotic,
To take up moral attitudes
Would be too idiotic,
Though nobody could be meeker
Than Uncle had been before
I bet today he's giving way
At practically every pore!

Poor Uncle Harry
Having become a missionary
Found the natives' morals rather crude.
He and Aunt Mary
Quickly imposed an arbitrary
Ban upon them shopping in the nude.
They all considered this silly and they didn't take
                                                it well,
They burnt his boots and several suits and wrecked
                                the Mission Hotel,
They also burnt his mackintosh, which made a
                                disgusting smell.
Poor Uncle Harry
After some words with dear Aunt Mary
Called upon the chiefs for a pow-wow.
They didn't brandish knives at him, they really
                                were awfully sweet,
They made concerted dives at him and offered him
                                things to eat,
But when they threw their wives at him he had to
                                admit defeat.
Uncle Harry's not a missionary now.

Poor dear Aunt Mary
Though it were revolutionary
Thought *her* time had come to take a bow.
Poor Uncle Harry looked at her, in whom he had placed
                                his trust,

His very last illusion broke and crumbled away to dust
For she'd placed a flower behind her ear and frankly
        exposed her bust.
Uncle Harry's not a missionary now.
He's left the island
But he's certainly not a missionary now.

•

"ALICE IS AT IT AGAIN"

In a dear little village remote and obscure
A beautiful maiden resided,
As to whether or not her intentions were pure
Opinion was sharply divided.
She loved to lie out 'neath the darkening sky
And allow the soft breeze to entrance her
She whispered her dreams to the birds flying by
But seldom received any answer.

Over the field and along the lane
Gentle Alice would love to stray,
When it came to the end of the day,
She would wander away unheeding,
Dreaming her innocent dreams she strolled
Quite unaffected by heat or cold,
Frequently freckled or soaked with rain,
Alice was out in the lane.
Whom she met there
Every day there
Was a question answered by none,
But she'd get there
And she'd stay there
Till whatever she did was undoubtedly done.
Over the field and along the lane
When her parents had called in vain,
Sadly, sorrowfully, they'd complain,
"Alice is at it again."

Though that dear little village
Surrounded by trees
Had neither a school nor a college
Gentle Alice acquired from the birds and the bees
Some exceedingly practical knowledge.

The curious secrets that nature revealed
She refused to allow to upset her
But she thought when observing the beasts of the field
That things might have been organized better.

Over the field and along the lane
Gentle Alice one summer's day
Met a man who was driving a dray
And he whisked her away to London.
Then, after many a year had passed,
Alice returned to her home at last
Wearing some pearls and a velvet train,
Bearing a case of champagne.
They received her
Fairly coldly
But when the wine had lifted the blight
They believed her
When she boldly
Said the Salvation Army had shown her the light.
When she had left by the evening train
Both her parents in grief and pain
Murmured brokenly, "More champagne—
Alice is at it again!"

Over the field and along the lane
Gentle Alice would make up
And take up—her stand.
The road was not exactly arterial
But it led to a town near by
Where quite a lot of masculine material
Caught her roving eye.
She was ready to hitchhike
Cadillac or motorbike,
She wasn't proud or choosy,
All she
Was aiming to be
Was a prinked up,
Minked up
Fly-by-night floozy.
When old Rajahs
Gave her pearls as large as
Nuts on a chestnut tree
All she said was, "Fiddle-de-dee,

The wages of sin will be the death of me!"
Over the field and along the lane
Gentle Alice's parents would wait hand in hand,
Her dear old white-headed mother wistfully
                      sipping champagne
Said, "We've spoiled our child—spared the rod,
Open up the caviar and say Thank God,
We've got no cause to complain,
Alice is at it,
Alice is at it,
Alice is at it again."

The prim Miss Martin soon refused to sing "Alice." "It wasn't right," she said, "for a girl from Texas to make her London debut with this scandalous song . . . Now I know that I should have sung it. It would have stopped the show every night." She recalled that "Noël was sweet and said he would write me another."

Noël's own recollection was slightly different. He reminded her that it was all very well to be lyrically virginal but hadn't she made her reputation with Cole Porter's "My Heart Belongs to Daddy"? And what did she think *that* was about—filial affection?

The show was not a happy experience and he was glad to put "Dreary Lane" behind him.

·

Over the years Noël's patriotism was largely expressed through his songs or his verse. With the exception of elements in *Cavalcade* and *This Happy Breed* he did not make his feelings overt in the plays. With two exceptions . . .

In Singapore in 1930 he had been the guest star playing the part of Stanhope in a local production of *Journey's End*. In the ship on the way home, he recalled . . .

During that voyage I wrote an angry little vilification of war called *Post-Mortem*. My mind was strongly affected by *Journey's End,* and I had read several current war novels one after the other. I wrote *Post-Mortem* with the utmost sincerity; this, I think, must be fairly obvious to anyone who reads it. In fact, I tore my emotions to shreds over it. The result was similar to my performance as Stanhope: confused, underrehearsed, and hysterical. Unlike my performance as Stanhope, however, it had some very fine moments. There is, I believe, some of the best writing I have ever done in it, also some of the worst. I have no deep regrets over it, as I know my intentions to have been of the purest. I passionately believed in the truth of what I was writing; too passionately. The truths I snarled out in that hot, uncomfortable little cabin were all too true and mostly too shallow. Through lack of detachment and lack of real experience of my subject, I muddled the issues of the play. I might have done better had I given more time to it and less vehemence. However, it helped to purge my system of certain accumulated acids.

Typical of the "vehemence" was the ghost hero's big speech about those who gave their lives, addressed to those who stayed at home and would now like to forget there ever was a war . . .

They're free from your hates and loves and small, pitiful prayers, for eternity . . . They've escaped—escaped. You'll never find them again, either in your pantomime hell or your tinsel heaven. Long live war! Long live death and destruction, and despair. Through all that \there may be a hope, a million-to-one chance for us somewhere, a promise of something cleaner and sweeter than anything your bloody gods have ever offered. Long live war.

The play was unproduced for several decades, and he showed it to few people. One of them was a new friend, T. E. Lawrence, who wrote . . .
"I have read your play twice. It's a fine effort, a really fine effort.
"You know better than anyone what sort of play it is; I fancied it hadn't the roots of a great success. You had something far more important to say than usual, and I fancy that in saying it you let the box office and the stalls go hang. As argument it is first rate. As imagination magnificent: and it does you great honour as a human being."
After World War II ended, Noël's sentiments were precisely the same but his expression less hysterical.
In 1946 he started to write a play to be called *Might Have Been,* taking the idea from a 1913 story by one of his literary idols, "Saki" (H. H. Munro), which supposes that the Germans have actually won the war and Britain has become an occupied nation.
Saki's story—"When William Came"—was clearly a warning, about a war that was yet to be. Noël's, written from a disrupted peace, was more of a "What if?" In an ironic reference to his old antihero, Neville Chamberlain, he later changed the title to *Peace in Our Time.*
The setting is a typical English pub, The Shy Gazelle, run by Fred Shattock and his wife, Nora. We are initially lulled into a sense of false security by the usual pub banter with some of the regulars until they hear an announcement on the radio . . .

The Military Parade will move off from Hyde Park Corner at 9:30 a.m. precisely . . . After passing the reviewing stand at Buckingham Palace, the Parade will be followed at 9:43 precisely by a procession of State carriages escorted by a guard of honour. In the first open landau will be seated the Führer. The carriages following will contain Air Chief Marshal Goering, Dr. Goebbels and high-ranking Army, Navy and Air Force officers. *The lights fade.*

PEACE IN OUR TIME

CAST

FRED SHATTOCK	BERNARD LEE
ALMA BOUGHTON	HELEN HORSEY
ALBRECHT RICHTER	RALPH MICHAEL
NORA SHATTOCK	BEATRICE VARLEY
GEORGE BOURNE	KENNETH MORE
CHORLEY BANNISTER	OLAF POOLEY

DIRECTED BY ALAN WEBB

UNDER THE SUPERVISION OF THE AUTHOR

PRODUCED AT THE LYRIC THEATRE, LONDON, JULY 22, 1947

The difference in *Peace in Our Time* is that Noël brings a greater degree of disillusion. When he began to write it, he had just returned from his first postwar visit to Paris—a very different Paris from the one he had left so precipitately in 1940.

There was an air of shame and evasion. Which of one's friends might have collaborated with the occupying Germans? It didn't do to ask too many questions. It left Noël wondering whether—despite the eternal optimism Frank Gibbons had expressed in *This Happy Breed*—his fellow Britons would have all held firm in similar circumstances.

In The Shy Gazelle, Fred and Alma debate the issue . . .

FRED: I'm just trying to see things clearly, to get my mind straight. I hate the bastards, same as everybody else does, there isn't any argument about that.

ALMA: On the contrary there is a great deal of argument already about just that.

FRED: Not here there isn't.

ALMA: Are you sure?

FRED: I can't be answerable for my customers' opinions, can I?

ALMA (*turning away*): Oh, Fred.

FRED: Well, can I, now?—be fair—

ALMA: It isn't a question of being fair—it's a question of holding on to what one believes in—what one has always believed in.

FRED: I've always believed in one thing, Mrs. Boughton, and that was that the people of this country were the finest people in the world.

ALMA: Don't you still believe that?

FRED: Of course I do—in a way, but you see—

ALMA: I don't see.

FRED: Now listen, Mrs. Boughton.

ALMA: I'm listening.

FRED (*with a tremendous effort*): As I see it, it's like this. We were the finest people in the world—see . . . but we were getting too pleased with ourselves. We all swore in 1918 that we'd never have another war. Then gradually, bit by bit, we allowed our politicians and our newspapers and our own selfishness to chivvy us into this one. Even as late as 1938 we were dancing in the streets because a silly old man promised us "Peace in our time." We knew bloody well there wasn't a dog's chance of "peace in our time." Then suddenly in 1939 we woke up and found ourselves in the soup, no guns, not enough aeroplanes, half the Navy we should have had. Then what happens? In spite of blood and toil and sweat and fighting on the beaches and in the streets, we get licked. See! We lost the Battle of Britain—not because our flying boys didn't do their best but because of our—stupidity, they hadn't got a chance. They got shot down—my son and hundreds of other people's sons. Now we've been conquered. Do you see now why I don't any longer quite believe all the things I was brought up to believe? Do you, Mrs. Boughton?

ALMA: That was very bitter and impressive, Fred. But it didn't impress me.

FRED: I don't want to impress anybody.

ALMA: Do you think it would have been better for us if we had won the Battle of Britain?

FRED: Of course I do.

ALMA: I don't.

FRED: Mrs. Boughton!

ALMA: It might have been better for America and the rest of the world, but it wouldn't have been better for us.

FRED: Why not?

ALMA: Because we should have got lazy again, and blown out with our own glory. We should have been bombed and blitzed and we should have stood up under it—an example to the whole civilized world—and that would have finished us. As it is—in defeat—we still have a chance. There'll be no time in this country for many a long day for class wars

and industrial crises and political squabbles. We can be united now—
we shall have to be—until we've driven them away, until we're clean
again. I think I'd like another brandy.

FRED (*pouring them*): You know the trouble with you women is, you're too
emotional.

ALMA: Are you so sure that intellectual thinking is so vastly superior to
emotional thinking?

FRED (*handing her her brandy*): I'm dead sure it is.

ALMA: I often wonder. I should think on the whole that emotion has contributed more over the centuries to the world's happiness than intellect.

FRED: To the world's trouble too.

Later there is a discussion among Fred, Norma and two of Fred's regulars with Albrecht Richter, the German who acts as their "minder" and
who now faces them with what he considers the new reality of their
situation . . .

FRED: Do you think that our Dominions overseas and our friends in America are going to allow you to occupy this country indefinitely?

ALBRECHT: They will have no choice in the matter. If only you British had
trained your minds to be less insular and more realistic you would
understand that your friends in America are a small minority. Three-
quarters of the United States are not in the least concerned today as to
whether Great Britain survives or not. Before you were conquered you
were still a potent force in the world. Now you are not. America is fully
occupied with a war against us in the Atlantic and the Japanese in the
Pacific. Both these she will eventually lose—

FRED: Is that inevitable too?

ALBRECHT: Quite. (*Preserving his suavity.*) You mentioned—a trifle opti-
mistically—your Dominions overseas. Taking them in order of their
possible importance to you. Canada is the nearest; but Canada is too
closely allied to the United States both geographically and ideologically
to move independently. Australia is thirteen thousand miles away. New
Zealand is equally far and equally negligible. South Africa will support
your cause only for as long as General Smuts holds the reins. His succes-
sor will support ours. That we have already arranged. There remain a
few scattered Colonies. Malaya and Borneo which will be under Japanese domination within a few weeks. India which, as usual, is in a state
of racial and economic chaos—I am not painting this gloomy picture
maliciously, Mr. Shattock—I am merely trying to convince you of the
actual facts of the case.

FRED: Like so many foreigners, Mr. Richter, you speak English much better than you understand it.

ALBRECHT: I see that I have failed.

FRED: Even supposing all you say is true—even if we are in the soup up to our necks—what do you expect me to do about it? What's all this in aid of?

ALBRECHT: I know that you are too stubborn to believe me, Mr. Shattock, but I assure you that my intentions are friendly.

FRED: All right—so what?

ALBRECHT: I asked you just how long, in your opinion, would it take ordinary, decently educated, hardworking people like yourself to become reconciled to the situation.

FRED: Never, Mr. Richter. Nor our children after us, nor their children's children.

ALBRECHT: Admirable. That is exactly what I hoped you would say. That is just the quality in the British that we Germans have always saluted, that infinite capacity for holding true to an idea. We, too, believe utterly and completely, individually and collectively in our idea. We believe that it is our destiny to rule the world and by doing so make it a better place. We have always believed that and that is why—at last it is coming true. We are also, Mr. Shattock, a great deal more intelligent than your countrymen gave us credit for. You, for instance, I am sure were convinced that when we invaded you and conquered you, we should immediately embark on a considered programme of organized murder, rape, pillage and destruction. Is not that so?

FRED: Yes.

ALBRECHT: Have we done so?

FRED: Not yet.

ALBRECHT: And why do you suppose we have been so restrained?

FRED: I should think you were waiting to see which way the wind blows.

ALBRECHT: Not at all. We know that already. Our policy in this country—contrary to all expectations—is essentially a friendly one. In that lies the genius of Hitler; the psychological intuition which enables him not only to dominate the human mind but to understand the human heart as well. Believe me the Führer is fully aware of the inherent greatness of this nation.

NORA: Very nice of him, I'm sure.

FRED: Nora!

ALBRECHT: The Führer believes that the spirit of this country is indestructible. He believes—in spite of what you said just now, Mr. Shattock—that ultimately, in so many years, Great Britain will become reconciled to the inevitable, not through any weakening of her spirit but through the strengthening of her innate wisdom and common sense. As soon as that innate wisdom and common sense reasserts itself, as soon as you are willing to renounce your imperialistic convictions and cut your losses sensibly and courageously, then we can stand firmly together—your country and mine who have so much in common—and combine to drive the evil forces of Jewry and Communism from the face of the earth.

GEORGE: That was a very excellent speech, Mr. Richter.

FRED: Do you believe it, Mr. Bourne?

GEORGE: The important point is, Fred, that Mr. Richter believes it.

CHORLEY: It's rather a shock, isn't it, Fred, to be made to realise that we in England haven't got the monopoly of ideals?

FRED: Do you think that what the gentleman said just now represented an ideal?

CHORLEY: It's an intelligent and consistent policy for the future of civilization.

FRED: There are lots of Jews in England, Mr. Richter, and lots of Communists too—what's going to happen to them?

ALBRECHT (*sharply*): The former will be liquidated or deported. The latter will change their views.

FRED: Liquidated?

ALBRECHT: A certain amount of ruthlessness is unavoidable when the end justifies the means.

FRED (*turning away*): I knew there was a catch in it. Last orders, please.

As the play proceeds, it becomes clear that an underground resistance movement is growing, as it did in the occupied European countries, and by the end the forces of liberation are literally at the door.

Peace in Our Time enjoyed only a modest run, and it seems clear in retrospect that in writing it, Noël had broken one of his own precepts that he'd

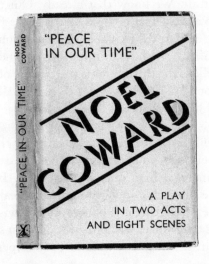

"PEACE IN OUR TIME"

NOËL COWARD

A PLAY IN TWO ACTS AND EIGHT SCENES

defined as far back as *The Vortex:* "The greatest thing in this world is not to be obvious—over *anything!*"

The British paying public, battered by over five years of war, had no appetite to consider an even worse alternative.

They'd won the war. Now it was time to concentrate on winning the peace.

"VICTORY?"

During the years of peace, in that other life that we have almost forgotten, luxurious British commercial liners—without fear of night attack, U-boats, bombs or torpedoes—used to ply to and fro across the seven seas. It was a convention in these ships, an unwritten law, that on the last evening before the end of the voyage there should be a disciplined celebration, the Captain's Dinner. On these occasions the stewards solemnly placed balloons, rattles, squeakers, crackers and little net bags of coloured paper balls on every table; the ship's orchestra played gay tunes with verve and a certain valedictory abandon, and the passengers, many of whom had not spoken to one another throughout the trip, surrendered obediently to the gala atmosphere, ordered more wine than usual, pulled the crackers, donned the paper caps, exploded the balloons with cigarette ends, whirled the rattles, blew the squeakers and vivaciously hurled handfuls of the coloured paper balls into the faces of complete strangers.

We are a law-abiding, docile people; orders are orders, and it was the Captain's Dinner. We are still, in spite of the ordeals we have endured, a law-abiding, docile people; orders are still orders and it is Victory Day. A day which, after years of tragedy, defeat, suffering, humiliation, fortitude and imperishable courage, has at last dawned for us. Having agreed to write an article commemorating this tremendous occasion I find myself faced with an insuperable obstacle and that obstacle is that I don't believe it.

Victory Day! The slogan seems too facile, its implications too final and too absolute. One day set apart in time, presumably to be revived year after year ad infinitum, one day bracketed annually for legitimate exultation: out with the flags, rattles, squeakers and paper caps—here we are again— let's have a party and remember and get drunk and try to forget. The voyage is over, or rather the first part of the voyage is over; perhaps we can afford to be noisy and a little silly; surely we have reason enough for celebration? Perhaps we may be forgiven if we cheer and shout and throw our paper caps in the air. The relief is immense. We can go to sleep in peace. There will be no more earsplitting sirens to drag us awake, no more impersonal violence and sudden fear, no more urgent demands made upon our courage and endurance and will to survival. We can, as Fred Astaire once sang, "Pick ourselves up, dust ourselves down and start all over again!"

At least it looks as if we can. The skies are clear: all our elderly gentlemen are full of promises and our soldiers, sailors and airmen, some of them, will be coming home again. Certainly on the face of it we have enough reason for celebration, or at any rate for tentative celebration but somehow the word Victory seems too overwhelming, too complete and surely a great deal too premature. We have conquered the Nazis in war; defeated their armies on land, their ships on the sea and their Luftwaffe in the air. Their ambition to dominate the world, to impose their "new order" of tyranny and subjugation upon free peoples has been shattered. The might and determination of the United Nations has forced them back into their battered and devastated Fatherland, where presumably, all they have left to do is to lick their wounds and howl for mercy. It is certainly victory over the Nazis and deserving of a few flags and bugles, but the triumph is not final. We have not yet conquered the Japanese, and it remains to be seen whether or not we have really conquered the Germans!

Above all, and before our victory can be set in history whole and complete, we shall have to do a little conquering of *ourselves*. This is indeed a great opportunity, probably the greatest our country has ever had. For five dreadful years the people of Britain have endured intense personal suffering and loss, and the violence of air bombardment on their undefended cities. They have also, and this has perhaps been more difficult, put up cheerfully with the countless minor discomforts of war: food, fuel and clothes rationing; fewer and fewer transport facilities; the soul-destroying, endless dreariness of the blackout; the months of anticlimax when apparently nothing was happening at all and the end of the war seemed so far away as to be almost inconceivable.

All this has been endured with stoicism and our deep-rooted, indestructible humour, and it has, of course, done us a power of good. Archaic class distinctions have been broken down; the poor are no longer the poor, the rich are no longer the rich and the middle classes (always the most rigid social autocrats) have sent their insular prejudices whistling down the wind and relaxed into an unself-conscious gregariousness from Cheltenham to Maida Vale and from Kensington to Peckham Rye; they have even, since the influx of American and Dominions troops, been known to speak to strangers in railway carriages. In addition to these marked improvements in our national character there appears to be on the part of most people a healthy desire to participate in the affairs of the country, a desire which was dismally lacking in the black years immediately preceding the war. We have assuredly learned a lot but our victory will not be proved and consolidated unless we have learned enough; and I hope, I so profoundly hope that we have.

Speaking personally, I know that during this war I have been more fortunate and privileged than most civilians. I have travelled many hundreds of thousands of miles and have had the opportunity of watching events from many different angles. I have returned to this country several times, stayed awhile and then gone away again and have therefore, I think, been able to see the various moral and psychological changes in clearer perspective than those who have remained at home all the time. Above all, I have been lucky enough to have been in close contact over and over again with the men who are fighting for us. Being neither a statesman, a politician, a government official, a military strategist nor even a journalist, my observation has been untrammeled by any particular urgency or prejudice. This perhaps is sufficient reason for me to tell you a little of what I learned about ourselves as a nation and a Commonwealth of Nations in relation, not only to our enemies but to our allies as well.

It is time, I feel, for at least one Britisher to discard temporarily our age-old tradition of understating our achievements, and I would like to warn any of my readers who still cherish intellectual illusions of world democracy and equality of nations and peace-in-our-time, that they are going to disapprove profoundly of what I am about to say.

First of all, I do not believe that genuine peace in our time is possible, probably, or in the long view, even desirable. If we grab too eagerly at peace in *our* time and compromise again with our ideals and betray again our warriors, there will be no hope of peace for our children or our children's children. The far future is more important than the immediate future; maybe not for us but certainly for those who follow after. The immediate future is more, much more important than the present and in this we can participate, for this we can work and try to see clearly and remain vigilant until the end of our days.

Let us, for God's sake, or rather for the future's sake, not be deceived by our Victory Day. The physical war is perhaps nearly over but the moral war is only just beginning. We as a race are capable, like all other races, of prevarication, muddled thinking, sentimentalism, untimely arrogance and most untimely self-deprecation but we are also capable, in adversity of greater qualities than any other race in the world. Must adversity always be our only spur? Can we not this time, with so many bitter lessons learned, be brave and strong and vigilant in comparative peace as well as in total war? Let us try with all our concentrated will to maintain the spirit that upheld us in 1940. Let us remember, disregarding political tact and commercial expedience, that it was our inherited, stubborn integrity that gave the future of the civilized world a chance and a glimmer of hope. It was our soldiers who fought on the land, our young airmen who cleared the skies and our sailors who kept the sea routes open. Then we had no allies. We had much sympathy from other parts of the globe and much sincere admiration but we had no allies and we stood alone in the path of the most powerful and menacing onslaught in the history of mankind. A menace not only to ourselves and our much decried British Empire, but a menace to all those who are now fighting side by side with us.

It may be considered by many "bad taste" to emphasize so insistently this immeasurable achievement but we live in an age of advertisement, publicity and specialized propaganda and now, amidst the rather deafening cacophony of trumpets, one or two gentle fanfares on British bugles should not strike too sharp a discord. This is Victory Day, but there were greater Victory Days in 1940 for us and for the world because then it was the beginning and now it is still a long way from the end.

CHAPTER FIVE
THE 1950s

It is dull to write incessantly about tramps and prostitutes as it is to write incessantly about dukes and duchesses and even suburban maters and paters, and it is bigoted and stupid to believe that tramps and prostitutes and underprivileged housewives frying onions and using ironing boards are automatically the salt of the earth and that nobody else is worth bothering about. It is true that a writer should try to hold the mirror up to nature, although there are aspects of nature that would be better unreflected.

—"A WARNING TO PIONEERS"
(*SUNDAY TIMES*, LONDON, 1961)

There may be bad times just around the corner . . . but I shall twitch my mantle blue and rise above them.

NOËL SAW LITTLE to encourage him at this time. As he wrote to his friend Joyce Carey, "We won the war but my concern is—how shall we win the *peace?*" What idiot could honestly say "Happy Days Are Here Again," when it was perfectly obvious that . . .

"THERE ARE BAD TIMES JUST AROUND THE CORNER"

They're nervous in Nigeria
And terribly cross in Crete,
In Bucharest
They are so depressed
They're frightened to cross the street,
They're sullen in Siberia
And timid in Turkestan,

They're sick with fright
In the Isle of Wight
And jittery in Japan,
The Irish groan and shout, lads,
Maybe because they're Celts,
They know they're up the spout, lads,
And so is everyone else.
Hurray! Hurray! Hurray!
Trouble is on the way.

There are bad times just around the corner,
There are dark clouds hurtling through the sky
And it's no use whining
About a silver lining
For we *know* from experience that they won't roll by,
With a scowl and a frown
We'll keep our spirits down
And prepare for depression and doom and dread,
We're going to *un*pack our troubles from our old kit bag
And wait until we drop down dead.

There are bad times just around the corner,
The horizon's gloomy as can be,
There are blackbirds over
The grayish cliffs of Dover
And the vultures are hovering round the Christmas tree.
We're an *un*happy breed
And ready to stampede
When we're asked to remember what Lincoln said,
We're going to *un*tense our muscles till they sag, sag, sag
And wait until we drop down dead.

They're morbid in Mongolia
And querulous in Quebec,
There's not a man
In Baluchistan
Who isn't a nervous wreck,
In Maine the melancholia
Is deeper than tongue can tell,
In Monaco
All the croupiers know
They haven't a hope in Hell.
In faraway Australia

Each wallaby's well aware
The world's a total failure
Without any time to spare.
Hurray! Hurray! Hurray!
Suffering and dismay.

There are bad times just around the corner,
We can all look forward to despair,
It's as clear as crystal
From Brooklyn Bridge to Bristol
That we *can't* save Democracy
And we don't much care.

At the sound of a shot
We'd just as soon as not
Take a hot-water bag and retire to bed
And while the press and the politicians nag, nag, nag
We'll wait until we drop down dead.

There are bad times just around the corner
And the outlook's absolutely vile,
You can take this from us
That when they Atom bomb us
We are *not* going to tighten our belts and smile,
                                        smile, smile,

We are in such a mess
It couldn't matter less
If a world revolution is just ahead,
We'd better all learn the lyrics of the old "Red Flag"
And wait until we drop down dead.
A likely story
Land of Hope and Glory,
Wait until we drop down dead.

•

Noël was always convinced—or, at least, *said* he was always convinced—
that things would always turn out well for him personally.

"Like Mother Goddam, I shall always survive . . . I shall always pop out
of another hole in the ground. I shall twitch my mantle blue, tomorrow to
fresh woods and pastures new."

In October 1951 he popped out of a hole neither he nor just about anyone else could have anticipated.

He was invited to appear in cabaret—a form of entertainment he had never tried before.

In fact, that is not exactly true. In 1916 he had appeared as part of a duo with a young lady called Eileen Dennis at the Elysée Restaurant (which later became the Café de Paris). He was not a marked success. Attempting a solo number, he forgot the words and had to make an undignified exit murmuring, "La-la-la" to the puzzlement of the patrons.

This time things were very different, but only at the very last minute.

In the afternoon rehearsal at the Café de Paris—everything perfect except my voice, which is failing fast . . . This is the cruelest luck. I feel fine, the microphone is perfect, all London fighting to get in to see me—and now this happens. I am heartbroken.

—DIARIES (OCTOBER 26, 1951)

Enter Noël's throat specialist, and on the following Monday . . . "Went to the Café feeling slightly tremulous. Really triumphant success—tore the place up." It was to be the start of a whole new career.

Noël "tears them up" at the Café de Paris.
Norman Hackforth at the piano.

Noël with "our legendary, lovely Marlene"

He played there for several seasons and was on hand when Marlene Dietrich, a friend since the 1930s, made her own cabaret *début* in June 1954.

He introduced her . . .

"TRIBUTE TO MARLENE DIETRICH"

We know God made trees
And the birds and the bees
And the seas for the fishes to swim in
We are also aware
That he has quite a flair
For creating exceptional women.
When Eve said to Adam
"Start calling me Madam"
The world became far more exciting
Which turns to confusion
The modern delusion
That sex is a question of lighting
For female allure
Whether pure or impure
Has seldom reported a failure
As I know and you know

From Venus and Juno
Right down to La Dame aux Camélias.
This glamour, it seems,
Is the substance of dreams
To the most imperceptive perceiver
The Serpent of Nile
Could achieve with a smile
Far quicker results than Geneva.
Though we all might enjoy
Seeing Helen of Troy
As a gay cabaret entertainer
I doubt that she could
Be one quarter as good
As our legendary, lovely Marlene.

Although Marlene would prove to be a lifelong friend—she was on his arm at his last public appearance in New York shortly before he died— Noël was under no illusion about her. The lady was an emotional hypochondriac. He held her hand (metaphorically) through a string of love affairs and it's difficult not to see aspects of her—among others—in . . .

"LOUISA"

Louisa was a movie queen.
Before she'd achieved the age of sweet sixteen,
Long before Cagney threw those girls about,
Little Louisa tossed her curls about.
Later when the talkies came
The whole world
Resounded with her fame,
Each time she married
Every daily paper carried
Headlines blazing her name.
Not only headlines
But photographs and interviews,
Everything she did was news
That held the world in thrall.

Some said she read lines
Better than Marlene could,
No other entertainer could

Compare with her at all.
But regardless of the fact
That she could sing and dance and act
And owned furniture that wasn't "Little Rockery,"
And regardless of her gems,
Which were hers, not MGM's,
Her life was one long mockery.

Louisa was terribly lonely,
Success brought her naught but despair.
She derived little fun from the Oscars she'd won
And none from her home in Bel Air.
She declared she was weary of living
On a bestial terrestrial plane.
When friends came to visit their hands she
                            would clutch
Crying, "Tell me, why is it I suffer so much?
If only, if only, if only
My life wasn't quite such a strain."
And soon after that she was terribly lonely,
All over again.

Louisa was terribly lonely,
Louisa was terribly sad.
It appears that the cheers that had rung in her ears
For years had been driving her mad.
She sobbed when men offered her sables
And moaned when they gave her champagne.
She remarked to her groom on their honeymoon night
As he tenderly kissed her and turned out the light,
"If only, if only, if only
I'd thrown myself out of the plane . . ."
The very next day she was terribly lonely,
All over again.

Louisa was terribly lonely
(The girl had no fun),
Louisa was tired of it all
(Not a call from anyone),
She gazed like a dazed belated Sphinx
At her hundred and eight mutated minks
And she wrung her hands and she beat her breast
Crying, "My, my, my, I'm so depressed."

Nobody knew the trouble she'd seen,
Nobody knew but you know who.

The tribulations of a movie queen.
So farewell to lovely Louisa
(Who just let her life tease her),
Let's leave her seeking in vain
(To find someone to explain)
Why destiny should single her out to be only lonely,
Over and over again!

Great big glamorous stars can be very tiresome . . . God preserve me in future from female stars. I don't suppose He will.

—DIARIES (1956)

It was in 1955 that the real breakthrough came. One evening the previous November at the Café de Paris he had a visitor . . . "A character called Joe Glaser flew in from New York to sign me up for Las Vegas. A typical shrewd, decent, sharp agent type. The discussion was satisfactory financially, everything being contingent on whether or not I like Las Vegas, so he is escorting me there for a couple of days so that I can case the joint and decide which room I prefer to appear in, if any. Joe Glaser watched my performance at the Café and was obviously bewildered as to why the audience liked it so much. We are getting together in New York."

The tax-free fee soon swept aside any reservations Noël might have had, and June 1955 found him the king of the "fabulous madhouse."

"I have never had such an ovation in my life . . . also I have never known such generosity. Judy Garland was in tears and told me that she and Frank Sinatra decided that I was better than anyone they had ever seen and could give them lessons, which couldn't have been more comforting or more sweet. If you note a slight egocentric strain in this letter you will have to forgive it because it was a rather dangerous challenge and has turned out to be successful beyond my wildest dreams."

The discipline of cabaret also inspired some of his best comedy songs.

In the great tradition of Mrs. Worthington he gave us another comic *femme noire*—the born-again bibulous Mrs. Wentworth-Brewster, she of the Bar on the Piccola Marina . . .

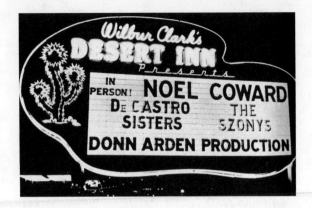

"A BAR ON THE PICCOLA MARINA"

I'll sing you a song,
It's not very long,
Its moral may disconcert you,
Of a mother and wife
Who most of her life
Was famed for domestic virtue.
She had two strapping daughters and a rather dull son
And a much duller husband, who at sixty-one
Elected to retire
And, later on, expire.
Sing Hallelujah, Hey nonny-no, Hey nonny-no, Hey
    nonny-no!

He joined the feathered choir.
Having laid him to rest
By special request
In the family mausoleum,
As his widow repaired
To the home they had shared,
Her heart sang a gay Te Deum.
And then in the middle of the funeral wake
While adding some liquor to the Tipsy Cake
She briskly cried, "That's done.
My life's at last begun.
Sing Hallelujah, Hey nonny-no, Hey nonny-no,
                      Hey nonny-no!
It's time I had some fun.
Today, though hardly a jolly day,

At least has set me free,
We'll all have a lovely holiday
On the island of Capri."

In a bar on the Piccola Marina
Life called to Mrs. Wentworth-Brewster,
Fate beckoned her and introduced her
Into a rather queer
Unfamiliar atmosphere.
She'd just sit there, propping up the bar
Beside a fisherman who sang to a guitar.
When accused of having gone too far
She merely cried, "*Funiculi!*
Just fancy me!
Funicula!"
When he bellowed *"Che Bella Signorina!"*
Sheer ecstasy at once produced a
Wild shriek from Mrs. Wentworth-Brewster,
Changing her whole demeanour.
When both her daughters and her son said,
"Please come home, Mama,"
She murmured rather bibulously, "Who d'you think
                you are?"
Nobody can afford to be so lahdy-bloody-da
In a bar on the Piccola Marina.

Every fisherman cried,
"Viva, Viva" and *"Che Ragazza."*
When she sat in the Grand Piazza
Everybody would rise,
Every fisherman sighed,
"Viva, Viva, che bell' Inglesi,"
Someone even said, "Whoops-a-daisy!"
Which was quite a surprise.
Each night she'd make some gay excuse
And beaming with goodwill
She'd just slip into something loose
And totter down the hill
To the bar on the Piccola Marina
Where love came to Mrs. Wentworth-Brewster,
Hot flashes of delight suffused her,
Right round the bend she went,

Picture her astonishment,
Day in, day out she would gad about
Because she felt she was no longer on the shelf,
Night out, night in, knocking back the gin
She'd cry, "Hurrah!
Funicula
Funiculi
Funic yourself!"
Just for fun three young sailors from Messina
Bowed low to Mrs. Wentworth-Brewster,
Said "*Scusi*" and politely goosed her.
Then there was quite a *scena.*
Her family, in floods of tears, cried,
"Leave these men, Mama."
She said, "They're just high-spirited, like
                                all Italians are
And most of them have a great deal more to offer
                                                than Papa
In a bar on the Piccola Marina."

•

SÉBASTIEN: I don't think anyone knows about painting anymore. Art,
like human nature, has got out of hand.

—NUDE WITH VIOLIN (1956)

In later life Noël became an enthusiastic painter. Another hardy amateur, Winston Churchill, weaned him from tepid watercolours into oils,
pointing out with shrewd logic that with oils you could always change
your mind and paint over your mistakes.

Noël described his own personal style as "touch and Gauguin." In fact,
he made himself into a creditable primitive painter, but he was never a
slavish admirer of modern art. After reading Wilenski's *Lives of the Impres-
sionists,* he wrote in his *Diaries . . .*

Really, no burlesque, however extravagant, could equal the phrases
he uses to describe the "abstract" boys . . . He talks a great deal of
"emotive force" and "lyrical color" and "constant functional forms,"
etc., and after he has described a picture in approximately these
terms you turn to a colored plate and look at a square lady with three
breasts and a guitar up her crotch.

In 1956 he turned his skepticism into a play . . .

NUDE WITH VIOLIN

CAST

SÉBASTIEN	JOHN GIELGUD
CLINTON PREMINGER JR.	JOHN STERLAND
JACOB FRIEDLAND	DAVID HORNE
ISOBEL SORODIN	JOYCE CAREY
COLIN (HER SON)	BASIL HENSON
JANE (HER DAUGHTER)	ANN CASTLE
LAUDERDALE	NICKY EDMETT

DIRECTED BY JOHN GIELGUD

PRESENTED AT THE GLOBE THEATRE, LONDON, NOVEMBER 7, 1956

Paul Sorodin, the world-famous painter, has just died, and his estranged family gather in Paris to attend his funeral and hear the details of his will. While they are still at the funeral, Sébastien—his longtime servant and a distinctly questionable Mediterranean Machiavelli—receives a visit at Sorodin's studio from a rather ingenuous American reporter.

At this moment CLINTON PREMINGER JR. comes tentatively into the room. He is an earnest-looking young American in his late twenties or early thirties.

CLINTON (*laboriously*): *Excusez-moi.*

SÉBASTIEN: Monsieur?

CLINTON: *Parlez-vous anglais?*

SÉBASTIEN: Yes, monsieur.

CLINTON: Thank God.

SÉBASTIEN: This is a house of mourning, monsieur.

CLINTON: I know. That's why I'm here—I mean I have to see Madame Sorodin, it's business—urgent business.

SÉBASTIEN: Madame Sorodin has not yet returned from the funeral and when she does I feel that she will be in no mood to discuss business, however urgent.

CLINTON: I guess you're Sébastien.

SÉBASTIEN: Your guess is correct, monsieur.

CLINTON: I have some notes on you.

SÉBASTIEN: Have you indeed?

CLINTON: I represent *Life* magazine.

SÉBASTIEN: It is in questionable taste to force *Life* magazine into a house of death, monsieur.

CLINTON: My name is Clinton Preminger Junior.

SÉBASTIEN: It would be all the same if you were Clinton Preminger Senior.

CLINTON: Now see here, I'm not an ordinary press reporter out for scoop headlines, I'm a serious writer.

SÉBASTIEN: I am delighted to hear it.

CLINTON: For over two years I've been assembling material for a comprehensive study of Sorodin and his paintings. It's to be called "Triton Among the Minnows."

SÉBASTIEN: Most appropriate.

CLINTON: I came by sea to give myself time to get all my notes in order and when I landed at Cherbourg I found that he had died. You can imagine the shock!

SÉBASTIEN: It was a shock to the whole world, monsieur.

MARIE-CELESTE (*entering from service door with a jar of pâté*): *Il est beau gars, qu'est-ce qu'il dit?*

SÉBASTIEN (*crossing to* MARIE-CELESTE *and taking the pâté*): *Rien d'importance . . . sauve-toi!*

MARIE-CELESTE: *Bon. Je me sauve.*

She goes out.

SÉBASTIEN: You say you have some notes on me? What sort of notes?

CLINTON: Merely factual. I have them here in my file—just a moment. (*Looks in file.*) S-S-Sébastien.

SÉBASTIEN: I sound like an Atlantic liner.

CLINTON: Sébastien Lacreeole. Is that right?

SÉBASTIEN: Not quite. There should be an accent on the first *e* in Lacréole.

CLINTON: My French isn't too good.

SÉBASTIEN: You must persevere.

CLINTON (*consulting his notes*): You entered the service of Paul Sorodin in July 1946 in the capacity of valet.

SÉBASTIEN: Correct.

CLINTON: You don't talk like a valet.

SÉBASTIEN: You can't have everything.

CLINTON: You are of mixed parentage.

SÉBASTIEN: You have a genius for understatement, monsieur.

CLINTON: Born in Martinique, date uncertain.

SÉBASTIEN: My whole life has been uncertain.

CLINTON (*still at his notes*): Deported from Syria in 1929. No offence specified.

SÉBASTIEN: The Syrians are terribly vague.

CLINTON: Imprisoned in Saigon 1933. Offence specified.

SÉBASTIEN (*reminiscently*): I remember it well.

CLINTON: Resident in England 1936.

SÉBASTIEN: The happiest time of my life.

CLINTON: Landed in Los Angeles 1937.

SÉBASTIEN: The saddest.

CLINTON: Married in Rio de Janeiro 1939. Wife living.

SÉBASTIEN: With a customs officer.

CLINTON: From 1942 to 1946, proprietor of a rooming house in Mexico City.

SÉBASTIEN: Your delicacy does you credit, monsieur.

CLINTON (*closing file*): Those are all my notes on you up to date.

SÉBASTIEN: Quite accurate as far as they go.

CLINTON (*earnestly*): I'd like you to understand that by reading them to you I had no intention of embarrassing you.

SÉBASTIEN: Thank you. You didn't.

CLINTON: I despise moral attitudes. I believe that life is for living, don't you?

SÉBASTIEN: It's difficult to know what else one could do with it.

CLINTON: Personally I have no inhibitions. I took a course of psychiatry at Yale.

SÉBASTIEN: That explains everything.

CLINTON: I've studied Jung and Freud and Adler and Kinsey and all the big boys.

SÉBASTIEN: Mr. Kinsey himself studied quite a number of the big boys.

CLINTON: What I mean to say is that nothing shocks me. I think that every man should do what he wants to do.

SÉBASTIEN: A tolerant philosophy but apt to lead to untidiness.

CLINTON: Where did you learn to speak such good English?

SÉBASTIEN: The Esplanade Hotel, Bournemouth.

CLINTON: What were you doing there?

SÉBASTIEN: Looking after an elderly lady. No offence specified.

CLINTON: You liked working for Paul Sorodin?

SÉBASTIEN: Very much indeed, monsieur. He was a great man.

CLINTON: Was he difficult, temperamental? I mean did he fly into violent rages?

SÉBASTIEN: Frequently.

CLINTON: Did he ever strike you?

SÉBASTIEN: No. He once threw a pork chop at me but it only broke the clock.

CLINTON (*scribbling a note*): Excuse me.

SÉBASTIEN: I really think, Monsieur Preminger, that as Madame Sorodin may return from Père Lachaise at any moment, it would be tactful of you to leave now. The presence here of a stranger would be an intrusion on her grief.

CLINTON: Grief? Just a moment— (*He searches through his file, finds a paper and scans it.*) Sorodin deserted her in 1926, didn't he?

SÉBASTIEN: 1925.

CLINTON: And she hasn't seen him since?

SÉBASTIEN: I believe that they once met by accident in the Galeries Lafayette.

CLINTON: I shouldn't imagine she'd be suffering much grief after all those years.

SÉBASTIEN (*reprovingly*): He was her husband and the father of her children.

CLINTON: Why did she never divorce him?

SÉBASTIEN: She is a woman of the highest principles, and a Catholic.

CLINTON: Can you beat that?

SÉBASTIEN: People have tried, monsieur, but seldom with unqualified success.

CLINTON: Tell me. Did he hate her?

SÉBASTIEN: Not at all. He once painted a moustache on her photograph but only in a spirit of fun.

CLINTON (*rising*): You know, I like you, Sébastien.

SÉBASTIEN: Thank you.

The family returns, accompanied by Sorodin's agent, Jacob Friedland.

One aspect of Sorodin's work that had always intrigued art critics the world over was the way he had moved through three distinct periods. Jacob explains them to the others . . .

JACOB: The first, what is now described as his "Farouche" period, lasted from 1927 until the early '30s. His first exhibition caused an uproar. There were jeers and catcalls. One elderly art critic struck at one of the canvases with his umbrella. A lady from Des Moines, Iowa, fainted dead away and had to be taken to the American hospital.

ISOBEL: Poor thing. That's where they took poor Edith Carrington when she had that dreadful rash.

JACOB: The "Circular" period was an evolution and a reaction at the same time. Through the dark years of the war I had no message from him. Indeed I imagined he must be dead. It was not until he returned to Paris in 1946 that I realized the full significance of the private war he had been waging with his own genius, a struggle that resulted in the greatest victory of his career. The "Jamaican" period.

COLIN: All those fat Negresses?

JACOB (*sharply*): Yes, all those fat Negresses, all that primitive simplicity and glorious colour as well. The first painting he showed me on that fabulous day is now in the Louvre.

JANE: *Girl With Breadfruit?*

JACOB: No. *Boy With Plantain. Girl With Breadfruit* is in Prague.

ISOBEL: That was the one we used for our Christmas cards the year before last, you remember, Colin? Your Aunt Freda wrote "Indecent" on it in red ink and sent it back.

Instead of a will Sorodin has left a letter, which Sébastien reads to them. It ends:

In consideration of the fact that when this letter is ultimately made public I shall be in my grave, I feel it to be only fair that the world of Art, to which I owe so much, should receive from me one final and unequivocal statement, which is that, with the exception of a water-colour of a dog executed at Broadstairs when I was eleven years old, I have never painted a picture of any sort or kind in the whole of my life.

As the play continues, Sébastien introduces them to the real Paul Sorodin—an itinerant Russian "princess" (the "Farouche" period), an English tart (who painted the "Circular" period when in her cups) and a Jamaican religious fanatic (the "Jamaican" period). Sorodin had paid all of them for the rights to their work and their guaranteed silence on the subject. The family is now obliged to do that all over again.

But there is one more surprise to come. The world's art critics are descending on Paris to view Sorodin's last great masterwork. Sébastien now reveals that the *chef d'oeuvre* was painted by his young son, Lauderdale. He also gives them a lesson in artistic *realpolitik* . . .

JACOB: Do you mean to tell me that that child painted that picture unaided?

SÉBASTIEN: Yes, monsieur. Under my supervision. His colour sense is not as yet fully developed and his draughtsmanship still leaves a lot to be desired, but he is a diligent boy, and when he grows up and matures, he should go far.

COLIN: No farther than Wormwood Scrubs.

SÉBASTIEN: The other canvases of course are more abstract.

JACOB: Other canvases?

SÉBASTIEN: Yes. About thirty, all told. Mr. Sorodin signed them all.

JACOB: This is grotesque!

SÉBASTIEN: He described them as his "Neo-Infantilism" period. He dearly loved a good joke. (*He laughs.*)

JACOB: Where are they?

SÉBASTIEN: In a warehouse in Passy, monsieur.

COLIN: They must be destroyed immediately.

SÉBASTIEN (*crossing to* COLIN): I think not, monsieur. That would be a futile gesture of vandalism. If judiciously placed on the market during the next few years they should fetch anything up to a hundred thousand pounds. I have already insured them for eighty thousand.

JACOB: *You* have insured them?

SÉBASTIEN: Yes, monsieur. They are my property. Naturally enough really, considering that my son painted them. Mr. Sorodin saw the justice of that, which is the reason he assigned them to me to dispose of as I saw fit. He suggested that you and I might come to some sort of arrangement.

JACOB: I'll see you damned first! I'll expose the whole abominable swindle!

SÉBASTIEN (*suavely*): Wouldn't that be a little inconsistent, seeing that you have already paid off Princess Pavlikov, Miss Waterton and Mr. Lewellyn? I really do advise you to think carefully, Mr. Friedland. If you expose the whole abominable swindle, as you call it, you also expose yourself to the ridicule of the world.

COLIN (*rising*): On behalf of my mother and my family I would like to say that I entirely agree with Mr. Friedland. The scandal must be exposed and we must face the consequences. Don't you agree, Mother?

ISOBEL: Yes—I suppose so—but—

COLIN (*sitting again*): But what?

ISOBEL: I was thinking of that dear little boy—after all that work—he'll be dreadfully disappointed.

SÉBASTIEN: Not only will *he* be disappointed, the whole world of modern painting will be humiliated and impoverished. The casualties in Hollywood alone will be appalling. The bottom will fall out of the market and thousands of up-and-coming young artists will starve. It will be a cataclysm! Many of the great masters too will be flung into disrepute, their finest pictures will be viewed with suspicion and distrust. If the news leaks out that the great Sorodin's masterpieces were painted by a Russian tart, an ex–Jackson Girl, a Negro Eleventh Hour Immersionist and a boy of fourteen, the rot will spread like wildfire. Modern sculpture, music, drama and poetry will all shrivel in the holocaust. Tens of thousands of industrious people who today are earning a comfortable livelihood by writing without grammar, composing without harmony and painting without form, will be flung into abject poverty or forced really to learn their jobs. Reputations will wither overnight. No one will be spared. Not even Grandma Moses.

ISOBEL: I see no reason to drag in the Old Testament.

SÉBASTIEN: Pause and consider, Mr. Friedland, before you unleash this chaos. It will not only be ridicule that you have to fear, it will be crucifixion! Your colleagues alone will see to that. (*The front doorbell rings.*) Here are two of them now.

JANE: What are you going to do, Jacob?

SÉBASTIEN (*to* JACOB): Is our little secret to be kept inviolate, monsieur, or laid wide open?

JACOB: Come to my office this afternoon. We'll discuss it there.

SÉBASTIEN: And Sir Alaric and Mr. Riskin?

JACOB (*despairingly*): Show them in.

SÉBASTIEN: Very good, monsieur. (*He bows to* ISOBEL, *then to* JACOB, *and opens the double doors.*)

THE CURTAIN FALLS.

•

The play ran for well over a year, but once again, the critics remained steadfastly unimpressed. By now Noël expected nothing less.

Theatre critics had become his lifelong *bêtes noires*. He frequently claimed that he ignored them, but the evidence—particularly in later years—indicated otherwise . . .

Understudy meets understudy. John Gielgud had understudied Noël in *The Vortex* in 1924. Now in 1956 he creates the part of Sébastien in *Nude With Violin*, in London. Noël would play the part later in New York.

If I had really cared about the critics, I would have shot myself in the '20s.

—*PLAY PARADE*, VOLUME 4 (1954)

•

I have always been fond of them . . . I think it is so frightfully clever of them to go night after night to the theater and know so little about it.

•

I can take any amount of criticism, as long as it is unqualified praise.

—PRESS INTERVIEW

•

By the late 1950s English theatre was awash with unwashed, angry young actors and actresses up to their elbows in Kitchen-Sink drama presented by the likes of John Osborne and Arnold Wesker. This, declared the critics, was the theatre we'd been waiting for, a true reflection of urban society today.

Noël—firmly relegated to the wings at this point for his irrelevance—couldn't have disagreed more and said so in a series of articles for the *Sunday Times* (London) under the heading of "Consider the Public."

He had words of warning for both actors and critics . . .

•

"CONSIDER THE PUBLIC"
"A WARNING TO ACTORS"

Having, in a previous article, delivered a measure of warning and advice to our pioneer playwrights, I should like, in this essay, to give a few pointers to our young actors and actresses. Before I begin laying about me however I must say in all fairness that the standard of acting among the youth of our New Movement in the theatre is, within its limits, remarkably high. Nevertheless, "within its limits" is the operative phrase, for these limits, imposed principally by left-wing socialism, are dangerously narrow.

To perform small grey plays in small grey theatres with the maximum of realism and the minimum of makeup is a great deal easier than to play classic drama or modern comedy with enough style and technical assurance to convince an audience of fifteen hundred to two thousand people.

The fact that wit, charm and elegance have been forced into temporary eclipse by our present-day directors and critics, many of whom would be incapable of recognizing these qualities if they saw them, does not mean that they will not return. The wind and the weather will change: it always does, and, when this happens, some of our young scratch-and-mumble-school players will find that their hitherto circumscribed training and experience have ill equipped them to perform in *milieux* to which they are totally unaccustomed.

This is largely the fault of contemporary playwrights and directors but not entirely. It is also the fault of the actors themselves for they should realise that *one* approach to the mastery of their medium, however intelligent that approach may be, is not enough. The duty of every young actor, regardless of what political beliefs he may hold, or what particular class he comes from, is to widen his views and his scope as much as possible.

Many of our greatest and most distinguished actors and actresses have come from humble beginnings and one of the principal contributory causes of their later greatness and distinction was the fact that they were not content to stay as they were. With determination, hard work and concentration they strove during their early years to improve themselves. They studied dancing, fencing and elocution; they banished from their speech, both on the stage and off it, the telltale accents of their early environments; they trained their ears and their tongues to master alien dialects, and to many of them the most alien of these was the speech of the educated. In fact they rigorously disciplined themselves to a point where they could play Kings and Queens, North Country farmers, foreign diplomats, Cockney cabdrivers, Irish colleens, Welsh miners and average middle-class businessmen, without strain and with equal authenticity. I have noticed few signs of this deliberately and painstakingly acquired versatility today. It can be argued, of course, that there is no longer any demand for it, and this up to a point is true, but it must be remembered that when the pendulum begins to swing back again, there will be.

Theatrically, one of the more depressing aspects of the present transition phase through which the civilized world is passing, is the monotonous emphasis on the lot of the Common Man; for the Common Man, unless written and portrayed with genius, is not dramatically nearly so interesting as he is claimed to be. A glance at the list of currently successful plays in London will show that the public, on the whole, prefer to see extraordinary people on the stage rather than ordinary ones; fantastic situations rather than familiar, commonplace ones, and actors of outsize personality and talent rather than accurately competent mediocrities.

I am quite prepared to admit that during my fifty-odd years of theatre going, I have on many occasions been profoundly moved by plays about the Common Man, as in my fifty-odd years of restaurant going I have frequently enjoyed tripe and onions, but I am not prepared to admit that an exclusive diet of either would be entirely satisfying. In this I am fully convinced that the general public is in complete agreement with me.

From the acting point of view, of course, the Common Man is the easiest and most immediately rewarding assignment in the theatre, particularly in straight, down-to-earth plays where no comedy values are involved. For any experienced actor who has mastered the poetic nuances of Shakespearean verse and the intricate subtleties of modern high comedy, "Dear Old Dad" in a kitchen-sink drama is the equivalent of a couple of aspirin and a nice lie-down. Some years ago when I was giving alternate performances of *Present Laughter* and *This Happy Breed* at the Haymarket Theatre I can remember to this day the relief I used to feel when, after a matinee of the former with its tension and tempo and concentrated timing, I returned in the evening to play Frank Gibbons in *This Happy Breed.* To wander about in shirtsleeves, take off my boots, pick my nose and drink cups of tea was so infinitely less demanding than dashing about at high speed in coloured dressing gowns and delivering comedy lines accurately enough to reach the back of the gallery.

I am well aware that this confession will probably bring forth howls of derision from my younger, more dedicated colleagues, but the fact remains that it always has been and it always will be easier to play realistic drama than artificial comedy. That this is not generally accepted by our modern pseudo-intellectual groups, merely proves that they don't know nearly so much about the theatre as they think they do.

This brings me, with a slight yawn, to what is colloquially known as The Method.

A number of years ago Vladimir Ilyich Lenin was conveyed, in a sealed compartment, across Europe to Russia. This furtive adventure resulted in a great deal of trouble for a great many people. A few years later, whether in a sealed compartment or not I have no idea, a book by Konstantin Stanislavsky found its way to America where it, in its turn, caused a great deal of trouble to a great many actors, actresses, directors and, ultimately, to the unfortunate public. The only ones who benefited from it being a few performers who, having proved themselves dismally inadequate on the stage, decided to set themselves up as teachers.

Actually there were two books, *My Life in Art* and *An Actor Prepares,* in both of which Mr. Stanislavsky states his views on the art of acting. In the former, which is autobiographical, he explains without humour but in merciless detail, his psychological, spiritual and technical approach to every part he played in the course of his distinguished career. These esoteric soul-searchings are accompanied by a series of photographs which prove at least that he was a great one for the nose-paste and crepe hair and not above a comical posture or two when the role demanded it.

In *An Actor Prepares* he is more objective and, under the thin disguise of a director called Tortsov, he sets out to explain his theories to a group of embarrassingly earnest young drama students. That this book should become a sort of theatrical bible in Russia is quite understandable. It is written by a Russian for Russians with, naturally enough, a proper appreciation of the Russian temperament, but that it should be regarded as holy writ to the theatrical youth of the Western world is less understandable and to my mind excessively tiresome.

It would be foolish to deny that among Mr. Stanislavsky's analyses of acting there are not a few simple and basic truths concealed beneath his labored and tortuous verbiage, but these truths are so simple and so basic that I doubt if they would have called forth more than a casual grunt of agreement from the late Sarah Siddons.

There is quite a lot to be said in favour of certain aspects of The Method. It stresses a few essential "musts" such as the necessity of finding the correct psychological values of the part to be played and concentrating first on the interior truth of a character before attempting the exterior projection of it. As this however is what every experienced actor I have ever met does automatically, I cannot entirely welcome it as a dazzling revelation. In my opinion The Method places too much emphasis on actual realism and too little on simulated realism. To Be, up to a point, and Not To Be, over and above that point, is the whole art and craft of acting. Every intelligent actor realises the impossibility of *genuinely* feeling the emotions necessary to his part for eight performances a week over a period of months or even years. His art lies in his ability to re-create nightly an accurate simulation of the emotions he originally felt when he was first studying and rehearsing it. If acting were actually a state of "Being," anybody playing a heavy dramatic role in a smash success would be in a mental home after a few weeks. In any event, emotion on the stage without the technique to project it and the ability to control it merely results in mistiming and untidiness and has nothing whatsoever to do with acting.

Technique, although a much despised word nowadays, is, beyond a shadow of doubt, indispensable. It is impossible to give a consistent and continued performance without it. However progressive and revolutionary a young actor's theories may be and however many rules, conventions and traditions he may hold in contempt as being "ham" and old-fashioned, he would be well advised to learn these rules, conventions and traditions before attempting to break them. It is as palpably foolish for an actor to try to play a major role, or even a minor one for that matter, without first learning to move about the stage and speak audibly, as it would be for a budding pianist or violinist to embark on a concerto without first having mastered his scales. And it is here that I feel that The Method, as a method, breaks down. I myself have heard a famous Method teacher in

New York inform a student that audibility was unimportant compared with "the moment of truth!" This lofty statement of course evaporates immediately when even cursorily examined, for how can fifty moments of truth be of the faintest significance on the stage if no one in the auditorium can hear what the actors are talking about?

In addition to a large number of grimy, introspective megalomaniacs, The Method has undoubtedly produced a small number of brilliant actors. But then so has the Royal Academy of Dramatic Art, The Old Vic Drama School and every other sort of acting school down to "Miss Weatherby's Shakespeare In Twelve Easy Lessons, 36, Station Approach, Sidcup."

Genuine talent can profit from or survive any given system of instruction, although unquestionably the best training of all is acting to paying audiences either in touring companies or repertory companies. Audience reaction is of paramount importance to learning the job, for without it, the acting, however brilliant, has no point. To perform to a handful of fellow students and relatives in a small fit-up studio theatre is a waste of time and not even good practice; in fact it is very often bad practice because the reaction, both from teachers and prejudiced spectators, can be misleading. The aim of every budding actor should be to get himself in front of a paying audience, no matter where, as soon as he possibly can.

This salutary experience might conceivably rub off a little of the solemn, dedicated gloom that Mr. Stanislavsky and his disciples have imposed on our hitherto cheerful and fairly ramshackle profession. The Theatre may be regarded as an Art with a capital letter, a craft, a means of earning a living or even a showcase for personal exhibitionism, but it is not and should not be a religion. I am all in favour of actors taking their work seriously, in fact on many occasions I have been accused of being a martinet in this respect. But I am definitely not in favour of every member of the company embarking on endless, ego-feeding, quasi-theological discussions of the possible reactions and motivations of the parts they have to play. If they have studied the play intelligently and learnt the words they should *know* the necessary reactions and motivations already and not waste my time and their own in gabbing about them. All this tedious argument, recapitulation and verbose questing after "Truth," apart from giving the individual actor an overblown opinion of his own intellectual prowess, is pretentious nonsense and not to be tolerated for a moment by a director of integrity. The director of a play is analogous to the Captain of a ship, and few ships' Captains in moment of crisis lend a benign and tolerant ear to the suggestions of every minor member of the crew.

Another, to my mind, dangerous assumption on the part of the Method teachers is that actors are cerebral and can be relied upon to approach the playing of a part intellectually. In my experience, the really fine actors whom I have known and admired and often worked with have been, in varying degrees, intelligent, shrewd, egotistical, temperamental, emotional and, above all, intuitive, but never either logical or intellectual. Their approach to their work, according to their respective characters and techniques, is guided almost mystically by their talent.

It is this that has propelled them up from the ranks of small part players into the position of loved and envied stardom. It is this, combined with every trick and technical device they have acquired on the way, which enables them on a nerve-strained, agonized opening night to rise supremely to the challenge and sweep the play into success. And it is this, curiously enough, in which most of them have the least confidence and for which they require the most reassurance. However much self-confidence they may appear to have, this basic uncertainty is their most valuable and endearing asset. It is also the hallmark of the genuine article. I have encountered few fine actors and few real stars in the true meaning of the word who, beneath God knows how much egotism, temperament and outward flamboyance do not possess a fundamental humility.

Alas and alack, I have encountered quite a number of our young actors and actresses of today who, sodden with pretentious theories and trained to concentrate solely on their own reactions and motivations to the exclusion of their fellow actors and the audience, have not even a bowing acquaintance with humility. They apparently despise the far past as thoroughly as they despise the immediate past. They arrogantly condemn the "commercial" theatre, which in essence means the public that they must hope ultimately to please, thereby, it seems to me, spitting in the eye of the golden goose before it has even met the gander.

It is this innate contempt for the values of other days which accounts, I presume, for their physical slovenliness on the stage. I have watched, with Edwardian dismay, these talented young creatures arriving at a rehearsal. The boys, unshaven, wearing grubby open-necked sweaters and stained leather coats, and with dark fingernails. The girls, in stained jeans, equally grubby sweaters, with their hair unwashed and unbrushed or twisted into unalluring ponytails. Admittedly this very young sartorial defiance is perfectly consistent with most of the parts they are called upon to play, but my point is that if they are really to succeed over the years they will be called upon to play all sorts and kinds of parts and that all this initial grubbiness will suddenly turn out to be a severe handicap. There is, after all, no theatrical law decreeing that an actor should identify himself off stage with whatever he is going to play on stage. In point of fact it is a dangerous and confusing premise. Slovenliness of appearance all too often indicates slovenliness of mind and no actor can afford to have that.

I do not wish to imply by the above that I am so advanced in my dotage as to be entirely out of sympathy with the facile defiance of the young. I was young myself once; defiant, pushing and self-confident—outwardly at least—and, like most intelligent, ambitious youngsters, I imagined I knew a great deal more than I actually did. But never, in all my youthful arrogance, was I idiotic enough to allow myself to be influenced by any current political creed, nor conceited enough to curl my lip contemptuously at the "great" of the theatre because they happened to be commercially successful.

On the contrary, I was deeply in awe of them and blushed with pride whenever one of them deigned to speak to me. I had only two presentable suits, but these were daily pressed within an inch of their lives. I would never have dreamed of attending even an understudy rehearsal, and in those days I attended many, without going to immense pains to look my very best.

The theatre should be treated with respect. The theatre is a wonderful place, a house of strange enchantment, a temple of illusion. What it most emphatically is not and never will be is a scruffy, ill-lit, fumed-oak drill hall serving as a temporary soapbox for political propaganda.

The theatre still spells magic for many millions of people and that magic should be a source of deep pride to all those who are privileged to serve in it.

•

"CONSIDER THE PUBLIC"
"A WARNING TO DRAMATIC CRITICS"

In the long history of the arts there have been almost as many harsh things said by artists about critics as there have been by critics about artists. Byron, Pope, Dryden, Coleridge, Hazlitt, to name only a few, have all, in their time, lashed out when driven to exasperation by the carping of those they considered, rightly, to be their inferiors.

Like the cobra and the mongoose, the artist and the critic have always been and will always be Nature's irreconcilables. Occasionally a temporary truce may be established, based insecurely on a sudden burst of enthusiasm from the latter for the work of the former, but these halcyon interludes are seldom of long duration. Sooner or later a dissonant note is sure to be sounded and back we tumble again into the dear old basic status quo.

> For never can true reconcilement grow,
> When wounds of deadly hate have pierced so deep.

My personal attitude to the dramatic critics, after fifty years of varying emotions, has finally solidified into an unyielding core of bored resignation. Every now and then the outer edge of this fossilized area in my mind can be twitched into brief sensitivity by an unexpected word of praise or a stab of more than usually vicious abuse, but these occasions are becoming rarer and rarer and the core remains, hardening imperceptibly with the passing of time until, presumably, it will achieve absolute invulnerability.

However, before this state of Nirvana finally sets in, I feel an impulse to rise up, gird my loins and have just one valedictory bash at my natural enemies. Not, I hasten to say, on my own account; I have never been attracted to lost causes—but on behalf of the love of my life which is the theatre.

The Theatre, in all its diverse aspects, fascinates and enchants me today as much as it did when I first became a professional actor at the age of ten. A fine play impeccably acted or a good musical well sung and danced can still send me out into the street in a state of ecstatic euphoria, just as a mediocre play indifferently acted can depress me utterly and rob me, temporarily, of all hope and ambitions.

Naturally, I do not expect dramatic critics to scale such heights of enjoyment or plumb such depths of despair, for in order to do so they would have to know a great deal more than they do about playwriting and acting. And if they did know a great deal more about playwriting and acting, it is highly probable that they would be playwrights or actors themselves and not critics at all, for either of the above occupations are more attractive and financially remunerative, when successful, than journalism.

A dramatic critic is frequently detested, feared, despised, and occasionally tolerated, but he is seldom loved or envied. The awareness of this must, in course of time, lower his morale and corrode his spirit, either consciously or subconsciously. Some of them, of course, seek compensation by making small names for themselves, usually by the use of sensational vituperation, but alas, both the vituperation and the names are soon forgotten.

The well-worn cliché that most critics are frustrated artists has, like most clichés, a certain basis of truth, and this truth, from time to time, has been fairly dismally proved when one or other of them, rendered mad by the monotony of his nightly calvary, has attempted to free himself from his bondage and write a play. With a few notable exceptions, these sporadic bids for freedom have been painfully abortive. Unfortunately, I cannot recall any occasion in England when a dramatic critic decided to become an actor, but there is still hope in my heart and my fingers are crossed. Mr. Kenneth Tynan, we know, started as an actor, but was soon forced, by managerial and public apathy, to desist.

In earlier years it was customary for critics, after they had given their opinions of the play and the leading actors, to mention some of the lesser members of the cast. This provided a certain encouragement to supporting players, if only to the extent of bringing their names to the attention of the public and to other managements. That this custom, of late, seems to be gradually dying out is perhaps regrettable, but only up to a point, for the critic is yet to be born who is capable of distinguishing between the actor and the part. A minor actor playing a brief showy role, however ineptly, can always be sure of good notices, whereas a popular favourite, using all the subtle resources of long experience to bring life to a long, unrewarding part, is dismissed with a caution.

In the course of an interview some months ago with Mr. Robert Muller, whose Teutonic earnestness is finely matched by his lack of humour, I was horrified to learn of the circumstances in which the critics of today have to work, particularly those who write for the daily newspapers. These poor beasts are apparently allowed only a brief half an hour, and sometimes even less, in which to collect and correlate their views of an opening performance and get them down on their typewriters. Now this would be a formidable assignment even for men of lightning perceptiveness, and none of our present crop could honestly be credited with that.

Apart from this cruel time limitation, it appears that they are also crushed into a position of cowed subservience by an omniscient being called a Sub-Editor. This Sub-Editor, whose knowledge of the Theatre is probably limited to his local Odeon, holds all these fearsome oracles in deadly thrall. It is he who has the power to slash their columns to pieces and he who is responsible for those sensational headlines which are so often entirely irrelevant to the reviews they preface. Thousands of members of the public I believe seldom read further than these headlines and so when they are confronted by large black-lettered phrases such as "Not This Time, Sir Laurence" or "Noël Flops Again!" they automatically follow their own instincts and go out to book seats.

In consideration of these circumstances, therefore, it is perhaps unfair to blame critics too much for their lack of selectiveness. They have to sit night after night in different theatres, staring glumly at what is put before them, haunted by the spectre of the Sub-Editor waiting for them, and aware that Time's Wingèd Chariot is goosing them along towards their deadline. All they can do really is to scribble a few hurried notes onto their programmes and run like stags to their desks as the final curtain touches the stage.

For most Theatre people, however, both the Sub-Editor's headline and the criticisms beneath them have an importance far out of proportion to their actual significance. Most playwrights, stars, actors, directors and managers devour avidly every review from the *Times* down to the *Express,* and allow themselves to be either depressed or elated, according to what they read. What few of them seem to realise is that an average member of an average audience seldom takes more than one or, at most, two newspapers, and even then he is more than likely to turn to the latest crime or the sporting page before casting his eye over the theatrical news.

There is no doubt, however, that a unanimously unfavourable press can sometimes do considerable damage to a production, particularly if the play in question happens to have no famous name on the bill, either author or star, to attract the public. Just as a unanimously enthusiastic press can ensure good business for two or three weeks. If the play is good and worthy of the praise it has received, it will run. If not, the public, within a comparatively short space of time will discover that it has been duped and stay away.

This has occurred with increasing frequency of late because the public has become wise to the fact that most of our contemporary critics tend to favour "dustbin drama" to the exclusion of everything else. The prevalent assumption that any successful play presented by a commercial management in the West End is automatically inferior in quality to anything produced on a shoe string in the East End or Sloane Square is both inaccurate and silly. It also betrays an attitude of old-fashioned class consciousness and inverted snobbism which has now become obvious even to the ordinary playgoer, who gives little thought to "movements" or "trends" and merely goes to the theatre expecting to be entertained.

It is quite apparent that "The New Movement in the Theatre," with all its potential talent and genuine belief in its own significance, is failing. And it is failing because it has been so shrilly oversold, not only to the public but to itself. For young, aspiring playwrights and actors to be consistently overpraised because what they write and act happens to coincide with the racial, political and social prejudices of a handful of journalists, can only have a disastrous effect on their creative impulse. Very few beginners, however talented, can be expected to survive indiscriminate acclaim without becoming complacent and over-sure of themselves. The wise ones among them will, of course, after a little while, compare their notices with their royalties and decide that they still have a great deal to learn. But alas, such wisdom is usually the fruit of experience and in this the majority of them are, naturally enough, lacking.

To state that the dramatic critics of today are doing a grave disservice to the Theatre and to the public is a sweeping generalization that needs qualifying, although in my far from humble opinion, it is very largely true. However I will qualify it to the extent of saying that those who write for the more respectable newspapers such as the *Times,* the *Daily Telegraph,* the *Sunday Times* and the *Observer,* can at least be relied upon to treat an author or an actor with courtesy. But then, being men of reasonable integrity, they presumably do not allow themselves to be bedevilled either by ignorant sub-editors or the dubious policies of overlords.

The critics of the *Daily Mail,* the *Daily Express,* the evening papers and the picture papers, however, have, of late years, flung all thought of courtesy to the winds and devoted themselves, with increasing virulence, to witless and indiscriminate abuse. Being myself one of the principal victims of this vulgarity, I feel perfectly justified in pointing out that they are making cracking idiots of themselves and proving nothing beyond the fact that they are entirely out of touch with the public they are supposed to be writing for.

It surely cannot be good for the reputation of a popular newspaper for its dramatic critic to be proved dead wrong over and over again. I am aware of course that the Lords Beaverbrook and Rothermere are not particularly interested in the Theatre, but even so it must dawn on them that quite a number of their readers are. And that these readers should be continually misled and misinformed about even so trivial a matter as a new play, cannot in the long run redound to the credit of the paper they represent.

In conclusion, I would like to suggest that our contemporary critics, if they wish to retain an atom of respect from their readers and the theatrical profession, should rid themselves of their more obvious personal prejudices, endeavour to be more objective and, if possible, more constructive.

In any event they should mend their manners.

•

The articles created a considerable furor. Kenneth Tynan, the leading critic of the day, who felt most assailed, sneered that the deck of a sinking ship was hardly the best vantage point from which to take an objective view.

But at least the ice was broken, and it wasn't long before Noël had developed warm relationships with Osborne, Wesker and, particularly, Pinter. There was even a rapprochement with Tynan, when he persuaded Olivier, as head of the new National Theatre, to invite Noël to direct a revival of *Hay Fever* in 1964—the first such revival by a living English playwright.

•

America continued to restore his fortunes, both professional and financial.

CBS offered him $450,000 for three live TV specials, which turned out to be *Together With Music* with Mary Martin, *Blithe Spirit* and *This Happy Breed* with Noël starring in all of them. The amount of money involved caused him to have a serious reappraisal of his circumstances. It was time to save for his old age, "which starts on Tuesday."

First came the reunion with Mary Martin. They had long since made up their differences over *Pacific 1860* and were clearly glad to be . . .

"TOGETHER WITH MUSIC"

Together with music,
Together with music,
We planned this moment long ago,
Many a year we've sighed in vain
For both of us knew
Many a moon would wax and wane
Before this dream came true.
Together with music,
Together with music,
The thought of it enchants us so,
When those first chords crash out
We know beyond a doubt
That everything's going to be divine
Watch us rise and shine
Riding as high as a kite
Our hearts are fancy free
Because at long long last we happen to be
Together, with music tonight.

Bear with us, bear with us please,
If we look a bit wild and overwrought,
But we're dreaming a dream we never thought
Would ever quite come true for us,
Share with us, share with us please
The excitement of standing hand in hand
While this very select exclusive Band
Plays a personal Tattoo for us.
For many a year and many a day
We've laid our plans away
For many a day and many a year
We've prayed that somewhere, sometime we'd appear . . .

Together with music,
Together with music,
Now suddenly our hearts feel gay,
Ever since that first day we met
We both of us guessed

NOEL
COWARD

MARY
MARTIN

"Together with Music"

An archive recording of
the entire brilliant television
event made during the
actual television broadcast.

Many a sun would rise and set
Before we coalesced

Together with music
Together with music
At last the Gods have said Okay,
When those first notes we hear
A million stars appear.
Our personal world goes round and round
Gaily wired for sound
Everything's shining and bright
This is our jubilee
Because at long long last we happen to be
Together with music tonight.

"Television," he firmly stated, when it was all safely and successfully behind him, "is for appearing on—not looking at." And he proceeded to illustrate his own dictum by appearing on numerous TV interview shows for the rest of his life.

·

Reluctantly, he concluded it would be foolish to continue to be domiciled in England, with its penal tax system.

There was a brief sojourn in Bermuda, which proved to be too English Suburban, but then Jamaica proved to be "where my heart is."

"JAMAICA"

Jamaica's an island surrounded by sea
(Like Corsica, Guam and Tasmania)
The tourist does not need to wear a topee
Or other macabre miscellanea.
Remember that this is a tropical place
Where violent hues are abundant
And bright coloured clothes with a bright yellow face
Look, frankly, a trifle redundant.
A simple ensemble of trousers and shirt
Becomes both the saint and the sinner
And if a headwaiter looks bitterly hurt
You *can* wear a jacket for dinner.

Jamaica's an island surrounded by sea
(It shares this distinction with Elba)
It's easy to order a goat fricassee
But madness to ask for pêche Melba.
You'll find (to the best of this writer's belief)
That if you want rice you can get it
But visitors ordering mutton or beef
Will certainly live to regret it.
There's seldom a shortage of ackees and yams
Or lobsters, if anyone's caught them
But if you've a passion for imported hams
You'd bloody well better import them.

Jamaica's an island surrounded by sea
(It has this in common with Cuba)

Its national tunes, to a certain degree,
Are founded on Boop-boop-a-duba.
'Neath tropical palms under tropical skies
Where equally tropical stars are
The vocal Jamaicans betray no surprise
However off-key their guitars are.
The native calypsos which seem to be based
On hot-air-conditioned reflexes
Conclusively prove that to people of taste
There's nothing so funny as sex is.

Jamaica's an island surrounded by sea
(Like Alderney, Guernsey and Sark are)
Its wise not to drive with exuberant glee
Where large barracuda and shark are.
The reefs are entrancing; the water is clear,
The colouring couldn't be dreamier
But one coral scratch and you may spend a year
In bed with acute septicemia.
The leading hotels are extremely well run
The service both cheerful and dextrous
But even the blisters you get from the sun
Are firmly included as extras.

Jamaica's an island surrounded by sea
(*Unlike* Ecuador or Guiana)
The tourist may not have a *fromage de Brie*
But always can have a banana.
He also can have, if he has enough cash,
A pleasantly rum-sodden liver
And cure his rheumatic complaints in a flash
By shooting himself at Milk River.
In fact every tourist who visits these shores
Can thank his benevolent Maker
For taking time off from the rest of His chores
To fashion the Isle of Jamaica.

•

He got to know Jamaica just after the war, when fellow spy Ian Fleming rented Noël his own house, Goldeneye, at what Noël considered an exorbitant rent. Its somewhat monastic and clinical atmosphere caused him to rechristen it Goldeneye, Ear, Nose & Throat, but his thank-you note (in verse) paints a more affectionate picture . . .

"HOUSE GUEST"

Alas! I cannot adequately praise
The dignity, the virtue and the grace
Of this most virile and imposing place
Wherein I passed so many airless days.

Alas! I cannot accurately find
Words to express the hardness of the seat
Which, when I cheerfully sat down to eat,
Seared with such cunning into my behind.
Alas! However much I raved and roared,
No rhetoric, no witty diatribe
Could ever, even partially, describe
The impact of the spare-room bed—and board.

Alas! Were I to write till crack of doom
No typewriter, no pencil, nib nor quill
Could ever recapitulate the chill
And arid vastness of the living room.

Alas! I am not someone who exclaims
With rapture over ancient equine prints.
Ah no, dear Ian, I can only wince
At all those horses framed in all those frames.

Alas! My sensitivity rebels,
Not at loose shutters, not at a plague of ants
Nor other "sub-let" bludgeonings of chance.
But at those hordes of ageing, fading shells.
Alas! If only common sense could teach
The stubborn heart to heed the cunning brain,
You would, before you let your house again,
Remove the barracudas from the beach.

But still, my dear Commander, I admit,
No matter how I criticize and grouse
That I was strangely happy in your house—
In fact I'm very, very fond of it.

Noël's Jamaica consisted of a house by the water (Blue Harbour) and later, a bungalow (Firefly) on top of a mountain, to which he would retreat for complete privacy.

He wrote to his secretary, Lorn Loraine . . .

Last night we took a thermos full of cocktails up . . . and sat and watched the sun set and the lights come up over the town and it really was magical. The sky changed from deep blue to yellow and pale green and then all the colour went and out came the stars and the fireflies . . . The view is really staggering, particularly when the light begins to go and the far mountains become purple against a pale lemon sky.

There is a very sweet white owl who comes and hoots at us every evening. I don't think he does it in any spirit of criticism but just to be friendly.

•

When he, Graham and Coley were there together, painting became a shared passion.

We are all painting away like crazy. Little Lad [Graham], as usual, is at work upon a very large ruined cathedral. I can't think why he has such a penchant for hysterical Gothic. Perhaps he was assaulted in childhood by a South African nun. Coley is bashing away at a lot of thin people by a river while I, swifter than the eye can follow, have finished a group of Negroes and I am now busy with a crowded fair-ground with swings and roundabouts and what should be a Ferris wheel but looks like a steel ovary. The trouble with me is that I don't know the meaning of the word *peur.*

Little Lad has done a sort of "Rose Red City," which looks a bit like Golders Green. The effect is dashing but the architecture is a bit dodgy. I keep on doing lots of people walking about and I'm sick to death of them.

Little Lad is painting a large picture of a Priest and an Acolyte in acid moonlight. He suddenly changed the Priest into a lady in a red dress, which is better really but perhaps not better enough. She is very tall and the Acolyte is crouching. It is all a great worry.

The plumbing has proved to be a trifle eccentric and my lavatory hic-coughs and sprays my behind with cold water every now and then which is all very gay and sanitary.

When it decides to rain here there are no half measures about it. It comes down in a deluge and there is already some valuable Penicillin growing in all my shoes!

There are no dangerous insects or animals here but I have just found a beetle the size of a saucer nestling among a lot of three-halfpenny stamps. It seems fairly amiable but its expression does not inspire confidence. I have now thrown it over the veranda and I *think* it went into Graham's bedroom window.

I rather enjoy my morning shopping trips into Port Maria. Everyone is very amiable and their colours are graded from deep ebony to pale *café au lait*.

Mr. Philpot in the General Store is coal black with far more teeth than are usual and he always wrings my hand like a pump handle and we make little jokes. Then, of course, there is Madame Cecilia Chung, my Chinese groceress. She, having read in some obscure Chinese newspaper that I was renowned for being witty, goes into gales of Oriental laughter when I ask quite ordinarily for Colman's mustard or Worcester sauce!

The girls in the post office start giggling with anticipatory delight before I get out of my car so you do see that there is never a dull moment for anybody!

Oh la la! As I always say, having acted so prettily in the French language.

·

But he increasingly felt the need for a European base, too, and a Swiss search began in earnest. Shangri-la turned out to be Les Avants, high in the mountains behind Montreux. He flirted with the idea of calling it Shilly Chalet, but the locals decided for him. *Chalet Covair* (their approximation of Coward) they called it—and still do. Far from being an architectural gem, there was a touch of Eastbourne about it, Cecil Beaton's friends told him, though Rebecca West favoured Margate or Folkestone and thought its white wooden balconies should have been hung with drying bathing dresses. Nonetheless, it was "home" and "it worked."

It is eight o'clock in the morning and I am sitting up comfortably in bed in my own house at last. Outside it is still blue-dark but the sun is preparing to come up from behind the Rochers de Naye. The mountains are beginning to turn pink and the visible world is white with snow. The house is really beautiful, much more so than I would have believed.

—DIARIES (DECEMBER 21, 1959)

"WORLD WEARY"

When I'm feeling dreary and blue,
I'm only too

Glad to be left alone,
Dreaming of a place in the
  sun.
When day is done,
Far from a telephone;
Bustle and the weary crowd
Make me want to cry out
  loud,
Give me something
  peaceful and grand
Where all the land
Slumbers in monotone.

I'm world weary, world
  weary,
Living in a great big town,
I find it so dreary, so dreary,
Everything looks grey or brown,
I want an ocean blue,
Great big trees,
A bird's-eye view
Of the Pyrenees,
I want to watch the moon rise up
And see the great red sun go down,
Watching clouds go by
Through a Winter sky
Fascinates me
But if I do it in the street,
Every cop I meet
Simply hates me,
Because I'm world weary, world weary,
I could kiss the railroad tracks,
I want to get right back to nature and relax.

Get up in the morning at eight,
Relentless Fate,
Drives me to work at nine;
Toiling like a bee in a hive
From four to five
Whether it's wet or fine,
Hardly ever see the sky,
Buildings seem to grow so high.

Maybe in the future I will
Perhaps fulfill
This dream of mine.

I'm world weary, world weary,
Living in a great big town,
I find it so dreary, so dreary,
Everything looks grey or brown,
I want a horse and plough,
Chickens too,
Just one cow
With a wistful moo,
A country where the verb "to work"
Becomes a most improper noun;
I can hardly wait
Till I see the great
Open spaces,
My loving friends will not be there,
I'm so sick of their
Goddamned faces,
Because I'm world weary, world weary,
Tired of all these jumping jacks,
I want to get right back to nature and relax.

—THIS YEAR OF GRACE! (U.S., 1928)

So he *didn't* get a "bird's-eye view of the Pyrenees"—he had to make do with the Alps. But he certainly did have the "great big trees" and a safe haven for the rest of his days.

He also had "a spectacular view overlooking an absolutely ravishing tax advantage."

CHAPTER SIX
THE 1960s

MAUDIE: Who was it who said there was something beautiful about growing old?
HELEN: Whoever it was, I have news for him.

—WAITING IN THE WINGS (1960)

It is said that old age has its compensations. I wonder what
they are?

—DIARIES (1967)

Noël × 3

T IME'S WINGÈD CHARIOT," Noël told his diary in 1959, "is beginning to goose me."

Age was beginning to preoccupy him increasingly as the decade
wore on. As early as 1949 he had written, "As one gets older people begin
to die and when each one goes a little light goes out."

Even theatre folk were apparently not immune when the Grim
Reaper—Noël's favourite pseudonym for Death—called their cue to exit.
Many of Noël's longtime female colleagues, though, enjoyed remarkably
long runs, even if they were no longer the stars they had once been.

He was remarkably loyal to them, always managing to find a small part
for one or more of them in his later plays. In many cases of personal hardship his help was often financial, too—a fact that only came to light years
later in the privacy of his letters.

His tribute to elderly actresses came in the form of his 1960 Chekho-
vian play, *Waiting in the Wings.*

The Wings is a home for retired actresses, and their personal relationships are every bit as dramatic as anything the ladies did onstage.

By an ironic twist of their own personal plot, two former leading ladies,
Lotta Bainbridge and May Davenport, find themselves thrown together.
May's former and now deceased husband had left her for Lotta. They have
not spoken to one another for some thirty years. Finally, there appears to be
a crack in the ice . . .

CORA (*pulling herself together and getting up*): Are you coming up, May?
MAY: No. I'm going to stay by the fire for a little.
LOTTA (*cheerfully*): So am I.

MAY looks at *LOTTA* sharply and then looks away again. *CORA* stares at
them both for a moment, then, without another word, she goes upstairs
and disappears. There is a long silence. *MAY* takes up her work bag, which
is by her chair, and takes out her embroidery frame. She shoots *LOTTA*
another swift look and, fumbling in her bag again, produces her wool, needle and spectacle case. She gives a little grunt of satisfaction. *LOTTA* sits
quietly staring in front of her. The silence continues.

MAY (*at last*): They were here all the time. (*LOTTA without replying looks at
her inquiringly.* MAY *meets her eyes and forces a wintry little smile.*) My
glasses. They were here all the time—in my work bag.

LOTTA (*gently*):

> And frosts were slain and flowers begotten
> And in green underwood and cover
> Blossom by blossom the Spring begins.

MAY: The fire's nearly out.

LOTTA: There's enough heat left, really. It's not very cold.

MAY: Were you happy with him?

LOTTA: Yes. I was happy with him until the day he died.

MAY: That's something gained at any rate, isn't it?

LOTTA (*lightly*): He was a monster sometimes, of course. Those black Irish rages.

MAY: Yes. I remember them well. (*She looks at* LOTTA *curiously and says, without emotion.*) Why did you take him from me?

LOTTA: I didn't. He came to me of his own free will. You must have known that. He wasn't the sort of character that anyone could take from anyone else.

MAY (*dispassionately*): You were prettier than I was.

LOTTA: You know perfectly well that that had nothing to do with it. The spark is struck or it isn't. It's seldom the fault of any one person.

MAY: Any one person can achieve a lot by determination.

LOTTA: Would you like a scrap of accurate but rather unpleasant information?

MAY: What do you mean?

LOTTA: I can tell you now. I couldn't before. You never gave me the chance anyhow.

MAY: What are you talking about?

LOTTA: There was somebody else.

MAY: Somebody else?

LOTTA: Yes. Between the time he left you and came to me.

MAY: I don't believe it.

LOTTA: It's quite true. Her name was Lavinia, Lavinia Parsons.

MAY (*incredulously*): Not that dreadful girl who played Ophelia with poor old Ernest?

LOTTA: That's the one.

MAY: Are you telling me this in order to exonerate yourself?

LOTTA (*with a touch of asperity*): No, May. I'm not apologizing to you, you know, not asking for your forgiveness. I see no reason to exonerate myself. Charles fell in love with me and I fell in love with him and we were married. I have no regrets.

MAY (*drily*): You are very fortunate. I have, a great many.

LOTTA: Well, don't. It's a waste of time.

MAY: What became of your first husband, Webster Whatever-his-name-was?

LOTTA (*evenly*): His name was Webster Bennet. After our divorce in 1924 he went to Canada and died there a few years later.

MAY: You had a son, didn't you?

LOTTA: Yes. I had a son.

MAY: Is he alive?

LOTTA: Yes. He went to Canada with his father. He is there still. He has had two wives, the first one apparently was a disaster, the second one seems satisfactory. They have three children.

MAY: Does he write to you often?

LOTTA: I haven't heard from him for seventeen years.

MAY (*gruffly*): I'm sorry, Lotta, very sorry.

LOTTA: Thank you, that's kind of you. I was unhappy about it for a long time but I'm not anymore. He was always his father's boy more than mine. I don't think he ever cared for me much, except of course when he was little.

MAY: Why did you come here? Was it absolutely necessary?

LOTTA (*looking down*): Yes, absolutely. I have a minute income of two hundred pounds a year and nothing saved; the last two plays I did were failures and—and there was nothing else to be done, also I found I couldn't learn lines anymore—that broke my nerve.

MAY: That's what really finished me, too. I was always a slow study at the best of times, the strain became intolerable and humiliating, more humiliating even than this.

LOTTA: I refuse to consider this humiliating. I think we've earned this honestly, really I do.

MAY: Perhaps we have, Lotta, perhaps we have.

LOTTA: Bonita's left her bottle of whisky. Would you like a sip?

MAY: A very small one.

LOTTA (*going to the table and pouring out two drinks*): All right.

MAY (*ruminatively*): Lavinia Parsons. He must have been mad!

LOTTA (*handing her her drink*): She was prettier than you and prettier than me and a great deal younger than both of us.

MAY (*thoughtfully*): I must buy a bottle of whisky tomorrow in Maidenhead. What is really the best sort?

LOTTA: Oh, I don't know. There's Haig and Black and White—they're all much of a muchness unless one happens to be a connoisseur, and we're neither of us that.

MAY (*rising and holding up her glass*): Well, Lotta—we meet again.

LOTTA: Yes, May dear, we meet again. (*She also holds up her glass.*) Happy days!

MAY: Happy days!

They both drink and then stand quite still for a moment looking at each other. In their eyes there is a glint of tears.

CURTAIN.

Even though these "senior" ladies are in every sense waiting in the wings to be called onstage for that Final Exit, there are times when the far-distant past becomes present for a while. Someone presents them with champagne at Christmas—and what memories *that* triggers off . . .

BONITA (*meditatively*): There's always something glamorous about champagne, isn't there? I wonder why.

DEIRDRE: Because it's a devil's brew and very expensive.

BONITA: When did you first taste it, May, can you remember?

MAY: Certainly I can. It was at my brother's wedding in Wimbledon in 1898. I was a bridesmaid and it gave me hiccoughs.

ALMINA: When I was at the Gaiety with Millie James she used to have a magnum in her dressing room every night. That was in 1904.

MAY: Poor Millie. The results were only too apparent in 1905.

PERRY: When was your first go at it, Bonita?

BONITA: Before a dress rehearsal of *Aladdin* in Manchester when I was sixteen. The assistant stage manager brought some to the digs and we all got soused.

ESTELLE: What were you playing?

BONITA: The Spirit of the Lamp and I fell into the orchestra pit, lamp and all.

MAUDIE (*breaking into song—at the piano*):

> Champagne—Champagne—Champagne
> So sublime, so divine, so profane
> It fizzes and bubbles
> And banishes troubles
> Champagne—Champagne—Champagne!

BONITA: That's a common little lyric if ever I heard one.

MAUDIE: It's the waltz from *Miss Mouse*—Poor Dolly Drexell sang it at the end of the second act, she had a big headdress of ostrich feathers and they kept on getting into her mouth.

LOTTA: Play the other one, Maudie—the one I like—

MAUDIE: Oh dear—I can't remember much of it—wait a minute— (*She pauses for a second and then plays a few chords and begins to sing.*) "Won't you come and live in my house—Miss Mouse?"—Now you all have to repeat "Miss Mouse"—let's start again. "Won't you come and live in my house—Miss Mouse?"

ALL (*singing*): "Miss Mouse."
MAUDIE: "It's as neat as any apple pie house—Miss Mouse."
ALL (*singing*): "Miss Mouse."
MAUDIE (*singing*):

> I will give you honey from the bees
> Bread and milk and lovely bits of cheese
> Please please please please please please please
> Come and live in my house—

All together—
ALL (*singing*):

> "Come and live in my house."

MAUDIE (*singing*):

> "Come and live in my house—Miss Mouse!"

Everyone laughs and applauds.

—Now once more—all together.

She repeats the refrain and they all join in with a will.

LOTTA (*laughing*): That really is the most idiotic song I ever heard.
MAUDIE: Come on, Bonita—"Over the hill I'll find you."
BONITA: Good God, no—it's too long ago—I couldn't.
MAUDIE: We'll sing it with you—come on. (*She plays some introductory chords.*)
BONITA (*starting to sing, in a husky, uncertain voice*):

> Over the hill I'll find you
> There by the murmuring stream.

(*Speaking.*) Help me somebody—
MAUDIE (*prompting*): "And the birds in the woods—"
BONITA (*continuing*):

> And the birds in the woods behind you
> Will echo our secret dream.
> There in the twilight waiting
> Gentle, serene and still
> All the cares of the day
> Will have vanished away
> When I find you—over the hill.

Everybody applauds.

DEIRDRE: Sentimental poppycock.
MAY: The words are a little sugary but it's a very pretty tune.

Noël was particularly fond of period pastiche and used it frequently in early revues. In *Waiting in the Wings* the age of the ladies provided him with the opportunity to pay affectionate tribute to the songs from the music hall and operetta of his youth. Yes, they are "idiotic" and "sentimental poppycock," but they evoked a long-lost pace and grace of living and he still regretted their passing.

"Cheap music" remained for him extraordinarily potent to the very end.

The prospect of old age might not be exactly encouraging but, in one of Noël's favourite maxims, one must "rise above it." In each of the Seven Ages of Man there was satisfaction to be found. It was a matter of looking for it . . .

"LATER THAN SPRING"

Have no fears for future years
For sweet compensation you may find,
Make your bow
To the moment that is now
And always bear in mind:

Later than Spring
The warmth of Summer comes,
The charm of Autumn comes,
The leaves are gold.
Poets say
That the blossoms of May
Fade away
And die.
Yet, don't forget
That we met
When the sun was high.
Later than Spring
Words that were said before,
Tears that were shed before
Can be consoled.
Realize that it's wise to remember

Though Time is on the wing,
Songbirds still sing
Later than Spring.

—SAIL AWAY (1961)

As the 1960s began, he found "sweet compensation"—though neither of them might have put it quite that way—in discovering a new star: Elaine Stritch.

The last musical over which he was to have total control was *Sail Away*, and it began life on Broadway in 1961.

It was set on a cruise ship, and Mimi Paragon (Stritch) was the Cruise Hostess, who just happened to hate her job and shared a conviction Noël had reached over a lifetime of travelling—alone or in company—the seven seas . . .

"WHY DO THE WRONG PEOPLE TRAVEL?"

Travel they say improves the mind,
An irritating platitude
Which frankly, *entre nous,*

Is very far from true.
Personally I've yet to find
That longitude and latitude
Can educate those scores
Of monumental bores
Who travel in groups and herds and troupes
Of various breeds and sexes,
Till the whole world reels
To shouts and squeals
And the clicking of Rolleiflexes.

Why do the wrong people travel, travel, travel,
When the right people stay back home?
What compulsion compels them
And who the hell tells them
To drag their cans to Zanzibar
Instead of staying quietly in Omaha?
The Taj Mahal
And the Grand Canal
And the sunny French Riviera
Would be less oppressed
If the Middle West

Would settle for somewhere rather nearer.
Please do not think that I criticize or cavil
At a genuine urge to roam,
But why oh why do the wrong people travel
When the right people stay back home
And mind their business,
When the right people stay back home
With Cinerama,
When the right people stay back home,
I'm merely asking
Why the right people stay back home?

Just when you think romance is ripe
It rather sharply dawns on you
That each sweet serenade
Is for the Tourist Trade.
Any attractive native type
Who resolutely fawns on you
Will give as his address
American Express.
There isn't a rock
Between Bangkok
And the beaches of Hispaniola,
That does not recoil
From suntan oil
And the gurgle of Coca-Cola.

Why do the wrong people travel, travel, travel,
When the right people stay back home?
What explains this mass mania
To leave Pennsylvania
And clack around like flocks of geese,
Demanding dry martinis on the Isles of Greece?
In the smallest street
Where the gourmets meet
They invariably fetch up
And it's hard to make
Them accept a steak
That isn't served rare and smeared with ketchup.
Millions of tourists are churning up the gravel
While they gaze at St. Peter's dome,
But why oh why do the wrong people travel
When the right people stay back home

And eat hot doughnuts,
When the right people stay back home
With all those benefits,
When the right people stay back home?
I sometimes wonder
Why the right people stay back home!

Why do the wrong people travel, travel, travel,
When the right people stay back home?
What peculiar obsessions
Inspire those processions
Of families from Houston, Tex.,
With all those cameras around their necks?
They will take a train
Or an aeroplane
For an hour on the Costa Brava,
And they'll see Pompeii
On the only day
That it's up to its ass in molten lava.
It would take years to unravel—ravel—ravel
Every impulse that makes them roam
But why oh why do the wrong people travel
When the right people stay back home
With all that Kleenex,
When the right people stay back home
With all that lettuce,
When the right people stay back home
With all those Kennedys?
Won't someone tell me
Why the right
I say the right people stay back home?

—SAIL AWAY (1961)

Mimi decides that, as the cruise director, she had better keep at least one step ahead of her charges. They will soon be in Italy so, alone in her cabin, she studies a somewhat outdated Italian phrase book . . .

"USELESS USEFUL PHRASES"

When the Tower of Babel fell
It caused a lot of unnecessary Hell.
Personal "rapport"

Became a complicated bore
And a lot more difficult than it had been before.

When the Tower of Babel fell,
The Chinks and the Japs
And the Finns and Lapps
Were reduced to a helpless stammer,
And the ancient Greeks
Took at least six weeks
To learn their Latin grammar.
The general wheeze
Of the Portuguese
Filled the brains of the Danes
With horror,
And verbs, not lust
Caused the final bust
In Sodom and Gomorrah.

If it hadn't been for that
Bloody building falling flat
I would not have had to learn Italiano
And keep muttering "*Si, si*"
And "*Mi chiamano Mimi*"
Like an aging Metropolitan soprano!

I should not have had to look
At that ghastly little book
Till my brain becomes as soft as mayonnaise is,
Messrs. Hugo and Berlitz
Must have torn themselves to bits
Dreaming up so many useless useful phrases.

Pray tell me the time,
It is six,
It is seven,
It's half past eleven,
It's twenty to two,
I want thirteen stamps,
Does your child have convulsions?
Please bring me some rhubarb,
I need a shampoo,
How much is that hat?
I desire some red stockings,

My mother is married
These boots are too small,
My Aunt has a cold,
Shall we go to the opera?
This meat is disgusting,
Is this the town hall?

My cousin is deaf,
Kindly bring me a hatchet,
Pray pass me the pepper,
What pretty cretonne.
What time is the train?
It is late,
It is early,
It's running on schedule,
It's here
It has gone,
I've written six letters,
I've written no letters,
Pray fetch me a horse,
I have need of a groom,
This isn't my passport,
This isn't my hatbox,
Please show me the way
To Napoleon's Tomb.

The weather is cooler,
The weather is hotter,
Pray fasten my corsets,
Please bring me my cloak,
I've lost my umbrella,
I'm in a great hurry,
I'm going,
I'm staying,
D'you mind if I smoke?
This mutton is tough,
There's a mouse in my bedroom,
This egg is delicious,
This soup is too thick,
Please bring me a trout,
What an excellent pudding,
Pray hand me my gloves,
I'm going to be sick!

Sail Away made Elaine Stritch a star—if a sometimes wandering one—and Noël occasionally felt the need to correct her course . . .

Darling Stritchie,
I hope that you are well; that your cold is better; that you are singing divinely; that you are putting on weight; that you are not belting too much; that your skin is clear and free from spots and other blemishes; that you are delivering my brilliant material to the public in the manner in which it *should* be delivered; that you are not making too many Goddamned suggestions; that your breath is relatively free from the sinful taint of alcohol; that you are going regularly to confession and everywhere else that is necessary to go regularly. I also hope that you are not encouraging those dear little doggies to behave in such a fashion on the stage that they bring disrepute to the fair name of Equity and add fuel to the already prevalent suspicion that our gallant little company is not, by and large, entirely normal. I also hope that you are not constantly taking those silly Walter Kerrs and Agnes B. de Mille to the Pavillon for lunch every day. They only exhaust you and drain your energy and, however much you want to keep in with them, you must remember that your first duty is to me and the Catholic church—in that order.
I remain yours sincerely with mad hot kisses.

•

Although Noël was spending little time in England at this point, its manners and *mores* at home and abroad never ceased to fascinate him.
"The British Empire was a great and wonderful social, economic and even spiritual experience and all the parlour pinks and eager, ill-informed intellectuals cannot convince me to the contrary."
Even when the Empire was in full retreat, he managed to conserve a fictional corner of it.
The island of Samolo is one of the last British possessions in the South Seas. Noël created it in the 1930s, revisited it in *Pacific 1860* and then—in 1960—made it the setting for his only published novel, *Pomp and Circumstance.* By this time it was showing distinct similarities with his beloved Jamaica.
"My novel is so light," he wrote to his American publishers, "that you will have difficulty capturing it between hard covers."
"It is gay and irreverent and with little sentiment and *no* significance . . . I know that my greatest gift is comedy and this gives me wonderful opportunities for all sorts of irrelevancies, because my heroine has a light mind and through her I can have a lot of fun with all the colonial types."

Noël's cover design for his only published novel

The story is narrated by Griselda ("Grizel"), the wife of a local planter and an old friend of Lady Sandra Shotter, the Governor's wife.

A Royal Visit to the island has been scheduled. Naturally, those on the island who consider themselves part of the elite—which is *everyone*—are determined to take part in a suitably magnificent event in honour of their visitors.

And, naturally, there must be a committee meeting to decide who does what . . .

•

POMP AND CIRCUMSTANCE

The meeting of the SADS [Samolan Amateur Dramatic Society] took place in the back room of the Art Institute. I arrived a few minutes late, having had the usual difficulty of finding somewhere to park the car. Everybody was standing about gossiping, and a long table was impressively set out with pads and pencils and individual ashtrays. I greeted Buddha and Dusty and Cuckoo Honey, who was wearing a tiny hat with a knob on the top, like the lid of a jar of preserved ginger. Alma Peacock, impressive in a flowing print with an eye-searing pattern of white pineapples on a pink background, took the chair and we all arranged ourselves around the table. Alma is an admirable character in many respects. She is kindly, resolute, enthusiastic, and industrious. Under her ebullient leadership the SADS, which she started from scratch many years ago, has certainly achieved some creditable if occasionally overambitious productions. There is, however, something about her personality, a certain incongruous schoolgirlishness, which always makes me want to laugh whenever I look at her. On the other hand Ivy Poland, who runs a dancing school in Queen Street and has achieved local fame with her "Ivy Poland Dancers," without whose ardent modern posturing no annual pantomime is complete, retains no endearing aura of long-ago School Theatrics. She is professional to the core, sharp as a needle, and is reputed, when unduly irritated, to fly into ungovernable rages. Her mouth droops a trifle at the corners, and it is not difficult to envisage her whacking the shins of the I. P. Dancers with a cane when their jetés and coupés are clumsily executed. It is difficult however, looking at her now, a small grey woman in her middle forties, to imagine her in her far-off heyday as a ballroom dancer floating glamorously into the Palm Court of the Grand Hotel, Folkestone, on the arm of some agile and suitably betailed male partner, and more difficult still to picture her in even earlier years flitting through the enchanted forest of "Where the Rainbow Ends" as a will-o'-the-wisp. Nevertheless that, we are led to believe, is her authentic background and it would ill become any of us in our distant colonial isolation to question it. It is scarcely necessary to add that there exists between her and Alma a state of decently veiled hostility which only on very rare occasions has been permitted to blaze into open warfare. The rest of the committee, apart from Buddha, Dusty, Cuckoo, and myself, consists of Peter Glades and Esmond Templar, who landed hand in hand on the island in 1949 and set up an antiques shop, Michael Tremlett, Brinsley Martin, and Keela Alioa. Brinsley Martin is our main character actor and is chiefly remarkable for his prowess at elaborate makeup. He has seldom appeared in any production, wigged, padded, lined, and crepe-haired, without a spontaneous round of applause at his first entrance. On one or two occasions, however, his passion for visual characterization has led to disaster as on the famous night when he was playing the inquisitor to Letty Togstone's St. Joan and his entire nose fell with a soft thud into her outstretched hands. Michael Tremlett, although lacking any outstanding histrionic ability, is an efficient stage manager; Peter Glades and Esmond Templar are enthusiastic but occasionally petulant artistic supervisors, and Keela Alioa, our star turn as an actor, is on the committee in an honorary capacity as representative of Samolan interests. He is in his mid-twenties and extremely handsome, and his performance of *Hamlet* in modern dress was the talk of the island. It was an all-Samolan production, and as their idea of modern dress consisted mostly of brilliantly coloured sarongs the visual effect was quite enchanting.

When we were all seated and the buzz of conversation and the scraping of chairs had died down, Alma whacked the table with a little hammer and embarked on a lengthy speech which glowed with royalist enthusiasm and was peppered with splendid phrases such as "Allegiance to the Crown" and "Our Imperial Visitors" and "Showing the Flag," etc. When she had finished and sat down amid a few grunts of assent and muttered "hear hears" everyone began talking at once until she had to whack the table again for silence.

There is something about well-intentioned, amateur committee meetings that induces in me a feeling of claustrophobia, I feel trapped and hopeless and quite incapable of constructive thought or concentration, and this one was no exception to the rule. It droned on for two solid hours, during which time I drew hideous faces on the piece of paper in front of me . . . Hot sunlight filtered through the slats of the venetian blind, and outside in the street the noise of gears changing and dogs barking and klaxons hooting made it difficult at moments to catch what anyone was saying, and everyone, as usual, was saying a great deal. It was finally decided after many impracticable suggestions had been put forward and discarded that an ordinary theatrical production in the local Playhouse would be inadequate and that what was needed was something on a much larger scale. At this point Cuckoo Honey sprang to her feet and delivered a stirring eulogy of a military tattoo she had seen in Darjeeling when she was a little girl—"It really was magnificent," she said, her nose growing quite pink with remembered emotion. "The cavalry came charging through a gap in the hills and all the people who had been besieged in a fort for weeks cheered and cried and then the fort went up in flames and everyone sang 'Abide With Me.' "

"A curious moment to choose," said Buddha in a loud whisper, but Cuckoo ignored this and went on. "What I really mean is," she said, "that it made a tremendous impression on the natives, and I do honestly think that we should try to do something on those lines. After all we *are* a British colony and we have got the Royal Shropshires."

"We have also got several gaps in the hills," said Dusty, "but I still don't think a military tattoo is quite the answer."

"Speaking as the only 'native' present," said Keela with gentle acidity, "I cannot feel that my brother Samolans at this present time would be so easily impressed by sudden chargings and flames and a great display of British militancy. It would puzzle them, and when Samolans are puzzled they laugh."

"It was only an idea." Cuckoo sat down rather crossly.

"What about a lovely medieval pageant?" suggested Esmond Templar. "With the Knights of the Round Table and everybody in armour and wimples and that sort of thing."

"I should think that would puzzle the Samolans into hysterics," said Dusty.

Alma rose to her feet authoritatively. "Our main object," she said sternly, "is not only to entertain the inhabitants of our island but to give pleasure to our royal visitors."

"Hear hear," murmured Peter Glades and giggled. Alma shot him a disapproving look and continued, "I have, as you know, given this matter a lot of thought and I am aware that we have very little time at our disposal, but I am convinced that what we really should do is to present Her Majesty with something that she could see nowhere else, something indigenous to our island and entirely Samolan. Ivy is in complete agreement with me over this . . ." She smiled at Ivy Poland, who nodded austerely. "We discussed it yesterday after the Bleekers' cocktail party, and as the idea was originally hers I now take pleasure in asking her to explain it to the committee." Alma sat down and there was a slight pause while Ivy blew her nose delicately and rose to her feet.

"The idea is this," she said modestly. "A historical water pageant." She paused, unfortunately long enough to allow Buddha to mutter "Good God!" and then went on. "We thought of telling the story of the island beginning with the legend of FumFumBolo in which my girls could do a ballet as water sprites. Then the landing of Captain Cobb and the missionaries and so on right up to the present day. We also"—she smiled encouragingly at Cuckoo—"thought of enlisting the aid of the Royal Shropshires, in fact I have already telephoned Colonel Shelton warning him that we might call on him to help us. They are a fine body of men and would do splendidly for pirates in the earlier scenes . . ."

"Where on earth do you propose to do all this?" interrupted Buddha.

"Cobb's Cove," replied Ivy triumphantly. "It would make an ideal setting. We have it all planned in our minds. We could have grandstands built around the semicircular beach and the two headlands would provide wonderful wings for entrances and exits. The Samolan Electrical Company and the Royal Shropshires between them could organize the floodlighting. We also propose to ask Kerry Stirling to write the libretto, probably in blank verse, and persuade dear Inky Blumenthal to compose a score based on traditional Samolan folk music—you all know how brilliant he is at that sort of thing—and we thought, as a grand finale, that the church choir, which we've got to use anyway, could come sailing in on a barge singing, while the Royal Shropshires, having changed back into their uniforms, would march down that path from behind the Turlings' bungalow and assemble on the beach and do a sort of Trooping of the Colours!" She paused, smiling expectantly, and then rather abruptly sat down. There was silence for a moment or two, which was broken by Esmond Templar clapping his hands and crying enthusiastically that it was a marvelous idea.

"It's not 'Trooping *of* the *Colours,*'" said Buddha. "It's Trooping the Colour.'"

"I remember being taken to see it for the first time when I was a tiny little girl," said Cuckoo. "Daddy had six months' leave and we stayed at the Hyde Park Hotel and I cried my eyes out!"

"The Hyde Park Hotel can be depressing," murmured Dusty.

"Come, come," cried Alma firmly, "to our muttons!"

From then on everyone began talking at once and the noise was deafening.

·

Eventually, inevitably, the great day arrives—the dress rehearsal.

Presently, when the excitement had died down a little, the band of the Royal Shropshires, which was huddled, a trifle insecurely, I thought, on a wooden rostrum under an umbrella of wild almond trees, began to tune up with little irrelevant trills and glissandi on the trumpets and woodwinds and intermittent bangings on the drums. Ever since I was taken to my first pantomime at the age of nine this particular sound has enchanted me. It evokes nostalgic memories of warmth and plush and gold; of squeezing sixpences into slots to release tiny pairs of opera glasses; of sudden, thrilling darkness followed by footlights glowing on red velvet curtains; of feverish anticipation, excited wriggling, and chocolates in silver paper. I have never outgrown this special joy, although the present-day theatres of our welfare state with either no music at all or a panatrope scratching away in an empty orchestra pit concealed by dusty greenery have dampened it considerably and provide little prelude to glamour. However, I managed to recapture a small whiff of it sitting there looking out over the dark sea with the band tuning up and the lights glimmering in the trees.

The audience reseated themselves on their chairs and benches amid a babble of conversation which was drowned out by the band embarking briskly on a selection from *The Pirates of Penzance.*

"The dear Royal Shropshires," said Sandra. "They're always right up-to-the-minute, aren't they?"

"Inky Blumenthal's overture isn't orchestrated yet," I said, leaning forward. "The only alternatives to this were *The Indian Love Lyrics, The Gondoliers,* and *William Tell.*"

"We shall probably get the lot before the evening's over." Sandra produced her glasses from her bag and studied the programme. "I'm afraid it's going to be a long job."

At the end of the overture the lights in the trees went out all except one which stayed on, resolutely pinpointing Mrs. Innes-Glendower, who was sitting in the front row wearing a multicoloured Chinese coat and a glittering Spanish comb embedded in her bright blue hair. She fidgeted unhappily in the glare and shaded her eyes with her hand. There were some muffled shouts, and Alma's voice rang out authoritatively from the darkness. "If it won't go out by itself somebody must climb up and *turn* it out!" There was a short pause and the sound of further argument until a small boy dashed out onto the sand, shinnied up the tree like a monkey, and wrestled valiantly with the lamp. He managed to shift it slowly round so that it illuminated each of the occupants of the front row in turn, including old Sir Albert, who shrank back in his seat and placed a handkerchief over his head. Finally the poor boy, obviously in the grip of mounting panic, shook the lamp violently with the result that it broke away from its moorings and fell with a dull thud onto the beach where it was pounced upon by two policemen who staggered away with it into the shadows. The little boy slid down the tree to vociferous applause and the band struck up the opening bars of Inky Blumenthal's water music.

While this was going on, Captain Gedge and Lieutenant Proctor of the Royal Shropshires, both of whom had had previous experience of Military Tattoos at Aldershot, switched on two searchlights from each side of the cove and Keela Alioa was discovered standing facing the sea with his back to us with his arms outstretched to the stars. The small waves were breaking over his feet and he turned slowly, with exquisite grace, and walked out of the sea towards us. He was wearing a short silver tunic, and in the bright light his dark skin shone like polished mahogany. He began to speak, but his first words were lost in a spontaneous burst of applause. We were all well used to Keela's good looks, but the picture of this handsome young Samolan standing there against the night was suddenly breathtaking.

"Well," said Sandra, clapping vigorously. "It's started with a nice sexy bang at any rate, hasn't it?"

Keela certainly spoke the prologue resonantly and well but alas, the lines themselves fell a good way below his rendering of them. Kerry Stirling, although he was Samolo's literary lion and had written a number of successful novels reeking with local atmosphere, obviously had no more than a nodding acquaintance with the poetic muse. His verse, hovering uneasily between Scott, Macaulay, and Ella Wheeler Wilcox, was at its best merely serviceable and at its worst almost excruciatingly banal. There was a great deal of heavy-handed allegory interspersed with flowery rhyming couplets such as:

> Long long ago in Time's primeval dawn
> This island paradise, in fire, was born

And fire and water, striving hand in hand
Wrought, on this desolate, small coral strand
Strange music where, as yet, no birds had sung
And whilst the ancient universe, still young,
Gazed down upon a sea of azure blue
Amazed to see a miracle come true,
Far out, beyond the breakers' thundrous boom,
Other small islets born of Neptune's womb
Rose up like jewels from the deeps below
Thus to create our archipelago.

"Fancy Neptune having a womb!" whispered Sandra. "I always saw him as rather a hearty type."

When the prologue ended, Keela, with his arms still raised in a gesture of invocation, turned slowly, walked into the sea, and with a graceful dive disappeared from view. The lights went out, and in a silence after the applause had died away we distinctly heard Alma's voice say "Now!" in a piercing whisper. There was the sound of whispering and scuffling in the darkness; the lights came on again, and from down the gangways on each side of the grandstand Ivy Poland's sprites bounded onto the beach where they arranged themselves, a little breathlessly, into a stylized tableau. They were dressed in diaphanous sea-green chiffon, long flowing green wigs to represent seaweed, and necklaces of coral-pink shells. They held the tableau gallantly for a long time, occasionally shooting anxious glances at the band, which remained discouragingly mute. Finally, after some audible hissing in the direction of the bandstand, the music began and they started their dance. It was a pretty enough dance although not startlingly original and they executed it charmingly, but it didn't really come to life until Tauhua Tali suddenly appeared from the outer darkness glittering like a dragonfly in peacock blue and did a quite enchanting pas de deux partnered by Kokoano, Juanita's head beach boy, who wore nothing but gilded bathing trunks and looked like a dusky Greek god who had been touched up by Gauguin. This brought forth storms of applause and they were recalled over and over again.

One of the principal difficulties in the original planning of the pageant was the almost monotonous tranquillity of Samolan history. Whereas other Pacific islands had had their full quota of wars, invasions, human sacrifices, and bloodshed, the Samolan archipelago had basked peacefully and cheerfully in its eternal sunshine for centuries. True, there had been a gentle whisper of incipient revolution in 1791 when it had been considered advisable to ask King Kopalalua III to abdicate, but this had been swiftly hushed by the willing cooperation of Kopalalua himself, who after a feast lasting for three days and nights, made a public announcement to his subjects. This announcement stated candidly and with dignity that, as he found no personal satisfaction in intercourse with the opposite sex and could therefore contribute little to the future of the dynasty, he thought it wiser to retire with his private entourage to the island of Tunaike and leave the ruling of Samolo to his nephew, young Prince Kefumalani, who, although still in his teens, had already proved that his procreative capabilities were beyond question. Esmond Templar and Peter Glades had enthusiastically voted that this historical incident should be included in the pageant but had been sharply overruled by the rest of the committee.

As it was, the pageant had been divided into two parts, the first of which dealt mainly with fantasy and the ancient legends, including the famous eruption of FumFumBolo. This, although technically complicated, went smoothly and was most effective. Tauhua Tali and Kokoano played FumFum the goddess of fire and Bolo the god of water, respectively. An enormous raft with the volcano built onto it was towed, under cover of darkness, from behind the left headland and, when suddenly illuminated by searchlights, erupted entirely satisfactorily. When the applause for this had died away the lights were swivelled back onto the beach again and the Royal Shropshires, dressed picturesquely as pirates, came whooping and shrieking down the two side gangways and engaged each other in a tremendous battle with pikes and cutlasses, eventually, as the lights faded, leaving many of each other for dead. This was enjoyed, not only by the audience, but very much indeed by the Royal Shropshires.

The finale of the first half was the historic landing of Captain Evangelus Cobb with his cargo of missionaries and their reception on the beach by King Kefumalani and his retinue. It had originally been intended to show the actual shipwreck with *The Good Samaritan* breaking up on the rocks. But this idea had been abandoned when Peter Glades had pointed out that for a ship to break up on rocks in perfectly calm water would not only be expensive and difficult to do, but would inevitably cast a slur on the heroic Captain Cobb's skill as a navigator. It had therefore been decided that the wreck must be *presumed* to have taken place out of sight behind the headland and that the survivors, battered and exhausted by a *presumed* tempest, should appear out of the darkness in one of the ship's boats.

All this went according to plan except that poor Letty Togstone, who had made a striking success last season as Mrs. Alving in *Ghosts,* was stricken down by malignant fate in what should have been her moment of triumph. As Mrs. Brunstock, the chief evangelist missionary, she had to spring onto the prow of the boat when it was only a few yards from shore, clad in a long white shift with a bloodstained bandage around her head, and declaim exultantly with arms outstretched:

Land—Land! The Blessed Land at last.
The storm is over and the tempest past.
Thanks be to Thee, dear Lord, our faith sufficed
To carry to these isles the Word of Christ!

This dramatic moment had been meticulously directed by Alma Peacock and, at the last few rehearsals with the band playing "Nearer My God to Thee" in the minor and Letty Togstone giving the full force of her voice, many onlookers, including Madame Alice and the Fumbasi brothers, had been reduced to tears. Tonight however, owing to nerves, perhaps, she miscalculated her leap onto the prow and teetered dangerously on the edge. Michael Tremlett, who was navigating the boat slowly from the stern with a muffled outboard motor, perceiving poor Letty's plight, suddenly, in a misguided effort to help, slammed the engine into reverse, whereupon she tumbled head foremost into the sea. Even then the situation might have been saved if she hadn't unfortunately repeated the word "Christ!" as she struck the water.

There was a horrified gasp from the audience and then, as she surfaced, an uncontrollable roar of laughter. She disregarded this with magnificent presence of mind, waded ashore, and sank gracefully at the feet of King Kefumalani, who, bending forward to lift her up, struck her sharply on the head as he did so. With a loud cry of pain she fell back onto the sand again and from that moment on the scene went to pieces. Michael Tremlett, unnerved by his previous error, switched the engine to full speed ahead and the boat shot forward and grounded on the beach with such force that Captain Cobb and the missionaries fell into a heap. The audience's laughter rose to a hysterical pitch, the band played a crashing chord, and all the lights went out. Unhappily they came on again a moment or two later disclosing the missionaries clambering out of the boat, Letty Togstone in floods of tears, and Alma Peacock in a gold lamé dress, up to her knees in water, gesticulating furiously at Michael Tremlett.

After this debacle there was a twenty minutes' interval during which we retired to the anteroom behind the royal box.

•

Presently the lights flickered on and off, there was a long roll of drums from the band, and we all returned to our seats.

"Hold on to your hats," said Sandra. "We're off again."

The lights dimmed and went out and suddenly, from the two headlands, the little bay was brilliantly illuminated. In the middle of it, a few yards from shore, was moored the raft that earlier on had held the erupting volcano. It now held the Ladies' Church Choir in full strength. The singers were arranged in three tiers and stood immobile, staring fixedly at their leader, Mrs. Lamont, who, vast in black satin, was standing, baton raised, in a small flat-bottomed dinghy just below their eye line. The dinghy was kept in position by two Samolan boys, one in the bow and one in the stern, each clasping an oar.

Owing to a slight miscalculation the Royal Shropshires hadn't quite finished playing the *William Tell* "Overture" when the lights came on. Realizing this, the bandleader, Sergeant Major Brocklehurst, increased the tempo violently, but there was still an appreciable time lag before the music crashed to an untidy conclusion, during which Mrs. Lamont shot baleful looks over her shoulder at the bandstand.

To Mrs. Lamont the Ladies' Church Choir was the be-all and end-all of existence, the sum total of her dreams and the golden apple of her eye. She rehearsed it interminably year in year out; fought tigerishly in defense of its rights and monotonously insisted on its appearance at any and every public function where it could conceivably be appropriate. For this occasion Alma Peacock had suggested that the choir's routine costumes of plain white Mother Hubbards banded with red, blue, and violet ribbons to distinguish the sopranos, mezzos, and contraltos, should be abandoned in favour of native dress. But Mrs. Lamont, deaf to all entreaty, had stood firm. Vainly had Alma and Ivy pleaded that as the scene represented the first burgeoning of Christianity on the island which took place early in the nineteenth century, the coloured sarongs and gay brassieres of the period would not only be effective but a great deal more accurate from the point of view of atmosphere, but Mrs. Lamont had remained obdurate. The Ladies' Church Choir was primarily a religious body, she argued, and as such could not be expected to jettison the insignia by which it was so justly famed and impair its high dignity by romping about in the wanton apparel of a pagan age. Finally, after much heated discussion and a lot of acrimonious correspondence, Alma and Ivy were forced to give in and Mrs. Lamont won the day. So here they were, those serried ranks of white-covered bosoms and exalted brown faces, looking as they had always looked and standing as they had always stood, except that on this occasion a slightly ambulant raft had been substituted for the more familiar terra firma of the Town Hall.

At the long-awaited end of the overture there was a short pause, Mrs. Lamont raised her baton still higher, Sandra gave an audible groan, and the Ladies' Church Choir burst forth.

The oratorio, "Blessed the Hearts That Suddenly See," was, in Inky Blumenthal's opinion at least, the high spot of his musical score. He had worked over it laboriously for weeks, and poor Kerry Stirling had been driven to the verge of a nervous breakdown by having to rewrite the verses no less than eleven times. Not that he need have bothered, because the Ladies' Church Choir in all their years of triumph had never been known to enunciate a single word that was even remotely comprehensible. However, the sounds they made were generally considered to be of high quality, and when they all opened their mouths together and let fly, as they were required to do in the opening bars of Inky's opus, the impact was considerable.

There was no escaping the fact that "Blessed the Hearts That Suddenly See," musically speaking, was a pretentious hash-up of Handel, Elgar, and Verdi with, alas, none of the melodic quality of any of them. It was also far far too long. We sat there battered into a state of hypnotic resignation watching glumly the rows of bosoms rising and falling, the numberless mouths opening and shutting, and Mrs. Lamont flailing the air with her arms and rocking the dinghy dangerously with her feet. After a while I closed my eyes and tried to shut my ears and my mind to what was going on and concentrate on something entirely different. Suddenly, however, I became conscious of an extra sound over and above the incessant booming and trilling. A queer, metallic whining noise that seemed to be growing in volume. I opened my eyes again and saw that the raft was rocking alarmingly. At this moment, with a shriek and a roar, the storm struck. There were a few screams from the audience and a panic-stricken rush for the exits. The skies opened and a curtain of rain, shining like glass spears in the searchlights, crashed down onto the sea obliterating completely the raft, the choir, Mrs. Lamont, and even the palm trees a few feet away from us. We all instinctively rose from our seats and crowded up into the back of the grandstand to get as much cover as we could, but it was of little avail because the wind was blowing straight into the cove and within a few seconds we were all drenched to the bone.

"This," said Sandra through chattering teeth, "comes under the heading of 'An Act of God,' and I must say I'm on His side."

There we stood, huddled into a sodden little group waiting for the first violence of the storm to die down. After what seemed an age there was indeed a slight lull. The force of the wind lessened and the density of the rain thinned out.

"Oh Lord!" cried Sandra. "Look at the church choir!"

We all looked, and the sight that met our eyes will be emblazoned on my memory forever and a day. On the first impact of the storm the raft had broken loose from its moorings and begun to drift away towards the open sea. At the same moment, apparently, the dinghy had capsized and was now floating upside down with Mrs. Lamont lying across it like a large black seal supported on each side by the two fisherboys. The choir itself, Samolan-born and -bred from the biggest contralto to the smallest soprano and therefore as at home in the water as on dry land, appeared, at the same moment to arrive at a unanimous decision. In almost perfect unison they tore off their coloured ribbons, whipped their white robes over their heads, and in varying states of nudity dived into the turbulent waves and struck out firmly for the shore. At this moment the wind struck again with a renewed shriek, and a fresh deluge of rain blotted the scene from view.

"If only they'd done that in the first place," said Sandra, "it would have brought the house down."

•

While it was relatively easy to ensure that the sun never set on a fragment of empire of your own invention, the real situation at home struck a rather different note.

In 1963 he attended the annual Battle of Britain Dinner in New York and wrote in his diary . . .

What was it that I so minded about twenty-three years ago? An ideal? An abstract patriotism? What? . . . I wanted suddenly to stand up and shout . . . "Let's face the truth. The England we knew and loved was betrayed at Munich, revived for one short year in 1940 and was supreme in adversity, and now no longer exists." That last great war was our valediction. It will never happen again.

"THE BATTLE OF BRITAIN DINNER, NEW YORK, 1963"

I have been to the Battle of Britain dinner.
Held at the Hotel Shelbourne on Thirty-seventh Street
    and Lexington
And there they were, a few survivors
Of that long-dead victory
And there they were too, the non-survivors
Somewhere in the air above us,
Or at any rate in our hearts
The young men who died, humorously, gaily, making
    jokes
Until the moment when swift blazing death annihilated
    them.
And there we were, raising our glasses to them
Drinking to their intolerable gallantry
And trying to make believe that their sacrifice

Was worthwhile
Perhaps it was worthwhile for them, but not for us.
They flew out of life triumphant, leaving us to see
The ideal that they died for humiliated and betrayed
Even more than it had been betrayed at Munich
To those conceited, foolish, frightened old men.
Today in our country it is the young men who are
    frightened
They write shrill plays about defeat and are hailed
                        as progressive
They disdain our great heritage. They have been labeled
                        by their dull
Facile contemporaries as "Angry Young Men"
But they are not angry, merely scared and ignorant,
Many of them are not even English
But humourless refugees from alien lands
Seeking protection in our English sanity
And spitting on the valiant centuries
That made the sanity possible.
These clever ones, these terrified young men
Who so fear extinction and the atom bomb
Have little in common with the men we were
    remembering tonight.
Whatever fears they had remained unspoken. They flew
    daily and nightly into the sky
Heavily outnumbered by the enemy and saved us for
                        one valedictory year
Gave us one last great chance
To prove to a bemused and muddled world
Our basic quality. All that was done.
The year was lived alone and then
Conveniently forgotten and dismissed
Except for just one night in each long year.
We raised our glasses sentimentally
An Air Vice-Marshal made a brief, appropriate speech
And then we chatted a little, oppressed by anticlimax
And finally said good night and went our ways.

·

I continue to tell foreigners how great we are. Before I die, I would like once again to be able to believe this myself.

—SUNDAY EXPRESS (1965)

In 1965 Noël decided to fluff out his "bedraggled wings" (as he put it) and write a play in which he would make his farewell appearance on the stage—first in London, then in New York.

In fact, *Suite in Three Keys* turned out to be a trilogy of one full-length and two one-act plays: "A Song at Twilight," "Shadows of the Evening" and "Come Into the Garden, Maude."

"A Song at Twilight" was particularly significant, since it was to be the only time he touched upon the subject of homosexuality in his work. It was generally known, of course, that he himself was homosexual, but as his friend Rebecca West said of him, "He was a very dignified man . . . There was an impeccable dignity in his sexual life which was reticent but untainted by pretence."

What gave him the idea was an incident described by Lord David Cecil in his biography of Max Beerbohm. Beerbohm was visited in extreme old age in his fastness in Rapallo by a former lover, the actress Constance Collier. The actual incident was more humorous than acutely embarrassing but, Noël admitted, "my play is more sinister, and there is Maugham in it as well as Max."

In Noël's early career as a playwright, Somerset Maugham had been a role model and friend, but the years had taken their toll and by the time Maugham died in 1965, the affection had soured. Maugham to Noël was "that scaly old crocodile."

All three plays take place in a luxury hotel in Lausanne, Switzerland. In "A Song at Twilight," Noël plays Sir Hugo Latymer, a writer who spends three months of every year there with his wife and former secretary, Hilde. He is visited by Carlotta Gray, a failing actress, who was once his mistress.

SUITE IN THREE KEYS (1966)

"A SONG AT TWILIGHT"

CAST

HILDE LATYMER	IRENE WORTH
HUGO LATYMER	NOËL COWARD
CARLOTTA GRAY	LILLI PALMER

DIRECTED BY VIVIAN MATALON
QUEEN'S THEATRE, LONDON, APRIL 14, 1966

CARLOTTA GRAY comes into the room. She is an attractive woman who at first glance would appear to be in her late forties or early fifties. She is

"A Song at Twilight," from *Suite in Three Keys,* 1966. Hugo Latymer (Noël), a distinguished writer—a combination of Max Beerbohm and Somerset Maugham—is visited by a former mistress, Carlotta Gray (Lilli Palmer).

heavily made up and her hair is expertly tinted. She is wearing expensive costume jewellery, perhaps a little too much of it. Her dinner dress is simple and well cut and she carries a light coat over her arm.

CARLOTTA goes to the box, takes a cigarette and lights it.

HUGO comes out of the bedroom. He is wearing an emerald-green velvet smoking jacket over dark trousers. He has a cream silk shirt, a black tie and his slippers are monogrammed in gold.

CARLOTTA rises and looks at him for a moment. Then she goes to him.

CARLOTTA: Hugo! What a strange moment this is, isn't it? I had planned so many things to say and now they've gone clean out of my head. Do we embrace?

HUGO (*with a slightly self-conscious smile*): Why not? (*He kisses her formally on both cheeks.*)

CARLOTTA (*drawing away*): How well you look! Slim as ever and so distinguished. White hair definitely becomes you.

HUGO (*with splendid chivalry*): The years seem to have forgotten you, Carlotta.

CARLOTTA: Oh no my dear. It isn't that they have forgotten me, it's that I have remembered them and taken the right precautions.

CARLOTTA strolls over to the window.

CARLOTTA: How lovely it is with the lights glittering in the distance. I went over to Evian the other evening on the little steamer and won nearly a thousand francs.

HUGO (*slightly shocked*): Can you afford to play so high?

CARLOTTA: Oh yes, I have a certain amount put by. I also still get alimony from my last husband.

HUGO: Have you had many others?

CARLOTTA: Two before this one. They both died. One in an air crash and the other in the war.

HUGO: Did you love them?

CARLOTTA: Oh yes. I shouldn't have married them if I hadn't.

HUGO: Have you any children?

CARLOTTA: Yes. I had a son by my second husband. He's twenty-four now and very attractive. You'd love him. He's an entomologist.

HUGO: I don't believe I've ever met an entomologist. That's insects, isn't it?

CARLOTTA: Yes. There's a great deal more in insects than meets the eye.

HUGO: I'm sure there is. Personally I've never felt particularly drawn to them.

CARLOTTA: I expect you thought that the bombardier beetle shoots compressed air from its intestines, whereas in actual fact it is highly explosive rocket fuel which it produces in two of its glands.

HUGO: I must admit that has been baffling me for some time.

CARLOTTA: And grasshoppers! You must like grasshoppers!

HUGO: I'm sorry to disappoint you, but I don't.

CARLOTTA: They converse by rubbing their back legs together.

HUGO: I'm beginning to wish we did.

CARLOTTA: Am I to drink alone?

HUGO: Too much alcohol is bad for me.

CARLOTTA: Too much alcohol is bad for everyone. Just pour yourself a teeny weeny one to keep me company.

HUGO: Really, Carlotta, you're too absurd.

CARLOTTA: She's nice, your wife. I like her.

HUGO: I'm so glad.

CARLOTTA: I don't think you quite did her justice in your book. But then, you weren't very nice about anybody in your book, were you?

HUGO: You were under no obligation to read it.

CARLOTTA: There was no warning on the cover. You take a fairly jaundiced view of your fellow creatures, don't you, on the whole?

HUGO: Perhaps. I prefer to see people as they are rather than as more sentimental minds would wish them to be. However, I am a commentator, not a moralist. I state no preferences.

CARLOTTA: Admirable!

HUGO: I would hate you to imagine that I am unaware of the mocking expression in your eye.

CARLOTTA (*with a smile*): Don't worry. I would never suspect you of missing a trick. Except perhaps the most important one of all.

HUGO: And what might that be?

CARLOTTA: The knack of discovering the best in people's characters instead of the worst.

HUGO: Without wishing to undermine your radiant self-confidence I must break it to you that that has been said often before. Usually by ardent lady journalists.

CARLOTTA: "One, two! One, two! And through and through. The vorpal blade went snicker-snack."

HUGO: My dear Carlotta. I had no idea you had such a thorough grounding in the classics. You were virtually illiterate when we first met.

CARLOTTA (*laughing*): It was you who set my stumbling feet upon the path of literature, Hugo. It was you who opened my eyes to many wonders.

HUGO: Don't talk such nonsense.

CARLOTTA: You worked assiduously on my virgin mind. And now I come to think of it you didn't do so badly with my virgin body.

HUGO (*turning away*): Please don't talk like that, Carlotta. I find it distasteful.

CARLOTTA (*gently*): Try not to be so easily cross with me. It's almost too reminiscent. You always told me I was vulgar. According to your lights that is. But your lights are so bright and highly placed that they bring out the bags under my eyes and the guttersnipe in my character. They always did and they always will. There's really nothing I can do about it, except perhaps go away. Would you like me to go away, now, this very minute? I promise I will if you truly want me to. You don't even have to answer. A valedictory little nod will be enough.

HUGO: Of course I don't want you to go away. With all my faults and in spite of my "jaundiced" view of my fellow creatures, I am seldom discourteous.

CARLOTTA: I would like it to be something warmer than your courtesy that wishes me to stay.

HUGO: I fear I can offer you little more at the moment, Carlotta, except perhaps curiosity, which is even less complimentary. I have reached a stage in life when sudden surprises stimulate me less agreeably than they might have done in my earlier years. I am what is called "set in my ways" which at my age is not entirely to be wondered at.

CARLOTTA: It implies resignation.

HUGO: Resignation has much to recommend it. Dignity for one thing, a quality, alas, that is fast disappearing from our world.

CARLOTTA: I think I know what you're up to.

HUGO (*still secure on Olympus*): I am open to any suggestions.

CARLOTTA: You are remodelling your public image. The witty, cynical author of so many Best Sellers is making way for the Grand Old Man of Letters.

HUGO: Supposing your surmise to be accurate, do you consider such a transition reprehensible?

CARLOTTA: Of course not, if the process is inevitable and necessary. But aren't you jumping the gun a little?

HUGO (*patiently*): No, Carlotta. I am not jumping the gun, or grasping Time by the forelock, or rushing my fences.

CARLOTTA: You must be prepared for a few clichés if you invite retired actresses to dinner.

HUGO (*ignoring her interruption*): I am merely accepting, without undue dismay, the fact of my own mortality. I am an old man and *I* at least have the sense to realise it.

CARLOTTA: Don't be waspish, my dear. Just as we are getting along so nicely. At least you can congratulate yourself, on having had a fabulously successful career. How wonderful to have been able to entertain and amuse so many millions of people for such a long time. No wonder you got a Knighthood.

HUGO: I'm beginning to suspect that you are here as an enemy. I hoped for a friend.

CARLOTTA: Did you, Hugo?—Did you really?

HUGO: Perhaps I was wrong?

CARLOTTA: No. You were not wrong. I think I am more friend than foe, but I suppose there must still be a little bitterness left. After all we were lovers once, for two whole years actually. Our parting was not very happy, was it?

HUGO: Fairly inevitable at any rate.

CARLOTTA: I really was very much in love with you.

HUGO: And I with you.

CARLOTTA: How convincingly you said that.

HUGO (*turning away irritably*): Oh really, Carlotta! Shall we stop sorting out our dead emotions now? I dislike looking at faded photographs.

CARLOTTA: Why did you write so unkindly about me in your memoirs?

HUGO: Aha! Now I'm beginning to understand.

CARLOTTA (*cheerfully*): Oh no you're not. You're merely jumping to conclusions. That was always one of your most glaring defects.

HUGO: Why can't we concentrate for a moment on some of my glaring assets? It might lighten the atmosphere.

CARLOTTA: We will, when you've answered my question.

HUGO: My autobiography was the assessment of the events and experiences of my life up to the date of writing it. I endeavoured to be as objective and truthful as possible. If in the process I happened to hurt your feelings, I apologize. There was no unkindness intended. I merely wrote what I thought to be true.

CARLOTTA: Your book may have been an assessment of the *outward* experiences of your life, but I cannot feel that you were entirely honest about your inner ones.

HUGO: Why should I be? My inner feelings are my own affair.

CARLOTTA: In that case the book was sailing under false colours.

HUGO (*nastily*): And all this because I described you as a mediocre actress.

CARLOTTA (*laughing*): Did you really say that? I'd forgotten. How catty of you.

HUGO: I've already said I was sorry.

CARLOTTA: No, my dear. You apologized. It isn't quite the same thing.

HUGO (*a little guilty*): I'm sorry then. There—will that do?

CARLOTTA: Yes. That will do for the moment. Are you working on anything now?

HUGO: Yes, a novel. Unfortunately I have been a little ill lately which halted progress for a time, but now I am back again to more or less my normal routine.

CARLOTTA: Your self-discipline was always remarkable.

HUGO: It was less constant when we knew each other. (*He smiles*) There were too many distractions.

CARLOTTA: Did you think I was a mediocre actress then?

HUGO: How could I? I was in love with you.

CARLOTTA: It was later, when you laid aside your rose-coloured glasses, that you saw through me?

HUGO: It isn't exactly that I saw through you. It was that I realized that, in spite of your vitality and charm and outward "allure," there was some essential quality missing.

CARLOTTA: You mean you guessed that I would never really become a star?

HUGO: I sensed it rather than guessed it.

CARLOTTA: Anyway your diagnosis was accurate. I never did become a star, a real star, but my career hasn't been altogether a failure, you know. I've played interesting plays and travelled the wide world. My life has fascinated and amused me all along the line. I'm seldom bored and I have few regrets.

HUGO: But the one abiding one is that you would rather have been great than merely competent.

CARLOTTA (*serenely*): You don't happen to have any parchment lying about, do you?

HUGO: Parchment?

CARLOTTA: Yes. When zoological experts extract the venom from snakes they force them to bite on parchment.

HUGO (*with a thin smile*): I accept your rebuke.

CARLOTTA: How generous of you.

HUGO: It's curious that you should still be able to arouse hostility in me.

CARLOTTA: Not really. As a matter of fact it was always there, just below the surface.

HUGO: When two young people are passionately in love, a certain amount of bickering is inevitable. It even has charm, up to a point. But when the old indulge in it, it is merely tiresome.

CARLOTTA: Speak for yourself. You are the one who has decided to be old. I haven't yet, maybe I never shall. Some people remain young until they're ninety.

HUGO: You see no point in dignified withdrawal, in "growing old gracefully"?

CARLOTTA: There is little grace in growing old, Hugo. It's a dreary process that we all have to deal with in our different ways. To outside observers my way may seem stupid and garish and, later on perhaps, even grotesque. But the opinion of outside observers has never troubled me unduly. I am really only accountable to myself. I like slapping on the makeup and having my body massaged and my hair tinted. You've no idea how much I enjoy my long, complicated mornings. I admit I'm liable to cave in a bit by the late afternoon, but a short snooze fixes that and then I have all the fun of getting ready again for the evening.

HUGO: And does the evening really justify so much effort?

CARLOTTA: As a general rule, yes. I have many friends, some of them quite young. They seem to enjoy my company. I like to watch them dancing.

HUGO: I detest the young of today. They are grubby, undisciplined and ill-mannered. They also make too much noise.

CARLOTTA: Youth always makes too much noise. Many of the ones I know are better informed and more intelligent than we were. Also their world is more shrill than ours was. You really must make allowances.

HUGO: I'm too old to make allowances.

CARLOTTA: Oh Hugo! You're positively stampeding towards the quiet grave, aren't you?

HUGO: Shall we change the subject? Shall we try to discover some general theme on which we can both agree?

CARLOTTA: Your indestructible elegance is flustering me and making me talk too much.

HUGO (*without malice*): You always talked too much, Carlotta.

CARLOTTA: Ah yes. It's a compulsive disease. Useful at dinner parties but fatal in the home.

HUGO: As this is neither, you can afford to relax.

CARLOTTA: There's so much I want to know about you, about what's happened to you during these long years, and here I am talking you into the ground. Will you forgive me?

HUGO: Why is there so much that you want to know about me? Why are you so suddenly curious about what has happened to me during these long years? Some motive must have impelled you to come here, some spark must have been struck. What was it?

CARLOTTA: All in good time.

HUGO: I think you will agree that that is an extremely exasperating reply.

CARLOTTA: Yes it is, isn't it? Again I must ask you to forgive me.

HUGO: If our first evening together after so many years is to be devoted entirely to mutual apologies, it may become tedious.

CARLOTTA: I think I can guarantee that whatever the evening may become it will not be tedious.

HUGO: Do I detect an undercurrent of menace? Is it in your mind to revive our dead and forgotten sex duel?

CARLOTTA: Is that how you remember it? How sad.

HUGO: Carlotta! What is it that you want of me?

CARLOTTA: At the moment, dinner.

HUGO (*with irritation*): Carlotta!

CARLOTTA: I only had a salad for lunch and I'm famished.

HUGO (*resigned*): Very well. Have it your own way. I am prepared to play any game you wish to play, up to a point. But do remember, won't you, that I tire easily.

(*He rings the bell.*) The dinner is ordered anyhow. I even remembered that you liked caviar.

CARLOTTA: That was sweet of you. The first time I ever tasted it was with you. You took me to Ciro's for supper after the show.

HUGO: Was I still wooing you then, or had I won?

CARLOTTA: You'd already won, more or less, but I think the caviar clinched it. I can remember what we had after the caviar too.

HUGO: What was it?

CARLOTTA: A filet mignon with sauce béarnaise and a green salad and the— (*She thinks for a moment.*) Then a chocolate soufflé.

HUGO: Did we by any chance have pink champagne as well?

CARLOTTA: Yes. I believe we did.

HUGO: You will see in a moment with what nostalgic charm history can repeat itself.

CARLOTTA: I don't believe you're really old at all.

There is a knock at the door.

HUGO: *Avanti.*

FELIX wheels in the dinner table.

FELIX: Good evening, madame.

CARLOTTA: Good evening.

FELIX (*as he comes in*): The table in the usual place, sir?

HUGO: Yes please, Felix.

FELIX (*seating* CARLOTTA *at the table*): Madame.

CARLOTTA: Thank you.

FELIX goes to open vodka.

HUGO: You can leave the vodka, we will serve ourselves.

FELIX: *Bien, monsieur.* (*He gives a quick glance at the table to see that everything is all right, then, with a bow, goes out of the room.*)

CARLOTTA: How handsome he is, isn't he? He has just a slight look of my first husband, Peter. Poor Peter. His feet trod the world lightly and alas, all too briefly.

HUGO: He was the one who was killed in an aeroplane?

CARLOTTA: Yes. He was studying to be a pilot in San Diego. I was trying out a new play in San Francisco. They had the sense not to tell me until after the matinée.

HUGO (*a little embarrassed by tragedy*): How dreadful for you.

CARLOTTA: Yes. It was my first real sorrow. We'd only been married for eighteen months, too soon for the gold to rub away. Then a little while afterwards I had a miscarriage. That was my second real sorrow. It was quite a year. San Francisco is a divine city and I love it, but I always seem to have bad luck when I play there. In 1957 I lost my last remaining tooth in the Curran Theatre.

HUGO (*with a shudder of distaste*): Carlotta!

CARLOTTA: It was a gallant old stump that held my lower plate together. I remember saying to my understudy one day, "Sally, when this is out, you're on!" And sure enough, a week later, it was and she was.

HUGO: I don't wish to sound fussy, Carlotta, but I really don't care to discuss false teeth during dinner.

CARLOTTA (*cheerfully*): Why ever not? That's when they're a force most to be reckoned with.

HUGO: Nevertheless, I should welcome a change of subject.

CARLOTTA: Dear Hugo. I am so sorry. I remember now, you always hated spades being called spades. What shall we talk about? Perhaps you would like some further vignettes from my rather ramshackle career?

HUGO: Provided that they are general rather than clinical.

CARLOTTA: Well let me see now. I married my second husband, Vernon Ritchie, in the Spring of 1936. He was my leading man in a ghastly play about the Deep South which ran for ages.

HUGO (*without much interest*): Was he a good actor?

CARLOTTA: No, terrible. But he made up for his performances on the stage by his performances in (*she hesitates*) in the boudoir. I didn't say bed in order to spare your feelings.

HUGO: Thank you. I appreciate your delicacy.

CARLOTTA: He was a sweet man and I was very fond of him. He was the father of my son David and then, soon after Pearl Harbor when the war came to us in America, he joined the navy and was killed in the Pacific in 1944.

HUGO: Was that another "great sorrow"?

CARLOTTA: No. Just a sadness.

HUGO: What decided you to make your life in America rather than in Europe where you were born?

CARLOTTA: Because I happened to be there I suppose. I went there originally on account of you. It was your play, if you remember, that first deposited me on the Great White Way, where it ran exactly ten days.

HUGO (*loftily*): That was no surprise to me. I never thought they'd understand it.

CARLOTTA: Do you know, Hugo? I have a terrible feeling that they did.

HUGO: Let me help you to some more caviar.

CARLOTTA: Thank you.

HUGO (*serving her and himself*): And your third husband?

CARLOTTA: Dear old Spike.

HUGO: Dear old what?

CARLOTTA: Spike. Spike Frost. Lots of people are called Spike in America. As I told you he's a movie agent, and a very successful one too. He handles a lot of the big stars.

HUGO: That sounds vaguely pornographic.

CARLOTTA (*delighted*): Hurray! A little joke at last. Almost an off-colour little joke too. Things are looking up.

HUGO: And you've never appeared in the London theatre since, since my first play?

CARLOTTA: Oh yes, twice.

HUGO: I don't remember hearing about it.

CARLOTTA: Why should you? As a matter of fact on each occasion you were away, in the Far East I believe, on one of your excavating expeditions.

HUGO: Excavating expeditions?

CARLOTTA: Yes, digging for treasure trove in the trusting minds of the innocent.

HUGO: You have a malicious tongue, Carlotta.

CARLOTTA: Yes. I really should learn to keep it between my false teeth. Let's stop talking about me now. Tell me about Hilde.

HUGO: I really see no reason to discuss Hilde with you.

CARLOTTA: Your loyal reticence does you credit, but it is a little overdone, almost defensive. After all I'm not a newspaper reporter.

HUGO: You might easily be, judging by the tastelessness of some of your questions.

CARLOTTA: It's no use trying to intimidate me, Hugo, because it won't work. If you remember it never did work. You have asked me questions about my husbands and I didn't snap your head off. Why shouldn't I ask you about your wife?

HUGO: The analogy is a trifle strained.

CARLOTTA: I truly want to know, not from idle curiosity, but because I liked her. She has wisdom and repose and her eyes are kind, a little sad perhaps, but kind. I suspect tragedy in her life.

HUGO (*giving in*): There *was* a tragedy in her life. She managed to escape from Nazi Germany in 1940, soon after the Phony War began. She left the love of her life behind, a young poet called Gerhardt Hendl. He died two years later in a concentration camp. Now are you satisfied?

CARLOTTA: Satisfied is not quite the word I would have chosen. But I am pleased that you told me.

FELIX comes in wheeling a table on which are the covered dishes for the next course.

FELIX: Am I too early, sir?

HUGO: No, we have finished. You'd better open the wine.

FELIX: *Bien, monsieur.*

CARLOTTA: Champagne! Oh Hugo, I have a feeling that it is going to be pink.

HUGO: It is.

CARLOTTA: How disarming of you to be so sentimental. It must be that evanescent nostalgia. Do you remember the cottage at Taplow and driving down together on summer nights after the Show?

HUGO: Yes. Yes, I remember.

CARLOTTA: And how cross you were that night at the Grafton Galleries, when I appeared in a red sequin frock that Baby Briant had lent me. You said I looked like a Shaftesbury Avenue tart.

HUGO: You did.

FELIX, having cleared away the first course and opened the bottle of champagne, pours a little into *HUGO's* glass. *HUGO* sips it and nods his approval. *FELIX* then fills both their glasses and proceeds to serve the filets mignons, salad, etc.

CARLOTTA: And the weekend we went to Paris, and I got back to the Theatre on the Monday night exactly seven minutes before curtain time. My understudy was all dressed and ready to go on . . . I often wonder why you didn't write any more plays. Your dialogue was so pointed and witty.

HUGO: You flatter me, Carlotta.

CARLOTTA: I've read everything you've ever written.

HUGO: You flatter me more than ever.

CARLOTTA: I only said that I'd read everything you've ever written. I ventured no opinion, flattering or otherwise.

HUGO: The statement alone is flattering enough.

CARLOTTA: Yes. Yes, I expect it is. I suppose Ciro's isn't there anymore? (*She sighs.*) Oh, dear!

HUGO: That was a pensive sigh.

CARLOTTA: I've been in America too long. It's so lovely to see a steak that doesn't look like a bedroom slipper . . .

FELIX bows and leaves the room.

CARLOTTA: He really is most attractive, isn't he? Those glorious shoulders.

HUGO: I've never noticed them.

CARLOTTA: They're probably padded anyhow. Life can be dreadfully treacherous.

HUGO (*he laughs quite genuinely*): You really are extraordinary, Carlotta. You don't look a day over fifty.

CARLOTTA: I should hope not. After three cellular injections and two face-lifts.

HUGO (*pained*): Carlotta!

CARLOTTA: It's wonderful how they do it now. You can hardly see the scars at all.

HUGO: What on earth possessed you to tell me that?

CARLOTTA: Oh dear. Now I've shocked you again.

HUGO: Aesthetically yes, you have.

CARLOTTA: I am sorry. Just as we were making such progress.

HUGO: As the object of such operations is, presumably, to create an illusion, why destroy the illusion by telling everybody about it?

CARLOTTA: Quite right, Hugo. As a matter of fact you could do with a little snip yourself. Just under the chin.

HUGO: I wouldn't dream of it.

CARLOTTA: It would do wonders for your morale.

HUGO: My morale is perfectly satisfactory as it is, thank you.

CARLOTTA (gaily): Long may it remain so.

HUGO (after a slight pause): Why did you come here, Carlotta?

CARLOTTA: I told you. I'm having a course of injections at Professor Boromelli's clinique.

HUGO (frowning): Professor Boromelli!

CARLOTTA: Yes. Do you know him?

HUGO: I know of him.

CARLOTTA: You look disapproving.

HUGO: His reputation is rather dubious.

CARLOTTA: In what way?

HUGO: The general consensus of opinion is that he's a quack.

CARLOTTA: Quack or no quack he's an old duck.

HUGO: Don't be foolish, Carlotta.

CARLOTTA: There's no need to stamp on my little joke as though it were a cockroach.

HUGO: Well? (he smiles a faintly strained smile) I'm still waiting to hear the reason that induced you suddenly to make this, shall we say, rather tardy reappearance in my life? It must be a fairly strong one.

CARLOTTA: Not so very strong really. It's only actually an irrelevant little favour. Irrelevant to you I mean, but important to me.

HUGO: What is it?

CARLOTTA: Prepare yourself for a tiny shock.

HUGO (with a note of impatience): I'm quite prepared. Go on.

CARLOTTA: I too have written an autobiography.

HUGO (raising his eyebrows): Have you? How interesting.

CARLOTTA: There's a distinct chill in your voice.

HUGO: I'm sorry. I was unaware of it.

CARLOTTA: It is to be published in the Autumn.

HUGO: Congratulations. Who by?

CARLOTTA: Doubleday in New York and Heinemann in London.

HUGO (concealing surprise): Excellent.

CARLOTTA (with a trace of irony): I am so glad you approve.

HUGO: And have you written it all yourself? Or have you employed what I believe is described as a "ghostwriter"?

CARLOTTA: No, Hugo. I have written every word of it myself.

HUGO: Well done.

CARLOTTA: On an electric typewriter. You really should try one. It's a Godsend.

HUGO: I have no need of it. Hilde does my typing for me.

CARLOTTA: Of course yes—I'd forgotten. Then you can give her one for a birthday present.

HUGO (*after a slight pause*): I suppose you want me to write an introductory preface.

CARLOTTA: No. I've already done that myself.

HUGO (*with a tinge of irritation*): What is it then? What is it that you want of me?

CARLOTTA: Permission to publish your letters.

HUGO (*startled*): Letters! What letters?

CARLOTTA: The letters you wrote to me when we were lovers. I've kept them all.

HUGO: Whatever letters I wrote to you at that time were private. They concerned no one but you and me.

CARLOTTA: I agree. But that was a long time ago. Before we'd either of us become celebrated enough to write our memoirs.

HUGO: I cannot feel that you, Carlotta, have even yet achieved that particular distinction.

CARLOTTA (*unruffled*): Doubleday and Heinemann do.

HUGO: I believe that some years ago Mrs. Patrick Campbell made a similar request to Mr. George Bernard Shaw and his reply was, "Certainly not. I have no intention of playing the horse to your Lady Godiva."

CARLOTTA: How unkind.

HUGO: It would ill become me to attempt to improve on Mr. George Bernard Shaw.

CARLOTTA (*helping herself to some more salad*): You mean you refuse?

HUGO: Certainly. I most emphatically refuse.

CARLOTTA: I thought you would.

HUGO: In that case surely it was waste of time to take the trouble to ask me?

CARLOTTA: I just took a chance. After all, life can be full of surprises sometimes, can't it?

HUGO: If your forthcoming autobiography is to be peppered with that sort of bromide it cannot fail to achieve the best-seller list.

CARLOTTA: You can turn nasty quickly, can't you? You were quite cozy and relaxed a moment ago.

HUGO: I am completely horrified by your suggestion. It's in the worst possible taste.

CARLOTTA: Never mind. Let's have some more champagne. (*She takes the bottle out of the bucket and pours herself some. She holds it up to him enquiringly.*)

HUGO: Not for me, thank you.

CARLOTTA: There's quite a lot left.

HUGO: Finish it by all means.

CARLOTTA: Professor Boromelli will be furious.

HUGO: I gather he doesn't insist on any particular regime. What sort of injections does he give you?

CARLOTTA (*enjoying her steak*): Oh it's a formula of his own. Hormones and things.

HUGO: The same kind of treatment as Niehans?

CARLOTTA: Oh no, quite different. Niehans injects living cells from an unborn ewe, and as long as he doesn't pick a non-U Ewe, it works like a charm.

HUGO: Have you been to him as well?

CARLOTTA: Oh yes, ages ago. He's an old duck too.

HUGO: You seem to regard Switzerland as a sort of barnyard.

CARLOTTA (*raising her glass to him*): Quack quack!

HUGO (*crossly*): Don't be so childish.

CARLOTTA (*laughing*): You used to enjoy my jokes when you and I were young love and all the world was new.

HUGO: Flippancy in a girl of twenty-one can be quite attractive, in a woman of more mature years it is liable to be embarrassing.

CARLOTTA: Like bad temper in a pompous old gentleman.

FELIX reenters, wheeling a table on which is a chocolate soufflé.

CARLOTTA: Perfect timing, Felix. I congratulate you.

HUGO (*testily*): That will be all for the moment, Felix. Please bring the coffee immediately.

FELIX: *Subito, signore!* (*He bows, smiles at* CARLOTTA, *and leaves.*)

HUGO: I hate familiarity with servants.

CARLOTTA: Oh eat up your soufflé for God's sake and stop being so disagreeable.

HUGO (*outraged*): How dare you speak to me like that!

CARLOTTA: Dare? Really Hugo. What have I to fear from you?

HUGO: I consider your rudeness insufferable.

CARLOTTA: And I consider your pomposity insufferable.

HUGO (*icily*): I should like to remind you that you are my guest.

CARLOTTA: Of course I am. Don't be so silly.

HUGO: And as such I have the right to demand from you at least a semblance of good manners.

CARLOTTA: "Semblance of good manners"! Talk about clichés. That's a clanger if ever I heard one.

HUGO (*quivering with rage*): Once and for all, Carlotta—

CARLOTTA: For heaven's sake calm down. Your wife told me earlier on that it was bad for you to overexcite yourself. You'll have a fit in a minute if you don't stop gibbering.

HUGO (*beside himself, shouting*): I am not gibbering!

There is a silence for a moment. *CARLOTTA* continues to eat her soufflé. *HUGO* rises majestically.

HUGO (*with superb control*): I think, Carlotta, that as we really haven't very much more to say to each other, it would be considerate of you to leave as soon as you've finished eating. As I told you, I have been rather ill recently and it is my habit to retire early. I also feel that I have reached an age when I no longer have to tolerate being spoken to as you spoke just now.

CARLOTTA: If you are determined to decline so rapidly you'll soon reach an age when nobody will be able to speak to you at all.

HUGO: I am sorry if I appear to be discourteous but after all, it was you who forced us both into this—this rather unprofitable meeting. I have done my best to receive you kindly and make the evening a pleasant one. That I have failed is only too obvious. I am sorry also that I was unable to accede to your request. I am sure, after you have given yourself time to think it over, that you will realise how impertinent it was.

CARLOTTA: Why impertinent?

HUGO: Not having read your book I have naturally no way of judging whether it is good, bad or indifferent. I am perfectly aware, however, that whatever its merits, the inclusion of private letters from a man in my position, would enhance its value considerably. The impertinence I think lies in your assuming for a moment that I should grant you permission to publish them. We met and parted many years ago. Since then we have neither of us communicated with each other. You have pursued your career, I have pursued mine. Mine, if I may say so without undue arrogance, has been eminently successful. Yours, perhaps less so. Doesn't it strike *you* as impertinent that, after so long a silence, you should suddenly ask me to provide you with my name as a stepping-stone?

CARLOTTA (*looking at him thoughtfully*): Am I to be allowed a cup of coffee before I leave?

HUGO: Of course. He will bring it in a moment.

CARLOTTA: Poor Hugo.

HUGO: I am in no need of your commiseration.

CARLOTTA: Think carefully and you may not be quite so sure.

HUGO: I haven't the faintest idea what you are implying nor, I must frankly admit, am I particularly interested.

CARLOTTA: I am implying that a man who is capable of refusing a request as gracelessly and contemptuously as you have done can be neither happy nor secure.

HUGO: Happy and secure? My dear Carlotta, I salute the facility with which you have picked up the glib, sentimental jargon of American women's magazines.

CARLOTTA: Look out, Hugo. You are riding for a fall. Your high horse may suddenly buck and throw you.

FELIX enters with the coffee.

FELIX: Coffee, *monsieur?*

HUGO: For Madame only. You can put it over here and take away the dinner table.

FELIX: Very good, sir.

CARLOTTA: You are afraid of not sleeping?

HUGO (*coldly*): I never drink coffee in the evening.

CARLOTTA: What about a nice cup of cocoa? Inelegant but soothing.

FELIX: That will be all, *monsieur?*

HUGO: Yes thank you.

FELIX: Good night, sir—madame.

CARLOTTA: Good night, Felix. The dinner was delicious and the service impeccable.

FELIX: Madame is most kind. (*He bows and wheels the table out of the room.*)

HUGO (*pouring out a cup of coffee*): Do you take sugar?

CARLOTTA: Yes please, a little. How long have I got before the curfew sounds?

HUGO (*ignoring this*): Here's your coffee.

CARLOTTA: The letters really are very good, Hugo. It's disappointing that you won't allow me to use them. They *are* love letters of course up to a point and brilliantly written. The more ardent passages are exquisitely phrased although they do give the impression that they were commissioned by your head rather than dictated by your heart.

HUGO: I have no wish to discuss the matter any further.

CARLOTTA: It seems a pity that posterity should be deprived of such an illuminating example of your earlier work.

HUGO: I really am very tired, Carlotta. I feel that my age entitles me to ask you to leave me alone now. Perhaps we may meet and talk again within the next few days.

CARLOTTA: My wrap is in your bedroom. Hilde put it there. May I fetch it?

HUGO: By all means.

CARLOTTA goes into the bedroom. *HUGO* lights a cigarette and then immediately stubs it out again. He is obviously seething with irritation. He opens the table drawer, takes two white tablets out of a bottle and crunches them.

CARLOTTA returns.

CARLOTTA: Good night, Hugo. I am sorry the evening has ended so . . . so uncozily.

HUGO: So am I, Carlotta. So am I.

CARLOTTA (*turning, on her way to the door*): To revert for a moment to the unfortunate subject of the letters. You may have them if you like. They are of no further use to me.

HUGO: That is most generous of you.

CARLOTTA: I'm afraid I can't let you have the others though. That would be betraying a sacred promise.

HUGO: Others? What others?

CARLOTTA: Your letters to Perry.

HUGO (*visibly shaken*): My letters to Perry! What do you mean?

CARLOTTA: Perry Sheldon. I happened to be with him when he died.

HUGO: What do you know about Perry Sheldon?

CARLOTTA: Among other things that he was the only true love of your life. Good night, Hugo. Sleep well.

CURTAIN *as* CARLOTTA *turns upstage exiting through the door.*

•

In the event, the plays had to be postponed to a 1966 opening. Having written them, Noël took time off—for once really travelling alone—to visit the Seychelles. There he contracted amoebic dysentery and belatedly returned home a very sick man indeed. The episode undoubtedly permanently undermined his health and shortened his life.

He managed the London run to great acclaim, but he noticed telltale signs that humiliated him. He, who had always insisted on word perfection from his actors, was having to be prompted with words that he had written himself.

He canceled the following year's Broadway commitment. The "temple of dreams" had seen him for the last time.

•

Noël was perpetually fascinated by the subject of stars and the nature of stardom. "I don't know what it (star quality) is, but I've got it," he once said, but he frequently tried to define it.

What is it that stars have that others haven't? Is it an earthy quality or a spiritual quality? Is it concrete, abstract, animal, vegetable or mineral? There will obviously never be a satisfactory answer. A young girl decides to go on the stage. She is strikingly beautiful and by no means untalented. She is adequately taught at an acting school or by the better method of playing small parts in a repertory company. After a year or so she procures a job in London for which she receives honorable mention in the *Sunday Times* and an "Among others" in the *Daily Telegraph*. She at once acquires an agent, or has one thrust upon her, and her future is shining with promise. Twenty years later, having played two leading parts, one on tour and one in the West End in a play that ran only a fortnight, bits in movies, snippets on the radio and an endless succession of heroine's friends, she one day looks at herself in the mirror and, if she is wise, notes that she is not quite so strikingly beautiful as she was, marries a well-disposed dentist in Kettering and is heard of no more. If she is not wise she sticks doggedly to the Theatre and finally has to be assisted to the grave by the Actors' Benevolent Fund.

This, I admit is a gloomy picture but it is not an unusual one . . .

This extra "something" is an amalgam of various elements; vitality, sex appeal, an intriguing voice (nearly all big stars have distinctive voices), an individual style of movement and some sort of chemical emanation, of which she may or may not be conscious, which places her on a different plane from her possibly more talented colleagues. The balanced mixture of all these ingredients is recognized as "personality" or, in other words, "Star Quality." Very very occasionally this "Star Quality" may be acquired by years of experience, determination and the assurance of polished technique, but as a general rule it is something that people either have or have not and when they have, it is unmistakable.

In any event this fortunately endowed creature, whoever she may be, is hailed, within a relatively short space of time, as a Star, and it is in this glorious moment that the rot usually starts to set in. Her hitherto unblemished character begins, subtly at first, to suffer that "sea change—into something rich and strange." The name in lights, tumultuous applause, hosts of admirers, acres of first-night flowers and extravagant publicity all contribute their insidious magic until, a few years later, we see, bowing graciously to us on an opening night, a triumphant, assured, fascinating, adored, ripsnorting megalomaniac.

The grim fact must be faced: that the majority of the theatre-going public would rather pay their money to see an extraordinary creature than an ordinary one. An extraordinary actress playing a relatively ordinary part may indeed lay waste the author's original intentions, but she will bring to that part a certain quality, a composite of her own personal magnetism, her reputation and her acquired technique which will hypnotize the audience into loving her. An ordinary, possibly better actress, playing the same part honestly and with loyal adherence to the author's text, will usually succeed in being little more than accurate. She will, of course, be effusively thanked by the author, director and the management and, if she happens to be an understudy, cheered to the echo by the gallery, but the business will drop steadily until the star returns to the cast. From the point of view of the dedicated drama enthusiasts this is indeed a desperate injustice as is the world outside it.

—"HOW I WONDER WHAT YOU ARE" (ESSAY)

•

"Poor darling glamorous stars everywhere, their lives are so lonely and wretched and frustrated. Nothing but applause, flowers, Rolls-Royces, expensive hotel suites, constant adulation. It's too pathetic and wrings the heart," he confided to his diary in 1955.

A dozen years later in his last completed play, *Star Quality,** adapted from his short story of the same name, he tackled the subject again.

STAR QUALITY (1967)

Star Lorraine Barrie has agreed to appear in *Dark Heritage,* a play by new playwright Bryan Snow. Miss Barrie is notoriously temperamental, but Bryan sees no sign of it as readings begin. Tony Orford, the director's assistant—who has witnessed the phenomenon more times than he cares to recall—enlightens him . . .

BRYAN: You're not being very encouraging.
TONY: Cheer up—it's all part of life's rich pattern.
BRYAN: Oh, shut up.
TONY: The whole thing is primarily biological and it began way back in the beginning of the world when the Almighty, for personal reasons best known to Himself, arranged that ladies should be constructed differently from gentlemen.
BRYAN: I don't know what you're talking about.

*The text is taken from Noël's original version, which has never been produced. An adaptation by Chris Luscombe with Penelope Keith as Lorraine Barrie was staged at the Apollo Theatre, London, on August 8, 2001.

TONY: All temperamental scenes made by all temperamental female Stars since the theatre was first invented have been based on that inescapable fact. It is drummed into their fluffy little heads from infancy onwards that they possess something unique and infinitely precious that every man they meet desires more than anything else. They receive cartloads of flowers on opening nights whereas the poor leading man considers himself lucky if his cousin gives him one carnation wrapped in damp cellophane.

BRYAN: Aren't male actors ever temperamental?

TONY: Only very rarely. They cannot afford to be. They can be morose, nervous, wretched and miscast and sometimes tearful but that is as far as it goes. They must press on gallantly and stand aside for the leading lady, present her graciously to the audience and dress in a less comfortable dressing room. They must give up cheerfully many privileges their talent has earned them, all to feed the already overweening vanity of some gifted, self-indulgent, domineering harridan whose every thought and feeling is motivated by sex-consciousness, treachery and illusion.

BRYAN: You make it a little too obvious that you don't care for women.

TONY: Don't be silly. I adore women, but not in what is known as "that way." Some of my best friends are women and they're a damn sight more loyal and sweet to me than they are to each other. Above all, I love great big diamond-studded glamour stars. They fascinate me. I love all their little tricks and carry-ons; their unscrupulousness, their inflexible determination, their courage, their magnificent dishonesty with themselves and with everyone else. I love and pity their eternal gullibility and their tragic, silly loneliness. In our darling Lorraine, for instance you have a glittering example of *bona fide,* sizzling megalomania. She could only exist in the theatre or the film studios. No other career, not even that of a brilliantly successful courtesan, could ever provide enough food for her ravening ego.

BRYAN: You seem to have left out one very important thing—her talent.

TONY: Oh no, I was leaving that to the last. That's the payoff, the definitive answer to all the silly riddles. That's her basic power, her superb natural gift for acting. I don't suppose she has ever acted really badly in her life. I don't believe she could if she tried. That is her one reality, the foundation upon which the whole structure of her charm and personality rests, and, believe you me, it's rock solid.

BRYAN: I'm glad you admit that at any rate.

TONY: Calm down, there's a good boy. You've missed the entire point.

BRYAN: I certainly have, and a bloody good job too.

TONY: You helped me up onto my favourite tub and I started thumping it too soon. It's silly to issue storm warnings when the sky is clear and we haven't even left the harbour. Am I forgiven?

BRYAN: There's nothing to forgive. But I still don't quite believe you when you say you're devoted to Lorraine.

TONY: Perhaps "devoted" is overstating it a little. But I like her more than you think I do and I admire her for something that is beyond definition and beyond praise, her star quality. Whether she was born with it, or how and where she managed to acquire it, I neither know nor care, but it's there all right. It's there as strongly in comedy as in tragedy. I once caught her at a matinée in Manchester. The play was lousy, the fort-night's notice was up on the board and the audience so dull that I thought half of them must be dead. That was during the first act.

Suddenly you are aware that you are in the presence of something very great indeed—something abstract that is beyond definition and beyond praise. Quality—star quality plus. It is there as strongly in comedy as in tragedy, magical and unmistakable, and the hair will rise on your addled little head, chills will swirl up and down your spine and you will solemnly bless the day that you were born. All this, of course, only applies if you happen to love the theatre, and I suspect that you might learn to if you stick around a bit.

BRYAN: You're just as stagestruck as I am.

TONY: And you need never again accuse me, in that prim disapproving voice of yours, of not liking women, because it just doesn't make sense. Nobody can love the theatre without liking women because they are the most fascinating, unpredictable and exciting part of it.

Here endeth the first lesson.

•

If you're a star, you should behave like one. I always have.

—SUNDAY TIMES, LONDON (1969)

•

Although it wasn't immediately obvious, "Dad's Renaissance" (as Noël called it) had quietly begun.

In late 1963 there was a little-heralded revival of *Private Lives* at the new Hampstead Theatre Club in London. Critics—many of whom were too young to have seen it before—found it "the funniest play to have adorned the English theatre in this century." Noël found it particularly satisfying that this should have happened in Hampstead, the scene of his first major success—*The Vortex*—almost forty years before.

Early the next year Sir Laurence Olivier—now running the new National Theatre—invited him to direct a revival of *Hay Fever* with a cast "that could have played the Albanian telephone directory." It was the first time a living playwright had been so honored. "So you've been nationalized at last," Terence Rattigan wrote to him, and critic Ronald Bryden dubbed him "demonstrably the greatest living English playwright."

Noël noted, "Such (almost) unanimous praise has not been lavished upon me for many a long year and to pretend that I am not delighted by it would be the height of affectation."

·

There was one more play—begun but never completed. A pity, because it is vintage Coward.

Almost *Fallen Angels II,* it has three ladies now well into middle age, who were "girls together" and will remain "girls" to each other until that wingèd chariot carries them off. Every year they meet to gossip and reminisce over a drink or two . . . or three . . .

AGE CANNOT WITHER (1967)

(UNFINISHED)

CAST

NAOMI KEMBLE	SALLY ANN HOWES
STELLA MILVERTON	HAYLEY MILLS
JUDY CRAVEN	ROSEMARY HARRIS

FIRST PERFORMED IN CONCERT IN AN ABRIDGED VERSION AT THE PLAYERS CLUB, NEW YORK, DECEMBER 10, 2002

MRS. ROTHWELL flings open the door.

MRS. R. (*announcing*): Mrs. Craven.

JUDY CRAVEN enters. Of the three ladies she is the most chic. She is expertly dressed, dyed and made-up. Not a hair is out of place. MRS. ROTHWELL withdraws, closing the door behind her.

JUDY (*kissing* NAOMI): Dearest Naomi—Here we go again. (*She kisses* STELLA) I can hardly believe a year has gone by since last time. It might have been last Tuesday.

NAOMI (*admiringly*): Well! I must say you certainly do look—

JUDY (*holding up her hand*): Don't say it. I know perfectly well I look wonderful. If I didn't after all I've been through, I'd shoot myself.

NAOMI: How do you mean—"all you've been through"? *What* have you been through?

JUDY (*dramatically*): The full treatment! Face-lift, breast lift, the lot. I had to suck Ovaltine through a straw for four whole days. It was hell.

STELLA: You don't mean to say you really—?

JUDY: I certainly do, and what's more I wouldn't go through it again if my chin fell down to my knees. It was perfectly beastly and I loathed every minute of it.

STELLA (*starry-eyed*): You always were the brave one at school. Do you remember striking Miss Lockhart with a hockey stick?

NAOMI: Never mind about Miss Lockhart and hockey sticks for the moment. This is serious. (*To* JUDY.) When did all this happen? How long ago?

JUDY: Seven months ago. On the fifth of November, as a matter of fact. Gunpowder, treason and plot.

NAOMI: Where?

JUDY: Vienna. It was just one long dreamy waltz.

NAOMI: Why didn't you write and tell us?

JUDY: I wanted it to be a surprise.

STELLA: Well, you got your wish. It most emphatically is.

NAOMI: What did Robert say?

JUDY: He said—"What's the matter, old girl, you look a bit seedy?"

STELLA: Oh, Judy! How discouraging. After all that trouble!

JUDY: I suppose it was in a way. Not that I expected him to rush at me in a frenzy of sudden, uncontrolled lust, but I would have liked a casual comment like—"That hat suits you" or "Your trip to Vienna certainly seems to have done you good." But not a bit of it. He just went back to his *Times* crossword and asked me for a dismissive verb starting with B in six letters.

STELLA: I can think of several in four letters.

NAOMI: Well, all I can say is that I think you've been downright underhand, underhand and crafty.

JUDY: Believe me, "understand" is the last word to describe the operation. He snipped and stitched away at me for three and a half hours.

NAOMI: *Who* did the operation?

JUDY: Professor Krindling, of course.

NAOMI (*horrified*): Professor Krindling! You must have been mad. He's well known to be the biggest charlatan in the business.

JUDY: Charlatan or no charlatan, you've got to admit he did a wonderful job on me.

NAOMI: You took a terrible risk.

JUDY: Nonsense.

NAOMI: He was the one who was responsible for Mary Kinnerton's strawberry chin.

JUDY: Mary Kinnerton's chin was always a worry anyway. Whatever he did to it couldn't have made all that much difference.

STELLA: Fancy knowing somebody who's actually been to Krindling! What's he like?

JUDY: Absolutely hideous with tufts of black hair bursting from his ears but gentle as a dove.

NAOMI: He sounds a horror.

JUDY: Well, he isn't a horror—he's an angel. And he's an absolute fanatic over his job, a hundred percent dedicated. He used to sit on my bed and tell me the most fascinating things. You've no idea what you can have done to you nowadays, if you really put your mind to it. You can even have your sex changed at the drop of a hat.

NAOMI: King's Road, Chelsea, must be knee-deep in discarded bowlers.

JUDY: It's all very fine to laugh and make silly jokes.

NAOMI: I'm not laughing, not really. Actually, I'm thoroughly shocked and horrified. I hate the whole idea of this undignified scampering after Youth. I intend to grow old as gracefully as I can and let nature take its course.

JUDY: Then you'd better give up those blue rinses to start with and eat a lot of chocolate éclairs.

STELLA (*laughing*): Touché!

NAOMI (*crossly*): I don't know what you mean by "touché." I see nothing wrong in trying to make the best of oneself. A little self-discipline never hurt anybody. But I draw the line at plastic surgery, unless it's a medical necessity.

JUDY: Well, I find it a medical necessity to look at least ten years younger than I really am, so you can come off your high horse and stop being so pompous.

NAOMI: I don't mean to be pompous, really I don't. It's just that I can't bear the idea of mutton dressed as lamb.

JUDY: Do you think *I* look like mutton dressed as lamb?

NAOMI: No I can't honestly say that I do. But is it really worth the effort? I mean does it really make you *feel* younger and happier and more able to cope with everything?

JUDY: Yes, it does. It most certainly does.

STELLA: The sad thing about the whole business is that nobody's really fooled.

JUDY: That's not the point. I don't give a hoot whether other people are fooled or not. I shan't care when everybody knows perfectly well that I'm eighty-five, so long as I don't *look* it. It's a question of personal satisfaction. I should hate to get out of my bath and look in the glass and see everything hanging about.

NAOMI: Even now there must be a certain amount hanging about.

JUDY: That's just where you're wrong, there isn't, thanks to the dear professor. A snip here and a tuck there have worked wonders. I'll show you if you like.

NAOMI: Not before lunch, dear.

JUDY: Really, Naomi. You should try not to be so prim and hidebound.

NAOMI: It's nothing to do with being prim and hidebound. I just don't want Mrs. Rothwell to come in and see you prancing about stripped to the waist.

JUDY: I hadn't planned on doing the dance of the seven veils.

NAOMI: I also feel that to examine scar tissue just before Steak Béarnaise might be a bit off-putting.

JUDY: All right—all right—have it your own way. I merely thought you might be interested.

NAOMI (*soothingly*): But I *am* interested. I also think it was frightfully brave of you to have it done at all. A little sly perhaps to have been so secretive about it.

JUDY: You could hardly expect me to put an announcement in the *Times*.

STELLA: What I want to know is—did it *hurt?*

JUDY: No, not really. It itched a bit and I felt as if I'd been scalped but it soon wore off. My face swelled up, of course, and looked like a vast Victoria plum for several days. Every time I looked in the glass I got the giggles and that *did* hurt like hell, I must say.

STELLA: Do you think *we* ought to have it done?

NAOMI: What do you mean "we"? Speak for yourself. Personally, I have no intention of being tampered with.

JUDY: What a ghastly expression. It's only little girls on Wimbledon Common who get tampered with.

STELLA: Oh no, it isn't. Muriel Bailey gets tampered with every time she goes in the tube.

NAOMI: Poor Muriel. She's always been terribly unpunctual. Perhaps that explains it.

STELLA (*to* JUDY): Did you tell Robert you were going to have it done?

JUDY: Of course I told him. I always tell Robert everything.

STELLA: What did he say?

JUDY: "Anything for a change"!

NAOMI: Has it made any difference to his feeling for you?

JUDY: If by that you mean what I think you mean, you ought to be ashamed of yourself.

NAOMI: I only wondered.

JUDY: Robert and I haven't indulged in any of that sort of thing since 1945.

STELLA: Victory year.

JUDY: And we wouldn't have then, if Mrs. Anstruther hadn't been in the Isle of Wight.

NAOMI: That horrible woman! I can never remember her first name.

JUDY: Neither can Robert, I asked him only the other day. He thinks it was Hermione but he wouldn't take a bet on it.

STELLA: Did you mind at the time? About Mrs. Anstruther, I mean?

JUDY: Of course I did. I was heartbroken. I even hired a private detective to follow them everywhere.

NAOMI: And did he?

JUDY: Yes, but without very satisfactory results. According to his report they went into the New Gallery Cinema and never came out.

STELLA: Perhaps it was *Ben-Hur*.

NAOMI (*with a luxurious sigh*): Isn't it lovely getting old? I wouldn't care now if Jonathan slept with a different woman every night.

JUDY: It's possible that *they* would.

NAOMI: That was a very bitchy thing to say. Jonathan is still a very attractive man.

JUDY: Yes, but not really in that way.

NAOMI: Certainly in "that way." He's particularly alluring to the young. Debutantes fall for him in droves. Only the other day the eldest Hatherton girl asked him point blank to take her to Paris for the weekend.

JUDY: If he had, I expect "point blank" would have been the operative phrase.

NAOMI: If you're trying to insinuate—

JUDY: I'm not trying to insinuate anything. I'm merely rejecting your fanciful image of dear old Jonathan as a rampaging Casanova. He'll be sixty-eight next birthday. I know that because Robert's is the day before and they always send each other cards.

NAOMI: There's no accounting for the sex urge. Ninon de L'Enclos went on having lovers until she was pushing ninety.

JUDY: Then she must have been a conceited old ass.

NAOMI (*going to the drinks table*): Would anyone like another nip?

STELLA: Yes, please. I'm looking forward to the day when I don't have to worry whether I look nice or not.

JUDY: When that day dawns, it will be your last.

STELLA: Do you really think that when I'm a gnarled old crone of ninety-five that I shall still fuss about my hair?

JUDY: Certainly. If you've got any left, and if you haven't, you'll fuss about your wig. Old habits die hard.

STELLA: Oh, God!

JUDY: It's nothing to be depressed about. On the contrary, it shows a certain spiritual nobility. My Aunt Esther died on her eighty-ninth birthday painted up to the eyes.

NAOMI: Had she led a very giddy life?

JUDY: Lord, yes. Three husbands and strings of lovers. One of them was rumoured to be the station master at Kettering.

STELLA: You mean she was a natural sexpot?

JUDY: She certainly was. We were none of us allowed to see her until after we'd been confirmed.

STELLA (*seriously*): But she really liked sex for sex's sake? I mean it was necessary to her?

JUDY: I suppose it must have been.

STELLA: Well, it isn't to me. It never was.

JUDY: But you must have liked going to bed with people when you were young?

STELLA: I never went to bed with people when I was young. I was occasionally mauled a bit at dances and I once had a set-to with my cousin Stephen in the maze at Hampton Court.

NAOMI: How dreadful. There isn't even anywhere to sit down!

JUDY: All right. We'll settle for the fact that you were a virgin until you married Robert. But what happened then?

STELLA: How do you mean "what happened then"? The usual thing, I suppose.

JUDY: You were in love with him, weren't you?

STELLA: Of course I was. I was dotty about him.

JUDY: Then didn't you *enjoy* it?

STELLA: Not at first, I was too agitated. Later on I got sort of used to it. I suppose it *is* rather habit-forming.

JUDY: Oh, Stella—really!

STELLA: There's no need to look so shocked. I just don't happen to be a voluptuary.

JUDY: It certainly takes more than thirty years of marriage and one set-to in the Hampton Court Maze to make a voluptuary.

STELLA: I really do rather resent your tone of patronage, Judy. We can't all go about swooning over men years younger than we are and working ourselves into states and plunging our heads into gas ovens.

JUDY: It's mean of you to bring that up. It happened years ago and I only put my head in a little way to see what it felt like but it made me sneeze, so I took it out again.

NAOMI: That was Derek What's-his-name, wasn't it?

JUDY: Yes. That was Derek What's-his-name, all right. He certainly was a killer.

NAOMI: He had no back to his head.

JUDY: I never noticed the back of his head. I was always too busy looking at the front. As a matter of fact, I saw him in the Ritz Bar only a few months ago.

STELLA: How did he look?

JUDY: Bright red and bald as an egg.

NAOMI: Oh dear—it does seem sad, doesn't it?

JUDY: Not to me it doesn't. I was absolutely delighted.

NAOMI: Did you see who was with him?

JUDY: Not very clearly. They were right at the other end of the bar near the door.

NAOMI: Perhaps it was Mildred.

JUDY: Not unless she's recently joined the Navy.

NAOMI (*fascinated*): Oooh, just fancy! Derek of all people. Upper deck or lower?

JUDY: Upper, but only just.

STELLA: It's no surprise to me, I always had my suspicions about Derek. There was something in the way he played the piano.

JUDY: Come now, Stella. He did at least play the piano beautifully.

STELLA: Too much Debussy.

NAOMI: None of the men in my life have been able to play a note on anything. Jonathan did buy a ukelele soon after we were married but it gave him a blister on his thumb and he threw it into the fire.

STELLA: Like that beastly roman Emperor and those little boys.

JUDY: What on earth are you talking about?

STELLA: I can't remember his name offhand but I know he used to throw little boys into the fire after he'd had his way with them.

JUDY: Italians are naturally cruel, I'm afraid. Look how they whack away at those wretched donkeys in Capri.

STELLA: This drink's terribly strong. If lunch doesn't happen soon, I shall fall down.

NAOMI: It should be ready any minute.

JUDY: Couldn't you ring a bell or something?

NAOMI: Good Heavens, no. Mrs. Rothwell would have a fit. She's terribly highly strung.

JUDY: One should never allow oneself to be dominated by servants.

NAOMI: That feudal attitude won't wash nowadays, Judy. If anything upset Mrs. Rothwell, I should be done for. Also, when the bell rings in the kitchen, it really is deafening. Enough to give anyone a nervous breakdown.

JUDY: That could be fixed by wedging in a bit of rag.

NAOMI: Then it wouldn't ring at all, so we should be back where we started.

STELLA: Wouldn't it be awful if we really were?

JUDY: Really were *what*?

STELLA: Back where we started. On the threshold of life—young and eager and oversexed.

NAOMI: Speak for yourself. I wasn't oversexed.

JUDY: What about Miss Mowforth? You were barmy about her.

NAOMI: That had nothing to do with sex, it was a spiritual relationship.

JUDY: You kept a snapshot of her in fencing bloomers in your handkerchief drawer.

NAOMI: What about you and Dr. Pringle? I remember you fainting dead away when he sounded your chest.

JUDY: That wasn't passion. I was sickening for mumps.

STELLA: You were too old for mumps.

JUDY: Nevertheless, I had them all right. Is mumps *them* or *it*?

NAOMI: It must be *them.* You can't have a mump all by itself.

STELLA: Isn't it lucky that we're all reasonably healthy? Considering our ages I mean.

JUDY: I'm not reasonably healthy. I'm a martyr to practically everything. I cough and sniffle from November to May and in June I get hay fever, which torments me until the end of September.

NAOMI: At least you have October to look forward to.

STELLA (*earnestly*): I still maintain that we're fantastically lucky. We might be bedridden or crippled with arthritis or bent double like croquet hoops. Instead we're all three sound in wind and limb and ready for anything.

JUDY: You always exaggerate so. We're far from being ready for anything, except lunch. And it doesn't look as if we're ever going to get that.

NAOMI: You must be patient, it's a cheese soufflé. She couldn't possibly start it until you'd both got here. You might have been stuck in a traffic jam and it would have sunk like a stone. Would you like another little nip?

JUDY: If I had another little nip I shouldn't be able to tell the difference between a cheese soufflé and a steak and kidney pudding.

STELLA: At least nothing agitating is likely to happen to any of us now, we're too old. Except getting ill and dying, of course.

JUDY: Do stop harping on how old we are. It's undermining. I'm beginning to feel as though I couldn't get out of this chair without help.

NAOMI: I doubt if you can. It's a perfect beast, like a hip bath. Even quite young people get stuck in it.

STELLA: I'd hate to get ill but I don't believe I shall mind dying all that much.

JUDY: It's easy enough to say that now but just you wait until the time comes. You'll probably be in the most awful frizz.

STELLA: I don't know why you should assume that. Lots of people are calm as cucumbers on their deathbeds and think up lovely memorable things to say to comfort everybody.

JUDY: I doubt if I shall. I'm more likely to be in a tearing rage and insult people right and left.

NAOMI (*thoughtfully*): I shall cry, I expect. Not the boo-hooing, snuffly kind of crying, but just gentle, helpless tears, because everyone is being so kind to me.

JUDY: Perhaps they won't be.

NAOMI: Of course they will. People are always kind at deathbeds. They smooth your pillows and keep putting their fingers to their lips and tiptoeing about the darkened room.

JUDY: That would drive me mad to start with.

STELLA: Why don't we change the subject to something more cheerful? Lunch, for instance!

NAOMI: I wish you'd shut up about lunch. It'll be ready in a minute.

STELLA: I'm famished and it's nearly a quarter to two.

JUDY: Perhaps Mrs. Rothwell has had some sort of accident.

NAOMI: Mrs. Rothwell could never have an accident. You only have to look at her.

STELLA: I wish I could look at her. I've never wanted to look at anybody so much in my life.

JUDY: Three grandmothers! It really does seem grotesque, doesn't it? Almost indecent.

NAOMI: What's indecent about it? I don't know what you mean.

JUDY: The way we behave and dress and carry on. It's all so unsuitable somehow.

STELLA: What on earth are you talking about?

JUDY: I think nineteenth-century grandmothers were far more attractive and impressive than twentieth-century ones. They were yellowish and frail and infinitely more understanding and smelt vaguely of lavender water.

STELLA: Mine didn't. She had a voice like a foghorn and smelled dreadful.

NAOMI: What of?

STELLA: Mothballs, principally, but there was something else as well, I can't quite describe it—

JUDY: Well, be a dear and don't try.

NAOMI: Actually, I do rather see what Judy means. Nobody seems to get comfortably old anymore. I'm sure we should all three of us find life far less agitating if we'd given up at fifty and were content to sit about clanking with cameo brooches.

JUDY: "Old and gray and full of sleep / And nodding by the fire."

STELLA: I'd rather sit in Antoine's, where at least there's someone to nod to.

JUDY: I still maintain that we present the wrong image.

STELLA: Who to?

JUDY: The world in general and our grandchildren in particular. How can we expect them to rush to us with their tiny troubles when we're always having our hair set and our nails done?

STELLA: You're getting your generations mixed, dear. My granddaughter's last tiny trouble had to be dealt with by that very dubious doctor in St. John's Wood.

NAOMI: Jennifer *is* an exception, Stella. You must admit that.

STELLA: I don't admit anything of the sort. The majority of the Young today are morally irresponsible. Jennifer was just a bit careless. She was always vague as a child.

NAOMI: I think to become pregnant at the age of eighteen and a half is carrying vagueness a little too far.

JUDY: She inherits a lot of it from her mother.

STELLA: I resent that, Judy. Harriet was a bit forgetful, I agree, but she had a brilliant mind.

JUDY: She left two bull terrier puppies in the ladies' lavatory at Paddington. If that isn't vague I should like to know what is.

NAOMI: Oh, poor things! What happened to them?

JUDY: The usual routine. Lost Property Office, Battersea Dogs' Home, advertisements in the *Daily Telegraph*. She got them back eventually.

NAOMI: Thank God for that. I can't bear to think of dogs being left about and forsaken. They must suffer so dreadfully not being able to explain anything to anybody.

STELLA: I don't suppose abandoned babies on doorsteps have too good a time, either.

NAOMI: At least they don't run the risk of being put into strange kennels and getting bitten by other abandoned babies.

STELLA: I don't care what you say about us presenting the wrong image, Judy. I still think we have every reason to congratulate ourselves.

JUDY: What on earth for?

STELLA (*vehemently*): Because we've survived! We've cleared all the hazards and hurdles and ditches. All we have to do now is to canter serenely down the home stretch.

NAOMI: Your phraseology is overebullient, Stella, it always was. We're none of us capable of cantering anywhere. It's as much as I can do to stagger from the top of Sloane Street to Harrods.

STELLA: You know perfectly well what I mean. We've all three of us been through the mill in our different ways and at last, at long last, we can afford to put our feet up and relax. There really isn't much that can happen to us now.

JUDY: For God's sake, touch wood!

STELLA: I wouldn't dream of touching wood. In my opinion all those foolish old superstitions encourage disaster rather than prevent it.

NAOMI: That's a superstition in itself.

STELLA: I don't in the least mind being thirteen at table and I can't wait to walk under ladders.

In an evening dedicated to Noël on the occasion of his seventieth birthday, Richard Attenborough presents him with a book of his lyrics signed by the cast of the special performance (*A Talent to Amuse*) at London's Phoenix Theatre.

NAOMI: I'm afraid you'll have to until after lunch. Unless I can persuade Mrs. Rothwell to set up the kitchen steps outside the dining-room door.

MRS. ROTHWELL enters.

MRS. R. (*announcing*): Luncheon is served, Madame.

MRS. ROTHWELL withdraws, leaving the door open. *NAOMI* ushers the others out.

CHAPTER SEVEN
ENVOI . . . THE 1970s

Whenever I reflect with what alarming rapidity I am trundling toward old age and the dusty grave, I find it comforting to count my blessings. And although the future, like the late Mrs. Fiske, is heavily veiled, my blessings, up to date, have been considerable.

—PAST CONDITIONAL (1965)

A world weary Noël enjoys another room with a view—this one in Jamaica. ("I want to get right back to Nature and relax.")

"THE PARTY'S OVER NOW"

The Party's over now,
The dawn is drawing very nigh,
The candles gutter,
The starlight leaves the sky.
It's time for little boys and girls
To hurry home to bed
For there's a new day
Waiting just ahead.
Life is sweet
But time is fleet,
Beneath the magic of the moon,
Dancing time
May seem sublime
But it is ended all too soon,
The thrill has gone,
To linger on
Would spoil it anyhow,
Let's creep away from the day
For the Party's over now.

—WORDS AND MUSIC (1932)

For Noël the party *was,* to all intents and purposes, over.

There would be another couple of film roles—a sideline that had become a significant source of income—and that would be that. Our last view of him is as Mr. Bridger, the master criminal, accepting the acclaim of his fellow prisoners on the successful completion of *The Italian Job* (1968). It was a fitting public exit.

Strangely, for someone of so many accomplishments, Noël frequently worried that he would be forgotten. To the end of his days the past was always part of his present.

"Those I have really loved are with me in moments of memory—whole and intact and unchanged."

"I can enjoy retrospective laughter again and again, but retrospective tears, never."

"WHEN I HAVE FEARS"

When I have fears, as Keats had fears,
Of the moment I'll cease to be
I console myself with vanished years
Remembered laughter, remembered tears,
And the peace of the changing sea.

When I feel sad, as Keats felt sad,
That my life is so nearly done
It gives me comfort to dwell upon
Remembered friends who are dead and gone
And the jokes we had and the fun.

How happy they are I cannot know
But happy am I who loved them so.

The critical praise and the honours flowed unabated, culminating in the long-delayed knighthood in the 1970 New Year's Honours List. There was nothing left to do. Noël even stopped writing his diary.

He made his last public appearance in New York at a special performance of the revue *Oh, Coward!* Graham and Coley were there with him. Marlene was on his arm, though it was not entirely clear who was supporting whom.

Had he enjoyed the show? "One does not laugh at one's own jokes." Then he relented. "But I *did* leave humming the songs."

•

He left behind a manuscript for an unfinished novel, *Beyond These Voices,* which he began in 1956. Like several of his plays and stories, it is set in his mythical South Sea Island, Samolo.

It sounds almost as though both the author and the narrator, Kerry Stirling, were taking their leave. It begins . . .

I have come home again, this time, I suspect, for good. The years that are left to me I intend to pass here on the island where the winds are soft and the climate temperate and where, except for a few weeks twice a year in the rainy season, there is always sunshine.

This thought fills me with gentle pleasure for I am tired. Not physically tired, for I am in the best of health and look and feel a great deal younger than I am, but spiritually a little under the weather. This is not a disagreeable sensation; on the contrary it is rather pleasant, for there is space around me and time ahead of me, time enough at least to enable me to give myself up to my quiet malaise and wait, without agitation, until the unhurried days smooth it away.

By the time he arrived in Jamaica that last time, there were, as it turned out, only days left to Noël. He died peacefully in the early morning of March 26, 1973.
And, indeed, the winds that day were soft . . .
The marvelous party was finally over.

I would prefer fate to allow me to go to sleep when it's my proper bedtime. I never have been one for staying up too late.

—DIARIES (1967)

"I'M HERE FOR A SHORT VISIT ONLY"

I'm here for a short visit only
And I'd rather be loved than hated.
Eternity may be lonely
When my body's disintegrated
And that which is loosely termed my soul
Goes whizzing off through the infinite
By means of some vague, remote control.
I'd like to think I was missed a bit.

·

When asked what he would like as an epitaph, Noël replied,

"He was much loved because
he made people laugh and cry."

"He was much loved because
he made people laugh and cry."

ACKNOWLEDGMENTS

"Age cannot wither nor custom stale [his] infinite variety."

Yes, I know Shakespeare said that about Cleopatra first but he might have held that thought back, if he'd known that The Master would be coming along three hundred short years later.

Thank you to my publisher and editor, Victoria Wilson, who knows full well that when she says—"Let's do it" she neatly removes an author's every excuse, leaving him determined to justify that trust!

Thanks, too, to her two "enablers" at Knopf, Kathy Zuckerman and Carmen Johnson. Always a pleasure doing business with you, ladies.

To Dany Dasto (who looks after the Coward Estate exactly as Noël would have wished) for continuing to give me unlimited access to the Archive and his support—not to mention his friendship—in this, as in so many other Coward ventures, over the years.

To Alan Brodie, agent for the Estate (my help in ages past and hope for whatever years may be to come), for encouraging me to present the many remarkable talents of a truly remarkable man . . . without for one moment forgetting his team of formidably charming and charmingly formidable ladies—Harriet, Lisa, Clare and Kirsty . . .

To Geoffrey Johnson—Noël's friend and U.S. business representative—and now, I like to think, my friend, too . . .

To Rosalind Fayne, who has typed more of The Master's words—as well as my own—than she probably cares to remember . . .

To Coco, my pal posing as a miniature poodle, whose expression frequently says—"Surely you're going to put in the bit about . . ." (It's in. It's in!)

And always to Lynne, my support and inspiration in everything I set my hand to. And much that I don't.

BARRY DAY
2010

INDEX

Page numbers in *italics* refer to illustrations.

PERMISSIONS ACKNOWLEDGMENTS

Grateful acknowledgment is made to the following for permission to reprint previously published and unpublished material:

Methuen Drama: Excerpts from *Design for Living*; excerpts from *Easy Virtue*; excerpts from *Fallen Angels*; "The Kindness of Mrs. Radcliffe"; "Me and the Girls"; "Mr. and Mrs. Edgehill"; excerpt from *Nude With Violin*; excerpt from *Pomp and Circumstance*; excerpts from *Present Laughter*; *Red Peppers*; *Shadow Play*; excerpt from *Suite in Three Keys*; excerpts from *Tonight at 8:30*; excerpt from *The Vortex*; excerpts from *Waiting in the Wings*; and "What Mad Pursuit" by Noël Coward. Reprinted by permission of Methuen Drama, A & C Black Publishers Limited.

N.C. Aventales AG: Excerpt from *Age Cannot Wither*; "Alice Is at It Again"; "A Bar on the Piccola Marina"; "The Battle of Britain Dinner, New York, 1963"; excerpts from *Blithe Spirit*; "The Boy Actor"; excerpts from *Brief Encounter*; "Bronxville Darby and Joan"; "Canton Island"; "Come the Wild, Wild Weather"; "Dance Little Lady"; "Don't Let's Be Beastly to the Germans"; "Epitaph for an Elderly Actress"; "Forbidden Fruit"; "Green Carnations"; "Has Anybody Seen Our Ship?"; excerpts from *Hay Fever*; "House Guest"; "I Am No Good At Love"; "I Knew You Without Enchantment"; "I Like America"; "I Travel Alone"; "I Wonder What Happened to Him?"; "If Love Were All"; "I'll Follow My Secret Heart"; "I'll See You Again"; "I'm Here for a Short Visit Only"; "I've Been to a Marvellous Party"; "I've Got to Go Out and Be Social"; "I've Just Come Out From England"; "Jamaica"; "Later Than Spring"; "Lie in the Dark and Listen"; "London Pride"; "Louisa"; "Mad About the Boy"; "Mad Dogs and Englishmen"; "Men About Town"; "Mrs. Mallory"; "Mrs. Worthington"; "Notes on Liaison"; "Parisian Pierrot"; "The Party's Over Now"; "Personal Note"; "Personal Reminiscence"; "Play, Orchestra, Play"; "Poor Little Rich Girl"; excerpts from *Peace in Our Time*; excerpts from *Private Lives*; "A Room With a View"; "Sail Away"; "Social Grace"; "Someday I'll Find You"; "Something Very Strange"; excerpt from *Star Quality*; "The Stately Homes of England"; "Then"; "There Are Bad Times Just Around the Corner"; excerpt from *This Happy Breed*; "This Is a Changing World"; "This Is to Let You Know"; excerpts from *Time Remembered*; "Together With Music"; "Touring Days"; "Tribute to Marlene Dietrich"; "Twentieth Century Blues";" excerpts from *The Unattainable*; "Uncle Harry"; "Useless Useful Phrases"; "What Is Love?"; "When I Have Fears"; "When You Come Home On Leave"; "Why Do the Wrong People Travel?"; "Why Must the Show Go On?"; "World Weary"; and "You Were There" by Noël Coward, copyright © N.C. Aventales AG. Excerpts from *In Which We Serve* by Noël Coward, copyright © Granada International. Reprinted by permission of Alan Brodie on behalf of N.C. Aventales AG.

ILLUSTRATION CREDITS

Barry Day Collection: 9 *(both images)*, 30, 37, 162, 175, 252, 253 *(bottom)*, 255 *(both images)*, 259, 357 *(both images)*, 474, 483, 497, 519, 582
Cecil Beaton: 369
Coward Estate Archives: ii, 4, 25, 27, 94 *(top)*, 104, 115, 125, 132 *(top)*, 136, 146, 149, 153, 177, 179, 181, 185, 304, 346, 348, 356, 374 *(top)*, 379, 425, 426, 433, 438, 448, 454, 455, 458, 479, 488, 526, 527, 533, 547, 578 *(bottom)*, 579, 584
Faber Music: 42, 142, 146, 151, 154, 166, 172, 184, 195, 198, 354, 363, 480, 510, 516
Geoffrey Johnson, Noël Coward Collection: 484
Mander and Mitchenson Archive: 94 *(by Sasha)*, 128 *(top and bottom)*, 278, 453
Max Beerbohm: 155
Photofest: 305 *(both images)*, 578 *(top)*
Roundabout Theatre Company: 374 *(bottom)*
The Executor of Lady Lancaster: 196
Ten Chimneys Foundation: 253 *(top)*, 262
University of Birmingham Special Collection: 132 *(bottom)*, 361, 428

A NOTE ON THE TYPE

*The text of this book was set in Garamond No. 3. It is not a true copy
of any of the designs of Claude Garamond (ca. 1480–1561),
but an adaptation of his types, which set the European
standard for two centuries. This particular version
is based on an adaptation by Morris Fuller Benton.*

COMPOSED BY
*North Market Street Graphics,
Lancaster, Pennsylvania*

PRINTED AND BOUND BY
*Berryville Graphics,
Berryville, Virginia*